STATE, ECONOMY AND

GREAT DIVERGENCE

CW01020216

STATE, ECONOMY AND THE
GREAT DIVERGENCE

GREAT BRITAIN AND CHINA, 1680s−1850s

Peer Vries

Bloomsbury Academic
An imprint of Bloomsbury Publishing Plc

B L O O M S B U R Y
LONDON · NEW DELHI · NEW YORK · SYDNEY

Bloomsbury Academic

An imprint of Bloomsbury Publishing Plc

50 Bedford Square	1385 Broadway
London	New York
WC1B 3DP	NY 10018
UK	USA

www.bloomsbury.com

BLOOMSBURY and the Diana logo are trademarks of Bloomsbury Publishing Plc

First published 2015

British Library Cataloguing-in-Publication Data
A catalogue record for this book is available from the British Library.

ISBN: HB: 978-1-4725-2193-4
PB: 978-1-4725-3022-6
ePDF: 978-1-4725-2918-3
ePub: 978-1-47252-640-3

Library of Congress Cataloging-in-Publication Data
A catalog record for this book is available from the Library of Congress.

Typeset by Deanta Global Publishing Services, Chennai, India
Printed and bound in Great Britain

I want to dedicate the book to the memory of John F. Richards,

a great scholar and a great person

CONTENTS

PREFACE

A year and three months before I finished this manuscript, I finished another one, entitled *Escaping Poverty. The Origins of Modern Economic Growth* (Vienna and Göttingen, 2013), which also appeared in German as *Ursprünge des modernen Wirtschaftswachstums. England, China und die Welt in der Frühen Neuzeit* (Göttingen, 2013). That book dealt extensively with the origins of modern economic growth and thus also with the Great Divergence and the role of the state in it. Inevitably, Great Britain and China and their states were also discussed in that book. In this book I explicitly and exclusively focus on the role of the British and Chinese states, but of course build upon earlier work, in particular on Part Two Chapters 10, 12, 16 and 20-6 and the chapter 'Why Not China?' of my *Escaping Poverty* and, when it comes to public finances in Great Britain and China, on my 'Die Staatsfinanzen Chinas und Großbritanniens im langen 18. Jahrhundert. Ein Vergleich' in Peter Rauscher, Andrea Serles and Thomas Winkelbauer (eds), *Das 'Blut des Staatskörpers'. Forschungen zur Finanzgeschichte der Frühen Neuzeit, Historische Zeitschrift. Beiheft* 56 (Munich, 2012), 209–57. (This article has also been published, in English, as a working paper (no. 167/12) on the website of the Department of Economic History at the London School of Economics and Political Science: http://www2.lse.ac.uk/economicHistory/workingPapers/economicHistory/home.aspx.) A certain overlap with previous work, which I refer to in the Bibliography, was inevitable, but I considered it more efficient, for myself and the reader, and better for the flow of the arguments in the book, to not repeatedly refer to older texts but to partially include or paraphrase them, often with adaptations and changes. But at a time when one can be accused of 'auto-plagiarism', it may not be superfluous to acknowledge that one as an author of course builds upon previous work. I had already finished my manuscript when I read Sven Beckert's *Empire of Cotton: A New History of Global Capitalism* (New York, 2014), so I could not integrate its findings and claims in my manuscript. I do, however, want to point out that in that publication too the author time and again emphasizes the fundamental role of active state intervention in the Great Divergence. According to Beckert that divergence and more in general the 'rise of the West' simply cannot be explained without reference to the state and its intervention in and manipulation of the economy, or to the coercion and violence endorsed or even actively used by that same state.

INTRODUCTION

Perfect markets are for the poor.

Erik S. Reinert, *How Rich Countries Got Rich ... and Why Poor Countries Stay Poor,* 18

One of the most lively and interesting debates in global economic history is that on 'the Great Divergence', that is the emergence of a huge gap in the levels of wealth, development and growth between various parts of the world in the eighteenth and nineteenth centuries.[1] In that debate, comparisons between Western Europe – in particular Great Britain – and China play a prominent role. Why did Great Britain first industrialize instead of China? Why did Great Britain not develop like China? The fact that such questions have stirred up such an ongoing and fertile debate is a clear sign that in Western historiography over the last decades the image of China in the early modern era, that is roughly from the late fifteenth century to the first decades of the nineteenth century, has gone through some radical changes. In economic history, the field that I will concentrate on in this text, many authors no longer picture China during the high Qing[2] as a completely different – that is, at least as compared to the Western world – underdeveloped and poor part of the world. They now, in contrast, emphasize that looking at China and the West at that time they see 'a world of surprising resemblances'.[3] This so-called 'Eurasian similarity-thesis', to use an expression by Perdue, and the accompanying tendency 'to transcend the hoary insistence on East-West dichotomies' have become quite popular.[4] The American sociologist and historian Goldstone even coined a term, 'the California School', to refer to a growing group of scholars who claim that in the early modern era levels of wealth, development and growth at the two extremes of Eurasia were quite similar and that the supposedly unique character of Western society at the time to a very large extent is only a figment of the imagination of Eurocentric historians.[5] Some revisionists, like Frank, Hobson and Marks, go even further and claim that Europe as compared to East Asia in the early modern era has to be considered 'backward'.[6]

---

[1] The term became popular thanks to Pomeranz, *Great Divergence.*
[2] The Qing ruled China from 1644 to 1911. The period of the High Qing runs from the 1680s to the end of the eighteenth century.
[3] This now popular expression actually is the title of the first part of Pomeranz's *Great Divergence.*
[4] For the Eurasian similarity-thesis see Perdue, *China Marches West,* 536–42. This wish to transcend 'dichotomies' also figures in recent publications by Goody (even somewhat obsessively), by Lieberman and much more even-handedly in Darwin's *After Tamerlane.* I refer to the Bibliography. For the expression 'hoary insistence on East-West dichotomies' see Lieberman, *Beyond binary histories,* the backflap.
[5] For the California School, its members and ideas see my 'California School and beyond'.
[6] See for their publications the bibliography.

Serious scholarly attention to the economic history of Ming (1368–1644) and Qing China was long overdue in Western historiography. For too long prejudiced clichés had abounded. In the new and booming field of global economic history, China deserved not only serious study but clearly also some rehabilitation. The negative, primitive image of China that was reproduced time and again, especially by people who hardly knew anything about China's imperial past, definitely needed correcting. But I am afraid that, as is so often the case in scholarship, a tendency has emerged to err in the opposite direction. The healthy wish to break with a tradition of focusing almost exclusively and even somewhat obsessively on what 'the East' lacked in contrast to 'the West', must not, as now often is the case, lead us to ignore major differences that *did* exist. Scholars who systematically focus only on the similarities between Western Europe and China, in the end will be more or less forced to explain the undeniable Great Divergence of the nineteenth century by referring to 'contingency', 'accident', 'fortuitous circumstances' and the like, as indeed many of them do.[7] Personally, I don't think that is a very satisfactory way of explaining major historical divergences. Although undoubtedly contingency plays a big role in history, explaining major transformations normally implies referring to major underlying conditions. In the case of major *persistent* divergences, that normally means major differences in initial conditions.[8] I recently published a book, *Escaping Poverty* that tried to provide an overall analysis of the emergence and possible explanations of the Great Divergence. The underlying goal of this text is to point at one such specific major difference that very well *may* have been an important cause of the Great Divergence.

The importance, role and function of the state: The cases of Great Britain and China

That really major difference would be the importance, role and function of the state. In studying the Great Divergence, as in many other fields of global history, it has become increasingly popular to no longer take states and their territories as point of departure and as obvious 'setting' for one's analysis. In many fields of study there indeed exist good reasons to stop doing so. There also, though, exist good reasons to not err in the opposite direction, as now happens in many texts on global history, and almost completely ignore the state. In a study like this, where one wants to investigate what exactly were the characteristics of various states and how they impacted on economic development, one evidently and by necessity *has* to take existing states as basic unity of analysis. To find out things about states one has to study states.

What I intend to do in this text, is to show how fundamentally *different* Great Britain (and, more in general, Western Europe) and China were in these respects. My reason

---

[7]See for a great number of examples my *Escaping Poverty*, 53–5.
[8]See for further explanation my *Escaping Poverty*, 44–53.

for 'only' focusing on Great Britain and China is that I am convinced that using a simple dichotomy of 'the West' versus 'the Rest' normally obscures more than it helps to explain. My thesis is that when it comes to the way in which the state impinged on economic life in these extremes of Eurasia, it is not surprising *resemblances* but surprising *differences* that catch the eye. Geographically, the focus of the text will be on Great Britain that clearly has its idiosyncrasies but will also refer quite regularly to other western European states to show how exceptional *or* non-exceptional that British case is. Chronologically, my analysis will focus on what one could call 'the very long eighteenth century'. For Great Britain that would be the period from 1688, when with the Glorious Revolution many important changes in the organization of the British state were either introduced or institutionalized, to 1849, when with the formal repeal of the Navigation Acts a new era in British economic policy started.[9] For Qing China the period discussed will be from the 1680s when, with the end of the Three Feudatories War, the Qing dynasty began to effectively rule over the whole of mainland China, and on top of that incorporated Taiwan, to the 1840s, when with the First Opium War (1839–42) China was 'opened' and a fundamentally new phase in its economic history began. My focus on Great Britain during the very long eighteenth century needs no further explanation: that is the period in which the country took off and became the world's first industrial nation. For China my periodization is far less obvious. I choose the period of Qing rule to the Opium Wars basically because that is the period that up until now has been discussed by virtually all the participants in the debate on the Great Divergence and that is the debate that I want to analyse, interpret and evaluate from the perspective of the role of the state. It may very well be true that actually China came closer to taking off under Song rule (960–1279) than it ever did under the Qing, but systematic comparisons between that period and Europe in the early modern era are still extremely scarce, which means that I as yet lack sufficient material for writing a book like this focusing on Song China.[10]

For me the Great Divergence is caused by the emergence of modern economic growth in a specific part of the world and its absence in the rest of it. In my *Escaping Poverty* I have extensively discussed the specific characteristics of modern economic growth and its overall causes. Doing that again in this book would just become repetitive. I will here explicitly focus on the role the state may have played in the emergence of such growth in Great Britain and in its non-emergence in China during the very long eighteenth century. This is the first study in which these two polities are systematically compared from this angle. Therefore the bulk of my research had to be devoted to charting similarities and differences, which left me less room for

---

[9]See for the debate on continuity versus discontinuity in a strictly institutional sense: Braddick, *Nerves of the State*; He, *Paths toward the Modern Fiscal State*, ch. 2; O'Brien, 'Fiscal exceptionalism'; Stasavage, *Public Debt*, and Sussman and Yafeh, 'Institutional reforms'. For a recent general interpretation of '1688' that emphasizes how *revolutionary* it was, see Pincus, *1688*. In recent publications by North, Wallis and Weingast and by Acemoglu and Robinson, the Glorious Revolution is presented as an event of world-historical dimensions. See the Bibliography.

[10]See, for the thesis that Song China would have been more advanced economically than Qing China, Deng, 'Demystifying growth'; Jones, *Growth Recurring*, 73–84, and Liu, *Wrestling for Power*.

the question of what all these similarities and differences might imply. Many of their effects are quite obvious. In some respects, however, determining their *exact* effects would require a separate new and extensive analysis – here I can only suggest the main questions it should deal with.

Considering the fact that Qing China is a huge continent, whereas Great Britain is only a medium-sized state, a critic might point out that my comparison does not make sense and that I should compare Europe or at least Western Europe to China. I nevertheless decided to focus on (Great) Britain. I did so for several reasons. First because even 'Western Europe' in this context would not always be a very useful category as in various respects there existed substantial differences between states in that part of the world. Even if Great Britain might in several respects be regarded as a typical Western European state, although almost always in some extreme sense, in other respects it clearly was exceptional. It, moreover, was the first and in many respects for a couple of decades, the *only* major industrial nation. This book is definitely not meant as the umpteenth Whiggish effort to defend the 'peculiarity of the British', but, as the text will show, in various respects Britain indeed *was* different, sometimes even *very* different. To simply proceed as if there was such a thing as '*the* (Western) European state' during the early modern era would be, as we will see time and again, seriously misleading.[11] A clear convergence of different models of state-formation only became apparent *after* the French Revolution and its impact; before that there were striking varieties. Charles Tilly (1929–2008), one of the major specialists in the study of state-formation, actually set out to answer the following question: 'What accounts for the great variation [*sic*] over time and space in the kinds of state that have prevailed in Europe since AD 990?'[12] In the early modern era 'the western European state' did not (yet) exist. It is mistaken to speak in such terms not just because quite substantial differences existed between various polities, but also because they were engaged in almost permanent competition and, quite often, even wars with one another. Europe's history in the early modern era was characterized by permanent wars in which Europeans fought Europeans. Millions of Europeans were killed by other Europeans. Let me only give one, it being the worst example: 'During the Napoleonic period, France alone counted close to a million war deaths. ... The toll across Europe may have reached as high as five million deaths.'[13] In that respect Europe clearly was a collection of very distinct, different and competing, even combative entities. I will, nevertheless, often refer to other European states to broaden my comparison and to show that notwithstanding the substantial differences between states in Western Europe that I just alluded to, it can *in some respects* indeed make sense to compare China with Western Europe *as a whole*. For the staggering amount of literature in which one can read

---

[11]See Appendix A for literature that discusses in what respects Great Britain was different from other (Western) European countries and in what respects it was not.

[12]See the flap of Tilly, *Coercion, Capital, and European States*. Compare Epstein: 'One of the most historically pregnant aspects of pre-modern Europe was its variety of political types, and the fact that economic leadership did not stay with one type of regime or country for very long'. Epstein, 'Rise of the West', 252.

[13]Bell, *First Total War*, 7.

about the differences and similarities between states in Europe during the early modern era I refer to the bibliography.[14]

That of course does not exclude that many of these competing and fighting European states may have been be quite similar. One may even, with Tilly, claim that this competition, that very often implied emulation and the borrowing of best practices of the states in the state system, was the main reason that *in the end* their state structures became more and more similar. As competing parts of one state system they were constantly watching, analysing and emulating each other. Governments and many subjects were very keen on figuring out the relative strength and potential of their countries and they definitely would have grasped the logic and value of the comparative analyses that I present here. It was quite normal to compare the economic, political and military systems of various 'Great Powers' and to then try and learn from these comparisons and adopt best practices. The history of early modern Europe is a history of competing states that permanently benchmark, borrow, imitate and emulate.[15] Britain, France, the Dutch Republic, 'Germany', 'Italy', Portugal and Spain, for example, all clearly were part of a (Western) European state system and in the end this indeed had 'equalizing' effects on their state structures. But that did not mean they had similar histories: differences at times were enormous, depending, for example, on how one organized for competition and on whether one was successful or not. Being part of the European state system, to focus on what is at stake in this book, in any case did not imply *ipso facto* that the economic history of a state and its level of development and wealth would be similar to that of the other states in that same system. One need only compare Spain and Portugal on the one hand with Great Britain and the Dutch Republic on the other. Many economic historians would claim that the differences between these European states, in, for example, terms of wealth may have been bigger than those between say Great Britain and the Dutch Republic on the one hand and China on the other hand. So one would be well advised to not look at states in Europe in isolation but also be cautious to not exaggerate and 'standardize' the impact of Europe's state system. One should in any case be wary of undifferentiated references to the assumedly 'salutary' effects of the European or Western state system and its plurality on 'Europe' or 'the West'.

In this context I think it is also important to point out that states in early modern Western Europe in many respects were much more 'porous' than they were to become

---

[14]See for example: Black, *Kings, Nobles & Commoners*; Blockmans, *History of Power*; Downing, *Military Revolution*; Ertman, *Birth of the Leviathan*; Tilly, *Coercion, Capital, and European States*, and Tilly and Blockmans, *Cities & the Rise of States in Europe*. Finer, *History of Government* provides a brilliant global analysis of systems of government from the ancient monarchies and empires to the coming of modern states. For information with regard to the fiscal-military state that will figure so prominently in my text, I refer to, in alphabetical order: Bonney, *Economic Systems and State Finance*; Bonney, *Rise of the Fiscal State*; Cavaciocchi, *Fiscalità nell'economia europea*; Cardoso and Lains, *Paying for the Liberal State*; Conway and Torres, *Spending of States*; Dincecco, *Political Transformations*; Karaman and Pamuk, 'Ottoman state finances'; O'Brien and Yun, *Rise of Fiscal States*; Rauscher, Serles and Winkelbauer, 'Blut des Staatskörpers'; Storrs, *Fiscal-Military State*, and Torres Sánchez, *War, State and Development*.

[15]See, e.g. Hont, *Jealousy of Trade*; Sophus Reinert, *Translating Empire* and 'Rivalry'; Scott, 'Fiscal-military state' and the literature about mercantilism referred to in Chapter 6 notes 2–11.

in the nineteenth century after the French Revolution, when rulers were resolved to have a more exclusive grip on their people and resources and the distinction between domestic/national and foreign became much strictly defined and enforced. Their armies and the personnel of their navies could to a very large extent consist of foreigners, as could the people who worked for their chartered companies. Very often their rulers were foreigners too.[16] The highest layers of the aristocracy were quite transnational. Foreign merchants were present in great numbers in every important trading centre.[17] Moreover, there already existed something like international finance. Financiers from the Dutch Republic, for example, subscribed to British public debt, while in 1764 and 1774 investors from that same country held over 30 per cent of stocks of the English East India Company.[18] In monetary matters, too, borders still could be quite porous. Foreign coin could be an important element in local currency, particularly when there was little local coinage produced or when a small-scale issuer bordered a more prolific and important neighbour. In Ireland, English, Scottish and other foreign coins, mostly Spanish issues, were used; in Russia one used Western coins, in Poland coins from Sweden and Saxony.[19] In many respects European states in the early modern era still were quite distinct from modern states, as they became the 'norm' during the nineteenth and twentieth centuries.[20]

The text will consist of eight chapters. It opens with a long introduction, providing some historiographical background, methodological comments and caveats, and some basic empirical information. Then there are four chapters that deal with the 'hardware' or 'infrastructure' of the British and Chinese states, with many references to other European countries. Here revenue (over-)expenditure, finance and money, and personnel are discussed. The final four chapters are dedicated to the military and the economy, economic policies, economy and empire and finally to state- and nation-building. A large part of my text will be quite descriptive, as I think it is very important to try and determine *precisely* and where possible *in quantitative terms* how big and fundamental the differences between Britain – and other European countries – and China actually were. So many different views are presented about the role of the state in the rise of the West, especially in 'grand narratives', and so many of these views have so little solid empirical underpinnings that an endeavour to find out 'how it actually was' is long overdue and highly relevant. I hope to show beyond reasonable doubt that any serious

---

[16]For foreigners in (Great) Britain's army, navy and chartered companies see e.g. Thomson, *Mercenaries, Pirates & Sovereigns*, 29, table 2.1, here reprinted on page 279 and Chapter 4 notes 92–3. Europe's aristocracy almost by definition was transnational. For the period 1689 to 1702, Britain and the Dutch Republic had the same ruler, the man who became known as William III, King of Britain.

[17]For foreign merchants/bankers in London see e.g. Chapman, *Merchant Enterprise*, and more specifically for the period of the Napoleonic Wars, Beerbühl, 'Supplying the belligerent countries'.

[18]For Dutch subscribers to British public debt, see Van Zanden and Van Riel, *Strictures of Inheritance*, 99, table 1.3. For foreign capital and capitalists going to Great Britain, see also Cassis, *Capitals of Capital*, ch. 1; Knight, *Britain against Napoleon*, ch. 13, and O'Brien, 'Contributions of warfare'. For Dutch investors in the English East India Company, see Bowen, *Business of Empire*, 112.

[19]Eagleton and Williams, *Money*, 167.

[20]See for some further comments pages 40–51.

analysis of the causes of the Great Divergence must pay attention to these differences. The impact of these differences – in other words, an analysis of what differences these differences may have made – will be briefly discussed in the conclusion. I really want to emphasize the importance of description in this text. One should first describe a state of affairs as precisely as possible, which as will become evident in this text already is quite an endeavour, before one makes assertions about its impact. In this text I will primarily refer to publications in English and try to show 'the state of the art' with regard to my topic in Western scholarship. It would be very interesting to confront that with the state-of-the-art expertise, as it exists in China.

HISTORIOGRAPHICAL INTRODUCTION: TRADITIONAL VIEWS AND ALTERNATIVE PERSPECTIVES

The persistence of the traditional view: Britain as an emerging free-trade economy

Many readers probably will be surprised by my intention to show that the differences between early modern China and Western Europe, when it comes to the importance, role and function of the state in the economy, were big and deserve close scrutiny. Have these differences not always figured very prominently in studies of 'the rise of the West' and 'the decline of the East' in the early modern era? Have not numerous scholars always emphasized the contrast between the state of early modern and especially industrializing Britain that was supposed to become ever leaner and cleaner till it only functioned as a kind of night-watchman and China's 'oriental despotism'? Whom am I trying to convince of what? To make that clear, I have to start my text with a historiographical introduction in which I briefly present 'traditional' and 'alternative' views on the topic of my research.

Adam Smith (1723–90) is claimed to have said: 'Little else is required to carry a state to the highest degree of opulence from the lowest barbarism, but peace, easy taxes, and a tolerable administration of justice.'[21] His impact has been enormous, even, as so often is the case, among people who have never read a word of his texts. Many scholars have claimed – and many still do – that Smith's ideas with regard to the role of the state in economic development – i.e. *as they interpreted them* – were correct. Many scholars have defended the thesis that the history of the rise of the West, first and foremost that of Britain, the first industrial nation – again, *in their interpretation* of his ideas – has proved that Smith was right. In their opinion the West rose *when* and *because* Western rulers took Smith's frowning on state intervention and mercantilism very seriously.[22] Let

---

[21]This is claimed by Adam Smith's friend Dugald Stewart. See Hall, 'States and economic development', 154.
[22]Smith was *not* always taken seriously by his contemporaries and even for quite some time after his death. In particular not when it came to his ideas about free trade. See, e.g. Magnusson, *Nation, State and the Industrial Revolution*, 14–15.

us not debate what Smith actually said,[23] but deal with what 'Smithians', his latter-day adherents, think about growth in general and the rise of the West in particular, focusing on the role of the state. One can discuss what exactly Smith wants the state to do and abstain from doing *in practice*. But it is clear that *in principle* he, and his followers, want to confine its role to creating and sustaining the circumstances in which the market can function as a well-oiled mechanism. The economic function of the state would be to 'serve' the market. In their view, it implies that government should create and sustain free and fair competition, so that the invisible hand can do its work. That in any case means it has to take care of defence, a system of transparent and efficient law and law enforcement – in particular when it comes to protecting property rights – and of the necessary material and institutional infrastructure that private enterprise cannot profitably provide for itself. What it should in any case abstain from is *intervening* in the market, allowing monopolies to exist or even creating them, and protecting and supporting certain producers and consumers against fair competition. In brief, all the things that Smith detested in the 'mercantile system' of his times.

In the 'Smithian' interpretation of British economic history, that fits in quite neatly with the Whig interpretation of Britain's overall history, the primacy of Britain and its industrialization are by and large regarded as the culmination of a long process in which Britain's economy increasingly became characterized by free and fair competition and in which government increasingly tended to behave according to 'Smithian' logics. The following quote by Arnold Toynbee, who coined the expression 'Industrial Revolution' in the 1880s, puts it very neatly:

> The essence of the Industrial Revolution is the substitution of competition for the medieval regulations which had previously controlled the production and distribution of wealth.[24]

Some hundred years later this view was still quite popular, as is shown in this quote by Rosenberg and Birdzell in their book about how the West grew rich:

> Between 1750 and 1880, the respect of Western governments for the autonomy of the economic sphere became virtually an ideology. Apart from such sporadic

---

[23]There are at least two elements in Smith's work that are not very 'Smithian', in the sense that the bulk of the people who claim they stand in his tradition would *not* endorse them. The first one is illustrated most clearly in the fact that Smith did *not* oppose the Navigation Acts. He thinks they were 'not favourable to foreign commerce, or the growth of that opulence which can arise from it' but nevertheless calls some of the regulations 'as wise … as if they had been dictated by the most deliberate wisdom' and explicitly indicates why: 'As defence, however, is of much more importance than opulence, the Act of Navigation is, perhaps, the wisest of all the commercial regulations of England.' Smith, *Inquiry into the Nature and Causes*, 464–5. Please note that Smith explicitly refers to 'nations' in the title of his book and claims that 'the great object of the political economy of every nation is to increase the riches and power [*sic*] of that country'. Ibid., 372. The second element is that Smith held the view that sustained, substantial economic growth is impossible, in particular in a situation where population increases. See for an analysis of this element in Smith's work Wrigley, 'Classical economists'.
[24]Toynbee, *Toynbee's Industrial Revolution*, 58. This basically is also the thesis defended in Polanyi, *Great Transformation*.

intrusions as the British Factory Acts and Bismarck's system of social insurance, governments were content to assist only when asked.[25]

McNeill wrote about the wealth and dynamism of 'such conspicuously undergoverned lands as Holland and England', claiming that welfare and warfare are bad for economic development.[26] This idea, that economic growth and the Industrial Revolution as a special case of economic growth in the end can best be explained by reference to 'the market', is still predominant, in particular with the wider public.

Of course, one finds all kinds of nuances and adaptations and, especially in British 'Whig historiography', a long tradition that focuses on British 'exceptionalism' and its claim that Great Britain had been quite different from the rest of Europe from quite early on and had shown the rest of Europe how best to modernize. However that may be, the view that in the end more than anything else it was the market mechanism that lay at the root of economic primacy and predominance of the West has always been and still is very popular.[27] Let me give a couple of examples and start with Eric Jones's claim that: 'Economic history may be thought of as a struggle between a propensity for growth and one for rent-seeking.'[28] According to him, in premodern states, and in most modern ones too, 'politics mean rent-seeking or pie-slicing behaviour.'[29] I guess this means, that the market, if left to itself, would be the ideal mechanism to create growth. An almost perfect and apparently extremely appealing example of this line of reasoning is provided by Landes' bestseller *The Wealth and Poverty of Nations*.[30] His explanation of why Western Europe, or rather Protestant Western Europe, and first and foremost Protestant *Britain*, industrialized is multifaceted. But his view on the role of the state in the process is quite outspoken, as shown in his extensive, separate discussion of why Britain became the first industrial nation. According to him, that could only happen because its government ensured that the market functioned as free and 'thus' as efficiently as possible.[31] He places the market at the heart of 'European exceptionalism'. When he wonders what was at the basis of the European cultivation of invention, that in his view was uniquely European and the main precondition for industrialization, he concludes:

> In the final analysis … I would stress the market. Enterprise was free in Europe. Innovation worked and paid and rulers and vested interests were limited in their ability to prevent or discourage innovation.[32]

---

[25]Rosenberg and Birdzell, *How the West Grew Rich*, 145.
[26]McNeill, *Global Condition*, 122.
[27]See for just some examples Baechler, Hall and Mann, *Europe and the Rise of Capitalism*; Bernstein, *Birth of Plenty*; Crone, *Pre-Industrial Societies*; Ferguson, *Civilization*; Gellner, *Plough, Sword and Book*; Hall, *Powers & Liberties*; Jay, *Road to Riches*; Jones, *European Miracle*; idem, *Growth Recurring*; Landes, *Wealth and Poverty*; Macfarlane, *Riddle of the Modern World*; idem, *Invention of the Modern World*; Powelson, *Centuries of Economic Endeavor*; Ringmar, *Why Europe was First*; Rosenberg and Birdzell, *How the West Grew Rich*.
[28]Jones, *Growth Recurring*, 1.
[29]Jones, *Growth Recurring*, 47.
[30]Landes, *Wealth and Poverty*.
[31]Landes, *Wealth and Poverty*, ch. 15.
[32]Landes, *Wealth and Poverty*, 59.

In his view, too, the function of government is to create and sustain the preconditions that enable the 'invisible hand' to do its job.

We still find this classical mainstream economist's view that the 'rise of the West' in general and of Great Britain in particular equalled the rise of the market and the dismantling of what Adam Smith called the 'mercantile system'. This is what John Nye wrote about this system:

> When one factors in deadweight inefficiencies of high taxation and large government with the cost of administering and defending the colonial empire, it is likely on both theoretical and empirical grounds that such large-scale expansion was on net, costly to the nation.[33]

In his view Great Britain would have been better off without its intervening and interventionist state:

> Absent a theoretically sound economic argument about the ways in which empire promoted overall economic development, accompanied by appropriate empirical evidence, the economists' presumption that such intervention is globally ineffective should be seen as decisive. At best it might be argued that the nature of political incentives was such that no more efficient policy was feasible. But that is simply an observation about the ways in which politics constrained productive behaviour; in which case it becomes even more interesting to ask how Britain developed *despite* [italics in original] such inefficient interventions.[34]

Deirdre McCloskey is very outspoken and quite unrestrictedly opposes the idea that mercantilism and its fiscal-military state apparatus might have had major positive effects for Great Britain's economy. Everyone who thinks otherwise, including all the contemporaries, is simply mistaken: '[P]eople *thought* that mercantilist aggression was good for them. ... But it is not sound, then or now, whatever people believe.'[35] In her words, 'No ceaseless struggle for survival, prosperity, and predominance backed by ships and men and money, by jingo, explains British economic success, now or in 1792 or in 1790. Innovation enabled by bourgeois dignity and liberty does.'[36] The suggestion that imperialism may have had a positive role in helping trade and so in helping industrialization, in her view, implies the counterfactual that a 'pacific and free trade Britain would *not* [italics added] have benefited from European engagement with the rest of the world'. Which she thinks is 'an odd assumption, since European places like Denmark did benefit, with trivial overseas colonies. Sweden and Germany and Austria benefitted, with few or none.'[37] Great Britain's economy in her view could have done just

---

[33]Nye, *War, Wine, and Taxes*, 24.
[34]Nye, *War, Wine, and Taxes*, 24 and 25. See also the quotation on page 427.
[35]McCloskey, *Bourgeois Dignity*, 215.
[36]McCloskey, *Bourgeois Dignity*, 216.
[37]McCloskey, *Bourgeois Dignity*, 223–4.

as well with much less military effort and expenses and much less mercantilism, as shows in the following quotes:

> A Britain with a little Tudor-style navy devoted to coastal defence would have remained independent for a long time … .

> A Quaker United Kingdom … would have gotten the same prices and opportunities as the actual Britain, allowing for the transhipment costs through Amsterdam or Le Havre.

> … if Manchester had been the right place to spin cotton before the invention of air conditioning, then European events would have put it there, regardless of whether Britain won at Plassey or Québec or Trafalgar or Waterloo.[38]

We will of course come back to Great Britain's mercantilism and fiscal-militarism time and again in this book. Here I will confine myself to saying that I consider these claims extremely naïve. In my view they completely ignore the harsh realities of 'competition' in the early modern world.

Joel Mokyr in his book on the economic history of Britain from 1700 to 1850 explains much of its development and growth by the fact that 'by the time of the ascent of Queen Victoria to the throne', the country had become 'as much of a laissez-faire economy as can be expected on this earth' and that rent seeking there 'was approaching extinction'. For him the transition to the free market, 'the mother of all institutional changes', is a necessary precondition for economic growth to become 'the norm rather than the exception'.[39] He clearly rejects the thesis that Great Britain's fiscal-military state would have had a positive impact in this respect: 'Some scholars seem to forget that the huge expenses of the Hanoverian foreign wars were costs, not benefits', and claims there perhaps is a certain 'naiveté' of supposing that the eighteenth-century state provided public goods 'such as infrastructural investments and national defence'.[40] The state primarily did one thing: waging wars and raising the revenue to pay for them. Its other main activity, according to Mokyr, was redistributing wealth and income.[41] As an expert in British economic history, he of course knows and admits that 'before the end of the eighteenth century, Britain remained on the whole committed to protectionist and mercantilist doctrines', but claims that, 'after 1815 the new liberalism was slowly gaining ground'.[42] On the eve of the Industrial Revolution, therefore, according to him, Britain still in many ways was 'a protectionist and regulated economy', in which growth took place '*despite* rather

---

[38] For these three quotes see McCloskey, *Bourgeois Dignity*, 224–5.

[39] All these quotes are from page 8 of his *Enlightened Economy*. This thesis is defended throughout the book.

[40] Mokyr, *Enlightened Economy*, 159 and 392. Mokyr himself seems to forget that someone's costs are someone else's income.

[41] Mokyr, *Enlightened Economy*, 392.

[42] Mokyr, *Enlightened Economy*, 153.

than *because* of the institutional preconditions'.[43] It nevertheless was 'better situated and equipped by comparison' than other European nations.[44] One may synthesize his view in the claim that Britain's economy in the very long eighteenth century initially developed and grew *notwithstanding* mercantilism, only to develop and grow faster once mercantilism had disappeared.[45] According to him, 'It is the changing balance between wars and the provision of public goods that is at the heart of the economics of the public sector in Britain between 1700 and 1850.'[46]

This 'classic' story of how the West grew rich has always been underpinned by the fundamental tenet of classical or neoclassical mainstream economics that the invisible hand of free and perfect competition would be a guarantee for economic success. In the last couple of decades, the so-called 'new institutional economics' is having a substantial impact on Western economic thought. This impact can also be traced in economic history, although economic historians of course have always continued to be much more aware of the role of institutions than most 'hard-core' economists. Douglass North, the main exponent of new institutional economics, has been very active as an economic historian and has published widely on the rise of the West and on Britain's economic development.[47] His ideas and those of his co-authors and supporters therefore have to be taken on board in my analysis. It will not come as a surprise that he claims that this rise was caused by more efficient Western economic institutions. In all of his work an almost direct and, in any case, very smooth connection is assumed between the right institutions, economic development and economic growth including industrialization. There tends to be a heavy emphasis on the development of well-described and state-enforced property rights. Having described how – in their view – England after 1688 acquired an efficient system of property rights (including a patent law that implied private property in knowledge), North and his co-author Thomas in 1971 ended their book on the rise of the Western world claiming: 'The stage was now set for the Industrial Revolution.'[48] In his *Structure and Change in Economic History,* published in 1981, North claimed that 'better specified and enforced property rights and increasingly efficient and expanding markets' are 'the most convincing explanation for the Industrial Revolution' in Britain.[49] In his *Violence and Social Orders* from 2009, a book co-authored with Wallis and Weingast, post-1688 Britain figures as the first society that clearly set itself on the way

---

[43]Mokyr, *Enlightened Economy*, 25.

[44]Mokyr, *Enlightened Economy*, 12. See also ibid, 68: 'None of this is to suggest that Britain had a society perfectly designed for economic growth and technological progress. Yet compared to the rest of Europe, its advantages seem obvious.'

[45]That puts him in a similar position as Nye (page 10) and to some extent Jack Goldstone who wonders: 'Might it be that modern economies emerged despite, rather than because of, the growth of modern states?' See Goldstone, 'A historical, not comparative method', 270.

[46]Mokyr, *Enlightened Economy*, 392. Figures with regard to public expenditure in my view do not exactly support that claim. See page 185.

[47]I refer the reader to the Bibliography. During his long career North has often and at times fairly drastically changed his opinions. See my *Escaping Poverty*, 120–1, note 335.

[48]North and Thomas, *Rise of the Western World*, 156.

[49]See there, page 166.

to become a so-called 'open-access-order' society. Such societies are defined as 'societies with widespread political participation, the use of elections to select governments, constitutional arrangements to limit and define the powers of government, and unbiased application of the rule of law'.[50] To reach this stage certain preconditions have to be fulfilled. These so-called 'doorstep conditions' are the existence of a rule of formal law for elites, of perpetually lived organizations and of a consolidated control of the military.[51] In a society like post-1688 Britain, rent seeking is eroded and growth promoted. Let me just give a couple of other examples of this institutionalist perspective. For the famous political scientist-economist Mancur Olson, 'a few decades after stable and nationwide government had been established in Britain [i.e., after 1688], the Industrial Revolution was on its way'.[52] In their widely acclaimed *Why Nations Fail* Daron Acemoglu and James Robinson repeatedly postulate a *direct* connection between the Glorious and the Industrial Revolution. The dynamics that led to industrialization in their view were 'unleashed by institutional change that flowed from the Glorious Revolution'.[53] Chapter seven of their book, dealing with the Glorious Revolution, is called 'The turning point: how a political revolution changed institutions in England and led to the Industrial Revolution.' All one needs for modern economic growth, so it seems, are the right 'inclusive' institutions and those emerged in Britain in 1688. The authors distinguish between political institutions and economic institutions and provide the following descriptions.[54] Inclusive political institutions are institutions that 'distribute political power widely in a pluralistic manner and are able to achieve some amount of political centralization so as to establish law and order, the foundation of secure property rights and an inclusive market economy.' Inclusive economic institutions are institutions that 'enforce property rights, create a level playing field, and encourage investments in new technologies and skills.' Extractive political institutions 'concentrate power in the hands of a few who will then have incentives to maintain and develop extractive economic institutions for their benefit.' Extractive economic institutions are 'structured to extract resources from the many by the few and ... fail to protect property rights or provide incentives for economic activity.'

Institutionalists strongly tend to look on state governments as 'predators', or at least, as in Olson's term, as 'stationary bandits' when they are not held in check.[55] In their view rulers almost without exception must have hindered rather than promoted growth. Economist John Bradford DeLong is so convinced that high taxes and public debts are bad for an economy that he concludes that Great Britain's industrialization must have been an

---

[50]See North, Wallis and Weingast, 'Violence and the rise of open-access orders', abstract.

[51]See their *Violence and Social Orders*, ch. 5.

[52]Olson, *Rise and Decline*, 128.

[53]Acemoglu and Robinson, *Why Nations Fail*, 197.

[54]Acemoglu and Robinson, *Why Nations Fail*, 429–30. See for several other, often slightly varying, descriptions under 'extractive institutions' and 'inclusive institutions'.

[55]For Olson's description of the state as a stationary bandit see his *Power and Prosperity*, under 'Bandits'. For the claim that states are predatory, see also Bonney, in his introduction to Bonney, *Rise of the Fiscal State*, 4; Levi, *Of Rule and Revenue*, and North, *Structure and Change*.

'extraordinary event', due to a 'fortunate combination of causes'. The country, so he thinks, was simply 'lucky'.[56] The first exceptions to this rule of predating emerged in the course of the early modern era in Western Europe. For the rest, if they were not actually hampering growth, most governments are regarded as too indolent, unknowing or ill-equipped to bring it about.[57] Acemoglu and Robinson stress the fact that the state has to be strong in the sense of having a monopoly on violence.[58] But apart from that they confine its role to creating and supporting inclusive institutions and 'facilitating' market mechanisms. They clearly do not believe a state can successfully implement a developmental strategy. What is lacking so far in most analyses by institutionalist economists are explicit, systematic thoughts on any potential *positive* effects on economic life of proactive, interventionist government policies that are not focusing on 'getting the prices right'.[59]

The persistence of the traditional view: China as a despotic, 'oriental' empire

In the study of the economic history of imperial China too, traditional (i.e. mainly nineteenth-century) perceptions persist. For those who endorse them, the predicament of imperial China, that it did not industrialize, has always been quite easy to explain. They only need to refer to the 'fact' that China was characterized by some kind of 'oriental despotism'. This notion has a long pedigree whose beginnings can be traced back at least to Marco Polo.[60] In the nineteenth and twentieth century it was 'elaborated' and 'systematised' to become part and parcel of a scholarly consensus that used it and concepts like 'hydraulic state' and 'Asiatic mode of production' as obvious explanations of China's economic underdevelopment.[61] Scholars from different intellectual, national and political backgrounds like Hegel, Mill, or Marx, and to a much lesser extent Weber, contributed to the creating of this negative image.[62] For the historiography of China it turned out to be very consequential that the founding fathers of historical materialism, Marx and Engels, believed many of these clichés, if they were not actually creating and promoting them. Marx, for example, in a letter dated 2 June 1853, approvingly refers to

---

[56]Bradford DeLong 'Overstrong against thyself', 164–7. According to him Britain's strong population growth was the most important fact that enabled the country to industrialize because it meant a lower per capita public debt. I fail to see how this can explain industrialization.

[57]See e.g. Jones, *Growth Recurring*, 126 and 132.

[58]See e.g. Acemoglu and Robinson, *Why Nations Fail*, 80–1. The political institutions they call 'inclusive' are 'sufficiently centralized and pluralistic'. See there 81.

[59]For clear examples of the influence of new institutionalist thinking among historians see e.g. pages 8–14. That influence is also obvious in Ferguson, *Civilization*, and idem, *Great Degeneration*.

[60]For this idea and other images of China before the Great Divergence see Lach, *Asia in the Making of Europe*; Rubiés, 'Oriental despotism', and Spence, *Chan's Great Continent*.

[61]See for these concepts Blue, 'China and Western social thought', and Hung, 'Orientalist knowledge'. For a detailed analysis of the Asiatic mode of production, see Brook, *Asiatic Mode of Production*. For the classic description of Oriental despotism see Wittfogel, *Oriental Despotism*.

[62]For the view of Weber see Schluchter, *Max Webers Studie über Konfuzianismus und Taoismus*. For the views of Hegel and Marx (and Weber), see Song, *Bedeutung der asiatischen Welt*.

the seventeenth-century author Bernier who had written that 'in all the various parts of the Orient – he speaks about Turkey, Persia and Hindustan – there was no private property. That is the real key to understanding the Orient'.[63] Engels, in a letter to Marx, fully agrees: 'The lack of property in land indeed is the key to understanding the entire Orient'.[64] It was not at all self-evident that this would become the dominant image of imperial China. In early modern Europe, in particular during the eighteenth century and especially among enlightened Europeans, the image of China, including its system of rule and its economy, had often been quite positive. In various respects it was even considered as a model for Europe. Voltaire had written about China's system of government: 'The human mind certainly cannot imagine a government better than this one'.[65] In post-Napoleonic Europe such 'Sinophilia' became exceptional. A bleak and negative image began to take over to become the almost universally accepted cliché in the second half of that century.[66]

Even now we still find plenty of publications where Qing China is described as 'despotic', 'absolutist' and 'backward'. Interestingly enough, in this respect differences in Western historiography between scholars with more Smithian and scholars with more Marxist leanings have continued to be relatively minor. Like in the nineteenth century, when the traditional negative view of China's history became dominant, many scholars from *both* ends of the political spectrum still regard the Chinese state under the Qing as despotic or even totalitarian and are convinced that, whatever else it may have been doing, it was *not* promoting growth, let alone capitalism. Many Western scholars still think it was rather the opposite. Landes, to begin with a non-Marxist example, is just as traditional when it comes to describing why 'the West' rose as when it comes to describing why 'the East' did not. In his work, Qing China appears as a despotic, even totalitarian regime. In his view, Qing China, or rather imperial China during its entire history, was ruled by the elite that opposed invention and innovation, 'strangled initiative, increased the costs of transaction, diverted talent from commerce and industry' and that, with its 'intellectual xenophobia', kept the country closed to external influences. It is obvious that he thinks that in all these respects it compared very badly to Western Europe.[67] Landes is strongly influenced by the views of sinologist Etienne Balazs.[68] This

---

[63] *Marx Engels Werke* (Berlin 1990) Volume 28, page 254. The translation is mine.

[64] *Marx Engels Werke*, Volume 28, page 259. The translation is mine. It is striking that Marx and Engels so casually switch from those 'various parts of the Orient', to 'the Orient' and even 'the entire Orient'. For the comments on the situation in China that Marx wrote in the *New York Daily Tribune*, see Torr, *Marx on China*.

[65] I found this quote in Paine, *Sino-Japanese War*, 14–15.

[66] For this seventeenth- and eighteenth-century European 'Sinophilia', see e.g. Maverick, *China. A Model for Europe*. There of course never was an absolute dichotomy with a sharp caesura. See for nuances Jacobsen, 'Chinese influences or images?' and Millar, 'Revisiting the Sinophilia/Sinophobia dichotomy'. Not everyone in the nineteenth century had become negative about imperial China. For positive comments on the country and its economy until way in the second half of the century, see Murphey, *Outsiders*, ch. 9. With the Sino-Japanese War of 1894–5 positive remarks about the Middle Kingdom came to an abrupt end. See Paine, *Sino-Japanese War*, ch. 1.

[67] Landes, *Wealth and Poverty*, 56–7 and 341. For a comparison, or rather juxtaposition, of Europe and China, see chapters 2 and 21.

[68] Balazs, 'China as a permanently bureaucratic society' and 'Birth of capitalism in China'.

scholar has also had a pervasive influence on the man who in the West is often regarded as the most influential historian of the twentieth century, to wit, Fernand Braudel. In his work too, all the classic clichés appear to portray Qing China as 'unchanged' and 'unchanging' and claim that it had an overpowering, anti-capitalist state apparatus. According to him, in China capitalism was 'deliberately *thwarted* by the state' [Italics in the original].[69] In a popular book from 1989, his colleague Alain Peyrefitte still referred to China as 'the immobile empire' and to the British Macartney mission to China in 1792–4 as exemplifying a 'collision of civilisations'.[70] In his book on the European miracle Jones approvingly cites this quotation: 'Property is insecure. In this one phrase the whole history of Asia is contained'.[71] According to Westad, the Qing state 'aspired to control every aspect of the lives of their subjects'. He points at the 'pervasiveness' of their state and even calls it a 'police state', writing that, 'their [the Qing's] immense brutality when threatened had been seen over and again in China for more than 200 years'.[72] North, Wallis and Weingast in their *Violence and Social Orders* never refer to Qing China but it is quite clear that it would not satisfy their criteria for making the transition to an open-access-order society. Acemoglu and Robinson in their *Why Nations Fail* describe without exception Qing China as 'absolutist'.[73]

Marxists as a rule endorse this view. Immanuel Wallerstein in many respects clearly is a *neo*-Marxist, with ideas that go against the grain of orthodox classical Marxism. In his highly influential books on the modern world system, though, he takes all the classic clichés for granted when he explains why empires, of which China in his eyes is a clear example, did not develop the dynamic type of capitalism that according to him emerged in the West in the sixteenth century:

> The political centralisation of an empire was at one and the same time its strength and its weakness. Its strength lay in the fact that it guaranteed economic flows from the periphery to the centre by force (tribute and taxation) and by monopolistic advantages in trade. Its weakness lay in the fact that the bureaucracy made necessary by the political structure tended to absorb too much of the profit, especially as repression and exploitation bred revolt which increased military expenditures.[74]

As we will see later on in this text this quotation seriously misrepresents what was going on in Qing China. We even see a similar perspective in the work of Needham, the historian who has done more than anyone else to *change* the perception of China's history,

---

[69]Braudel, *History of Civilizations*, part three, ch. 2; idem, *Civilization & Capitalism, II*, 588–9; idem, *Civilization & Capitalism, III*, 520, from where I took the quote. For a critical analysis of Braudel's ideas on China see Elvin, 'Braudel and China'.

[70]Peyrefitte, *Empire Immobile*.

[71]Jones, *European Miracle*, 165. The quotation, dating from 1925, is from Reade, *Martyrdom of Man*, 108. To be fair to Jones, in the first edition of his *European Miracle* he also had positive things to say about a more 'pro-active' state and he has adjusted his perspective in later books like *Growth Recurring*.

[72]Westad, *Restless Empire*, 8–9, 20 and 50.

[73]See Acemoglu and Robinson, *Why Nations Fail*, under 'China'.

[74]Wallerstein, *Modern World-System, I*, 15.

in his specific case the history of science and technology. He was strongly influenced by historical materialism and accordingly blamed the stunted development of science in China on its 'system of bureaucratic feudalism'.[75]

Historians inspired by Marxist thought like Brenner and Isett, Gates or Mazumdar, continue to pay attention to the, in their view very big, differences between China and, in particular, Britain when it comes to their modes of production, their property relations, their agrarian class systems and the role their governments played in guaranteeing or upsetting the existing social order.[76] Their perception of differences between China's mode of production and that of Britain has been strongly influenced by the work of scholars, first and foremost Huang, who claim that China's economy was dominated by a petty peasant-household mode of production. Huang does not deny that China's economy went through a process of widespread commercialization under the Ming and especially the Qing. But in contrast to Smith and Marx, whose focus on modes of producing he, as such, shares, he thinks that because of the predominance of those peasant households as productive units this at best leads to some growth for some time, but not to development. Commercialization and the extension of the market in such a setting, so he claims, only lead to an intensification of the production process. That implies a consolidation or even a strengthening of the household mode of production instead of its dissolution. This process of intensification is bound to, in the end, lead to decreasing returns to labour inputs, a process he calls 'involution', and thereby to an economic *cul-de-sac*.[77] In the end, in this view too, China's economy is static and unable to industrialize on its own, being stuck in what Elvin has called its 'high-level equilibrium trap'.[78] Marxist analyses of various sorts, of course, find ample support in China. The persisting influence of classical Marxist ideas on the history of China, there, for example, clearly shows in the so-called 'sprouts of capitalism debate', a debate that can only be understood against the background of Marx's evolutionary view on history as a fixed succession of modes of production and that therefore focused on finding sprouts of capitalism in 'feudal' China and discovering why these sprouts never fully developed into a new mode of production.[79] The state, in all these analyses, is seen as a guarantor of the existing mode of production.

Alternative perspectives: Fiscal-militarism and mercantilism in Britain and benevolent agrarian paternalism in China

Considering the massive amount of recent research on the history of Britain as well as China, it is surprising that so many clichés from the nineteenth century continue to

---

[75]Needham, *Grand Titration*, 197. For information on Needham, see Findlay, 'China, the West, and world history', and Winchester, *Bomb, Book & Compass*.

[76]Brenner and Isett, 'England's divergence'; Gates, *China's Motor*; Isett, *State, Peasant, and Merchant*, and Mazumdar, *Sugar and Society*.

[77]Huang, *Peasant Economy and Social Change*, and idem, *Peasant Family and Rural Development*.

[78]Elvin, *Pattern of the Chinese Past*, in particular ch. 17, and idem, *Another History*, ch. 2.

[79]See Dirlik, 'Chinese historians'. For an analysis of such 'sprouts of capitalism', see Xu and Wu, *Chinese Capitalism*.

be repeated so un-critically. At least part of the explanation must be, as I have already pointed out, that they fit in so neatly with deeply held convictions of mainstream economists and politicians on what 'good governance' and an 'efficient economy' would look like. The 'Smithian' approach, however, with its focus on the market mechanism, private property and private enterprise, has never had a monopoly among Western scholars interpreting the rise of the West. It always had to compete with a more 'Marxist' approach in which 'primitive accumulation' and 'coercion', at home and abroad, figured prominently. There have always been scholars in whose work the 'visible hand' and thus, by implication, an interventionist state was regarded as a quintessential element in any explanation of the nature and causes of Western wealth. Just think of scholars like Williams, who claimed that talking about British capitalism implies talking about slavery,[80] or scholars who, to put it in Wallerstein's terms, connected the development of 'the centre' in 'the West' to the underdeveloping of 'peripheries' in 'the Rest'.[81] It was not by accident that Hobsbawm called his book on the social and economic history of Britain between 1750 and 1968 *Industry and Empire*.[82] When Patrick O'Brien claimed that in the history of Britain there have been inseparable connections between trade, economy, fiscal state and the expansion of empire, he was voicing an opinion that has been held and is still held by many. He also made it clear that one need not be a die-hard Marxist or conspicuously left-wing scholar to hold this view.[83] In particular since the publication of John Brewer's *The Sinews of Power*, the thesis that in the 'very long eighteenth century' the impact and role of the state in Britain's economy would have been fairly small has become highly contested. I have the impression that support for contesting views that regard Britain, to put it in Brewer's terms, as a fiscal-military state are on the increase.[84] In the end, of course, all states might be called fiscal-military, as a state without any economic and coercive means would not be viable. What I refer to here is the specific configuration as it existed in early modern Britain and various other parts of Western Europe, where the state first and foremost was a war machine, absorbing on a systematic basis unheard-of amounts of resources for warfare.[85] Many authors have begun to analyse British state-formation along lines similar to Brewer, which does not necessarily mean they entirely share his interpretation and evaluation, and often in a

[80]Williams, *Capitalism and Slavery*. For a discussion of William's views see Solow and Engerman, *British Capitalism and Caribbean Slavery*, and Solow, *Slavery and the Rise of the Atlantic System*. For the revival, often in a somewhat mitigated and adapted form, of the Williams thesis see, for example, Blackburn, *Making of New World Slavery*; Blaut, *Colonizer's Model*; Drayton, 'Collaboration of labour'; Frank, in most of his earlier work but also in his *ReOrient*; Inikori, *Africans and the Industrial Revolution*, and, with a particular twist, also Pomeranz, *Great Divergence*. See, for example, its introduction. The thesis that Europe 'unfairly' acquired a large part of its wealth on the back of the rest of the world has found ample support in 'textbooks' like Hobson, *Eastern Origins*; Marks, *Origins of the Modern World* and Ponting, *World History*.
[81]Wallerstein, *Modern World-System. Four Volumes*.
[82]Hobsbawm, *Industry and Empire*.
[83]O'Brien, 'Inseparable connections'.
[84]Brewer introduces the term in Brewer, *Sinews of Power*, XVII.
[85]For a discussion of the meaning of this term and of various alternatives, see Storrs, 'Fiscal-military state', 2, 9–10, 17, 47–8 and 52, and Torres Sánchez, 'Triumph of the fiscal-military state'.

certain sense have 'rehabilitated' mercantilism or rather British mercantilism in doing so. For example, Findlay and O'Rourke in their book on power and plenty are clearly torn between the, in their view, theoretical supremacy of *laissez-faire* economics and the harsh realities of early modern competition. But in the end they more or less willy-nilly conclude that mercantilism and fiscal-militarism must have paid for Great Britain:

> Universal free trade would presumably have been even better for Britain than trade with its colonies, based on costly military victories, but this was hardly a realistic alternative during the early modern period. ... To contend that the expenditures and policies of the Hanoverian state that secured this outcome [unalloyed triumph for the British in the European struggle for imperial and politico-military] nevertheless reduced the welfare of the British people seems somewhat academic, and is in any case not provable.[86]

They add that 'it seems reasonable to conclude that British military success overseas played an important role in explaining why Britain, rather than France, was so successful and precocious an industrializer.'[87] They basically endorse Ormrod's view that 'the limits to growth in the premodern period were determined by geopolitics: by state power and the extent of naval protection available for merchant shipping in distant waters.'[88] William Ashworth is very explicit and convinced:

> If there was a unique English/British pathway of industrialization, it was less a distinct entrepreneurial and technocentric culture than one predominantly defined within an institutional framework spearheaded by the excise and a wall of tariffs.

> An industrial policy revolving upon protection and the excise, coupled with the extraordinary rise of lightly taxed or untaxed goods of cotton, iron and pottery, and with rich resources of coal, had put Britain into a seemingly invincible industrial and commercial position.[89]

Elsewhere we find this quotation in which he describes Britain's industrial development as

> less the result of a distinctive indigenous mentality and the gift of mutating 'natural inquiry' into mastering nature; instead, it can be argued that it owed more to a policy of nurturing domestic industry behind a wall of tariffs, skill in imitating and subsequently transforming foreign (especially Asian) products, unparalleled exploitation of African slave labour, rich resources of coal, a monopoly of trade

---

[86]Findlay and O'Rourke, *Power and Plenty*, 351–2.
[87]Findlay and O'Rourke, *Power and Plenty*, 352.
[88]Ormrod, *Rise of Commercial Empires*, 340.
[89]See for these quotations Ashworth, *Customs and Excise*, 379 and 382.

with British North America, aggressive military prowess and, not least, a relatively efficient body for the collection of inland revenues.[90]

This is a striking, recent comment by Patrick O'Brien:

Our rhetorical and debateable speculation is that in significant respects the First Industrial Revolution can be plausibly represented as a paradigm example of successful mercantilism and that the unintended consequences of the revolution in France [massive long-lasting wars won by Britain] contributed positively and perhaps 'substantially' to its ultimate consolidation and progression.[91]

From a quite different background and perspective Prasannan Parthasarathi in his *Why Europe Grew Rich* also comes up with a rather 'positive' interpretation of the effects of mercantilism on Britain's economic development: 'The British path was a coming together of global competitive pressures, ecological shortfalls and a mercantile state.'[92]

Some social scientists hold similar views. We will see that sociologist-economist Giovanni Arrighi in 2009 in his *Adam Smith in Beijing* (and in 1994 in his *Long Twentieth Century*), in many respects harking back to ideas of Braudel and Wallerstein, assumes a prominent, active role for the state in the Western path of economic development. Political scientists Hobson and Weiss in the 1990s defended the thesis I will defend here, that '"strong" states … are vital for national economic development and industrial transformation'.[93] Industrializing Great Britain would be a clear example of such a (infrastructurally) strong state. They find support in Michal Mann's publications about the sources of social power. Even some (historical) economists are now rejecting the predominant neoclassical and neo-institutionalist perspectives on the role of the state in economic development.[94] Ha-joon Chang, Erik and Sophus Reinert are the most outspoken and the ones with the broadest historical perspective, but they certainly are not alone.[95] Several other economists have published books in which they show the fundamental importance of growth-promoting policies by states, in particular so-called developmental states.[96] Their critique is fundamental. According to Joe Studwell, founding editor of the *China Economic Quarterly*, mainstream (in his words neoclassical) economics is all but irrelevant when it comes to explaining how the developed countries in

---

[90]Ashworth, 'Revenue', 1047.
[91]See the Conclusion of O'Brien, 'Contribution of warfare'.
[92]Parthasarathi, *Why Europe Grew Rich*, 263.
[93]Weiss and Hobson, *States and Economic Development*, 1.
[94]Differences between those perspectives actually are quite marginal and much smaller than their fundamental similarities.
[95]I refer to the Bibliography for their publications.
[96]Just a personal selection of recent literature, *apart* from the literature directly referred to here: Amsden, *Rise of the 'Rest'*; Johnson, *Japan: Who Governs?*; Lindert, *Growing Public*; Mazzucato, *Entrepreneurial State*; Porter, *Competitive Advantage*; Schwartz, *States versus Markets*; Stanislaw and Yergin, *Commanding Heights*; Wade, *Governing the Market*, and Woo-Cumings, *Developmental State*.

the world actually took off.[97] In his analysis of development and non-development of Asian economies he claims

> there is no significant economy that has developed successfully through policies of free trade and deregulation from the get-go. What has always been required are pro-active interventions.[98]

'Mercantilist' policies, according to him, have played a major role during the industrialization of *all* societies that have taken off so far. No society ever became rich just confiding in *laissez-faire*. That several historians have always known this makes Studwell claim this insight presents 'the victory of the historians' over mainstream economists.[99]

In this context the role of war and violence in economic development is also receiving more attention. It is not by accident that Ronald Findlay and Kevin O'Rourke call their book on trade, war and the world economy in the second millennium *Power and Plenty*. They explicitly posit that 'no history of international trade can ignore the causes or the implications of military exploits.'[100] The greatest expansions of world trade, so they write, have tended 'to come … from the barrel of a Maxim gun, the edge of a scimitar, or the ferocity of nomadic horsemen', adding that 'For much of our period the pattern of trade can *only* [italics in original] be understood as being the outcome of some military or political equilibrium between contending powers.'[101] Some scholars claim, more specifically, that industrialization and growth in Great Britain would be closely and positively connected. In many of his studies about the fiscal-military state O'Brien seems to imply this and in various recent quotes he seems to explicitly endorse this thesis.[102] The quotes by Beckett and Turner and Neal on page 311 also are quite outspoken. The contrast with the traditional claims that wars, and in particular, the Revolutionary and Napoleonic Wars, would have crowded out growth in Great Britain could hardly be bigger.[103] Whatever one may think of these claims, N. A. M. Rodger, I think rightly, admonishes: 'It is surely time that war was ranked as an economic activity of pre-industrial Britain at least equal in importance to agriculture and foreign trade.'[104] He reminds scholars of the fact that 'At a critical early stage in the Industrial Revolution Britain fought a world war lasting almost a quarter of a century' and that 'it seems scarcely credible that the French Wars, which bore at least as heavily on the British economy as the Second World War, had no major economic consequences, or that Britain's economic and military successes were entirely unconnected.'[105] In the

---

[97]Studwell, *How Asia Works*, e.g. 59–84 and 223–6.
[98]Studwell, *How Asia Works*, 226. The author means interventions by the government.
[99]Studwell, *How Asia Works*, Part Two.
[100]Findlay and O'Rourke, *Power and Plenty*, XIX.
[101]Findlay and O'Rourke, *Power and Plenty*, XVIII and XIX.
[102]See e.g. the quote on page 20.
[103]See page 214.
[104]Rodger, 'War as an economic activity', 18.
[105]Rodger, 'War as an economic activity', 2 and 17.

social sciences too we see increasing attention to the role of violence in economic life. We will focus in this text on the ideas of Arrighi.[106]

Many historians who study early modern Western Europe tend to no longer minimize the impact and active role of the state in the economic history of that part of the world. Even authors like James Bradford DeLong, Niall Ferguson, Jack Goldstone, Deirdre McCloskey, Joel Mokyr or John Nye, who are much less positive about the growth-enhancing potential of mercantilist policies by fiscal-military states, admit that early modern Britain indeed was such a state, at least till the end of the Napoleonic Wars.

Among historians studying Qing China one also finds shifting opinions. Here we see a development in the 'opposite' direction: to wit, a tendency to picture the role of the (Chinese) state as *less* important, which means, in this particular case, less oppressive and less opposed to economic development. The old standard view of China as an 'oriental' society ruled by a despotic elite that was constantly interfering in societal life, including the economy, is becoming less popular. Several scholars were already aware decades ago that imperial China under Ming but especially Qing was not at all suffering under an oriental despotic regime but was rather under-governed.[107] Many scholars no longer believe that the rulers of Qing China were 'anti-trade' and 'anti-traders' and had turned China into a kind of 'command-economy'. What we witness is major shift. As far as I can see, the *dominant* interpretation has now become one in which the policies of China's central government can best be described as a kind of 'agrarian paternalism'.[108] According to this view, China's domestic economy, with its many small producers and consumers, its extremely large number of markets and its substantial level of market integration, basically operated along 'Smithian' lines. China during the long eighteenth century is considered to have been a commercialized market economy – or as Adam Smith would say, 'a commercial society' – with government only interfering in the market mechanism when it feared that 'people's livelihood' was endangered.[109] It is now claimed in the work of Bin Wong, to mention one example among many, that when it comes to economic life, China's government was not erratically despotic but 'benevolent' and quite efficient. It did have a certain agenda and certain priorities, first and foremost agriculture, in which security and wealth of the people prevailed over individual freedom, and it undoubtedly wanted to control or at least monitor and 'manage' certain aspects of public life. But when

---

[106]See e.g. pages 212–16 and 315–17.

[107]See Jones, *European Miracle*, second edition, ch. 11, and *Growth Recurring*, ch. 8, for that thesis and for references.

[108]Many people held this view before the big change in the European image of China in the nineteenth century. In their view China came much closer to a '*laissez-faire* economy' than Europe. See Gerlach, 'Wu-wei in Europe' and Jacobsen, 'Chinese influences or images?'. For 'agrarian paternalist' interpretations of the Qing state, I refer, in alphabetical order, to Antony and Leonard, *Dragons, Tigers, and Dogs*; Deng, *China's Political Economy*; Dunstan, *State and Merchant* and *Conflicting Counsels*; Leonard and Watt, *To Achieve Security and Wealth*; Pines, *Everlasting Empire*; Will, 'Chine moderne' and 'Développement quantitatif'; Will and Wong, *Nourish the People*, and, Wong, *China Transformed*; idem, 'Taxation and good governance' and, together with Rosenthal, *Before and beyond Divergence*. The view that Qing China was not a 'totalitarian', 'absolutist', oppressive state but rather 'benevolent' and later on 'weak' has found its way into many 'textbooks'. See e.g. Crossley, *Wobbling Pivot*; Deng, *China's Political Economy*, and Rowe, *China's Last Empire*.

[109]For Smith's concept of a commercial society, see Macfarlane, *Riddle of the Modern World*, part II.

its main priorities were not in danger, its economic policy is believed to have normally been one of 'leaving well alone'. Proponents of this view seem to admit that this basically implied a conservative attitude, which was more oriented towards preservation than change. Will admits this strategy, in all probability, would lead to 'quantitative growth' rather than to 'qualitative development', whereas according to Wong, 'The Chinese state aimed for and to some degree achieved its goal of static efficiency; that is, spreading the best techniques available across a vast area'. This goal, according to him, made sense 'in a world of limited possibilities' even though it contrasted with what Europeans wanted 'competition and growth'.[110] At times, however, revisionists go further in their claims. Peter Perdue claims: 'The capabilities of the Qing to manage the economy were powerful enough that we might even call it a "developmental agrarian state."'[111] In their *Before and Beyond Divergence*, published in 2011, Rosenthal and Wong write, 'Early modern Chinese political economy was more explicitly intended to foster economic growth than European political economies' and go even as far as claiming 'if there was a state that sponsored economic development anywhere in the eighteenth century, it was the Qing state, not Britain, France or any other European state'.[112] In that same book they dedicate an entire chapter (chapter 3) to explaining that China's informal mechanisms would be just as efficient as the formal mechanisms highlighted in stories about Europe's economic rise and indicate, as many scholars do at the moment,[113] that property was far less insecure in China than is always suggested in classic stories about 'oriental despotism'.

An integral part of the standard Western view of the role of China's imperial government in economic life was the conviction that this government preferred to keep China's economy closed to foreign goods and people, especially when they came from the West. No one, of course, has ever denied that China had extensive economic relations with other countries. But the dominant interpretation has long been that (much of) the exchange of goods that did take place between China and other countries should not be regarded as normal 'trade' but rather as 'tribute'.[114] Now that supposed difference too is strongly disputed. Many publications dealing with this topic claim that what went by the name of, or under the cover of, 'tribute' often simply was trade.[115] That does not mean, though, that the 'tribute system' concept would have completely disappeared. There are several influential scholars who clearly think it refers to an important reality in the history of early modern China.[116] The idea that China's imperial government would

---

[110]Wong, *China Transformed*, 280.

[111]Perdue, *China Marches West*, 541.

[112]See also Wong's recent 'Taxation and good governance'.

[113]See pages 64–6.

[114]See for this classic view Fairbank and Teng, 'On the Ch'ing tributary system'.

[115]Many scholars no longer believe in the existence of a Chinese tribute system. See, in alphabetical order, Blussé, *Visible Cities*, 11; Millward, *Beyond the Pass*, under 'tribute system'; idem, *Eurasian Crossroads*, 70–4, and Perdue, *China Marches West*, 402. For helpful comments see Deng, 'Foreign staple trade'.

[116]For a description of the working of the Chinese tribute system by a scholar who does believe it exists, although he is much less outspoken than Fairbank and Teng in contrasting and separating trade from tribute, see the work of Hamashita as compiled by Grove and Selden and his 'Introduction', written together with Arrighi and Selden. See further e.g. Kang, *East Asia before the West*, and Wang, *White Lotus Rebels and South China Pirates*.

constantly interfere in foreign trade is rejected as well. That view is now increasingly regarded as a consequence of the almost exclusive focus on Sino-Western contacts in Western scholarship. A tendency to intervene, supervise and sometimes even control those contacts may indeed have existed. But one should realize that very often there was a wide gap between words – that is official policies – and reality. More importantly, Sino-Western trade was only a (small) part of China's total trade and the rest of that trade is claimed to, overall, have been fairly free from government interference. Again, revisionism is quite radical. According to Roy Bin Wong 'The Chinese state in contrast [i.e. to states in Western Europe,] did little to impede either domestic or foreign trade.'[117] He claims 'the Chinese state's policies toward long-distance trade, both domestic and foreign, promoted Smithian growth in ways that exceeded contemporary European practices.' He even goes as far as to suggest that merchants in the West were more heavily taxed and preyed upon than their Chinese counterparts.[118]

In mainstream historiography the (presumed) closed-door policy of China's government has long been regarded as a simple 'extension' of that government's xenophobic and closed world-view in which autarky and self-centredness figured prominently. In almost every Western text on the subject, one came, and often still comes, across the famous words of the Qianlong Emperor, in the letter he sent to King George III in the wake of the Macartney Mission. They are supposed to epitomize China's rejection of foreign goods: 'The productions of our Empire are manifold, and in great abundance; nor do we stand in the least need of the produce of other countries.'[119] An edict by the same emperor to King George III, moreover, read: 'we have never valued ingenious articles, nor do we have the slightest need of your country's manufactures.'[120] One can easily collect many similar quotes.[121] It is not by accident that, for example, Landes and Peyrefitte extensively refer to the failure of this mission. Now various Western historians writing about Qing China deny that China would have been self-centred and closed, even when it comes to people and ideas from the West. Joanna Waley-Cohen, for example, writes: 'From the late sixteenth to the late eighteenth century, then, Chinese were extremely interested in Europe and all it had to offer.'[122] John Hobson in a way goes even further and now claims that what we see in the

---

[117]See his 'Role of the Chinese state', 20.

[118]See his 'Role of the Chinese state', 18.

[119]See for this translation Morse, *Chronicles of the East India Company*, II, 248.

[120]See Cranmer-Byng, *Embassy to China*, 340.

[121]Let me just give a couple of extra examples. In the preface to a volume on geography in *Notes on All Documents in the Qing Dynasty*, edited during the Qianlong period, it reads: 'China is located at the centre of the earth and surrounded by seas. Overseas countries are considered to be marginal ones.' See for this quotation Zhuang, *Tea, Silver, Opium and War*, 21. By the same Qianlong emperor there also is this quotation: 'The Celestial Court possesses all things in prolific abundance and lacks nothing within my territory. The reason that I permit foreigners to come to trade in my country is only because I wish to display my kindness to the people from remote regions' (ibid., 165). For more examples of sinocentrism by Chinese rulers see ibid., 15.

[122]Waley-Cohen, *Sextants of Beijing*, 128. See also her 'China and western technology', and Zurndorfer, 'Sinologie immobile'.

early modern period is not a 'closed' China refusing to learn from a superior Europe, but on the contrary, a backward Europe that borrowed many things from a China that indeed was 'superior' and did not *need* any 'support' from Western civilization.[123]

Further revisionism: Early modern parallels in state-building and the creating of empire

Among specialists a much more varied, if not outright confusing, picture of the British and Chinese states in the early modern world has emerged. At least two quite differing pictures of Britain's state can be discerned: one that shows Britain at the time as a state clearly *heading* for *laissez-faire*, another one emphasizing that what really characterized Britain until the 1840s were its extended fiscal and military apparatus and its mercantilist policies.[124] When it comes to China, the idea of an Oriental despotic state certainly lingers on in some circles, but here the idea of China as an 'agrarian paternalist' polity has become increasingly popular, not to say dominant, at least among sinologists. Roy Bin Wong, who without any doubt is one of the most influential authors when it comes to describing China's political economy in agrarian paternalist terms, actually does so in a sustained effort to focus on the *differences* in state-formation between Western Europe and China, while subscribing to the 'Californian' view that differences in the level of economic development between advanced regions in Western Europe and advanced regions in China were minimal. In his view, and in that of many other scholars, institutional differences did not make much of a difference for the economies of the two regions *before* industrialization. He and Rosenthal in their *Before and Beyond Divergence* do admit that clear institutional differences existed but they fiercely oppose the suggestion that there might have been anything 'superior' in Western cultural or institutional arrangements and explicitly favour an approach that 'eliminates all possible arguments that make European cultural or political arrangements superior to those found in China'.[125] In their view 'early modern Chinese political economy was more explicitly intended to foster economic growth than European political economies'.[126]

When it comes to state-formation and nation-building, Evelyn Rawski points to what she sees as clear parallels; according to her in both Western Europe and China during the early modern era there occurred an increase in state revenues, territorial consolidation, administrative centralization and cultural convergence.[127] In his *China Marches West*, Peter Perdue writes that it is not very enlightening to, as has long been the case, contrast early Qing China as an isolated empire with Europe as an expanding system of states: 'The early Qing Empire, then, was not an isolated, stable, united "Oriental empire", but an

---

[123]Hobson, *Eastern Origins*.
[124]Great Britain's state actually had *two* faces, depending on whether one looks at the way it handled domestic affairs or at the handling of matters that pertained to Britain's position in Europe and the wider world.
[125]Rosenthal and Wong, *Before and Beyond Divergence*, 101.
[126]Rosenthal and Wong, *Before and Beyond Divergence*, 209.
[127]Rawski, 'Qing formation'.

evolving state structure engaged in mobilisation for expansionist warfare.'[128] According to him it would be a mistake to continue to use 'the models that argue for distinctive features of a European state system, marked by pluralism, competition, or special core-periphery structures' and then 'draw an oversimplified contrast between Western Europe and the rest of the Eurasian world.'[129] For the period up until the 1750s, he sees similar interactions between commercial exchange and military force across the entire Eurasian continent. It is only from then onwards, so he claims, that developments in China and the West did indeed begin to diverge and clear differences did become visible. With the delimitation of a fixed border with Russia and the elimination of the Zunghar Mongol state in the 1760s, according to him, China's rulers felt they had finished their state-building project and it was only then that, while no longer facing threats from the Central Eurasian steppe, that their empire lost dynamism and flexibility.[130] John Darwin in his book on the global history of empire is also keen to point out that differences between what went on in Europe and in Asia were not that big: 'State-building and cultural innovation were striking features of Eurasian, not just European, history in the early modern era.'[131] Wenkai He in his comparison of institutional development in the field of public finance in England (1642–1753), Japan (1868–95), and China (1850–1911) also tends to lean towards emphasizing resemblances rather than differences. He clearly is aware of existing differences and focuses on different outcomes: the emergence of a modern centralized fiscal state in England and Japan in contrast to its non-emergence in Qing China. But he starts with a pages-long introduction focusing on the comparability of England, Japan and China in terms of their state-formation.[132] Among the 'revisionists' Goldstone seems to hold a minority view with his claim that the British state became something quite exceptional and that this did matter a lot.[133]

The functioning of China's bureaucracy too seems to be undergoing re-evaluation. As with so many aspects of the history of late imperial China, it has been described in surprisingly dissenting terms and been the object of surprisingly differing assessments, ranging from often quite positive ones in the early modern era, to negative ones during most of the nineteenth and twentieth centuries, and again much more positive ones during roughly the last twenty years. In the eighteenth century, at the height of Enlightenment 'Sinophilia', China's system of rule by gentry scholars had been widely admired in certain circles and regarded as much more rational, or if you like 'modern', than Western systems of administration. In Europe, overall, by far the majority of 'public' jobs were still firmly in the hands of 'non-professionals': aristocrats who claimed their jobs by birth; people who had bought them and often managed to pass them down to one of their children; or, especially on a regional and local level, people who did some public work without any or with hardly any remuneration and qualification, just as a kind of 'civic

---

[128]Perdue, *China Marches West*, chs 15 and 16n. The quotation is on page 527.
[129]Perdue, *China Marches West*, 527.
[130]Perdue, *China Marches West*, 550–1.
[131]Darwin, *After Tamerlane*, 104.
[132]He, *Paths toward the Modern Fiscal State*, ch. 1.
[133]Goldstone, *Why Europe*, ch. 6.

duty' or 'civic honour'. It can hardly come as a surprise that, as compared to the highly *un*-professional system that characterized most of *Ancien Régime* Western Europe, many Europeans regarded China's system as superior. There, at least, people were employed who had to qualify for their jobs and who actually worked for the government instead of for themselves. Many Europeans thought China's civil administration examination system was an example to be imitated.[134]

This positive image did disappear with the disintegration and erosion of Qing rule that became increasingly obvious with the passing of the nineteenth century. Among scholars it was probably Max Weber's analysis in particular that put China's officials in a less positive light through his claim that, some appearances notwithstanding, according to his ideal-type, they were *not* 'real' bureaucrats and China's system of administration *not* a 'real' bureaucracy. Weber clearly was aware that China's administration with its examination system presented a break with feudalism and characterized it as a 'patrimonial bureaucracy' in which social rank, at his time for already twelve centuries, was determined 'more by qualification for office than by wealth'. He even goes as far as to claim that, in strictly formal terms, China had been 'the most perfect example of a typically modern pacified and bureaucratic society'.[135] He, however, was quite adamant that, as he calls it – probably not very helpfully – 'the spirit' of bureaucratic work differed widely in 'the East' and in 'the West'. The Confucian gentlemen who ruled China were not and did not want to be specialists. They did not receive specialist education and were not trained to become professionals in a rational, utilitarian organization. They, still according to Weber, did not function in a system with a clear division of labour and a clear delineation of competences. The bulk of their income was irregular; that is it did not consist in official remunerations. What in his view is even more important is that they clearly were not operating in a rational legal system.[136] Weber's views became extremely influential. Many comparisons have been made between China and Europe that use his ideas as point of departure or even as a measuring rod and they all tended to conclude that China indeed was different and 'less' bureaucratic than Western countries.[137] Weber, so to say, studied the *theory* of Chinese administration and found it defective. Authors who were more interested in its *practice* also became less impressed. They began to refer to a lack of efficiency and widespread corruption. The alternative image of imperial China as an inefficient and corrupt polity clearly gained in popularity with the passing of time.

Here too the tide has, again, turned. A recent example is the book by Alexander Woodside on the bureaucratic politics of pre-industrial China, Vietnam and Korea with

---

[134]See for the way in which those exams were regarded in Western public opinion Jacobsen, 'Chinese influences or images', 632–4. For actual Chinese influence on the reform of Britain's civil service see Chang, 'China and English Civil Service reform', and Wong, *Deadly Dreams*, 161. A report presented in 1853 finally led to the adoption of examinations for entry into the civil service of the United Kingdom. They were based on knowledge of the Roman and Greek classics and mathematics.

[135]These quotations are respectively from the opening sentence of chapter 5 in his *Religion of China* and from page 610 of his *Wirtschaft und Gesellschaft*. The translation of the second quotation into English is mine.

[136]For Weber's point of view I refer to his *Religion of China*, in particular Part Two, and to his *Wirtschaft und Gesellschaft* under 'China'. For an analysis, see Van der Sprenkel, 'Max Weber on China'.

[137]See Reed, *Talons and Teeth*, ch. 1, and Yang, 'Some characteristics'.

the revealing title *Lost Modernities*. In this book the author, as he claims, sets out to recover one of (what he claims are) the multiple sources of modernity and finds it in the way in which these countries were, already in the early modern era, looking for – and to an unprecedented way even actually creating – a merit-based bureaucracy. He claims that China, and Japan and Korea, were 'postfeudal' long before Western Europe and had rationalized their system of government by training their government officials long before any effort was made to create a merit-based administrative structure in the West. This makes him conclude that 'rationalization', a phenomenon that, ever since Weber, plays such a central role in studies dealing with global history, is a manifold process that can take different shapes in different contexts. Processes of rationalization, moreover, may occur independently of each other. According to him, the existence of what he calls 'East Asian mandarinates' shows that the differences between the 'traditional' and the 'modern' have been exaggerated and ought to put an end to one civilization's (i.e., of course, the West's) historical self-centredness. This obligatory and ritualistic attack on the self-centredness of the West, which always leaves me somewhat bewildered when it is performed by people who study 'the Middle Kingdom' or 'all under heaven', does not mean that Woodside would ignore the hazards and weaknesses of the 'mandarinate' system. Quite the contrary, he gives us a very informative and insightful analysis of, in particular, its feeble capacity to mobilize the population for collective purposes. But overall his tone is one of showing East Asia's precocious political modernity and of proudly pointing at its education-based governments of talents.[138] Peter Perdue apparently agrees and claims Woodside's book 'punctures Western pretensions by showing that East Asian societies anticipated contemporary controversies over bureaucracy, meritocracy and social welfare'.[139] Roy Bin Wong, too, has no qualms about describing Qing China's administration as a bureaucracy and in his *China Transformed* explicitly writes about the 'bureaucratic' way in which the empire was ruled.[140] On top of that, according to him, China's bureaucracy was not just like any other bureaucracy at the time. He claims that it 'certainly [was] the world's largest eighteenth-century civilian state operation'.[141] In that respect he and Wensheng Wang, who is much less positive about its actual functioning, seem to agree. Wang describes Qing China under the Yongzheng and Qianlong emperors as a 'highly interventionist state' with a 'vast bureaucracy'.[142] As such, that of course need not imply it was efficient and powerful. Wong, however, clearly thinks it was: 'The Chinese state developed an infrastructural capacity to mobilize and disburse revenues quite beyond the imagination, let alone the abilities, of European state makers at the moment.'[143] In his view it would be a major mistake to regard Qing

---

[138]Woodside, *Lost Modernities*, 'Introduction' and 'Conclusion'.

[139]See for this comment the back flap of Woodside's book.

[140]See e.g. Wong, *China Transformed*, 134, 157 and 282.

[141]Wong, 'Changing fiscal regime', 14. For a comparison with several European states that does not corroborate Wong's claim see chapter 4.

[142]Wang, *White Lotus Rebels and South China Pirates*, 257. See also ibid., 33.

[143]Wong, *China Transformed*, 132. See also Epstein, who writes about the 'apparently high degree of fiscal efficiency in pre-modern China'. Epstein, 'Rise of the West', 248.

China as something of a 'failed bureaucratic state' (or for that matter as an example of oriental despotism). He, time and again, claims that the Qing state showed 'commitments to material welfare beyond anything imaginable, let alone achieved, in Europe'[144] and that 'The ambit of Chinese imperial authority and power stretched far beyond those of European states in spatial scale and substantive variety.'[145] He is impressed in particular by imperial China's state-sponsored granaries for famine relief and claims: 'To think of state concerns for popular welfare as a very recent political practice makes sense only if we again limit ourselves to Western examples.'[146] In his co-edited volume with Will (1991), he had already written: 'European states failed to promote granaries and other food supply policies found in China to ease subsistence anxieties.'[147] On top of that, he suggests that in Europe states lacked a 'deep concern with elite and popular education and morality … and … [an] invasive curiosity about and anxiety over potentially subversive behaviour.'[148]

Almost all quotations in the previous paragraph were from Wong's *China Transformed*, but Wong clearly has not changed his opinions since and continues to claim that social government expenditures in Qing China were substantially higher than was usual in Europe until the late nineteenth century and that this was caused by its many 'paternalistic' practices.[149] In his recent *Before and Beyond Divergence*, he and Rosenthal still claim 'the rulers of the Middle Kingdom seem to have spent considerably more resources on public goods than any European ruler.'[150]

What makes these views interesting and relevant is that they have become widely accepted as unquestioned truths. It will not come as a surprise that Pierre-Étienne Will agrees with his one-time co-author. Before publishing *China Transformed*, Wong, together with Will and a couple of other authors, had already written a book on civilian granaries and food redistribution in Qing China. In that book, they both were quite optimistic about the capacities and efficiency of China's administrative system when it came to food distribution for the largest part of the eighteenth century.[151] One can also encounter this positive view in two articles Will wrote for the famous French journal *Annales* in 1994.[152] In the first one, on modern China and sinology, we find a critique of Max Weber for having denied other civilizations the aptitude to create institutions capable of rendering services similar to those provided for by bureaucracies in the West and with the potential to evolve in a similar direction. Will points at various parallels, convergences and structural similarities in the construction of modern states

---

[144]Wong, *China Transformed*, 98–9.

[145]Wong, *China Transformed*, 103.

[146]Wong, *China Transformed*, 98–9.

[147]Wong on page 521 in a contribution of his to Will and Wong, *Nourish the People*.

[148]Wong, *China Transformed*, 103 and 101.

[149]See e.g. Wong, 'Relationships between the political economies', 30–1, and idem, 'Politiques de dépenses', 1408.

[150]Rosenthal and Wong, *Before and beyond Divergence*, 173.

[151]I refer to Will and Wong, *Nourish the People*. Before that, Will had already written, in the same vein, *Bureaucratie et famine*.

[152]Will, 'Chine moderne et sinologie' and 'Développement quantitatif'.

in China and in Europe at the level of institutions and regulations and thinks it was not by accident that up until the nineteenth century and, in some cases even longer, China's state had been praised as rational. China's early modern state reminds him of the '*état technocratique*' of France after the French Revolution. He does not recoil from calling China's state and economy 'modern' from the beginning of the sixteenth century onwards. Here too we find the claim that when it comes to economic security and social protection early modern China had developed institutions that have to be regarded as precursors of arrangements that states in Europe were only to develop much later.[153] The comments made so far were from Will's first article in *Annales*. In his second publication he appears to be somewhat less 'optimist' about the actual grip of central government on China's society at large and suggests that the actual administrating of that society in most respects was done primarily at the local level. But even so the impression he gives of the situation in the eighteenth century is one of an administration that clearly is not so much defective as simply setting itself different goals and working under differing constraints – external as well as self-imposed – than governments in the West. What he wants to bring across is an image of a basically conservative government that does its best to improve society without basically changing it, not an image of plain inefficiency and corruption.[154]

Woodside in his recent study of East Asian 'mandarinates' explicitly and in full agreement refers to the statements by Wong that I quoted earlier.[155] Hoffman, Postel-Vinay and Rosenthal, writing about the early modern period, claim, as if it is a matter of proven fact and referring to Will and Wong: 'China spent … more [than Europe] on what we might call public welfare. … [It] devoted far more of its resources to famine relief … than did European states.' Their additional comment that Imperial China had developed a tax bureaucracy that transferred tax revenues 'on a scale unheard of in Europe' can hardly come as a surprise.[156] Martin Jacques in his recent book on the rise of the Middle Kingdom fully endorses every claim Wong has made about the efficient, bureaucratic welfare state of the Qing.[157] Kent Deng, who rejects many claims of the Californians, does not hesitate to refer very positively to the 'proto-welfare systems' of the Qing state in its heydays.[158] Robert Marks in this context writes about 'an impressive state relief system' and claims that: 'Given [its] impressive relief credentials, it probably never occurred to the Qing state that the preservation of forests could function as a life preserver for the rural population in times of crisis.'[159] Mathias Heinrich, in an article on welfare and public philanthropy in Qing China, writes: 'the Qing government

---

[153]All these rather upbeat characterizations do not imply that Will would be indifferent to differences. He emphasizes that Qing China did not develop into a fiscal-military state and that taxation was and continued to be strikingly low and strikingly stable. The implications of that fact, however, are not addressed.

[154]Will, 'Développement quantitatif'. I refer the reader interested in the practice of China's bureaucracy also to Will, 'Bureaucratie officielle et bureaucratie réelle'.

[155]Woodside, *Lost Modernities*, 56. See also Woodside, 'Ch'ien-lung reign', 307.

[156]Hoffman, Postel-Vinay and Rosenthal, *Surviving Large Losses*, 16.

[157]Jacques, *When China Rules the World*, 81–6.

[158]Deng, *China's Political Economy*, 19–24.

[159]Marks, *China. Its Environment and History*, 254.

created a complex system of social welfare which dwarfs those of Western pre-modern states.'[160] In 2001 Peter Perdue had written: 'In some ways imperial policies then look precociously modern. Qing China's welfare policies, for example (orphanages and famine relief) and price regulation with ever-normal granaries, exceeded those of most European states until the mid-twentieth century.'[161] Let me give one last quotation, by Jeremy Black, who makes this comment on early modern states: 'Central government meant, in most countries, the monarch and a small group of advisers and officials. The notion that they were capable of creating the basis of a modern state is misleading, although an exception may be suggested for China where the resources and scale of government were greater.'[162]

The system of rule of Qing China is now often described in more positive terms. Madeleine Zelin, for example, in the *Cambridge History of China* writes: 'The policies undertaken during the Yung-cheng reign [1723–35] laid the foundations for the development of a strong, modern state apparatus in the eighteenth century.'[163] Patricia Thornton agrees that those policies were important and innovative, but thinks their impact was not lasting.[164] William Rowe in his book on Chen Hongmou describes Qing China as 'a Confucian, imperial, centralized bureaucracy'.[165] Scholars, however, who quite some time ago were positive about the organization of the Qing state and its performance, normally tended to become far more pessimistic when discussing the period from the end of the reign of the Qianlong emperor. Many, if not most, scholars used to share the opinion that in the beginning of the nineteenth century China's administration was in disarray.[166] Voices have been raised that even this view would be too bleak.[167]

Even the infamous 'country clerks' and 'runners' of the Qing administration are to a certain extent rehabilitated. In as far as our sources, which normally have been written by members of the gentry and officials who tended to look down upon them, can be trusted, they were widely despised and hated during the Qing reign and as a rule regarded as corrupt, inefficient and rapacious. 'All the recent suffering under Heaven is caused by clerks,' a nineteenth-century commentator wrote.[168] It became a standard trope in Qing bureaucratic discourse to describe them and the runners as 'millions of tigers and wolves'. The problem of disciplining this 'sub-bureaucracy' became perhaps the single central theme of all Qing administrative writing.[169] In historiography they fared

---

[160]Heinrich, 'Welfare and public philanthropy', 126.

[161]Perdue, 'Empire and nation', 301.

[162]Black, *Power of Knowledge*, 122. See also ibid, 166.

[163]Zelin, 'Yung-cheng reign', 228.

[164]Thornton, *Disciplining the State*, 69.

[165]Rowe, *Saving the World*, 326.

[166]For the standard 'declinist' view on the history of China from the end of the rule of the Qianlong emperor onwards, see Mann Jones and Kuhn, 'Dynastic decline'.

[167]See for an overview Wang, *White Lotus Rebels and South China Pirates*, and the literature referred to there on pages 1–34.

[168]Reed, *Talons and Teeth*, 1.

[169]I paraphrase Rowe, *Saving the World*, 339.

hardly any better for a long time: 'the evil clerk or runner [figured] as the stock villain on the stage of local government.'[170] Now, dissenting voices make themselves heard, in particular in Bradley Reed's book.[171] This author of course cannot deny that most of what they did in the literal sense of the word probably was 'illegal' and that various forms of what we would now call 'corruption' were rife. But he points at the fact that those runners and clerks simply had to find ways of earning their income. As a rule they did not receive an official salary and, as they did not have an official job with all the rules and regulation that we associate with that, they simply had to improvise and behave 'extra-legal' or 'a-legal'. Moreover, whatever their exact position and behaviour, they simply were indispensable. Reed describes them as 'illicit bureaucrats' and writes about their activities in terms of 'the legitimacy of the indispensable'.[172]

A final example of the 'upgrading' of China's state, in this case to a large extent by 'downplaying' what had happened in Europe, can be found in the book by Victoria Tin-bor Hui on war and state-formation in ancient China and early modern Europe. Although she only refers to the situation in ancient China (i.e. China from 656–221 BC), this book too can be seen as part and parcel of a 'rehabilitation' of China's process of state-formation in that period and later on. She presents – to me quite surprising – the claim that state-formation in early modern Europe would have been characterized by what she calls 'self-weakening' expedients. The most important of those expedients are the use of military entrepreneurs and mercenaries, of tax farming and the sale of public offices. Her rehabilitation, so to say, primarily is *a contrario*. She claims that what was happening in early modern Europe was not exactly impressive and clearly fell short of what had been happening in China for many centuries. She characterizes developments in early modern Europe as state *de*formation. She suggests that in early modern Europe central authority would have been increasingly eroded by intermediate power-holders and thus monopolization of the means of coercion proved to be impossible, the rationalization and nationalization of taxation got derailed and bureaucratization of administration was negated. This definitely is a highly original interpretation of the history of the state in Europe between the later Middle Ages and Waterloo.[173]

Some authors would even want to include imperialism in their list of 'striking [Eurasian] resemblances'. This would imply that Qing China was quite successful when it comes to the wielding of power against other countries. Here too one comes across examples of radical revisionism. Jeremy Black, expert in the field of military history,

---

[170]Reed, *Talons and Teeth*, 252.

[171]Reed, *Talons and Teeth*.

[172]Reed, *Talons and Teeth*, ch. 7.

[173]Hui, *War and State Formation*, 49, table 5. The author declares she has written her book to challenge the presumption that Europe was *destined* to enjoy checks and balances while China was *preordained* to suffer under a coercive universal empire. See page III. (The italics are mine.) I have never read a text containing those presumptions. Perdue describes her book as a 'superb demonstration of how comparative analysis of Europe and China can point the way to more adequate theories and better-informed history'. See his review.

in a book about warfare in the eighteenth century, makes the following claim: 'The most dynamic state and the most successful military power in the world, on land, was China.'[174] Evelyn Rawski does not recoil from explicitly claiming that Qing China, again just like Western nations, was imperialist: 'In the early modern historiography, the omission of the expanding empires, such as the Habsburgs in Eastern Europe, the Russian Empire, or the Qing Empire, reflects a persistent western Eurocentric bias.'[175] She even complains that an 'odd historiographical bias that assigns "imperialism" and "colonialism" to Europe and "empire building" to the Chinese, Zulus and others' privileges Europe. That would be because 'colonialism is deemed to be one of the global forces that have defined the modern age [whereas] empires are seen as modes of state expansion that are increasingly anachronistic in an era of industrialization and high technology.'[176] Paraphrasing Adas, she writes, that 'Manchu (Qing) imperialism shared many parallels with the British, French and Dutch colonialism in South and Southeast Asia.'[177] Darwin seems to agree: 'It would be a mistake to draw too sharp a distinction between "European" methods and "Asian".'[178] When comparing the Qing Empire to the Mughal, Muscovy-Romanov, Ottoman and British empires, Rowe claims: 'We are now struck less by the differences than by the common features of their imperial ambitions.'[179] Laura Hostetler writes that she wants 'to highlight the similarities between the methods, technologies and ideologies that the Qing Empire employed in extending its geographical reach, and those used by European colonial powers during the same period'.[180] Arrighi in his *Adam Smith in Beijing*, while pointing out several important differences between the European and the East Asian interstate system nevertheless calls them both 'state-systems' and considers them similar enough to make a comparison of them analytically meaningful.[181] Qing imperialism and the relations between Manchus, Han and other inhabitants of the Qing Empire have become very popular subjects.[182] Even though authors like Adas and Arrighi in their work emphasize that some quite substantial differences existed between Qing China's imperialism and that of the nations of Western Europe, the tendency to focus on similarities at the moment is predominant.

---

[174]Black, *Warfare in the Eighteenth Century*, 31.

[175]Rawski, 'Qing formation', 209.

[176]Rawski, 'Qing formation', 220.

[177]Rawski, 'Qing formation', 221. She refers to Adas, 'Imperialism and colonialism'.

[178]Darwin, *After Tamerlane*, 493.

[179]Rowe, *China's Last Empire*, 73. On page 7 of that book he calls those empires 'effectively similar'.

[180]Hostetler, *Qing Colonial Enterprise*, 30. She refers to the eighteenth century.

[181]Arrighi, *Adam Smith in Beijing*, 314–5.

[182]For further examples see, in alphabetical order: Christian, *History of Russia, Central Asia and Mongolia*; Dabringhaus, *Qing-Imperium*; Dai, *Sichuan Frontier and Tibet*; Giersch, *Asian Borderlands*; Herman, *Amid the Clouds and Mist*; Isett, *State, Peasant, and Merchant*; Lee, *Political Economy of a Frontier*; Millward, *Beyond the Pass* and *Eurasian Crossroads*; Perdue, 'Erasing the empire'; idem, 'Nature and nurture'; idem, *China Marches West*; Richards, *Unending Frontier*; Rhoads, *Manchus and Han*; Shepherd, *Statecraft and Political Economy*; Siu and Sutton, *Empire at the Margins*, and Teng, *Taiwan's Imagined Geography*. For review articles see Guy, 'Who were the Manchus?' and Supdita, 'New frontiers'.

BRINGING THE STATE BACK IN

Abandoning the notion of universally grasping authoritarian regimes that quashed all prospects of growth … we arrive at the possibility that pre-modern regimes were too indolent, unknowing and ill equipped to bring about growth.

Jones, *Growth Recurring*, 132

Capitalism only triumphs when it becomes identified with the state, when it is the state.

Braudel, *Afterthoughts*, 64–5

'Bringing the state back in' has been quite popular for some time now.[183] In classic social science it of course has never been completely absent. Both Marx and Weber considered the state as a fundamental ingredient in the emergence and persistence of capitalism that in their view epitomized Western economic exceptionalism. For them its role was certainly not confined to that of a night-watchman. In *Capital* Marx emphasized the importance of actions taken by the state in the process of 'primitive accumulation' that according to him is at the basis of the emergence of capitalism, and in the *Communist Manifesto* he explicitly referred to the role of government as 'a committee for managing the common affairs of the whole bourgeoisie'.[184] Max Weber repeatedly pointed at the fact that capitalism and the modern bureaucratic state presupposed each other and went as far as to make the following claim:

This competition [between competing national states] created the best chances for modern capitalism in the West. Every single state had to compete for the mobile capital that dictated the conditions under which it was willing to bring it to power. This enforced alliance with capital produced the national citizenry, the bourgeoisie in the modern sense of the word. Therefore it is the closed national state that guarantees capitalism its chances of continued existence: as long as it does not cede to a global empire, capitalism will exist too.[185]

Braudel, who also has become a classic over the decades, was very outspoken too, as the quote at the start of this section shows. All three of them, moreover, agreed that the state of imperial China was not exactly helpful when it came to promoting modern growth and development, if it was not actually hampering it. Wallerstein, not yet a 'classic', would agree on both accounts.

In (neo)classical mainstream economics the rational *homo economicus* as a free individual clearly occupied centre stage ever since its practitioners started thinking they

---

[183]This expression was coined by Evans, Rueschemeyer and Skocpol, *Bringing the State Back In*.
[184]See Marx, *Capital, I*, chs 26–33, and Marx and Engels, *Communist Manifesto*, 82.
[185]Weber, *Wirtschaftsgeschichte*, 288–9. The translation is mine.

were scientists. In their view the ideal role of the state could hardly be regarded as other than 'facilitating'. Economists like Rostow and, even more, Gerschenkron, who actually studied development, never lost sight of the actually far bigger importance of the state for economic development. In current debates most economists seem to agree that, at least when it comes to long-run development and growth, institutions 'rule'.[186] That suggests a very important, though in the end mostly still only facilitating, role for the state. I have already pointed at two recent books, *Violence and Social Orders* by North, Wallis and Weingast and *Why Nations Fail*, the immensely successful blockbuster by Acemoglu and Robinson, that put an all-but-exclusive emphasis on institutional explanations of economic development and non-development and in doing so almost inevitably focus on the state.

Among (global) historians over the last two decades a very broad spectrum of explanations have been suggested for the emergence of the great divide between poor and rich countries in the global economy, ranging from contingency, geography, factor endowments in the widest sense of word, the (non-)existence of a sophisticated market mechanism and specialization, accumulation, changes in industriousness and consumption, to innovation and 'culture' and everything in between. Reference to institutions are not lacking – in the work of several scholars they are quite prominent. Some scholars explicitly reject institutionalist explanations. Andre Gunder Frank, for example, simply denies the state – or any other institution – any independent causal role in the economic development of East and West. To him, the role of institutions like the state in economic history is only derivative. Fundamental economic forces drive human history and institutions just respond to them. Gregory Clark, who also has extensively written about the Great Divergence, also thinks the role of institutions in it is quite minor. Rosenthal and Wong, to give a last example, emphasize the role of factor prices and war and deny the existence of inherently superior institutions in the West. Overall in current debates on the Great Divergence, references to contingency, geography, accumulation and the market abound.[187]

As we have seen, references to 'the state' are not exactly lacking in the many comparisons that have recently been made of early modern China and early modern Europe either. In debates on the Great Divergence, however, explicit claims that it would have played an important role have become much *less* prominent than they were when most scholars simply 'knew' that '*laissez-faire*' Britain was bound to be more successful economically than 'despotic' China. Those claims, moreover, tend to be quite 'underspecified'. As a rule what is said about differences and similarities between states in the West and in the (Far) East tends to be not very concrete – one misses a solid, preferably quantitative foundation for the claims that are made, just as one misses a systematic comparative approach. What one does come across, by and large, are rather offhand general comments. That critique

---

[186]For that expression see Rodrik, Subramanian and Trebbi, 'Institutions rule', and for further explanation my *Escaping Poverty*, ch. 9.

[187]For discussions about the role of institutions in explanations of the Great Divergence see my *Escaping Poverty*, chs 20–7.

also applies to the studies by North, Wallis and Weingast, and Acemoglu and Robinson. Whatever their general merits, for the empirical economic historian it continues to be rather unclear how exactly their very general claims regarding property rights, the rule of formal law, representation and inclusion, perpetually lived impersonal organizations and the like might explain the actual emergence of the Great Divergence between West and Rest.

Pomeranz, a key figure in the Great Divergence debate, clearly and explicitly acknowledges the importance of the state in providing an explanation of the diverging of Europe and China. He does so, in particular, in his claim that early modern China lacked 'capitalism' in the specific sense in which Braudel, Wallerstein and Arrighi use that term.[188] In their interpretation of early modern capitalism, which, not by accident, has often been called '*mercantile* capitalism', capital is accumulated in long-distance trade in a setting where markets are neither free nor perfect but, on the contrary, monopolized or at least manipulated. Such an economic system cannot exist without a strong 'visible hand' – that is, without an interventionist and supportive state. In the work of Pomeranz 'non-Smithian capitalism' clearly is present when it comes to his claim that in explaining Britain's economic growth and primacy a fundamental place must be accorded to its peripheries. He regards the fact that Britain in – and outside – its colonies had created a kind of periphery that Qing China lacked as an equally important precondition for its industrialization as the fact that it was so successful in exploiting coal. It will be obvious that concepts like 'colonies' and 'peripheries' or 'non-consensual trade' and their importance cannot be discussed without paying serious attention to the nature of the state. In this respect Pomeranz's Great Divergence is right on track but it could do with more detailed descriptions and in-depth analyses. Its author does not expand on the exact mechanisms by which governments would promote or hamper economic growth in Western European countries and China and, importantly for this text, he does not go into much detail when it comes to showing exactly *what* governments did and *how* different states were. In a later publication he again indicates to be fully aware of major differences between the political economy of Qing China and that of most Western countries 'the regime [i.e. the Qing regime] did have an enduring set of priorities, rooted in (its) orientation toward reproducing empire that made it indifferent or even hostile to overseas colonization and mercantilism.'[189] But again, this claim is made without being extensively discussed when it comes to its ramifications.

In Wong's *China Transformed* differences between Western Europe and China when it comes to state-formation are the main focus of attention. Wong wrote the book with the explicit purpose of showing how *different* these regions were and how wrong it would be to simply measure state-formation in China by a European yardstick. This, as indicated, does not make him refrain from suggesting that the differences that *did* exist between the process and logic of state-formation in China and Europe *did not* have much economic

---

[188]Pomeranz, *Great Divergence*, chs 2 and 4. For Arrighi's view see his *Long Twentieth Century* and *Adam Smith in Beijing*. Braudel and Wallerstein present their theories of capitalism in, respectively, *Civilization & Capitalism* and *Modern World-System*.
[189]Pomeranz, 'Without coal?', 266.

impact *before* industrialization and did not in any way *cause* industrialization.[190] His comparison is certainly very knowledgeable and subtle, but what is striking is his scarce and rather unsystematic use of *quantitative* data. We find very few figures, especially figures that are systematically *compared*, with regard to topics that are quintessential in his study, like government income and expenditure, especially for social policies, or number and quality of civilian and military government personnel. In that respect it is also quite unfortunate that Wong – though the same applies to almost all the China specialists whose work we will discuss in this book – is rather vague when it comes to indicating what exactly is meant by 'Europe' or for that matter 'the West'. One looks in vain for any distinctions between various countries in his book.[191] Considering the huge differences that existed between countries, even in Western Europe, that can have unwarranted consequences. In *Before and Beyond Divergence*, Wong and his co-author Rosenthal, as we saw, explicitly favour an approach that 'eliminates all possible arguments that make European cultural or political arrangements superior to those found in China'.[192]

Similar comments apply to the book by Hui. She constantly refers to 'Europe' without any clear specification of time and place and writes as if state-formation in that part of the world would have been characterized by self-weakening expedients: the most prominent of them being the use of military entrepreneurs and mercenaries, tax farming and the existence of the sale of public offices. In Britain, however – not a minor European state during the last century of the period she discusses – after 1680 tax farming and venal offices no longer existed. Private entrepreneurs providing for the military remained very important. But they no longer had the independent position of the 'military entrepreneurs' that Fritz Redlich describes in his classic book.[193] At various places in the text she clearly shows that she is aware that Britain does not fit her model. But in many respects neither do Prussia, Sweden or Russia. Differences between various parts of Europe and over time were immense, as she could have found out herself in Charles Tilly's work.[194] So what exactly does she mean by 'early modern Europe'? Her claim that what we see in early modern Europe is state *de*formation could clearly do with some more empirical underpinning. Are there really trustworthy and firm indicators that, in the period under discussion, the processes of monopolization of the means of coercion, rationalization and nationalization of taxation, and bureaucratization of administration, made no headway but, if we have to take the term *literally*, would have even been reversed?[195]

---

[190]Wong, *China Transformed*, ch. 6. See e.g. page 151: 'European political economy did not create industrialization, nor was the European political economy deliberately designed to promote industrialization. Instead, European political economy created a set of institutions able to promote industrialization once it appeared.' Please note the undifferentiated reference to a *European* political economy.

[191]Wong, *China Transformed*.

[192]Rosenthal and Wong, *Before and Beyond Divergence*, 101.

[193]Redlich, *German Military Enterpriser*. For literature, Harding and Solbes Ferri, *Contractor State* and Fynn-Paul, *War, Entrepreneurs, and the State*. For the situation in Britain see Chapter 1 note 299.

[194]I refer again to the text on the flap of Tilly, *Coercion, Capital, and European States*: 'Thus the central question for Tilly is this: "What accounts for the great variation over time and space in the kinds of state that have prevailed in Europe since AD 990?"'

[195]Hui, *War and State Formation*, ch. 1.

Talking about the state and comparing the West and China inevitably means talking about bureaucracy and thus about Max Weber. In Will's work and that of Woodside, Weber's name pops up every now and then but his 'ghost', so to say, is permanently present, even though I suspect both authors never really read Weber's relevant texts on bureaucracy.[196] That, in any case, would be the simplest explanation for why they try to profile their 'revisionist' perspective via attacks on what actually is a straw man. Woodside's rehabilitation of China's 'bureaucracy' focuses entirely on showing its meritocratic traits. Everyone who has actually read Weber knows that Weber never denied the existence of such traits in China's administrative system. He explicitly mentions them. Nor did Weber deny that Qing administrators undertook efforts at rationalization. But in the end these efforts failed or were not taken far enough to 'satisfy' him. What Weber claimed is that Qing China was not a *modern* – that is a fully and systematically *rationalized* – bureaucratic state. Neither Woodside nor Will really engage with the arguments actually presented by Weber and his followers. A simple comparison of Weber's ideal-type, which is reproduced in a somewhat abbreviated form in this book on pages 267–8, with China's structure of administration makes it quite clear that, in China under the Qing, mandarins in various respects were *not* like Weberian bureaucrats and the setting in which they operated in various respects was *not* a Weberian bureaucracy. The discrepancies between China's administrative system and Weber's 'ideal' bureaucracy are already substantial when we look at the *principles* of the system. What really matters of course is the way it functioned in *practice*. Here, as we will see, those discrepancies are simply staggering. Neither Woodside nor Wong and Will ever discuss the education and training received by those mandarins; their incredibly low number; the absolutely insufficient funding of local government and the far too low salaries of officialdom; the essential role of extra, unofficial income and of clerks, runners and private secretaries who were not in government service; the absence of a formal legal system; or corruption. We will discuss all these points later on and find enormous differences.

If one takes Weber's ideal-type seriously, one not only has to conclude that early modern Qing China was not a bureaucratic state: the same then goes for all states in Western Europe up until at least the first decades of the nineteenth century. There no longer is any serious historian or social scientist that would characterize *any* state in Europe in the *early* modern era as bureaucratic. Modern bureaucratic rule as a system of administering an entire society that encompasses all elements of administration is definitely a *post-Napoleonic* phenomenon. Before the big reforms that were directly or indirectly touched off by the changes in Revolutionary and Napoleonic France, what we see is 'islands of bureaucracy' in the midst of a sea of all kinds of less rational systems of rule.[197] Michael Mann calls it 'bizarre' that some historians are attracted to use the

---

[196]Woodside in his *Lost Modernities*, 122, note 34, refers to two pages of Weber's *Religion of China*. Will in his article on modern China and Sinology refers to Weber's introduction to his book on the Protestant ethic. That is strange: Weber's main systematic analysis of bureaucracy is in his *Wirtschaft und Gesellschaft* and his main comparison between the situation in Western Europe and that in China in his *Religion of China*.

[197]See, for what is currently the accepted view, Finer, *History of Government, III, 1473–1651*, and Mann, *Sources of Social Power, II*, chs 10–14.

word 'bureaucracy' to describe the administration of eighteenth-century France.[198] When it comes to the relative 'modernity' of European bureaucracy, Weber never claimed in his work that Western European states in the early modern era were already full-blown bureaucracies. His description of the characteristics and preconditions of bureaucratic society, as he sees it, makes it absolutely clear that it is a modern (i.e. post-French and post-Industrial Revolutions) phenomenon. He focused on the nineteenth and twentieth centuries.[199] Of course, there were developments that pointed in the direction of an increasing bureaucratization of government in various countries, and some specific sectors of government in some specific countries, most of all Britain's system of tax collecting, that might indeed be already described as bureaucratic. But no early modern European state's administrative system can be described as such. It would be silly to claim Weber spoke the last word. But that gives only more reason to systematically compare what *actually* happened in China to what *actually* happened in various Western European countries at the time. I am afraid that revisionists are not doing justice to Weber's intentions and analysis *and* not really taking on board recent empirical studies.

Let me finally refer to Peter Perdue. In his latest book he may not systematically refer to Weber, but he also clearly 'brings the state back in', gives it a central role in his analysis and refers to its role in the Great Divergence. But again, what is lacking is a *systematic* comparison with systematic, *quantitative* foundations. That very probably will be the reason that he can defend, in my eyes incorrect, the thesis that until the second half of the eighteenth century differences between states in Western Europe and the Chinese state were only marginal and did not really make a difference.[200] The same goes for Evelyn Rawski, who, as we have seen, also makes quite far-reaching claims with regard to the similarities between developments in Western Europe and China and voices the opinion that these regions can both be called 'early modern'.[201]

What we need to be able to judge all these widely different and often contradicting statements with regard to the state in Western Europe and in China in the early modern era is an analysis that is *systematic*, where possible *quantitative*, *comparative* and focusing on *practice* rather than on norms and ideals, while being *sensitive to time and place*. The Qing state under the Yongzheng emperor (r. 1722–35) functioned quite differently from that under the Daoguang emperor (r. 1821–50). The fiscal-military state of Britain during the Napoleonic Wars was quite different from the *laissez-faire* state that began to develop after those wars. Whereas it had been something of a bureaucratic frontrunner in the late-eighteenth century, Britain became a laggard in the nineteenth century and the thesis has been, I think correctly, put forward that in the second half of that century it had turned into a relatively under-developed, *weak* state suffering from 'disadvantages of

---

[198]Mann, *Sources of Social Power, II*, 453.
[199]Weber's analysis in *Wirtschaft und Gesellschaft*, chs III and IX, makes it quite plain that according to him an encompassing system of bureaucratic rule can only exist in modern industrialized societies.
[200]Perdue, *China Marches West*, ch. 15.
[201]Rawski, 'Qing formation'.

priority'.[202] My analysis will be closest to that of Michael Mann, John Hobson and Linda Weiss, but as I focus on only two countries, China and Britain, and on a much briefer period, I can provide more detail and go more in-depth than they do.[203] My conclusion will be that the differences in importance, role and function of the state between China and Britain are so fundamental and incisive that they simply *must* have had important consequences for economic development in both countries.

States: Modern and premodern

This book is about states. It permanently analyses, compares and discusses them, so some conceptual and empirical clarification certainly is in order here. The following general, open and broad definition will be my point of departure. A state is:

1. A differentiated set of institutions and personnel embodying
2. centrality in the sense that political relations radiate outwards from a centre to cover
3. a territorially demarcated area, over which it exercises
4. a monopoly of authoritative binding rule-making, backed up by a monopoly of the means of physical violence.[204]

The state as we nowadays, according to the definition just given, define is a modern, post-French Revolution phenomenon. Before that revolution, Great Britain and Qing China, surprisingly enough, were probably the polities in the world that came closest to it. In their ideal-type version, modern 'Weberian' states have a clearly defined and clearly confined, fixed territory and clearly defined subjects/citizens. Sovereignty in them is undivided, not overlapping, and it is exclusive. It no longer is, to use Perry Anderson's term, 'parcellized'.[205] There is only one source of sovereignty and no indirect, only delegated, rule that is on the basis of laws which apply equally to all. Such states are characterized by a monopoly of legitimate violence, rule and taxation. They have a circumscribed definition of sovereignty and legitimacy and, especially since the rise of nationalism, tend to create or instrumentalize a sense of 'national' identity among its subjects/citizens.[206]

---

[202]See for an introduction into this thesis Moers, *Making of Bourgeois Europe*, 171–82. According to its defenders, Britain did not become as thoroughly modernized, bureaucratic and impersonal as many continental states in the course of the nineteenth century because its bourgeoisie had failed to oust the aristocracy from its position of power and distinction.

[203]I am referring here to, in chronological order, Mann, *Sources of Social Power, II*; Weiss and Hobson, *States and Economic Development* and Hobson, *Eastern Origins*.

[204]Mann, *State, War and Capitalism*, 4.

[205]Anderson, *Passages from Antiquity to Feudalism*, 147–72.

[206]A compact introduction into the peculiarities of premodern and modern states, highly influenced by Weber's thinking, can be found in Poggi, *Development of the Modern State*.

Modern states first and foremost are territorial rather than jurisdictional or personal. They have clear borders instead of vague frontier zones. They abhor enclaves and exclaves. They are defined by abstract homogenous space, not by a collection of concrete places or people. In that respect the emergence and enormous spread in the West of maps based on a Ptolemaic world-view using geometric coordinates was highly consequential. Territorial sovereignty can be mapped; personal overlapping sovereignty cannot. The logic of modern Western cartography certainly is co-responsible for the logic of modern Western state-formation. Paraphrasing Charles Tilly, one might say: 'States make maps and maps make states.' Governments clearly were interested in that cartography, but for a long time they just used the existing commercial cartography. It was only in the seventeenth, and even more, the eighteenth century that they became prominent in instigating big cartographic projects and organizing space, often so that the maps produced were much more clear-cut and systematic than reality on the ground.[207]

What does it mean for our analysis that states in the period discussed in this book did have boundaries but that those often were zones rather than lines and that their sovereignty often still had jurisdictional (i.e. personal) traits and was not exclusive and undivided but overlapping and parcellized? The most important consequence, to my view, is that the distinction between the 'public' and the 'private', which is at the very heart of our current thinking about the state, from our modern perspective at least, is rather blurred. The frequent existence of parcellized and overlapping sovereignty meant that the central government in premodern states did not have exclusive monopolies on violence, public rule and taxation. There still was plenty of private possession and use of means of violence – for example, the position of many aristocrats and military entrepreneurs, the system of hiring mercenaries and privateering. There still was plenty of indirect rule, in which the central government could not directly reach all its subjects who often were ruled by local elites and in which privileges, immunities, 'beneficia', sinecures and the selling and owning of offices were quite normal. When it comes to tax collection we see non-governmental levies like feudal duties or tithes but also tax exemptions and tax farming. A 'national' system of law and a 'national identity' were often lacking or only quite rudimentary.

The fact that the distinction between the private and the public was so unclear also means it is difficult to decide who actually counted as government officials doing a public job and who a private person. All the problems and un-sharp boundaries referred to can be clearly illustrated in the context of this book by referring to so-called chartered companies that, as private companies, basically received 'sovereignty' from their state over certain parts of world where they acted as governments (i.e. concluded treaties, waged war, had armies and officials of their own, collected taxes and so on). The Dutch East India Company, for example, according to her original charter, was allowed to 'make war, conclude treaties, acquire territories and build fortresses'. Other chartered companies acquired similar rights.

---

[207]For the information and claims in this paragraph see Branch, *Cartographic State.*

To avoid interrupting the flow of my arguments too much later on, I will here provide some basic clarification of these companies' structure and history, using the most important company for my book, the English East India Company, as example. Its original charter implied that government sold a monopoly of trade in the Eastern hemisphere to a group of traders.[208] Those traders pooled their risks in such a way that, from 1657 onwards, one can speak of a real joint-stock company. The company was not *founded* as a quasi-national endeavour. In principle it was set-up as an autonomous company that – which is quite telling in this context – was allowed to have armed vessels. The company's focus was to be entirely on trade and profit, not on conquest and colonization. One, however, can see clear shifts in that focus. With a series of five acts around 1670, King Charles II provisioned it with the right to autonomous territorial acquisition, to mint money, to command fortresses and troops and form alliances, to make war and peace and to exercise both civil and criminal jurisdiction over acquired areas. By 1689, the company was arguably a 'nation' on the Indian mainland, independently administering the vast presidencies of Bengal, Madras and Bombay and possessing a formidable and intimidating military strength. From 1698 it was entitled to use the motto 'Auspicio Regis et Senatus Angliae', meaning 'Under the patronage of the King and Parliament of England.' This implied that 'acquisition of sovereignty by the subjects of the Crown is on behalf of the Crown and not in its own right'.

Understandably, not everyone was enthusiastic about the granting of monopolies to select groups of people. It was controversial almost from the very beginning. The company was often fiercely attacked and went through some severe crises in which its continued existence was threatened and its structure changed. At the very end of the seventeenth century, we even see the founding of a 'new' company next to the old one. But this did not come to fruition and in 1709 the 'old' and 'new' companies merged in a United Company of Merchants trading in the East Indies. Overall, till the 1760s, state interference was minor and mainly showed in certain legal and constitutional requirements, especially the granting and renewing of the charter. The increasing political power of the company overseas, and especially the corruption and mismanagement that went with it, created major problems and fierce criticism *in patria*. It caused the company's 'fall from grace', to put it in the words of Philip Lawson.[209] In 1784, government came to oversee its political and diplomatic functions. The company was no longer to decide independently over war and peace and was now officially 'bound to conform to his majesty's pleasure'.[210] In the new legislation of 1784, it was explicitly inserted that 'to pursue schemes of conquest and extension of dominion in India are measures repugnant to the wish, the honour and the policy of this nation'.[211]

---

[208]I have taken the general information on the East India Company from Kumagai, *Breaking into the Monopoly*; Lawson, *East India Company*; Robins, *Corporation that Changed the World* and Webster, *Twilight of the East India Company*. For specific information regarding the company as a business, see Bowen, *Business of Empire*.

[209]Lawson, *East India Company*, ch. 6.

[210]Lawson, *East India Company*, 125.

[211]Lawson, *East India Company*, 128.

Nevertheless, in India the company, after some time, again behaved in daily practice like a military, territorial power that was fairly independent from Britain. Its territory only grew and its army only increased, as did its debts and the critique it incurred. In the end this led to a slow dismantling of its privileged position and to the loss of its last trade monopoly, that of China in 1834, after having lost that of India in 1813. It, however, continued to rule over huge tracts of lands in India, almost like a full sovereign, till the British Crown assumed direct government. That only occurred in 1858. So in the end from a *company*, though one that from the very beginning mixed business with matters of sovereignty and the wielding of violence, it had evolved into a major military, economic and political *power* that actually ruled over a country that was much bigger and much more populous than Britain and enormously important for Britain's economy.[212] Or as Bowen puts it: 'The Company had once presided over a vast empire of business, but it entered its final decades devoted exclusively to the business of empire.'[213] This shift was not something unique to this company. According to Jan de Vries, European trading companies 'step by step, beginning with the English in 1757 and continuing into the nineteenth century … were transformed into colonial rulers and/or replaced by their national states'. He claims that both the Dutch and the English East India companies sought to compensate for the decline of trading profits by cultivating territorial power.[214] As I will show later, the English East India Company was a formidable military power and it behaved as such. [215]

When it comes to ruling over a huge territory one cannot, for Great Britain, leave the Hudson's Bay Company unmentioned. This company received a charter in 1670 for a trade monopoly of over a region of 3.6 million km^2, over which *de facto* it also ruled. In 1821, it and the North West Company of Montreal were forcibly merged by intervention of the British government. Their combined actual trade territory covered more than 7.7 million km^2. This new company was only definitely dissolved as a chartered company in 1869. After rejecting an offer by the American government of $10 million, the company approved the return of Rupert's Land and the North-Western Territory to the United Kingdom, which gave it to Canada, which in return had to pay £300,000 to the United Kingdom so that it could compensate the Hudson's Bay Company for its losses. Even after that, the company retained its most successful trading posts and one-twentieth of the lands surveyed for immigration and settlement.[216] The examples just given will have made clear that for the early modern European context it is anything but simple to pinpoint where sovereignty actually resides. I will not try and solve this problem on an abstract level but just deal with it every time it is relevant for my analysis for all countries involved.

---

[212]See for this information the articles dealing with India in Marshall, *Oxford History of the British Empire. The Eighteenth Century* and Porter, *Oxford History of the British Empire. The Nineteenth Century.*

[213]Bowen, *Business of Empire*, 298.

[214]See De Vries, 'Limits of globalization', 731 for the quotation. For further comments see also idem, 'Connecting Europe and Asia', 88 and 91.

[215]See page 287.

[216]I took these basic data for the Hudson's Bay Company and its history from Bown, *Merchant Kings*, ch. 5 and from internet references to the history of the Company.

That fact that private violence was not 'expropriated' by central government and that, on the contrary, governments often explicitly allowed or even encouraged private people to use violence against subjects of other states means that one also cannot draw a sharp distinction between peaceful, private economic activities and public violence. Power, politics, violence and economics of course have never been neatly and completely separated but in the period discussed here they often were really inseparable and almost undistinguishable. I can do no better than quote Marx: 'In actual history, it is a notorious fact that conquest, enslavement, robbery, murder, in short, force, play the greatest part. In the tender annals of political economy, the idyllic reigns from time immemorial.'[217] Economic historians have again become much more aware of this fact recently.[218] Here too I will not try to provide general, theoretical distinctions and principles but deal with the problems I encounter case by case, on a more pragmatic level.

Gauging the macroeconomic impact of 'the state' requires knowing the size of countries one discusses and the size of their populations. Let us begin with the country that together with China will hold centre stage in this book. Just like almost *all* states in Europe, Britain, Great Britain and later on the United Kingdom of Great Britain and Ireland, though to a lesser extent than most other European states, was a 'composite state', in this case a 'composite monarchy' (i.e. a state composed of a number of separate territories with distinctive senses of identities and often differing rights, regulations, institutions and ways and levels of control by the centre).[219] 'Was' is very important for the topics that are central to our analysis: states in the early modern era as a rule were not economic unities to the extent they are now, as Table 1 shows, in which the 'peculiarity' of, in this case, England again clearly stands out.

Here is one example to show how fragmented European states could still be economically at the end of the *Ancien Régime* (for further examples I refer to Dincecco's book from which I took Tables 1 and 2): 'In France, at least 1,500 internal river tolls were estimated to exist in 1789, for all Colbert's attempts at elimination.'[220]

The composite character of polities like the Habsburg Empire or the Spanish Empire at the time is obvious. The Habsburg monarchy has been described as the very antipode of a modern state.[221] But we must not lose sight of the fact that even their heartlands that

---

[217]Marx, *Capital*, I, 874.

[218]See Chapter 5.

[219]These concepts acquired wider currency via Koenigsberger, 'Dominium regale' and 'Crisis of the seventeenth century'. In 'Dominium regale', 12, Koenigsberger gives the following, quite loose, description: 'Most states in the early modern period were composite states, including more than one country under the sovereignty of one ruler. These composite states or monarchies could consist of completely separated countries, divided by sea or by other states, such as the dominions of the Habsburg monarchy in Spain, Italy and the Netherlands, those of the Hohenzollern monarchy of Brandenburg-Prussia or, indeed, England and Ireland, or they might be contiguous such as England and Wales, Piedmont and Savoy or Poland and Lithuania.' For a more analytical approach see Elliott, 'Europe of composite monarchies', where one also finds the expression 'multiple kingdoms', and Nexon, *Struggle for Power*, under 'composite states'. The author presents a very helpful description on pages 6 and 7. One can also come across the expression 'polycentric state'. See Grafe, 'Polycentric states'.

[220]Branch, *Cartographic State*, 161. For further information on the failure to create an integrated market in France see Bosher, *Single Duty Project*.

[221]See e.g. Hochedlinger, 'Habsburg Monarchy', 56–7.

Table 1 Average internal customs zones as percentages of sovereign areas, 1700–1815

	1700	1750	1788	1815
England	100	100	100	100
France	22	22	22	100
Netherlands	14	14	14	100
Spain	16	94	94	94

Source: Dincecco, *Political Transformations*, 16, Table 2.1.

Table 2 Average sizes of internal customs zones, 1700–1815, in km²

	1700	1750	1788	1815
England	151,000	151,000	151,000	151,000
France	118,000	118,000	118,000	544,000
Netherlands	5,000	5,000	5,000	34,000
Spain	302,000	467,000	467,000	467,000
Overall	150,0000	182,000	182,000	375,000

Source: Dincecco, *Political Transformations*, 18, Table 2.3.

normally, for the sake of convenience, are referred to as 'Austria' or the 'Habsburg Lands' or 'Spain', were not exactly modern *unified* states with one uniform administration. That also applies to the tiny state we call 'the Dutch Republic' and to the big state we call 'France'. Even Prussia, that presumed prototype of a bureaucratic centralized state, in the eighteenth century still was far from a fully integrated and uniformly ruled, modern territorial state. The territorial, centralized and uniform state as we now know it only emerged with and after the French Revolution, with the exception – I would claim – of Great Britain. But even in discussing 'Britain' during the early modern era, one has to differentiate between four different regions which, at one time or another, were part of it. Those regions were England, Wales, Scotland and Ireland. Their approximate respective sizes are shown in Table 3. In 1801 the United Kingdom of Great Britain and Ireland was founded. That comprised all four regions just mentioned. England and Wales had been united since the Late Middle Ages. Formal incorporation of Wales in the English system of government took place in 1536, although for fiscal purposes this unity was only implemented in 1576.

The four regions that came to form one 'composite state' were not equals. England clearly was the most important one. In a sense Great Britain and later the United Kingdom were an English Empire, a term that has been used as a way of indicating that

Table 3 Size of the four parts of the United Kingdom of Great Britain and Ireland

England	130,000 km²
Wales	20,000 km²
Scotland	79,000 km²
Ireland	70,000 km², of which Ulster is about 15,000 km²

Table 4 Population of the four parts of the United Kingdom of Great Britain and Ireland, in millions

	1700	1750	1800	1850
England/Wales	5–6*	6–6.5*	9	18
Scotland		1.3	1.6	2.9
Ireland		2.5–3	5.2	6.6–6.8

Source: Mitchell, *British Historical Statistics*, 7–12.

*Only England. The figures for Ireland are approximations.

England in one way or another ruled over all the other three 'nations'.[222] England and Wales to all relevant intents and purposes formed an entity during the entire period that will be discussed here. As indicated, Scotland was officially united with England and Wales in 1707 in one United Kingdom with the name of Great Britain, having one (Protestant) ruler, one legislature and one system of free trade. This, however, does not mean that a fully thoroughgoing political union was achieved.[223] With regard to taxation, the expenditure of revenue and the servicing of national debt, Scotland was often treated differently from England and Wales. Until the very beginning of the nineteenth century taxes paid by the people of Scotland hardly ever ended up in London in any substantial amount – in the first five decades after 1707 some 15 to 20 per cent at best.[224] So my figures for that period will normally only refer to the situation in England and Wales. In most matters of public finance, Scotland was only really integrated into Great Britain during the nineteenth century. Scotland's highly developed system of banking continued to be different for quite some time too. The realm had its own bank and bank notes, which did make a difference.[225] Whereas the Bank of England handled much government business, the Bank of Scotland was expressly forbidden to lend to the state. After 1707 the monetary systems of England and Scotland may have been integrated, but the value

---

[222]Elliott, *Empires of the Atlantic World*, 120. For the thesis that Britain colonized its fringes see Hechter, *Internal Colonialism*.

[223]See, for example, Colley, *Britons*, 12–13, and passim under 'Scotland'.

[224]Devine, 'Scotland', 397.

[225]For the history of Scotland, see Devine, *Scottish Nation*.

of money in Scotland continued to be indicated in Scots currency.[226] Scotland's system of poor relief, to mention another example, also continued to be different from that of England for a very long time. Although Scotland may indeed have contributed relatively little to Britain in fiscal terms, it was of crucial importance in other respects.[227]

The Act of Union of 1801 that terminated Ireland's formal status as a dominion and united it with Great Britain actually did not create a real unity nor was it based on equality.[228] Most Irish people considered the status of their country rather like that of a semi-colony than a full member of a federal state.[229] It had long functioned as a colony of Great Britain in the original meaning of the word; it received some 200,000 immigrants from England, Wales and Scotland during the first seventy years of the seventeenth century.[230] In the eyes of these colonists and many other Great Britons, the Irish clearly were strangers, or to put it in the words of a contemporary: 'The wild Irish and the Indians do not much differ.'[231] Ferguson correctly claims that 'Ireland was the experimental laboratory of British colonization and Ulster was the prototype plantation.'[232] Whatever the juridical niceties, Ireland had clearly long been dealt with as if it was a colony. In the 1690s, for example, there was concerted action in England to make export of foreign (Irish) cattle, sheep and pigs to Britain impossible. Powerful British wool manufacturers managed to get a suppression of Irish wool exports to Britain. The Irish were forcibly advised to build a linen industry.[233] What is quite interesting for our analysis is the fact that the Navigation Acts basically were British. They had an unfavourable effect on the Channel Islands, Scotland (before the Act of Union of 1707) and especially Ireland by excluding them from a preferential position within the system.[234] Ireland continued to have a special status after 1801 for quite some time. Actual fiscal integration only took place in the period 1817 to 1819. Free trade between Ireland and Britain was only enacted in 1824. Before that, trade with Ireland counted as foreign trade. Separate currencies existed for another two years and excise duties and taxation remained sharply at variance until 1853. In many statistics of the United Kingdom, Ireland continued to be regarded as a foreign country. The Catholics of Ireland obviously did not feel very much at home in 'their' Protestant nation. The former British and Scottish Protestants that had settled in their country probably did.

---

[226]Eagleton and Williams, *Money*, 185–6.

[227]See e.g. Whatley and Patrick, *The Scots and the Union*.

[228]For an effort to connect, integrate and compare the history of the four nations that became the United Kingdom of Great Britain and Ireland see Kearney, *British Isles*.

[229]For the position of Ireland in the United Kingdom after 1801 see Fitzpatrick, 'Ireland and the empire'.

[230]Canny, 'English migration', 62.

[231]The Englishman Hugh Peter, who had been in Massachusetts, made this claim in 1646. He was not the only one, though, to make this comparison. See Elliott, *Empires of the Atlantic World*, 80.

[232]Ferguson, *Empire*, 64.

[233]See Hont, *Jealousy of Trade*, 222–33.

[234]For the different ways in which, in the various Navigation Acts, the different parts of what became the 'United Kingdom' were treated see Cullen, 'Merchant communities overseas' and Morgan, 'Mercantilism and the British Empire', 168–9.

The differences that undoubtedly existed and sometimes continued to exist must, however, not blind us to the fact that the Scots especially, and to some extent even the Irish, were incorporated in the 'United Kingdom', for better or for worse. The integration of the Scots in Great Britain in this respect looks quite successful. They fought side by side, for example, with English and Welshmen in various wars. They clearly were not aloof in the big wars between Great Britain and France between 1793 and 1815. In 1803 over 60,000 Scots were serving as rank-and-file members of volunteer regiments, some 17 per cent of the total number in arms throughout Great Britain. In 1804, 44 per cent of the eligible male population in Scotland was willing to serve, most of them in any part of Britain. That is a better rate of response than was to be found in England. Of course, these figures need not point at a Scottish infatuation with Great Britain per se; it could just as well be an indication of widespread poverty in parts of Scotland.[235] That definitely was the case after the so-called Jacobite Rising in 1745–6, when the British army forcefully integrated Scotland in Great Britain to function as a kind of military reservation.[236] Whatever may have been the exact reason, the Scots clearly tried their luck in joining the English and Welsh in creating and ruling an empire. In the 1750s little more than a tenth of the population of the British Isles lived in Scotland. Yet the East India Company was at the very least half-Scottish.[237] Scotland had its Enlightenment and its industrial transformation. One might even argue that Scotland by the middle of the nineteenth century had become *more* industrialized than Britain.[238]

The Irish situation was quite peculiar. On the one hand Ireland clearly was a kind of occupied territory. Britain's 'standing army' of some 12,000 troops was billeted there. Its costs were borne by the Irish out of taxes that were forced upon them by 'their' Anglo-Irish Parliament whereas its main task consisted in protecting Britain.[239] The government of that country in principle did not enlist people from Ireland, not even if they were Protestant, in this army. In the second half of the eighteenth century, demand for soldiers increased so much that men from Ireland, Protestants and even Catholics, could enlist for service outside their home country. Their contribution became quite important. With the passing of time the Irish became (over-)represented in the imperial army and bureaucracy and in migration to overseas colonies or former colonies. In that way, they too participated in England's empire. In the Bengal Army of the East Indian Company in the period 1825–50, no less than 48 per cent of the soldiers were Irish. In 1830 over 40 per cent of the entire British Army came from Ireland. That number, by the way, decreased over the nineteenth century to only some 10 per cent in 1900.[240] In the Royal Navy things were no different: in the 1790s, as a rule, 25 to 30 per cent of the sailors

---

[235]Colley, 'Reach of the state'.
[236]Way, 'Klassenkrieg', 100–1.
[237]For the Scots' role in empire-building see Colley, *Britons*, 117–32. For the claim that in the 1750s the East India Company was at least half-Scottish see Ferguson, *Empire*, 45.
[238]For an analysis of Scotland's economic history during the very long eighteenth century see Devine, 'Scotland'. The claim that Scotland became more industrialized than the rest of Britain is on page 400 of that article.
[239]Way, 'Klassenkrieg', 101–4.
[240]See for this thesis, and more figures, Leonard, 'Imperial projections', 37, with original references.

on board most of its ships were Irish.[241] All this clearly shows the Janus-face of Ireland, being colony as well as colonizer.[242] The empire clearly helped in forging at least three of the four nations into one. What originally had been described as the 'English Empire', after 1750 increasingly was referred to as 'British Empire'.[243] Of the 'British' army in America in the mid-eighteenth century; 30.3 per cent were English-born, 27.8 per cent Scots, 27.2 per cent Irish and the rest colonials and foreign-born residents of America.[244]

As this text is not confined to discussing 'Britain' but at times also comments on the situation in other Western European countries, some information regarding their size and population is in order. When it comes to size, I will here give the *current* size of a couple of Western European countries, just to give an idea of orders of magnitude, full well realizing that in the period we are discussing Germany, Italy and to some extent Belgium did not yet exist as such and that Austria was just (one of) the central region(s) of a large empire, not a small independent country. For the other countries, differences between their *current* size and that in the early modern period are rather small.[245]

If we take all these countries together, 'Western Europe' in its entirety (including Great Britain and all Ireland) would be about 2.3 million km². In 1700, the total population

Table 5 **The current size of the main Western European countries that are referred to in this text plus their highest populations during the very long eighteenth century**

	Size in km²	Population in million
Austria	83,000	±4
Belgium	32,000	4.5
France*	547,000	36
Germany	357,000	33
Italy	301,000	24
The Netherlands	41,000	3.1
Portugal	92,000	<4
Spain	504,000	15
Switzerland	41,000	2.4

*Only the European territory.

---

[241]Frykman, 'Seeleute', 61.

[242]For analyses whether and in what respects Ireland was a British colony and a victim of imperialism see Bush, *Imperialism and Postcolonialism*, 62–76 and Kenny, *Ireland and the British Empire*.

[243]Cain and Hopkins, *British Imperialism*, 670.

[244]See Way, 'Klassenkrieg', 100.

[245]That does not mean they are negligible. France measured 440,000 km² in 1600. That is some 100,000 km² less than in the present. A large part of this territorial expansion occurred in 'the very long eighteenth century'. See Braudel, *Identité de la France. Seconde Partie*, 45–7.

of the Western European countries mentioned in Table 5 was about 75 million people; in 1820 that number had increased to about 125 million, in 1870 to some 175 million.[246] Specific information for specific periods and specific countries will be given where and when helpful.

In the actual analysis no references will be made to 'Germany' and 'Italy', as in the early modern era these were basically only 'geographical expressions', to borrow a quote from Metternich. Information about the current size of Germany and Austria is not very informative when it comes to the size of their 'precursors' in the very long eighteenth century. So some further information is in order. The German Empire, of which in the end Prussia became the core, measured about 541,000 km² in 1871. Its population was some 40 million people then. The Habsburg Empire, of which what we now call Austria and later Austria and Hungary formed the core, under Francis Joseph I was some 675,000 km² and in the first decade of the twentieth century in its then extension had somewhat over 50 million inhabitants. To get an idea of the order of magnitude, I give the size of some other empires at their maximum size and with their maximum population (Table 7).

Please note that I have *not* included the overseas territories or colonies here and only refer to the actual motherlands. Information with regard to size and population of the

Table 6 The size of Prussia

Prussia	1688	111,000 km²
	1740	119,000 km²
	1786	195,000 km²
	1806	347,000 km²

Source: North, 'Finances and power', 158.

Table 7 Some empires with their maximum size and their maximum population during the very long eighteenth century

	Size (in million km²)	Population (in million)
Mughal empire	4	150–200
Ottoman empire	5.2	30
Russian empire	15	>150

Note: For information on the maximum size of all these empires see Turchin, 'Theory for formation of large empires', Table 2. Information about their population is in every textbook.

---

[246]Maddison, *World Economy*, 183.

empires of Great Britain and several other Western European countries will be given on pages 383–4.

The size of a country as such need not mean much. For pre-industrial societies total agricultural land might be a better indicator of their potential, as might location. Trying to measure total available agricultural land and using that as an indicator of a country's 'potential' is fraught with difficulties. Arable land in Britain between the end of the seventeenth century and 1850 increased from 40,000 to 60,000 km[2].[247] On average, for the period discussed, on top of that, no less than 60,000 km[2] of land were used to feed animals. In 1850 about two-thirds of Britain's entire surface was used as agricultural land, which in this case means as arable, meadow or pasture. What all these figures exactly mean is hard to determine because of the different ways in which land might be used and because the different yields of various crops. In France, around the 1600s, land used as arable or meadow amounted to 180,000 km[2]. That is about 40 per cent of the total surface of France at the time. In 1859, land used as such amounted to 280,000 km[2], over 60 per cent of the total surface of France at that time.[248]

What would the data for China in these respects look like? Early modern China is usually described as 'an empire', very probably in the quite specific meaning of a country being ruled by an emperor. For the sake of convenience I will follow this tradition, although I think Pierre-Étienne Will has a point in stressing that till its expansion in the eighteenth century, China resembled *a state* more than *an empire*. Up until then, it still was basically identical to China Proper and could not yet be considered as a group of countries, colonies or peoples, which, according to English dictionaries, would be characteristic of empires.[249] I would, however, refine Will's position somewhat. First, because the eighteen provinces of China Proper included provinces in the southwest like Hunan, Hubei, Guangdong, Guangxi, Guizhou, Sichuan and Yunnan, of which, in the words of Madeleine Zelin, 'Prior to the 1720s, large areas … were inhabited by non-Han people over whom the state exercised only limited political and no social control.'[250] Second, because the realm of the Qing, apart from China Proper, from the very beginning included *parts of* Mongolia and, more importantly, Manchuria, which both were regions with a special status. Manchuria may have been quite empty for a long time but it was a huge territory. Until the Qing lost a big part of it to the Russians in the 1850s, it measured over 1.2 million km[2]. Currently, the three so-called 'North-eastern provinces' that traditionally were the heart of Manchuria cover some 800,000 km[2]. Third, there is the fact that Taiwan, with a size of about 36,000 km[2], was conquered and added to the Qing realm in the 1680s. Whatever exact description one

---

[247]Vries, *Via Peking back to Manchester*, 93–4, note 86.

[248]Braudel, *Identité de la France. Seconde partie*, 45–7.

[249]See Will, 'Chine moderne et sinologie'. I looked up this definition in *Longman Webster English College Dictionary*. I will not enter the complex debate here about what exactly would be the difference(s) between 'state' and 'empire'. I refer the reader to Burbank and Cooper, *Empires*, in particular 8–11.

[250]The quotation is from Zelin, 'Yung-cheng reign', 221. For the 'integration' of these regions see this article; Woodside, 'Chi'en-lung reign', and the texts I refer to notes 175–82 of the Introduction.

wants to give of the realm over which the Qing ruled, from the very beginning it also had traits of a composite polity. With the passing of time these became ever more prominent.

Systematic extension of their rule by the Qing had already started at the very end of the seventeenth century when what then was called 'Outer Mongolia' also became part of the Empire. The Manchu's had already conquered Inner Mongolia when they entered China in 1644. We are talking about huge regions here. Inner Mongolia currently measures 1.2 million km². The current People's Republic of Mongolia – that is about the same region as former Outer Mongolia – measures over 1.5 million km². The region that now is called Qinghai also became part of the Qing Empire during the eighteenth century. It currently measures 720,000 km². Xinjiang, the enormous 'New Frontier' region that was subjected during the eighteenth century, currently, with somewhat changed frontiers, measures 1.6 million km². In that very same eighteenth century China's influence and power in Tibet clearly increased. The current size of that region is over 1.2 million km².[251] The 'composite' structure of the Qing Empire with the passing of time became ever more obvious, with various parts of the reign under Qing rule or supervision having different administrative arrangements and the differing ethnic groups living there not necessarily having the same social and legal status.[252] The situation would become even more complex if we took into consideration the position of the various tribute states of the empire. We will return to this topic later on (pages 394–6) when we compare the imperialism of Britain and Qing China. There I will also go into more detail with regard to the size of the population of all these regions outside China Proper. At this stage of the text it suffices to say that they were almost empty. Even in the highest estimates their population around 1800 will have been much less than 10 per cent of the total population of the Qing Empire.

We have already referred to the size of various parts of what we, in shorthand, will call 'China' in this book. At the moment, China is a country of about 9.3 million km².[253] China Proper, the territory of the eighteen provinces that has always been regarded as 'the heartland' of China and whose population has always consisted overwhelmingly of Han Chinese, measures less than 4 million km².[254] During the eighteenth century Qing China evolved into a huge 'empire'. For the size of that empire at its maximum, I have found quite differing estimates, very probably depending on what regions are included and which ones aren't. I simply present them to give an impression of orders of magnitude. According to Turchin, it reached its maximum size in 1790, measuring 14.7 million km². Finer claims that at the time of its biggest extension – that he dates in the first half of the nineteenth century – it was almost 13.5 million km². According to Deng,

---

[251]I collected this information from Benewick and Donald, *State of China Atlas*, 94; Fletcher, 'Ch'ing Inner Asia' and 'Heyday of the Ch'ing order'; and Naquin and Rawski, *Chinese Society*, 213.

[252]For a description of these arrangements see *Cambridge History of China*, Volumes Nine, Ten, and Eleven.

[253]Benewick and Donald, *State of China Atlas*, 102.

[254]I calculated the size of China Proper on the basis of information in Benewick and Donald, *State of China Atlas*.

it measured more than 11.5 million km² in 1812.[255] In contrast to the empires of Western Europe, China's extensions, apart from Taiwan, were not located overseas. The hundreds of thousands of Chinese that settled overseas were *not* part of it. The regions with which China had tribute relations are *not* included here as they were not in any way part of the Chinese state. In my view the grip of China on those states was too loose to justify such an inclusion.

We have not yet made any comments on the size of the China's population. In this respect, too, differences between China and the various states in Europe are huge. We are again talking about completely different orders of magnitude. In the 1680s, the recovery

Map 1 China Proper and Qing China as an empire.

[255]See Turchin, 'Theory for formation of large empires', 202; Finer, *History of Government*, III, 1130, and Deng, 'Sweet and sour Confucianism', 16. These of course are estimates. The borders of regions, which often were not exactly drawn anyhow, sometimes changed. It is not always exactly clear when, if ever, the Qing effectively ruled over certain regions. For maps see: Barraclough, *Times Atlas of World History*, 174–5; Ebrey, *Cambridge Illustrated History of China*, 223 and 241, and Herrmann, *Historical Atlas of China*, 51.

after the Ming–Qing transition began. The population figures that one comes across in the literature for that moment in time are amazingly diverse. They range from some 50 million (according to Deng) to some 140 million (according to, among others, Lee and Wang) to far over 200 million (according to Heijdra).[256] Estimates for the end of the period discussed (i.e. the 1840s) are all of the same order of magnitude, to wit somewhat over 400 million people.[257] Again, one has to realize that in the period under discussion China, a very big country, greatly expanded by conquering or incorporating various very large regions. Most of those regions, however, were and *continued* to be quite empty.

In the Chinese case, too, simply referring to the size of the country may not be very informative. So here also one may ask about the total amount of available agricultural land. From various estimates, I gather that the amount of land used for agriculture in China in the period between the end of the seventeenth century and about 1850 increased from somewhere between 400,000 and 500,000 km^2 to somewhere between 700,000 and 800,000 km^2.[258] Meadows and pasture played only a minor role, as animal husbandry was relatively unimportant. In Britain at the time, the size of agricultural land, including meadows and pastures, which amounted to about half of it, was about

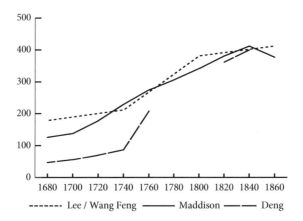

Graph 1 Estimates of China's population in millions.

Sources: Deng, 'Unveiling China's true population statistics', Appendix 3; Maddison, *Chinese Economic Performance*, 169, and Lee and Wang Feng, *One Quarter of Humanity*, 28.

---

[256]For various estimates see: Deng, 'Unveiling China's true population statistics'; Heijdra, 'Socio-economic development'; Kolb, 'About figures and aggregates', 245; Lavely and Wong, 'Revising the Malthusian narrative', and Lee and Wang, *One Quarter of Humanity*. Deng's very low estimates have not found much support among colleagues. Heijdra – on page 440 of his text – estimates the population of China at the end of the Ming period, *before* the serious population decline due to the Ming–Qing transition, at 230 to 290 million people. His estimate is supported by Mote, *Imperial China*, 743–7. Myers and Wang opt for an estimated population of 150 to 200 million around 1700 in their 'Economic developments', 565–6. The figures by Lee and Wang at the moment, overall, are regarded as the most credible.
[257]See the literature in the previous note.
[258]Vries, *Via Peking Back to Manchester*, 93–4, note 86.

120,000 km². That means that, per inhabitant, roughly three times as much agricultural land was available there as in China. Per agriculturalist the difference will have been even more pronounced in favour of Britain. Total agricultural land in China at the time amounted to less than 10 per cent of its total surface. Considering the popularity of the thesis that China would have been over-populated, that may not seem much, but one has to realize that huge tracts of China's surface were not suited for agriculture and much extra land was needed to provide actual arable land with water and fertilizer. What this exactly means for our comparison of Britain and China is difficult to assess because of the big differences in the agricultural systems of both countries, especially between the many Chinese regions where rice was the staple crop and regions where – like in most of Britain – grains like wheat and rye and animal husbandry were at the core of agricultural production. What, however, is beyond any serious doubt is the fact that in Western Europe much more agricultural land was available per capita than in China.[259]

These huge differences in the actual size between the various countries that we are discussing here and in the number of their inhabitants – and of their empires – could raise the question whether with regard to their 'administration' there are certain economies or diseconomies of scale connected to size or number of inhabitants. Or to put it in less abstract terms: does a small state in terms of size or population *ceteris paribus* need more and more expensive or less and cheaper government per km² or per capita than a big one? There is no clear, unequivocal answer to this question. And even if there was, there simply is no *ceteris paribus* when we compare, for example, early modern Britain with early modern China. A country with a huge population as compared to its neighbours only needs an army that is relatively small as compared to its total population to still overwhelm its potential enemies. When it is also big, however, that might be counterbalanced by the fact that it has such extended borders. Monitoring a big country from the capital will easily be more expensive and cost more effort than monitoring a small country. Costs of infrastructure per km² and per capita, as a rule, will be lower in a densely populated small country than in a thinly populated big one. An island in certain respects will be easier to govern than a big continental landmass. There simply are too many variables involved and too many factors to be taken into consideration to be able to give one general answer. Personally, I tend to think that when it comes to cheap and efficient government, an island like Great Britain, that is relatively small, relatively densely populated, urbanized and relatively accessible, has an advantage over a huge landmass with enormous differences in population density and less urbanization like China.

---

[259]For a comparison of the number of agriculturalists working per acre in various regions in the world in the year 1700 see Bairoch, *Révolution industrielle*, 140–3. Compare Clark, *Farewell to Alms*, 141–2: 'In 1801 England, then just moderately densely populated by European standards, had 166 people per square mile. … (T)he coastal regions of China attained … higher population densities: Jiangsu in 1787 had an incredible 875 people per square mile. It may be objected that these densities were based on paddy rice cultivation, an option not open to most of Europe. But even in the wheat regions of Shantung and Hopei Chinese population densities in 1787 were more than double those of England and France.'

The concept of state strength

In my text references to the 'strength' or 'power' of states abound. Therefore some further clarification as to what these concepts (can) mean is in order. It might be helpful to differentiate between various dimensions of state power and in that respect follow Linda Weiss and John Hobson.[260] The main difference they make is that between 'despotic power' on the one hand and 'infrastructural' or 'organic power' on the other. These distinctions are not theirs: Michael Mann introduced the concepts 'infrastructural' and 'despotic' power, and John Hall writes about 'organic' state power.[261] Despotic power concerns the range of actions which rulers can undertake without resorting to routine, institutionalized negotiation with civil society groups. It basically concerns the extent to which rulers can do as they please with their subjects. This should be distinguished from 'infrastructural' or 'organic power', which can be defined as the capacity of rulers to actually penetrate civil society and to implement political decisions logistically throughout the realm. We are talking about two quite different kinds of power that tend to stand in an inverse relationship to each other: as a rule a state with strong despotic powers have been infrastructurally weak and vice versa.[262]

When it comes to 'infrastructural' or 'organic' state power, Weiss and Hobson in the introduction of their book make further differentiations and come up with a useful distinction between three varieties. To begin with, there is what they call *penetrative power*: the ability of a state to reach into and directly interact with the population. Then there is *extractive power*: the ability of a state to extract resources, both material and human, from society. For such extractive power to be stable, routinized and enduring, it presupposes negotiation with the social power groupings. Third, they refer to the *negotiated aspect of infrastructural power*. Here we are dealing with a form of power that implies a rudimentary reciprocity between political and economic power actors. They, I think correctly, claim that an embedded but autonomous state apparatus can create more economic and social energy, to the extent that it has more supportive social linkages. That would mean that a state's strength increases with the effective *embedding* of its autonomy, whereas state weakness ensues from abrasion against society. What is very important in the context of our analysis, where there is a clear tendency to talk in terms of 'states *versus* markets' or 'public *versus* private', is that one should *not* automatically think in terms of a zero-sum game where the state's loss is society's gain and the other way around. This opposition of the public and private sector indeed, as Mazzucato writes, often is 'a myth'.[263] In its 'highest stage', infrastructural, organic power may imply a capacity to coordinate and totally transform the economy. Infrastructural power is about societies' abilities to get things

---

[260] See their *States and Economic Development*, 6–8.
[261] Mann, 'Autonomous power'; idem, *Sources of Social Power*, and Hall, *Powers & Liberties*, 133–44.
[262] Mann, 'Autonomous power', 113.
[263] Mazzucato, *Entrepreneurial State*.

done'.[264] In our comparison of the situation in China and Britain and other parts of Western Europe the distinctions discussed above will prove to be highly relevant and informative. They provide good measuring rods for the ways in which a state can have power and influence.

I want to emphasize that talking about 'state strength' is not just a hobby of contemporary social scientists and historians – far from it. As indicated, people in Europe, in particular of course rulers and big merchants, in the long eighteenth century were fascinated by state power and constantly compared, for example, their wealth, armies, navies, bureaucracies or tax systems with those of other states.[265] Such comparisons were also drawn with non-European states. Many ways of measuring state strength were suggested and tried. They knew that strength was not simply a function of available resources or despotic power. Central to the idea of the fiscal-military state was the recognition that international power rested on the ability to *extract* resources rather than on the level of resources per se, which means that strength was primarily based on internal coherence and organization.

SOME COMMENTS ON METHODS, MEASUREMENTS AND MONEY

The fallacy of misplaced precision is an empirical statement which is made precise beyond the practical limits of accuracy.

Fischer, *Historians' Fallacies*, 61

Money plays the largest part in determining the course of history.

Karl Marx and Friedrich Engels in *The Communist Manifesto*

My book tries to be systematically comparative and empirically precise. It is extremely important, however, not to succumb to 'the fallacy of misplaced precision' in the comparisons I make – that is, not to try and be more precise and firm than the available information allows. It cannot be emphasized enough that what I give in this text are *orders of magnitude*, *estimates* and sometimes even mere *guesstimates*. What I am looking for are orders of magnitude that are sufficiently certain and precise to be used as ingredients for a comparison, not absolute certainty and precise hard data, which is simply lacking. We are discussing a pre-statistical period. Often we lack even basic information about extremely important matters like population size, size of arable land, wages and prices, tax revenue, other government revenues, numbers of people in army, navy, bureaucracy and so on. The data we do have often are scarce, imprecise, unreliable and difficult to

---

[264]See Morris, *Why the West Rules*, 24. The expression thus has a much broader meaning than that used in Guldi, *Roads to Power*, where the author discusses Britain as an *infrastructure* state, i.e. a state that takes care of material infrastructure.

[265]See Introduction note 15.

compare. There are major problems of definition and categorization. The geographical entities we are talking about often were subject to change.

Even when it comes to public finance of early modern governments, the sinews of their power, we often are badly informed. Those governments did not have what we would *now* call real 'budgets'.[266] Surprising as it may sound, at the level of central administration it normally was anything but clear exactly how much revenue came in and how much of it was spent on what. China's rulers did not have a real budget until the beginning of the twentieth century.[267] Chen in his book from 1914 on the system of taxation in China under the Qing duly informs his readers that his book is 'by no means satisfactory from a statistical standpoint … because no one can solve the mystery of the financial conditions in all the provinces of China owing to the inefficiency of the financial control'.[268] At the very end of the *Ancien Régime*, in 1781, Necker, the minister of finance of France, to put it in modern terms, announced a surplus of revenue over expenditure of 10 million livres whereas Calonne, who was to become his successor, argued that there was a deficit of over 46 millions livres.[269] This difference appeared to be partly due to a misunderstanding, but such a discrepancy nevertheless indicates how hard it was, even for experts, to find their way in 'public finances' at the time. In that light it will not come as a surprise that a specialist in the history of early modern France wrote: 'The complexities of the fiscal system almost defy description'.[270]

Lack of transparency was often created on purpose. A specialist in Dutch history, Van Deursen, wrote that it almost seems as if the financial administration of the Dutch Republic was made as chaotic as possible to make sure that no one was able to get a complete survey, not even the highest officials themselves.[271] According to Dickson, an expert in the public finances of the Habsburg Empire in the eighteenth century, 'revenue figures were often little more than guesses, were not always from the year stated, were sometimes averages, [and] were not always added up correctly'. On top of that, revenue was often paid in arrears.[272] What we see in (Western) Europe is often a mix and overlap of what we would nowadays call 'the public' and 'the private', in the field of finance as well as in matters of administration or warfare. According to Bosher 'there were very few phases in the management of government funds which could properly be described as *public* finance'.[273] Again, apart from *parts* of Britain's administration, this probably applies to all European countries discussed in this text. Even in Britain it took until the Napoleonic Wars for the first transparent overview of annual public expenditure

---

[266]For some comments on the meaning of the term and on when such 'budgets', with or without double-entry bookkeeping, were introduced in various parts of Europe see Scott, 'Fiscal-military state', 26–9.

[267]Stanley, *Late Ch'ing Finance*, 4.

[268]Chen, *System of Taxation*, 8.

[269]Bosher, 'French administration', 590.

[270]Hoffman, 'Early modern France', 230. See further for the intricacies of France's fiscal-financial system, Soll, *Reckoning*, chs 6 and 9.

[271]I found this quote in Veenendaal, 'Fiscal crises', 136. See also the text by Soll referred to in the previous note.

[272]Dickson, *Finance and Government, II*, 90.

[273]Bosher, *French Finances*, 6.

to be published.[274] In China's system of rule there was much less of a legacy of feudalism with its parcellized sovereignty and indirect rule than in most of Europe. In principle, China was a centralized state; in practice, though, it definitely was not and here too the private and the public often were 'mixed'.

There are serious problems of definition. What exactly must be counted as tax and what not? How to differentiate, if at all, between taxes and other kinds of government income? The accent in this book will be on taxation, but where possible other sources of central government revenue will be included. Even if one would be able to get a clear overview of the official data, one can be almost certain there will have been big differences between those quota and the amounts that were *actually* paid. To claim corruption, fraud, embezzlement and leakage were not unknown, is an understatement. In this respect there are problems for the historical researcher when it comes to the income-side of the equation as well as the expenditure-side. On top of that, differences between regular and irregular revenues and expenditures could be huge, as could be the differences between times of peace and times of war. This makes it hard to find out what averages mean and what figures would be representative.

In contemporary society a major part of government expenditure is on people working for government as personnel. Here too the situation in early modern times was complicated as the difference between 'public' and 'private' was anything but clear-cut. Difficulties are legion when it comes to analysing how many people were actually working for government as civilians or in the military, what official remuneration (if any) they received and what exactly (if anything!) they did. Especially in Western Europe, there were people exerting, what we would nowadays call 'public functions', who were not public servants in the contemporary sense of the word, as they owned their position via inheritance or had bought it. There were others who were officials in name but held their jobs as sinecures and did not do any actual work at all. Remuneration for public services quite often was not or not only in the form of a salary paid in money. Many jobs, in particular on a regional and 'municipal' level, were just honorary and there was no, or very little, salary involved. Often, 'officials' had to improvise methods to get some income out of their 'job', if it didn't actually cost them money. In China there were many people who worked for officials and did 'public' jobs without being in any way in the service of the state and without being paid by the state. As a matter of fact, they formed the bulk of those who provided public services. Those officials that were employed by the state supplemented their official income with all kinds of fees and charges, but on the other hand also paid a lot of public expenditures out of their own pockets.

The historian in this respect can only try to be as clear, consistent and prudent as possible. What I look for in this text is 'orders of magnitude'. I am under no illusion of precision but hope to get a more solid *basis* for a serious comparative analysis of the role of government in China and various states in the West in promoting or hindering economic growth in general and in causing the Great Divergence in particular. That is

---

[274]See Knight, *Britain against Napoleon*, 389.

the main goal of my overarching research project for which in this text I try to collect and construct essential empirical data.

A note on money and silver

Government revenues, expenditures and debts will play a key role in my analysis. These are expressed in the monetary units of the various countries at the time: for Britain, that unit was the pound sterling and, for China, the tael. To put the data that I will present in perspective, one needs to know the relative value of these two 'currencies'. I have put the term 'currencies' in brackets as both the pound sterling and the tael were moneys of account – money units whose value was expressed in terms of a certain amount and purity of silver but that were not actual (silver) coins. China did not have any official silver coins at all. Reference to Chinese silver here, in principle, means reference to un-coined silver. The pound sterling and the official (kuping) tael were just 'measures'. Britain did have silver coins, but the pound sterling was not one of them. The country was *de facto* on a gold standard for most of the period we discuss here, with the value of the pound normally being expressed in terms of gold. For China, I will refer to the official kuping tael. In fact there were many different taels with differing weights and purities.

The question of the relative value of pound and tael is not difficult to answer, at least as long as we take the official (kuping) tael as our point of departure and look at the amounts of silver that tael and pound represented. A kuping tael was one ounce of Chinese silver, or in Western terms 37.3 grams of silver, with (officially) 99 per cent purity.[275] It was what the national treasury that used to measure receipts and payments and was the nationwide standard for paying taxes.[276] Weight and purity of course both matter. Actually there were many different taels with different weights and purities. Even when it comes to the weight of the official kuping or treasury tael experts apparently do not fully agree.[277] References to taels in this text will always be to kuping taels unless indicated otherwise. In connection with foreign trade, from 1858 there also was a Haikwan or custom tael with a slightly different value: to wit 1.14 Chinese ounces of silver.[278] During the period we discuss here, the value of a pound sterling was somewhat over 111 grams of pure silver and officially equalled 3 taels, each of one Chinese ounce of silver. In the direct trade of the English

---

[275]One Chinese ounce of silver is called a liang, the currency of account with that value is called a (kuping) tael. See Lin, *China Upside Down, XXIII*. For an introduction to China's complicated monetary system see in alphabetical order: Deng, 'Miracle or mirage'; Horesh, *Chinese Money*; Kahn, *Currencies of China*; King, *Money and Monetary Policy*; Lin, *China Upside Down*; Ma, 'Chinese money and monetary system'; Morse, *Trade and Administration*, ch. 5; Peng, *Monetary History*; Von Glahn, *Fountain of Fortune*; idem, 'Money use in China', and Wang, 'Evolution of the Chinese monetary system'.

[276]I paraphrase Peng, *Monetary History*, 669.

[277]According to Deng, 'Miracle or mirage', note 23, it weighs 37.5 grams and according to Hsü, *Rise of Modern China*, XXIX, 37.8 grams. Peng, *Monetary History*, 669–70, gives figures in the same order of magnitude and points out that Canton had a tael that weighed a Canton ounce which was slightly different from the official treasury ounce.

[278]Peng, *Monetary History*, 669.

East India Company with China, that exchange rate showed some fluctuations.[279] In this text I will systematically convert figures in pounds sterling into taels and the other way around at this 'exchange rate'. When referring to other currencies like guilders or livres, I will also give their 'exchange rate' against taels and other 'currencies', in principle, on the basis of the amount of silver they represent. As we will see, however, silver equivalents need *not* always indicate actual 'exchange rates'.

In this way, just as we express the value of money in US dollars today, for example, I hope to create certain comparability between all my data. This comparability is not just a scholarly figment. Silver *was* traded all over the globe: or rather, in terms of value, it was the *most important* commodity in early modern global trade. That is not all: according to a very popular point of view in current global history, China played a major role in that trade and is even supposed to have functioned as 'the global silver sink' during most of that era. This means, according to scholars who adhere to this view, that a very substantial amount – estimates differ from half, to two-thirds and in an extreme case even three-quarters – of all traded silver from Latin America ended up in China till roughly the 1820s, when a net silver drain out of China started. Huge amounts of that Latin American silver are supposed to have reached China from Europe via the sea route along the Cape or, more indirectly, overland. On top of that, apart from a substantial domestic production, China's economy was also supplied with silver from Annam and Vietnam and Burma, with silver coming from Latin America over the Pacific and via Manila and, very important at times, with silver from Japan. I will discuss this thesis later on.[280] Whatever the actual merits of this silver-sink thesis, silver was traded all over the globe and it did function as the basis of actual currencies or as money of account across the world. In this context one simply has to refer to the Spanish/Mexican silver dollar, at the time almost a global currency that was not only used in Latin America but also, until far in the nineteenth century, was (legal) tender in the United States, in Europe and in parts of Asia. In China these dollars became an important money of account and in various regions even a very important 'real' currency.[281] In principle, silver coins imported into China had to be turned into ingots and could not function as legal tender but in practice they very often did. Here too weight and purity have to be taken into consideration. According to Lin, dollars produced in Mexico weighed about 27 grams in the period discussed in this book and amounted to some 24 grams of pure silver. In pure silver they thus contained about the equivalent of two-thirds of a tael, whereas one tael contained about the equivalent in silver of 1.43 dollars.[282] This is the exchange

---

[279]Mui and Mui, *Management of Monopoly*, 57–61. To be precise: a pound sterling equalled 111.35808 grams of pure silver. For further explanation see Lin, *China Upside Down*, Explanatory note, XXIII–XXVI.

[280]See the index under silver-sink.

[281]For some examples of the use of Spanish/Mexican dollars in China see Hao, *Commercial Revolution*; Irigoin, 'End of a silver era'; King, *Money and Monetary Policy*; Lin, *China Upside Down*; Peng, *Monetary History, II*, ch. 8.1.4, and Von Glahn, 'Cycles of silver' and idem, 'Foreign silver coins'.

[282]Lin, *China Upside Down*, XXII–XXIII. According to Deng, 'Miracle or mirage', note 23, a Mexican dollar weighed between 24.25 and 25.56 grams, with a purity (from 1555–1820) of between 89.6 and 93.1 per cent. Taking an average weight and an average purity, one kuping tael in that case equalled some 1.6 dollars. That is the same order of magnitude we find in Hsü, *Rise of Modern China*, XXIX, who claims that one kuping tael equalled 1.57 Mexican dollars. I will use Lin's exchange rate knowing that there is an upward margin of some 10 per cent.

rate I will use throughout this book. Many different weights, purities and values existed but differences overall were not so big as to substantially impact on the gist of my claims.

In brief, silver not only was exchanged as a *commodity* all over the world, it also was actually used as *money* in all continents. In China it was not coined, nevertheless functioned as 'money'. One could and often *had* to pay with it and it functioned as a means to express values. The ingots one used passed as a bullion currency, with the value determined at every transaction between payer and payee as to the fineness and weight of the silver. In Britain, money as a rule was convertible into silver, at a rate of about 111 grams per pound sterling. So here too one could pay with silver and express values in it. In Western Europe as well as in China paper money was known and used. However, a prevailing belief existed that paper money could only function effectively if it was convertible on demand into gold or silver coin – and of course shortage of coin was often the very reason for the issue of paper money. In that respect it really was a matter of emergency when, in 1797 in Britain, convertibility was suspended and only fully restored in 1821.

The conversion of currencies into silver and the other way around of course has to be done with utmost care. It would certainly be a mistake to pretend that silver functioned in early modern international and intercontinental trade like, for example, the American dollar did under the Breton Woods system. Of every piece of silver that changed hands in international trade, whether it was un-coined or coined, the exact weight and purity had to be determined. But that was no different from what one had to do in domestic transactions. Even in the case of coined silver one had to be very careful: the actual silver weight of coins could be changed officially – that is, coins could be debased. The weight could be tampered with. It could simply change because of wear and tear. In this book I have invariably used the official silver weights of various moneys.[283] Silver (coins) in Western Europe and American dollars normally were between 85 and 95 per cent pure. In China *sycee* silver officially was supposed to be (close to) 100 per cent pure. In practice it often was much less. Weighing and assaying were not always up to standard: pure silver was not by all means pure, but pure according to standard of purity. The Imperial government probably accepted silver ranging in touch from 95 to 100 as pure.[284] If one wanted to turn loose pieces of silver into an accepted ingot, one always lost some silver in the process. In the case of tax payment, central government collected the so-called 'melting fees' or 'meltage fees', as each year with collecting taxes it incurred an actual loss of silver in the process of re-melting and recasting chunks and bits of un-minted silver into oval shaped ingots.[285] We find examples of cases where *sycee*

---

[283]For the period 1450–1750 see Braudel and Spooner, 'Prices in Europe', 458. They do not provide information on the Prussian thaler. From 1764 onwards, its value was 16.7 grams of silver. For more detailed general information covering the period from 1660 to 1775, see McCusker, *Money and Exchange*.

[284]King, *Money and Monetary Policy*, 78.

[285]There often were huge differences between official rates, accepted 'customary' rates and extraordinary rates that were simply forced on people.

shoes, with an official weight of 50 taels, especially when certified, passed at a premium over bullion, just like coins did over un-coined bullion.[286]

The actual exchange rate of the pound sterling versus the tael that I mentioned earlier on (1 pound equals 3 taels) was indeed based on the amounts of silver they represented. There, however, are many examples of certain coins having a so-called 'premium' over other coins or over bullion. Clear examples are the dollars from Spanish America that were exchanged in certain parts of China at a value that was higher – and at times also lower, but we will not expand on that – than would be 'justified' on the basis of their silver weight and purity. In King's words, 'the Chinese at times and in certain regions accepted dollar coins by weight only, placing primary importance on the quantity of metal the coin contained; in other areas and at other times the Chinese accepted coins by count or tale without reference to their intrinsic value.'[287] Apparently dollar coins often were regarded as more trustworthy, as being of a higher standard and, in particular, easier to use, than simple pieces of silver with a similar weight. They therefore could fetch a higher price. According to one source, at the very end of our period this premium could be as high as 50 per cent. That may have been exceptional, but substantial premiums were quite normal.[288] Foreign silver dollars were very much sought after. In that respect several scholars point at the striking fact that, in particular, at the time of the famous silver drain, China *imported* foreign silver coins that were traded with a substantial premium over their silver value, whereas it *exported* silver ingots.[289] Actually matters were even more complicated; there also were differences between *different* dollars when it came to the premium they might fetch in China.[290] It would be a major mistake to think in terms of one undifferentiated category called 'money' based on directly and smoothly interchangeable monetary substrates of, in our case, (precious) metals. Gold, silver and copper – to confine us to these metals – could have quite different functions as money and their mutual exchange rates could fluctuate substantially. A difference between the actual exchange rate and the silver content ratio also existed between the silver dollars and the pound sterling. Spanish/Mexican dollars as a rule exchanged, certainly till 1814, for one fourth of a pound sterling, whereas they were some 24 grams of pure silver and the pound about 111. After 1814 there could be small deviations.[291] The US dollar is taken to be equal in value to the Mexican one, although there actually was a tiny difference in value.

This means that expressing the value of revenues, expenditures and debts of the central government in various countries in terms of 'moneys of account' whose value is expressed

[286]King, *Money and Monetary Policy*, 31 and 73.

[287]King, *Money and Monetary Policy*, 46.

[288]For that premium of 50 per cent see Kahn, *Currencies of China*, 129. See for other examples of sometimes quite high premiums Hao, 'Commercial revolution', 35–44; Irigoin, 'Trojan horse'; King, *Money and Monetary Policy*, under 'dollar, Chinese attitude toward'; Peng, *Monetary History*, 672–8, and Von Glahn, 'Foreign silver coins'.

[289]See Hamashita in Grove and Selden, *Takeshi Hamashita*, 27–38 and 114–44; Horesh, *Chinese Money*; Irigoin, 'Trojan horse'; and Von Glahn, 'Cycles of silver'.

[290]For *different* premiums for *different* dollars see e.g. Burger, 'Coin production', 180–6; Irigoin, 'Trojan horse'; Peng, *Monetary History*, 672–8, and Von Glahn, 'Cycles of silver', 52–3.

[291]Lin, *China Upside Down*, XXIV, note 8.

in terms of silver, as will be done in this text, is not as straightforward a procedure as it may seem and needs to be done with care. If we manage to get a clear view on the orders of magnitude involved in terms of silver, we have relevant information concerning those questions where the absolute and relative amounts of silver (equivalents) that a country disposes of matters, for example, in matters of international exchange or transfer. That information, however, would not be very helpful in providing answers to a number of questions that are of the utmost importance in the context of our research. To be able to judge how 'present' the state was financially in the national economies under review, one also has to express revenues, expenditures and debts in per capita terms and as percentage of GDP. To know the impact of payments to and from the state one would have to compare them with real incomes and thus also look at income and price levels. As far as possible, I will try and come up with these different measures to provide specific, and sometimes different, angles on the importance of the state in economic life.

TWO TOPICS THAT WILL NOT BE DISCUSSED EXTENSIVELY: PROPERTY RIGHTS AND LAW

As far as possible my analysis will be quantitative, structural and systematically comparative. I will start with a description of what one might call the 'hardware' of the states under discussion; that is their revenues, expenditures, debts, personnel and institutions. In the next part of my analysis, I will focus on their economic policies. Overall my analysis will be somewhat biased in its explicit attention given to the state's 'hardware' and take much of its inspiration from the work of Michael Mann on the sources of (social) power.[292] I do, however, realize that the most important government activities in terms of money and people involved need not be the ones that actually have the biggest impact on economic development.[293] Government implements all kinds of policies that directly or indirectly impinge on economic life even if they are not or not primarily 'economic'. One must be wary not to neglect the very important role of the state as an institution that provides all kinds of public goods and that makes a society, to put it in James Scott's terminology, 'legible'.[294] Where possible and where I feel acceptably competent, I will take them into consideration. To keep things manageable, I will not *extensively* discuss property rights and law, to mention just two topics that would need to be dealt with more thoroughly in an analysis that wants to be exhaustive. There has always existed a tendency to claim that in these respects differences between Western Europe and China in the early modern era were huge.

References to property rights, including patents, from the very beginning played a central role in debates on Western economic development and its supposedly unique

---

[292]For Mann's ideas on power see his *Sources of Social Power, I*; idem, 'Autonomous power', and idem, 'Response'.
[293]For critical comments with regard to Mann's tendency to focus too exclusively on the state's 'hard power' see Braddick, 'Early modern English state'; Epstein, 'Rise of the West', 247; and He, *Paths toward the Modern Fiscal State*, 18–20.
[294]See Scott, *Seeing Like a State*, 2.

'capitalist' economic order. They received a boost in the work of new institutionalist economists and social scientists like North and his various co-authors and, at the moment, in particular Acemoglu and Robinson, who present them as a necessary and at times even sufficient precondition for sustained development and growth. Their importance for stable economic situations and for a society's potential to develop and grow is fairly obvious but their explanatory value when it comes to actually explaining the Great Divergence, in my view, is highly debatable or, rather, I would claim very weak. I will succinctly present my position here and refer the reader to further literature on the topic.[295] Great Britain certainly was not the first society with property rights. Basically all societies in history have always known some kind of protection of property. To me it is not clear in what sense Britain would be different here. I, moreover, see no concrete direct links between changes in property rights and the emergence of modern economic growth during industrialization in Britain, or rather I do not see any major changes in that respect just before and during take off. In several respects property rights in Britain after 1688 were *not* better protected, as a strengthened central government had acquired *more* power to interfere with them on the basis of national interest. More in general, one has to realize that, as will be discussed later on, the history of Western Europe was not exactly lacking examples of 'expropriation' and that well protected, entrenched property rights including patents can also be an obstacle to growth.[296] Unsurprisingly many scholars who studied the actual process of British industrialization, the essence of the emerging Great Divergence, like Allen, Clark, Crafts, Findlay and O'Rourke, Jones and McCloskey, therefore are not at all convinced that property rights were the factor that made the key difference.[297] A recent volume dedicated to property rights, land markets and economic growth in the European countryside from the thirteenth century onwards shows that many regions in pre-industrial Europe with 'imperfect' or 'multi-layered' property rights nevertheless had economic growth. Its authors found no direct, clear link between certain property rights and industrialization.[298] It is very important in this complex field to differentiate. For Great Britain, for example, after 1688 small peasant property clearly was much less protected (as shows in the continuing process of enclosures) than aristocratic estates that via all sorts of rules of 'entail' and (strict) settlement often continued to be all but completely protected, that is protected *against any sale and division*.[299]

When it comes to property rights in Qing China some more specific comments are in order. All the literature that I have studied strongly suggests that private property actually

---

[295]For debates on the importance of property rights and my position see my *Escaping Poverty*, 323–32. I here also want to refer to Everest-Phillips, 'Myth of "secure property rights"', that I only read after finishing that book.

[296]Watt's patent, in several respects was an *obstacle* to further development of steam power. See Macleod, *Heroes of Invention*, 85–6 and 107. For debates on the importance of patents and my position see my *Escaping Poverty*, under 'patent' and in particular, for the situation in industrializing Britain, Mokyr, 'Intellectual property rights'.

[297]See for references my 'Does wealth entirely depend on inclusive institutions and pluralist politics?', note 21. For Jones' view see his 'Economics without history' that appeared after my *Escaping Poverty*.

[298]Béaur, *Property Rights, Land Markets and Economic Growth*.

[299]See e.g. Daunton, *Progress and Poverty*, under 'settlement' (inheritance).

was quite normal there, indeed even the rule. Some important differences between China and Western Europe, however, did exist. Let me focus on Chinese land rights, the most important form of property. It is not easy to make firm and valid general statements about them. We are dealing here with an extremely complex topic, so complex that an expert in the field concluded: 'Complexity is the only feature of the pre-Taiping land-tenure system (i.e. the period before 1850) that can be noted with assurance.'[300] What contributed to this complexity was the quite current distinction between topsoil and subsoil rights (i.e. between ownership rights and cultivation rights) over one and the same tract of land. The form of actual co-ownership this implied made eviction all but impossible, even more so as rents that often became fixed in monetary terms could only be raised by landlords with great difficulty, if at all, because of strong social pressure and 'custom'. As long as a tenant paid that fixed rent he could feel pretty sure that he could continue to till 'his' land. What complicated matters even more is the fact that those landowners who owned a substantial amount of land rented that out, as a rule, in many separate, often quite dispersed plots, whereas the tiny farms of ordinary peasants often consisted of various separate lots. Overall, it seems to me that in China individual, absolute property rights were less common than in Western Europe. Property rights there tended to be more restrictive and 'collective' and were more burdened with duties and obligations.[301] The concept of 'conditional sale', moreover, continued to be important.[302]

When it comes to law, most experts now agree that written contracts were quite normal in early modern China and their 'juridical' status not fundamentally different from that in Western Europe.[303] If one wanted to prove one's ownership of a piece of land, for example, one needed a 'real' contract (i.e. a contract with an official seal that could only be given by a state official). Receiving such a seal implied one had to pay taxes over the land, which then turned into proof one officially owned it. This could lead to a situation where people 'volunteered' to pay taxes to thereby show land was theirs.[304] Although I guess the opposite: people preferring *not* to officially own land because that

---

[300]Bernhardt, *Rents, Taxes, and Peasant Resistance*, 14. For general analyses and examples see Bernhardt's book; Huang, *Peasant Economy and Economic Change* and idem, *Peasant Family and Rural Development*, in particular ch. 6, and the literature in the next note.
[301]See e.g. Linklater, *Owning the Earth*, 156–7, where the author claims that: 'in China ownership of land was burdened with duties. It was the reverse of the English belief that attached rights to property'.
[302]For the thesis that individual property rights and individual freedom of enterprise were more restricted in Qing China than in Britain at the same moment in time, see Gates, *China's Motor*; Linklater, *Owning the Earth*, ch. 9; Macauley, 'World made simple'; Mazumdar, *Sugar and Society*; Schurman, 'Traditional property concepts', and Wakefield, *Fenjia*. For the view that in fact there was not much difference, see Pomeranz, *Great Divergence*, 69–107. Buoye, *Manslaughter*, gives an analysis of the conflict between various perceptions with regard to property and ownership in eighteenth-century China and points at the existence *and* the erosion of a moral-economy perspective. Isett, *State, Peasant, and Merchant* contains a lot of information on property relations in Manchuria and China. For the most recent overview see Kishimoto, 'Property rights'. For the British situation with respect to property rights in land, see Daunton, *Progress and Poverty*, chs 3 and 4.
[303]For the role of contracts in China's early modern economy see, Zelin, Ocko and Gardella, *Contract and Property*.
[304]Osborn, 'Property, taxes and state protection of rights'.

implied paying taxes will have occurred more frequently.[305] Debates on the role of law in economic history have a strong tendency to focus on property rights, but the importance of what one may call 'the rule of law' of course is much broader. It is not by accident that Max Weber in all his publications on 'Western exceptionalism' was so keen on finding out whether systems of law were rational and formal and how they actually functioned. In his view 'predictability, continuity, trustworthiness and objectivity of legal order are all essential for … capitalism on a large scale.'[306] I will not go into this interesting topic in this text and refer the reader to existing literature.[307] I only want to point at one interesting fact here and that is that England continued to have a system of common law. It never took, as Weber himself indicates, Roman law as the basis of its juridical system. Its common law system was a system of case law that operated on the basis of persuasive authority. This means that conscious action and interpretation by law makers and judges, elements that Weber thinks should be eliminated as much as possible in any full-blown,[308] *rational*-bureaucratic system of law, continued to be very important in what is so often described as the first modern state. Alan Macfarlane, who lays a very strong emphasis on Britain's system of law as an explanation for its extraordinary economic development, strikingly enough, apart from the principle of the rule of law, that he too considers fundamental, focuses on its flexibility, its attention to context and the role of juries in it.[309] In this context interesting debates are being waged on the legal origins of property rights and on the possibly differing effects on economic development of common law and civil law legal systems.[310]

Weber's 'rationality' and 'predictability' of law as a rule is connected to its formal, impersonal character. North, Wallis and Weingast consider that a fundamental precondition for (a possible transition to) an open-access order.[311] Here again Wong and Rosenthal, as indicated, take an anti-Eurocentric stance. They claim that the informal personal mechanisms as they prevailed in China's *domestic* juridical arrangements, at least when it comes to trade, in particular long-distance trade in China, were just as efficient as the formal arrangements that prevailed in Western long-distance trade *between* countries.[312] Even if that were true, informal arrangements will become quite problematic when one has to come to terms with real outsiders – that is, people operating in another legal and political system. Then informality simply no longer functions. The more China was opened the more obvious this became. As far as I can see there as yet is

---

[305]See Elvin, 'Why intensify?'

[306]I quote directly from the English translation of Weber, *Wirtschaft und Gesellschaft*, 1095.

[307]For China I refer to Bernardt and Huang, *Civil Law*; Huang, *Civil Justice*, and idem, *Code, Custom and Legal Practice*; for Britain see Introduction note 309.

[308]See for a somewhat different interpretation Cotterell, 'Development of capitalism'.

[309]See Macfarlane's numerous comments on law in Britain in his *Invention of the Modern World* and Mokyr, *Enlightened Economy*, ch. 16, where Mokyr emphasizes the importance of trust, confidence and *informal* rules in British society.

[310]For some introductory comments and literature see Helpman, *Mystery of Economic Growth*, 119–22.

[311]See North, Wallis and Weingast, *Violence and Social Orders*, ch. 5.

[312]Rosenthal and Wong, *Before and Beyond Divergence*, ch. 3.

insufficient literature in which the connection between law and economic development is tackled on a level that is concrete as well as generalizable enough to allow scholars to make firm general statements about law's concrete role in the Great Divergence. I am personally convinced that role is substantial and will be explored more in future. At the moment the best I can do is refer to two recent publications to show 'the state of the art'.[313]

---

[313]Cooter and Schäfer, *Solomon's Knot,* and Ma and Van Zanden, *Law and Long-Term Economic Change.*

CHAPTER 1
REVENUE

Revenue at the disposal and discretion of central government

Taxes upon every article that enters the mouth, or covers the back, or is placed under the foot – taxes upon everything which is pleasant to see, hear, feel, smell or taste – taxes upon warmth, light, locomotion – taxes on everything on earth, and the waters under the earth – on everything that comes from abroad or is grown at home – taxes on the raw material – taxes on every fresh value that is added to it by the industry of man – taxes on the sauce which pampers a man's appetite, and the drug that restores him to health – on the ermine which decorates the judge, and the rope which hangs the criminal – on the poor man's salt and the rich man's spice – on the brass nails of the coffin, and the ribbons of the bride – at bed or board, couchant or Levant, we must pay. The school-boy whips his taxed top; the beardless youth manages his taxed horse with a taxed bridle, on a taxed road; and the dying Englishman pouring his medicine, which has paid seven per cent, into a spoon that has paid fifteen per cent, flings himself back upon his chintz bed, which has paid twenty-two per cent, makes his will on an eight pound stamp, and expires in the arms of an apothecary, who has paid a licence of a hundred pounds for the privilege of putting him to death. His whole property is then immediately taxed from two to ten per cent. Besides his probate, large fees are demanded for burying him in the chancel. His virtues are handed down to posterity on taxed marble, and he will then be gathered to his fathers and taxed no more.[1]

> Reverend Sidney Smith (1771–1845) in the *Edinburgh Review*
> of which he was one of the founders, January 1820

The first thing to be reformed in China is its taxation. No government can exist without money and China cannot improve so long as her officials have no better way of getting funds than at present.

> Sir Robert Hart (1835–1911) Inspector General of the Imperial Maritime Customs
> in a letter to Customs Commissioner E. D. Drew, 4 June 1869

Let us begin our actual analysis with what many people will probably consider to be the most important, and probably the most resented, way in which government makes its presence felt in economic life: taxation and other government levies. As Tocqueville

---

[1] I found this quotation in Davies, *History of Money*, 299–300.

wrote in his analysis of Europe's *Ancien Régime*, there are hardly any public affairs that are not based upon taxes or that in the end do not result in taxes.[2] In Western states they have always been at the heart of the political process, with the budget as 'the bare skeleton of the state ruthlessly stripped of all misleading ideology'.[3] According to Schumpeter, a scholar who chooses to analyse the fiscal history of a state 'discerns the thunder of world history more clearly than anywhere else'.[4] I will therefore start my analysis by looking at government revenue. What I will try and compare here are taxes collected *for* and, directly or indirectly, spent *by* central government.

The reference to *central* government is quintessential. This text will not deal with revenue that is never put at the disposal of central government as it is collected *and* at the discretion of authorities other than those of the central state. The point is that central government in Europe, at least normally, was not in (full) control of local spending, so it would be misleading to add locally spent money to its budget. The situation in China was less clear-cut as we will see. What Hofmann in the following quote writes about *Ancien Régime* France applies to practically all the European countries discussed in this book: 'Since so much tax revenue was spent in the provinces, the monarchy had to wrestle control over its funds from local elites, who had their own ideas about how the money should be spent. The result was to reduce the portion of tax revenues at the king's disposal.'[5] The distinction between central and local is not always neat, sometimes it even is fairly arbitrary, often the nature of the available information does not even allow making it. But as it is so important I will try to make it as consistently as possible.

Again, the focus is on Britain and China, but I will also present data for other (Western) European nations. As my thesis is that taxes and, more in general, government income was much higher – on a per capita basis and at times even in absolute terms – in Britain than in China, I will, to not be accused of special pleading, systematically 'minimalize' figures with regard to Britain (use lower-bound estimates) and 'maximize' figures with regard to China (use upper-bound estimates). I will do the same with regard to government expenditures. For Britain most of the comments will be on the situation from roughly 1688 to 1850 or somewhat earlier, depending on the available data. For my 'sources', I refer to the literature in the notes.[6] For China I will refer to roughly the

---

[2]Tocqueville, *Ancien Régime*, 159.

[3]The reference to 'the bare skeleton' is originally from the Austrian scholar Rudolf Goldscheid (1870–1931) in his *Staatssozialismus oder Staatskapitalismus*, 128. The translation is mine.

[4]I took this quotation from the reprint of his article on the crisis of the tax state in Swedberg, *Economics and Sociology*, 100–1.

[5]Hoffman, 'Early modern France', 231.

[6]There is a massive literature on the history of taxation in (Great) Britain at the time. I used, in alphabetical order: Beckett and Turner, 'Taxation and economic growth'; Bonney, 'Towards the comparative fiscal history of Britain and France'; Brewer, *Sinews of Power*; Capie, 'Origins and development of stable fiscal and monetary institutions'; all the publications by Daunton referred to in the Bibliography; Harling and Mandler, 'From "fiscal-military" state to laissez-faire state'; Horstman, 'Taxation in the Zenith'; Kozub, 'Evolution of taxation'; Mathias, 'Taxation and industrialization'; Mathias and O'Brien, 'Taxation in Britain and France'; all the articles by O'Brien dealing with taxation and fiscal affairs referred to in the Bibliography; Schremmer, 'Taxation and public finance'; and Weiss and Hobson, *States and Economic Development*. Finally I refer to the articles by O'Brien, Hoppit, Capie, Daunton and Peden in Winch and O'Brien, *Political Economy of British Historical Experience*, and to the edited volumes referred to in Introduction note 14 that contain many articles dealing with the situation in (Great) Britain.

same period in time, again depending on the available data. Here too I refer to the notes for my 'sources'.[7] A preliminary general remark is in order here; for the sake of comparability, I will systematically calculate and present amounts of money in terms of amounts of silver. This does not imply that all the payments I refer to *actually* were made in silver. For the period covered here that is helpful and sensible. The position of silver as a general measure of wealth, because of its substantial change in value as compared to gold, became quite different from the 1840s onwards, but that, by and large, is outside 'our' period.

Let us begin by presenting two quite rough indicators, the total and per capita revenues of central government for several European countries, expressed in amounts of silver (Tables 8a and 8b).

Table 8a Average annual tax revenue of central government in grams of silver per capita in selected European countries as estimated in recent publications

	Britain*	Dutch Rep.	France	Prussia	Austria	Spain
1650–59	31	114	56	9	11	57
1700–09	92	211	43	25	16	29
1750–59	109	189	49	53	23	46
1780–89	172	228	78	35	27	59
1820–29	300	144	131	69	47	47
1850–59	250	170	180	95	69	117

Sources: Karaman and Pamuk, 'Ottoman state finance', for the period to 1800, and Dincecco, *Political Transformations*, for the period from 1800 to 1850. Karaman and Pamuk give their figures in terms of silver, Dincecco in gold. I have expressed his figures in terms of silver too, using an exchange rate of gold to silver of 15 to 1. This is an approximation that is not entirely exact, but for the story I want to tell here it is not problematic.

*In the calculations made here for 'Britain', Scotland is included from 1707 onwards and Ireland from 1801 onwards. I think in matters of taxation that is misleading. Fiscal integration took place much later than official (partial) political integration. My personal estimates for British (England and Wales) per capita tax payments are substantially higher. See pages 104–10.

Table 8b Average annual tax revenue of central government in grams of silver per capita in selected European countries as estimated in recent publications

	United Kingdom	Former Dutch Rep.	France	Prussia	Spain
1810–15	>300->400	180	140–200	22–75	10–18

Source: Dincecco, *Political Transformations*, Appendix A.1.

---

[7]Most of my information with regard to China's taxes is from Beal, *Origins of Likin*; Chen, *System of Taxation*; Bernhardt, *Rents, Taxes, and Peasant Resistance*; Deng, 'Continuation and efficiency'; idem, *China's Political Economy*; Feuerwerker, 'Presidential address'; idem, *State and Society*; idem, 'The state and the economy'; He, *Paths towards the Modern Fiscal State*; Hsü, *Rise of Modern China*; Huang, *Broadening the Horizons*, 242–54; Lee, *Political Economy of a Frontier*; Liu, *Wrestling for Power*; Ma, 'Rock, scissors, paper'; Sng, 'Size and dynastic decline'; Wang, *Land Taxation*, and Zelin, *Magistrate's Tael*.

In Table 8a, no information is included for the period of the Revolutionary and Napoleonic Wars, for which it is not easy to produce similar trustworthy and thus comparable figures. What is clear is that taxes in this period of war and inflation increased substantially. Table 8b presents estimates based on recent work by Dincecco for the period at the height of the Napoleonic Wars, that I think can better be presented separately. In my text I will, for the European side of the equation, focus on the case of Great Britain, with ample references – to put that case in perspective – in particular to the Dutch Republic, France and Prussia.

In the years immediately after the War of Spanish Succession (1702–13) had ended, *net* tax revenue of the Exchequer in Britain was less than £6 million. In per capita terms, this would boil down to about 110–120 grams of silver. By 1790, still *before* the major increase caused by the French Revolutionary and Napoleonic Wars, it had increased to £16 million, or the equivalent of almost 1,800 million grams of silver. These had to be paid by somewhat less than 10 million people, *even* if we would include Scotland.[8] Per capita that would be some 190 grams. What we discuss here is tax income as it was *actually received* by the Exchequer (the central treasury). As gross payments are estimated to have been some 10 per cent higher, actual average payments per capita will have been about 210 grams.[9]

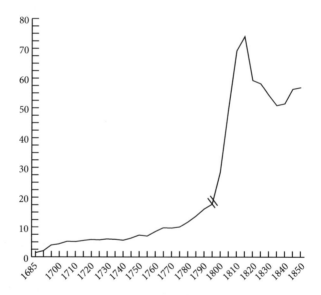

Graph 2 Net government tax income, excluding loan income, of Britain, 1688–1800, and gross public income of the United Kingdom, 1800–50, five years' averages centred on indicated years, in £ million.

Sources: O'Brien, 'Political economy of British taxation', 3, and Mitchell, *British Historical Statistics*, 581–2.

---

[8]According to O'Brien till the beginning of the nineteenth century hardly any Scottish tax money ever reached the Exchequer. See O'Brien, 'Political economy', 3, under Notes and sources.
[9]I base these figures on O'Brien, 'Political economy'.

During the period from the beginning of the 1790s till the end of the Napoleonic Wars, according to O'Brien net tax revenue *received* by the central treasury increased from some £16 million to over £62 million in 1815.[10] That is (about) the highest amount for the *entire* period we are discussing here. Gross total revenue of central government was even higher, peaking at almost £80 million according to several sources.[11] Those £62 million of net tax income would amount to some 6,900 million grams of silver. Divided between the population of England and Wales that would amount to over 600 grams of net tax revenue per capita, including Scotland to over 500 grams. If we take the highest *gross* income of almost £80 million that would boil down to a per capita payment for England and Wales of about 800 grams of silver. Including Scotland, although the Scots continued to send very little of their taxes to London over the entire period to 1815, that would still be almost 700 grams. Average gross income over the period 1801–16, and thus average gross payment, was some £60 million. It might be objected that we are dealing with highly unrepresentative figures because they refer to the end of a period of almost 'total' war and inflation. But even if we would take (the rather low) inflation into account, as we will do later on, the increase still is substantial.[12] Besides, the period from the late 1780s to the 1820s is quite a long period. In roughly four decades quite a lot can and *did* happen. It, moreover, is a period of fundamental importance for the debate on the Great Divergence as it is the period when Britain began to become the first industrial nation. And finally, I want to point out that, even considering the decrease in taxation from the 1820s onwards, we continue to be talking about completely different orders of magnitude from those in China.

In the period from directly after the Napoleonic Wars to the 1850s, taxes indeed declined substantially in Great Britain/the United Kingdom as can be seen in Graph 2. Per capita at least, Britons started to pay less taxes and the share of taxes in their GDP declined. The huge administrative expansion and expense of the Napoleonic Wars had pumped the fiscal-military state to the point of bursting. Public hostility had spread quickly. Most of the additional taxes raised between 1793 and 1815 had fallen on the consumption and income of the wealthy as the limits of endurance of the ordinary taxpayer had been reached. In the words of Harling and Mandler: 'The fiscal-military state was the ultimate casualty of the French Wars because the public was no longer willing to pay the price of maintaining it.'[13] In the second quarter of the nineteenth century total net government income in Great Britain/the United Kingdom hovered between £50 million and £60 million. That still is between 5,600 million and 6,700 million grams. In 1821, the United Kingdom of Great Britain *including* Ireland in total had some 21 million inhabitants; in 1850 that number had increased to 28 million. That means that per capita over the entire realm people paid some 250 grams of silver in 1821 and some

---

[10]O'Brien, 'Political economy', 3.
[11]According to Mitchell, *British Historical Statistics*, 581, gross government income of Great Britain peaked in 1816, with £78.6 million.
[12]See page 107.
[13]Harling and Mandler, 'From "fiscal-military" state to laissez-faire state', 52.

240 grams in 1850, which would be quite optimistically low, as the people in Ireland at that time continued to live under a different tax system and contributed less than the national average.[14] As the figure had certainly been more than £6 during the very height of the Napoleonic Wars, this meant a sharp decrease to less than £3. To determine what this development actually meant for the ordinary tax payer, one of course has to consider that the general price level tended to decrease substantially in Great Britain in the second quarter of the nineteenth century,[15] plus the fact that for most of this period there was no – or in any case no substantial – direct income tax, as had been the case during the French Wars. It is not at all certain that for most 'ordinary' people tax pressure actually decreased. What is clear is that with the passing of time (Great) Britain, the country with the highest taxes in Europe over most of the eighteenth century and the beginning of the nineteenth century, became a low-tax country later on in that century if we measure that in terms of tax revenue as a percentage of GDP.[16]

This brief and rather 'rough' preliminary overview nevertheless yields some quite interesting and, to many people, probably quite unexpected results, the most striking being the fact that taxes in Britain were so high, higher than any place else. Among experts this has become a known fact for quite some time, but one still comes across references to Britain as a low-tax state.[17] What is also striking is the fact that, as will be the case so often in our analysis, differences between various (Western) European states and differences over periods of time could be quite substantial. Finally it shows that, all differences notwithstanding, from a global perspective, central governments in Western Europe, overall, in the early modern era managed to collect large amounts of revenue.[18]

Other forms of government revenue in (Western) Europe

In this text for Western Europe the focus has been and will continue to be on tax income. One must realize, however, that as a rule this was not the only kind of revenue of governments in Europe or elsewhere. They *could* and often *did* have other sources of income. Some of these provided a regular income; others did so irregularly; some were

---

[14]Fitzpatrick, 'Ireland and the Empire', 495: 'Excise duties and taxation [of Great Britain and Ireland] remained sharply at variance until 1853. … Until 1853 Irish taxation and excise duties were relatively light.' According to O'Brien, the British government was not concerned with tax collection in Ireland at all until 1817. See O'Brien, 'Political economy of British taxation', 3, Table 2, Notes and sources. Things, however, clearly changed to the worse for the Irish over time.

[15]See page 107.

[16]For the level and structure of government income and expenditure of Britain in the long nineteenth century, see Daunton, 'Trusting Leviathan'; idem, 'Creating legitimacy'; Harling and Mandler, 'From "fiscal-military" state to laissez-faire state'; Hoppit, 'Checking the Leviathan', and Peden, 'From cheap government to efficient government'.

[17]Clark, in his *Farewell to Alms*, 148, writes that pre-industrial societies generally were low-tax societies and claims that England in particular was an extremely lightly taxed nation. For the period discussed in my book this claim certainly is untrue.

[18]See O'Brien and Yun-Casalilla, *Rise of Fiscal States*, and my 'Governing growth', which contains a comparison of matters related to taxation in Western Europe and in the Ottoman, Mughal and Qing Empires.

even one-offs. Such irregular, somewhat one-off kinds of government income for rulers in Western Europe tend to be overlooked in general surveys. I will not discuss them extensively but it would be highly incorrect not to point them out.[19]

Again, differences in Europe and even in Western Europe were so big that it is quite misleading to speak of 'the European state'. In Western Europe and especially in Britain and the Dutch Republic almost all government income was tax income, almost if not entirely paid in money, or it was raised via borrowing. In Central and Eastern Europe substantial parts of government income were not collected as tax but came, for example, from government properties or rights, whereas many payments here were in kind or labour. To get a good overview of total government income in the early modern era one cannot confine oneself to tax revenue. A classic form of *regular* income for governments all over the world, the origin of which normally was older than taxation, was revenue from domain land. In this respect substantial differences existed in Europe.[20] In Central Europe, the role of domain land remained quite important. In Prussia in 1740, 45 per cent of total state income supposedly came from state domains. In 1800, that would have been 40 per cent.[21] In Austria in the last decades of the eighteenth century, as much as about 20 per cent of total government income might have come from state property, in this case income from domain land but also from mines and coinage.[22] For these countries, income from state properties is always included in estimates of total government revenue. They were too important and too structural a part of total revenue to be ignored. In Saxony, in the period 1478–1844, and Brandenburg-Prussia, in the period 1653–1913, 'public operating surplus' were very important – that is, 'all kinds of net revenues that emerge from princely and public economic activities beyond mere tax- or fee-collecting. Typical items are revenues from domains and forests, but also from regalian rights like revenues from mines, salines or other monopolies'.[23] It is my guess that this also applies to various other regions of Central and Eastern Europe.

For governments in Western Europe state property or 'regal rights' were less important as a source of income. Over the eighteenth century, on average less than 5 per cent of state income in Britain came from domains or other properties. In calculations for this region, authors as a rule focus on taxes, although other sources of incomes, all quite tiny, might be included, often without being explicitly referred to. Kozub does explicitly refer to them and claims that non-parliamentary revenues (in this case sale of monopolies and land, income of the Mint) in Britain after 1688 never amounted to more than 3 per cent of the

---

[19]For different *kinds* of government income in Europe and their evolution over time see Bonney, 'Revenues'. For changes in thinking about government income see idem, 'Early-modern theories'.

[20]For some general, comparative information see Hartmann, *Steuersystem der europäischen Staaten*, 314–36, and Spoerer, 'Revenue structures', 790, for the middle of the eighteenth century, and Mann, *Sources of Social Power, II*, 382, table 11.6 for the period 1760–1910.

[21]Gorski, *Disciplinary Revolution*, 82. Compare Bonney, 'Revenues', and Henderson, *Studies in the Economic Policy*, 66.

[22]Mann, *Sources of Social Power, II*, 382. See for further information Capra, 'Eighteenth century. I'; Dickson, *Finance and Government, I*, and Otruba and Weiss, *Beiträge zur Finanzgeschichte Österreichs*.

[23]Spoerer, 'Revenue structures', 784.

Table 9 Percentage of state revenue coming from direct and indirect taxation and from state property, 1760–1850

Year	Great Britain			France			Austria			Prussia		
	Dir.	Ind.	S.P.	Dir.	Ind.	S.P.	Dir.	Ind.	S.P.	Dir.	Ind.	S.P.
1760	26	69	4	48	45	7	53	35	12			
1770	16	70	4				48	33	19			
1780	20	71	5	41	49	10	41	37	23			
1790	18	66	9	35	47	18	27	36				
1800	27	52	12				29	45				
1810	30	57	11				30	42				
1820	14	68	16				44	50	6+	36	33	30
1830	10	73	17	40	22	38	39	45	16			
1840	8	73	19	c30			25	49	29	24	34	41
1850	18	65	16	c28			29	44	22	22	32	46

Source: Mann, *Sources of Social Power, II,* 382. See for further explanation Mann, *Sources of Social Power, II,* 387–9.

total income of the realm.[24] Whatever may have been the exact figure, its importance was not substantial and tended to decrease with the passing of time. In France, on average, it was some 5 to 10 per cent, less at the very beginning of the eighteenth century but some 12 per cent just before the Revolution.[25]

In the nineteenth century, after the ending of the Napoleonic Wars, we see an important change. Revenue derived from state property then became quite substantial (again) in almost all European countries. But it now no longer came primarily from domains and the like but from a variety of different sources: from 'regalian' rights that the population had to pay for to the government that held them as monopolies or privileges; from shares of profits of ports and mines, and from government enterprises like the postal office and railroads. In late nineteenth-century Prussia, railway profits became so important for central government that it has even been called 'a railway state'.[26] The figures in Table 9 indicate how big this increase actually was.

Another way in which governments in Western Europe could collect revenue was by selling 'offices'. In France, the state had two main employment statuses. Only a minority of those working for it were 'commissaires' – salaried and working employees. It is estimated that in 1784 these amounted to only roughly 20 per cent of all officials.[27] Most officials were 'officiers'. This meant that they actually owned their 'job', usually

---

[24]Harris, 'Government and the economy', 215.
[25]Morineau, 'Budget de l'état', 314.
[26]Thier, 'Steuergesetzgebung und Staatsfinanzen', 316.
[27]Mann, *Sources of Social Power, II,* 452.

because they had bought it or because they inherited it directly or indirectly from someone who had done so. Corporate bodies protected their property rights. Most of the 'officiers' who 'owned' a job did not do any actual work and on top of that did not pay taxes. Being 'officier' meant having acquired noble status. The number of such people must be counted in the many tens of thousands. The moment they bought their jobs, they provided the state with a substantial income. But that was only a short-term 'windfall'. As government could no longer tax these newly created 'officiers', who instead began to receive some remuneration, it lost leverage over its 'bureaucracy'. Selling offices was especially popular at the end of the Thirty Years War and at the end of the rule of Louis XIV. It was only abolished in France with the Revolution. Lots of money could be involved. During the War of the League of Augsburg (1689–97), to just give one example, 61 per cent of royal expenditures were raised by taxation and 39 per cent by the creation of new venal offices. It is estimated that the French monarchy raised roughly 700 million livres tournois by creating offices between 1689 and 1713 alone.[28] In our calculations of French government income we have included this source of revenue. In Britain, at least when we compare its yields to total government income, it was irrelevant.

Income from domains had been of the utmost importance in the days when a ruler was still supposed 'to live of its own'. In those days, gifts and services had been yet another source of income for rulers. In the eighteenth century in Western Europe, governments as a rule began to make fewer such demands on their subjects. In France, however, they were not negligible, as shown in a debate that was waged in the 1780s about the value of corvee labour for transport infrastructure. Necker, then France's minister of finance, estimated it at 20 million livres tournois, not including the Generality of Paris and all the *pays d'état*. Total government revenue at the time was in the order of magnitude of 500 million to 600 million livres tournois. At the very end of the *Ancien Régime* this corvee was, in principle, substituted by payment in silver.[29] Up until 1836, nevertheless, French peasants were required by government to contribute three days' work per year to the maintenance of roads.[30]

A very important way in which governments all over Europe requested labour of their subjects was the 'conscripting' of people for army and navy. This strategy was particularly popular in those parts of Europe like Prussia, the Habsburg Empire and Russia that harboured great power-ambitions but lacked capital. In these 'coercion-intensive states', to put it Tilly's terms, governments frequently resorted to extracting men, grain and animals from the population. That could be a very heavy burden. Native conscripts in these countries, for example, had to serve for life. During the War of Austrian Succession, 1701–14, more than 280,000 recruits were demanded by Vienna. During the period 1734–9, when the War of the Polish Succession and the Turkish War were waged, the number was 145,000. Whereas cadres increasingly enlisted voluntarily, for the rank and

---

[28]Stasavage, *Public Debt*, 87–8.
[29]Conchon, 'Resources fiscales', 1060.
[30]Osterhammel, *Verwandlung der Welt*, 982.

file there continued to be conscription until 1868. In Prussia, to give just two examples, in 1756 half of the soldiers were conscripts and in 1763 two-thirds.[31]

The *levée en masse* in 1793 in Revolutionary France, normally considered as the beginning of modern mass conscription, was an emergency measure. It was formalized in 1798. Under the system that was then introduced, two to three million men, in principle, could be called to serve. In France and Prussia experiments with 'massive' conscription went furthest during the Napoleonic Wars. Quite some time would pass before *universal* conscription was actually introduced as a permanent policy: in Italy only in 1862 and in the German Empire only in 1871. In Britain there officially was no conscription. That would only come into existence in 1915. In a situation of crisis, however, the state could compel men to join the services. The use of force was quite normal in recruiting personnel for army and navy. One would have to be quite an optimist to call it 'voluntary', even in Britain, where the situation was better than in most of the rest of Europe and many people chose to enlist. In principle they did so for a period that was so long it could be called 'lifetime'; in practice often 'only' as long as the war lasted or their commanders needed them.[32] Poverty and lack of alternatives were the most important reasons to opt for the military. It is clear that we are talking about very substantial amounts of adult male labour requisitioned by the state in this way. One must not forget that military personnel, apart from actual fighting, were used to do all kinds of work, particularly in the colonies, like building roads or fortresses.

All this still does not exhaust the ways in which rulers in Europe might appropriate labour of their subjects. One can also include the labour of people that had been put in the workhouses or the forced labour of convicts.[33] Those convicts often were sent to colonies. Pre-Revolutionary France sent seven times as many convicts to the colonies as it executed.[34] Countries that had no colonies could sell their convicts to others. In the eighteenth century German authorities sent some of their prisoners to North America as slaves, while somewhat later Prussia sent convicted felons to Russia to labour in Siberia.[35] I will return to this topic in detail when discussing the role of un-free labour for the specific case of Britain and its economy on pages 333-9. I will also present quantitative data there to give an indication of the importance of this type of labour recruitment.

Rulers were constantly on the lookout for skilled workmen and 'experts'. They tried to entice them from elsewhere with all kinds of special offers and in some cases even kidnapped them. It was regarded as quite normal to prevent people who had a certain scarce expertise leaving the country. There are also various examples of people who happened to have capital or expertise being forced to *leave* a country, after which they

---

[31]See for the figures in this paragraph Hochedlinger, 'Habsburg Monarchy', 81–4; Lucassen and Lucassen, 'Mobility transition revisited', 365–9, and Wilson, 'Prussia as a fiscal-military state', 119.

[32]See for recruitment practices in Western Europe Black, *European Warfare*, 178–86; Parrott, *Business of War*, passim, and Tallett, *War and Society*, passim. For the situation in Britain see pages 335–7.

[33]For information on workhouses in Europe see Lis and Soly, *Worthy Efforts*, under 'workhouses'. For general information on convict labour, see De Vito and Lichtenstein, 'Writing a global history of convict labour'.

[34]Thomson, *Mercenaries, Pirates, & Sovereigns*, 46.

[35]Weisser, *Crime and Punishment*, 140–1.

were often welcomed in other countries. The most well-known examples here are the Jews and the Moriscos who were kicked out of Spain before the time period discussed here or the Huguenots who had to leave France at the very beginning of our very long eighteenth century. But one could also think of the 20,000 Protestants leaving Salzburg for Prussia in 1732.[36] When rulers thought they had too many unruly *and* 'useless' mouths to feed, they might try and ban them. When the idea prevailed that a large population meant a large labour force, and thereby wealth, this practice was far less popular.[37] Forced migrants often provided a windfall for the economies of other countries. Of those Huguenots, for example, an estimated 40,000 to 50,000 went to England, whereas some 50,000 to 60,000 are supposed to have gone to the Netherlands. These Huguenots were not the only people who left France for 'political' reasons in the early modern era. About 130,000 clerics and nobles left the country in the course of the revolution that started in 1789. The tens of thousands (often wealthy) Protestants who left the Southern Netherlands when these were occupied by Spanish troops during what came to be known as 'the Dutch Revolt' – in total probably as much as 150,000 – were another very important example of a group of people forced to leave one country and transferring their money, networks and skills to another one.[38] Such transfers involved lots of expropriation, official and actual, which brings us to yet another source of income.

In comparing the economic history of Europe with that of Asia there is a strong tendency, especially among historians and economists who firmly believe in the beneficiary effects of the market, to contrast the 'sanctity' of private property in 'the West' with its 'insecurity' in 'the East'. This view is based on a fairly benevolent reading of the history of Europe. Actually, the expropriation of various types of property, in particular privileged property (land and other property owned by aristocrats and the Church) was an integral part of that history. A first and very important example is the secularization of Church property during the Age of Reformation. The lands of the Catholic Church that were taken over by the English Crown between 1536 and 1552, and consequently sold, amounted to about one-fifth to one-quarter of total agricultural land in England at the time. The Crown, for that matter, took it upon itself to provide for subsistence for the ex-monks.[39] The fiscal relations between Church and Crown were fundamentally altered during the process, with clerical taxation becoming an integral part of Crown finance, providing on average about one-sixth of total direct tax income of central government in the period from the 1550s to 1642.[40] After the Civil War in Britain in the 1640s, lands with a value of over £5 million were confiscated. Fines imposed on royalists to avoid confiscation of

---

[36]Clark, *Iron Kingdom*, 141–4.

[37]See for some general comments and information, especially about the British Atlantic, Morgan and Rushton, *Banishment in the Early Atlantic World*.

[38]The figures in this paragraph are from Gorski, 'Little Divergence', 170–5, and Lucassen and Lucassen, 'Mobility transition revisited'.

[39]For information see Habakkuk, 'Market for monastic property'; Knowles, *Religious Orders in England, III*; Woodward, *Dissolution of the Monasteries*; Youings, 'The Church', and idem, *Dissolution of the Monasteries*. For the final result see Overton, *Agricultural Revolution*, 168.

[40]See for further information Sheils, 'Modernity, taxation and the clergy', 745–56.

their lands raised £1.3 million.[41] After the Glorious Revolution the Crown lands were almost entirely sold for a very soft price or simply given away.[42] In the so-called South Sea Scheme of 1720 central government managed to seduce most of the holders of unredeemable annuities in government debt to change them into redeemable stocks in the South Sea Company. Stock prices first inflated – to which central government was not innocent – and then the bubble burst. Government had thus gotten rid of the bulk of its high interest, irredeemable annuities. This *de facto* amounted to a kind of defaulting.[43] One could of course also refer to the 'disappearance' of the bulk of the commons lands during the long-drawn process of enclosure and the usurpation of feudal and clan property. But one can probably do no better than simply quote Marx, who pointed at the enormous important kinds of 'primitive accumulation' that took place inside – and of course also outside – Great Britain during the early modern era.

> The spoliation of the Church's property, the fraudulent alienation of the state domains, the theft of the common lands, the usurpation of feudal and clan property and its transformation into modern private property under circumstances of ruthless terrorism, all these things were just so many idyllic methods of primitive accumulation.[44]

Even long after the Glorious Revolution, confiscation was not totally unknown in Britain: think for example of the implications of the abolition of the slave trade and even more clearly of slavery as such.[45] In times of war government did not hesitate to commandeer many private ships and their sailors. In what was to become the Dutch Republic, halfway through the sixteenth century, religious and charitable institutions in the main province of Holland owned at the very least 5 to 10 per cent of the land. During the revolt of the Dutch Protestants against Spanish Catholic rule from 1568 to 1648, this land was expropriated and taken over by the towns and provinces, to be used for all kinds of charitable goals.[46] In Sweden, ecclesiastical landed property amounted to about one-fifth of all agricultural land at the beginning of the sixteenth century. In 1560 it had all been liquidated for the benefit of the Crown.[47]

In the very long eighteenth century these huge transfers of ecclesiastical land in the process of ecclesiastical 'reformation' had become matters of a distant past. But that century too had its share of massive expropriations. In France, on the eve of the French Revolution, 'the Church', to use this somewhat simplistic shorthand, owned about

---

[41]Habakkuk, 'Public finance'.

[42]Marx, *Capital, I*, 884.

[43]See Brewer, *Sinews of Power*, 114–26.

[44]Marx, *Capital, I*, 895.

[45]Harris, 'Government and the economy', 230–1. The fact that compensation was paid does not change the fact that in the case of the abolition of slavery, to give but one example, property *was* expropriated.

[46]For the amounts of ecclesiastical land involved see Hoppenbrouwers, 'Mapping an unexplored field', 44. For what happened with the land, see De Vries and Van der Woude, *First Modern Economy*, 654–7.

[47]Heckscher, *Economic History of Sweden*, 67 and 126.

10 per cent of total landed property. About double was in the hands of aristocrats. Of the Church lands that were confiscated and sold during the Revolution, some 4 to 5 million hectares, *nothing* was returned. In Revolutionary France priests became government officials who had to swear an oath of loyalty to the Republican government. In all the Revolution cost the aristocracy about half of its land. The compensation received from 1825 onwards in the form of government stocks that became known as the 'émigrés billion', although their actual value was soon reduced to some 620 million francs, did not lead to a massive re-purchase of land.[48] Joseph II, the Habsburg ruler, closed one-third of the monasteries in his lands in the 1780s and sold their property. This earned him 60 million florins, about the tax income of an entire year. He only allowed the rest of the monasteries to continue to exist if they promised to do useful work in future.[49] In Spain, there was the long, complex and intermittent process of disentailment or 'desamortización'. It began during the reign of King Charles III (r. 1759–88) and lasted for about a century. In this process of converting privileged property into normal private property, in the period between 1836 and 1895 alone, some 615,000 properties, covering about 10 million hectares, changed hands. That was about one-fourth of total agricultural land.[50] The total value of land that was disentailed during the period 1798–1900 amounted to 12.808 million reales of 1.2 grams of silver.[51] Secularization of Church property did not mean that government was anti-Church per se or wanted to eliminate it. The costs for the state of maintaining the Church during the forty years when the income of disentail was at a maximum, by the way, were actually *higher* than the revenue earned from these sales.[52] Please note that I have only referred here to ways in which European rulers tampered with property rights at home; in 'their' colonies the rights of the natives were ignored almost as a matter of principle.[53]

Another way in which central governments in (Western) Europe 'expropriated' resources, in this case money of their subjects, was by defaulting on their debts. Here again we see huge differences between states like Britain or the Netherlands, with highly developed systems of borrowing and, in the case of Britain, even a system of managing a funded debt, and countries like Austria, Russia, Prussia and to a large extent also France, that on the eve of the Revolutionary and Napoleonic Wars still lacked monetary and financial institutions to efficiently deal with really big debts. In these countries government 'credit' often was just a euphemism for government non-payment. A default by government in the end is simply a forced payment to the state. The amounts of money involved therefore ought to be added to other more 'normal' and regular forms of government revenue. In Britain as a rule government paid its dues, as was the case

---

[48]See Asselain, *Histoire économique de la France*, 114–17, and Dupeux, *French Society*, 47–56 and 95–9. Among the aristocrats it was the *émigrés* who lost almost all of their land.
[49]Oppenheim, *Europe and the Enlightened Despots*, 102–6. For further examples and references see Sandgruber, *Österreichische Geschichte*, 144–7.
[50]Shupert, *Social History of Modern Spain*, 58–60.
[51]Tortella, *Desarollo de la España contemporanea*, 48.
[52]Tortella and Comín, 'Fiscal and monetary institutions', 171–2.
[53]For further examples see Lorenzetti, Barbot and Mocarelli, *Property Rights and their Violations*.

in the Netherlands, at least until the beginning of the nineteenth century. The French government of the Kingdom of Holland (1810–13) defaulted on its debts by reducing interest payments to one-third. In France itself government defaulted wholly or partially in 1559, 1598, 1634, 1648, 1661, 1698, and again in 1714, 1721, 1759, 1770 and 1788. The default of the first revolutionary government in 1797 affected fully two-thirds of the entire national debt. Government wrote off 2.6 billion livres owed to its creditors.[54] In Prussia, to give another example, in 1820 government declared its public debt of 180 million thalers 'a closed (account) for all time'.[55] For the Habsburg government too, at times debts proved too much. It 1811 and 1816, it was more or less declared bankrupt. Of the existing debt of 1811 in the end only a small part, about one-fifth, would be paid.[56] In Spain government defaulted on all or part of its debts no less than fourteen times between 1557 and 1696.[57] There is no lack of examples of government default in early modern Europe. Neither is there when it comes to debasing the national currency, which boils down to a hidden tax levy. This too was a quite popular strategy among governments. It enabled them to collect money from their subjects who had to pay seigniorage to have their coins re-minted and to 'short-change' those who did not notice the difference.[58] In this context one should also refer to all sorts of strategies by government to create inflation, including the use of the printing press, in that way to 'shrink away' debts. Again it has to be pointed out that Britain was 'special'. After the Great Re-coinage of 1694, silver and gold coins were no longer tampered with.[59] Of the three ways in which a government can get rid of debt, defaulting, inflating it away or austerity, none is without at least some pain for some of its subjects. None of them was actually implemented in Great Britain in the period under study.

A form of 'taxation', finally, that often is overlooked but that clearly is a 'payment' of the population to their state would be the billeting of troops. This could be a quite severe burden for the towns or villages concerned. Billeted troops lived from the land – preferably of course the land of the enemy but often the land of their 'own' state. Overall, in Western Europe, the frequency of billeting declined in the eighteenth century although, for example, the British continued to billet their standing army in Ireland.[60] In Central and Eastern Europe, however, governments continued to expect their populations to help provision troops stationed in their region. To keep costs within limits, those troops often were encouraged to take care of their own provisions as much as possible.[61]

Not all my examples were from the very long eighteenth century or from countries that play a cardinal role in my book but, in a way, that is not so relevant for the point

---

[54]Ferguson, *Cash Nexus*, 146–7. See also Bonney, 'Rise of the fiscal state in France'; Bordo and White, 'Tale of two currencies', and Félix and Tallett, 'French experience', 164.

[55]Clark, *Iron Kingdom*, 342.

[56]Sandgruber, *Österreichische Geschichte*, 222.

[57]Ferguson, *Cash Nexus*, 146–7.

[58]For examples see Sargent and Velde, *Big Problem of Small Change*.

[59]See for that re-coinage Davies, *History of Money*, 245–52.

[60]See for various ways in which armies could live off the country and exploit local resources Parker, *Military Revolution*, ch. 2, and Tallett, *War and Society*, 148–9.

[61]See e.g. Hochedlinger, 'Habsburg Monarchy' and Wilson, 'Prussia as a fiscal-military state'.

I wanted to make here: that encroaching on private property and manipulating the labour 'market' were not exactly exclusive specialities of Eastern despots. All this of course is not meant to deny that certain property was very well protected in Western Europe. The number of crimes punishable by death in England increased from fifty in 1689 to two hundred in 1800. Most of those crimes amounted to some kind of theft. As a specialist in the history of crime in the early modern era puts it, by 1800, at least in theory, 'English property was protected by the most comprehensive system of capital punishment statutes ever devised.'[62]

War reparations and prize money

War was almost a constant in the history of Western Europe. Later on we will deal with the enormous costs of it that dwarfed those in China. Those costs as a rule were borne because the stakes were so high. That implies that the gains could be very high too. Whatever may have been its final balance sheet in terms of costs and benefits, war also generated income – for the winner. Just think of booty, reparations payments, territories or privileges that were acquired and so on. The wider general question about the relationship between war and development and growth will be dealt with later on in chapters 2 and 5. Here I will only look at war as a direct source of government income. It would be impossible to even begin to chart the extra income generated by all the varying war spoils just mentioned. I will only comment very briefly on booty and on the paying of reparations in this context. I have already referred to the exploits of Napoleon's France, of which David Bell writes that it 'raised the practice of pillage to a fine art'.[63] For Napoleon, war had to feed war and pay for itself. The old method of pillaging increasingly came to be considered too haphazard. It was substituted by systematically forcing those one had defeated to pay large amounts of money or other indemnities as reparations.[64] The total amount of money that Napoleon 'collected' in Prussia between 1806 and 1812 is estimated at about half a billion francs. That means at least 225 grams of silver per inhabitant of Prussia.[65] It is claimed that between 1803 and 1814 French taxpayers paid 'only' 60 per cent of the costs of Napoleon's wars: of the total costs of 4,259 million livres tournois, no less than 1,743 million were levied from defeated regions.[66] Napoleon himself boasted that he had gained more than 2 billion francs by his conquests. He avoided credit as much as possible. He considered national debt 'immoral and destructive' and thought that 'silently undermining the basis of the state, it delivers the present generation to the

---

[62]Weisser, 'Crime and punishment', 139.
[63]Bell, *First Total War*, 17.
[64]For some examples of such exactions and some estimates of the total sums involved see Ferguson, *Cash Nexus*, 394–7, and Macdonald, *Free Nation*, 331–4. Napoleon, who only figures as an example here, was inventive when it came to finding money. In 1803, with the so-called Louisiana Purchase, he sold 2,140,000 km^2 of French territory to the United States. That is a tract of land about four times the size of France. Including interest and cancellation of debts, the United States paid $23,213,568 or some £5 million for the territory.
[65]See Macdonald, *Free Nation*, 333. Apart from having to pay financial reparations, Prussia also had to deal with the fact that its territory was more or less halved.
[66]Félix and Tallett, 'French experience', 165.

execration of posterity'.[67] After the final defeat of Napoleon, France itself was confronted with a burden of reparations of more than 1,800 million francs – that is 18–20 per cent of total GDP and more than 270 grams of silver per inhabitant.[68] The total amount of reparations that France had to pay in 1871, after losing the war against Germany, was 5,000 million francs, some 30 per cent of national income. Per inhabitant of France that was more than 500 grams of silver. The indemnity was paid without any problem before the set term.[69] Of course many more examples might be given.

There also were gains of war at an individual level that took the form of extra income for people working for government and that can count as government income, as it allowed government to pay lower wages to its personnel. Here is an example of how important such income could be. All those employed by the Royal Navy at sea were entitled to so-called 'prize money' – not to the same extent of course: people in high ranks received a manifold of the rank and file. Captured warships and merchantmen were considered prizes of war, which were sold at auction with their fittings and cargoes. The cash was then divided among the crews of the ships that had taken them. The sums involved were immense. The total value of prizes seized by British warships – *and* privateers, – between March 1744 and April 1745 was £4.92 million. Between 1803 and 1810 it reached £7 million. The total amount of prize money earned by British subjects during the Napoleonic Wars has been estimated at £30 million, a staggering amount of money, equal to the annual GDP of the Dutch Republic at the time.[70]

In the preceding paragraph reference was made to privateers. In international law privateering ships are defined as 'vessels belonging to private owners, and sailing under a commission of war empowering the person to whom it is granted to carry on all forms of hostility which are permissible at sea by the usages of war'.[71] Privateers were usually required to post a bond to ensure their compliance with the government's instructions, and their commissions were subject to inspection by public warships. In principle they have to be distinguished from pirates. By piracy one means 'acts of violence done upon the ocean or un-appropriated lands, or within the territory of a state through descent from the sea, by a body of men acting independently of any politically organized society'.[72] Here are a couple of examples to show how much money might be involved in this government policy to 'outsource' violence and increase its income in the sense of lowering its own costs.[73] During the War of Austrian Succession (1739–48), New York privateers captured more than 240 prizes, worth almost £620,000. The privateers who were then turned loose on the Dutch inflicted damages upon them to a sum of £1.3 million. Over the course of

---

[67]I found this quotation in Macdonald, *Free Nation*, 328. For Napoleon's claim of having collected more than 2 billion francs see ibid., 333.

[68]Bordo and White, 'Tale of two currencies', 315.

[69]See Asselain, *Histoire économique de la France*, 159–60, and Piketty, *Capital in the Twenty-First Century*, 132.

[70]See for figures Allen, *Institutional Revolution*, 120–3; Hill, *Prizes of War*, passim; James, *Warrior Race*, 328; Knight, *Britain against Napoleon*, under 'privateers', and Thomson, *Mercenaries, Pirates & Sovereigns*, 22–6.

[71]Thomson, *Mercenaries, Pirates & Sovereigns*, 22.

[72]Thomson, *Mercenaries, Pirates & Sovereigns*, 22.

[73]Thomson, *Mercenaries, Pirates & Sovereigns*, 22–6.

the entire war, an estimated 3,500 prizes were taken. During the first four years of the Seven Years War (1756–63) alone, after ships of neutrals trading with France had been declared 'fair game' too, English privateers took 1,000 French prizes and their French counterparts some 300 English ones. American privateers who supported the rebel cause in the War of Independence (1775–83) captured or destroyed 600 British vessels worth an estimated $18 million and captured 16,000 British prisoners. In total French privateers took 5,114 British merchantmen in the years 1803 to 1815.[74] In this context the following claim by Wang is quite relevant: 'China's imperial policy, in striking contrast, did not support government-sanctioned piracy or maritime military expansion.'[75]

There were other forms of lowering *immediate* costs – and as such increasing real income – for government. Many of them were another kind of outsourcing of 'violence'. Think of military entrepreneurs that took care of all sorts of activities that governments were not willing or able to take upon themselves. If mercenaries came from abroad, which governments often preferred, they could provide services that need not be provided by a state's own subjects who then might do something more productive instead. When chartered companies ruled or fought, governments need not do so. Those companies moreover provided all sorts of direct or indirect payments to governments. In the sphere of revenue collecting we see similar examples. One may assume that when government decided to have recourse to tax farming, it did so because that looked as the rational thing to do for the time being. I presume the same also applies to selling offices or privileges. I have to point out here that government in China in the very long eighteenth century also made ample and, according to some, *increasing* use of all sorts of 'privatization', often combined with 'liberalization' to outsource state activities to 'others' or 'the market'. My overall impression is that it increasingly, after the Qianlong reign, lost its grip on society.[76]

For scholars who think that what *is* somehow must be *right* otherwise it would have been wiped out by competition, it is very seductive to look at the activities described in the previous paragraphs only in terms of lowered costs, savings and direct or indirect incomes and profits. But of course it is not by accident that the strategies just referred to are so often connected with inefficiency and costs and a serious loss of sovereignty and control in the longer term. It is also not by accident that central governments, when they thought they were able to, preferably made an end to all sorts of such outsourcing only to find that it was often far from easy to eradicate the vested interests they themselves had created. From the perspective of central government it will in all probability normally[77] appear preferable to only give up control or sovereignty in case of necessity. The current debate on privatization of many activities that have long been regarded as public *par excellence*, or in any case by preference, shows that differences of opinion about (in-)efficiency in this context are not easily settled and very

---

[74]Knight, *Britain against Napoleon*, 627 note 43.
[75]Wang, *White Lotus Rebels and South China Pirates*, 84. British contemporaries would not have used the word 'piracy'!
[76]See for some comments Dunstan, 'Safely supping with the devil'.
[77]At least in a Western context.

probably do not have an unequivocal, general answer. Where relevant, I will comment on specific situations.

Income from the colonies and the outsourcing of violence and rule

Finally, there is the possibility that government *directly* (and of course also indirectly) extracted income from a country's overseas 'colonies'. The revenue it collected by, for example, taxing products coming from there or incomes earned there could be very substantial, but they are already included in ordinary tax revenue and discussed as such. In countries like Britain and the Dutch Republic, directly taxing 'colonial' income might have been a tempting option, but governments never resorted to it to the extent that Spain's government, for example, did. The chartered companies, which played such an important role in the overseas exploits of Britain and the Dutch Republic, were (semi-) autonomous entities, not royal companies. That means that in principle they worked on their own account and kept the profits that were made. That, however, doesn't mean that they didn't contribute to government revenue. Their biggest 'contribution' in that respect was that they basically *ruled* over 'their' territories, in that way saving their governments the costs of doing so. In practice, to confine us to that example, the British East India Company began to rule the Indian territories that *de jure* belonged to the Crown almost as if it was the government of an autonomous fiscal-military state. The amounts of money involved in its tribute-collecting, which became more and more intertwined with its trade, were too big for Britain's government to not, in the end, want to share directly in the spoils: after the company had become tax collector in Bengal it e.g. was forced, in the 1760s, into agreeing that it would pay £400,000 annually to the treasury as the state's share of that tax income. It also had to pay for each renewal of its charter. It often played a major role as subscriber to public debt by buying bonds on the stock market, in that way serving the interests of the state. Other companies like the Royal African Company and the South Sea Company played similar roles.[78] The state could of course also profit from the activities of the chartered companies in a more indirect way by taxing regulated trade. The amounts of money involved could be very substantial.[79] Massive amounts of incomes and profits were sent home to Britain. This income of course has already been discussed in as far as it was subsumed under total tax income. More will be said later on about the specific case of England chartered companies. Debates about the exact height of the 'India drain' have never stopped: what is beyond any doubt is that there is nothing comparable for the case of Qing China when it comes to monetary transfers from abroad during the period discussed here.[80]

---

[78]For background information with regard to the mutual financial and economic entanglement of state and chartered companies in Britain see, in alphabetical order, Bowen, *Business of Empire*, chs 2 and 3, with some concrete examples on pages 30–1; 't Hart, 'Mobilising resources'; Paul, 'Joint-stock companies'; Stern, 'Auspicio Regis', and Thomson, *Mercenaries, Pirates & Sovereigns*, 32–41.

[79]See e.g. page 342.

[80]See for that drain in the period from the 1770s to 1820 Cuenca-Esteban, 'British balance of payments'.

The Dutch East India Company did not last as long as its British counterpart. It became a debt-ridden liability that cost the state money and was declared officially defunct in 1799. That did not mean that the East Indies became less important for the public finances of what, after the French had left, would become known as the Kingdom of the Netherlands. When this kingdom received 'Indonesia' back from the British, the East India Company was succeeded by yet another monopolistic company, the Nederland's Handelmaatschappij (Dutch Trading Company), while under the so-called 'cultuurstelsel' (cultivation-system) peasants on Java were forced to grow crops for export. Government systematically supported development of the 'colonial complex' that after 1830 became far more important than ever for public finances. For the period from the 1830s to the 1870s, the 'batig slot' (colonial surplus) has been described as 'the cork upon which the entire Netherlands float.'[81] In the 1840s, it accounted for almost 40 per cent of tax income of the state. This percentage would be even higher in the 1850s and 1860s. This colonial surplus is included in my calculations.[82]

In the rest of this text the figures for central government income in Great Britain and various other European countries as presented in tables will be used as point of departure for analysis and comparison. The estimates presented are rather low, as not all categories of regular and irregular income are (fully) included. For the sake of convenience, however, I have decided to focus primarily on taxes when discussing government revenue for countries in Europe, except of course when indicated otherwise. It is now time to have a look at the situation in Qing China.

Taxes and other forms of government revenue in China during the entire period of the high Qing: General remarks

What was the situation like in Qing China roughly between the 1680s and the 1830s? I will deal with this entire period in one go because in China, as compared to Europe with its extremely expensive wars between 1792 and 1815, no fundamental break, acceleration or even change occurred in these 160 years. That is to say that we see hardly any changes in the amounts of official government income, the ways in which it was collected and the items that were taxed. A real rise in total income only set in after the 1860s and it was only in the 1850s that an important new tax was introduced. Special attention will nevertheless have to be paid to the period from the 1820s to the 1850s, when the exchange rate of silver appreciated sharply against copper, at times reaching a level of no less than 2,500 to 1. This was to have serious consequences for ordinary taxpayers who did not have any silver and who had to exchange ever-increasing amounts of copper into silver to be able to pay their taxes.

As far as I can judge on the basis of literature available in Western languages, information is scarcer and much harder to interpret than in the case of Britain. Which as

---

[81]Van Zanden and Van Riel, *Strictures of Inheritance*, 115–20 and 178–82. The quotation is on page 117.
[82]Van Zanden and Van Riel, *Strictures of Inheritance*, 99 and 180.

such already is telling: Qing finances were not exactly transparent, in particular, for the Han Chinese. The accumulated wealth in cash and kind in stores and vaults of the Board of Revenue and Public Works was exclusively in the hands of the Manchus. Before the last quarter of the nineteenth century no Chinese was employed in the Board of Revenue and the Board of Public Works as overseer. The Imperial Household too was closed to (Han) Chinese.[83] Revenues and expenditures of the empire remained a complete secret to the Han till then. Reading the literature, one gets the impression that we still lack systematic, serial information. Adoption of an annual budget was one of the abortive reforms of 1898. It was only in 1909 that the Chinese began to get an annual overview of their finances. By and large the system worked on the basis of centralized control of expenditures through allocation directives from the Board of Revenue (in the case of taxes) and decentralized methods of tax collection. Official figures here too, like in France, were not all inclusive. For example, allowances for the imperial clan were never published. This clan numbered some 2,000 people when the Qing took to the throne. At the beginning of the nineteenth century, it numbered no fewer than 30,000 people. We then must be talking about a sum of a couple of million taels. There were also other revenues and expenditures that were kept out of the 'official' surveys.[84] Not only were there two central collecting instances – the Hubu, Board of Revenue, and the Neiwufu, the Imperial Household, that played an important role in managing in customs bureaus, the salt monopoly and the imperial manufactories and that between 1662 and 1796 saw the number of its officials increase threefold[85] – but also we are confronted with a wide variety of sources of income. Let us begin with taxes. These were collected for the Board of Revenue. By far the most important tax during the period under discussion here was the land tax, or rather from 1713 onwards the combined land and poll tax. For the bigger part it was paid in money; the rest was paid in kind.[86] On top of that, there existed a couple of minor taxes, the main ones being a separate grain tribute, salt taxes and customs. The term 'customs' refers to both levies on internal trade and to the import and export duties collected on foreign trade in Canton. It was only in 1858 that a separate maritime customs administration for all open ports was founded.[87]

There are many differing estimates but the differences are not so substantial that they would change the outcome of my comparative analysis. Again, what matters are orders of magnitude. Those are fairly clear and not really up for debate. All the estimates I came across of official regular (tax-)revenue of central government in Qing China during the period 1750–1850 were between some 30 million taels in the lowest and some

---

[83]Chang, 'Economic role'.

[84]Will, *Bureaucracy and Famine*, 292. For further information see Chen, *System of Taxation*, 32–3.

[85]Wang, *White Lotus Rebels and South China Pirates*, 174–5.

[86]For a non-technical overview that revels in the complexity of China's tax system, basically focusing on the situation in the nineteenth century but also informative for earlier periods, see Morse, *Trade and Administration*, ch. 4. For an introduction into the intricacies of the Qing land tax system see Chen, *System of Taxation*, ch. 3, and Wang, *Land Taxation*.

[87]For the distribution of the Qing Custom Houses in the eighteenth century see Myers and Wang, 'Economic developments', 584–5. For the new Maritime Customs, which was actually run by foreigners, see Lyons, *China Maritime Customs*.

80 million taels in the highest estimate. I refer the reader for my sources to Appendix B. Of this money only a minor part[88] ever actually reached Peking, but by and large central government there decided on what most revenue would be spent and by whom.

I did come across one much higher estimate that was already made in the eighteenth century. It is by Lord Macartney, made on the basis of information provided to him by a spokesman. He estimates it would have been 200 million taels, some 100 million taels regular income and about the same amount of income from extraordinary sources. Of this total revenue, he claims only one-sixth was actually sent to the emperor's treasury in Peking. Most of the money, however, which was not sent to the capital, remained at the disposal of central government.[89] John Barrow, who was in China with Lord Macartney and later wrote about his travels in China, accepts this estimate and interestingly enough for the thesis of this book claims this would mean – taking the tax revenue for central government of Great Britain in 1803 to have been some £33 million and taking 3 taels to be one pound sterling – that people in Great Britain paid fifteen times as much taxes, in terms of silver, to their government as inhabitants of the Middle Kingdom.[90] In the period 1800–40s tax revenue continued to be at that level; in 1849 it was 42 million taels. In the 1850s, it started to increase substantially to reach 300 million in 1911.

In the literature taxes tend to be rather casually equated to *total* government income, as if government in Peking had no other revenues. That, however, clearly is incorrect. To begin with, one, as Wang shows in his book on land taxes, has to add a substantial amount of so-called 'surcharges' to these taxes.[91] He claims that for the year 1753 the official tax quotas in total amounted to over 56 million taels. According to his calculations almost 18 million taels have to be added to this as surcharges. That is an addition of over 30 per cent. Considering that by far the most important tax, the land tax, had been

Table 10 Ordinary, official government tax revenue in Qing China during the reigns of several emperors, in millions of taels

Kangxi emperor (r. 1661–1722)	± 35
Yongzheng emperor (r. 1722–35)	40
Qianlong emperor (r. 1736–95)	43–48
At the very end of the eighteenth century	43–44

Source: Hsü, *Rise of Modern China*, 59 and 61.

[88]See Chapter 1 notes 237–46.
[89]Cranmer-Byng, *Embassy to China*, 247–51.
[90]Barrow, *Travels in China*, 192.
[91]For an explanation of the concept of 'surcharges' see Wang, *Land Taxation*, 33: 'When the tax quota, even fully collected, could not meet the financial needs of the government, officials had to levy surcharges to finance public activities if the quota could not be increased. When surcharges were levied, the most convenient way was to have the quota as base.'

virtually fixed in the beginning of the eighteenth century, these surcharges actually became a normal levy, as regular income was always too low. Their height had to be determined by the magistrate at a level that was satisfactory to both the government and the people. This mostly meant that magistrates consulted local gentry and local elders or asked the provincial government for approval. The decision to diverge from the official tax rate could also be made by provincial government after being subjected to imperial approval.[92]

But this was not all. Wang also refers to what he calls 'contributions' and distinguishes two kinds. The first consists of the revenues of conferring offices, office patents, titles, ranks or degrees to people who made a contribution to the public cause. This method of collecting income or resources functioned under the Qing as a legally fully accepted 'contribution system' in which what was basically a sale was disguised as a reward. Wang provides some general information in this respect: at the end of the eighteenth century, according to him, government collected 3 million taels per year through the sale of nominal degrees, titles and ranks alone. Selling public offices could bring in sums varying from 2 million taels to more than 30 million taels at a time. Contributions for degrees, titles and offices became an important source of income, especially during the early nineteenth century. For the revenue collected via the sale of degrees and offices, Wang gives the following figures: during the Yongzheng period (1723–35), revenue collected in this way amounted to nearly 9 per cent total of total government revenue. During the Qianlong period (r. 1736–95), that figure had risen to nearly 17 per cent. When the Jiaqing emperor ruled (r. 1796–1820), this revenue would have amounted to no less than 54 per cent of government revenue. Finally, when the Daoguang emperor ruled (r. 1821–50), it would have amounted to 36 per cent, to decline further under the next emperor.[93] These percentages are very high, but one has to realize that government revenue here must, considering the absolute amounts referred to, have been defined as that part of total government revenue (excluding grain tribute) that actually arrived in Peking. As indicated, that was only a minor part of total government revenue. For the reign of the Daoguang emperor (1821–50), this is clearly shown by Elisbeth Kaske when she indicates that the *total* silver income of the Central Board of Revenue Treasury during that period never surpassed a sum of some 20 million taels.[94] The selling of the *jiansheng* title, (Student of the Imperial Academy), alone, at a cost of a little over 100 taels per title, yielded over 74 million taels during the period 1799–1850. Titles provided an entry ticket to offices. Of local officials, 22.4 per cent had bought their initial qualifications in 1764; 29.3 per cent in 1840 and 51.2 per cent in 1871. The direct sale of offices also was substantial. In 1798, 1,437 central offices and 3,095 provincial and local offices were sold. That certainly will have been exceptional and such sales were not annual affairs, but the figures are nevertheless striking.[95] Non-orthodox ways of making a career in which money was more important than academic attainment became increasingly important – in particular in times of

---

[92]Wang, *Land Taxation*, 33–4.
[93]Wang, *Land Taxation*, 9.
[94]Kaske, 'Price of an office', 291.
[95]I took all these figures from Ho, *Ladder of Success*, 34, 49 and 47.

crisis. Halfway through the nineteenth century the tables clearly turned. Whereas 'up to the outbreak of the Taiping Rebellion in 1851 the state had always made the examination system the primary, and the sale of offices secondary, channel of mobility',[96] it by and large was the other way around after that rebellion. During that rebellion selling offices yielded 4 to 6 millions taels annually.[97] For the period we discuss in this book, it seems safe to conclude that Wang's first type of contributions, in total, apparently did not yield more than, on average, a couple of million taels per year.[98] That is substantial, but not so much as to fundamentally change orders of magnitude of total government income.

The second kind of contributions Wang refers to are those made by merchants. According to him, the amounts of money involved were smaller, although they tended to increase. The figure he gives for the entire period from 1735 to 1820 is 40 million taels. He is solely referring to contributions by the big merchants in the salt producing areas and by the Hong Merchants in Canton.[99] This estimate strikes me as rather low.[100] He, moreover, immediately adds that it is doubtful whether the state's treasury did really gain from those merchant contributions. The merchants very often were in debt and only paid their contributions in name. On the basis of my reading, I have the impression that the fact that many people who officially had to contribute did *not* may have been more than compensated for by the fact that many contributions were made that were not official. China's government never had to compensate for these contributions, let alone pay any interest on them. This is all in sharp contrast to Western European governments.

One may of course discuss whether these contributions should be included in the same category as taxes or other kinds of regular government revenue. I think in principle they should. They were an integral and structural part of government revenue in China. They, moreover, could be quite substantial. This means that ignoring them would give us a distorted picture, even though I am under no illusion whatsoever about being able to even estimate their approximate volume. The argument that paying taxes would be obligatory whereas 'contributing' would be voluntary is too simple. Many contributors indeed were in no way coerced and got something that they eagerly wanted in return for their contribution – that is their gift was voluntary and there was 'reciprocity'. The examination-system was never really ousted by this paying of contributions in 'our' period but apparently there always were people willing to pay serious amounts of money in the hope of getting an office, even though that hope, at least when one wanted a real, official job, became increasingly unrealistic.

---

[96]Ho, *Ladder of Success*, 50.

[97]Swart, *Sale of Offices*, 110. See there for original sources.

[98]See for figures that would confirm this Ma, 'Rock, scissors, paper', page 25, figure 4.

[99]Wang, *Land Taxation*, 8–12.

[100]See, for example, Ho, *Ladder of Success*, 80, where the author claims the Liang-huai salt merchants contributed over 36 million taels to government between 1738 and 1804, not including many small contributions, and Naquin, *Millenarian Rebellion*, 360, where it is claimed that those merchants gave 12.4 million taels to government, almost all for river repair, between the fifth month of 1810 and the fourth month of 1814. For the contributions made by the Hong merchants in Canton see pages 355–9.

On the other hand, there are many cases where 'contributors' may not have been actually 'coerced' but were under enormous pressure to comply. That would be my conclusion, if one may generalize from the comments that Will makes with regard to the way in which government 'convinced' people to help victims of famine. The line between what we would call 'voluntary contributions' and 'forced contributions', as he describes it, must have been extremely thin indeed. According to him: 'The state relentlessly appealed for charity and generosity, condemned the egotism of the rich – albeit without ever going so far as to *order* [italics in the original] them to pay – and bestowed ranks and distinctions on those who had made voluntary contributions.' In his words, 'direct constraint was normally out of the question'. But he adds that those unwilling to contribute were officially brandished as 'devoid of altruism', a description that was very likely to attract popular retaliation, even though government let it be known, rather disingenuously, that it was forbidden to blackmail or persecute the people it had described as such.[101] Even a cursory look at the literature presents countless examples of severe pressure on the gentry-merchant classes of 'wicked merchants' and 'rich but not benevolent people', who were squeezed by government and *forced* to help the poor.[102] We find numerous, almost institutionalized examples of this when we look at the dealings of the state with salt merchants, members of the Hong, foreigners wanting to trade with Chinese and so on. Qing China may not have been as despotic as the old 'black legend' has it, but one should beware of erring in the opposite direction and only focusing on its benevolent side. From a macroeconomic perspective, however, all the sums referred to do not look substantial.

Wang, finally, also refers to rents, interests and profits from public enterprises. According to him their importance in the period under consideration was negligible. This reference to rents and interests in fact means talking about sources of revenue of the Imperial Household, not of central government as such. In total, those clearly were *not* negligible. Te-ch'ang Chang, who devoted an article to them, even goes as far as to claim that 'the immense magnitude of the imperial resources ... before the mid-nineteenth century as often as not exceeded the income of the Board of Revenue of the government'.[103] As most of the tax money was never actually sent to that Board in Peking this claim *might* be correct. Evelyn Rawski, though, I think correctly points out that secondary literature does not support Chang's estimate.[104] Neither do the examples presented in the book by Torbert on the Qing Imperial Household Department, a book to which Chang

---

[101]See for these quotations Will, *Bureaucracy and Famine*, 6, 59 and 60.

[102]See Hung, 'Contentious peasants', and idem, 'Agricultural revolution'.

[103]Chang, 'Economic role', 244. For further information on the Imperial Household and its economic importance see Torbert, *Ch'ing Imperial Household Department*. Lin, 'Shift from East Asia', 94, presents a graph that indicates that revenues and expenditure of the Imperial Household during the Qianlong reign were never higher than 3 million taels per year. Lai, 'Economic significance', Graph 2 comes up with a similar figure. Burger claims its budget in the beginning of the nineteenth century would have been some 10 million taels. See Burger, 'Coin production', 183.

[104]Rawski, 'Qing formation', 218. Ma goes as far as to claim that the Neiwufu took in a mere 1 per cent of the total budget of the Qing state. See his 'Rock, scissors, paper', 26, note 17.

[105]Torbert, *Ch'ing Imperial Household Department*. See also Lai, 'Economic significance', 11–12.

sometimes refers.[105] Strikingly enough even the evidence Chang presents himself fails to really support his rather strong claim. He does, however, prove that the early Qing saw very substantial increases in the size of their 'Privy Purse', just as he establishes that the Imperial Household provided for at least a *substantial* part of total government income. Chang mentions a broad range of sources of that specific imperial income: revenues derived from the imperial domain – that were really tiny compared to total government revenue – two kinds of tribute (native and vassal tribute), income derived from surplus quotas of customs, proceeds from the sales of the monopoly trade of ginseng and furs, incomes from 'fines' paid by officials and from confiscations. Over the period 1780–95, the Neiwufu collected 3.4 million taels income from so-called 'self-assessed fines'.[106] One could add income from moneylending to merchants, from imperial pawnshops and from urban real estate.[107] There is clear evidence that till the beginning of the nineteenth century, money from the Imperial Household was quite regularly used for financing various government activities.

Other sources of government income

If we were to believe the old 'oriental-despotism thesis', government in China would have owned most of the land, which would then of course have provided it with a huge income. There indeed was land that was directly in the hands of government or that had been reserved for banner troops. The total amount of land actually owned by the Qing government, however, probably was never more than a few per cent of total agricultural land.[108] The income of this land that went to the Imperial Household was tiny – again of course relatively speaking.[109] Public operating surpluses were very small in China and continued to be so after the 1850s, when their importance for government revenue in some European countries, for example Prussia/Germany, became fundamental. The Chinese state collected hardly any revenue from state properties or state monopolies during the period we discuss here and would be unable to profit from the exploitation of railway nets or postal offices as much as states in Europe did.[110] In *Western* Europe, as indicated, the amount of gifts or services asked by government from its people tended to decrease over the eighteenth century, to become almost nil at its end. In China the situation was and continued to be quite different. One may think here of corvee labour, of various forms of mass mobilization during special 'campaigns' and in particular of unpaid

---

[106]Wang, *White Lotus Rebels and South China Pirates*, 177. These fines were a form of extortion in which officals paid 'voluntarily' to assuage guilt for assumed offences.

[107]For further information on the importance of government pawnshops see Deng, 'Miracle or mirage?' and Stanley, *Late Ch'ing Finance*, 22–4.

[108]For land owned by China's government see Huang, *Peasant Economy and Social Change*, 87. Pomeranz, *Great Divergence*, 71, refers to this publication and concludes that crown land under the Qing never amounted to more than 3 per cent of total arable land. For public lands see also Chen, *System of Taxation*, 47–51.

[109]See Chang, 'Economic role', and Torbert, *Ch'ing Imperial Household Department*.

[110]For the concept 'public operating surplus' see page 75.

public services rendered by richer subjects.[111] These unpaid services often took the form of 'conspicuous philanthropies', gifts of the local gentry who volunteered to pay for all sorts of public works to show their benevolence and public-mindedness.[112] Officials could afford such donations and probably felt obliged to give something back to the public, as their total income from office was a multiple of their official income. Government very often resorted to these kinds of *ad hoc* measures and their importance must have been quite substantial. There, however, is no way to figure out how substantial.

Expropriation of land or other forms of wealth of course were not unknown in Qing China and one can easily be impressed by it when one looks at the amounts involved in some spectacular cases. But as compared to total government income, we are dealing with a quite tiny source of income here.[113] Defaulting did not occur, as government in China never borrowed. Neither did central government try to increase its income – or lower its costs – by debasing the currency. It could only have done so by manipulating copper coinages, as it did not coin silver or gold. Income from seigniorage therefore was relatively low. We have already indicated that government collected meltage fees, which basically were a kind of wastage allowance, similar to the allowances that were collected in grain to make up for loss and spoilage of taxed grain during transit.[114] These charges provided magistrates with a fiscal margin with which to fund their daily operations, public works projects or their own private needs. Widely regarded as the private prerogative of the individual magistrate and not previously regulated by the throne, they customarily ranged from 10 to 20 per cent of the official tax due. As usual big differences might exist between the 'official' and the 'real'. In some areas they rose to 50 per cent or more. Tolerated by early Manchu leaders as a necessary evil, the Yongzheng emperor resolutely prohibited their collection; or rather he tried to.[115] As far as I know, there are no examples of China's central government conscripting subjects or billeting soldiers in their homes. Forced labour of convicts was not unknown. They were employed in, for example, Xinjiang and Manchuria. Examples of what we would call 'corvee labour' abound.

China: A closer look at official quantities

Let us go into somewhat more detail and have a closer look at official tax revenue collected for central government in China, including surcharges, as our information here is much less clear than in the British case. By far the most important tax, the one on land, remained almost stable for the entire period of Qing rule that we are discussing

---

[111]See for these ways to mobilize resources and people Wong, 'Changing fiscal regime of Qing dynasty China', and idem, 'Taxation and good governance'. For some concrete examples of how governement commanded money and/or services see Mann, 'Liturgical governance', and Sun, 'Finance ministry'.
[112]See for examples Chang, *Income of the Chinese Gentry*, under 'Conspicuous philanthropies'.
[113]See Chang, 'Economic role', and Torbert, *Ch'ing Imperial Household Department*.
[114]See page 62.
[115]Thornton, *Disciplining the State*, 32.

here. It basically only increased somewhat with the extension of cultivated land. I did not find any estimate for the period till the First Opium War that was higher than 50 million taels. The yield of the rest of official taxes was and continued to be much smaller. It would not be widely off the mark to estimate total government tax income, including surcharges, at the end of the rule of the Qianlong emperor at some 100 million taels. I tend to think this would be a quite high estimate. But even this high estimate is only the equivalent of £33 million or, expressed in silver, 3,700 million grams of silver. Per capita of China's population, that would be about 11 grams.[116] I indicated earlier that the importance of various 'contributions' began to increase substantially at the end of the eighteenth century. It of course is not easy to know how much they actually yielded. But even if, at their height under the Jiaqing emperor (1796–1820), they would have been as important for total state income as official taxes and surcharges, which of course is a very bold hypothesis, that would still not have made the income of the Qing government, at that exceptional moment, higher than 200 million *taels*. Per Chinese, during the 1810s, that have been the equivalent of some 20 grams of silver. Then finally, there is the income of the Imperial Household. The only thing that is really clear here is that we lack the trustworthy series of figures that we need for our comparative analysis. But even if this income would have amounted to on average 100 million taels per year – which would be *twice* as much as government revenue from land tax – total government income of the Qing before the First Opium War would still not have been higher than 300 million *taels*. That is 11,190 million grams of silver. In the 1820s, when income reached that highest level, population amounted to some 380 million people. So per capita we are talking about some 30 grams of silver. I have never come across *anything near* such a high estimate in Western literature. Yet to strengthen my case that differences between Britain and China were big, I will use this very high estimate as the point of departure in my comparisons. These figures refer to the situation until 1820. In the period from 1820 to 1850 total official tax income *in terms of silver* did not increase. It may even have decreased somewhat.

That the estimate of 11,190 million grams is a very high one also shows in the fact that figures that one can find with regard to government *expenditures* never come even anywhere near 300 million taels. Figures I found for the period 1750 to 1840 never exceed *fifty* million taels – that is £17 million.[117] That would be less than a fifth of the annual spending of Britain's central government at the end of the Napoleonic Wars. Even an *extremely high* estimate of total income of China's central government, at its height, points at an *extremely low* revenue – and expenditure – compared to central government in Great Britain.

---

[116]In the 1790s China, in a fairly high estimate, had some 340 million inhabitants. Brandt, Ma and Rawski, 'From divergence to convergence', 56 note 23, claim that number was 385 million. That certainly is too high. Compare Deng, 'Fact and fiction', Appendix Three; Ho, *Studies on the Population*, 278; Lee and Wang, *One Quarter of Humanity*, 27. All estimates in Sieferle and Breuninger, *Agriculture, Population and Economic Development* on pages 35, 107, 245 also are much lower.
[117]See pages 187–90.

A more in-depth comparison of government revenue in (Great) Britain and China during the very long eighteenth century

I have never come across an estimate of the total value of *all* sources of income for China's government in recent scholarly literature in the West. One may wonder whether the information to make such an estimate will ever be available. According to my, admittedly rather wild and definitely quite high estimate, *total* central government revenue will never during the entire period discussed in this book have amounted to more than 300 million taels. This means that I will use a figure that is much higher than the figures suggested for 'government revenue' by authors like Elliott, Lee, Will and Wong, who all surprisingly enough think China was a fairly well-endowed state. Whatever may have been the exact figure, all the information I could gather clearly indicates that total central government *income* – let alone official taxes – expressed in grams of silver, per capita was much lower in China than it was in Western Europe, especially Great Britain. The difference when it comes to the amount of *taxes* paid per capita is really huge. This is not just a difference: it is a gap. There can be no doubt that taxes were much higher in '*laissez-faire* Britain' than in 'oriental despotic China'. Taking into consideration the various kinds of income of China's government apart from regular taxes does not alter our conclusion: compared to Britain's central government and to a somewhat lesser extent those of most states in Western Europe, China's central government did have very little disposable income.

The reader has to be attentive to the exact wording: we are talking about payments *actually* at the disposal of *central* government, including the money central government earmarked for local and provincial expenditure. Immense amounts of money were paid by the populace to people who provided what we would now call 'public services' of some kind, but who were not paid, or in any case not enough, by central government, nor by local government, and who therefore depended heavily or even completely on the 'fees' their 'customers' were willing to pay. If we were to add these payments to the official taxes – as in the end I think we should because we are talking here about payments for public goods and services – we would have to conclude that the 'tax' burden in China was far higher than official figures suggest. Of course we will never be able to find out how big these amounts of 'customary fees', as they were quite euphemistically called, actually were. As a rule the actual payments were determined on an *ad hoc* basis and resulted from bargaining between the parties involved. The possibilities for malfeasance, inefficiency and corruption were legion and will be discussed later on when we analyse China's bureaucracy more in detail. But even if we were able to determine the amounts of money involved in these payments, they were *not* made to central government, or rather not to any part of government at all, and therefore cannot be regarded as *disposable* government income, which is what this text in principle is about.

There existed a huge difference between *official* payments to government and *actual* payments made by the populace to all kinds of people in compensation for being 'governed' and 'administrated', just as there, as we will see, existed a huge difference between *official* expenditure by government and *actual* expenditure for public good and services. As the French would say, 'pays legal' and 'pays réel' were quite distinct in Qing

China. The consequences, in the end, were not positive, not for central government and not for the population. Basically what we see is something like a 'worst of both worlds' scenario with people paying a lot and government receiving little. Central government could easily be confronted with a disaffected population that felt exploited and victim of all kinds of corruption from which government as such did not 'profit'. Qing China in the very long eighteenth century, in various respects, was quite weak 'infrastructurally' as a state, in particular when it came to making long-term investments and their maintenance. Central government did not have much grip on society and in many respects lacked the capacity to actually penetrate it and logistically implement political decisions throughout the realm. The population paid lots of money to all kinds of (semi-)officials and their helpers for which it often did not receive any public goods in return. Such 'surplus' payments simply became extra private income for those to whom they were paid.

From a comparative perspective, it is important to note that with the passing of time the importance of all kinds of 'irregular *non-tax* income' – that is *excluding* regular state property income that became more important again with the passing of time – *decreased* very sharply in Great Britain and the Dutch Republic, to completely disappear in *all* of Western Europe with the reforms of government beginning with the French Revolution. In China in contrast, 'extra-ordinary', non-tax revenues apparently became *more* important during the first half of the nineteenth century. Government there improvised and increasingly resorted to all kinds of *ad hoc* measures to find money and resources, among them the selling of titles and offices that clearly undermined the legitimacy of the state. Taxation on land was basically fixed and would not have been very 'flexible' anyhow. It was only with the introduction of the new trade tax or *likin* after 1853 that China experimented with a new regular tax.[118] The contrast with Great Britain, where one sees constant debates on taxes and tax policies, and constant changes in those policies often connected to wider economic issues, could not be bigger. Here is one anecdotic but, to my view, striking example: by 1760, there were 800 separate Acts of Parliament affecting Customs duties alone.[119]

Let us now delve somewhat deeper into the Sino-British comparison. According to Wang, the government in Peking in 1753 collected, including surcharges, almost 74 million taels in taxes. Other sources of government income at the time, according to him, were still almost irrelevant.[120] So let us settle for a total of 90 million taels. That, in silver, would be the equivalent of £30 million. This would be somewhat over four times as much as the tax revenue of Britain's central government at the time. If this estimate is correct, it would mean that in the sixth decade of the eighteenth century Britain's central government received an equivalent of 25 per cent of China's tax income while Britain's population was only some 3 per cent of that of

---

[118]In Britain the type of contributions Wang refers to had already become irrelevant at the end of the seventeenth century. For the *likin* tax see the Index.

[119]Berg and Clifford, 'Luxury'.

[120]Wang does not include income of the Imperial Household in his consideration and I lack concrete information on that for this period.

China. Even if we were to believe Kent Deng's extremely low population estimate for China, Britain's population at the time still would have counted for only some 8 per cent of that of China. Just before the Revolutionary and Napoleonic Wars, the inhabitants of Britain paid their government effectively £16 million, or the silver equivalent of 48 million taels, in taxes. Per capita, in terms of silver, that is more than 200 grams and some twenty times as much as inhabitants of China, where regular tax income had not, or at best marginally, increased over the century.

As indicated before, at the end of those wars, total gross tax income of Great Britain's central government had risen to over £70 million, net tax revenue to over £60 million. Average gross tax income of central government over the period 1802–17 was some £60 million. Divided by the total population of Great Britain, that is of England, Wales and Scotland together, that would boil down to a per capita gross government income of the equivalent of roughly 550 grams of silver per year over that period. The difference with China, where at that time, in an extremely high if not simply far *too* high estimate, effective payments from the populace to central government per capita still were only 300 million taels divided by some 350–60 million people (some 30 grams of silver), is enormous. In the beginning of the nineteenth century, *total* gross revenue of the Qing government, expressed in silver-equivalents, would, even in an unduly 'optimist' estimate, have only been 60 to 70 per cent higher than that of the rulers of Great Britain. Per capita, government in London then would have received some *eighteen* times as much revenue from its subjects as its counterpart in Peking. This does not seem an extreme assumption: as indicated John Barrow, who made an estimate in 1803, claimed that at that time, on average, a Briton paid fifteen times as much tax as a Chinese.[121] I have no doubt that in fact the difference was even bigger. Please note that I am talking about '*effective* payments' – the amounts of money that actually were at the disposal of central government – not of *actual* payments – the amounts of money people had to pay in one way or another for being governed or, for that matter, in many cases simply for being squeezed. Whatever the exact figures will be, one thing is clear beyond any reasonable doubt: we are talking about completely different worlds. What we see are *surprising differences*. The period 1801–17 of course is exceptional. But over the entire period of 1802–51 annual gross income of the United Kingdom in no year was lower than £39 million. On average it annually was almost £60 million.[122] Even if we fully include Ireland in our calculation and divide that average sum by the average population of the entire United Kingdom plus Ireland over that entire period (some 22 million) we would still be talking about on average some 300 grams per year. For China per capita gross payments over that half-century were at best stable, almost certainly down.

The differences would become even more striking if we were to take estimates as our point of departure like those by Lee, which are in the orders of magnitude that the majority of scholars at the moment accepts. As a reminder, this scholar claims that China's government revenue before the First Opium War would never have been over

---

[121]See Barrow, *Travels in China*, 192.
[122]Mitchell, *British Historical Statistics*, 587–8 and 581–2.

60 to 80 million taels (the silver-equivalent of £20 million to £27 million). The interesting point of course is that several scholars who think the Qing managed to effectively tax their country have accepted these estimates. In particular the case of Wong stands out here as he, while accepting Lee's estimates, at the same time persistently claims that China's government managed 'to mobilise and disburse revenues quite beyond the imagination, let alone the abilities, of European state makers at the moment'.[123] For the eighteenth century and the part of the nineteenth century that we are discussing here this claim simply is untrue for *all* the Western European countries for which I have found information. It applies *least of all* to Great Britain, the most important European country in the Great Divergence debate. For the last decades of Qing rule it would also be untrue. The fact that in 1911 the Qing state had managed to collect almost 300 million taels in taxes seduces Wong into writing: 'Whatever the late Qing's state's weaknesses, raising money was not one of them.'[124] Those 300 million taels of government tax income would amount to between 2 and 3 per cent of net national product of China at the time. That is a surprisingly *low* percentage as compared to other countries *and* as compared to most periods in China's own past.

Government revenue and national income

China's government was not well funded. This did not escape contemporaries and some Chinese government officials complained that taxes were too low. Jin Fu (1633–92), for example, the Director General of the Grand Canal and the Yellow River from 1677 to 1688, regarded the low tax rate as one of the 'three great mischiefs' of China's political economy, the other two being the failure to undertake major water conservancy projects and the toleration of an excessively high ratio of consumers to producers.[125] Chen Hongmou (1696–1771), a Grand Secretary of the Qianlong Emperor and still very influential as a thinker after his death, in principle was in favour of low taxes, as were the majority of officials, but even he claimed: 'If long-term benefit to the people is at stake, we should not begrudge even the most massive spending.' He thinks of investments in waterworks, for example, and during his lifetime suggested policies that required substantial extra funding. The Qianlong emperor, however, was opposed to extra spending and very keen on showing how 'frugal' and 'benevolent' he was.[126] Chen Hongmou warned against 'fiscal caution', a kind of false economy that makes officials unwilling to embark on necessary undertakings and leads them to only act once the damage is done. This, according to

---

[123]Wong, *China Transformed*, 132.

[124]Wong, *China Transformed*, 156. The claim is repeated in Rosenthal and Wong, *Before and Beyond Divergence*, 201, and in Wong, 'Taxation and good governance', 373.

[125]Dunstan, *Conflicting Counsels*, 155.

[126]Rowe, *Saving the World*, 333 and 342. For statements that show that this emperor was in favour of low taxes see pages 122–3 of this book and Zelin, *Magistrate's Tael*, 262–3. To establish his reputation as a benevolent ruler, one of his first acts as emperor was to declare a tax amnesty for all taxes of over ten years' standing. See Dunstan, *State or Merchant*, 444–52.

him, was precisely the Sage's (Confucius') meaning when he included fiscal meanness as the last of the 'four evils'.[127]

For those who hold the view that in the very long eighteenth century Qing China was a poor country, the relatively low amount of government revenue will not come as a surprise. Even in a supposedly despotic state you simply cannot make poor people pay lots of 'taxes'. This is not the place to enter into the very lively and even fierce debate on how poor or rich China exactly was at the time.[128] What I can and *do* claim is that when we compare the shares of national income that were paid to central government in China and in Western Europe, we come to an identical conclusion: in that sense, too, government income in China was not high. It is far from easy to make the necessary calculations to firmly support this claim. That is true even for Britain, without any doubt the country whose economic and fiscal history has been studied more extensively and 'successfully' than that of any country in the world. Even here estimates are fraught with difficulties. These are only aggravated by the fact that the geographic regions referred to are not always identical. Estimates, however, do not differ so much as to make it impossible to be quite certain about the orders of magnitude.

So, what were the ratios of tax income, or rather *government* income, to 'national income'?[129] For the period from 1715 to 1812, Mathias and O'Brien have estimated Britain's ratio of taxes to national commodity output.[130] They claim it increased from a low of 16 per cent in the beginning of that period to a high of 36 per cent in the war period of 1803 to 1812 at its end. At the very end of the Napoleonic Wars, the figure was even higher.[131] In a later publication O'Brien estimated that the share of national income (of England and Wales) that was appropriated as taxation increased from 3.4 per cent in 1665 to 18.2 per cent in 1815.[132] Kozub, also talking about Britain, thinks that tax revenues as a percentage of national income fluctuated between 9 and 13 per cent throughout most of the eighteenth century. During the Napoleonic Wars this ratio rose to over 20 per cent.[133] Daunton, writing about the United Kingdom, claims that taxes amounted to 9 per cent of gross national product in the beginning of the eighteenth century to then reach a level of 23 per cent at their height in 1810.[134] Goldstone estimates that in 1789, when they were higher than ever before, but clearly not yet at their 'top', taxes amounted to 18.61 per cent of GDP in Britain.[135] After the Napoleonic Wars tax revenue as a percentage of (an increasing) Britain's GDP declined. In the 1830s, it amounted to some 10 per cent, in the 1840s to some

---

[127]Dunstan, *Conflicting Counsels*, 188–91. For further information see Yang, 'Economic justification' and Chen, 'Financial strategies'.

[128]For literature that does, see Chapter 1 notes 169–82.

[129]I use this rather vague term because actual calculations refer to *different* national aggregates like commodity output, national income and GDP.

[130]National commodity output is lower than national income. Exactly how much we do not know but considering the number of people working in services, at least about one-third, to my view, would be a reasonable guess.

[131]Bordo and White, 'Tale of two currencies', 304, Figure 1.

[132]O'Brien, 'Political economy', 3. Compare O'Brien, 'Fiscal and financial preconditions', 13, figure 5.

[133]Kozub, 'Evolution of taxation', 373.

[134]Daunton, *Trusting Leviathan*, 23.

[135]Goldstone, *Revolution and Rebellion*, 205 and 206.

11 to 12 per cent.[136] The estimates, not surprisingly, differ, but not so much as to not give us a good idea of orders of magnitude. We have to realize that in Great Britain and in most other countries in Western Europe government expenditures as a rule were substantially *higher* than government revenues.[137]

For France, a country for which our information is less unequivocal and reliable than we would want, one can nevertheless be certain that in the 1780s tax revenue as a percentage of national income will have been less than ten.[138] Here there was no linear, steady increase. Over the period from 1715 to 1808, according to Mathias and O'Brien, the ratio of tax revenue to national commodity output was lowest in 1770 and highest in 1735 when it was some 17 per cent (some 12 per cent of GDP).[139] After the Napoleonic Wars the ratio overall was lower. In 1840 after more than ten years of increasing taxes, it still was less than 10 per cent.[140] In the Dutch Republic, overall, taxes collected for central government amounted to some 10 to 15 per cent of national income during the eighteenth century.[141] During the first half of the nineteenth century that percentage hovered between some 10 and 12 per cent of GDP.[142] Dickson in a very rough estimate claims that for the parts of the Habsburg Empire that he has studied – the Austrian lands, the Hungarian lands, the Bohemian lands and Galicia – central government took between 12 and 15 per cent of national income in the 1780s, before war-expenditure caused a big increase in taxation.[143] For Prussia, that very probably was somewhat lower or in the same order of magnitude.[144] For both these countries too, total government income, taxes and other incomes, after the Napoleonic Wars amounted to a lower percentage (below 10 per cent) of GDP than during and just before those wars.[145]

Making claims in this respect for China is even trickier than it is for various countries in Western Europe. Actually, the figures we have about its GDP for the entire period before 1880 are no more than (sometimes even wild) guesses. These are the estimates I found in recent literature:

---

[136]See e.g. Kozub, 'Evolution of taxation', 373.

[137]See pages 205–12 of this book.

[138]I base this claim on information from Bonney, 'France 1494–1815'; Goldstone, *Revolution and Rebellion*, 204–5; Macdonald, *Free Nation*, 241 and 252; Mann, *Sources of Social Power, II*, 366–7; Mathias and O'Brien, 'Taxation in Britain and France', tables 3 and 4, and White, 'France and the failure to modernize macroeconomic institutions', 62.

[139]Mathias and O'Brien, 'Taxation in Britain and France', 613 and 611.

[140]Bonney, 'Apogee and fall', 89.

[141]I distil this from the literature referred to under tables 8a and 8b, page 71.

[142]See Van Zanden and Van Riel, *Strictures of Inheritance*, 99, for the period 1814–40.

[143]Dickson, *Finance and Government, I*, 133–7. Gorski, on the basis of quite different figures, claims that for Austria in 1789–90 the proportion of national income that was appropriated as tax was just below 12 per cent. See Gorski, *Disciplinary Revolution*, 81. Sandgruber, *Österreichische Geschichte*, 222, comes up with a similar tax-to-GNP ratio for the Habsburg state.

[144]Gorski, *Disciplinary Revolution*, 81–2. For some information on Prussia's 'national income' and tax levels at the end of the eighteenth century, see Krug, *Betrachtungen über den Nationalreichtum*; Riedel, *Brandenburgisch-preußische Staatshaushalt*, and Weitzel, *Entwicklung der Staatsausgaben*. For general information on the situation in the region that is nowadays called 'Germany', see Pierenkemper and Tilly, *German Economy*, ch. 2, and Ullman, *Deutsche Steuerstaat*, 13–39.

[145]See Spoerer, 'Evolution of public finances', and Pammer, 'Public finance in Austria-Hungary'.

Table 11 Some estimates of Qing China's GDP, in millions of taels

1750	952−1713[a]
1770	2,000[b]
Late eighteenth century	6,417[c]
1830s	±4,000[d]
1840	5,553[e]
1840	6,000[f]
Late 1880s	3,200−4,000[g]
Late 1880s	5,500[h]

Sources:
[a]Feuerwerker, 'State and the economy', 16.
[b]Guanglin William Liu, *Wrestling for Power*, 104.
[c]Brandt, Ma and Rawski, 'From divergence to convergence', 56, note 23. I consider this estimate very improbable as it is based on very implausible assumptions.
[d]In an unpublished paper called 'The Nanking Treaty System: Institutional change and improved economic performance', Kent Deng gave an estimate for 1833 of 3,931.8 to 4,325.0 million taels in 1839 price. At a workshop at the London School of Economics and Political Science on 5 June 2006 he claimed that China's GDP in 1830 amounted to 150,000 tons of silver or some 4,000 million taels.
[e]Broadberry, Guan and Li, 'China, Europe and the Great Divergence', Table 3.
[f]Ma, De Jong and Chu, 'Living standards in China', 17.
[g]Chang, *Income of the Chinese Gentry*, 196; Deng, 'Miracle or mirage', table 9, and Feuerwerker, *Chinese Economy, ca. 1870-1911*, 2.
[h]Calculated on the basis of Ma, De Jong and Chu, 'Living standards in China', 47.

Note: The estimates in T. Liu, 'Estimation of China's GDP' are so low that they simply are not realistic. For very preliminary but interesting findings see Shi Zhihong, Xuyi, Ni Yuping, and Bas van Leeuwen, 'Chinese national income'. In the most recent estimates there is a consensus emerging that real income in Qing China was decreasing during most of the period discussed here and was substantially lower than that in Great Britain.

Our figures for total government income are fraught with uncertainties too and differences between various estimates are huge. So figures that express the ratio of government income to national income can only be broad approximations. For the eighteenth century, estimates vary between 4 and 8 per cent.[146] For the first half of the

---

[146]See Feuerwerker, 'State and the economy', 16, where he gives his estimate of 4–8 per cent for c. 1750. Naquin and Evelyn Rawski in their *Chinese Society*, 219, write that in eighteenth-century China 'taxes garnered less than five per cent of the gross national product'. Thomas Rawski has argued repeatedly that even taking into account corruption, the Qing state never commandeered more than 5 per cent of GDP (Zelin, 'Modernization', 109, note 64). Liu thinks that in the 1770s government's tax income amounted to 2.8 per cent of GDP (Liu, *Wrestling for Power*, 104). According to Sng, 'Size and dynastic decline', 35, there was a steady lowering of the taxes/GDP ratio from almost 10 per cent in 1685 to 2 per cent in 1845. Some three-quarters of total tax income of the government were generated by the tax on land. According to Dunstan the norm for land taxation was set at about 10 per cent of the annual agrarian production. In reality, though, so she claims, it appears to have been lower. (Dunstan, *Conflicting Counsels*, 151). According to Perkins the percentage would be five to six (Perkins, *Agricultural Development*, 176). According to Wang, to give one final example, the Qing land tax burden showed a 'secular trend of lessening' and during the last quarter of Qing rule 'fell within the range between two and four per cent of the land produce in most districts and provinces' (Wang, *Land Taxation*, 126-8).

nineteenth century this percentage will certainly not have been higher. Combining my extreme high estimate of total government income in silver with Deng's estimate of China's GDP in the 1830s, referred to in Table 11, would suggest government in China then collected about 8 per cent of GDP. For the last decades of the Qing dynasty, when government's total *tax income* increased to some 300 million taels, it will have been *substantially* less than 10 per cent.[147] When we break the Chinese picture down regionally, the story becomes more complicated, and much to the disadvantage of the richest regions; nonetheless, it would be hard to see taxes in those areas as particularly harsh.

All these figures are very shaky. What *can* be claimed, however, is that the income of China's government as compared to that of governments in Western Europe, during the long eighteenth century, was very small in per capita terms. In relative terms, that is as compared to GDP, it clearly was smaller too. We can only conclude that taxes were a *major* factor in the economies of early modern Western Europe. It is difficult to understand how most of the Californians can compare Western economies with that of China without intensively studying them. In the two books that have done most to change our ideas with regard to the economy of early modern China, Pomeranz's *The Great Divergence* and Frank's *ReOrient*, there is not even an entry for 'taxation' in the index. Referring to percentages of GDP as such, however, can be somewhat misleading in this context. Not only because the figures we have for GPD of various countries – and for government income – in the early modern era are very shaky, but also because the impact of a specific tax rate can be quite different with differing incomes. The tax burden in Britain and the Dutch Republic, to only focus on the countries with the highest taxes, must have been experienced as extremely high, considering the much lower real income per capita of people at the time. Gross domestic product per capita in real terms in the United Kingdom and the country that is now called the Netherlands, in the beginning of the twenty-first century, is more than ten times as high as it was around 1800. For Western Europe as a whole, the increase in this period was no less than fifteen-fold.[148] Ordinary consumers needed a large part of their money to buy necessities. In that light the *impact* of any government levy must have been substantial.

Private incomes and government incomes in Great Britain

Critics could of course object that all the figures presented so far as such do not tell us much about the actual value of the amounts of money we are discussing. How do they compare to income? What could one buy for them? How long did one have to work to earn them? These are important points and I will try and deal with them. But I want to emphasize again that these comments, even though they are valid, do not imply that the

---

[147]See Bastid, 'Structure of financial institutions'; Deng, *China's Political Economy*, 17; Feuerwerker, 'State and the economy', 16; Liu, *Wrestling for Power*, 104; Ma, de Jong and Chu, 'Living standards in China', figure 3; Perkins, 'Government as an obstacle', and Wang, *Land Taxation*, 129–33. They all give percentages *far* below 10 and even *far* below 5 per cent.
[148]Maddison, *World Economy*, 246.

comparisons in terms of silver that have been made or the information with regard to percentages of GDP that have been given in this book up until now would be meaningless. For answering questions in which exchange rates between different countries or the sizes of their monetary stocks matter, for example, they are very useful and even essential. The figures with regard to percentages of GDP of course also have their value: they tell us something of presence and leverage of central government in the national economy.

For answering various questions more directly related to the *domestic* situation, the estimates made so far of course are *not* very informative and should at least be complemented by other indicators. The first one would be what the figures we have found of per capita tax payments mean when we compare them to wages at the time. Let us be more specific and look at daily wages of unskilled labour.

Table 12 again shows how misleading it can be to talk about 'Europe'. The figures for per capita payments to government and wages, in this case daily wages of ordinary 'average' labourers, enable us to determine how many days those labourers had to work to be able to pay their dues to government. Let us compare the average per capita tax payment over the first half of the nineteenth century with the average per capita nominal wage for unskilled labour in London. In the period 1800–15 it would have taken an unskilled labourer there, earning somewhat over 17.7 grams of silver, some thirty days to pay the average per capita gross tax in his country.[149] After their peak in the 1810s, wages continued to be fairly stable in terms of silver, with a tendency to decrease. In the 1840s my estimate would be that this same labourer would have earned somewhat less than the fifty years' average of 17.7 grams and had to work somewhat less than twenty days to pay his dues. Most British labourers earned less than their colleagues in London and probably would have had to work longer to be able to pay the average per capita tax rate for the country.[150]

Table 12 Nominal average wages of building labourers (grams of silver per day) over the periods 1750–99 and 1800–49

	1750–99	1800–49
London	11.5	17.7
Southern England towns	8.3	14.6
Amsterdam	9.2	9.2
Paris	5.2	9.9
Leipzig	3.1	4.4
Vienna	3.0	2.1

Source: Allen, 'Great Divergence in European wages', 416, Table 2.

---

[149]He of course also had to pay taxes for his dependents.
[150]See Allen, *British Industrial Revolution*, 43, for a comparison of wages in Oxford, York and London over the period 1500–1850.

There of course are no such people as *average* workers with *average* incomes in *average* times. In the previous paragraphs we discussed *daily* wages of male wage labourers. The number of days those labourers actually worked in a year, however, was not a constant. Very often more than one person contributed to the family income. Besides, during the period discussed here the number of people who sold their labour or in any case worked for a market tended to increase, and people tended to work longer and harder.[151] But let us nevertheless try and get at least an impression of orders of magnitude by means of some 'stylised facts'. The period we focus upon is that from 1800 to the 1850s, the time span that is at the heart of our analysis. As a reminder, per capita *averaged* tax payments to central government of Great Britain by Great Britons during that period amounted to a maximum of between 500 and 600 grams of silver per year (in the first two decades) and a minimum of some 250 grams, at the end of the period. For an average family these figures would have to be multiplied by four to five.

Graph 3 Per capita tax pressure in Holland, England and France, 1500–1800, expressed in the number of daily wages of an unskilled labourer in the construction industry.

Source: Van Zanden, *Long Road to the Industrial Revolution*, 218.

Table 13 Average estimated yearly wage in grams of silver during the period 1800–50, in London and in towns in Southern England

London		Southern England	
Unskilled labourer	5,000 grams	Unskilled labourer	4,000 grams
Building craftsman	8,000 grams	Building craftsman	>6,000 grams

Source: Allen, 'Great Divergence in European wages', 416, Tables 1 and 2. I have assumed people worked 300 days per year.

---

[151]See De Vries, *Industrious Revolution*, and the reactions it provoked.

The estimates by Allen are high and based on the income of rather well paid labourers who worked many days. If one bases estimates on figures by Feinstein, the yearly income of an *average* manual worker in the United Kingdom in the period from 1780 to 1850, assuming full employment, will have hovered between 2,100 and 3,700 grams of silver. Most of the time, it was about 3,000 grams of silver.

The male head of the family as a rule was not the only person in a British family who had an income. Overall, between 1787 and 1865, his income was somewhere between 70 and 80 per cent of total family income, with, of course, differences between sectors and over time.[152] Considering changes over time, Horrell and Humphries detected a pattern of gradually rising monetary contributions by wives and children to total household income from about 25 per cent in the late 1780s to more than 40 per cent up to the 1830s, followed by a decline in the difficult 1840s and a further decline in the 1860s.[153] To get a stylized average family income, we therefore have to add an average additional income earned by the rest of the family. Let us fix that at one half of average male income.

If we would add half to the income of Feinstein's average manual worker in the United Kingdom his family income over the period 1780–1850 would have been between some 3,400 and 5,500 grams of silver, in most years near 4,500 grams. These figures provide us with some benchmarks to get an idea how high *average* tax payments were in proportion to various *average* incomes.

All estimates by Allen are rather high. Most people will not have actually worked 300 days per year. An average of 275 to 300, or even somewhat lower in all probability, would be more realistic. At any moment in time, moreover, there were substantial amounts of people with no employment at all. The labour input by the rest of the family and its rewards – especially in the case of skilled labourers – is also set quite high. The actual *average* family income per year in Britain and Wales in the years 1801 to 1803 has been estimated at 10,000 grams of silver.[154] The income of an *ordinary* family in Britain, in

Table 14 Average estimated yearly family wage income in grams of silver during the period 1800–50 in London and in towns in Southern England

London		Southern England	
Unskilled labourer	7,500 grams	Unskilled labourer	6,000 grams
Building craftsman	12,000 grams	Building craftsman	9,600 grams

Based on: Allen, 'Great Divergence in European wages', 416, Tables 1 and 2. I have assumed 300 working days per year.

---

[152]Humphries, 'Household economy', 259. The categories that together count as total household income in my calculations are man's earnings, woman's earnings, children's earnings and other income; the sectors that were analysed were agriculture, mining, factory work, outwork and trades. See also De Vries, *Industrious Revolution*, 117–3 and ch. 5.

[153]See the synthesis of their ideas and exact references in De Vries, *Industrious Revolution*, 108.

[154]I found this figure in Floud and McCloskey, *Economic History of Britain, I*, 391. Here, too, exact figures are hard to get and if they are exact they can never be fully trusted.

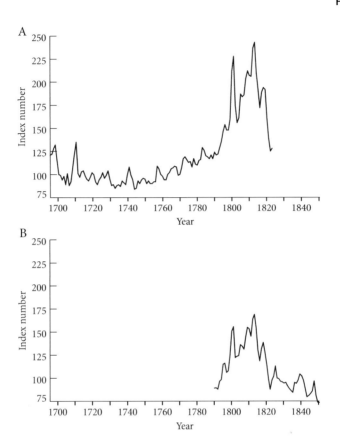

Graph 4 Costs of living in Britain.

A) Schumpeter-Gilboy price index for British prices for the period 1696–1823, for consumer goods (1701 = 100).

B) Gayer-Rostow-Schwartz index of British commodity prices (domestic and imported) 1790–1850 (monthly average, 1821–25 = 100).

Source: Mitchell, *British Historical Statistics,* 719–21.

this case in 1803, would have been £39 – the equivalent of somewhat over 4,300 grams of silver.[155]

The real value of the sums of money we are discussing either as tax payments or as income of course depended on (changes in) the costs of living. These are presented in Graphs 4 and 5. These figures are only meant to give an indication of how big the average 'tax take' of the state was compared to the average earnings of 'ordinary' people. My primary goal is to indicate how much 'abstract' labour government expropriated via taxes rather than how much concrete labour concrete people actually had to perform

---

[155]See for this figure Perkin, *Origins of Modern English Society,* 20–1, who derives it from Colquhoun, *Treatise on Indigence.*

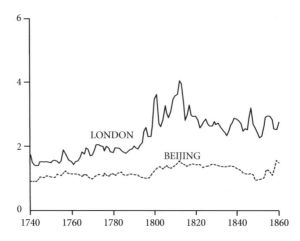

Graph 5 Cost of a 'subsistence basket of goods' in grams of silver per day.

Based on Allen, 'Wages, prices and living standards', 23. See for further explanation Allen, *British Industrial Revolution*, 35–42.

to pay their dues. Nevertheless a better approximation of real tax pressure showing how much specific people actually paid would be welcome. To get an idea of the actual tax incidence for varying groups of people, several facts have to be considered. First, that the bulk of taxes in Britain over the period 1780–1850 always consisted of indirect taxes, that is customs or excises, collected mostly on consumer goods that were not absolute necessities but that over time lost much of their status as luxuries. How much of these taxes one paid depended on how much of the taxed goods one consumed, which to a certain extent was a choice. The second relevant fact is that taxes related to income and wealth were not unknown.[156] 'Ordinary' Britons as a rule had no land and their income was too low to be liable to pay income tax. During the Napoleonic Wars, taxes on income and wealth could amount to about one-third of total tax income. Of the *extra* taxes collected to wage the wars against the French in the last decade of the eighteenth and the first two decades of the nineteenth century, wealthier Britons paid over 60 per cent, among others, via an income tax that was introduced in 1798, abolished already in 1816, only to be reintroduced in the 1840s.[157] Land tax and assessed taxes yielded an ever-decreasing amount of money after the end of the wars against the French. In 1840–9 they only amounted to some 8 per cent of total tax revenue, the newly reintroduced income taxes to some 6 per cent and customs and excises to about two-thirds. This means that although part of taxes – sometimes a substantial part – did not touch ordinary people, the bulk of them did. In the last decades of the period discussed here, that part did not decrease. As soon as the Napoleonic Wars were over, the rich

---

[156]See Figure 1 for the importance of land taxes, other assessed taxes and income taxes in the period from 1700 to 1850.

[157]See O'Brien, 'Triumph and denouement', 167–200.

stopped paying income taxes till the 1840s, which means that the decrease of average tax payments that set in at that moment will hardly have favoured the average Briton. Even more so as declining prices – and that is a third factor that has to be considered – meant that, *ceteris paribus*, the real impact of taxation *increased*.

How much tax such a wage earner actually paid in Britain at the time depended on his consumer habits. Here, too, substantial differences existed according to time, place and the exact amount of money one earned, as many heavily taxed goods had a high price-elasticity.[158] If one looks at various budgets, it becomes clear that a large majority of ordinary labourers could afford a 'respectable lifestyle basket of consumer goods' above subsistence and will have spent a substantial amount of money on heavily taxed goods like beer (taxed heavily until 1830), tobacco, tea, sugar, salt, fuel and other consumer goods whose consumption tended to increase with income.[159] Every Briton earning an income that allowed him to live above bare subsistence had to pay so much taxes on so many goods that their payment as a percentage of their income will easily have amounted to the national average. For all those with a decent income it will very probably have even been higher, in particular at times when taxes on income and wealth were low. Most excises were imposed on products holding the middle ground between necessities and real luxuries. That means that the so-called 'middling rank of people', with incomes between £50 and £400 per year, will have contributed disproportionately. In 1750 some 15 per cent of total population belonged to this group, in 1800 some 25 per cent.[160]

In that context the extreme inequality in income (and wealth) in Britain – and other Western countries of course – is highly relevant.[161] In Britain wage labour had become quite normal and its remuneration, over time, showed a tendency to become *higher* than that of the self-employed.[162] But according to Peter Lindert and Jeffrey Williamson, over the entire very long eighteenth century, the share of total national income earned by unskilled and skilled *wage* labour together – the types of income that almost all analyses of the standard of living focus upon – nevertheless never amounted to more than one-eighth of British GDP, even when one stretches the definition of 'working class'.[163] Income inequality in Britain was not only very high: when one looks at the share of total income earned by the top 5 per cent of personal incomes, it also tended to increase over the very long eighteenth century. What is also striking is that the group of

---

[158]For representative baskets of consumer goods see e.g., Allen, *British Industrial Revolution*, 25–56; Feinstein, 'Pessimism perpetuated'; Floud and Johnson, *Cambridge Economic History of Modern Britain, I*, the articles by Berg, Humphries and Voth; Hofman, 'Real inequality'; Horrell and Humphries, 'Old questions', and Mokyr, 'Is there still life in the pessimist case?'

[159]For more details on how heavily such consumer goods were taxed see pages 175–9.

[160]Berg and Clifford, 'Luxury', 1108.

[161]See my *Escaping Poverty*, 234–45, in particular 244 . For income inequality in Britain and various other parts of the West in the early modern era see Hoffman, 'Real inequality in Western Europe'. For interesting figures for the nineteenth and twentieth centuries in the 'capitalist' West see Piketty, *Capitalism in the Twenty-First Century*, passim.

[162]Mokyr, 'Is there still life in the pessimist case?', 87–90.

[163]See the income tables on Peter Lindert's website at University Davis California under 'Data and Estimates'.

wage-earning workers and labourers, including those in agriculture, exceptionally big as it was in Britain comparatively speaking, will never have been more than roughly one-third of the total labour force. This can only make one wonder why exactly this group of people and their income gets almost all the attention in discussions of 'the standard of living' in Great Britain as such or as compared to other nations.

Private incomes and government incomes in China

Figuring out how big a percentage of income was actually paid in taxes by 'ordinary people', whatever that may exactly mean, is even more problematic for the Chinese case. To begin with there are very few data with regard to wages. Not only are they scarce: they also are often hard to interpret when it comes to their exact meaning and representativeness. Moreover, even if we would be able to get a clear idea of wages levels, they do not tell us much about the standard of living of ordinary Chinese, as they, to an overwhelming majority, did not work solely or even primarily for wages. So one needs other ways of figuring out what their income was. The differing and changing exchange rates of copper and silver caused additional problems. They make it difficult to determine the actual value of payments expressed in one of these metals. This becomes a very serious problem in the 1820s. Finally, two more facts need to be briefly addressed or at least noted. First there is the fact that just like in Britain the distribution of incomes was very unequal in China. A disproportionate share of total income went to a quite small percentage of the population. In Changs' often-quoted study on the income of China's gentry, one finds the estimate that in the 1880s 2 per cent of the population would have earned 24 per cent of national income.[164] That is of course an estimate, but there are no reasons to believe that the gist of Chang's figures is wrong or that earlier in the very long eighteenth century the situation would have been very different. Second there is the fact that the bulk of tax revenue came from land taxes. In principle people owning land paid them, which of course already implies that averages are misleading when it comes to actual incidence of payment. They moreover varied enormously depending on region, quality of land and who actually owned it. There were huge differences in assessment between different qualities of land: there are examples of excellent land being taxed no less than twenty-five times as high as land on mountain slopes.[165] If we add this to the fact that our information with regard to government revenue is quite shaky, it is clear that we have to be very prudent and refrain from making firm statements.

How high was the tax burden for an 'ordinary' Chinese? Ordinary Chinese by and large did not work for wages. Wage labour was quite exceptional – only a very small part of the entire working population can be regarded as real 'proletarians'.[166] Let us nevertheless first discuss their income. In China in the second half of the

---

[164]Chang, *Income of the Chinese Gentry*, 326–32.
[165]Wagner, *Chinesische Landwirtschaft*, 136–42.
[166]See Chapter 1 note 171.

eighteenth century – it is only from then onwards that we find data that is more than anecdotic – an unskilled labourer, *payment in kind included*, as a rule certainly did not earn more than the equivalent of 3, in *very* exceptional circumstances 4, grams of silver per day.[167] On average, again very roughly, it will have been 2 to 3 grams. That was at a level similar to that of towns in Central and parts of Southern Europe. Whereas wages tended to rise in most parts of Europe in the next half century,[168] they, in terms of silver, barely changed in China. Anecdotal evidence suggests that many ordinary unskilled labourers had a wage at the lower edge of this estimate, or even below it.[169] Especially as compared to England, Chinese silver wages clearly were lower, which of course has its implications for the real impact of payments to the government.[170] Average tax payment in China – again in my extremely high estimate – amounted to the income of only some ten working days of a well-paid unskilled wage labourer. I admit that this comparison is not fair as wage labour in China was quite abnormal *and* badly paid.[171] The incomes of wage labourers in China were quite low as they were meant to only cover the personal subsistence costs of the labourers themselves, not those of wives and children which such labourers, as so-called 'bare sticks', were not supposed to have. An average, 'normal' Chinese, working on his farm, would certainly have a higher income than the wage labourer we referred to in our comparison. The income of someone renting land may have been twice as high; that of someone owning land even three times to, in exceptional cases, five times as high, at least according to Pomeranz.[172] We are then talking in orders of magnitude of 3–6 and 4.5–9 grams of silver. The number of working days required to pay taxes would of course decrease proportionately.

If wages – or any kind of income – were actually paid (entirely or partly) in copper cash, which for ordinary labour was the rule, one is confronted with the major and

---

[167]This estimate is in Allen et al., 'Wages, prices, and living standards'.

[168]See Table 12 and the source from which it is taken for more information.

[169]Broadberry and Gupta think silver wages in China in the Yangzi Delta at the time were less than 2 grams. See their 'Early modern great divergence'. Clark in his *Farewell to Alms*, e.g. 49, also is less optimistic about Chinese wages. For the middle of the eighteenth century see e.g. Pomeranz, *Great Divergence*, 319–20. For the 1790s–1810s see e.g. Hu, *Concise History of Chinese Economic Thought*, 509–10; Mazumdar, *Sugar and Society*, 54; Naquin, *Millenarian Rebellion*, Appendix 3, and Smith, *China's Cultural Heritage*, 302–3. For the first half of the nineteenth century see e.g. Gamble, 'Daily wages'.

[170]In China labour as a rule was paid in copper. The copper to silver rate could fluctuate wildly. Especially during the period of the silver drain, roughly the second quarter of the nineteenth century, the value of copper declined sharply as compared to that of silver. Allen and his colleagues have tried to take this into account in their estimates.

[171]For the entire period discussed here, I have never come across an estimate that claims that more than 5 per cent of China's labour force would have consisted of full-time wage labourers. Pomeranz himself recently wrote that even in the highly commercialized Yangzi Delta at most 15 per cent of the rural Chinese lived primarily on wages. Pomeranz, 'Ten years after', 23.

[172]Pomeranz, 'Institutions and economic development': and idem in his presentation at the German Historikertag on 24 September 2014 in Göttingen. For an effort to calculate the *income* of Chinese peasants (in the Yangtze Delta) in the period c.1620–1820 see Allen, 'Agricultural productivity', where the author claims that *peasant* families in that region in the 1820s earned about as much as a family of an *agricultural wage labourer* in England at the time, but that their income had decreased since the 1620s and was very unlikely to increase again as the Yangtze Delta had developed a 'surplus labour economy'. In England agricultural wages were much lower than those in the secondary sector of the economy.

sometimes insoluble problem that the exchange rate of copper with silver underwent enormous fluctuations and also varied from place to place. Official policy under the Qing has always been to fix the exchange rate between silver tael and copper cash at 1,000 to 1. In practice, however, the exchange rate always oscillated widely and varied locally. In the period from the late 1820s to the 1860s silver appreciated against copper to such an extent that at times the rate was more than 2,000 to 1. Again wide variations existed according to place and time. This appreciation had big implications that are not easy to calculate.[173] For the ordinary taxpayer, who had no silver, it meant a serious increase in

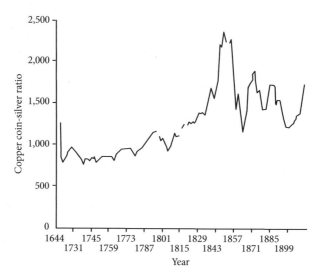

Graph 6 Copper to silver ratios, 1644–1911.

Source: Lin, *China Upside Down*, 3.

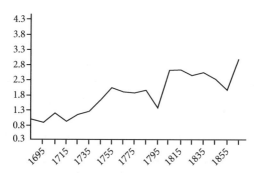

Graph 7 Rice prices in China, as measured in silver, in taels per shi 1685–1865.

Source: Lu and Peng, 'Research on China's long-term rice prices', 487. Other sources point in the direction of a somewhat clearer decrease of prices in terms of silver. See under Chapter 1 note 174.

---

[173]See the next note.

actual payment, as he had to exchange far more copper cash to get the required amount of silver to pay his dues, in a time when copper also was not in ample supply. As silver became more expensive prices of goods paid in silver fell: China faced deflation. From the second half of the 1810s onwards, silver prices tended to decline, having risen substantially during the previous decades.[174]

Overall, from the 1820s onwards, taxes in real terms increased sometimes substantially for all those people who received their income in copper and had to pay the taxman in silver. Even though government did not actually increase tax rates, in effect the population had to pay much more, especially in the 1840s. In 1849, according to an official, taxes were three times as heavy as during the reign of the Qianlong emperor (r. 1736–95) and his successor the Jiaqing emperor (r. 1796–1820). There is ample evidence of hardship caused by the increasing tax burden. Peasants had to relinquish much more of their crops in order to pay the same amount of taxes as before. They had to do so at a time when they faced sharply reduced incomes from selling their crops and from off-season employment. Everyone who was paid in copper faced a lowering net income.[175] Things only worsened because peasants often were also cheated in the process of exchanging copper for silver.

In real terms government income *ceteris paribus* must have increased. One should be careful though not to exaggerate that increase. Taxes in kind remained unchanged, as did taxes that were not commuted in silver. For many ordinary taxpayers from the 1820s onwards, because of the copper–silver exchange problem *and* increasing corruption and fraud, the actual tax burden indeed became much higher. That translated into increasing amounts of non-payments and arrears. The actual state income therefore must have been substantially lower than the official rates. Moreover, whereas total tax income in silver might have been fairly stable, population increased. That will probably have implied higher costs for government. We are dealing here with quite a complex situation. The problems were intensely discussed and there was no shortage of proposals to deal with them, but basically they were not solved.[176] In the 1850s, deflation came to an end and a new period in China's economic history began. That, however, is not the subject of this book.

Notwithstanding all these complicating factors, one may certainly conclude that official tax-payments in terms of silver, *on average*, must also in real terms have been far lower as compared to *average* income than they were in Great Britain. Finding out what this means for actual tax payment by various concrete groups requires an analysis that cannot be done in the context of writing this book, if it can be done at all. The bulk of taxes were land taxes: only people who owned land paid them and, for them, where

---

[174]For the history of prices in China over the very long eighteenth century see, in alphabetical order: Buoye, *Manslaughter*, ch. 2; Cheung, 'Copper, silver, and tea'; Deng, 'Miracle or mirage?'; Li, 'Grain prices'; Lu and Pang, 'Research on China's long-term rice prices'; Wang, *Land Taxation*, 114–5, and idem, 'Secular trends'.

[175]For a general analysis of the economic and social consequences of the appreciation of silver and the ensuing deflation see He, *Paths to the Modern Fiscal State*, chs 5 and 6, and Lin, *China Upside Down*, ch. 3. For an analysis at a regional level see Bernhardt, *Rents, Taxes, and Peasant Resistance*.

[176]See pages 251–63.

they lived and what their social status was could make a big difference. The incidence of so-called 'contributions' made to government of course also was quite different: the wealthy certainly will have 'contributed' more. As pointed out, from the 1820s onwards, taxes in real terms increased very substantially for those who received their income in copper and had to pay the taxman in silver. Last but definitely not least, there was the fact that actual payments were much higher than official ones. Adding all this up strongly suggests that, certainly in the first half of the nineteenth century, for many Chinese 'taxes' must have been far more of a burden than ever before, and maybe for those living on a tiny plot close to subsistence *more* of a burden than for the 'poor' Britons who mostly had a higher income to begin with and could to some extent, via their consumption, decide how much tax they actually wanted to pay.

The best one can do here is refer to abstract averages: that can nevertheless be quite instructive as it at least provides us with a point of reference to assess the incidence of taxation on incomes. Let us set total per capita payments to China's government for the first decades of the nineteenth century at 30 grams of silver, which is a very high estimate, some three-quarters of it collected as land tax. Let us very optimistically assume that, like in the British case, a wage labourer would work 300 days a year. He would then earn 900 grams of silver per year if he was well paid. An estimate of some 600 grams of silver would probably be more realistic. An average tax payment of 30 grams of silver per year would then amount to between 3.3 and 5 per cent of that income. This of course is a fairly unrealistic exercise. People living by wage labour alone – whose number in Qing China was almost negligible – in fact will hardly have paid any taxes at all. They did not pay any land taxes, nor will they have been hit hard by the various other taxes. For skilled labourers, taxes will have been even less sizeable. Land taxes were the bulk of all taxes. It was the owners of the land who paid them. What would it mean for them to pay the average tax? For a family of four, average tax-incidence would have amounted to the equivalent of 120 grams of silver per year, for one of five to the equivalent of 150 grams of silver per year.

Let us for the sake of argument assume that such a family consisted of four people and earned five times as much income as a wage labourer. Total annual household income would then be between 3,000 and 4,500 grams of silver. Its tax payments would then also to some 3 to 4 per cent of total family income. Of course these are all 'stylized' estimates, but the message I guess is clear: tax pressure was very low. Again, these are all abstract averages based on tentative estimates, but still the information they give is relevant. We do get an impression of how much government took in terms of income of its subjects and that is quite relevant for determining over how much resources it actually disposed.

Government levies and purchasing power

It is a priori highly unlikely that determining the real, domestic value of the revenue of Great Britain's and China's central government – that is, figuring out the purchasing power of their incomes – will lead to a refutation of the thesis that Britain was a high-tax country and Qing China a low-tax country. In the first decade of the nineteenth century an inhabitant of Great Britain on average had to annually pay the equivalent of roughly 600 grams of silver to government, the bulk of it in the form of indirect taxes. In China, that would certainly suffice to provide subsistence for an adult man for an entire year. At the time, a Chinese, in a very high estimate, on average, annually had to pay roughly 30 grams of silver to his government. In London at the time that would not even suffice to pay an unskilled labourer for two days' work! We referred to substantial regional differences in Britain but there will undoubtedly also have existed differences in China. That fact will certainly not change the gist of my thesis.[177]

What do we actually know about the purchasing power of a gram of silver in China as compared to its purchasing power in Britain? What does giving a gram of silver to the state mean for the person who pays in China? When we look at the costs of subsistence in terms of silver, 'China' clearly was cheaper than 'Britain'. Much of course depends on the exact time and the exact place, so one has to be very careful in making bold statements, even though in China differences between places and moments in time appear to be much smaller than expected. For the entire duration of the very long eighteenth century the claim that China would be a cheaper place to live in than Great Britain is beyond any reasonable doubt. What is much more difficult is to determine *how* much cheaper 'life in China' was than 'life in Great Britain'. Looking at the available literature, and with all the huge margins and reservations such a general statement requires, I think it is safe to conclude that subsistence in China in terms of silver was cheaper, but that the difference certainly was far too small to make up for the difference in tax level per capita.

I would claim that at the level of subsistence in the period 1790–1820 China was about two to three times as cheap – in terms of silver – as Great Britain.[178] The figures given by Allen presented in Graph 5 endorse this position. Anecdotal evidence too seems to support this, again very rough, estimate. John Barrow, who travelled in China in 1803, would, for what it is worth, agree: 'I should suppose, however, that a shilling in China generally speaking will go as far as three in Great Britain.'[179] Macartney in 1793 estimated that a Chinese peasant may maintain himself on fifty cash (roughly 1.8 grams of silver) per day.[180] According to Hong Liangji in that same year it would have been very hard to live with a family on 4 grams of silver per day.[181] According to Lin Zexu a

---

[177]See tables 12, 13 and 14.

[178]For comparisons of the costs of living and the standards of living in China and (parts of) Europe see Allen, Bengtsson, and Dribe, *Living Standards in the Past*; Allen, 'Agricultural productivity'; idem, *British Industrial Revolution*, 34, 39 and 40; Allen et al., 'Wages, prices, and living standards'; Broadberry and Gupta, 'Europe and Asia'; Gupta and Ma, 'Europe in an Asian mirror', and Van Zanden and Li, 'Before the Great Divergence?' As so often in this text, my claims are educated approximations, at best. For further, very recent estimates I refer to Sources under Table 11. For 1840 it has been estimated that the purchasing power parity of £1 was about 2 taels.

[179]Barrow, *Travels in China*, 192.

[180]Cranmer-Byng, *Embassy to China*, 244.

[181]I found this comment in Hu, *Concise History of Chinese Economic Thought*, 509. Hu refers to Hong Liangji's *The Conjectures. On People's Living*.

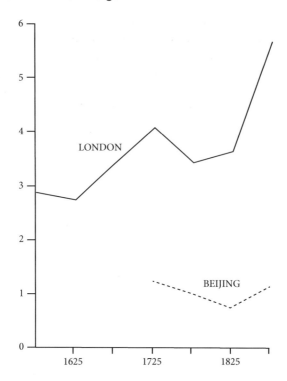

Graph 8 Subsistence ratios for unskilled labourers in London and Beijing.

Source: Allen, *Global Economic History*, 11.

medium-income family needed one-tenth of a tael (3.7 grams worth of silver) for daily expenses in 1838, when China was in the midst of great financial troubles, but overall knew somewhat lower prices.[182]

Graph 8, which presents a comparison of the height of real incomes in terms of the times it affords the purchase of a basic basket of subsistence, suggests a very important conclusion: even taking on board all the comments made so far, China's ordinary people apparently were poorer than their counterparts in Great Britain. In this respect too, I consider Pomeranz's 'striking resemblances-thesis' rejected. When in Great Britain industrialization started British ordinary labourers per capita were wealthier than their Chinese counterparts. This ensured that their government could in principle collect more revenue than China's government, which it actually did by taxing the consumption

---

[182]Lin, *China Upside Down*, XXIII. See also Chang, *Commissioner Lin*, 37, where Chang refers to Lin as claiming that in Suzhou and Wuhan the ordinary cost of living of a poor man in an average year was about four- to five-hundredths of a tael and that one-tenth of a tael would have been plentiful for every need. A poor man at the time thus would have needed about 1.5 grams of silver per day for subsistence. Compare Zhuang, *Tea, Silver, Opium and War*, 199, where it reads that according to Lin in 1839 the ordinary costs of living for a single common person would have been 18 taels – 670 gram of silver – per year. For estimates roughly in the same order of magnitude see Ma, De Jong and Chu, 'Living standards in China', 19.

of commodities that were not subsistence necessities. If my estimate of comparative costs of living is correct, that would mean that, at the beginning of the nineteenth century, in terms of 'overall', domestic purchasing power, Britain's government actually received on average at the very least *five* times as much money from each of its subjects as China's government. One may debate the exact figures but definitely not the overall gist of this claim. Considering my extremely high estimates for China's government's income, I would defend the claim that the difference actually was even much bigger.

Government's purchasing power

In this context, where we discuss the role of government in economic life, it matters to look not only – as is usually done – at the real tax burden for the populace by taking into consideration costs of living, but also – and in a certain sense even more – at *real* government income, that is to figure out what government could actually do with its revenue. To find that out information about the sheer amounts of money involved and general costs of living need not be very helpful. In the context of our interest we would need to know more about 'governmental purchasing power', which depends on what government actually purchased.

There is no need and no room to go into detail here, but a couple of general comments can and need to be made. By far the biggest expenditure by government, both in Britain and in China, was on the military. So we would need to know what that actually means in terms of purchases. Probably the first 'expenditure' that comes to mind would be weapons. In that respect, it would be helpful if someone were to do for China what Philip Hoffman did for England and France in the early modern era. He looked at the prices in those countries of artillery, handguns and gunpowder over the period between the fourteenth and the eighteenth century and claims that they declined, relatively speaking.[183] That means that a substantial, and in the context of 'the Rise of the West' quite relevant, part of expenditure of Western governments became relatively cheaper. Though clearly not negligible, we should, however, not overestimate the importance of this fact in strictly economical terms. Pay and provisions for soldiers and mariners comprised by far the largest item, indeed the large majority of the states' military expenditure. The bulk of the money needed to maintain armies as well as navies was spent on pay for the soldiers and on uniforms and food, *not* on weaponry and fortifications and the like. Data from countries as diverse as France, Venice, Spain and Russia for the period from the Renaissance to the late seventeenth century show that the costs of artillery and of fortifications were probably not more than some 4 to 8 per cent of total military expenditure each. For Great Britain for the years 1804, 1809 and 1810 together, the costs of military and navy have been calculated as follows: pay, 50 per cent; food, 16 per cent; shipbuilding and repairs, 15 per cent; charter of sea transport, 5 per cent; clothing, 4 per cent; arms and ammunition, 4 per cent; building and construction, 3 per cent; and

---

[183]Hoffman, 'Prices, the Military Revolution, and Western Europe's comparative advantage'.

horses, barrack stores and prisoners of war, one per cent each.[184] Armies were huge and expensive. In the seventeenth century, the Dutch army cost twice as much as the Dutch navy. Even in Britain, the leading naval power of the eighteenth century and an island, total expenditures on army and navy ran neck and neck.[185] For example, in 1811 the Royal Navy cost more than £19.5 million, the Army £23.8 million and the Ordinance over £4.5 million.[186] That of course does not mean that as such, for example, warships were cheap. The costs of hardware of fleets were substantial, as was their maintenance. Fifteen per cent of total military expenditure during the Napoleonic Wars went to shipbuilding and repairs alone.[187] In Western Europe infantry as a rule of the thumb was regarded as half as expensive as cavalry. Infantry accounted for most of the army's growth in absolute terms in the early modern period. It grew in absolute number as well as relative share. Cavalry, however, increased too.

In the end it turns out that information about the kind of ordinary expenditures that figure so prominently in calculations of 'cost of living' of ordinary consumers are also quite informative when it comes to figuring out *the bulk* of the costs of sustaining armies and navies. The expression 'cost of living' also applies to horses. Those were very important in the armies of both European countries and China. According to Von Creveld, in a normal army in Western Europe at the end of the seventeenth century there were 60,000 people to 40,000 horses.[188] Horses were not just important for cavalry, where their importance relatively speaking *diminished*, but also for transport, including transport of artillery, where their importance *increased*.[189] At Austerlitz the French cavalry alone numbered 20,000 in an army of 70,000. In 1812, at Borodino, 30,000 of Napoleon's soldiers were mounted men.[190] His Russian campaign cost the lives of 180,000 horses on the French side alone.[191] In the Prussia of Frederick the Great, to give just one other example, with the peace in 1763 that ended the Seven Years War, 37,000 horses were released from the army. According to Frederick himself, some campaigns during that war cost the country 20,000 horses.[192] Feeding horses probably was as important to early modern warfare as supplying oil in the age of tanks and large amounts of money were involved. The total number of horses in Western Europe, whether they were held for agricultural labour, for their manure, for transport, for fun or for war, or for a combination of these things, was enormous. According to Wrigley, there were 1.2 million horses in England and Wales alone in 1695 and 1.49 million in Great Britain in 1855. Here again Britain is something

---

[184] O'Brien, 'Impact of the Revolutionary and Napoleonic Wars'.

[185] See for this information Gat, *War in Human Civilization*, 469–71. Tallett, *War and Society*, 168–87, also points at the overwhelming importance of pay and provisions for soldiers and marines when it comes to maintaining an army in early modern Europe. Both texts refer to the situation quite early on in our period and sometimes even before that. For the situation later on see the literature about the contractor state under Introduction note 193 and Chapter 1 note 299.

[186] Hall, *British Strategy*, 16.

[187] O'Brien, 'Impact of the Revolutionary and Napoleonic Wars', 366–8.

[188] Van Creveld, *Supplying War*, 24.

[189] Parker, *Military Revolution*, under 'horses' and 'cavalry'.

[190] Johnson, *Napoleon's Cavalry*, 16.

[191] Black, *European Warfare*, 137. Bell, *First Total War*, 261, gives the even higher number of 200,000.

[192] See Hubatsch, *Frederick the Great*, 133, and Parker, *Military Revolution*, 148.

exceptional: no country in Europe had so many horses per capita. For France he claims there were 2.2 million horses in 1812 and 2.5 million in 1830.[193] These numbers already suffice to show that in Western agriculture large numbers of horses could be fed from *relatively* small tracts of land. The growing of all kinds of food crops for feeding animals in that respect paid. In the 1830s in Britain, five acres of land sufficed to maintain a horse over a year.[194] There are therefore very good reasons to think that buying and maintaining a horse was cheaper in Britain than it was in China in the early modern period. Denis Signor estimates that 120 acres of grazing land were required to support one horse for one year in Central Asia, where no food crops were grown.[195] Here the Europeans may very well have had an advantage over the Chinese.

In the Chinese case too, governmental purchasing power and private purchasing power in all probability will not have been very different, as there too, even more than in Europe, the bulk of military expenditure was absorbed by wages, provision of food for soldiers and animals, and clothing. It, however, is not easy to make a detailed and precise comparison of both regions, as the mode of payment and composition of their armed forces were quite different in various respects. A substantial part of China's soldiers, for example, basically lived off the land, something that no longer occurred in *Western* as in contrast to Eastern and Central Europe.[196] On the other hand, large amounts of money that went to 'the army' actually went to dependents of military men that were not military men at all.[197] In China's army, *as compared* to that of Britain and most other European countries, artillery and firearms definitely were less important. When it comes to cavalry, it is not easy to tell. The number of warhorses in China during the eighteenth century is estimated to have been between 1 million and 3 million. Per year some 25,000 to 50,000 new horses were required for the army. During the Qing regime, almost all these horses came from Central Asia. China's rulers kept a very close watch on all matters related to their supply. It was secured by the conquest of large parts of Central Asia in the eighteenth century, in particular during the reign of the Qianlong emperor.[198] It may well be that for China's army, cavalry was more important than it was in Western Europe. Considering the enormous 'militarization' of Western Europe, I doubt whether *in total* China had more military horses than Western Europe. What cannot be doubted is that in China, too, horses actually ate a quite substantial amount of the resources of the army.[199]

When it comes to material costs: the equipment used by banner men changed very little over time and when they did not receive it directly they received money to pay for it. In

---

[193]Wrigley, *Continuity, Chance & Change*, 37 and 40.

[194]Wrigley, *Continuity, Chance & Change*, 72.

[195]Sinor, 'Horse and pasture', 181–2. Sinor refers to the situation in the beginning of the second millennium. But there is no reason to believe things would have been different at the end of the early modern period when horses there still lived from natural pasturage.

[196]See my comments on monetization on pages 204–5 and 240–66.

[197]See Elliott, *Manchu Way*, 310, where it is claimed that the majority of banner expenses went to the support not of officers and soldiers but of their dependents and horses.

[198]For the information regarding war horses in Qing China see Gommans, 'Warhorse and post-nomadic empire'.

[199]Elliott, *Manchu Way*, 310–11.

the middle of the eighteenth century, an ordinary soldier received some 30 taels to pay for his equipment, an officer 600.[200] Their salaries in terms of money may not have been really high at the time but not bad as such. A capital banner man received 4 taels per month – roughly 5 grams of silver per day. A province banner man received 1 tael per month less, or somewhat over 3.5 grams of silver per day. On top of that, however, banner men received quite substantial food allowances. A banner man living in the capital received 22 shi of grain per year, a provincial banner man about 30. Average yearly consumption at the time is estimated at 3.6 shi for an adult and 1.8 shi for a child.[201] That means that these allowances could amply feed twelve or even sixteen people during an entire year. With the increasing number of mouths that most banner men had to feed, however, and with rising costs, things began to look much less rosy for them, especially as salaries did not increase or even decrease.[202] Their income, though declining in real terms however, as such continued to be much higher than that of ordinary Green Standard soldiers, whose equipment increasingly became less up to date, from a Western perspective.

When it comes to warfare on sea, the contrast could not be bigger: for Britain, and the Netherlands, the navy simply was the cornerstone of their military strength. For various reasons maintaining sea power was expensive, but it was also quite effective in terms of cost efficiency. China at the time had no navy to speak of. Talking about government expenditure in the West means talking about the 'contractor state'. In China government contracting certainly was not an unknown phenomenon but it never became as big and as complex as in Europe.[203] There finally are two other differences between Great Britain and China in the very long eighteenth century which are striking. One is that the Qing court normally was not an ordinary customer buying what it wanted on the market. It could order what it wanted from government workplaces that worked on its behalf. The other is that state production, especially of silk, was advantaged by the power of officials to demand quotas of raw materials or finished goods at below market prices.[204]

Increasing versus decreasing government revenues

Taxes in the West, especially in Britain, not only were much higher than in China. They also – we are talking here about an almost general tendency – showed a steady and steep increase. This increase was so steady and 'normal' that many Western scholars regard it as a 'law' or 'rule' that central governments are predatory – that is, always on the lookout for ways to increase their income.[205] The British example for the eighteenth century again

---

[200]Elliott, *Manchu Way*, 177–8.

[201]Will and Wong, *Nourish the People*, 21, and Appendix Table A1. A shi of, in this case, unhusked rice is between 65 and 70 kg.

[202]See page 204.

[203]See for an example Dai, 'Yingyung Shengxi'.

[204]Li, *China's Silk Trade*, 42.

[205]For this rule that, as we will see, does not apply to Qing China see under Introduction note 55.

may have been extreme, but figures with regard to the rest of Western Europe show that it was not so eccentric as to be fundamentally different.[206] Even if we correct for inflation *and*, as we already have done, for population increase, taxes in Britain between the beginning of the eighteenth and the beginning of the nineteenth century increased very substantially, being more than two times as high at the end of the Napoleonic Wars as they were a century earlier.[207] If we look at the situation from the 1680s onwards, the increase is even bigger. Tax income of Britain's central government between 1680 and 1815 increased from £2 million to over £60 million. Corrected for inflation it became some nine times as high: per capita, not including Scotland, in real terms it became more than four times as high during this period.[208] We see this tendency in most European countries. In France, for example, over the eighteenth century as a whole real tax pressure per capita increased.[209] The Dutch Republic, in this respect, was fairly exceptional: there the tax burden at the end of that century was more or less similar to that at the beginning.[210] In this respect the nineteenth century witnessed interesting changes after the big wars at its beginning. In Britain there emerged a strong conviction that taxation had become too high and we see a clear tendency to 'rationalise' and 'bureaucratise' the tax system in an effort to push back the role of the state. Per capita taxes (and expenditures) sharply decreased and their character changed.[211] In absolute terms, however, and in particular as compared to China, taxation and government expenditure continued to be very high.

In China, *in comparison*, increases in taxation between the 1680s and the 1830s were really minor, in particular when we look at their level per capita. If we only look at *regular* taxes of central government, their incidence per capita actually must have declined. When Evelyn Rawski claims that both in Western Europe and in China revenues increased, she is not, as such, making a false claim. But the differences in this respect between the increases during the very long eighteenth century in China and in Britain, in total and in particular per capita, are so huge that I would not call it very illuminating either.[212] In China during the reign of the Kangxi emperor, tax income of the government, the bulk of total government income at the time, was some 35 million taels.[213] All government income combined, in a very 'optimist' estimate, will *never* have been higher than 300 million taels per annum just before the First Opium War. We have seen that population estimates differ widely: but population in the very long eighteenth century must have increased at the very least from 130 million to 140 million to some 340 million in 1800 and some 410 million in 1840. Our information when it comes to price levels is less clear than it is for Britain. But all the information I did find shows a rate of inflation, at least for subsistence goods, that

---

[206]See Bonney, *Economic Systems and State Finance*; idem, *Rise of the Fiscal State*; Ferguson, *Cash Nexus*, and Mann, *Sources of Social Power, II*, ch. 11.

[207]Mathias and O'Brien, 'Taxation in Britain and France', 605.

[208]I have calculated these figures on the basis of information in O'Brien, 'Political economy', 3.

[209]See, for example, Goldstone, *Revolution and Rebellion*, 204–5, and Mathias and O'Brien, 'Taxation in Britain and France', 618.

[210]De Vries and Van der Woude, *First Modern Economy*, 97, table 4.3.

[211]See pages 72, 164 and 185.

[212]Rawski, 'Qing formation', 207–18.

[213]Hsü, *Rise of Modern China*, 59.

is comparable to that of Britain – that is, an increase in the order of 100 to 200 per cent when expressed in terms of silver over the period from the 1680s to the 1820s when, with the drain of silver, prices expressed in that precious metal started to decline.[214] This means that, *even when* we assume a very high absolute increase of government income, a very low population increase and a low inflation rate, total government income (i.e. not just taxes), in real terms and per capita, still *hardly* increased, *if at all*. Many scholars are convinced it *decreased* substantially.[215] Personally, I endorse that view. Again, it probably cannot be repeated enough: I am referring to official regular taxes received by central government. The amounts of money paid by people locally to officials and semi-officials can and does very well tell quite a different story.

It was not by accident that China's tax income relatively speaking was so stable. China's rulers were keen to keep taxes as low as possible and preferred cutting expenses over increasing income. Let me again quote Chen Hongmou who claimed that 'the good official is constantly attentive to keep taxes to a minimum' and thought that 'In managing wealth on behalf of the state, restraint and care are vital'. He therefore as a rule preferred to determine expenditure on the basis of income and regarded that as the 'naturally correct doctrine'. The Qianlong emperor himself shared that view: 'If the quantity of grain held by the government is too large, then that held by the people must be too small.'[216] Apparently this was a popular way of looking at national wealth: 'the realm has only so much wealth. If it is not accumulated with the sovereign, it will be dispersed among the people.'[217] It was widely regarded as the duty of the state to take care of 'the state's resources and the people's livelihood'.[218] To put it quite succinctly, in the words of Li Yesi, a seventeenth-century writer: 'The hallmark of good ruling is to keep the number of officials low; the hallmark of good government is to keep the burden of taxation light.'[219] The principle of 'preserving the wealth among the people' was considered very important.[220]

In line with this 'philosophy', official tax quotas and duties *in principle* were not high. In *practice*, payments to central government often were even lower than those quotas. We know of various occasions when government decided not to collect certain taxes at all or to remit tax arrears. The Kangxi emperor, to give one example, is supposed to have remitted the dazzling sum of 100 million taels, more than double the official annual tax income, during the first forty-nine years of his reign and decreed an empire-wide general amnesty that excused each province in turn from remitting its annual land

---

[214]See Graph 7.
[215]Scholars who explicitly make this claim are Deng, *China's Political Economy*, 16–18; Liu, *Wrestling for Power*, 88–108; Ma, 'Rock, scissors, paper', and Sng, 'Size and dynastic decline'.
[216]See for these quotations Rowe, *Saving the World*, 191, 332 and 260, and Dunstan, *Conflicting Counsels*, 189. For other quotations of Qianlong see Elliott, *Emperor Qianlong*, 143–53.
[217]See for this quotation Dunstan, *State or Merchant*, 445.
[218]Leonard, *Controlling from Afar*, ch. 2.
[219]I found this quotation in Dunstan, *Conflicting Counsels*, 151.
[220]See Dai, *Sichuan Frontier and Tibet*, 'Epilogue'.

tax once in a three-year cycle.[221] Famous and very consequential in this respect is his promise at the end of his reign in 1713 that the *ti* and *ting* taxes would be permanently based on the quotas of 1712. This so-called 'principle of eternally not increasing levies', in practice implied that after some time the poll tax became factually meaningless and began to merge into the land taxes.[222] There are quite a number of examples of 'tax holidays' and 'tax exemptions', often, but not necessarily, meant as a kind of disaster relief.[223] There also are examples of government grants. The Kangxi and Yongzheng emperors even had the habit of providing loans to merchants.[224] This practice stopped during the rule of the Qianlong emperor. The Kangxi and Qianlong emperors were proud to be frugal. Lillian Li refers to a, in her words, 'generous' estimate that the total amount of tax remission granted in the period from the early Qing through the Daoguang period, including both large and small cases, may have amounted to 150 to 200 million taels.[225] Please note, though, that we are talking about a period of more than 150 years.

On top of that, China's tax system, because of the predominance in it of land tax, was quite inflexible by nature. During the eighteenth century there was no necessity to fundamentally change it, so this wasn't a problem. The amount of land taxes collected was quite stable and there were no major changes in the system of assessment and collection. That does not mean that nothing changed. Government income did clearly increase via adaptations and small changes in the system of revenue collection. I think especially of the tapping of other sources of income, like the contributions I referred to earlier on, and of acquiring money via the Imperial Household. But China's tax system *as such* underwent no structural change at all until the 1850s, which of course is quite telling. Considering that its tax income in real terms was stable at best and very probably even decreased substantially, a Western observer can only be surprised to see that, nevertheless, expenditures normally were *lower* than income. Only in the last decades of the period discussed here do we see budget deficits. From a European perspective, they were very small. The treasury of central government – that is, the treasuries of the Board of Revenue – was never emptied. Till the very end of the reign of the Daoguang emperor in 1850, the Board of Revenue still had some reserves. Money from those reserves was often used for emergency relief or for helping to fund expensive military campaigns. Government never borrowed any money. The commitment to be frugal indeed was very strong. To systematically spend more than one collected in revenue, as became normal in the West, was simply out of the question. We will come back to that fundamental difference between Qing China and Western Europe later on in our analysis of public debt.

---

[221]Thornton, *Disciplining the State*, 31.

[222]Hsü, *Rise of Modern China*, 60.

[223]For tax exemptions *and* disaster relief see Deng, *China's Political Economy*, 20–4, and Myers and Wang, 'Economic developments', 603. For more anecdotal information see Dunstan, *State or Merchant* under 'land tax, universal remissions of', and Will, *Bureaucracy and Famine*, 292.

[224]See Chang, 'Economic role', 272, and Rawski, 'Qing formation', 217–18.

[225]Li, *Fighting Famine*, 448.

THE EFFICIENCY OF REVENUE COLLECTION

Centralization versus decentralization

Central government's (tax) revenue – that is what we have discussed until now – was never identical to the total amount of *official*[226] payments by the population to the centre, let alone to the sum of *all* payments by population to officials or their helpers. To begin with there is 'retainment': the amount of money or resources which it is officially agreed will *not* go to the capital and central government and will be spent where it is collected at local discretion. Its size in the end is a political decision and as such need not tell us something about the efficiency of a tax system. In principle, we are referring to a very important difference here. Even if much of what had been collected locally or regionally never went to the centre, that need not indicate a lack of efficiency of central rule. I here define 'efficiency' (from the perspective of central government) as the difference between gross and net income of central government in as far as it is caused by collection cost in the broadest sense of the term, that is the *official* costs of collecting, plus 'losses' or extra 'costs' in the process of collection caused by embezzlement, fraud, corruption and the like. There may have existed very good economic reasons for retaining money or resources. It may, for example, save the money and effort involved in collecting money, bringing it to the centre and from there again spreading it over the country. The point is that the money and resources that didn't leave the region where they were collected, in Europe at least, often were *not* actually at the disposal of central government. In Europe in many regions, according to law or custom, central government simply had no say in many affairs and could only rule indirectly. In China that *de facto* also was quite often the case, although 'on paper', considering its uniform bureaucratic structure, China Proper looked more like a centralized state with direct rule.

In Britain, retaining of taxes locally was almost negligible until the 1820s. Almost all taxes went to London – the delegation of day-to-day power to the local level did not include matters of the purse. Britain in this respect was undoubtedly the most centralized country of Europe. According to Peter Matthias, in the mid-eighteenth century local taxes totalled about 10 per cent of central government levies, rising to 14 to 15 per cent on trend between the 1770s and the 1830s.[227] Julian Hoppit gives a figure in the same order of magnitude for 1801: 'At a guess, British local government expenditure was £6 million or around eleven per cent of all public expenditure.'[228] However, he adds, local government often was un-monetized, as in much of the judicial system and minor road maintenance. We do see an increase here of local collection and spending after the Napoleonic Wars: in 1840 local expenditure amounted to 21.9 per cent of total government expenditure.

---

[226]I here refer only to those payments that were in accordance to the rules, not to the 'illegal', extra payments that were squeezed out of the population. I will discuss those later on in this text. See pages 151–8.
[227]Mathias, 'Taxation and industrialization', 117.
[228]Hoppit, 'Checking the Leviathan', 280.

In 1890, it had increased to 38.4 per cent and in 1910 to no less than 49.7 per cent.[229] In this respect, too, substantial differences existed between various Western countries. But what is common to them is that until far into the nineteenth century the bulk of taxes went to central government.[230]

When we have a brief look at some other countries in Western Europe, we again see similarities *and* differences. In literature on the French tax system the distinction between retaining taxes locally, subtracting costs and actual (in)efficiency in collecting them for central government, often is not made sufficiently clear: probably because in practice the distinction was far from neat. Let us begin with simply noting that during the eighteenth century a large part of collected revenues never reached the treasury. According to Weiss and Hobson, this would have been some 50 per cent.[231] Bosher claims that in 1788 the royal treasury received and paid scarcely more than half of the funds in the total budget of the state.[232] Richard Bonney claims that in that same year of 472 million livres tournois collected as 'ordinary' taxes, only 211 million were left after charges and costs had been deducted.[233] Philip Hoffmann looks even less 'optimist' and writes that in some instances the feeble receipts in the treasury documents formed only one-fourth of what was actually collected.[234] But he adds that, here too, appearances can be misleading; the central treasury did not record everything the government collected. The treasury accounts omitted from tax receipts large sums that were spent locally on assessment and collection costs, plus salaries and military expenses and certain disbursements and assignations. Much income that *was* under direct government control apparently was not included in treasury accounts. Much of the monarchy's credit was advanced by tax farmers and office holders who could deduct from the taxes they collected what was owed to them, as tax farmers, holders of debt or for other reasons. When it comes to central government expenses the official figures could be equally misleading.[235] As indicated earlier on, one must not only know who collects how much but also who actually decides on what the money will be spent.

Let us now turn to the fiscal organization of China. To keep things manageable, I will only comment on the collection of land taxes, by far the biggest part of all collected taxes.[236] I base my comments on information from Wang's book on land taxation in imperial China.[237] China's fiscal system in many respects was quite decentralized. The Board of Revenue in Peking only had a quite circumscribed power over public finance. It did not have the exclusive authority over the nation's fiscal policies and it did not collect

[229]Daunton, 'Trusting Leviathan', 342.

[230]See for figures on local expenditure in Britain, France, Austria, Prussia/Germany and the United States in the period 1780–1910 Tables 11.1, 11.2 and 11.3 in Mann, *Sources of Social Power, II*.

[231]Weiss and Hobson, *States and Economic Development*, 44. They refer to publications by Brewer, Levi and Mousnier to underpin their claim.

[232]Bosher, 'French administration', 586–7.

[233]Bonney, 'Introduction', 11. I refer to his introduction to his *Rise of the Fiscal State*.

[234]Hoffman, 'Early modern France', 236.

[235]Hoffman, 'Early modern France', 236–7.

[236]For general comments see He, *Paths toward the Modern Fiscal State*, chs 6 and 7.

[237]Wang, *Land Taxation*, 12–19.

taxes itself. Its power of controlling the nation's resources depended upon its authority of disposal over the taxes collected in the provinces, that is, save the portion reserved for the necessary provincial administrative expenditure. The device to achieve this control consisted of a series of regular communications between the Board and the provincial authorities. Each year the provincial authorities had to submit to the Board three kinds of financial report: an estimate of next year's expenditure in the province; two half-year reports on the state of the provincial treasure, and an annual report of revenue and expenditure. Basically what the Board did was set rates and approve and indicate expenditures. Taxes collected by or for local government were divided into two parts. One part, the so-called withheld or retained taxes, was retained locally for stipulated local expenses. The other part was to be delivered to the provincial authorities. Central government could keep a close watch there via its commissioner, who only ranked second to the governor in the provincial hierarchy and who was quite independent of the latter's control. At the provincial level, again, part was withheld for approved provincial expenses; the rest was left at the disposal of the central government. That could store it in treasures of provinces for further assignment from the centre, send it to the capital or, as happened often, to needy provinces. The actual transfer of government revenue and expenditures was conducted by transportation of silver bullion. That was extremely time-consuming. It therefore was only logical that central government did not aggregate all its annual income to Peking, but kept a large proportion at its disposal in treasuries at provincial level or even in prefectural governments in strategic locations. It may not have been in Peking but it was in Peking's hands. Almost as a rule the amount of taxes that was officially withheld for local expenditure was too low for actual expenses in general and much of it was earmarked for specific purposes. Funds provided for administrative expenses fell far short of actual needs at all levels of government.

Wang provides no figures as to how much of revenue was retained and how much ended up in Peking. I came across different estimates. Debin Ma claims that under the Qing usually only a third of fiscal revenue arrived at the coffers of the Board of Revenue in Peking. Even that seems a fairly high estimate. According to Zhihong Shi the central government up until the beginning of the nineteenth century collected some 25 to 33 per cent of total government revenue. Thereafter that percentage decreased to some 22 per cent over the period 1800–50 and even less afterwards.[238] In 1765, out of the total expenditure about one-fourth was spent by central government in Peking and the rest by local governments.[239] In the period 1862–74 (which of course strictly speaking is outside our period), 19 million taels tax revenue were remitted annually from the provinces to Peking; during the period 1875–93 that had increased to 63 million taels. That would in both cases be roughly one-fourth of total tax revenue.[240] According to Bastid, during the period 1887–1903, the share of revenue under direct control of the

---

[238]Ma, 'Rock, scissors, paper', 23. I took the figures by Shi from Ma, De Jong and Chu, 'Living standards in China', 17.
[239]Hsü, *Rise of Modern China*, 63.
[240]He, *Paths towards the Modern Fiscal State*, 157.

Board of Revenue in Peking varied between 18 and 27 per cent.[241] Again Macartney in his journal has somewhat different figures. According to him only one-sixth of tax money ever reached Peking. In his description all civil and military expenses and incidental and extraordinary charges are first paid on the spot out of the treasuries of the provinces where such expenses were incurred, after which the remainder is remitted to the Imperial Treasury at Peking.[242] According to Ma the best way to get insight into the actual working of China's fiscal system would be to determine the annual in- and outflows of revenue of the coffers of the Imperial Board of Revenue in Peking. For the period 1723–1867, he estimates them at, on average, some 11 million taels.[243]

It is not easy to give an exact figure for the amount of local availability of taxes in China. The figures I found suggest that some 20 per cent of the taxes collected in the provinces where *not* at the direct disposal of central government.[244] We are referring here only to percentages of the head and land taxes. We have to be careful in giving these percentages, as even of the locally retained and allocated tax money the bulk was *not* used for actual local expenses but to support government military activities and the imperial post. Madeleine Zelin in her book on tax reform in the eighteenth century presents figures that suggest that more than 80 per cent of locally retained money in that way was not available to local administrators. It will not come as a surprise that she concludes that local officers could not operate within the limits of this funding. Which means that they often had to try and get their resources on an *ad hoc* basis.[245] If we keep in mind this very important caveat, we might conclude that actually not more money was retained locally in China than in Britain.[246]

Tax (in)efficiency and what caused it: The case of Great Britain

Let us now discuss 'efficiency' in more detail. The difference between gross and net income shows us how much it cost central government to collect the revenue that in the end it actually had at its disposal. This difference will certainly not be unrelated to the following topics that I will discuss both for the British and the Chinese case, to wit the extent to which revenue collection was homogenized (i.e. having incidence that in principle is identical equal for all and everywhere); standardized (i.e. using the same procedures, methods and measurements); monetized, transparent and negotiated and, finally, subject to some sort of checks and balances. More often than not it is hard to exactly pinpoint

---

[241] Bastid, 'Structure of financial institutions', 75.

[242] Cranmer-Byng, *Embassy to China*, 247–8.

[243] Ma, 'Rock, scissors, paper', 23.

[244] See for information on the retaining of tax money in the provinces, Myers and Wang, 'Economic developments', 604–5. This text heavily draws upon Zelin, *Magistrate's Tael*, ch. 2. The figure of some 20 per cent is from Zelin's book, pages 28–9, and refers to the situation in 1685. I have no indication that during the period we are dealing with the rules with regard to tax retaining were changed.

[245] Zelin, *Magistrate's tael*, ch. 2.

[246] For further information see Chen, *System of Taxation*, 34–6.

the difference between actual retainment and all sorts of collection 'costs' or 'losses'. So in practice the distinction is often not made or consistently applied – for example, when one is dealing with tax farming. In my text too, I will not always be able to make the distinctions I would like, simply because my material does not enable me to do so.

In all probability the efficiency of revenue collection will increase with its homogeneity and standardization. Those are not only relevant in terms of 'technical' efficiency of revenue collection: they can also be relevant in a more indirect way by affecting its 'legitimacy' – that is, the extent to which it finds public 'support'. When it comes to homogenization and standardization, again, Britain is exceptional. In principle its tax system made no differences whatsoever according to place or social status. In practice, its land tax was collected somewhat *ad hoc*. That could and did result in regional differences. But for all other taxes, the country had *one* national system in which geographical location, status or rank made no difference. Please note that I am referring to Britain (i.e. England and Wales). When it comes to taxation, Scotland and Ireland continued to be quite different polities. I am moreover talking about *principles* of collection, not about *actual* incidence: that of course could depend very much on actual property, income and consumption. Standardization too had progressed quite far in Britain. Standard procedures require clear and uniform measures and methods. Government in Britain was concerned to come to a standardization of weights and measures, in particular from the 1790s onwards. Rather surprisingly, however, it was only in 1824 that common measures were created for the whole country.[247] A certain G. S. Keith in a book from 1817 claimed that throughout provincial England at the time there were 'about *two hundred and thirty*' (italics in original) different weights and measures, and in Scotland a further seventy.[248] Standardization of taxes and tax-collecting procedures increased the efficiency with which they could be collected. On the other hand, tax collectors often pushed for 'standardization' of the things they taxed to further increase that efficiency. In Britain, the Excise in particular was often instrumental in defining the method, materials and architecture of producing the commodities that were to be taxed. Taxing a good began to imply rendering it visible in terms of its ingredients and the way in which it was produced. The taxpayers, who wanted to be fairly and 'transparently' taxed, only pushed this process further. Excise and customs increasingly affected the shaping and regulating of production, the standardizing of weights, measures and packing, and also qualities, and it encouraged, if not monopolies, then certainly larger productive entities.[249] In that sense too taxation clearly was very instrumental in promoting certain methods of production, distribution and bookkeeping.

When it comes to homogenization and standardization, in the rest of Europe things often were quite different. On the Continent, we see big differences in revenue collection between regions and social groups when it comes to the amounts collected and the

---

[247]Hoppit, 'Reforming Britain's weights and measures'. For the nineteenth century see Velkar, *Markets and Measurement*.
[248]I found this reference in Ashworth, *Customs and Excise*, 285, note 11.
[249]See for these effects Ashworth, *Customs and Excise*.

methods of collection. Those could have an 'objective' basis in differences in income or structure of the economy. But often they did not and were the result of political arrangements. Whatever may have been the exact reason, regional differences were often immense. As a rule, 'core-regions' of a state contributed more than those in the periphery. It is estimated that at the end of the Old Regime, just before the outbreak of the French Revolution, the average fiscal burden for France as a whole was twenty-three livres tournois per capita. An inhabitant of the generality of Lyon, however, paid thirty livres, one of Rouen thirty-seven and an inhabitant of Paris over sixty-four.[250] Until its revolution at the end of the eighteenth century France continued to have various, differing tax systems and internal tolls. Even in the fairly small state of Prussia that is often regarded as the paradigm case when it comes to bureaucratization, homogenization was far from complete in the eighteenth century. In the beginning of the 1820s taxes still differed between various regions, and between town and country.[251] The Dutch Republic was even smaller. But there too regional differences existed. In 1790, the province of Holland, to give but one example, paid some 60 per cent of total Dutch taxes with little over one-third of the population.[252]

In Britain social distinctions in tax incidence were negligible, in the sense that no social status groups were privileged *as such*. They tended to be very important in most other parts of (Western) Europe. The conviction that all people are equal to the law, let alone the actual implementation of that principle, was an exception rather than the rule. The amount of taxes one paid was not normally directly connected to wealth and even less to income. In that sense, taxation clearly was not progressive. Rather the opposite. Even taxes that, in principle, are equal to all may, in practice, have a quite different impact on different people. Taxes on consumer goods were very important in Western Europe. That applies most of all to Britain, but they were also substantial in the Dutch Republic and France. As a rule such taxes, in practice, are regressive: they hit the poor harder than the rich, in particular when, as was normally the case, they were levied on fairly ordinary consumer goods.[253] But taxation on the European Continent – with the Dutch Republic as the major exception – was *not meant* to be socially homogenous. Many wealthy people were tax-exempt or in any case had special 'arrangements' implying all kinds of privileges. That is so fundamental a characteristic of the European *Ancien*

---

[250]Bonney, 'France, 1494-1815', 161.

[251]See for a brief description of differences in systems of tax collecting and tax incidence Henderson, *Studies in the Economic Policy*, ch. 3; Spoerer, *Steuerlast, Steuerinzidenz und Steuerwettbewerb*, ch. 2.2.1, and Wilson, 'Prussia as a fiscal-military state'.

[252]De Vries and Van der Woude, *First Modern Economy*, Table 4.3.

[253]O'Brien has published widely on the question of whether taxes in Britain were regressive or not. See his 'Political economy' and 'Triumph and denouement'. He is convinced that the British tax system was 'regressive' (in that it appropriated larger proportions of revenue from tax payers in lower rather than higher income bands) but he does also see 'some trends in legislation that probably moved towards progression'. See his 'Fiscal and financial preconditions', 33. Ashworth, *Customs and Excise*, 336, is quite outspoken in his view that the common people were disproportionally taxed, especially via the excises. Mathias holds a similar view. See his 'Taxation and industrialization', 127. For the Dutch Republic see De Vries and Van der Woude, *First Modern Economy*, 112, Table 4.7, and for France, Gross, 'Progressive taxation'.

Régime and its society of estates that it needs no extensive discussion. What, from the perspective of central government at least, made matters often even worse is that the rich not only contributed so little to the state's coffers but on top of that often pocketed very substantial amounts of money in the process of collecting taxes for government. 'Centralized' Britain, again, in that respect is rather exceptional. In Britain no one was exempt from taxation. That of course does not mean that all paid equally – the landed elites paid very little and the moneyed interest usually could see to it that their burdens were borne by others – but nevertheless there is a clear difference here. Tax farming had already been already abolished before 1688. The customs farm was cancelled in 1671, the excise farm in 1683 and the hearth tax farm in 1684. There was venality of several offices, especially in the army.[254] There were sinecures. But overall we clearly see an increasing professionalism. Seats in Parliament continued to be bought during the entire eighteenth century in 'rotten' or 'pocket' boroughs. But this problem too would be dealt with. In France, to focus on one country to illustrate my claim that Great Britain was exceptional, in contrast, wealthy people and institutions almost without exception paid no or relatively few taxes. Just think of the privileged members of the clergy, aristocrats and many bourgeois. Those, however, not only were often exempted and privileged in many ways, they also often profited directly or indirectly from the fact that other people were not exempted or privileged in this respect. The French Church as an institution was very rich. It may have owned as much as 10 per cent of all agricultural land in the country in the second half of the eighteenth century. It, however, hardly paid any taxes: on the contrary, it *collected* taxes that it kept to itself, the so-called tithes. For the year 1784, Necker estimated the income from these tithes at 110 million to 120 million livres tournois. That is more than central government collected as land tax. Total Church income at the time is estimated to have been 150 million to 300 million livres tournois. The contribution of the Church to total tax revenue of the state around 1750 is estimated to have been some 5 million livres tournois.[255] Some 20 per cent of agricultural land at that time was owned by aristocrats, among whom were many former bourgeois. As a rule aristocrats did not pay much in taxes. At the same time, though, they collected quite substantial feudal levies. Many wealthy bourgeois also profited from exemptions. They, and many aristocrats, moreover, were beneficiaries of the system of farming taxes and selling offices, which often were sinecures. When we add to all this that France's governments did at times default and debase the currency, that formal checks and balances on its policies were rare and that the existing financial and monetary systems were less developed, it is no wonder that those people in France who actually did pay taxes, including many internal customs that were non-existent in Britain, were dissatisfied and could feel 'much more oppressed by taxes than the people of Great Britain' to again quote Adam Smith, even if *on average* taxes were lower than in Britain.[256]

---

[254]See e.g. Swart, *Sale of Offices*, and James, *Warrior Race*, 32–337.
[255]Ferrarese, 'Problema della decima', 934, and Goubert, *Ancien Régime, II*, ch. 8.
[256]Smith, *Inquiry into the Nature and Causes of the Wealth of Nations*, 905.

Standardization of procedures but also of measures and weights was less developed in Western and Central Europe, let alone the rest of Europe, than in Britain. Ronald Zupko, for example, claims that *Ancien Régime* France knew no fewer than 250,000 different measures.[257] Prussia, to give another striking example, got one currency only in 1821. Overall, there are good reasons to expect that revenue collecting on the Continent was more decentralized, less homogenous and more 'improvised' than in Britain. So, if only for these reasons, one might expect less efficiency there with a bigger gap between what people paid and what government received.

In Britain taxes were paid in money. The 'success' of excises and customs suggests a very monetized economy. Taxes in kind were non-existent, as were forms of corvee or any other type of service. In the rest of Western Europe the picture is no different: monetization had become the rule. In market economies, like those that prevailed in most regions of Western Europe, it was clearly preferable for governments to collect payments in money rather than in kind or services.[258] The amounts involved were so high that basically only silver or gold could be used as payment. That is quite important for Britain's economy as a whole: central government there was the largest spender, employer and borrower. In less capital-intensive states, the situation could be quite different.[259] The Prussian government introduced the so-called 'canton system' in which military personnel might work when they were not on duty. Central government then need not take care of their livelihood. We are talking here about a system that involved about 7 per cent of the entire population of Prussia, so it could make a very substantial difference.[260] In the Habsburg Empire a similar approach was tried.

The efficiency of revenue collecting by government and the extent to which it is regarded as just – which in turn also has its impact on efficiency – is not unrelated to its transparency, the extent to which it is the result of actual bargaining between all involved, and the extent to which the tax payers can actually monitor and influence the entire process. When it comes to transparency, voice, and checks and balances at the central level, the situation in Britain looks better. Improvements here have always been associated with the Glorious Revolution. After that revolution, responsibility for public finances indeed ultimately devolved upon Parliament. Only Parliament could levy taxes and, from 1688 onwards, fiscal acts had to be discussed there annually. Public finance was an ever-present concern of its members. One has to be careful, however, in claiming that Parliament actually *controlled* government income and in particular government expenditure. To suggest, as is often the case, that after the Glorious Revolution Parliament in these matters 'ruled' would really be anachronistic.[261] The costs of the royal household and civil government, for example, for many years, till the 1780s, were a wholly private matter of the Crown, whereas national debt was regarded in terms of a contract between

[257]Zupko, *Revolution in Measurement*, 113.

[258]Western Europe was already covered by such a dense net of interconnected 'monetized' markets that every inhabitant of the region could participate in a market economy. See Bateman, *Markets and Growth*.

[259]For information in this respect on Prussia and the Habsburg Empire see Storrs, *Fiscal-Military State*.

[260]A substantial part of Prussia's military consisted of people coming from outside Prussia.

[261]See He, *Paths toward the Modern Fiscal State*, ch. 3.

the state and individuals. Expenditure, unlike revenue, was *not* subject to parliamentary supervision, even after the constitutional revolution. As late as 1780, Edmund Burke still argued that the First Lord of the Treasury could not 'make even a tolerable guess, of the expenses of the government for any one year', and if he could not, Parliament certainly could not.[262] In practice, there was an almost complete ministerial control of public finance initiatives and a clear primacy of the treasury. It was possible for Members of Parliament to scrutinize and collect information and debate it.[263] Considering that standardized and unitary bookkeeping practices in government departments were often lacking, that, however, was far from easy and, as far as the examples presented by Conway are indicative, Members of Parliament did not exactly make fanatical use of their rights.[264] According to present-day standards, government in eighteenth-century Great Britain can hardly be called accountable.[265] It was only in 1811 that the first printed, consolidated, easily understood table of annual public expenditure was published.[266] But overall, tax collecting was (becoming more) transparent and subject to certain checks and balances, which in turn would have helped in making it efficient and somewhat less 'unjust'. From the perspective of those who paid, the system of course was far from perfect, but in the end apparently they could bear with it. Many things would have played a role here: the fact that the country had a national, relatively speaking, good system of poor relief; the fact that it had a currency with a fixed unchanging value in terms of silver that was not, as occurred in many countries, occasionally or even frequently debased; the fact that its government did not default and took care that there was an ample and varied money supply; and finally the fact that, over time, there was a successful reduction of corruption.

As might be expected considering all the previous comments, efficiency in revenue collecting in Britain after the Glorious Revolution of 1688 was quite high – considering the norms of the time, of course, and irrespective of the big differences that existed between various institutions for tax collecting, like the quite efficient Excise and the quite inefficient Customs, and irrespective of the fact that the collecting of land taxes was basically delegated to the landowners and more or less fixed. Let me just synthesize Britain's strengths. Tax standards applied universally (i.e. for the entire country). Territorial or social distinctions were no longer made. In principle everyone was equal in the eyes of the tax collector. Central government was the only institution that in the end decided over taxes and tax revenue was almost entirely at its disposal. The country, moreover, was relatively small. It had a highly monetized, commercial economy with no internal customs and its laws and customs were quite uniform. Methods of tax collecting were quite standardized. All these factors must have had a positive impact on the efficiency of tax collecting and on the economy in general.[267] Adam Smith in any case thought so:

---

[262] I found this quotation in Harris, 'Government and the economy', 226.
[263] Hoppit, 'Checking the Leviathan'.
[264] See Conway, 'Checking and controlling', and Harding, 'Parliament and the British fiscal-military state'.
[265] See Soll, *Reckoning*, ch. 7.
[266] Knight, *Britain against Napoleon*, 389.
[267] Kiser and Kane, 'Revolution and state structure'.

This freedom of interior commerce, the effect of uniformity of the system of taxation, is perhaps one of the principal causes of the prosperity of Great Britain; every great country being necessarily the best and most extensive market for the greater part of the production of its own industry.[268]

Moreover, on a more concrete, practical level, many people were involved in tax collecting. In the 1780s, there were over 8,000 full-time employees working in England's fiscal bureaucracy.[269] That is roughly one such employee per 10,000 people then living in England and Wales. To simply refer to the number of people involved in collecting and managing taxes of course can easily be misleading. In France, for example, it is estimated that in the 1770s about 250,000 people were somehow involved in collecting revenue for the state. According to Michael Mann 'only' 35,000 of them did that full time and 'professionally', which here means that they depended on it for their livelihood.[270] When, however, we discount those people who did tasks that in Britain were carried out by the army, we end up with only 7,000 'real' fiscal bureaucrats in a country that had some three times as many inhabitants as Britain and was more than three times as big. If we only count the number of professional *fiscal* bureaucrats per head of the population, Britain in our period would be the most bureaucratized country of Western Europe, a fact that is still not recognized by many scholars.[271]

Britain not only had many bureaucrats when it came to collecting taxes: they were also employed efficiently. As indicated, there was hardly any venality of office, there were not many sinecures and tax farming no longer existed after 1681.[272] Many people involved in tax collecting continued to be sinecurists but venality of fiscal offices had become almost non-existent. Differences between various taxes were big. The most important taxes in Britain, at least from the 1710s until the 1830s, the excises, were collected by the very efficient and entirely state-run Excise Department. People working there were professional, full-time and trained officials, working exclusively for government. Britain's Excise in all probability was the closest thing to a real bureaucracy in the early modern world.[273] According to William Ashworth it was 'characterized by a well-trained army of officers subject to strict regulations, within a clearly structured hierarchy ... characterized by an element of merit, a regular wage, and an emphasis on a technical method of

---

[268]Smith, *Inquiry into the Nature and Causes*, 900.

[269]Brewer, *Sinews of Power*, 66, table 3.2. On top of that, there were thousands of local land tax collectors. Exactly how many, nobody knew.

[270]Mann, *Sources of Social Power, II*, 390.

[271]See Weiss and Hobson, *States and Economic Development*, 42–8, where on page 45 Britain is compared to France, the Netherlands and Prussia.

[272]It is not obvious that tax farming would always be less efficient for government than collecting taxes itself. See the comments with regard to the situation in France, Spain and Britain in the eighteenth century in Torres Sánchez, 'Triumph of the fiscal-military', 38–9. For more general comments see pages 136–7.

[273]Mann in his *Sources of Social Power, II*, 391, claims: 'The best organised government office of the eighteenth century was probably the British Excise Department.' For the working of the British tax bureaucracy and the characteristics of its personnel see Brewer, *Sinews of Power*, ch. 3; idem, 'Servants of the public', and idem, 'Eighteenth-century British state'.

revenue collection'.[274] He thinks the relative success of the Excise, in particular, was due to its eventual achievement in taxing goods at the point of production and encouraging, if not monopolies, then certainly larger and fewer producers preferably combining in a distinctive region.[275]

Estimates of the costs of collecting excises in Britain are surprisingly low – in contrast to what Hume claimed[276] – and those costs got significantly lower over time: 15.8 per cent of gross revenue in 1684; 7.7 per cent in 1730; 6.5 per cent in 1760, and in 1787 only 5 per cent.[277] Contemporaries were aware of this. Sir James Steuart in 1767 compared the situation in France with that in England and concluded:

> In France, the collecting of the branches of cumulative taxes, such as the general receipts, comprehending the taille, poll-tax, &c. costs the state no less than 10 per cent, or two sols in the livre, which is superadded to those impositions in order to defray that expenses. Whereas in England the expense of collecting the excise administered by Commissioners, who act for the public, not by farmers who act for themselves, does not cost above 5£. 12s. 6d. in the 100£.[278]

Britain's land taxes, and a couple of small other taxes, were assessed by lay commissioners. This happened on a far less bureaucratic and professional basis. But as land taxes were only a small percentage of total tax income and the amounts of money involved were much smaller, that happened not to be a serious problem. They were *de facto* fixed at the end of the seventeenth century and never really crossed the £2 million line until the 1790s. As such they had no relation to the actual value of land or agricultural produce.[279]

The system of collecting customs was quite complicated, still involved many sinecurists and was much less bureaucratic. In the eyes of various scholars, and contemporaries, it was quite corrupt and notoriously inefficient.[280] Nevertheless these taxes yielded about one-fifth to a quarter of total taxes in the eighteenth century. From the 1820s onwards, their importance increased steeply, amounting to more than one-third of total government revenue till the end of the period discussed here. In absolute terms we are then talking about very substantial amounts of money.[281] Income taxes were introduced in 1799, abolished after the Napoleonic Wars and reintroduced in the 1840s. In their collection there was a clear connection with actual income. In the first income tax of 1799, for example, incomes below £60 were exempted; those between £60 and £200 were

---

[274] Ashworth, *Customs and Excise*, 382.

[275] Ashworth, *Customs and Excise*, 262.

[276] See page 145.

[277] These figures are by Fine, *Production and Excise*. Relatively few people collected the money in operations carried out on a large scale. See Ashworth, *Customs and Excise*, 363.

[278] Steuart, *Inquiry into the Principles of Political Economy*, II, 697. I found this information in Ashworth, *Customs and Excise*, 344.

[279] See Beckett, 'Land tax or excise', and Evans, *Forging of the Modern State*, 413. For the way in which these taxes were collected see O'Brien, 'Taxation for British mercantilism'.

[280] Ashworth, *Customs and Excise*, Part III.

[281] For some figures see page 164.

graduated, and those over £200 paid a flat rate of 10 per cent.[282] When income tax was reintroduced in the 1840s, the principle that there had to be a connection with actual income was not forgotten.[283] Collection costs of these taxes were very low.

Overall, collecting costs must have been quite low. For 1788–1815, it is estimated that there was a difference of some 10 per cent between the gross sum of taxes collected and the net sum paid to the Exchequer.[284] Before that, the difference probably was bigger. Between 1800 and 1850 annual collection cost of government revenue hovered between the low of some £2.4 million and the high of some £4.9 million. Total expenditures of government in this period hovered between a low of £48.8 million and a high of £112.9 million.[285] They never were more than 10 per cent, as a rule clearly less. In all sectors of Britain's economy on average as compared to most other countries in the world – and definitely as compared to China – economic entities that were taxed were relatively large and centralized. That means that the tax collector, other things being equal, had to deal with fewer entities, which made his job easier and cheaper. As indicated earlier on, Britain's system of tax collecting often actively promoted the creation of larger units of production. In this respect too the contrast with China could hardly be bigger.

In the small, highly monetized Dutch Republic, where the government in the end disposed of impressive amounts of money, one would expect an efficient system of tax collecting. Collection costs in the first half of the nineteenth century are reported to have been 17 per cent, whereas in eighteenth-century Holland they were only 5.5 per cent. After the tax revolts of 1748, taxes were no longer farmed and taxation in any case in the province of Holland became more efficient.[286] Although it was one of the most heavily taxed states in Europe, the Dutch Republic had only a tiny fiscal bureaucracy, about 300 to 350 salaried officials at the end of the eighteenth century. If we would include the short-term representative office holders, the total would be less than 2,500, which in absolute terms may not be much but in relative terms, that is as compared to other countries at the time, is not exactly low either.[287]

When it comes to actual collection costs of tax revenue in France, O'Brien and Mathias give what turns out to be a fairly high estimate. They claim that the difference between gross and net taxation, including profits and costs of collection, in eighteenth-century France would have been about 20 per cent. They only refer to taxes collected by *fermiers généraux*.[288] Macdonald claims the actual costs of tax collecting were not higher than 15 per cent.[289] For the rest one can find some more anecdotic information in the

---

[282]For debates about, and functioning of, this income tax see O'Brien, 'Triumph and denouement'.

[283]For the functioning of that tax see Daunton, *Trusting Leviathan*, passim under 'income tax'. For the concrete tax rates see Evans, *Forging of the Modern State*, 413.

[284]See Mathias and O'Brien, 'Taxation in Britain and France', 642, and O'Brien, 'Political economy', 3.

[285]Mitchell, *British Historical Statistics*, 587–8. See here page 185.

[286]Fritschy, 'Taxation in Britain, France and the Netherlands', 71.

[287]Brewer, *Sinews of Power*, 127.

[288]Mathias and O'Brien, 'Taxation in Britain and France', 645–6.

[289]Macdonald, *Free Nation*, 254.

literature. In 1787, a contemporary expert estimated the costs of collection by venal tax officials at less than 8 per cent. That would be surprisingly low.[290] According to economic historian Riley, in 1752 no more than 14 per cent of crown revenues went to pay the cost of collection. In *pays d'état*, collection costs then amounted to 13 per cent of revenues if the expenses involved in negotiating with the estates – a charge only incurred once every four or five years – are deducted.[291] I already referred to the enormous amount of people that in one way or another was involved in tax collecting. Apparently this did not impact very much on efficiency. Actual collection costs were *relatively* low.

Not all European countries were that efficient when it came to acquiring income. Prussia with its strict, cheap and well-organized system of revenue collecting probably was. The fact that state-run domains often contributed as much as one-third of government revenue will surely also have played its part. But here too one must be careful to be not too optimistic when it comes to levels of bureaucratization and efficiency.[292] For Austria the difference between gross and net revenue over the period 1749–1784 has been estimated at between 15 and 34 per cent.[293] In 1782 Count Zinzendorf, president of the Austrian Hofrechenkammer, claimed that 26 per cent of the gross revenue of the Austrian Habsburg monarchy was either absorbed by collection costs or retained by provincial estates.[294] Over time there was a tendency here, as in all Western and Central European states, for collection to become more efficient. But overall, we must conclude that in most of Europe tax collecting from our contemporary perspective was not exactly efficient. Monitoring tax collection and sanctioning abuses clearly was far from easy in *all* pre-industrial societies. All sorts of exemptions and privileges made matters very complicated, as did regional and local differences. Tax farming and the selling of offices were quite common. To a modern observer they may look quite inefficient but considering the circumstances at the time, they may often have been the best viable strategy to collect revenue.

In all probability, selling offices and having taxes farmed will not be as efficient a way of collecting income as having a national, professional bureaucracy of salaried tax officials. But there often simply was no alternative, considering the difficulty of assessing taxes and of moving money from place to place.[295] Selling the right to collect taxes to the highest bidder, to focus on that strategy, moreover, need not by definition be a sign of weak or weakening state power. As long as abuses, which of course can easily arise, can be held in check, selling rights or positions can be a sensible expedient for the government of a pre-modern polity. This is true for *any* pre-modern government. It gets cash in advance and can easily take measures against a tax farmer, or any other 'official' who defaults, and sell his position to somebody else. Even in Britain farming taxes was not evidently inefficient: its abolition was more a matter of central government wanting

---

[290]Morineau, 'Budget de l'état', 318, note 83.
[291]Riley, *Seven Years War*, 60–1.
[292]See, for example, the articles about Prussia in Brewer and Hellmuth, *Rethinking Leviathan*.
[293]Dickson, *Finance and Government under Maria Theresa*, II, 88–9.
[294]Dickson, 'Count von Zinzendorf's "New Accountancy"', 24.
[295]See for the case of indirect taxes Hoffman, 'Early modern France', 232.

to be able to have a close, direct watch on its revenue than of inefficiency per se. The selling of offices can also function as a way of rewarding 'new' people and binding them to central government.[296] Black is even quite positive about it: 'Far from being a flawed aspect of government and information usage, tax farming was an effective way to raise revenue.'[297] Here again, we have to realize that the fully fledged bureaucratic state that is so dear to Weber only emerged very late in history.

What has again become evident are the striking differences between various countries in Western Europe. We see yet another clear indication that one has to be careful not to generalize too easily about 'Western Europe', let alone 'Europe'. Britain was far more centralized and more efficient than France. It actually had the most centralized and efficient system of tax collecting of Western Europe. In the light of what is said in the preceding paragraphs it is not a total surprise that French taxation before the revolution can be, and nowadays often is, pictured in somewhat less negative terms than has long been the case. But in the end, from the perspective of central government, it continued to be dogged by the persisting, fundamental problem that in this decentralized system it could not collect enough money efficiently for its purposes, whereas on the other hand actual taxpayers considered the existing system as highly unjust and taxes as high.

It would of course be extremely naïve and, more importantly, blatantly incorrect to suggest that Britain knew no corruption. On the contrary, what came to be called 'the system of old corruption' with its patronage, peculation and sinecures was notorious. Its fountainheads were the sovereign and his ministries. Venality and corruption were not unknown, far from in, for example, the British Navy.[298] We already referred to the patent inefficiency and corruption of the Customs Service. The British state continued to be reliant on contractors for matters as different as running prisons or naval and military victualling. Their role increased as the growth of the army outstripped the state's administrative machine to provide the supplies. Private sector actors continued to form an essential extension of the capabilities of the state and there of course were malpractices. But in contrast to what was often suggested at the time, the sector was not riddled with corruption. Competition between contractors was encouraged and administration tightened up.[299] 'Old corruption' in all its varieties was tackled, and from the 1780s onwards one can see some successful reforms. During the wars with France pressure to reform and improve became very urgent and many abuses were successfully tackled.[300] What is more important, the forms of corruption we are dealing with here, whatever their baneful effects, did not fundamentally undermine

---

[296]Wallerstein, *Modern World-System, I*, 133–8.
[297]Black, *Power of Knowledge*, 128.
[298]Baugh, *British Naval Administration*, chs 8 and 9.
[299]For such complaints see Conway, 'Checking and controlling'. For a more 'optimist' picture and (successful) efforts to do something against abuses see Bannerman, *Merchants and the Military*; Cookson, *British Armed Nation*; Knight, *Britain against Napoleon*, under 'contractors'; Knight and Wilcox, *Sustaining the Fleet*, and Morriss, *Foundations of British Maritime Ascendancy*.
[300]See e.g. Knight, *Britain against Napoleon*, ch. 11.

the administrative efficiency of the state in terms of having a major negative influence on its *income*. That, as we have seen, was to a very large extent collected via indirect taxes.[301]

Tax (in)efficiency and what caused it: The case of China

When it comes to centralization of Qing China's tax system, scholars now agree it was much less unified than has often been suggested in publications that dwell upon imperial China's supposedly oppressive central government. Basically, tax collection was organized at the provincial level with numerous provincial idiosyncrasies. It differentiated between rich and poor provinces and knew systems of transferring taxes from the richer to the poorer ones. Rich provinces paid much more than the national average.[302] Jiangnan's tax rates, for example, were roughly four times the empire-wide average per mu, while on top of that a far higher percentage of all cultivated mu was on the books there. The land tax could be 10 to 15 per cent in its most heavily taxed county but was only about 7 per cent for the province as a whole.[303] The tax system also differentiated between China Proper and other regions. Central government tended to adapt to local conditions. For example, the famous merging of the head/poll tax into the land tax that was announced in 1713 by the Kangxi emperor only covered most of China at the very end of the eighteenth century. Even then various peoples in provinces in the Southwest, like Yunnan, Guizhou and Guanxi, were still living under a different tax system, as was Tibet.[304] As in Western Europe, core regions yielded much more taxes than the periphery. On top of that, in China there were regional differences not only with respect to the tax burden, but also in disaster relief.[305]

In practice, there also were big differences between various social groups. The more substantial landowners and members of the local gentry quite often didn't pay any taxes at all. Members of the 'gentry' formed a privileged status group that enjoyed economic privileges. Yeh-chien Wang's authoritative analysis of the Qing land tax system shows enormous inequity in the amount of land tax paid by different people.[306] A 'gentry' household in the eighteenth century may have paid as little as about a third of the tax paid by an equivalent commoner household and it was always exempted from corvee. During the nineteenth century commoners may have paid twice to five times as much land tax

---

[301]For 'old corruption' see Harling, *Waning of 'Old Corruption'*. For some comments with regard to corruption and revenue collection see Ashworth, *Customs and Excise*, ch. 17.

[302]See Chen, *System of Taxation*; Dai, *Sichuan Frontier and Tibet*; Morse, *Trade and Administration*; Pomeranz, 'Institutions and economic development' and Wang, *Land Taxation*, ch. 5. Here too, in principle, these differences were supposed to have an objective basis in differing productivity. In practice, however, they became more and more arbitrary.

[303]Bernhardt, *Rents, Taxes and Peasant Resistance*, 44–6. For the term 'mu' see footnote 355 of this chapter.

[304]See for examples Dai, *Sichuan frontier and Tibet*, and Wagner, *Chinesische Landwirtschaft*, 136.

[305]See for example Deng, *China's Political Economy*, 20–4.

[306]Wang, *Land Taxation*, 34–48.

per mu as gentry landowners.[307] The gentry, by the way, were not the only privileged group in matters of taxation. Banner men, for example, paid less tax than commoners.[308] There was, moreover, massive tax evasion, for example, by falsely registering commoners' land under the name of a privileged magistrate and in that way sheltering it from taxation. The magistrate would of course expect some remuneration for that service. Another way in which rural elites might rig the tax system in their favour was by paying the taxes for poorer people and asking fees for that. Local elites could also use this strategy in dealing with officials who could not timely fulfil their tax quotas and therefore had to borrow money. In that way local gentry often acquired substantial leverage over Peking's representatives.[309] That the standardization of procedures was highly problematic hardly needs any explanation, considering the enormous differences that existed in measures, weights and moneys, the fact that taxes might be collected in silver, copper cash or kind, and of course China's huge size and complexity. In many recent Anglo-Saxon publications on Ming and Qing China the idea is often expressed that with the Single-Whip tax reforms of the late sixteenth century there had occurred a complete 'silverization' of taxes. Many scholars even go as far as to claim that this led to a complete 'silverization' of the domestic economy.[310] That is not true. One can only wonder how this claim can be repeated time and again in general literature, whereas all experts reject it. Silverization was never complete, not even when it comes to taxes. These often continued to be paid in copper cash or in kind.[311] Heijdra points out that this was the case under the Ming, when the process started.[312] But the same applies to the situation under the Qing. According to Deng even after the famous Single-Whip tax reforms only 40 per cent of central taxes were actually paid in silver, whereas 60 per cent were paid in another way. Besides, so he points out, during the entire Qing period there were big regional differences in the amounts of taxes that were paid in cash or in grain.[313] Lin points out that in 1657 it was regulated that 70 per cent of taxes be paid in silver and the other 30 per cent in copper cash and that many taxes continued to be actually paid in copper.[314] Probably the greatest expert on taxes in China during the period that we are discussing here, Wang, writes: 'As

---

[307]For gentry privileges and exemptions see, in alphabetical order: Chang, *Income of the Chinese Gentry*, 328–9 (for the nineteenth century); Ho, *Ladder of Success*, 17–40, and Hsü, *Rise of Modern China*, 72–5. For the situation in the Lower Yangzi region quite late in our period see Bernhardt, *Rents, Taxes and Peasant Resistance*.

[308]For a description of the privileges and exemptions of the Manchu military see Elliott, *Manchu Way*, ch. 4, where the banner Manchus are described as 'a privileged people'.

[309]See for ways in which members of richer, gentry households in China managed to lower their tax payments or to even entirely evade them, and often, on top of that, to feed on the tax payments of their compatriots, Kuhn, *Origins of the Modern Chinese State*, 80–100.

[310]This thesis originates with Flynn and Giráldez who repeat time and again that from the end of the sixteenth century onwards enormous amounts of silver were sucked into China because from then on all taxes there had to be paid in silver. See their *China and the Birth of Globalization*, passim.

[311]I refer to Chinese small currency as 'copper' and 'copper cash' in this text, although there are good reasons to use the term 'bronze' instead. See Chapter 3 note 162.

[312]Heijdra, 'Socio-economic development', 491–6.

[313]See e.g. his 'Miracle or mirage?', ch. 4.2.

[314]Lin, 'Shift from East Asia', 7, and idem, *China Upside Down*, 40–2. For reference to payments in copper see also Chang, *Commissioner Lin*, 243, note 86, and Chen, *System of Taxation*, 36–44.

is well-known, Ch'ing land tax quota was collected in silver or grain or both. From the middle of the eighteenth century, however, two distinct trends appeared in tax payment: commutation of the grain tax into money payment, and payment of the tax in cash instead of silver.[315] To give one final example, Ch'ü, expert on local government during the Qing, writes: 'As a rule, taxpayers were allowed to hand in copper coins in lieu of silver at a conversion rate which was established by the highest provincial authority in accordance with the current market rate, and which the magistrates were not permitted to exceed. However, the prevailing custom among the magistrates was to insist upon payment in copper coins in lieu of silver, and at a rate higher than the market rate.' In a note he adds that this practice became prevalent after the 1820s.[316] In short, till the very end of the very long eighteenth century – and even beyond that period – a substantial amount of taxes in China were not paid in silver but in copper, which was quite cumbersome. Even if government insisted on payment in silver ordinary people often paid their taxes in copper to intermediaries or officials who then paid the state, at least partly, in silver. When from the 1820s onwards silver began to leave the country, this became more frequent. A governor in the South of China observed just before the outbreak of the Taiping Rebellion (1850–64) that 80 to 90 per cent of the people in the country paid their land tax in copper cash.[317] A non-negligible part of taxes, to conclude, continued to be collected in kind (i.e. as grain or fodder). That not only was quite inefficient and thus expensive, it apparently also provided ample opportunities for embezzlement, fraud and corruption.[318] When it comes to the entire economy of Qing China, there can be no doubt whatsoever that this never became entirely silverized – far from it.

As compared to Britain, there clearly was much less government-induced monetization in Qing China: taxes were lower, and not only in cash, government had no debts and spent much less. Payment of taxes in money will have been more problematic than it was in Britain, as China's economy as a whole during the very long eighteenth century was less 'commercialized'; that is if we define commercialization in terms of the percentage of products that entered interregional trade. Britain as a country was more urbanized than China. The majority of people living on the land there did not own or rent any land that might help them to provide for their own subsistence. Landlessness was far more normal than in China's countryside. Market involvement or even market dependency must therefore have been more widespread than in China. A less commercialized society almost by necessity will also be a less monetized one.

Internal transport facilities in China in all probability also were less favourable to commercialization than in Britain. As in almost every pre-industrial economy, the extent

---

[315]Wang, *Land Taxation*, 60.
[316]Ch'ü, *Local Government*, 135.
[317]Wang, *Land Taxation*, 60.
[318]In the 1880s, payments in kind still amounted, in value, to more than 10 per cent of total land tax. See Beal, *Origin of Likin*, 154. In Wang, *Land Taxation*, 72, it reads that land tax in China in 1753, including the so-called surcharges, had a value of 54 million taels. Wang estimates the value of the land tax that was paid in grain (including 25 per cent surcharge) at over 16 million taels. For further information on the grain tribute, see Hinton, *Grain Tribute of China*. For information on fraud see Chapter 1 notes 325–6 and 388.

of long-distance trade as a percentage of total production was rather small as it depended so much on the availability of cheap transport, which in turn depended strongly on the availability of usable waterways. The waterway system of rivers and canals in South East China probably was denser and more efficient than in most of its counterparts in Western Europe before 1750. The country also had some big rivers that passed through much of the country but those were not always easily navigable – think, for example, of the Yellow River – and it of course was never easy to use them upstream. There moreover were serious problems of silting up and flooding. Its river system in any case was not as dense or as multi-directional as that of Britain. The country had many canals but those often did not have a good water supply and they often were not appropriate for the transport of bulky goods.[319] Where transport over water was impossible or problematic, for example, outside China Proper and in large parts of Northern China, costs of long-distance transportation must have been so high as to make regular long-distance trade in bulk goods almost impossible.[320] We must not forget that even 100 kms counted as a considerable distance in a pre-industrial context. Transport over land was highly problematic and problems of funding and maintenance increased.[321] To claim like Westad does that China's land and water transport compared favourably with that in the West certainly is one of the many revisionist exaggerations.[322] References that one comes across in the literature to Qing China as a highly integrated market economy strike me as optimistic and based on an idiosyncratic interpretation of the evidence that basically only looks at important towns near rivers and at towns that had an important administrative function, and at official instead of actual prices.[323] In the nineteenth century, China's transport system over land as well as over water deteriorated. Scarcity of materials like wood and iron played their part in this, in particular in the case of overland transport. But the weakness of central government is also at least partly to blame.[324]

---

[319]See for further information Tvedt, 'Why England?'

[320]It made a huge difference whether one was near a waterway in China or not. See Li, 'Integration and disintegration', and Ma, 'Modern economic growth'.

[321]For a general analysis see Kim, 'Transport in China'.

[322]Westad, *Restless Empire*, 35.

[323]See Shiue and Keller, 'Markets in China and Europe', and Wang, 'Secular trends'. Shiue and Keller claim that in Western Europe only Britain had markets that were somewhat better integrated than those in the Lower Yangtze-Region. Li, 'Market integration and disintegration' is much less optimistic about Qing China's market integration.

[324]See for figures with regard to the amounts of rice that were traded over large distances Isett, *State, Peasant, and Merchant*, 273–5. Pomeranz claims that in the eighteenth century in China at the very least 15 million people were fed with grain that had been transported 'over a long distance'. That on average is much less than 10 per cent of total population. Pomeranz, *Great Divergence*, 34–5. Compare Heijdra, 'Socio-economic development of rural China', 507–8, where it is claimed that in the seventeenth century 11 per cent of total food production was sold 'on a national market'. In the late eighteenth century still no more than 10 per cent of total acreage of China was used for cash crops. See Ts'ui-jung Liu, 'Rice culture', 135, and, for Jiangnan, Li, *Agricultural Development*, 33–5. Guangling William Liu estimates the value of interprovincial trade in domestically produced goods in the 1880s at 13 per cent of national income, and at some 17 per cent around the turn to the twentieth century. See Liu, *Wrestling for Power*, 248–51. According to Perkins, to give one last estimate, 'before 1910' some 5 to 7 per cent of total agricultural produce was transported over a distance of 100 miles and more, and only 1 to 2 per cent was sent abroad. Perkins, *Agricultural Development*, 136–7.

Overall, payment in money has some clear advantages over payment in kind. This is especially true in the case of high value 'currencies' like silver and gold: much less so in the case of very low value and thus bulky copper currency that was so important in China. Taxes in kind always involve high transportation costs. Transporting the tribute grain from Jiangnan to Beijing, for example, in the nineteenth century made its price double or treble. The entire expenditure had to be borne by the people, not by government.[325] Van Slyke in his book about the Yangtze claims that in the early nineteenth century, the Qing authorities may have been spending 15 million ounces of silver, according to him, nearly a quarter of their total income, for the transport and management of tribute grain.[326] Transport costs were also high when tax income, in the form of silver, actually was transferred to Peking. Government with good reason often tried to avoid that. Moreover, to refer to another advantage of monetary payment, money by definition can be put to different uses more easily than, for example, grain.

When it comes to checks and balances the situation in China was not very auspicious. I already referred to the fact that until the second half of the nineteenth century no Han Chinese were involved in the financial affairs of central government: those were exclusively a Manchu affair. The fact that various organizations, such as the Board of Revenue and the Imperial Household, dealt with financial affairs independently only made things more complicated. There was no 'independent' supervision of the way money was collected and handled, nor was there an institution like Parliament in Britain where tax policies were discussed and decided and that might take care of checks and balances. That would not have been an easy task anyhow: there was no 'budget' one could check. Taxes were low but not officially negotiated in an institutionalized setting. From a modern bureaucratic perspective one can only be surprised that the system functioned for so long and – at least at the central level – fairly satisfactorily at that.

In China, where taxation was meant to be cheap, tax collecting, at least in the case of land tax, consumed an estimated one-fifth to one-fourth of the total amount of taxes that were collected.[327] According to Susan Mann there basically were three ways in which taxes were collected: by government officials, by organizations of people who were allowed to tax themselves and by means of tax farming.[328] In none of those 'systems' of tax collecting was the *actual* collecting fully in the hands of professional bureaucrats employed and paid by government. Collecting at the local level was primarily done by what one may call 'sub-bureaucrats': people who were not themselves directly in government service and as a rule were not paid by the government. Sometimes they received some pay by the magistrates by whom they were hired. But most of the time they had to see to it themselves that they, one way or another, managed to make a living by performing tasks for the government, including tax collecting. The coordinating bureaucratic offices in Peking and in the provinces were really small. I only found figures for 1895, but I have

---

[325]Xue, 'A "fertiliser revolution"?', 220.
[326]Van Slyke, *Yangtze*, 74–5.
[327]Wang, *Land Taxation*, 72.
[328]Mann, *Local Merchants*, 3.

no indication that the situation a century earlier would have been very different. If for that year we count all the employees working for the Board of Revenue in Peking plus those employed in the provinces to manage taxes, the number of 'financial' officers for the whole of China was only 1,800. That is one for every 250,000 people.[329] In this respect it is important to realize how big the actual autonomy of the provinces was in matters of taxation and how big the differences of their actual tax systems, although central government took care via its classification of provinces as surplus- and deficit-provinces that tax income and tax spending were somewhat equalized. Actually at the local level in the countryside matters of tax collecting also were often delegated to two types of civil village organizations which grouped non-gentry villagers into blocks of households from which representatives were chosen to perform certain duties, the so-called *li-chia* that in principle were supposed to deal with matters of finance, including tax collecting and population registration, and so-called *pao-chia* that in principle had to deal with matters of public order, such as policing, population registration and crime, but that over time increasingly also took over the the functions of the *li-chia*. Those village-heads 'selected' to make their fellow villagers pay the taxes were often held personally responsible if those villagers did not come up with their payment. The *li-chia* system gave rise to a host of malpractices that I will not discuss here in detail and that certainly did not decrease when the work of the *li-chia* was taken over by *pao-chia*.[330]

As the workings of the administrative, 'bureaucratic' system of Qing China in its entirety will be discussed later on in this text,[331] I will confine myself here to comments that deal with tax collecting and, more in general, public finance. As we will see, China's official bureaucracy was very thin on the ground. The number of people officially paid to take care of locally administering China on behalf of central government amounted to only a couple of ten thousands *at best*. These magistrates received very little government funding and they hardly had any official staff – according to Will only some five to six sub-officials per official – whom they could pay an official, regular salary. They had to fall back on 'sub-bureaucratic' personnel: people who were *not* in official government service and did *not* receive an official government salary. Sometimes those people received some funding by the officials for whom they worked, but overall, they had to take care of their own income. This hardly strikes one as an efficient bureaucratic system. Nor, *in the end*, can it be qualified as 'light', as Wong does.[332] Taken over the entire empire, 'sub-official' clerks, runners or whatever exact name they got, not only those involved in tax collecting but *all* sub-bureaucrats together, must have numbered many hundreds of thousands during the eighteenth century. They all asked the populace's money or some other kind of remuneration for their services. How can we be sure that the populace got value for its money? Right at the beginning of the nineteenth century, Hong Liangji estimated that

---

[329]Bastid, 'Structure of financial institutions', 70.

[330]For an extensive discussion of the complicated histories of these household organizations and their relations, I refer the reader to Hsiao, *Rural China* under *Li-chia* and *Pao-chia*. I also came across the notation 'bao-jia'.

[331]See pages 271–6.

[332]Wong, *China Transformed*, 134.

there would be about 1,000 clerks in an important district, 700 to 800 in a medium-sized district and at least 100 to 200 in a small one. If one takes an arithmetical average of 500 clerks, their total then must have amounted to about 763,000 for the 1,526 districts and equivalent divisions (of China).[333] According to Wittfogel, who of course likes to expand on the despotic character of Qing rule, there must have been more than forty clerks per official in the provinces of China during Qing rule. He claims that 'during the last period of imperial rule' China had some 40,000 civil officials and more than 1,700,000 'underlings', as he calls the sub-official aides.[334] My reading of the literature suggests that up to a million 'un-official officials' had to be provided for by the populace. Chang claims that over the entire nineteenth century some 40 per cent of all members of the gentry rendered some kind of gentry service – some support in the management of local affairs. Considering the fact that he estimates there were some 1.5 million gentry in the country in the second half of the century, or rather in the 1880s, that would mean that this 'class' alone at the time provided some 600,000 'sub-officials'.[335]

Government officials as a rule were not financial experts and, even if they were, as incoming 'outsiders' they lacked the 'local knowledge' needed to efficiently and correctly run financial affairs in their provinces. The number of their *official* subordinates was very low. When it comes to real 'expertise', their clerks and runners do not seem to have been of much help, to put it mildly. So in this respect officials basically only had two options: one was to fall back on local gentry and the other was to privately hire and pay experts, who as a rule were members of the gentry themselves. Both 'solutions' of course can hardly be called efficient or fitting for a bureaucratic system. The local gentry had their own interests that, to put it euphemistically, need not necessarily be identical to those of the government official. They were a quite substantial group of people who locally were very powerful. Many, but not all of them, had passed an official exam. The second 'solution' to me is one of the many clear indicators that China's administration had fundamental weaknesses.[336] I think I need not expand on the fact that it is rather strange that government officials had to privately contract *and* pay personnel that was supposed to do very important public work without, however, in any way being integrated in any official hierarchy. What makes this situation even more 'inefficient' is the fact that the salaries that the 'mandarins' received and from which they, apart from their own livelihood, were expected to also pay many 'official' expenses were incredibly low. As a matter of fact one can say that government officials in the provinces simply *could not* do what was expected of them through sheer lack of funding. If they hired extra personnel, including qualified personnel, as a rule those people were not so much actually paid by

---

[333]Bastid, 'Structure of financial institutions', 71. For some other estimates see Ch'ü, *Local Government*, chs 3 and 4.
[334]Wittfogel, *Oriental Despotism*, 307. Folsom, *Friends, Guests and Colleagues*, 44–5, quotes Wittfogel as claiming that the ratio of provincial officials to underlings would have been one to thirty.
[335]Chang, *Income of the Chinese Gentry*, 69.
[336]For information on those privately hired specialists who mostly were experts in the field of taxes and law see Folsom, *Friends, Guests and Colleagues*. For legal specialists see also Chen, 'Legal specialists'.

their poor employers as given the possibility to earn their salary on the job, so to say, just like the clerks and runners. This, in practice, means they were given permission to extract their income one way or another from the population. We are talking about a substantial and increasing number of people. According to one estimate, in 1854 there were about 27,000 of these private secretaries functioning as experts. That is almost as much as the number of real officials.[337]

An intermezzo: Are some taxes easier to collect than others? Land taxes in China versus excises and customs in Great Britain

Let us delve somewhat deeper into the problem of tax efficiency and distinguish between what I call 'technical feasibility' – the extent to which it was technically feasible to collect certain taxes, measured in the amount of *planned* income that actually was collected – and 'political feasibility' – the extent to it was politically feasible to tap certain sources of revenue at all. Total efficiency then might be measured as the rate of total *realized* income to total *potential* income.

Charles Tilly, one of the greatest experts on the history of state-formation in the West, suggests that, overall, in a pre-industrial economy taxing land is more complicated and therefore has a lower efficiency than taxing goods.[338] If that were true the relatively low tax income of China's government might be linked to the prominent role of land taxes in that realm. Tilly is not the only one holding such a view. Norberg and Hoffman, in their survey of tax systems of various countries in early modern Europe, draw the following conclusion: 'When it was possible, both politically and administratively, early modern monarchs preferred to tax trade.'[339] Taxing trade in this context can mean collecting customs duties – which were nowhere as important as in Britain – or collecting excises – which were quite important in almost all European countries. In his essay *On Taxes* Hume wrote:

> The best taxes are such as are levied upon consumption. They seem in some measure voluntary; since a man may chuse how far he will use the commodity which is taxed: they are paid gradually, and insensibly; They naturally produce sobriety and frugality, if judiciously imposed: And being confounded with the natural price of the commodity, they are scarcely perceived by the consumers. Their only disadvantage is that they are expensive [*sic*] in the levying.[340]

---

[337]Lin, *China Upside Down*, 139. Chang, *Income of the Chinese Gentry*, 86, gives a number of 16,000 secretarial assistants to the higher-ranking officials alone in 1880.

[338]Tilly, *Coercion, Capital, and European States*, 87–91.

[339]Hoffman and Norberg, 'Conclusion', 302. Epstein, to just give one more example, claims that 'sedentary peasants and their wealth were easier to oversee than mobile merchants' and that 'therefore more highly centralized tributary states like China pursued policies favouring the former over the latter'. Epstein, 'Rise of the West', 248.

[340]Rotwein, *David Hume, Writings on Economics*, 85.

Adam Smith also points at an advantage – that is from the perspective of the taxman – of this method of taxation:

> The consumer, who finally pays them, soon comes to confound them with the price of the commodities, and almost forgets that he pays any tax.[341]

Not everyone, however, is convinced that Tilly and Hume, are right. Ertman, for example, thinks it is rather the opposite: taxing land would be easier than taxing trade.[342] He might have referred to Adam Smith, who claimed that 'the quantity and value of land which any man possesses can never be a secret and can always be ascertained with great exactness' adding that 'land is a subject which cannot be removed.'[343] Military engineer and tax reformer Vauban, on the other hand, complained about the difficulties of judging the value of land and assessing a land tax at the beginning of the eighteenth century.[344] I do not think the question at hand has an unequivocal answer. Much depends on the level of monetization of the economy in question, its size, the existence of a good cadastre and the way in which tax-assessing and -collecting were organized – not an easy job in *any* pre-industrial, pre-statistical society.

In Europe overall, taxes on trade and consumption played a much bigger role in total government revenue than in Qing China: these taxes were more flexible than land taxes and directly focused on monetized sectors of the economy. They also could be more easily collected at a few points of distribution or of production than land taxes. Britain's system of collecting excises indeed exploited these advantages and was quite efficient, considering what was possible at the time. Its Customs actually was not. In China customs income was regarded as quite irrelevant. Their collection was quite inefficient. Setting up a system of collecting excises on a massive scale would have been an enormous undertaking. The number of economic entities was so enormous, their scale normally so small and the country so big that taxing actual production and trade was a really major challenge as the history of the *likin* tax that was introduced in 1853 shows.[345] By far the most important indirect tax, the one on salt, was farmed to so-called salt merchants who received a monopoly from government. Taxes in China in the period we discuss here basically continued to mean *land* taxes.

I would, however, in the end consider the existing power relations of more importance in this respect than such fairly technical questions. They play a fundamental role

---

[341]Smith, *Inquiry into the Nature and Causes of the Wealth of Nations*, 895.

[342]Ertman, *Birth of the Leviathan*, 16: 'Far from requiring a minimum apparatus, the collection of commercial revenues in fact demanded a large number of well-trained personnel with advanced computational skills and a detailed knowledge both of the numerous commodities and of an array of complex regulations. On the other hand, land taxes were not difficult to administer because central government could dispense with the time-consuming business of wealth or income assessment and instead simply demand fixed amounts of each local area.' It is a fact that, as Ertman claims, in Britain as well as in Prussia *per capita* officials collecting land taxes collected more money than officials collecting customs or excises.

[343]Smith, *Inquiry into the Nature and Causes of the Wealth of Nations*, 848.

[344]Hoffman, 'Early modern France', 231.

[345]See He, *Paths to the Modern Fiscal State*, under 'lijin'.

in determining the 'fiscal constitution' of a country and in deciding *who* is to bear the brunt of taxation.[346] In Britain land taxes were levied *on* the landed classes *by* the landed classes.[347] They administered and hence controlled them. Excise officers levied the excise that was to become by far the most important tax. They were professional government officers. In principle, landlords were in favour of land tax over excises and borrowing *because* and *as long as* they controlled it. In practice, the importance of other taxes and borrowing increased quickly. In the process of land tax collection, land tax agents represented central government, which intervened very little: it was the landowners themselves who provided the information and in the end footed the small bill. It was the value of land, in terms of a notional assessed rent, and *not* the value of its products that was the basis for the tax assessment. The general land tax was collected every year between 1692 and 1798 without a surveyed or mapped base or even a comprehensive written register. In essence, till 1799, the assessment continued to be based on the evaluations that were made in 1694, which means that in practice there hardly existed any connection between the land's actual value and tax assessment. This in turn meant that the tax burden for wealthy agrarians was quite low and by and large decreased.[348] Incidence was not perfectly equal. Landowners in the North paid more than those in the South.

Neither central government, landowners nor the common people had any incentive to introduce a surveyed or mapped cadastre for collecting the land tax. Even the Ordnance Survey Maps of the 1850s were not real cadastral maps. Again, Britain, or in any case England, is distinct: 'England thus stands apart from the general European trend of levying land taxes on the basis of cadastral surveys in the eighteenth and nineteenth centuries.'[349] We are clearly dealing here with a political *decision*, not a matter of *incapacity* or a failure to see potential advantages. After its conquest by Cromwell, Ireland, as Ian Hacking puts it, 'was completely surveyed for land, buildings, people and cattle … in order to facilitate the rape of that nation by the English in 1679'.[350] The so-called Ordnance Survey, founding date 1791, could produce excellent maps of (parts of) Great Britain via triangulation when it saw fit, mostly for military reasons.[351]

Creating a central cadastre as a rule took a long time. Basically, such a cadastre was nowhere really implemented before (far into) the nineteenth century.[352] In *Ancien Régime* France, overall, the main exceptions being the Provence and the Languedoc, the land tax was based on the person, not the land, so what was needed were not plans or maps but lists of proprietors. In 1790 it was decided that all old taxes should be

---

[346]See for comments on the political economy of taxation Cain and Hopkins, *British Imperialism*, ch. 2, and Nye, *War, Wine, and Taxes*, ch. 8.

[347]The information on British land taxation and the history of Britain's cadastre in the next two paragraphs is distilled from Kain and Baigent, *Cadastral Map*, 257–61. See also Ward, *English Land Tax*.

[348]See Figure 1. Many landowners on the Continent, in particular aristocrats, often paid no or very little taxes.

[349]Kain and Baigent, *Cadastral Map*, 260.

[350]Hacking, *Taming of Chance*, 17. I found this reference in Scott, *Seeing Like a State*, 49.

[351]See for the history of the Ordnance Survey Hewitt, *Map of a Nation*.

[352]In my comments on various European countries, I again base myself on Kain and Baigent, *Cadastral Map*.

abolished and replaced by a single property tax that was to take into consideration the net productivity of the properties measured. In 1807, accordingly, a new land tax was introduced that was to be based on the size of the properties and the nature of land use. This would have to result in a *Cadastre Parcellaire*. It took until about 1850 before continental France, and even then not entirely, had been surveyed and mapped. The legacy of the French Revolution also gave a boost to cadastral mapping in what now is called 'the Netherlands'. Here one tried to create a system in which the land tax was based on the income the owner-user or owner-landlord derived from the land. The *Hollandse Cadastre* of 1795–1811 would become one of the first attempts at nationwide mapping by a body of surveyors working with strict and uniform regulations and measures. Let me give one last example: the Habsburg realm. The *Landeskontribution* (a land tax collected for the central treasury) was the main source of tax revenues for the army. Most of it was raised as tax on immovable property. Having a cadastre would thus would be very helpful for central government in assessing its tax base. Various efforts were made. Their success is not evident. It is claimed that in Maria Theresa's cadastre of 1756, 36 per cent of productive land escaped record. Joseph II wanted to set up a cadastre on which to base *one* tax on land to be paid by *all*. That plan was not realized, as was a plan to tax net income from the land. This simply proved too complicated and would take too long. So it was decided to tax gross income and then try to correct and adapt the outcome as far as possible. Making a cadastre proved an enormous challenge. Under Emperor Francis I, in 1817, mapping for a new cadastre got under way in Lower Austria. The cadastre for 'just' the Austrian part of the realm was only finished in 1861. The pricing system, on which its assessments were based, had become completely out of date and valuation no longer possible.

In China taxes on land were paid by the owner. That, as such, already is problematic. In Northern China, as a rule, it was the small peasant who was cultivator as well as owner of his plot. In the Yangzi Delta, for example, the situation was different. There the majority of the cultivators only rented the 'subsoil', which meant that it was the subsoil-*owning* landlord who had to pay the taxes, of course, seeing to it that he got his money back via the rent he asked from his peasants.[353] Moreover, many agriculturists had various separate plots of land; not only big landowners but even those cultivating very small tracts of land.[354] Assessing and collecting the land tax must have been a quite complex and huge undertaking. It departed from a standard classification of cultivated land in three main grades with each grade being subdivided in three sub-grades. In practice it became characterized by an enormous regional variety. On top of that, quite differing methods of assessment emerged in which officials in charge of the land tax fixed

---

[353]Huang, *Peasant Family and Rural Development*, 42. This text also provides information on the important distinction between sub-soil and soil. See under 'subsoil rights'.

[354]For bigger landowners see Bernhardt, *Rents, Taxes, and Peasant Resistance*, ch. 1. For farms in general, referring to the situation in the 1930s, see Buck, *Land Utilization*, where the author writes that the average size of farms that mainly grew rice or other grains in the case of owners was 4.2 acres and in the case of tenants 3.56 acres, with an average farm consisting of 5.6 plots.

a standard rate for land of diverse productivity, which they then expressed not in actual mus but in so-called fiscal mus.[355] There were major regional differences when it came to the amounts of land that were registered, the number of different qualities of land that were distinguished and the amounts of tax that had to be paid, depending on, for example, wealth or costs of transport. Rates of payment often differed with different social groups. All this of course created ample opportunity for fraud, evasion and extortion. Although central government in principle wanted to protect small tenants – and proprietors – and continued to be anxious that a class of big and powerful landlords might emerge, it increasingly tended to take the side of the landlords in cases of conflicts about rent payments. As a rule it became adamant that tenants paid their rents. In regions with high rates of tenancy, the government simply depended too much for its income on the landlords' ability to extract rents to let its policies be actually guided by the social considerations it liked to proclaim.

Under the Qing, under-registration of land was notorious. It clearly was the weakest link in the system of tax collecting. Till the 1850s, central government had no up-to-date cadastral surveys and no trustworthy information with regard to the land market and actual property relations. The last nationwide land census dated back to the years 1578–82, and the results, made into the 'base quotas' at the beginning of the Qing, were considered sacrosanct ever since for all practical purposes.[356] According to Osborne, much land, probably the majority of new reclamations after the establishment of the Ming quotas, remained unregistered. Of the land reclaimed in the eighteenth and nineteenth centuries in Guangdong, probably less than 20 per cent was registered.[357] Wang ventures a nationwide estimate and concludes that 'at least a third of the newly cultivated land in the first century of the Qing dynasty and about four fifths in the next one and a half centuries went unregistered.'[358] Imperial government apparently lost its interest in updating land data after the attainment of the original quotas. It was not keen on pushing the registered acreage beyond the 1,600 mark. At the local level, motives as well as means were lacking to do something about under-registration. The lower the tax quotas, the remoter the chance that the local official failed to meet them and the bigger the chance he could present a 'benevolent' image. Peasants of course were not interested in increasing their tax burden that, even if from a comparative perspective might seem low – at least officially – could still make a huge difference for all those living near subsistence. Reporting land acreage and land tax became a mere formality.[359]

As indicated, the land tax knew various grades, depending on the quality of the land. But it was only every now and then that land indeed was upgraded. Tax quotas were

---

[355]A mu is about one-sixth of an acre or one-fifteenth of a hectare.

[356]Will, *Bureaucracy and Famine*, 243.

[357]Osborn, 'Property, taxes and state protection', 154–5. For the reference to Guangdong, see Marks, *Tigers, Rice, Silks & Silt* under 'Guangdong'.

[358]Wang, *Land Taxation*, 26–7.

[359]See for the extent to which even fairly low (official) taxes could make a substantial difference for small peasants Elvin, 'Why intensify?'

not increased regularly. When tax revenue did increase, that normally was because of increases in the amount of taxed land. Keeping track of the prices of land and agricultural products and of their purchase and sale in a country as immense as China must have been too complicated for the underpaid and understaffed government officials, even if they would have wanted to, which they did not. Revenue from land taxation in that way was almost fixed and taxed farmers only on the area of land that they officially owned. According to Elvin this system of taxation may have had the consequence of putting a premium on intensification of cultivation.[360] This may be one of the reasons why, as a Jesuit report from the late eighteenth century noted, the lands of peasant proprietors were far more productive than large estates.[361] As we have seen, in Britain there was no good cadastre either. Or rather, there was no cadastre at all. But Britain's land taxes never in the entire period discussed here amounted to more than one-third of total tax income and their importance decreased sharply. In China, in contrast, land taxes over that period continued to be by far the most important source of tax income. The fact that its customs were not exactly efficient and the collecting of its salt taxes farmed, therefore, was fairly inconsequential. The 'inefficiency' in collecting land taxes, in contrast, must have had a major impact, even though that apparently was neither felt nor resented as such. This may have been due, at least to some extent, to the fact that in Qing China in fiscal as well as financial matters there was a great lack, at the central level, of transparency.

Strikingly enough Wong claims that states in Europe were particularly *inefficient* in taxing agriculture as compared to China.[362] He does not indicate which exact states he has in mind. Let us again focus on Great Britain. Land taxes there indeed did not amount to much. On average, *including* other assessed taxes, they amounted to some £2 million per year over the eighteenth century, reaching their highest annual average of some £8 million in the period 1810–19. But £2 million still is the equivalent of 6 million taels, collected in a country that, *including* Scotland, which kept its land taxes to itself at the time, was only some 230,000 km² and had only some 13 million inhabitants. Is that really 'inefficient' in comparison to the 40 to 50 million taels collected from over 300 million people in a country that, even if we only take 'China Proper', is some seventeen times as big? Correcting for the costs of living in both countries still does not provide solid support for Wong's thesis, nor does correcting for agricultural land. Besides, as indicated earlier on, the relatively low land tax revenue in Great Britain is a consequence of the fact that the main elite that actually ruled the country was powerful enough to use the state to limit its own tax payments and roll them off to others. It certainly as such is not a sign the country had a weak state.

---

[360]See Elvin, 'Why intensify?' This effect may have even been increased by the tendency to levy rents from tenants on the basis only of their main cereal crop and not of supplementary crops.

[361]See for this comment Elvin, 'Technology of farming', 14.

[362]Wong, *China Transformed*, 133: 'the Chinese tapped agricultural revenues so much more effectively than European rulers would'.

From inefficiency to malpractices and corruption

Up until now we have only discussed *official* payments to government by the populace. They of course need not have been identical to *actual* payments and they weren't. As has to be expected, some people paid *more* and others *less* than they officially had to and, as has to be expected, there existed all kinds of corruption. Let us begin with an analysis of the situation in China, where to my view problems were far more serious. To me it is obvious that the Chinese tax system simply *cannot* have been very efficient and is bound to have led to manipulation and fraud, as it indeed did. Too few officials had to do too much work. Many of them were not specialists and had to rely too much on underlings who received no official salary. When it comes to vulnerable spots in the system, this is not all. The drawbacks of the system of tax farming as it existed were fairly obvious and, with the further spread of this method of tax collecting over time, only tended to increase. The same goes for the 'outsourcing' of assessment and collection of taxes to various organizations that had to pay those taxes themselves, a method of revenue collecting that also tended to increase. It is also fairly obvious, though, that such ways of revenue collecting are not easily avoided in an enormous, pre-industrial country like Qing China. In the case of a government like that of the Qing that did not want or was unable to spend more money on creating a professional organization, they were inevitable.

When it comes to tax collecting, Chinese society was not very 'legible.'[363] Central government lacked information. A system of 'indirect rule' like the Chinese tax system did not only yield relatively little: central government did not even know how little, as it had no clear idea of the actual resources in its country. As tax collecting to a large extent was in fact semi-privatized, it was not very 'transparent' and lacked uniformity. It mostly worked by the principle that one should adapt to time and place, often because one simply did not have the power to do otherwise. In that way much tax collecting *de facto* was like tax farming. This refers to the collecting of land taxes but I would not want to call the way other kinds of revenue were collected 'bureaucratic', 'predictable' and 'transparent' either.[364] The same of course applies to the strategy of falling back on all kinds of contributions in times of need. That the efficiency of China's revenue collecting was not very high need not surprise us. Considering the huge problems that tax collectors faced, it actually was quite impressive.

Talking about (in)efficiency almost inevitably brings us to the subject of corruption. In discussing Qing China's bureaucracy the word pops up frequently. In every textbook on the history of Qing China we find extensive reference to all kinds of corruption. That does not mean it would be easy to indicate what exactly it refers to. Much was not laid down in written rules or laws but simply left to decide by the people who did the

---

[363]See for that term pages 416–17.
[364]For the Imperial Household see Torbert, *Ch'ing Imperial Household Department.* For some comments on the actual collection of customs see Huang, 'Chinese maritime customs'.

actual administration. Many people running the actual administration and rendering services that we would now call 'public' were *not* in fact public officials. Therefore much of what they did can perhaps best be described as '*extra*-legal' or '*a*-legal' without being necessarily '*il*legal' in the sense of not being in accordance with some existing rule or norm.[365] Much of what they did however also simply had to be done and in that sense 'the indispensable' was indeed 'legitimate', to use the phrase coined by Reed. As long as the fees asked for 'public services' were 'reasonable' and the procedures decent and efficient, the populace normally would have been willing to put up with them. But where, for example, do 'reasonable' customary fees end and where does 'extortion' begin? It will not come as a surprise that different parties tended to think differently about that. One simply cannot expect all those clerks and runners who received no salary at all, or all those officials whose salary evidently was too low, to not do something about their financial predicament. The imperial Chinese state in fact *relied* on extralegal sources of financial support in order to function – that clearly also applies to its officials who did receive a salary and whom it tended to blame and regard it as their moral failing when their 'improvising' did not work out.[366] Everyone knew that the regular income of officials, even if one included the 'honesty-nourishing allowances' and compensation for administrative expenses, was far too low and everyone knew they tried to remedy this situation. That was considered 'normal' – and inevitable – as long as the official did not abuse his powers. The temptation to do so was often too big, especially because what was not allowed was unclear and the chance that one might get away with all kinds of massive self-enrichment was fairly high. The following estimate by Chung-li Chang for the situation in the second half of the nineteenth century – in which really fraudulent income of course is not even included – shows how successful officials were in this respect. Earlier on the situation may have been less extreme but it certainly was not fundamentally different.

The regular income of officeholders totalled only 6,295,000 taels, while the extra income totalled about nineteen times as much as the regular income. The combined total income of gentry members from office holding was an estimated 121,000,000 taels annually. This large sum was shared by some 23,000 incumbent Chinese officeholders, who constituted about 1.6 per cent of the total gentry ranks in the late nineteenth century. On the average, the gross income of an officeholder amounted to more than 5,000 taels per annum.[367]

That means that a definition like Park's – 'corruption involves the deviant use of public office to achieve private gain' – may look quite helpful in theory but still is very difficult

---

[365]See Reed, *Talons and Teeth*, 'Introduction' and under 'corruption', and Thornton, *Disciplining the State*, chs 1 and 2.

[366]See Park, 'Corruption', and Thornton, *Disciplining the State*, chs 1 and 2.

[367]See Chang, *Income of the Chinese Gentry*, 42. According to Chang the total annual income of a labourer at the time was 5 to 10 taels, in addition to the food provided by his employer. Ibid., 12.

to implement in practice.[368] In many cases, however, there could be no doubt whatsoever that many people did make quite inappropriate use of their position.

The thin line between inefficiency, improvisation, malpractice and outright corruption was often crossed.[369] We hear of the use of various measures and of cheating taxpayers when they had to convert deliveries in grain into money payments or when they had to exchange copper cash for silver. Apart from that, there was ample opportunity to ask all kinds of extra payments, fees and bribes. Obviously, we can only guess at the amounts of money involved. But there can be no doubt that they were staggering. Let me give some examples. For the end of the nineteenth century actual levies are estimated to have been three to four times the professed returns.[370] The expert on Chinese military history and on late Qing China, Van de Ven, writes that it has been estimated that in the Late Qing no less than two-thirds of revenue collection took place 'informally'.[371] In 1854, a censor estimated that the costs of corruption by clerks and runners and of extra payments for private secretaries alone amounted to about 8 million taels, which according to him, would be one-fifth of the state's total annual revenue at the time.[372] One reads about grain tribute tax payments at that time that were 2.5 times the official, legal payment.[373] Wagner, in his book on Chinese agriculture, makes the following general claim, explicitly referring to the last decades of Qing rule but suggesting things would never have been fundamentally different: 'Only uninitiated people can believe the fairy tale that land tax would be low in China. In reality fairly high and in many cases even exorbitant sums are exacted.' He would not be surprised if actual land and poll tax payments would be six times as high as official taxes.[374] For the early nineteenth century, studies of provinces in the Lower Yangtze Valley suggest that the land tax collections reported to Peking were only a half or a third of the total actual payments by the population to the magistrate and his staff.[375] Apparently collecting salt tax also provided ample opportunities for enrichment. In the early nineteenth century, Lianghuai, the salt tax collection turned over to government, was a little over 2 million taels, while the actual tax collected was about 8 million taels, and the Linghuai transport merchants' outlay for that area's share of the salt trade was between 20 million and 30 million taels.[376]

---

[368]Park, 'Corruption', 968.

[369]For a more theoretical analysis of the phenomenon, with many examples, see Chen, 'Needham Puzzle reconsidered'; Kiser and Tong, 'Determinants of the amount and type of corruption'; Ni and Van, 'High corruption income'; Reed, *Talons and Teeth*, and Sng, 'Size and dynastic decline'. The reader interested in further examples is referred to Ch'ü, *Local Government*; Deng, *China's Political Economy*; Hsiao, *Rural China*, and Park, 'Corruption'.

[370]Bastid, 'Structure of financial institutions', 74.

[371]Van der Ven, 'Onrush of modern globalization', 180.

[372]Lin, *China Upside Down*, 138.

[373]Ch'ü, *Local Government*, 141.

[374]Wagner, *Chinesische Landwirtschaft*, 141. The translation is mine. Compare Morse, *Trade and Administration*, ch. 4.

[375]Feuerwerker, *State and Society*, 90–2.

[376]For this information see Murphey, *The Outsiders*, 115. He refers to a publication that I could not consult myself: Metzger, 'T'ao Chu's reform', 4.

Few people would want to deny that these things happened in China during the nineteenth century, especially in the second half of it. But the situation was already quite bleak earlier. Rumour has it that Ho-shen (or Hešen), the imperial bodyguard of the Qianlong emperor, bled the state for nearly a quarter of a century and amassed the incredible fortune of 800 million *taels*, which as my source in this respect, Hsü, adds 'reputedly [was] more than half the actual state income for twenty years'.[377] According to Hsü, Ho-shen was an acute *symptom* rather than the *cause* of the widespread corruption. In fact corruption was evident already before his rise to a position of power. Deng refers to several earlier major cases of corruption.[378] In the eighteenth century it was not uncommon for the taxes collected to be many times the official quotas and for ordinary peasants to be squeezed by the tax collector and the local gentry.[379] We already referred to the habit of collecting 'wastage allowances'. Here too, possibilities for overcharging abounded. They customarily ranged from 10 to 20 per cent of the official tax due. But in some areas that had risen to as much as 50 per cent of the regular tax quota. Early Manchu leaders regarded them as a necessary evil, but the Yongzheng emperor resolutely prohibited their collection and set in motion a scheme to legalize the meltage fee at a fixed rate – which, however, could be adapted to local circumstances – and then return it to the public coffers. Possibilities for magistrates to cheat and simply extort of course could never be fully eliminated.[380] Among all taxes in the Qing the most underreported was the group under the heading 'miscellaneous taxes'. For 1753 the amount that was actually collected was five times as big as the amount reported.[381] Judging by Tolbert's book on the Imperial Household Department, that institution too was rife with corruption.[382] Considering how Western traders were treated in Canton, one cannot escape the conclusion, even if one would take a lot of their complaints with more than a grain of salt, that China's 'Customs' too were rife with squeeze and corruption and the paying of numerous 'fees'.[383] Dai's book on the Sichuan-Tibet frontier region shows that in the eighteenth century this region was a 'fertile ground for corruption', where central government had no grip on expenditure and where fraud, embezzlement and tax evasion were rife. Government was afraid that tightening its grip and collecting more revenue to set up a decently paid bureaucracy would disturb the frontier.[384]

These comments are not 'Eurocentric', 'anachronistic' complaints. Chinese people at the time, members of the elite as well as the ordinary populace, were only too aware of malpractices, and one can find countless complaints and, increasingly, also

---

[377]Hsü, *Rise of Modern China*, 124–5. Compare for sometimes strikingly different estimates of Hešen's fortune Chang, 'Economic role', 267–8; Elliott, *Emperor Qianlong*, 157, and Nivison, 'Ho-shen and his accusers', 211.

[378]Deng, *China's Political Economy*, 15.

[379]Hsü, *Rise of Modern China*, 125.

[380]See Thornton, *Disciplining the State*, 32, and Zelin, 'Yung-Cheng reign', 206–13.

[381]Wang, *Land Taxation*, 71.

[382]Torbert, *Ch'ing Imperial Household Department*.

[383]See e.g. Huang, 'Chinese maritime customs'.

[384]Dai, *Sichuan Frontier and Tibet*, ch. 6. For the expression 'fertile ground for corruption' see page 185.

protests.[385] This is a comment by the same Hong Liangji to whom we referred earlier on, written at the end of the eighteenth century:

> What is really going on is that the magistrate is taking advantage of the authority vested in him by his superiors to extract money from the people: half of what he collects goes to the higher echelons but he keeps the other half to himself.[386]

The Qianlong emperor himself admitted in 1795 that 'only two or three-tenths of the governors are absolutely clean-handed and realizing the value of high principles actually live up to them'.[387] In the Qing *Veritable Records* for 1806 it reads:

> It has been reported that when the tribute grain is collected, the local officials in the provinces collect more than the amount sanctioned by law. They make arrangements to have gentry of bad character act as their agents in coercing payment. They first make enquiries as to who, among the gentry, are habitually fond of meddling. Then they bribe them in advance, granting them the right to contract a certain portion of the tribute grain. The rustics and the poor have a redoubled burden because these persons can levy an excess amount from them just as they please.[388]

In her article on corruption in *eighteenth*-century China, Nancy Park writes that observers, foreigners as well as Chinese, at the time believed corruption to be a ubiquitous and serious problem within the Chinese state. Even if those observers had all been mistaken, this would still indicate a major problem for the state as it shows an apparently enormous lack of trust among the population. The overarching picture that emerges from the Qing proverbs that she studied, among other things, is that of a bureaucracy riddled with corruption, presiding over a community of defenceless victims. Runners and clerks were almost uniformly despised, but a good bureaucrat apparently was also regarded as an exception rather than the rule. The Confucian ideal of the magistrate as the father and mother of the people, which was frequently trotted out in state commentaries on the bureaucracy, was not exactly reflected in the proverbial wisdom of the day. Ideals showed very little resemblance to reality. These negative images were not just figments of fantasy. Corruption in all forms could and did cause serious distress among the Chinese populace. The fact that, according to conventional wisdom, the bulk of official

---

[385]For criticisms by Chinese officials and scholars see e.g. Polacheck, *Inner Opium War*. Song Yun, an important official with a long and distinguished career, also pointed at the existence of widespread and serious corruption and regarded that as the main cause of the White Lotus Rebellion. See Dabringhaus, *Qing-Imperium*, 74. For criticism by Commissioner Lin, who played such an important role in the First Opium War, see Chang, *Commissioner Lin* under 'China, official corruption'.

[386]Mann Jones, *Hung Liang-Chi*, 176. Currently his name is written as Hong Liangji.

[387]Wang, *White Lotus Rebels and South China Pirates*, 30.

[388]Elvin, *Another History*, 15–16. Kent Deng claims that whereas the official rice tax for stipends for soldiers and officials was 4 million shi, in practice some ten times as much was collected. Deng, *China's Political Economy*, 28–9 and Appendix 5.

misconduct went unquestioned and unpunished did not help in improving trust in the administration. Problems were not confined to the civil bureaucracy. Long-term military operations offered splendid opportunities for enrichment, career advancement and embezzlement. The first three years of the White Lotus Campaign cost 100 million taels. The Board of Revenue calculated that only half of that amount was legitimately spent. Huge amounts of money might, for example, be allocated for hiring so-called temporary soldiers (who earned 2.4 to 3 taels per month, whereas a 'normal' soldier as a rule earned about 1 tael) who only existed on paper.[389] For most Chinese, corruption was an oppressive burden that exhausted the population. Dissatisfaction was extremely widespread. It did erupt into a major social conflict at the very end of the eighteenth century with the White Lotus Rebellion, which started as a form of tax unrest and anger about local maladministration and corruption in East Sichuan and spread to the provinces of Hubei and Shaanxi.

It was only the first of many uprisings, the next major one being the Eight Trigrams Uprising of 1813.[390] Park concludes her article with a sentence that deserves to be quoted literally:

> Thus the fiscal need for corruption compounded by the ineffectiveness of the criminal laws to prevent it and the professional benefits of engaging in it, contributed to the omnipresent corruption problem [sic] that plagued the eighteenth-century Chinese state and society.[391]

In that respect the Chinese state under the Qing increasingly began to present the worst of both worlds to its tax-paying population: very high payments and very few public goods in return. Trouble in these respects had already set in *before* the famous silver drain and *before* foreign intervention. Via their so-called 'conspicuous charities' officials did give back money to society that was used to provide for public goods, but one need not be a cynic to expect that those charities will have cost less than the extra revenues from which the official paid for them.

One can only conclude that during the long eighteenth century revenue collecting in China was much *less* efficient and much *more* mismanaged than in Great Britain. Wong's claims that the 'Chinese government developed routine, light, legitimate taxation of agricultural revenues mobilized by the state's bureaucratic infrastructure'[392] and that the 'Chinese state had routinely taxed its people in an organized bureaucratic fashion since the third century B.C.E.' are quite optimistic.[393] There is nothing wrong with characterizing taxation in China as 'light', at least where *official* taxes are concerned. But I would not want to describe tax collection in Qing China as 'organized', let alone as 'bureaucratic'.

---

[389]Wang, *White Lotus Rebels and South China Pirates*, 141–3. See also Dai, *Sichuan Frontier and Tibet*, ch. 6.
[390]See Hung, 'Contentious peasants', and Jones and Kuhn, 'Dynastic decline'.
[391]Park, 'Corruption', 999.
[392]Wong, *China Transformed*, 134.
[393]Wong, *China Transformed*, 282.

It was not. Nor would I claim China's imperial state sometimes outperformed early modern European states.[394] It certainly did not outperform Great Britain. The fact that one looks in vain for a word like 'corruption' in the index of Wong's *China Transformed* is telling. In *Before and Beyond Divergence* he and Rosenthal even claim that in Qing China: 'There were relatively few opportunities for rent-seeking and other forms of economic distortion that reduced the efficient allocation of resources and products.'[395] This is simply ignoring massive evidence to the contrary. Actually, the direct and indirect costs of corruption must have been enormous for China's economy.

These comments about the low level of taxation in China are not meant as simple value judgements. There may have been good or at least quite understandable reasons for the state of affairs in China. The fact that China's central government collected far less taxes than that of Britain to some extent clearly was a *choice*. Taxing the population lightly was regarded as a sign of good, benevolent rule that tied in neatly with the 'Confucianist' concept of the benevolent state that takes care of people's livelihood and does not take their money. Moreover, opting for such a policy can undoubtedly also be considered a *rational* and reasonable choice. It may to a large extent also have been *inevitable* as the Manchus were not more than a tiny foreign elite of a couple of million people, ruling over a huge, densely populated country with several hundred million inhabitants, that in fact was occupied by them. That their rule was less efficient and more 'corrupt' than that of Britain, at least in matters of public finance, to a large extent may also have resulted from a 'choice' made by the Qing: a government that is keen on hiring as few officials as possible and on providing them with a salary and funding that it knows to be insufficient may regret that all kinds of inefficiency and corruption develop, but it cannot really be surprised about that. To build one's hopes so strongly on the high moral standing of one's officials means building one's hopes very high indeed, if not simply too high. Here, too, politics play their part. The fact that there were so few officials was not unconnected to the fact that those officials in function wanted to stay 'scarce' and often opposed enlarging the number of mandarins in an effort to keep 'outsiders', first of all, the clerks and runners, whom they fiercely despised, at bay.[396] Sometimes it was central government that fiercely opposed incorporating the sub-county functionaries and turning them into real officials, as it feared expanding the formal system of administration might weaken the power of the state by increasing opportunities for clerical self-engrossment and subversion of central policies that did not favour powerful local interests.[397]

Most of the inefficiencies and malpractices that we, from a modern perspective, observe, in all probability simply were almost unavoidable, considering the huge size of Qing China, its large population and the state of technology at the time. To have ruled Qing China as a modern, bureaucratic and centralized state not only was impossible

---

[394]See, for example, Wong, *China Transformed*, 282.

[395]Wong, 'Taxation and good governance', 361.

[396]See for some further explanation, in alphabetical order: Folsom, *Friends, Guests and Colleagues*, 31–2; Kuhn, *Origins of the Modern Chinese State*, 23–4; Woodside, *Lost Modernities*, 51–2, and Yang, 'Some characteristics'.

[397]See e.g. Thornton, *Disciplining the State*, 49.

considering the actual power relations: it also was simply beyond the logistic and monitoring capacities, not just of China, but of *any* pre-industrial society. The Yongzheng emperor did try to turn his empire into something more resembling a modern bureaucratic state, but in the end he failed and his successor fell back to time-honoured informal rule in which control of local affairs was in the hands of local elites. Bureaucracy as a central agency simply never was strong enough to actually run the country.

Some general comments on the strength of the British and Chinese states

The previous remarks are a good introduction to some more general comments. The position of Britain's central government in British society was a very strong one, stronger than that of any government in the world at the time. It already had in the eighteenth century all the monopolies that are ascribed to a full-blown modern bureaucratic state *à la* Weber – that is, the monopolies of legitimate violence, of public administration and of the collection of public revenue. Britain's state no longer had *any* competitors in *any* of these public domains. There, at home, was no private property of means of 'military' violence and no significant private appropriation of parts of administration or public income. There were no feudal rights that might be exerted, no feudal exemptions, privileges, *beneficia* or immunities, and there was no trace of that blurring of the distinction between private and public that characterizes feudalism. Central government was sovereign when it came to all forms of public revenue collecting and could decide itself over the spending of the bulk of it. Aristocrats levied no feudal dues and in 1534 the right to collect 'first-fruits and tenths' had gone from the Pope and the monasteries to the Crown. Anglican bishops may sometimes have acted as collecting officials, but they did not keep the revenue. The rates of locally dispensed poor relief were decided by central government. No interest group could feed on the state and redirect public money to private coffers. Taxes were collected very efficiently, almost entirely by government officials, and with no exceptions: they were also almost entirely sent to the capital in the form of money. The country, moreover, was one market with no internal customs zones at all. All local self-government notwithstanding, the administration of the British state was centralized, 'centripetal', uniform and efficient. All those intermediate groups that, according to Wong, would have been entrenched in society and by their corporate power were supposed to weaken European states in the early modern era actually no longer existed in Great Britain during the period we deal with here; or rather they had taken over and become the state themselves after 1688.[398] Infrastructurally its state was very strong in terms of resources (money and civilian and military government officials) at its direct disposal. At the time of its economic take off, it clearly was the strongest in the world. It was certainly helped by the fact that it was a relatively small and

---

[398]See for scholars who in this respect agree with Wong, Hui, *War and State Formation*, and Jacques, *When China Rules the World*, 81–6.

homogenous island that, for government, was relatively easy to monitor, had no regional power bases since 1066 and was relatively rich and monetized. All the relevant elites were directly involved in ruling, which strengthened its legitimacy. Over time, many differences and conflicts notwithstanding, it developed a strong national identity.

When it comes to its 'hard' infrastructural power (i.e. its income and expenditure and its personnel), the Qing Empire can only look to be a rather weak state with a central government that only had a quite limited amount of resources at its disposal as compared to European fiscal-military states, first and foremost Great Britain. But calling it a weak state in a sense, of course, is rather weird. Everyone studying the history of China and comparing it to that of Western Europe can only be impressed by the continuity and longevity of the enormous Middle Kingdom with its huge population. Pines is right when he refers to the 'unparalleled durability' of Imperial China and claims that 'few if any premodern polities worldwide were able to provide such a fair degree of stability, peace and relative prosperity to so many people as did the Chinese empire'.[399] Qing rulers in China moreover also seemed differently motivated. Their motto of rule has been described as 'controlling from afar'.[400] Fei in his book *From the Soil* goes even further: 'In [Qing] China … the state does not exist as an organization.' In his opinion the main view in Qing China would have been that 'the ideal government should wuwei – do nothing' and 'not actively govern at all'.[401] In many respects at the local level there was no state, let alone as a formal organization. It was not much more than a thin administrative superstructure that left day-to-day business, and often much more, to the local elites. To claim on that basis that Qing China would have known a system of local self-government with a benevolent central government that confined itself to controlling from a distance would, in my view, be far too optimistic. Via its systems of mutual household surveillance that were under the control of local officials and its habit to think in terms of collective responsibility, central government could make villagers spy on each other and instil distrust and fear.[402] Where possible, however, rulers should accommodate. The following quote, dating from the Ming period, withstood the ravages of time and is repeatedly encountered even in nineteenth-century writings on administration:

> What is needed in administration at the present time is to keep troublesome business at a minimum, not to add to it; to preserve the rules, not to change them; to bring about tranquillity in all situations, not to stir them up; and to relax and simplify the control of the people, not to tighten and complicate it.

The same goes for the next quote: 'Maintenance of moral tradition is the main task of government.'[403] Apparently these sayings were regarded as good advice that had to be heeded. If they and many similar others are something to go by, governing apparently

---

[399]Pines, *Everlasting Empire*, 2 and 9.
[400]Leonard, *Controlling from Afar*, ch. 2.
[401]Fei, *From the Soil*, 29, 30, 113.
[402]See Chapter 1 note 330.
[403]Both quotes are from Yang, 'Some characteristics', 141.

was primarily about educating people and strengthening the social and moral order. It clearly was *not* about mobilizing the masses on behalf of state and nation. Wong and, for example, Thornton are right in emphasizing the moral foundations and logic of China's system of rule.[404] In the introduction to her book Thornton describes the state as '*the* moral agent … in modern Chinese history' and argues

> Without denying that mobilization for war has played a role in the extension and deepening of the power of the Chinese state, I argue instead that in modern China, state-making strategies … have been shaped at least as decisively by normative agendas as they were by military goals.[405]

Pines, rightly in my view, describes it as an 'extraordinarily powerful ideological construct'.[406]

In preparing for their examinations, China's rulers were all taught that they had to nourish and instruct the people. In office, they were constantly reminded of that duty. Let there be no mistake, they often used brute force. But Montesquieu was wildly exaggerating when he claimed that China was a despotic state whose principle was fear; where the ruler's authority was unlimited, and where the people, who could be made to do nothing without beatings, were groaning under tyranny.[407] The so-called 'mandate from heaven' did have a moral foundation. It had to be 'earned' and it might be 'lost' by the ruling emperor. The very length of the empire's existence and of the rule of various dynasties indicates that China's governments, overall, were quite successful in keeping their mandates and in holding their empire together. The numerous peasant revolts in China's history are a clear reminder that apparently not everyone was always convinced that government did a very good job.[408] But overall China's 'political system' was an enormous success: up until the Taiping no rebellious group came up with a real alternative for the existing imperial order in which, under patriarchal-monarchical rule, close connections developed between imperial officials and local elites in a system of cooperation, co-optation and complementarity that turned into a very strong mould.

We must be careful not to exaggerate Chinese exceptionalism when it comes to 'controlling from afar'. Actually Great Britain's state probably was more of an exception – also in Western Europe – than the Qing's state. Qing rulers in many respects were not that different from most rulers in the much smaller states of Western Europe before the French Revolution. Indirect rule and all it implied were the norm in most of Western

---

[404]See Wong, *China Transformed*, Part Two, and Thornton, *Disciplining the State*.

[405]For the quotations see Thornton, *Disciplining the State*, 1 and 2.

[406]Pines, *Everlasting Empire*, 3.

[407]These claims are made in Montesquieu's *De l'esprit des lois*. See for a description of Montesquieu's views Spence, *Chan's Great Continent*, 88–95.

[408]See, for example, Deng, *Premodern Chinese Economy*, ch. 4 and appendix J. The most frequent reasons for rebelliousness were economic. See also Pines, *Everlasting Empire*, 260.

Europe too, till the Napoleonic Era. Comparatively speaking, Britain's rulers at the time faced a task, at least at home, that was far easier than that of their Chinese and most of their European counterparts and, on top of that, who would want to sing an unmitigated song of praise for Britain's fiscal-military state, the solution they came up with? It of course is far easier for a central government in which all relevant elites are co-opted and involved to run a fairly small country than it is for a tiny elite of outsiders to run an enormous and very populous country.

On the other hand, in recognizing its overall 'success', one has to be careful – as I am afraid many revisionists studying early modern China are *not* – that one does not confound the 'high' principles of central government in Peking with the often 'low' practices of ruling groups in the provinces and overlook the clear signs of deterioration in the workings of the system. From the end of the eighteenth century, when the empire was bigger and more populous than ever before, signs of a developing crisis of confidence were clearly visible and a growing dissatisfaction with the ruling elites became evident. Such dissatisfaction need not result in actual revolt, although it increasingly did. It often manifested itself in a certain lethargy and apathy among the population. These were phenomena about which many officials and commentators at the time complained. They were to lead to dissolution of central rule along provincial fault lines.[409] Government's infrastructural power weakened as its resources became, relatively speaking, smaller and its tasks bigger. Even revisionists would have a very hard time denying that, at least from the last decades of the eighteenth century onwards, government was not only confronted with an increasing amount of problems, but also began to be less successful in dealing with them. Most scholars agree that China's government was in disarray during the last years of the Qianlong reign. Some claim that trouble had set in earlier.[410] Complaints about corruption increased, as did rebelliousness. Population pressure, over-extension of the empire, its growing diversity, ecological problems: they all made it harder to rule. In the area of bureaucratic initiative and morale, so Rowe writes, 'troubling signs appeared well before this date [1795]'.[411] This is what Madeleine Zelin writes about the situation at the end of the eighteenth century: 'Rational fiscal administration was dead, and informal networks of funding once again became the hallmark of the Chinese bureaucracy.'[412] In many respects the

---

[409]See for discussions of this lethargy and passivity of large parts of the 'excluded' population Kuhn, *Origins of the Modern Chinese State*, and Woodside, *Lost Modernities*. For dissatisfaction see e.g. Hung, 'Contentious peasants'. For the disintegration along provincial lines see Kuhn, *Rebellion and its Enemies*. Many Han Chinese began to no longer consider the Qing 'state' as 'their state'.

[410]The reign of the Qianlong emperor has long been regarded as the golden age of the Qing, apart from its end when the emperor's confidant Ho-shen actually ruled. One now also finds more ambivalent and sometimes even negative interpretations of this reign and of the emperor himself. As Wang puts it: 'Many recent studies recognize that the Qianlong reign, especially its latter part, might not have been as glorious as previously thought.' See Wang, *White Lotus Rebels and South China Pirates*, 8 and 9. See, further, for example, Dunstan, *State or Merchant*, 479, and Elliott, *Emperor Qianlong*.

[411]Rowe, *China's Last Empire*, 88.

[412]Zelin, *Magistrate's Tael*, 301.

Qing Empire in the last decades of the eighteenth century was already facing structural and wide-ranging problems. To again quote Rowe:

> It is undeniable that systemic failures within the Qing empire itself became manifest around the turn of the nineteenth century (Qing rulers and subjects themselves noticed these developments with alarm) which made the nineteenth-century divergence not merely a matter of being left behind by Europe in relative terms but also of an intrinsic and absolute loss of capacity.[413]

Central government during the first half of the nineteenth century did not manage to find a coherent set of strategies to provide lasting, workable solutions for its problems. The granary system started functioning less well, ecological problems became urgent and, related to that, problems in water management. Just when the Qing increasingly had to confront rebellion, it apparently became harder to find funding for the army and keep regional armies in check. Silver started to leave the country whereas opium entered it.[414] Most of those problems were primarily internal and started to become serious *before* Western interference made them worse.

Even in case one would want to describe the period of Jiaqing rule in terms of 'retrenchment after over-stretch' and not as as one of 'crisis' and 'deterioration', as Wang suggests,[415] one cannot avoid concluding that this retrenchment meant a clear diminution of the state's involvement in society – for example, when it comes to centralized operation of the granaries, of water control, defence and public order, and also in the selling of titles, degrees and public offices that now also began to take place at a provincial level. And even if one would not want to talk about retrenchment here, it would to my view be exaggerated to, as Wang does, claim that 'The Qing's final collapse should ... be attributed less to declining state power or deteriorating leadership qualities than to an inexorable process of transdynastic, transnational and global transformations'. The combination of problems China became confronted with was such that 'even the ablest ruler and the strongest government in the premodern world' would have been overwhelmed by them.[416] At least a substantial part of China's problems were homegrown and might have been solved.

If indeed the Qing regarded it as their main task to see to it that their people could 'live in security and wealth', one can only conclude that, from the end of the reign of the Qianlong emperor, they started to fail those people and no longer were up to their own standards. The minimal task of every government is to take care of law and order and deter foreign enemies. The Qing state increasingly failed to provide

---

[413]Rowe, *China's Last Empire*, 149–50.
[414]For brief analyses of the problems that confronted China in the last decades of the eighteenth century see Deng, *China's Political Economy*, ch. 3; Kuhn, *Origins of the Modern Chinese State*, 'Introduction'; Rowe, *China's Last Empire*; idem, 'Introduction: The significance of the Qianlong-Jiaqing transition', and Wang, *White Lotus Rebels and South China Pirates*, 'Introduction' and ch. 1.
[415]Wang, *White Lotus Rebels and South China Pirates*, 253.
[416]Wang, *White Lotus Rebels and South China Pirates*, 13–14.

even these public goods. We, again, are not dealing here with comments after the fact. Increasingly the 'mandate of heaven' of China's rulers became subject to doubt. Qing rule was increasingly attacked domestically. Its legitimacy was bound to be undermined even further when the Qing no longer managed to keep 'the foreign devils' out. As so often success had come with a prize. Their bureaucrats were not able and often not willing to break the hold of the local gentry – in the words of Rankin and Esherick, 'arguably the most unified (though not uniform) elite in the world' in late imperial times.[417] The Qing empire increasingly became an illustration of this claim by Patricia Crone: 'Pre-industrial states had considerable power to *prevent* things from happening, but very little to *make* them happen.'[418]

TAX SYSTEMS AND THEIR TRAJECTORIES

Great Britain as a European outlier

To be able to make meaningful statements about the importance and impact of taxation one needs to know what exactly is taxed and who exactly pays taxes. The main distinction made in this context is that between direct and indirect taxes. In this respect too, from a global perspective, early modern Britain after 1688 was fairly exceptional: indirect taxes had become much more important there than direct ones. Indirect taxes in this case meant excises and customs levied on a wide variety of goods; direct taxes were taxes on land plus various levies on property like windows, carriages, houses, riding horses or domestic servants. Land taxes, *including* other assessed taxes, never amounted to more than 20 per cent of total tax revenue after 1770. If we consider the level of inflation, the absolute amount of money paid by landowners as land tax basically was fairly stable.[419] Land was and continued to be by far the most important source of wealth and income.[420] Britain's landed interests had managed quite well to let other groups of the population shoulder the main tax burden.

Over the period from the beginning of the eighteenth century to the 1840s, no less than 70 to 75 per cent of all tax revenue in Britain was collected via indirect taxation. *Roughly* two-thirds of indirect taxes consisted of excises (50 per cent of total tax revenue) and one-third of customs (25 per cent of total tax revenue).[421] To know what those figures with regard to excise income actually mean, one of course needs to know what taxes counted as excise. An excise strictly speaking is a tax on goods manufactured or grown domestically. It is meant to be a duty on inland goods as distinct from customs levies on imported goods. However, and this is quite relevant for my analysis, this definition

---

[417]Rankin and Esherick, *Chinese Local Elites*, 338.
[418]Crone, *Pre-Industrial Societies*, 57.
[419]See Daunton, *Progress and Poverty*, 507–11.
[420]See e.g. Piketty, *Capital in the Twenty-First Century*, ch. 3.
[421]See Harris, 'Government and the economy', 218. Compare Evans, *Forging of the Modern State*, 411. From the 1820s onwards, the relative importance of customs increased sharply.

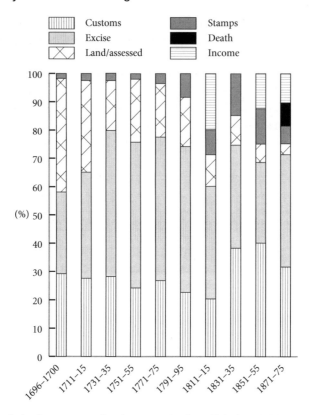

Figure 1 The relative importance of various taxes in Great Britain, 1688–1801, and the United Kingdom, 1802–75.

Based on: Mitchell, *British Historical Statistics*, 575–7 and 581–2.

does not always hold for the period surveyed in this book. Certain imports had come under the management of the Excise, a situation lasting from 1643 to 1825 when most of the excised imports were transferred to Customs. This is how Ashworth describes the changes:

> In 1825 former import excise taxes on wine, foreign, spirits, coffee, cocoa, pepper and tobacco were transferred to customs. This process continued throughout the 1830s until the customs accounted for forty-three per cent of all tax receipts between 1841 and 1845 and the excise a much-reduced rate of twenty-seven per cent.[422]

On the other hand, customs tariffs were reformed. In 1822 customs duties in total amounted to 63 per cent of the total value of imports; in 1825 that was only 38 per cent.[423]

---

[422] Ashworth, *Customs and Excise*, 374.
[423] Ashworth, *Customs and Excise*, 374.

Domestic goods as well as imports in that way became cheaper. Income taxes as we now know them are a latecomer in history. Britain saw their introduction in 1799. They were abolished in 1816, to be reintroduced again in 1842.

The figures with regard to the relative importance of various taxes in preceding paragraphs are rough averages over a long period of time. During major wars, direct taxes could become very important. In the first decade of the eighteenth century, during the War of Spanish Succession, they yielded over 35 per cent of total tax revenue. In the decade from 1800 to 1810, during the Napoleonic Wars, when Britain experimented with income taxes because there was a limit to what government could borrow, they amounted to over 30 per cent of total tax revenue and became known as 'the taxes that beat Napoleon'.[424] If the Napoleonic Wars indeed were, as is often claimed, fought for the defence of property, they were also to a substantial amount paid for *by* the propertied. Up to 60 per cent of all *additional* taxes raised between 1793 and 1815 probably came from the more affluent classes in Britain.[425] Overall excises and customs formed the bulk of Britain's tax revenue during the very long eighteenth century. Over time, one can see some clear shifts, though. The emphasis shifted roughly from land and other assessed taxes in the very beginning to customs then to excises and then to income taxes at the very end. Between 1816, when income tax was abolished, and 1842, when it was reintroduced, the British system was *more* dependent on indirect taxes than at any point since 1688. Income taxes quickly became important after their reintroduction in 1843. In the 1840s, they on average amounted to 6 per cent of annual tax revenue. In the 1850s that was 14 per cent and in the 1890s 15 per cent. In the twentieth century they became really prominent with already 30 per cent in the 1930s.[426]

In the Dutch Republic too, indirect taxes were very important, though less so than in Britain. In comparison to the previous century, when their share of total tax revenue at times had been as high as 70 per cent, their share during the eighteenth century decreased to less than 50 per cent. In 1790 it was 43 per cent.[427] In France, of total taxes collected over the entire eighteenth century, on average, roughly half were direct and roughly half indirect.[428] In Prussia customs and excise duties amounted to almost a third of total government revenue; taxes on salt and tobacco, both subject to a specific tax regime, to about one-tenth.[429] Their importance would increase sharply over the first half of the nineteenth century.[430] To varying degrees they were important all over Europe – almost without exception much more so than in China.

[424]Mathias and O'Brien, 'Taxation in Britain and France', 612.

[425]See O'Brien, 'Triumph and denouement'.

[426]Mathias, *First Industrial Nation*, 462.

[427]'t Hart, 'United Provinces', 320, and Ormrod, *Rise of Commercial Empires*, 22.

[428]Goldstone, *Revolution and Rebellion*, 202–9.

[429]See Henderson, *Studies in the Economic Policy*, ch. 3; North 'Finances and power', and Wilson, 'Prussia as a fiscal-military state'.

[430]Spoerer, *Steuerlast, Steuerinzidenz und Steuerwettbewerb*, 120.

But let us return to Britain and comment on the *absolute* amounts of money involved in various taxes. The most important source of government tax revenue in Britain consisted of excises. At the end of the seventeenth century excises collected by central government amounted to about £1 million. In the period 1781–85 that figure had risen to an annual average of about £6 million. In the period 1820–25 the figure was £29 million, almost five times as high. Then it began to decline: the annual average for the period 1845–50 was 'only' somewhat less than £15 million.[431]

The second important category of tax revenue of Britain's central government in terms of value was income from customs. These too were levied on consumer goods. Taxing *trade*, which is not identical to taxing *traders*, as traders by and large simply passed the costs on to their customers, played a very substantial role in Britain's state finance. I have already indicated that over the eighteenth century, on average, roughly one-quarter of total tax income came from customs. These customs were collected only on foreign trade, as Britain, in contrast to China, had no internal tariffs. In 1715 Britain's government collected about £1.5 million as customs. This figure increased with the passing of time. In the period from 1780 to 1800, on average, it was about £4 million per year. In the first half of the nineteenth century, after the Napoleonic Wars, customs became even more important as a percentage of total tax income and the amounts of money involved increased sharply. For the period between 1825 and 1850 we are talking about a figure of, on average, some £20 million – over 60 million taels.[432] It would of course have been impossible to collect such amounts of customs had not Britain been a very open economy – that is, one where international trade amounted to a substantial part of GDP.[433]

In this respect, too, one must be careful to not simply talk about (Western) Europe as if differences between countries would be irrelevant. In that other main trading nation in North-Western Europe, the Dutch Republic, for example, customs were very low.[434] For the period from 1700 to 1790 net customs revenue in Holland, its main trading province, rarely rose above 5 per cent of total revenue whereas in Britain that was between 20 and 28 per cent. For the Dutch Republic as a whole the sums involved were tiny, fluctuating around the equivalent of £100,000 to £250,000.[435] In principle this money was reserved to pay for the navy, which of course also set a certain limit to its size.

---

[431]The information for the end of the seventeenth century is taken from Daunton, *Progress and Poverty*, 523. The other figures are from Evans, *Forging of the Modern State*, 411.

[432]Evans, *Forging of the Modern State*, 411. The information for 1715 is calculated from Daunton, *Progress and Poverty*, 522–3.

[433]See for the ratio of imports and exports to GDP of the United Kingdom (and France) during the period 1820–1910 Nye, *War, Wine, and Taxes*, ch. 1. As indicated, in the 1820s import excises were turned into customs. One therefore has to be careful to not jump to conclusions with regard to the growth of British international trade too easily.

[434]See Fritschy, 't Hart and Horlings, 'Long-term trends', 58–9. This suggests that merchants had more leverage here than manufacturing interests.

[435]I paraphrase Ormrod, *Rise of Commercial Empires*, 25.

China: The continuing predominance of land taxes and the continued irrelevance of excises and customs

In contrast to Britain, and in fact most of Europe, the basis of China's tax system continued to be direct taxes, or, to be more specific, taxes on land that were paid by its owner. As indicated, over the entire period we do not see much upgrading of land or many changes in the assessments. By and large *nothing* changed in structure, principles and methods of land tax collection. In the seven years between 1650 and 1841 that Beal selected in his overview of tax collection in Qing China, land tax never amounted to less than 74.5 per cent of total official taxes. Until 1725, this percentage was never below 80. Of the official, regular taxes, those on land continued to be the bulk until far into the nineteenth century. The amounts collected were stable and basically only increased with the amount of land used as arable. Until the introduction of the so-called *likin* tax in the 1850s, trade was hardly touched by taxes, which makes a fascinating and extremely important difference with mercantile countries in the Western world, in particular Britain.[436] What we see are an agrarian state, China, supposed to be anti-merchant, that primarily taxes land, and a mercantile state, Britain, that primarily taxes trade.

When we talk about taxes on goods, for early modern China, salt is by far the most important. In 1650, taxes on salt yielded 2 million taels. In 1812, this figure had risen to its highest level for the period we discuss here, over 6 million taels or £2 million. As a percentage of total taxes, the tax on salt amounted to between less than 10 and almost 15 per cent.[437] The importance of salt for the Chinese state, however, resided not only in the salt taxes as such. Salt merchants were very prominent among those merchants who gave big contributions to government – or, maybe one should say, were expected to do this. According to Woodside these contributions 'provided the extra-budgetary revenues that sustained Chi'en-lung's [i.e. Qianlong's] war machine'.[438]

As Figure 1 shows customs were always an important source of revenue for Britain's government that, over the entire period discussed here, never yielded less than about one-fifth of total tax revenue and sometimes amounted to almost half of it. Considering what we have already said about government revenue in China, the importance of customs can only have been less there. For those who hold a traditional view of the economy of Qing China, the relative unimportance of customs revenue will not come as a surprise: in that view the economy of Qing China was closed. To a certain extent this is untrue. Complaints about China's 'isolation' mostly originate among Europeans who would have liked to trade more with a country they considered an interesting but stubbornly uncooperative trade partner. Complaints were often exaggerated. European trade from 1753 onwards was not, as the story normally goes, confined to Canton. There also were possibilities to exchange goods with Chinese traders in, for example, Macao and Amoy,

---

[436]See for the importance of different tax categories during Qing rule Beal, *Origin of Likin*, ch. 1; Lin, *China Upside Down*, 280, and Wang, *Land Taxation*, 72 and 74.
[437]Beal, *Origin of Likin*, 3.
[438]Woodside, 'Chi'en-lung reign', 272–3.

and of course in many places *outside* China. Moreover, trade of Europeans with China was only part of that country's foreign trade.[439] Its trade with other countries, though never completely unproblematic, often was more 'free' and more sizeable than that with Europe. I want to emphasize that I indeed mean 'trade' when I discuss China's foreign economic exchange. The traditional idea that this exchange would basically always have been a kind of tribute payment, although that definitely did exist, is a cliché that had better be forgotten.

Because so little is known about Chinese trade – in contrast to Great Britain's trade in the same period – some extra information might be welcome and helpful. Let's us start with overseas trade. Trade with Japan that had provided China with huge amounts of silver in the second half of the sixteenth and the first half of the seventeenth century, and next to that with copper, clearly diminished over the eighteenth century until it became quite irrelevant.[440] There was a lively trade with various parts of South Asia, from which China in particular imported food.[441] Then there was China's trade with Latin America. In particular, the bullion-versus-silk trade on the Manila galleons has aroused renewed interest among global historians who now tend to refer to it as quite substantial.[442] Trade with India, via British traders, became increasingly important. At first, from the 1780s onwards, China exported raw cotton to that country. Then increasingly opium became predominant in Sino-Indian exchange as India's main export product to China.[443] From the last decades of the eighteenth century onwards, the United States became an important trade partner for China. A very substantial part of their imports consisted of tea, although less so than in the case of Britain. They mainly exported silver and Turkish opium into China.[444]

To be 'complete', one must also include China's foreign trade over land. Trade with Russia over land, in principle, was strictly regulated and concentrated in one place, Kiakhta, in a way that strongly reminds of the situation in Canton, although the system there in effect was more relaxed. In principle this trade was meant to be barter, which implies that, at least officially, there were no precious metals or other kinds of money involved. It was conducted in a more amicable and respectful way than trade at Canton. China had a partner relation with Russia, the only country in the world with which it had made official treaties.[445] Furs were the most important exports from Russia to China.

---

[439]I will deal with this trade on the coming pages.

[440]See Cullen, *A history of Japan*, under 'foreign trade', and Deng, 'Foreign staple trade'.

[441]See Blussé, *Visible Cities*, and Lieberman, *Strange Parallels. Volume 1*.

[442]See for this trade Schurz, *Manila Galleon*, and for a later period Legarda, *After the Galleons*. For an analysis of exchange between China and Mexico see Schell, 'Silver symbiosis'. See also Deng, 'Foreign staple trade', that deals with a wider range of trade connections.

[443]See Bowen, *Business of Empire* under 'India' and 'China'. From the end of the eighteenth century onwards the India-China trade became the core activity of this company. For cotton in particular see Bowen, 'British exports of raw cotton'. For opium imports into China from the 1820s onwards see Wong, *Deadly Dreams*, ch. 16.

[444]See, for example, Dolin, *When America First Met China*; Irigoin, 'End of a silver era', and Mazumdar, 'Chinese Hong merchants'. For the rise of tea exports to the United States see Zhuang, *Tea, Silver, Opium and War*, ch. 3.4.

[445]For Sino-Russian (trade) relations see Fletcher, 'Sino-Russian relations'; Hsü, *Rise of Modern China*, 107–22, and Mancall, 'Kiakhta trade'.

At the end of the eighteenth century, they accounted for 75 per cent of total Russian exports to China. Before that, this share had even been higher. Over the first decades of the nineteenth century woollens became more important. In 1850, they amounted to 65 per cent of total exports, whereas the percentage of furs then had declined to only 23 per cent. In the other direction, the major export from China to Russia had been cotton. Silk exports had also been substantial but declined from 24 per cent of total Chinese export to Russia to only 12 per cent at the end of the century. The Chinese also exported substantial amounts of rhubarb to Russia. But as in China's export to the West, the main item was to become tea. Over the period 1760–1785, 15 per cent of Russia's imports from China consisted of tea; by 1825 this figure had risen to 87 per cent and in 1850 it was 90 per cent. There were trade contacts with regions in Central Asia.[446] Finally, there was overland trade with Tibet, to which country the Chinese exported mainly tea from Yunnan in return for horses that went to Yunnan and Sichuan;[447] with Burma[448] and with Siam[449] from where cotton was imported; with Vietnam,[450] and with Korea, a country with which there were long-lasting tribute relations.[451] There was a specific relation with what we in the West call 'Manchuria'. Trade between 'China proper' and Manchuria was considered like foreign trade, with tariffs and checks.[452] As Lord Macartney writes in his journal, goods imported from or through Manchuria to China were taxed with a moderate custom whereas exports from China to 'Tartary' were duty free.[453] Only in 1772 did the Qing government definitely abolish all restrictions – that were meant to protect Manchurian consumers – on transporting soybeans and bean cakes by sea out of their 'homeland'.[454]

China was not 'closed': it exchanged commodities with many parts of the world. The economic historian of course would like to know the value of that trade. According to Deng, China's exports during the 1820s and 1830s amounted to 9.8–9.9 million taels per year. That would be 1 gram of silver per capita.[455] Quite recently Sugihara produced some interesting figures.[456] According to him total exports from Guangdong in 1840 would

---

[446]See for some figures Perdue, *China Marches West*, 259–62 and 306. See for background information Millward, *Eurasian Crossroads*.

[447]See e.g. Giersch, *Asian Borderlands*.

[448]See for a first general introduction Lieberman, *Strange Parallels. Volume One*, ch. 2 and its references.

[449]See Cushman, *Fields from the Sea*.

[450]See for a first general introduction Lieberman, *Strange Parallels. Volume One*, ch. 4 and its references.

[451]See Chun, 'Sino-Korean tributary relations'; Hamashita, 'Tribute and treaties'; Larsen, *Tradition, Treaties and Trade*, and Lee, 'Re-evaluation of the Choson Dynasty's trade relationship'.

[452]See e.g. Isett, *State, Peasant, and Merchant*, chs 8 and 9.

[453]Cranmer-Byng, *Embassy to China*, 250.

[454]See Xue, 'A "fertiliser revolution"?', 202 and 209. For intervention in Manchuria's trade and economy see e.g. Isett, *State, Peasant, and Merchant*, chs 8 and 9. We will discuss the situation in Manchuria extensively later on. See pages 403–5.

[455]Deng, 'Miracle or mirage?', paragraph 2.1 and table 11. For figures in the same order of magnitude see Lin, *China Upside Down*, 65; Morse, *Gilds of China*, 82, and Wong, *Deadly Dreams*, 371. According to a contemporary estimate China's total exports in 1837 amounted to 35 million dollars. See Hu, *Concise History of Chinese Economic Thought*, 524.

[456]Sugihara, 'Resurgence of intra-Asian trade'.

have been worth less than £4 million. Total intra-Asian trade in that same year, measured by estimates of the trade between six main ports in six main regions in Asia, in his broad and optimistic estimate had a value of £24.55 million, whereas (overseas) exports to the West at that time had a value of £18.70 million. Sugihara wants to use these figures to show that intra-Asian trade was big or at least not insubstantial. I think he fails to do so. Foreign trade, including re-exports and trade with Ireland, of Great Britain alone, with some 25 million inhabitants, in that year amounted to some £125 million.[457]

Most calculations of China's international trade focus on its overseas trade. Including overland trade would definitely not change the overall picture. There are estimates of the value of trade with Russia, for example, for various moments in time. In the 1770s it had a total turnover of 2.5 million roubles. In 1800, that had increased to 7.5 million roubles. In the period from 1824 to 1830 it varied from 5.5 million to 7.8 million roubles per year. In the middle of the nineteenth century it had increased further to 16 million roubles per year.[458] As a rouble at the time was roughly half a tael in terms of silver weight, even in the 1850s total trade between Russia and China amounted to only 8 million taels, or less than £3 million. These figures are not impressive. Central Asian trade was even less. Here the value of traded goods really was tiny, at least for the first half of the eighteenth century for which I found figures: its 'normal' value can be expressed in terms of tens of thousands of taels. I did not come across a year in which it was over 200,000 taels. Overland trade with Tibet, India and Korea also was of minor importance, relatively speaking.[459] The conclusion is inescapable that *as compared to total GDP* the total value of its foreign and especially its intercontinental trade was quite small. In that respect Qing China *did* have a fairly closed economy. Whatever the exact figures may have been, as a percentage of GDP foreign trade in Qing China was and continued to be minimal till the very end of the dynasty's rule. For total foreign trade we have to think in terms of 1 or 2 per cent of GDP at best.[460] In the end that need not come as a real surprise considering the enormous internal market of the country with a couple of hundreds of millions of inhabitants, the low level of wealth of all the countries involved and the very high transportation costs.

---

[457]Evans, *Forging of the Modern State*, 415–6.

[458]See Kahan, *The Plow, the Hammer and the Knout*, 234–5, and Avery, *Tea Road*, 132. According to Fletcher, Sino-Russian trade peaked in 1819 with 16 million roubles. See his 'Sino-Russian relations', 319.

[459]Qing rulers thwarted efforts by the British to create trade relations with Tibet and China. See Dabringhaus, *Qing-Imperium*, 188–9, and Teltscher, *High Road to China*, passim.

[460]For structure, size and importance of foreign trade in Qing China, especially with Europeans, till the country was 'opened' see, in alphabetical order, Dermigny, *La Chine et L'Occident*; Eastman, *Family, Fields and Ancestors*, 123–39; Feuerwerker, *Studies in the Economic History of Late Imperial China*, 11; Greenberg, *British Trade*; Huang, 'Chinese maritime customs'; Hsü, *Rise of Modern China*, 139–220; Hung, 'Imperial China and capitalist Europe'; Lee, 'Trade and economy'; Liu, *Wrestling for Power*, 251, table AD16; Murphey, *Outsiders*, chs 7 to 12; Osterhammel, *China und die Weltgemeinschaft*, chs 7 and 11; Sugihara, 'Resurgence of intra-Asian trade'; Van Dyke, *Canton Trade* and *Merchants of Canton and Macao*; Wills, *China and Maritime Europa* and Xu and Wu, *Chinese Capitalism*, 395–9. For specific information on the eighteenth century see Mazumdar, *Sugar and Society*, ch. 2, where she – against her own intentions! – shows that China's overseas trade was very small as compared to total overseas trade of Western nations. For figures for the period after its 'opening' see Chapter 1 notes 467–8.

Again, people at the time knew that China's trade was big in absolute but small in relative terms. Marjoribanks, a former president of the Select Committee of Supercargoes at Canton, who had lived in China for seventeen years, declared in 1830 that the 'Chinese were as independent as any government in the world of foreign trade'.[461] He was not the only expert holding this opinion. In the early 1830s, a certain John Phipps estimated the value of the *entire* foreign trade of China, including the junk trade, at $70 million to $80 million per year. That would be less than £20 million or some 50 million to 60 million taels. Per Chinese this would amount to some 5 grams of silver.[462] Régis-Évariste Huc (1813–60), a French missionary who travelled through China and Tibet, in the 1840s regarded international trade, and in particular international trade with Westerners, as completely irrelevant for the Chinese empire as a whole. In his view it would not have any lasting effects on the country's economy if the trade with Westerners would stop from one moment to the other. In all probability, so he claims, people in its interior would not even notice.[463] In the 1790s tea had already become by far the most important export product of China. Sir George-Leonard Staunton, who accompanied Macartney on his mission, nevertheless thought that: 'People in China drink so much tea that the prices on Chinese markets would hardly decline when the Europeans would stop drinking it'.[464] At the end of the 1840s, Robert Fortune, who had travelled through China for various years, could still claim: 'But as it is with tea, so it is with silk – the quantity exported bears but a small proportion to that consumed by the Chinese themselves.'[465] In 1880 when, to be fair, exports were much higher, they amounted to some 40 per cent of total production according to Chang.[466] After China's 'opening', foreign trade overall clearly increased and in certain sectors there even was strong growth.[467] But even so, China's international trade still was quite marginal at the end of the nineteenth century. I fail to see examples of a systematic policy of government to increase it.

A modicum of common sense would suffice to see that intercontinental trade taking place on a couple of tiny ships per year, with a tonnage that in total did not surpass a couple of hundred thousand at the utmost – or for that matter overland trade with China – is not very likely to have had a fundamental impact on an economy of hundreds of millions of people. It was small in whatever way one wants to measure it. Let me again present some figures to put things in perspective: Great Britain's exports in 1840 had a value of about £50 million – some $200 million. Its imports had a value of some £75 million – some $300 million. Great Britain then had a population of about

---

[461]Greenberg, *British Trade*, 43.

[462]Phipps, *Practical Treatise*, 272. I found this reference in Greenberg, *British Trade*, 16.

[463]Huc, *L'empire Chinois*, 348.

[464]I found this comment in Peyrefitte, *L'empire immobile*, 337. The translation is mine.

[465]Fortune, *Tea Districts, I*, 12. For the year 1840 the total value of tea exported from China is estimated at no more than, at best, 0.3 per cent of China's GDP. I base this figure on estimates provided by Fang, 'Growth of commodity circulation', 175.

[466]Chang, *Income of the Chinese Gentry*, 304.

[467]See Deng, *China's Political Economy*, 107–14; Keller, Li and Shiue, 'Evolution of domestic trade flows'; Lyons, *China Maritime Customs*, and Maddison, *Chinese Economic Performance*, 88 and 165–7. Imports overall grew much faster than exports.

16 million. If wants to add Ireland to the calculations, its population at that time was about 8 million. China at the time, with, if we accept Phipps' estimate that is higher than that by Deng and Sugihara, a total *overseas* foreign trade of at best $80 million, counted more than 400 million inhabitants. Whereas the value of China's foreign overseas trade in this high estimate was some 5 grams of silver per capita, the value of the foreign trade of the United Kingdom at the time amounted to some 550 grams of silver per capita. China's junk trade in the 1830s has been estimated at 80,000 tons by John Crawfurd, according to Sugihara 'one of the best informed Westerners' at the time. Sugihara then adds, to underpin his thesis, that this is more than 'the total tonnage of English East India Company's ships [that] entered into Canton'.[468] That may very well be the case but total shipping tonnage registered in Britain at the time amounted to some 2.5 million tons.[469] In the same article Sugihara points out that total inter-Asian trade would have amounted to £53.25 million in 1840, clearly suggesting that is very substantial.[470] Here too a more explicitly comparative and global perspective would have been helpful. Of a total world population in 1840 of about 1.1 billion people, some 750 million were living in Asia.[471] That means that this intra-Asian trade, part of which actually was in Western hands, amounted to some 8 grams of silver per Asian. All these rough estimates point in the same direction and their overall outcomes are impossible to refute by more precise figures and calculations. All this of course need not mean much for China's customs revenue. Small amounts of trade can yield a lot of it, whereas large amounts of trade do not mean much if they are hardly taxed. In that respect the situation in China again was very different from that in Britain. It was only in 1858 that a special, separate organization was introduced for maritime customs on foreign trade. Before that, internal customs and those collected in Canton on foreign overseas trade had been combined. As is always the case in economic history of the early modern era, we come across differing estimates in the literature. But – and this is what matters for our argument – they all are *very* low as compared to figures we have for Britain. The various, differing estimates of *total* customs income, that I found, all are in the same order of magnitude. For the period from 1753 to the end of 1840s, they all hover between 4 million and 6 million taels.[472] Most customs revenue was collected on coastal and riverine junk trade. Part of it was levied at stations at several overland routes. The bulk was collected on internal, domestic trade.[473] Gernet claims that at the end of the eighteenth century commercial taxes on internal trade reached 4 million taels as against 650,000 taels for the revenue of the maritime customs.[474] If we may believe Zhuang, up to the eve of the Opium War

[468]Sugihara, 'Resurgence of intra-Asian trade', 147.

[469]Evans, *Forging of the Modern State*, 412.

[470]Sugihara, 'Resurgence of intra-Asian trade', 166. See also Yuping, 'Steady customs duties', 85–87.

[471]Maddison, *World Economy*, 175.

[472]See e.g. Beal, *Origin of likin*, 3; Deng, 'Continuation and efficiency', 345; Hsü, *Rise of Modern China*, 61; Lin, *China Upside Down*, 280; Wang, *White Lotus Rebels and South China Pirates*, 194–5, and Wang, *Land Taxation*, 72 and the information in note 790.

[473]For the organization of China's Customs at the time see Huang, 'Chinese maritime customs', and Lin, *China Upside Down*, 140–1.

[474]Gernet, *History of Chinese Civilisation*, 485.

the annual duty of the Canton customs authority was about 1.5 million taels, which, according to him, was about 3 per cent of the annual revenue of the Qing government.[475] If one wants to look at it from a broader perspective, one might claim that official duties on goods were not the only government revenue generated by trade. Van Dyke in his first book on the Canton trade writes that duties collected on imports rose from 780,000 taels in 1828 to over 1.2 million taels in 1832, while duties collected on exports increased too. He, however, also refers to over 450,000 taels that were collected as port fees under the Canton system in the 1830s.[476] What matters here is that from a macro, GDP perspective, these sums are all tiny. Trade with Russia in Kiakhta was supposed to be duty free and did not yield the Qing government any income. In the tea trade with Tibet, government collected some revenue via the sale of licences.

The figures given with regard to custom revenue refer only to 'regular' levies. Besides these levies – and sometimes *instead of* them – there were the so-called 'surplus quotas' that were paid directly to the Imperial Household. Here again I can only give some 'isolated' figures. In the period from 1796 to 1821, the emperor and his household gained 855,000 taels from the Canton trade. At that time, all surplus-quotas together, those on internal trade as well as those on coastal trade, annually amounted to some 2 million taels.[477] On top of that there will have been every kind of squeeze and extortion.[478] To show how complicated matters actually were, I can probably do no better than extensively quote from a book published in 1918 by the man who knows more about the topic than anybody else, Hosea Ballou Morse, referring to the situation in Canton in 1837:

The present author has made a careful calculation on the basis of the rates of duty reported to Sir H. Pottinger, of the amount of duties collected on goods imported and exported by British and American ships in 1837 and has found it to amount to just over 6,500,000 Tls; if we allow Tls 500,000 for the legal trade under other foreign flags, and the very moderate estimate of 1,000,000 for opium, which was never included in statistics or in report we have Tls 8,000,000 as a safe estimate of the amount collected by the Hoppo from the trade under foreign flags alone. We may, further, estimate a sum of Tls 2,000,000 for the receipts from Chinese shipping at the ports of Kwantung, including besides Canton such busy marts as Wuchow Chaochowfu (Swatow) Kongmoon, Tinpak, Kiungchow (Hoihow) and Limchowfu (Pakhoi). The resultant total, ten million taels, includes only customs duties. To it must be added the port dues and gifts constantly demanded from the Hong merchants who enjoyed the monopoly of foreign trade and their innumerable gratuities to be paid to smaller officials, who might find means to block the smooth course of trade, and who must in turn gratify the Hoppo, if they would retain their posts. In short, we may confidently declare that, while the official assessment of the

---

[475]Zhuang, *Tea, Silver, Opium and War*, 16. For lower estimates see Xu and Wu, *Chinese Capitalism*, 395–9.

[476]Van Dyke, *Canton Trade*, 33 and 113.

[477]See Chang, 'Economic role', 256–9, and Torbert, *Ch'ing Imperial Household Department*, 96–103.

[478]For examples see Morse, *Trade and Administration*, ch. 9, and Van Dyke, *Canton Trade*, under 'corruption'.

Hoppo's post was less than one million taels a year, the distribution fund must have much exceeded ten million taels.[479]

We lack the unambiguous data we would like to have. But all the data we do have with regard to total official 'customs revenue', in the widest sense of the word, and all circumstantial evidence points in the same direction. As compared to British customs revenue that rose to a couple of tens of millions of pounds sterling annually, China's customs revenue, that never exceeded a couple of million taels, the bulk of which was levied on internal and coastal trade, was really tiny but higher and more than of a nuisance than in Great Britain, where internal customs were unknown. In the case of the taxes collected on salt 'the demarcation line of salt districts tended to overlap with rigid, far-fetched political boundaries that were dictated by topography and overlooked such economic factors as production and transportation costs' and show a 'conspicuous lack of market rationality'.[480] Here customs certainly hampered consumption. Adding the total amount of money that was involved in the tributes paid by vassal states, by the way, does not change the picture. Compared to total GDP they were absolutely irrelevant.

Britain was a fairly small island with a fairly small population and China a huge country with relatively less direct access to overseas trade and with an immense population. So, other things being equal, it need not come as a surprise that foreign trade would have been less important for its economy than for that of Britain. But on top of that, and very importantly, as we will see, the governments of both countries had quite differing views on the function and importance of foreign trade. In China government was less occupied with foreign trade. Often it was also less positive about it, which, however, as we saw, did not show in the level of the customs it levied. Fang is right: 'Customs revenue was regarded as hardly worthy of notice, and trade with foreigners little more than a gracious concession.'[481] Foreign trade was closely watched and regularly interfered with but we see no *systematic* effort to maximize revenue or to manipulate it via tariffs, as was the case in mercantilist countries. It makes no sense to call the Qing's foreign trade policies 'mercantilist' as, for example, Westad does.[482] Import taxes appeared somewhat arbitrary and were often changed without rational calculation, but as a rule import tariffs were low.[483] According to Chang, exports were not taxed at all during the Qing period.[484]

---

[479]Morse, *International Relations of the Chinese Empire. II*, 5–6.
[480]Wang, *White Lotus Rebels and South China Pirates*, 67.
[481]Fang, 'Retarded development', 396–7.
[482]Westad, *Restless Empire*, 37.
[483]I can here refer to all the references to 'Duty' in Morse's *Chronicles of the East India Company* and his *International Relations of the Chinese Empire*. See, for an example, Zhuang, *Tea, Silver, Opium and War*, 18, where it reads that the duty European merchants had to pay on their goods on average was about 4 per cent of their value. On top of that, there was a tax for vessels of about 3,000 taels or £1,000. Then finally there was a category called 'additional taxes' of about 2,000 taels per ship plus a charge of 3 per cent destined for the guild of the Hong. In 1809 that charge *in total* yielded 700,000 taels. Of course, as always, one ought to know what was actually charged *on top of* these official levies and that did not go to central government.
[484]Chang, 'Evolution of Chinese thought', 63.

That certainly is somewhat too 'optimist'; in any case in the middle of the nineteenth century there was an export duty on tea of (officially) some 10 per cent.[485]

Some further comments on indirect taxes in Great Britain

Considering the predominant role of excises and customs in Britain's tax system – both taxes on goods – it might be useful to have a closer look at the *kind* of goods that were taxed. I already indicated that it was basically consumer goods. That still is a very broad category. For our analysis of government intervention in the economy it is relevant to have more precise information about what kind of goods were taxed; how heavily were they taxed; how important these taxes were for total government revenue, and what the philosophy was behind collecting them.[486] We can get a clear and fairly representative idea of the *kind* of consumer goods that were taxed and of their relative importance in total tax revenue by looking at data for the period 1788–92.[487] During that period 40 per cent of *total* tax revenue was yielded by taxes on beer, malt, hops, wine, liquor and tea. The importance of alcohol is striking. Foreign spirits were heavily taxed: on rum, in the period from 1788 to 1792, on average a custom tax was collected of 60 per cent. The tax on sherry was 27 per cent.[488] Overall, tariffs on French wines were virtually prohibitive from the last quarter of the seventeenth century onwards. Domestic beverages were not spared though. During the Napoleonic Wars, excises accounted for more than 40 per cent of the price of beer in London.[489] Beer consumption was massive. In England and Wales during the period from 1800 to 1830 it was on average some thirty gallons per year per capita. For the United Kingdom the figure was some twenty gallons for the period from 1830 to 1850.[490] Excises and tariffs on sugar, some 3 per cent of total tax revenue, to a large extent also were a tax on alcohol as sugar was massively used in the production of alcoholic beverages like rum. That would bring taxes on alcoholic beverages even closer to half of all taxes.[491] In 1841, to give an example near the end of our period, taxes on spirits amounted to 15 per cent of total tax revenue, taxes on malt and sugar both 10 per cent, those on tea 8 per cent and finally those on tobacco 7 per cent.[492] Beer duties had been abolished in 1830.[493] But overall, it is striking that tax

---

[485]Wong, *Deadly Dreams*, 343 and Lyons, *China Maritime Customs*, 32–3. Wong thinks that taxes on imports and exports were an important source of revenue for the government. See that same page. Morse claims that 'at the end of the monopoly days' (i.e. of the East India Company) actual levies on tea *exports* were much higher and could be as high as 30 per cent of the ordinary cost price in Canton. See Morse, *International Relations of the Chinese Empire. Volume One*, 80–1.

[486]For general comments about the topics discussed in the coming paragraphs see, Horstman, 'Taxation in the Zenith'; O'Brien, 'Political economy', and idem, 'Triumph and denouement'.

[487]See O'Brien, 'Political economy', 11. Almost all taxes were very substantially increased in the course of the wars with France. For those increases see idem, 'Triumph and denouement'.

[488]O'Brien, 'Political economy', 11.

[489]Mathias, 'Taxation and industrialization', 125.

[490]Burnett, *Plenty and Want*, 27,

[491]Nye, *War, Wine, and Taxes*, 72–3.

[492]Horstman, 'Taxation in the Zenith', 135–6.

[493]Mathias, 'Taxation and industrialization', 128.

revenues were and continued to be concentrated heavily on a few items among which alcohol remained very important.[494] Great Britain, by the way, was not the European state that to a large extent ran on alcohol. Government in Russia garnered on average one-third of its revenue from liquor between 1767 and 1863. Its defence budget was so dependent on the income of liquor tax farming that the country has been called an 'alcoholic empire'.[495]

Other products apart from alcohol that were popular in the eyes of most Western European tax-collectors were salt, imported food drugs like sugar, tea, coffee or cocoa, and tobacco. Salt is a commodity that was always taxed heavily all over the globe in pre-industrial times. Britain in this respect was no exception. In the period 1788 to 1792, to return to that same example, excise on salt in Britain was no less than 70 per cent.[496] Salt duties were abolished in 1825.[497] Sugar was heavily taxed. In the period from 1788 to 1792, on average, 34 per cent customs were collected on muscovado sugar, which was the basis of rum. That, as we saw, also was heavily taxed.[498] It nevertheless became much cheaper with the passing of time.[499] Together taxes on salt and sugar yielded almost 10 per cent of total tax revenue at the time. Then of course there is tea. In the eighteenth century tax dominated its retail price.[500] Up to 1784, the customs duty on tea ranged from 75.9 per cent to 127.5 per cent *ad valorem*. Then with the famous Commutation Act of 1784, it was lowered to 12.5 per cent. Nevertheless, it had become cheaper over the century: its price after tax between 1725 and the early 1770s, more than halved.[501] What normally gets less attention is the fact that only twenty years after that famous act, the duty had again risen to 100 per cent, an increase that was not revoked after the Napoleonic Wars. In the period from 1815 to 1850 the tea duty on average was even somewhat over 100 per cent.[502] The 1840s were the period with the heaviest taxation in the whole history of tea in Britain, in any case, when we look at the flat-rate duties paid per weight on Bohea and Congou tea, the latter generally drunk by the working classes. They amounted to 350 and 280 per cent of the prime costs.[503] All this did not deter the British from drinking their favourite beverage. The fact that its overall price nevertheless tended to decline will certainly not have been innocent to that: over the period 1787–1820 the price on average was some 30 per cent below that of 1725.[504] Over the period

---

[494]See for figures for 1788–92, 1792–1815 and 1841 absolute figures in money O'Brien, 'Political economy', 11; O'Brien, 'Triumph and denouement', 169–72, and Horstman, 'Taxation in the Zenith', 135–6.
[495]Herlihy, 'Revenue', 188.
[496]O'Brien, 'Political economy', 11.
[497]Mathias, 'Taxation and industrialization', 128.
[498]O'Brien, 'Political economy', 11.
[499]See Shammas, *Pre-Industrial Consumer*, 81: 'Over the course of the seventeenth century, the price [of sugar] went down by half and between 1700 and 1750 the price went down by another third.'
[500]Harley, 'Trade: discovery, mercantilism and technology', 183–4. For further information on tea, coffee and chocolate, see Burnett, *Liquid Pleasures*, and Schneider, 'Neuen Getränke'.
[501]Harley 'Trade: discovery, mercantilism and technology', 184.
[502]Wong, *Deadly Dreams*, 344–5.
[503]Burnett, *Plenty and Want*, 23.
[504]Zhuang, *Tea, Silver, Opium and War*, 127.

1820 to 1860 it almost halved inclusive duty.[505] The amounts of money we are talking about are huge. Over the period 1711–1810 Britain's government in total collected £77 million as tax revenue on tea.[506] Duties on tea in the United Kingdom in the 1830s yielded, on average, some £3 million. Over the period 1840–1860, on average, this figure had increased to over £5 million per year. That was over 8 per cent of tax revenue of the United Kingdom and a sum of money large enough to cover two-thirds of the costs of the Royal Navy.[507] After the 1850s, tea from the colonies India and Ceylon began to become important on the British market. In a couple of decades it almost completely wiped away tea imports from China.

Coffee, which might have become an important drink in Britain too and which at times was drunk in large quantities, in the end was not to become as 'English' as tea. Its consumption increased sharply in the first decades of the nineteenth century and almost caught up with that of tea in the beginning of the 1840s, when they both were about one pound per head per year for the entire United Kingdom. But we then see a sharp increase of tea consumption to nine pounds per capita in 1930, whereas coffee consumption per capita declined to less than one pound.[508] It too was taxed, though in the end less than tea and yielded much lower total revenue.[509] Taxing tobacco also became, and for quite some time continued to be, an important source of income for government in Britain. Over the entire period from 1793 to 1815, it provided over £11 million in tax revenues on a total of tax revenue for that period of £542 million.[510] Customs on tobacco were very high. In the period, for example, from 1788 to 1792, they averaged 83 per cent. In Britain, just like in the Dutch Republic, government collected its levies on tobacco via all sorts of taxes on the product. In the rest of Europe it often did so via monopolies that were farmed to private collectors. That was the case in, for example, Portugal, Castile, various regions in Italy, France and Austria. There taxing the product as such occurred only late in our period: in Austria only in 1784, in France in 1810 and in Italy only in 1862. Between 1750 and 1788, tobacco 'taxes' amounted to 4.6 to 6.5 per cent of income of the government of France. On average for early modern European states this percentage hovered between 3 and 6 per cent.[511] Notwithstanding heavy taxation tobacco too became much cheaper. Between 1600 and 1700, for example, the price of a pound of tobacco in Britain decreased from 30 to 40 shillings per pound to less than 1 shilling.[512]

Let me, as final examples of overseas imports from other continents, refer to raw silk and porcelain. Adam Smith already pointed out that raw silk was heavily taxed.[513] During the entire period of the Revolutionary and Napoleonic Wars customs duties

---

[505]Wong, *Deadly Dreams*, 344–5.
[506]Macfarlane and Macfarlane, *Green Gold*, 77.
[507]See Wong, *Deadly Dreams*, 343–55.
[508]Burnett, *Liquid Pleasures*, 81, figure 4.1.
[509]O'Brien, 'Triumph and denouement', 170. During the Revolutionary and Napoleonic Wars coffee taxes yielded only about £3 million, about one-tenth of taxes yielded by tea.
[510]O'Brien, 'Triumph and denouement', 169.
[511]See for this information with regard to tobacco Schmidt, 'Tabacco', 599–600.
[512]Piuz, 'Effets du commerce d'outre-mer', 940.
[513]Smith, *Inquiry into the Nature and Causes of the Wealth of Nations*, 906.

on its imports yielded £1.8 million.[514] Porcelain imported by the East India Company, at the beginning of the eighteenth century, was subject to an import duty of 12.5 per cent. In the 1770s that was over 33 per cent and by the end of the century, a duty was levied of half of the auction value.[515] The *number* of pieces imported was staggering. In 1721, when it reached its highest point of the first half of the eighteenth century, 2 million pieces were imported. The *duties* this yielded, however, were surprisingly low. They amounted to £104,370. Porcelain simply was not an expensive product and it became even cheaper. Bulk imports of 'Chinese wares' by the East India Company ended in 1791. It was no longer a significant source of tax revenue. Taxes on it yielded less than £500,000 during the entire period of the Revolutionary and Napoleonic Wars.[516] European porcelain was hit by import prohibitions. Those lasted until 1775. After that date, government started to collect import duties: On French porcelain they initially were no less than 150 per cent. After 1786 they were reduced to 12 per cent of sale value, which meant serious competition from France. Japanese and Chinese lacquer-ware also was heavily taxed to enable British substitutes to conquer the domestic market.[517] If we add up direct taxes and taxes on alcohol, salt and tropical imports, we have almost covered all tax revenue of British government at the end of the eighteenth century. The remaining 10 per cent came from taxes on simple manufactured products like candles, leather, soap, glass and printed ware. All in all, in the period 1788–92 taxes on *consumer goods* yielded more than £11 million, which was almost two-thirds of total tax income and almost as much as total land tax revenue for all China at the time.

What is striking about the goods mentioned is that they were neither absolute necessities nor – or in case of the imported tropical goods one should probably say *less and less* – real luxury goods. That is in line with the prevailing tax philosophy that read that in principle necessities of life should not, or only lightly, be taxed.[518] In Britain most taxes were collected on the sale of fairly ordinary products. That so much of them could be collected shows that Britain already was a fairly monetized, open and rich economy. According to Jan de Vries a *lower*-class household in Britain in the second half of the eighteenth century might already have spent as much as 15 per cent of its income on non-European import goods.[519] They were becoming more 'normal' over time. Increases in customs income on tropical goods were more indicative of the fact that population, and thereby total consumption, increased than of increases in per capita consumption. Per

---

[514]O'Brien, 'Triumph and denouement', 170.
[515]For the information with regard to porcelain see Berg and Clifford, 'Luxury', 1107.
[516]See O'Brien, 'Triumph and denouement', 169–71.
[517]Berg, *Luxury and Pleasure*, 79.
[518]See e.g. Berg and Clifford, 'Luxury'.
[519]De Vries, 'Industrious revolution and economic growth', 59. Compare De Vries, *Industrious Revolution*, 162, where the author claims that the new non-European products absorbed some 10 per cent of annual income of lower-class households in England by the late eighteenth century. For consumption of goods like beer, tea, coffee and sugar, see Burnett, *Plenty & Want*, part 1. For an analysis of the importance of exotic goods for consumers in Western Europe see McCants, 'Exotic goods'.

capita the consumption of tea, sugar and tobacco, in contrast to that of coffee, remained almost unchanged between 1800 and 1850.[520]

It is of course interesting to find out who actually in the end paid these taxes. Indirect taxes to a large extent were passed on to the consumer. In the case of excises that is fairly obvious. To quote John Brewer: 'Excises might have pinched more cruelly: there was no tax on clothing, or on basic foodstuffs apart from salt, and cheap candles and cheap soap paid duties at a lower rate. But the conclusion seems inescapable that excises hit the pockets of most consumers rather than just the purses of the prosperous.'[521] It was the merchants who paid the customs. But those, obviously, tried as best they could to pass them on to their customers. One could also try to not pay them at all and engage in smuggling, which happened to be an extremely popular strategy.[522] A substantial part of the costs of living in Britain, in contrast to the situation in China, actually consisted of (indirect) tax payments on consumer goods. Had Britain had a tax system like China, Britons would have been able to buy *substantially* more consumer goods. In that respect, it is misleading to pronounce on the wealth of Britons and Chinese by simply comparing the amounts of consumer goods they actually were able to buy.

---

[520]Mokyr, 'Is there still life in the pessimist case?', 75.

[521]Brewer, *Sinews of Power*, 217. For further information see that book, pages 211–17. See also Nye, *War, Wine, and Taxes*, 75: 'the excises were most likely passed on to the great mass of British consumers'.

[522]See Brewer, *Sinews of Power*, 211–13. The most famous example is tea that was smuggled in enormous amounts up until 1784, but one might also think of tobacco. It is estimated, that at times as much as two-thirds of the tobacco consumed in Great Britain had been smuggled into the country. See Mokyr, 'Is there still life in the pessimist case?', 85.

CHAPTER 2
(OVER-)EXPENDITURE

EXPENDITURE

The military preparations of all our neighbours compel us to follow their example.

The Great Elector of Prussia at the eve of the Great Northern War (1655–60)[1]

I have never been able to get this business of loans and interest into my head. I have never been able to understand it.

Philip II to his Minister of Finance[2]

Each little bit of (tax) burden that can be spared the common people … represents a corresponding contribution to their basic productive capacity.

Chen Hongmou, a Chinese official in the eighteenth century[3]

The curse of China is the small and insufficient pay of the officials, and from that has sprung forward a crop of what may be styled 'flowers and thistles' – the thistles being downright extortion and peculation, the flowers being *presents* to people in office.

Sir Robert Hart, journal entry, 22 November 1864

In Europe, between the thirteenth and nineteenth centuries, the enlargement of the fiscal system was expenditure-driven. Expenditure patterns were determined more or less independently of tax revenue. The problem then was how to raise sufficient funds to cover them.[4] Increased spending was the rule and, as we will see later on, so was substantial indebtedness. Almost without exception an opposite logic was at work in China. 'Measuring income to make expenditures' was regarded as 'the essence of fiscal management'.[5] The Qing rulers were very keen on ruling on the cheap. Funds provided for administrative expenses fell far short of actual needs at all levels of government, although we have to realize that figures about its expenses do not necessarily tell us much about actual total expenditure, or rather about total government activity. Discrepancies between statutory expenses and actual expenses were huge.[6] Officials in government

---

[1] I found this quote in Porter, *War and the Rise of the State*, 111.
[2] I found this quote in Macdonald, *Free Nation*, 128.
[3] I found this quote in Rowe, *Saving the World*, 332.
[4] I paraphrase Bonney, 'Introduction' of his *Economic Systems and State Finance*, 13.
[5] See for this information and this quote, that dates from 1887, Stanley, *Late Ch'ing Finance*, 86–9.
[6] See for differences between statutory expenses and actual expenses during the late Qing, Wang, *Land Taxation*, 53–7.

service receiving salaries were few in number. Those would did receive salaries, did not receive much. Many people delivered services that we would consider 'public' without receiving any official remuneration at all. A substantial number of soldiers were expected to, at least to a substantial extent, provide for their own sustenance and that of their dependents on tracts of land that were allotted to them. In the end this policy was not very successful, even though the amount of land we are dealing with was not negligible either. Local officials had to privately pay many expenses that simply were not covered by their *official* salary, not even if we include the so-called 'integrity-nourishing allowances' that could be many times as high as that official salary.[7] One can think here of the salaries they had to pay their privately hired advisers. These civilian experts, especially in the fields of law and taxation, were not appointed to any government office and therefore the officials had to pay them entirely out of their own pockets.[8] When it comes to the personnel that government gave them, officials received at best some insufficient funding for some of them. As a rule government officials were not able to provide any of their 'personnel' a decent income, neither out of their official allowances nor out of their own pockets, which meant they had to more or less give them free reign to take care of their own income. The bulk of the clerks and runners, without whom they simply could not even begin to do their job, were *not* paid out of government funds at all.

All this, of course, in practice meant that this personnel, experts as well as clerks and runners, had to make the population pay (in the case of the clerks and runners so-called 'customary fees') for all the services (they claimed) they rendered. Obviously, this created ample opportunity for extortion and corruption. The fact that officials were also expected to fulfil many tasks like repairing and building city walls, roads, embankments and so on and so forth, for which they received no funding, did not improve matters. Madeleine Zelin succinctly described the predicament of China's officials working in the provinces:

> In the end if local officials were to do their jobs, they had only two options. Either they siphoned off funds allocated by the central government for other purposes or earmarked for remittance to the central treasuries, or they squeezed the necessary revenue from the people in the process of collecting taxes. In fact, they did both.[9]

To be able to fulfil everything that was expected from him a magistrate indeed, as Balazs indicated, had to be a genius: which of course he very rarely was.[10] This was all the more problematic as deficits in treasuries or granaries or failures to meet certain quotas were

---

[7]See for these allowances that are also called 'anti-corruption fees' or 'honesty-fostering allowances', Hsü, *Rise of Modern China*, 62.

[8]See for these privately hired experts Chapter 1 note 336.

[9]Zelin, 'Yung-cheng reign', 207.

[10]Balazs, *Political Theory and Administrative Reality*, 54.

often effectively redefined as moral failures and placed squarely at the doorstep of the local bureaucrat's office.[11]

Of course, none of all this 'improvising' can be found in official accounts and it is not at all clear to what extent the income it provided could *in any way* be regarded as government income. It simply was not in any way at government's disposal, but on the other hand it enabled government to *spend* so little and in that sense was a sort of income. For a complete picture of expenditure of central government we would also have to take into consideration expenses by the Imperial Household and expenses paid out of taxes that were locally retained.[12] I did not come across any systematic information about those expenses either.

A closer look at expenditures: The overwhelming importance of the military

In his famous book on the history of state-formation in Europe, Charles Tilly claimed that in early modern Europe war made states and states made war.[13] Overall, he was right. All over Europe war was by far the biggest expenditure of government in the early modern era: that means paying for wars that were actually waged or that that might be waged in the future *and* paying off the debts incurred in previous wars. That servicing of war debts could easily be overlooked. It should not: it always was a very substantial part of total expenditure for most Western European governments. In the literature, estimates of the percentages of total expenses due to warfare often differ according to whether one only counts current expenditures or includes debt servicing on the premise that, as a rule, paying debts simply meant paying for the extra costs one had incurred sometime in the past because of war. Niall Ferguson estimated that during the eighteenth century European monarchies *on average* spent 54 per cent of their total budgets on warfare. He does *not* include debt service in that figure.[14] For the period from the 1760s to the 1840s, Michael Mann came up with figures in the same order of magnitude for Austria, Prussia–Germany, France and Britain, with, of course, substantial differences between periods of peace and periods of war.[15] In his text, too, debt servicing is *not* included in the category 'military expenses'. Reading the most recent publications on the fiscal-military states in Europe in the long eighteenth century, one can only conclude that indeed war at the time was their main expenditure by far.[16]

---

[11]Thornton, *Disciplining the State*, ch. 2.
[12]For expenses directly covered by the Imperial Household see Chang, 'Economic role', 270–1.
[13]Tilly, *Coercion, Capital, and European States*, ch. 3.
[14]Ferguson, *Cash Nexus*, 43.
[15]Mann, *Sources of Social Power, II*, 373.
[16]See O'Brien and Yun-Casalilla, *Rise of Fiscal States*; Storrs, *Fiscal-Military State* and Torres Sánchez, *War, State and Development*.

Prussia, up until the first decade of the nineteenth century, *never* spent less than 70 per cent of its budget on the military. Sometimes this figure was as high as 90 per cent.[17] Considering the fact that government systematically extended the so-called 'canton system', in which soldiers, as far as possible, had to take care of their own subsistence, this apparently still was not enough. In the Dutch Republic, to mention an important Western European state that is not discussed in several publications on the fiscal-military state, military expenditure amounted to 87 per cent of total government expenditure in the beginning of the 1640s. At that time, only 4 per cent of the total budget was used for debt servicing. In 1801, actual military expenditure as such amounted to 'only' 45 per cent of the budget, but now the percentage of the budget used for debt service had increased to 41. That 45 per cent of current expenditure on army, fortifications and navy alone, boiled down to over 30 million guilders (the equivalent of some 10 million taels).[18] There is no need for an in-depth analysis of the situation in all (Western) European states, suffice to say that it was overall quite similar. That also goes for Central and Eastern Europe. Prussia's name as military state has become legendary. In the case of the Habsburg Empire the famous proverb: 'Let others wage war, thou happy Austria … marry' has too long been taken seriously as a description of reality. Actually the military history of the Habsburg monarchy was quite similar to that of Prussia: war and all it implies played a major role in it.[19]

Let us again, as in the rest of this book, focus on Britain. Brewer undoubtedly was right when he called it a 'fiscal-military' state during the eighteenth century although the expression 'fiscal-naval state' would have been even more adequate. It continued to be one until the 1820s. The money of central government was largely used for the military. He claims that over the eighteenth century between 75 and 85 per cent of annual government expenditure was devoted to paying for the army, navy and ordinance, and to servicing debts incurred in earlier wars.[20] Eckhart Schremmer comes up with an estimate that is even somewhat higher: he assesses current and consolidated military expenditure in Britain in the eighteenth century at between 80 and 90 per cent of total government expenditure, closer to the first at the beginning and to the last at the end of the century.[21] Other estimates are in the same order of magnitude.[22]

After the Napoleonic Wars military expenditures decreased sharply, not only in absolute terms but also as a percentage of total government spending. The period from 1815 to 1914 would know far fewer expensive wars *in Europe* than the period from

---

[17]See Gorski, *Disciplinary Revolution*, ch. 3 and Mann, *Sources of Social Power, II*, 373. In contrast to almost all other European governments, Prussia's central government during almost the entire eighteenth century did not spend more than it 'earned'.

[18]'t Hart, 'United Provinces', 312.

[19]See Hochedlinger, 'Habsburg Monarchy'.

[20]Brewer, *Sinews of Power*, 40.

[21]Schremmer, 'Taxation and public finance', 325.

[22]See Ferguson, *Cash Nexus*, 43–51; Harley, 'Reassessing the industrial revolution', 218; Mann, *Sources of Social Power, II*, 373–4; O'Brien, 'Political economy'; idem, 'Power with profit', 12, and Weiss and Hobson, *States and Economic Development*, 113–21.

Table 15 Total net expenditures of central government of Great Britain, 1688–1801; total gross expenditure of central government of the United Kingdom, 1802–50, in thousands of £

	1700	1710	1720	1730	1740	1750
Debt charges	1,251	1,754	2,276	2,289	2,102	3,218
Civil government	699	857	980	935	846	1,016
Army & Ordnance	432	4,479	1,073	1,326	1,605	1,566
Navy	819	2,422	1,181	1,033	1,607	1,385
Collection costs	NR	NR	NR	NR	NR	NR
	1760	1770	1780	1790	1801	1810
Debt charges	3,372	4,836	5,995	9,370	16,479	24,200
Civil government	1,152	1,223	1,251	1,703	2,072	5,200
Army & Ordnance	1,031	1,781	8,540	2,742	16,900	28,900
Navy	4,539	2,082	6,329	2,482	14,707	19,400
Collection costs	NR	NR	NR	NR	NR	3,600
	1820	1830	1840	1850		
Debt charges	31,100	29,100	28,900	29,200		
Civil government	5,400	5,400	5,600	7,000		
Army & Ordnance	10,300	9,300	8,500	9,000		
Navy	6,400	5,900	5,300	5,700		
Collection costs	4,400	4,000	3,800	5,000		

Source: Mitchell, *British Historical Statistics*, 579–80 and 587–8.

Note: NR = not reported.

1688 to 1815. Now, overall, civilian expenditures, in particular those on infrastructure and education, became more prominent. Which has to be put in in perspective; they had always been very tiny. Again the situation in Great Britain is different. There they continued to be surprisingly low whereas the importance of debt service continued to be surprisingly high. For the period 1816–50, almost without exception, it was more than 50 per cent of the annual budget. But its importance was not a recent development. With the War of Spanish Succession (1702–13) debt payments reached a level of 50 per cent of total expenditure. That figure would not become lower than 35 per cent during the period from then to 1790.[23]

The decreasing importance of military expenditure after the French Wars to a certain extent is an optical illusion, considering the continuing importance of debt servicing. The debts that had to be paid back were due primarily to the costs of wars in the

---

[23]See for the first period, Brewer, *Sinews of Power*, 117, and for the second Ferguson, *Cash Nexus*, 140–1.

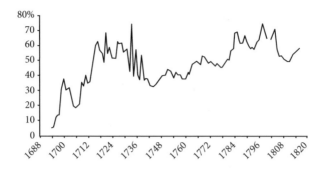

Graph 9 Debt servicing ratios as a percentage of total taxes, Great Britain, 1688–1815.

Source: O'Brien, 'The history, nature and economic significance of an exceptional fiscal state', 31.

Table 16 Average annual expenditure on army and navy by Great Britain during main periods of war

War of Spanish Succession (1702–13)	>£7 million
Seven Years War (1756–63)	>£18 million
American Wars (1776–84)	>£20 million
During the 1790s	>£20 million
1800–15	>£40 million

Sources: Brewer, *Sinews of Power*, 25–64; Evans, *Forging of the Modern State*, 412 and O'Brien, 'Political economy', 2.

past. Finally I want to point out the tendency for taxes and expenditure of government to *decline* as a percentage of GDP until at least the 1870s or 1880s.[24]

To be able to get a concrete idea of the existing differences, let us also look at the *absolute* amounts of money involved. In particular the costs of the Revolutionary and Napoleonic Wars were staggering. In the period from 1780 to 1830, a crucial period in global history, Great Britain, on average, spent about £20 million per year on its army and navy. In silver-equivalents that is as much, or almost as much, as *total* regular tax income of the Qing government of China, a country with thirty times as many inhabitants. We of course have to realize that there were years when

---

[24]Mann, *Sources of Social Power, II*, ch. 11, in particular Tables 11.2 and 11.3. See page 368: 'The trend is striking and surprising. Contrary – I am fairly confident – to most readers' expectations, state activities *decreased* [italics in the original] as a proportion of national economic activity between the mid-eighteenth and the early twentieth century'. Britain is a somewhat peculiar case: whereas its taxes and expenditure till the 1820s clearly were *above* the Western European average, from then on they both decreased and ended up *below* the average of Western Europe. Besides, from the 1820s onwards, the importance of indirect taxes *decreased* and that of direct taxes *increased*, whereas in the rest of Western Europe it was just the other way around. See Daunton, 'Trusting Leviathan', 323–4.

Table 17 British wartime expenditure and revenue, 1688–1815

Inclusive years	Total expenditure	Total income	Balance raised by loans	Loans as % of expenditure
1688–97	£49,320,145	£32,766,754	£16,553,391	33.6
1702–13	£93,644,560	£64,239,477	£29,405,083	31.4
1739–48	£95,628,159	£65,903,964	£29,724,195	31.1
1756–63	£160,573,366	£100,555,123	£60,018,243	37.4
1776–83	£236,462,689	£141,902,620	£94,560,069	39.9
1793–1815	£1,657,854,518	£1,217,556,439	£440,298,079	26.6
Totals	£2,293,483,437	£1,622,924,377	£670,559,060	33.3

Source: Kennedy, *Rise and Fall of the Great Powers*, 81.

Table 18 British borrowing to pay for war, 1689–1815

War	Cost £ millions	Borrowed %
League of Augsburg (1689–97)	31	53
Spanish Succession (1702–13)	51	56
Austrian Succession (1740–8)	40	71
Seven Years' War (1756–63)	73	78
American Independence (1776–84)	112	82
Revolutionary War (1793–7)	100	89
Napoleonic Wars (1798–1815)	772	49

Source: Macdonald, *Free Nation Deep in Debt*, 339. In calculating war costs, allowance is made for the normal peacetime spending on defence.

total expenditures were far above average. It is not much use to separately discuss the situation in other Western European countries. The results would be similar to what we see in Britain: the costs of warfare were huge and escalated.

When we look at government expenditure in China we again are in a world of striking differences. I did not come across any estimate in which central governement is supposed to have spent more than somewhat over 45 million taels per year at any moment during the period under discussion here.[25] Between 1802 and 1851, gross expenditures of central government of the United Kingdom were always above £48 million per year. *Average* annual gross expenditures over that period were some £65 million. For China, annual

---

[25]For a general overview see Ma, 'Rock, scissors, paper', figure 3. See also Hsü, *Rise of Modern China*, 61–3; He, *Paths toward the Modern Fiscal State*, chs 5 and 6 with a focus on the period after 1850; Rosenthal and Wong, *Before and Beyond Divergence*, 201. All the information with regard to total official income and reserves in the treasuries points to a very low level of expenditure.

official government expenditure at the time on average amounted to some 35 million taels. If we assume that the purchasing power of these taels would be three times as high in China than as in Great Britain this would be the equivalent of £35 million. This means that on average central government of Great Britain/the United Kingdom spent almost twice as much in terms of domestic purchasing power as China's government. Per capita, in domestic purchasing power, that would be some more than thirty times as much.[26] Even if we would be willing to double the figures for China, because actual expenditures will certainly have been higher, the gap is enormous. In that respect it seems quite strange to claim, as Wang does, that Qianlong, whom he considers a big tax-collector and spender, was unable to overcome 'a fundamental limitation to premodern political development: the worsening ratio of organizational resources to population size'.[27]

In China, too, government spent most of its money on the military, easily over half of total official expenditures, if we may believe the experts in the field. As always the figures one finds in this context have to be handled with care. I will differentiate between *official* and *regular* cost and *campaign cost* to then say something about *total costs*. In all the estimates that I have found of official and regular military expenditure, 'point of departure' was an estimated official and regular government revenue of no more than 60 to 80 million taels. Official and regular military expenditure, during roughly the period 1750–1850, is then estimated to have amounted to an annual average between, at the very least, 25 million and, at its highest, 32 million taels.[28] Bin Wong claims that in the middle of the eighteenth century, current military expenditure per year amounted to about 18 million taels, which, surprisingly, in his eyes shows how strong the Qing state was.[29] Again, Lord Macartney also provides information on this topic. In this calculation, which is based on information he obtained from a Chinese army officer, it is assumed that China's army consisted of 1 million infantry and 800,000 cavalry. He claims that this, in peacetime, would result in 74 million taels as regular costs and the same amount as extra, irregular costs. Together that would be three-quarters of what he considers to be total government revenue.[30] The figure of 1.8 million troops is much higher than one comes across in any recent scholarly analysis and it seems quite exaggerated. The total costs of such an army would simply be too high, especially considering the fact that Macartney is referring to peacetime costs and says he does not include the costs of a large number of Tartar troops stationed 'beyond the Great Wall'. It may well be that the very high number

---

[26]This, of course, is a rough estimate. I have estimated the average population of the United Kingdom over the 50-year period at 23 million people and that of China at 375 million people. As always, I only want to show orders of magnitude.

[27]Wang, *White Lotus Rebels and South China Pirates*, 22.

[28]I base this figure on my reading of Elliott, *Manchu Way*, 308–10; Lee, *Political Economy*, Table 1.6, and Van der Ven, 'Onrush of modern globalization', 179–80. For the middle of the nineteenth century, there is the calculation by Sir Thomas Wade, who claimed that the disbursements of the Board of War amounted to 30,874,540 taels, almost equally divided over the Banner Forces and the Army of the Green Standard. See Wade, 'Army of the Chinese empire'. I found this reference in Powell, *Rise of Chinese Military Power*, 19.

[29]Wong, 'Politiques de dépenses sociales', 1407.

[30]See Cranmer-Byng, *Embassy to China*, 255–6. The total of 150 million taels would still only be less than half a tael per Chinese.

Macartney gives is exaggerated and includes many soldiers who actually were not active soldiers, but simply included in the army, and who did not personally receive any or much remuneration.[31]

What about *irregular*, extra costs? Those, such as campaign expenses, for example, often were paid from reserves. According to a calculation by Peter Perdue, the major Qing campaigns between 1747 and 1805, in total, cost about 300 million taels.[32] Of course, in some years spending was higher than in others. The amounts in Table 19 look impressive but *on average* we are only talking about some 5 million taels per year. There, of course, had been campaigns before 1747. The seven-year campaign of the Yongzheng emperor (1723–35) against the Zunghars, according to a high estimate, cost nearly 130 million taels – that is £43 million in total or £6 million per year.[33] In the first half of the nineteenth century the costs of military campaigns appear to have decreased substantially. The costs of the Qing defence campaigns during the First Opium War till the Treaty of Nanking (1842) were 30 million taels or £10 million in total.[34] The total recorded amount of money spent by the Qing central government to repress domestic rebellions in the period between 1850 and 1868, by way of comparison, was 300 million taels of silver.[35]

The figures presented so far show two things. First that, as compared to Great Britain, China's military expenditure – ordinary *and* extraordinary expenditure

Table 19 Military campaigns that cost more than 10 million taels in eighteenth-century China

1st Jinchuan campaign (1747–9)	>10
Zunghar-Turkestan campaign (1754–61)	33
Burma campaign (1767–9)	13
2nd Jinchuan campaign (1771–6)	70
Taiwan campaign (1787–8)	10
2nd Gurkha campaign (1791–2)	11
Repression of the White Lotus Rebellion (1797–1804)	150

Source: Perdue, 'China's environment', table 1. I must again emphasize we are dealing here with estimates. In the literature one can find many somewhat differing estimates for specific campaigns. The biggest difference I found was in Wang, *White Lotus Rebels and South China Pirates*, 141, where it is claimed that the costs of repressing the White Lotus Rebellion in total amounted to some 200 million taels. But again what matters to me are rough orders of magnitude.

---

[31]See for critical comments in this vein Barrow, *Travels in China*, 193–5.
[32]Perdue, China's environment', table 1.
[33]Bartlett, *Monarchs and Ministers*, 121–2.
[34]Deng, 'Sweet and sour Confucianism', 28.
[35]He, *Paths toward the Modern Fiscal State*, 131. For a much higher estimate of costs see Deng, *China's Political Economy*, 33. In my view the figures there do not add up.

combined – was quite low. Over the period from the 1740s to the beginning of the nineteenth century that Perdue covers, annual regular costs on average were, if we take a high estimate, some 32 million taels. We then have to add some 5 million taels on average per year for additional campaign costs. In total that makes 37 million taels per year, which in terms of domestic purchasing powers has have about the same value as £37 million in Britain. With roughly twenty times as many people, China, in real terms, only spent roughly 1.8 times as much on the military as Britain did in the period from the 1760s to the 1820s. That means that *per capita* in *real terms* Britain spent more than *ten* times as much on its army and navy than China. These figures also point to another quite interesting fact: military spending apparently was much higher during the campaigns of the Qianlong emperor in the eighteenth century than during, and directly after, the First Opium War. Chinese commentators in the middle decades of the nineteenth century, who claimed they were living in peaceful times, were not as mistaken as Westerners, who are convinced that China must have been shaken by that war, may think. Under the Daoguang emperor military expenses were only 70 per cent of those of the early Jiaqing period and only 50 per cent of those of the late Qianlong era.[36] In the light of the figures presented here on the costs of waging war and on pages 234–6 with regard to the height of war reparation payments, it is not exactly convincing to suggest as Rosenthal and Wong, and the less outspoken Westad, do, that the problems of China in the nineteenth century would have been triggered by its high costs of preparing and fighting (and losing) conflicts with foreigners.[37] To be completely fair, in this comparison one would have to take into consideration that at least part of the real costs of China's military were hidden from view as a substantial number of China's soldiers, especially among the banner men, provided at least partly for their own livelihood, and were able to do so, as the government had provided them with land *and* often with people who tilled that land for them.

Non-military expenditures in Great Britain and China: Was Qing China indeed more of a 'welfare state' than Great Britain?

Military expenditures in Great Britain as well as in China were the most important single category of expenditures, but they were not the only ones. If we look at the overall situation in Western Europe we see that most governments also spent (a tiny!) part of their money on civil affairs like administration and the court. But that, with *some* expenditure on infrastructure, was about it until the 1820s. Whereas spending on things like infrastructure, transport and communication, education and social security, would

---

[36]Lin, *China Upside Down*, 286 and 295.
[37]See Rosenthal and Wong, *Before and Beyond Divergence*, 200–7. For Westad's emphasis on external reasons for China's troubles see his *Restless Empire*, 25, where he claims that 'almost none' of the many disasters that befell China in the nineteenth century 'seem to have originated from built-in weaknesses in the development of empire. Quite the contrary, they were the products of misrule, foreign invasion, wars, and rebellions'. See also the comments by Wang here on page 235.

dominate budgets in the twentieth century, it hardly existed, if at all, during the very long eighteenth century.

In China, the main expenses were similar: the military (*and* their dependents), the court, and salaries for officials. Two kinds of expenditure are interesting from our comparative perspective. To begin with those involved in what I would call 'water-management' – that is facilitating transportation over water, irrigation, and the prevention of flooding – considering the fact that this specific state-activity has so often held centrestage in stories about China as a 'hydraulic state', the amount of money of central government money actually involved in it, was rather small.[38] If total costs and importance of water-management would be an indicator to go by, the Dutch Republic would have been a better candidate for the designation 'hydraulic' state. The bulk of the costs there, however, *as in China*, were borne at the local level. The total burden of 'water-management' became heavier and more cumbersome in China with the passing of time. But whereas *maintenance* costs increased steadily and became an ever more prominent part of total costs, spending on *extension or innovation* became smaller: possibilities to extend and innovate had simply been all but exhausted. In this respect too, to put it in Mark Elvin's terms, China had reached a 'high-level equilibrium trap', in this case more specifically a kind of 'ecological lock-in'. There were serious problems in keeping open the Grand Canal and preventing the Yellow River from flooding and changing its course. Various parts of the country began to suffer from deforestation and exhaustion.[39]

Then there are the costs involved in running the state granary system. In its effort to procure for 'people's livelihood' China's government not only could decide to 'ask' merchants for contributions or intervene in the market if and when it saw fit but also kept its own granaries. Much is made of this granary system by authors like Will and Wong. According to estimates in their *Nourish the People*, the grain *stored* in government granaries towards the end of the eighteenth century, amounted, at its peak in 1791, in a very high, optimistic estimate, to almost 46 million *shi*. If following Wong, we take the average monthly consumption to have been 0.3 *shi* for an adult and 0.15 *shi* for a child, the stored grain would have sufficed to feed some fifteen to 20 million people, or roughly some 5 per cent of the population, for an entire year.[40] Actual *distribution* of course is another matter. Wong claims that 5 per cent of China's population received

---

[38]For some references to the absolute and relative sums of money involved see e.g. Hsü, *Rise of Modern China*, 63, and Wong, 'Politiques de dépenses sociales'. Central government in China had so little revenue as compared to governments in Western Europe and spent so much of it on the military that it simply cannot have spent a lot on water-management.

[39]For Elvin's comments on the increase of maintenance costs of water works, 'ecological lock-in', and the role of the state in ecological matters, see Elvin, 'Three thousand years of unsustainable growth'; idem, *Retreat of the Elephants*, and Elvin and Liu, *Sediments of Time*. See for the Grand Canal, Leonard, *Controlling from Afar* and Pomeranz, *Making of a Hinterland*. For the Yellow River see Dodgen, *Controlling the Dragon*. For a general overview see Marks, *China. Its Environment and History*, chs 5 and 6.

[40]I take this information from Will, Wong and Lee, *Nourish the People*, 21, and Appendix Table A1. Deng in his *China's Political Economy*, 21, claims, that the Qing granary system maintained a stockpile amounting to some 7 per cent of annual grain output.

some 15 per cent of their grain via distribution from those ever-normal granaries. That would mean that 0.75 per cent of total grain consumption would be provided for by the granaries. Via a somewhat different estimate he comes to basically the same result. According to him, distributed grain would amount to roughly 7 per cent of all marketed grain. As only 10 per cent of all grain in China was marketed, that is according to an estimate by Wu (that Wong supports), this can only mean that *distributed* grain indeed would account for some 0.7 per cent of all grain consumption, or the equivalent of the rice consumption of over 2 million people.[41] Even if these figures look already much less impressive, we still are confronted with a stunning achievement, considering the size of the country and the daunting logistical problems. As such this specific system indeed had no parallel in Western Europe.

To provide for 'people's livelihood' government not only ran the granaries-system and all that implied. When it saw fit, it also, as a kind of disaster relief, remitted taxes or exempted people from paying them. It distributed land, often tax-exempt, among poor people. It ran all kinds of charitable institutions like orphanages, poorhouses, schools, and so-called benevolent halls.[42] In this context one could and should also point at the position of the banner men. They were provided for from cradle to grave and held a hereditary privilege from which an ever-increasing number of people tried to profit. A very large part of the money set apart for the army in actual fact was used to take care of their dependents. Elliott goes as far as to claim that they indeed lived in a kind of welfare state.[43] He, correctly, points out that they made a very specific kind of 'welfare' provisions here:

> That one-fourth to one-fifth of state revenues were set aside every year to pay the living expenses of a conquest military caste that was less than 2 per cent of the population was certainly one of the more remarkable features of late imperial fiscal structure.[44]

The group of people profiting from government support in this case was confined to a small, circumscribed 'elite', but if Elliott is right the amount of resources distributed may have been of a similar order of magnitude as in the case of the granary system. In no way would I want to detract from the fact that the Qing rulers clearly did care about the welfare of 'their' people. But the point is that authors like Wong and Will, and others following in their footsteps, want their readers to believe that European governments during the early modern era did (next to) nothing for the welfare of their subjects and in that respect stood out in stark contrast to China's paternalist rulers. We have seen

---

[41] See Wong in Will and Wong, *Nourish the People*, 483–4. According to Deng 30 per cent of China's grain would be marketed annually.
[42] See, for example, Rowe, 'Social stability', 546–50.
[43] Elliott, *Manchu Way*, 311.
[44] Elliott, *Manchu Way*, 311. As indicated on page 204, their total payment per capita was about three times as high as that of Green Standard soldiers. See also pages 119 and 139.

that Wong claims that Imperial China's state-sponsored granaries for famine relief represented 'official commitments to material welfare beyond anything imaginable, let alone achieved, in Europe'[45]

In many texts by Wong it is suggested that in (Western) Europe – again this general, often misleading term is used – central government would be uninterested in public welfare and remain inactive. It would in any case be *less* interested and involved than in China. That suggestion, that is widely believed, really is unjustified. Overall, in early modern Europe substantial amounts of money were spent in bringing relief to the poor, which of course implies there must have been an enormous amount of paupers and pauperism.[46] Differences according to place and time were too big to generalize, but as such it is telling that on the basis of a survey of many local, regional and national studies, it has been concluded that the proportion of the population receiving relief at various times and various places in early modern Western Europe ranged between 3 and 25 per cent.[47] Again, revisionism, in this case with its focus on the benevolence of Chinese authorities versus the harsh nature of Western government, is really pushing things too far.

Let us go into some more detail. To begin with, systems of grain storage were not unknown in Europe. One could refer to Prussia-Brandenburg for example. In 1740, the total storage capacity of granaries there sufficed to feed 200,000 people, which was 9 per cent of total population, for a year.[48] In contrast to China, this storage system indeed was primarily intended to supply the army with food. But it also began to perform an important role in stabilizing the domestic grain market and it was part of a broader policy. Frederick II, for example, spent the equivalent of two entire years' total tax income on distributing free grain, fodder and livestock under his subjects after the Seven Years War (1756–63).[49] At the end of his reign, when Prussia's total population amounted to some 5 million, his grain magazines contained 120 million kg of grain, while enough cash was held in reserve to purchase an equal amount. In total, that sufficed to provide over a million people with grain for an entire year, according to consumption standards at the time. Prussia's magazines did not only serve the army. They were also ready to distribute grain and flour to the population and repeatedly did so.[50] There also were granaries in Spain, as Wong indicates himself, and, for example, in Amsterdam,

---

[45]Wong, *China Transformed*, 98–9.

[46]For a still highly informative analysis of poverty and economic development in Western Europe in the early modern era, see Lis and Soly, *Poverty and Capitalism*.

[47]For a general overview of poor relief in (Western) Europe in the early modern era see Jütte, *Poverty and Deviance* and for the period from the eighteenth century onwards, Lindert, *Growing public*. Focusing on Britain but with a comparative angle are, Harris, 'From poor law to welfare state?'; Innes, 'The state and the poor'; idem, 'Distinctiveness of the English Poor Laws'; Patriquin, *Agrarian Capitalism*; and Solar, 'Poor relief and English economic development'.

[48]Schmoller and Naudé, *Getreidehandelspolitik und Kriegsmagazinverwaltung*, 278. See also Clark, *Iron Kingdom*, 92–3.

[49]Oppenheim, *Europe and the Enlightened Despots*, 42–5.

[50]Hubatsch, *Frederick the Great*, 60. Pages 55–72 of this book provide information about all kinds of 'social' measures by this Prussian ruler.

which he apparently does not know.[51] Granaries were in any case less uniquely Chinese than Wong and others suggest.

Far more important is the fact that it will not do to simply take the presence or absence of a system of ever-normal granaries as a decisive indicator whether rulers of certain societies cared about the livelihood of their subjects. Nor does it make much sense, to come back to that point, to speak about 'Europe' in this context. What, during the very long eighteenth century, we see in *Western* Europe, to confine ourselves to that region, are differing strategies, differing challenges, and different rates of success in implementing those strategies, according to time and place. Great Britain and the Dutch Republic undoubtedly were the countries where government relied most on the market – *and* on poor relief systems – when it came to provisioning the population with its necessities. But even in the Dutch Republic in the eighteenth century, government regularly resorted to policies like price-fixing or subsidizing the production of bread, when, in an effort to avoid disturbances, it saw fit.[52] In France till the very end of the period discussed in this book, and even later, government continued to interfere in the grain market, as subsistence was regarded as too important to leave it to an invisible hand.[53] There indeed were times when physiocrat, *laissez-faire* rhetoric could be heard, but that never put an end to an incredibly varied and complex set of policies to protect the customer. When Montesquieu wrote in 1748 that the state owes all its citizens regular means of subsistence, he was expressing what all but a tiny minority of French people took to be a truism.[54] Whether the French state was very successful in its policies, is another matter. It quite often was *not*.

The firm statements by Wong and others on the absence of governmental social policies in early modern Western Europe actually are quite puzzling. Thousands of studies have been devoted to the emergence of exactly such policies in that very period of time. The fact that secular authorities in Western Europe, to quite differing degrees, often did trust in the workings of the market does not mean that they would not support forms of poor relief and charity – quite the contrary, England and Wales, to again focus on the *British*[55] case, had a *national* system of poor relief financed from taxation ever since their first Poor Law was enacted at the end of the sixteenth century. The rates were supposed to be paid by the *entire* population. In practice only those judged to be able to pay, a third to one-half of the population, did so. As a rule, poor relief was distributed in cash. Although there were other forms of spending on the poor, rate-based expenditure was undoubtedly the single largest component of Britain's relief expenditure throughout the eighteenth century. The British approach was quite distinctive, as is emphasized by experts like Lindert, Patriquin and Solar: it was centralized, with a strong emphasis on relief in the countryside – the scale of

---

[51]See Wong in Will and Wong, *Nourish the People*, 516, and De Vries and Van der Woude, *First Modern Economy*, 656–60.
[52]De Vries and Van der Woude, *First Modern Economy*, 654–64.
[53]Miller, *Mastering the Market*.
[54]Miller, *Mastering the Market*, 1.
[55]Scotland had its own system of poor relief.

Table 20 Poor rate receipts in England and Wales, 1748–1850

Years	Annual poor rates receipts in £m.
1748–50*	0.7
1776	1.7
1783–5*	2.2
1803	5.3
1813	8.7
1814–18*	8.0
1819–23*	8.1
1824–8*	7.3
1829–33*	8.3
1834–8*	6.6
1839–43*	6.3
1844–8*	7
1849–53*	7

Source: Mitchell, *British Historical Statistics*, 605.

* annual averages.

relief paid there was higher there than anywhere else in Europe.[56] The amount of money involved was quite substantial. The sums of money collected sufficed to keep some 3.5 per cent of the population provided with bread in the mid-1690s. In the mid-eighteenth century that percentage had doubled. By 1802–3 it had increased to about 14 per cent.[57]

All these figures provide us with the opportunity to actually try and compare Chinese expenditures on poor relief with those in Britain to find out whether Wong's claims hold water. They apparently do not. There are various ways of showing that. I here just endorse the estimates by Lindert, who makes it quite plausible – *using information from publications by Wong and Will* – that the grain from China's famous granaries that was provided to the population during the eighteenth century in terms of money never amounted to as much as 0.5 per cent of China's GDP. To be more precise: he claims it would have amounted to 0.36 per cent in 1735, and, according to another estimate, 0.17 to 0.26 per cent over the period 1735–80.[58] At the end of the eighteenth century the system began to

[56]See Lindert, *Growing Public*, chs 3 and 4; Patriquin, *Agrarian Capitalism* and Solar, 'Poor relief and English economic development'.
[57]Innes, 'The state and the poor', 229 and 226. In Sokoll, 'Armut und Familie', 58 and 62, we find even higher figures.
[58]Lindert, 'De bonnes idées', 1422–3.

Table 21 Poor relief expenditures expressed as a percentage of the GDP or GNP of England and Wales

Year	% GDP/GNP
1688	1.22
1749	0.99
1776	1.59
1783–5	1.75
1801–3	2.15
1811–3	2.58
1820–1	2.66
1830–2	2.00
1840	1.12
1850	1.07

Source: Lindert, 'Poor relief before the welfare state', 114. In Patriquin, *Agrarian Capitalism*, 204, one finds even somewhat higher figures with a peak in 1817 when expenditures are claimed to have amounted to £9.3 million, which he considers to be 3.1 per cent of GNP. Expenditures of course were lower than revenue because of the costs incurred.

function less well and from then on the percentages will certainly have been even lower. According to an estimate made by Will and Wong themselves, granary-system costs in the eighteenth century accounted for 0.5 to 2 per cent of annually generated government revenues, which they estimate at 60 to 80 million taels per year. In the highest estimate that would be 2 per cent of 80 million taels, which is 1.6 million taels.[59] According to Lillian Li the total amount of famine relief from the early Qing through the Daoguang period, may in an extremely high estimate have amounted to 446 million taels.[60] As such the sum looks impressive – on average per year it is relatively tiny, roughly the equivalent of £1 million. Deng, who is very positive about Qing famine relief, estimates that it in total, in terms of money, amounted to some 48 million taels over the period 1666–1877, roughly the equivalent of some £75,000 per year.[61] For Britain's poor relief we are talking about far higher orders of magnitude, in absolute terms as well as in percentages of GDP. In the period 1800–50, poor rate receipts hovered between £5.3 million at the lowest and £9.3 million, gross government between income £39 million at the lowest and £79 million at the highest.[62] The number of people who received relief in 'work houses'

[59]Will and Wong, *Nourish the People*, 494.
[60]Li, *Fighting Famine*, 248.
[61]Deng, *China's Political Economy*, 23. Differences when it comes to figures considering early modern China often are very disheartening!
[62]Mitchell, *British Historical Statistics*, 605 and 581–2.

for the poor was very substantial. In 1776, there were 1,970 such houses in England and Wales, excluding London, capable of housing almost 90,000 persons.[63] In 1850, the number of people receiving relief in workhouses (123,000) or elsewhere (885,696) amounted to 5.7 per cent of the population.[64] To show how active the Qing state was, the German author Mathias Heinrich points out that up until 1850, it established 362 poor houses and 567 orphanages and then claims that in the year 1850 there would have been one 'national' poor house per 1.1 million people and one 'national' orphanage per 694,000 people. Historians of social welfare in Western Europe in the early modern era will not be impressed. The idea to create a network of hospices in counties and districts was abandoned by the Qing government because of fraud and corruption.[65]

In an effort to show how *irrelevant* poor relief and charity were as a source of income transfer in the Dutch Republic, De Vries and Van der Woude come up with the estimate that at the very beginning of the nineteenth century, in total, would have amounted to 'only' eight to ten million guilders. That would be some four to five guilders, that is, the equivalent of some 40 to 50 grams of silver, per capita. GDP per capita per year at the time was estimated at about 120 guilders. So we are discussing a transfer of money to the poor of over 3–4 per cent of Dutch GDP. This clearly is *not* less than the Chinese government spent on relief via its granaries or other means.[66] Other figures too point in the direction of quite substantial poor relief in what is now called the Netherlands. In 1807 as well as in 1817, the number of people receiving poor relief was more than 10 per cent of total population.[67] This of course is only one more indication that the success of the market in relieving poverty in the West was very relative. Without massive poor relief the situation there at times would have been quite grim although I doubt whether the Dutch Republic and Britain then would have been confronted with real famines.

At various places in his work Wong is willing to admit that Western governments too did care about the food supply of their subjects. But he then claims that care would only extend to the cities, whereas nothing would have been done for the countryside.[68] That simply is not true. Poor relief in both Britain and the Dutch Republic during the eighteenth and nineteenth centuries covered the *entire* country, cities as well as villages.[69] Again, in particular, the British situation does not fit Wong's model. Let me just give two quotes from Peter Lindert's book on the history of social spending: 'The English gave relatively more relief in the poor and declining countryside, whereas the rest of the world gave more relief in the towns and cities'; and: 'Why was poor relief so rural in England and Wales, and so urban on the Continent…?'[70] Patriquin explicitly claims that the emergence and continuity of the Poor Law system can best be understood

---

[63]Daunton, *Progress and Poverty*, 471.

[64]Evans, *Forging of the Modern State*, 426.

[65]Heinrich, 'Welfare and public philanthropy', 126.

[66]De Vries and Van der Woude, *First Modern Economy*, 600.

[67]Van Zanden and Van Riel, *Strictures of Inheritance*, 122.

[68]Wong, 'Qing granaries and world history', 519–20.

[69]Lindert, *Growing Public*, 56–8.

[70]Lindert, *Growing Public*, 56 and 58.

in terms of the early development of capitalist social relations within England's *rural* economy. Payments to the poor had to be relatively high, as those receiving help were landless or semi-landless. The system may very well have been functional to capitalism by stabilizing the labour market and dampening social unrest.

Wong posits a second major difference: 'There was no Chinese parallel to the European distinction between providing charity to the poor, the task of the Church, and provisioning urban centres, the task of the state.'[71] Apart from the fact that making a strict distinction between Church and state in this context is clearly anachronistic for Protestant (and, by the way, to a very large extent also for Catholic) countries in early modern Europe, this claim too, at least for Britain and the Dutch Republic, simply is not true. The British system of poor relief may have been organized on a parish base, but it rested on *national* and *secular* legislation. It was a compulsory charity paid out of taxation on property that was locally collected in Britain's 15,000 parishes, and it was also spent locally. But it was determined by *Parliament* that set the rates. Poor relief was a shared project of Church and state in most Protestant countries, although, as Lindert stresses, this was the case *only* there.[72] In England the parishes acted as local government agencies. In the Dutch Republic, the Church – that was not really an official state church – had a leading role in actually administering poor relief, while civil authorities held a close watch, being in the last instance responsible.[73] Private relief, in practice highly decentralized, was mandated by and chained to government relief administration.[74] The Dutch Republic always also knew a purely civilian, non-Church organized poor relief, the importance of which clearly increased.

If one would really want to stress *differences* in this context between government policies in Qing China and in Western Europe, one should not focus so much on quantities, that I think clearly were *higher* in Britain and the Dutch Republic than in China, as on the reasons governments had for providing relief and the criteria that qualified people for actually receiving it. Here there indeed existed major differences between China's government and those of, for example, Britain and the Dutch Republic, to again focus on these two European countries. Reasons of public security and combating unrest were of course important for every ruler. But what is very prominent in Britain and the Dutch Republic, and in most of Western Europe, and what is almost completely lacking in China, is the tight connection between providing relief and 'disciplining', 'moralising', 'reforming' or whatever term one wants to use, the persons receiving that relief. In Western Europe, there almost always were strings attached to actually receiving help. To put it in a nutshell: social policy there was as much if not more about *discipline*, often a very specific, that is 'economic', discipline, than about *support*.

---

[71]Wong, 'Qing granaries', 518. Wong is not the only historian of China who writes as if the state in Western Europe in the early modern era was secular. See also Antony and Leonard, 'Dragons, tigers and dogs: an introduction', 4, and Thornton, *Disciplining the State*, 23.

[72]Lindert, *Growing Public*, 43–4.

[73]De Vries and Van der Woude, *First Modern Economy*, 656.

[74]De Vries and Van der Woude, *First Modern Economy*, 654–66.

In this respect it is quite telling and not accidental that in debates on how to take care of the poor, there is that constant reference to different kinds of poor who had to be treated differently. In the context of the British Poor Laws, for example, we see the following distinctions:

> The impotent poor could not look after themselves or go to work. They included the ill, the infirm, the elderly, and children with no one to properly care for them. It was generally held that they should be looked after. The able-bodied poor normally referred to those who were unable to find work – either due to cyclical or long-term unemployment in the area, or a lack of skills. Attempts to assist these people, and move them out of this category, varied over the centuries, but usually consisted of relief either in the form of work or money. The vagrants or 'beggars', sometimes termed 'sturdy rogues', were deemed those who could work but had refused to. Such people were seen in the sixteenth and seventeenth centuries as potential criminals, apt to do mischief when hired for the purpose. They were normally seen as needing punishment, and as such were often whipped in the market place as an example to others, or sometimes sent to so-called 'houses of correction'. This group was also termed the idle poor.[75]

As will be discussed later on, Western Europe became covered with hundreds of houses where poor people were put to work.[76] Nowhere in Europe were such workhouses of whatever kind self-supporting, let alone profitable. In England it soon became apparent that it was much cheaper to maintain people on outdoor relief in the form of cash payments. Their main function apparently was to create apprehension among the poor and make them keep their capacity for labour.[77] As a contemporary observer said: 'The true profit of parish labour is to form industrious habits'.[78] Those in charge of the poor tried to monitor and, if they saw fit, change their behaviour and were very keen on differentiating between 'worthy' and 'unworthy' poor. Peter Lindert presents an interesting list of offences from a village in Essex for the period 1823–8, indicating circumstances in which people were *not* or no longer entitled to receive relief. Number one on that list was the failure to attend church the preceding Sunday.[79] Then came failure to report earnings accurately to the parish overseer and refusal to work for a low pay for local farmers. Even having a pet could be regarded as a serious transgression.[80] For the Dutch case, but the same applies to most of Western Europe, De Vries and Van der Woude point out that taking care of the poor played a structural part in the regulation of urban and, quite often, also rural economies.[81] 'Charity' went hand in hand with the prohibition of begging and with running 'houses of discipline' or 'poor houses', where

---

[75] I took this description from http://cs.mcgill.ca/~rwest/wikispeedia/wpcd/wp/p/Poor_Law.htm. Consulted 16 December 2014.
[76] See pages 421–6.
[77] Lis and Soly, *Worthy Efforts*, 477–8.
[78] See for this quotation by a contemporary, Patriquin, *Agrarian Capitalism*, 139.
[79] So much for the separation of Church and State!
[80] Lindert, *Growing Public*, 48–51.
[81] I paraphrase De Vries and Van der Woude, *First Modern Economy*, 658.

'criminals', 'vagrants', 'beggars' and others were simply put to work. We will return to these efforts of the state and various societal elites to discipline the population, and in particular the labouring population, later on in Chapter 8.

How successful were social policies in combating crises?

If success is what matters, and that clearly is what Wong *cum suis* imply, the British and Dutch cases are quite interesting, and contradicting their theses. Overall and increasingly, governments in Britain and the Dutch Republic, the countries with the most liberalized internal markets of Europe, indeed acted on the assumption that 'the market' was to solve problems of food provisioning, in particular when it came to civilian consumption. I think one can only conclude that by and large their assumption proved to be correct and that 'the market' in combination with their measures was able to do just that. In 1671, to give but one example, merchants in a couple of towns in Holland had stored so much grain that they could meet domestic needs for ten to twelve years.[82] In the Dutch Republic the phenomenon of serious, *life-threatening* famine had already become extinct decades before. In the *magnum opus* by De Vries and Van der Woude on the Dutch economy in the period from 1500 to 1815, we find no reference at all to deaths by famine.[83] They refer to various 'subsistence crises' during the eighteenth century, but never to famines and indicate that during those crises government did intervene, be it on a fairly restricted scale and often in a decentralized way. The last serious famine in Great Britain was in Scotland in the years 1697–9, although 1710 was a very difficult year there too, like in the rest of Europe.[84]

Far be it for me to want to paint a rosy picture of the situation in Western Europe, but Wong's claim 'that it is uncertain that such crises [that is, serious famines that raised mortality] set (early modern) China apart from Europe' is not very helpful and somewhat misleading. They *did* set apart China from *Britain* and the *Dutch Republic*.[85] In these two Western European countries central governments did not choose China's 'solutions', as they simply did not face China's 'problems' – among other reasons because they simply were substantially wealthier. This obviously does not mean that those regions would not have known poverty, dearth, or years of serious distress – far from it. What 'better' proof could one wish for than the really stunning number of people receiving assistance of any sort over time? But, here again, *differences* between various European countries are extremely important. France, in the very heart of Western Europe, to give but one example, had no less than sixteen nationwide famines in the eighteenth century.[86] There

---

[82]Barbour, *Capitalism in Amsterdam*, 89.

[83]De Vries and Van der Woude, *First Modern Economy*.

[84]Daunton, *Progress and Poverty*, 56 and 410. For further information on England see Wells, *Wretched Faces*. For information on the famine in Scotland, see Devine, *Scottish Nation*, ch. 3.

[85]Wong, *China Transformed*, 25–7.

[86]See Daunton, *Progress and Poverty*, 56. Life expectancy at birth in France on average was some seven years lower than in Britain during the period from 1740 to 1810. See Livi Bacci, *Population of Europe*, 135.

was a serious subsistence crisis in many parts of the Western world in the years 1816–17. The second half of the 1840s was a period of very severe dearth, and many deaths, in many parts of Europe, with an absolutely disastrous famine in Ireland, formally part of the United Kingdom at the time, which claimed more than a million lives, most of them, again, perishing from diseases rather than from sheer starvation.[87] It would not be until after 1850 that provisioning the population with food would be fairly unproblematic – except of course during situations of crisis, for example, due to war – in the whole of Western Europe.

When it comes to the *need* of poor relief, the conclusion must be that in China during the eighteenth century the combination of increasing market integration and government policies to distribute grain in times of crisis certainly led to a decreasing incidence of 'famine' but not, I would think, to its actual disappearance. In that respect a tendency has emerged to paint a somewhat *too* rosy picture of material life in China at the time and to somewhat over-enthusiastically speak, even for the late eighteenth century, as Pomeranz does of 'a slowly but steadily rising standard of living' or as Deng does of 'the advancement in the Qing human development index, regarding life expectancies, adult literacy rates, standards of living and so forth'.[88] Food shortage continued to be a serious problem. This is what William Rowe writes in his biography of the famous official Chen Hongmou (1696–1771): 'Many times throughout his long provincial career [that brought him in many different regions of eighteenth-century China] Chen Hongmou was confronted with dearth or famine.'[89] Barrow, to whom we already referred earlier on, in his book from 1804, writes there were rarely three successive years without a famine in one province or other.[90] This of course is only quite impressionistic information, but, one might also look at the work of Will who, in his enthusiasm to show that China's government during the eighteenth century did a lot to fight famine of course has

Table 22 Life expectancy at birth, in years, for males and females combined, in England

1760	34.2
1780	34.7
1800	35.9
1820	39.2
1830	40.8
1850	39.5

Source: Wrigley, *English Population History*, 614.

---

[87]See Donnelly, *Great Irish Potato Famine*; Ó Gráda, Paping and Vanhaute, *When the Potato Failed* and Post, *Last Great Subsistence Crisis*. In the case of the Irish famine there are good reasons to believe that government in London was not willing or interested to help its 'second-class' subjects in Ireland.
[88]See Pomeranz, 'Without coal?', 249 and Deng, *China's Political Economy*, 23.
[89]Rowe, *Saving the World*. For the quotation see page 167.
[90]Barrow, *Travels in China*, 191.

to show that there was a lot of famine, and even famines that were life-threatening, to be fought.[91] The idea that people in China's most advanced regions lived as long and as good, or even longer and better, than people in Western Europe, which is quite popular in much of the revisionist literature, to my view has been refuted.[92] In the Lower Yangtze Valley life expectancy at birth in 1800 for females was 27.2 years and for males 28.4 years. Even if we take life expectancy at the age of one, the situation there certainly was *not* better than that in Britain.[93] The Chinese lived shorter lives and were poorer than inhabitants of Great Britain. Not by accident were China's rulers obsessed with food and famine. China is a huge country with many regions that were prone to bad harvests, especially outside the heart of China Proper, and many densely populated regions that were dependent on food imports, especially in the heart of China Proper. The supply of food certainly was more of a problem in China than in Britain during the very long eighteenth century.

Did China's rulers solve it? One should be wary of quick generalizations and differentiate according to place and, in this case especially, time. Overall, it seems that in China the situation deteriorated from the beginning of the nineteenth century when the granary system and, more in general, government policy became less efficient. During the eighteenth century, *overall* food supply was still 'sufficient'. That does not mean that food shortages were absent. On the contrary, they occurred quite frequently. In the nineteenth century a completely different situation emerged, in particular in the second half when the country became known as 'land of famines'.[94] In that respect it is helpful to differentiate between various types of food shortages and reserve the term 'famines' for crises that cause an increase in mortality.[95] An overall evaluation of the situation is very difficult because of differences in space and over time. The most extensive, impressively well-documented and even-handed study in this respect, the one by Lillian Li, analyses the situation in (various regions in) North China, in particular, in Zhili. The point of course is how representative her findings are. Zhili was one of the poorest provinces of the entire country. It, however, is near Manchuria, a grain-exporting region at the time, and near Peking, a city that received massive grain tributes that could be diverted to elsewhere. Li concludes that during the High Qing, that is, until the end of the eighteenth century, food shortages did not turn into 'true' famines with elevated mortality. Moreover, as compared to the worst famines in Europe, price rises were fairly moderate. Reports about death from starvation at the time were practically nil. Even

---

[91]Will, *Bureaucracy and Famine*. For a less optimistic picture see, for example, Kuhn, *Soulstealers*.
[92]See e.g. Pomeranz, *Great Divergence*, the chapter 'Living longer? Living better?'. For critique on the 'living-longer-thesis' or, more in general, the optimist picture of Qing China's demography, see Bryant, 'The West and the rest revisited', 421–33, and Wolf and Engelen, 'Fertility and fertility control' and the next note. For efforts to refute the claim that many Chinese would have been 'living better' see Chapter 1 notes 178–82.
[93]Elvin and Fox, 'Marriages, births, and deaths'.
[94]For the disastrous situation in the second half of the nineteenth century, but also for a quite gloomy picture of the situation in various parts of China already in the second half of the eighteenth century, see Davis, *Late Victorian Holocausts*, 64–79 and ch. 11. See also, for the situation in Hubei province, 1644–1911, Ho, *Studies on the Population*, Appendix IV.
[95]See for some distinctions Li, *Fighting Famine*, 8.

the mentioning of severe hunger was very exceptional. She thinks that in particular the combination of multi-cropping and state intervention prevented true famines and writes: 'The overall conclusion that famine relief … was fairly effective seems undeniable.'[96] Deng is far more outspoken and thinks that famine/disaster relief in China saved between 166.6 million and 251.3 million lives between 1666 and 1877. It, however, is not entirely clear to me how he came to these figures and he does not really expand on how successful Qing policies in the end were in *eliminating* hunger.[97]

Li explicitly points at the fact that hunger and malnutrition were quite frequent, with female infanticide being a sign of poverty and state activism helping to avert major mortality crises without, however, eliminating hunger and a marginal existence.[98] Which means it was not that successful after all. But again, we should be wary about being too optimistic about the situation in most parts of Europe too. Moreover, so she continues, the very success in fighting famine over the eighteenth century caused vulnerability in the nineteenth and twentieth centuries. The increase in population, made possible by an adequate provisioning of food, in the long run only helped to increase problems. The building of dykes and channels, undertaken to increase food supply, provided safety against flooding, but brought farming ever closer to rivers. Interference in the river system hastened its silting up which in turn was to cause flooding.[99] On the other hand, the efficiency of the institutions that had to combat famine, especially the system of granaries, over time decreased, as did their funding; corruption and fraud in contrast increased. The system of state-run civilian granaries began to function less well from the last decades of the eighteenth century with stocks decreasing just when, overall, the need became more urgent. Charity became more localized, as the central state needed more money for the military, especially after 1820, when local defence and law and order became priorities. Private philanthropy had to step into the breach. Of the three kinds of granaries – the ever-normal, charity and community granaries – the last two had always been more local but with government monitoring; that monitoring stopped after 1799. Whatever may have been the merits of China's rulers' 'agrarian paternalism', when it comes to food supply their policies became less efficient from the last two decades of the eighteenth century onwards.

The strategies China's government used to combat famine and poverty differed from those used in Britain. In comparing them we have to realize that the governments of both countries had quite different views of what their public role should be, so that one should be wary not to simply compare those strategies and their success out of context.[100] But even if one takes that into account, I fail to see how one can claim that China's government would be doing *more* for the material well-being of its subjects in terms of providing relief than that of Britain and how one can suggest it would have been more

---

[96]Li, *Fighting Famine*, 247. For her conclusions with regard to the situation under the High Qing, see 246–8.
[97]Deng, *China's Political Economy*, 23.
[98]Li, *Fighting Famine*, 382.
[99]Li, *Fighting Famine*, 'Introduction'.
[100]In chapter 6 we will look at those policies somewhat more in detail.

successful in eliminating famine. On top of that the conclusion seems inescapable that whereas the state in Britain became more involved and more efficient in planning and implementing various social policies, we see the opposite in China.

A brief comment on monetization of expenditure

When discussing government revenue in Great Britain we discussed whether government received its revenue in money or in kind. Let us ask the same question when it comes to expenditure. In Britain the government not only wanted payments to be in money: it also paid in money. Army and navy personnel increasingly were paid in hard and good money, as was the rule in *Western* Europe, and payment became more regular with the passing of time. In Britain payments by and to the state always were in silver or gold. Even allowances to the poor were mostly distributed in cash. Payments in kind were almost non-existent.[101] In China too, the biggest expenditure of central government was for the army. As compared to what was normal in Western Europe, that army was small. Basically it consisted of two parts: the Green Standard Army and units of so-called 'banner men'. The Green Standard troops received a salary. The 'active' banner men received a salary plus support for themselves and their dependents in the form of rice stipends.[102] The ratio of active to inactive among the banner men deteriorated substantially. During the eighteenth century, active banner men counted for only one-fourth of the total active army, but their stipends were three times as high as those of a normal Chinese Green Standard soldier, again an indication that Han and Manchu's were not equals in Qing China. Paying the banner men a salary was increasingly regarded as too heavy a burden on the treasury. So we see a tendency to 'pay' them in land that could be tilled for them by Chinese labourers. The highest-ranking banner men were provided with manors including the necessary labour. Isett estimates that the number of 'rusticated' banner men, that is banner men who had tracts of land and increasingly lost even the appearance of active soldiers, grew to be as high as 1 million. Whatever the exact figures, many people 'working' for government were not paid in money. Besides, *if* soldiers were paid a wage, that quite often was partly or even completely in copper coins, often at the official copper to silver exchange rate that need not have much connection at all to the actual 'exchange' rate, in particular in the second quarter of the nineteenth century.[103] This means wages often effectively were much lower.[104]

---

[101]Innes, 'The state and the poor', 229 and 241–3. For the amounts of money involved see page 195.
[102]For an analysis of 'the banner system' see Elliott, *Manchu Way* and Isett, *State, Peasant, and Merchant*, passim. Isset discusses the history of banner troops in Manchuria and Northern China. For information on the way in which soldiers were supposed to make a living when stationed in Xinjiang, basically on state farms and in colonies, see Millward, *Eurasian Crossroads*, 98–105.
[103]Lin, *China Upside Down*, e.g. 5 and 12 and passim under 'soldiers' in the index.
[104]Lin, *China Upside Down*, 130. See also, for a decline of real income of soldiers in the period from the seventeenth through the nineteenth centuries, Liu, *Wrestling for Power*, Appendix B 170–190. For a similar claim when it comes to agricultural incomes in the Yangtze Delta, see Allen, 'Agricultural productivity'.

The amount of money involved in paying public servants, too, was very small, comparatively speaking. The number of government officials in China was very low in comparison to Europe, as we will discuss later on in this text, and so was their official salary.[105] In the 1880s, for which we have an extensive calculation, the added official salaries of all 23,000 military and civilian officials together amounted to an ample 6 million taels. That is 270 taels or some 10,000 grams of silver (the silver equivalent of only some £90!) per capita.[106] Higher-ranking officials as a rule were paid in silver, but subordinate officials and officials' allowances at the provincial level were paid in copper. Funding for public works and transportation fees, too, were in copper.[107] Expenditures for poor relief and disaster relief by China's government were substantial. They are normally discussed primarily in terms of grain distributions from the so-called ever-normal granaries. But relief was rarely distributed in kind in its entirety. The usual rule seems to have been to give half the relief in kind and half in money.[108] All in all government clearly did contribute to the monetization of China's economy but it did so to a much smaller extent than was the case in Britain and also to a much smaller extent than scholars who refer to the epochal effects of the single-whip reforms like to claim.

OVER-EXPENDITURE

Whether the credit of the public funds be not a mine of gold to England?

Bishop George Berkeley (1685–1753) in 1735, from
The Works of George Berkeley, III, 172

... either a nation must destroy public credit, or public credit will destroy the nation.

David Hume (1711–76), *Essays, Moral, Political and Literary*,
II. IX, 28: Of public credit

If government deficits and arrears were the result of evil deeds by evil men, all that was needed was the intensification of moral exhortations and the punishment of the worst offenders.

Zelin, *Magistrate's Tael*, 25, on the traditional Chinese attitude towards
deficits incurred by rulers

---

[105]See pages 271–6.

[106]Chang, *Income of the Chinese Gentry*, 42. That may look substantial but Chinese government officials had to make all sorts of 'official' payments out of their private pocket. See pages 143–5. Compared to official incomes of Britons working for government, average official salaries of Chinese 'mandarins' were really tiny. See for examples of British salaries Knight, *Britain against Napoleon*, Appendix 1 and Ni and Van, 'High corruption income', Part Two. In the regulation Act of 1773 the salary of the Governor General of India of the English East India Company was set at £25,000 per year. Robins, *Corporation that Changed the World*, 112.

[107]See, for example, Lin, *China Upside Down*, 5 and 12.

[108]See Will, *Bureaucracy and Famine*, 133. I refer to official relief by government. Relief provided by individual gentry often was in kind. See ibid., 139.

It is beyond any reasonable doubt that central government's disposable income during the very long eighteenth century was much higher in Western Europe than in China, no matter how one would want to determine that difference. It was highest in Britain and the Netherlands. But that is not all. There were also huge contrasts between Western Europe and China when we look at government *expenditure*. Not so much the kind of things money was spent on – with all the differences in accent, those were fairly similar. The main difference was one of amount. Notwithstanding the fact that Western governments, relatively speaking, collected so much more money than those of China, that apparently still was not enough. They almost as a rule ran formidable budget deficits that accumulated into big debts.[109] Again, we have to realize the existence of big differences between mercantile countries like Britain and the Dutch Republic and the rest. Britain and the Dutch Republic had far better, institutionalized arrangements to deal with borrowing and the handling of loans and debts than other European countries. Public debts were quite common; institutional arrangements to effectively deal with them weren't. Averaged over the entire eighteenth century, about 30 per cent of the money Britain's governments spent was borrowed. That means they, on average, spent 40 per cent more than they received in revenue.[110]

Gross public expenditure for the period before 1850, reached its all-time high in the direct aftermath of the Napoleonic Wars. It then amounted to over £100 million.[111] That means that government in Britain spent a very substantial part of Britain's national

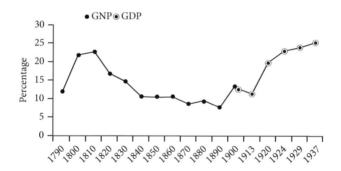

Graph 10 Total government expenditure as a percentage of gross national and domestic produce of Britain, 1790–1937.

Source: Daunton, 'Thrusting Leviathan: the politics of taxation', 321. See for several estimates that, although using different measures and calculations, come up with figures of a similar order of magnitude, Mann, *Sources of Social Power, II*, 366–7 and 373, and Weiss and Hobson, *States and Economic Development*, 114.

---

[109]See Ferguson, *Cash Nexus*, sections one and two; Körner, 'Expenditure' and 'Public credit'; Macdonald, *Free Nation*, 148–399, and Mann, *Sources of Social Power, II*, 358–509.
[110]See Schremmer, 'Taxation and public finance', 319, for the entire period. For periods of war, see Kennedy, *Rise and Fall of the Great Powers*, 81.
[111]Mitchell, *British Historical Statistics*, 587, gives a figure for total gross government expenditure at its height in 1815 of £112.9 million.

income. Here too varying estimates have been presented, but I will not be far off the mark in saying that this proportion, at its highest, in the beginning of the nineteenth century, will have reached a level of some 25 per cent of GDP.

Such massive spending resulted in a huge national debt. Of course, here too there are different estimates, but at its highest level, between 1815 and 1825, public debt was very near and in most estimates clearly *over* £800 million.[112] As this comparison to GNP shows, that is an enormous sum. A debt of £800 million is the equivalent of 88.8 billion grams of silver or 2.4 billion taels. This figure is for the United Kingdom and thus in principle includes Ireland. Per capita it would then amount to about 4,200 grams of silver. *Excluding* Ireland, which financially only became really integrated in the United Kingdom in the 1820s, we are talking about a sum of over 6,300 grams of silver per capita. This was a phenomenal burden for society and for government, even though the amount of money actually borrowed was substantially lower, as many bonds were sold at a discount.[113] Directly after the Napoleonic Wars over 60 per cent of taxes went

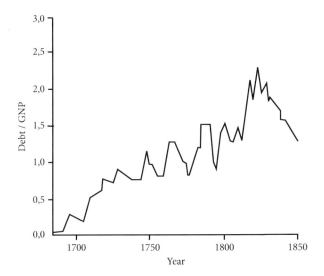

Graph 11 National debt of Great Britain/United Kingdom, 1690–1850, as compared to GNP.

Source: Macdonald, *Free Nation Deep in Debt*, 355. As indicated in Chapter 2 note 112, there exist higher estimates than the one by Macdonald.

---

[112]As always there are different estimates: Ferguson, *Cash Nexus*, 129 claims the United Kingdom's national debt reached its peak in 1821 with 268 per cent of GDP, which would be some £780 million; O'Brien claims that peak was £834 million in 1819. See his, 'Fiscal and financial preconditions', 23; Schremmer claims the country's national debt reached its peak with £848 million in 1820. See his 'Taxation and public finance', 354; Macdonald, *Free Nation*, pages 350 and 509–10, claims the peak was reached in 1821 with £856 million; Davies, to give one last figure, claims it was as high as £902 million (£816 million of funded debt and £86 million of floating debt) in 1816. See Davies, *History of Money*, 300. For the figures normally used see Mitchell, *British Historical Statistics*, 600–1.

[113]See for figures Macdonald, *Free Nation*, 350. He refers to a calculation that between 1794 and 1817 a debt had been created of £569 million in exchange for only £396 million in cash.

to servicing national debt. Default looked inevitable, but it did *not* occur. It was not just that the growth of the economy made even such a huge burden manageable: all the big creditors who obviously were interested in getting their money back were represented in Parliament.[114] The Napoleonic Wars brought national debt to an unprecedented level, but between 1760 and 1860 Great Britain's national debt was *never* lower than 100 per cent of GNP. For around two-thirds of that century – from approximately 1780 to 1845 – it was *never* lower than 150 per cent of GDP![115] In 1850 it still was some £800 million.[116] Budget deficits then, however, had become a thing of the past.

A good way to show the actual size of the amounts of money we are talking about is to compare them to China's GDP at the time. We have already referred to estimates of China's GDP for the 1750s, the 1830s and the 1880s. The estimate for China's GDP that is closest in time is the high estimate for 1833 of over 4 billion taels.[117] In grams of silver that is roughly 150 billion grams. As indicated, the United Kingdom's national debt of a rounded £800 million was the equivalent of 88.8 billion grams of silver. Whatever the exact value of the estimate of China's GDP, the United Kingdom, with a population substantially lower than that of various Chinese provinces, in the first half of the nineteenth century managed to keep its economy afloat *and* start industrializing, while having a debt that, expressed in silver, was more than half of China's total GDP at the time. If we look at them in per capita terms, the figures become even more astounding. As indicated, in the beginning of the 1820s, national debt for the entire United Kingdom, that is Great Britain *and* Ireland together, amounted to some 4,200 grams per capita. If we would not include the Irish under the debtors, the figure would be some 50 per cent higher. Let us assume for the sake of argument, that at that time GDP of China would have amounted to 4 billion taels. Considering the fact that there were some 400 million Chinese, this would amount to roughly 10 taels or about 375 grams of silver per Chinese. In brief: national debt per capita, expressed in silver, in the United Kingdom of Great Britain and Ireland was more than eleven times as high as average annual earnings per Chinese, expressed in silver. Of course, these are estimates at best and the fact that one could buy more for a gram of silver in China than one could in Britain would have to be taken into consideration. But even if our figures would be more precise and better comparable, the gist of my argument would certainly *not* collapse: in real terms and per capita, Great Britain's government spent *far more* than its Chinese counterpart, accumulated an enormous debt, got away with it, and did so while its economy took off. That is striking. Even more so considering the recent claim by economists Reinhart and Rogoff that across both advanced countries and emerging markets high public debt/GDP levels (which they define as 90 per cent and above) are

---

[114]Britain saw some examples of government trying to opt out of paying back its debts. But, overall, its track record from the Glorious Revolution onwards is impeccable as compared to that of, for example, France or Spain. For some comments, see Ferguson, *Cash Nexus*, 146–7.

[115]I took this information from Macdonald, *Free Nation*, 348–55. I paraphrase his text. Compare Clark, *Farewell to Alms*, 158, figure 8.8.

[116]See Mathias, *First Industrial Nation*, 463.

[117]See page 102 for estimates of China's GDP.

associated with notably lower growth outcomes.[118] Their claim has been contested.[119] But even those contestants would have to admit that the public debt of Great Britain at the very moment of its industrialization was extraordinarily high and would normally be expected to cause very serious trouble.

The other paragon of European mercantile capitalism, the Dutch Republic, also incurred a huge national debt. In the eighteenth century, crises were sometimes only narrowly averted, but it was not financial or fiscal problems that caused its collapse. The Dutch Republic presented a picture of almost unbelievable financial stability.[120] It never became ungovernable because of debts and it was not short of liquid money. Even in a very prudent estimate, foreign loans in 1790 amounted to at least 500 million to 650 million guilders. That is at a time when the Dutch Golden Age was supposed to have been already over for more than a century.[121] Nor did the Kingdom of Holland later became ungovernable or impoverished because of these huge debts on which government – that is the French king who ruled at the time – in 1810 *did* default. It reduced the interest payments on its debts to one-third and turned the rest of its debt into deferred

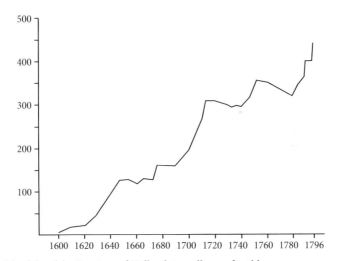

Graph 12 Public debt of the Province of Holland, in millions of guilders.

Source: De Vries and Van der Woude, *First Modern Economy*, 117, graph 4.2. Holland was by far the most important and wealthiest of the seven provinces of the Dutch Republic. A guilder was some 10 grams of silver.

---

[118]Reinhart and Rogoff, 'Growth in a time of debt', 578.

[119]Cecchitti, Mohanty and Zampolli, in their 'Real effects of debt', think that a public debt of over 85 per cent of GDP becomes a drag on economic growth. For critique see Herndom, Ash and Pollin, 'Does high public debt consistently stifle economic growth?'.

[120]Veenendaal, Jr., 'Fiscal crises and constitutional freedom'.

[121]De Vries and Van der Woude, *First Modern Economy*, ch. 4, 144.

debt. After the French left in 1813, this measure was not revoked.[122] In the 1820, the enormous debts notwithstanding, according to available estimates, the Netherlands was still one of the wealthiest countries in the world and invested enormous amounts of money abroad.[123] In the beginning of the nineteenth century, Dutch investors annually derived more than 50 million guilders as income from foreign investments. That is roughly 25 guilders per capita at a time when national income per capita amounted to 150 to 200 guilders. Total *foreign* investment per capita at that time was an estimated 1.75 times as big as GDP per capita. Total investment in domestic and foreign government debts, to give another indicator of Dutch liquidity, amounted to more than 1.5 billion guilders or, in silver, 400 million taels, substantially *more* than China's government income at that time.[124]

The fact that the Dutch Republic no longer acted as a great power after the War of the Spanish Succession and kept its real per capita tax levies fairly constant over the entire eighteenth century, clearly is not a sign of *overall* financial exhaustion, but rather of reticence of moneyed interests to finance a great power policy. Indirect taxes had already reached their limit early in the eighteenth century and substantial increases of taxes on income and wealth could only be realized if the elites were willing to comply: they only were to a limited extent. The fact that the Netherlands industrialized quite late in the nineteenth century is not due to a lack of private wealth either. Budget deficits, though, continued to be quite normal and at times quite high during the reign of the first Dutch King William I (1814–40).[125]

Table 23 **Public debt and interest payments of the Dutch Republic (to 1805)/the Netherlands, in millions of guilders**

Year	Public debt (guilders)	Interest payment (guilders)	Public debt/ GDP %
1795	766	22.7	160
1800	975 (±)	34.3	204
1805	1145	33.9	240
1810	1232 (±)	41.5	258
1815	1726	14.7	341
1840	2250	35.5	348
1850	1230	35.0 (±)	199

Source: Pfeil, Tot redding van het vaderland, 351.

[122]Veenendaal, 'Fiscal crises and constitutional freedom', 133. See also Van Zanden and Van Riel, *Strictures of Inheritance*, 90–106.
[123]According to Maddison, *The World Economy*, 264, the Netherlands were still the richest country in the world in 1820.
[124]De Vries and Van der Woude, *First Modern Economy*, ch. 4.3.2.
[125]See Van Zanden and Van Riel, *Strictures of Inheritance*, 99.

Britain and the Dutch Republic had extremely high debts. In France, as a percentage of national income, they clearly were lower. But they still were huge. Experts hold different strikingly different opinions when it comes to *how* huge. Richard Bonney estimates total French public debt in the beginning of the 1780s at an equivalent of 56 per cent of GNP.[126] Bosher suggests it was over 80 per cent in 1787.[127] Macdonald claims that in 1788 it amounted to 65 per cent.[128] Braudel thought it was no less than 150 per cent in 1789.[129] It is not easy to decide what to make of this, as the figures for the size of national debt *and* those for GDP that these authors use are so strikingly different. There seems to be consensus that the French National Assembly in 1789 inherited a public debt of approximately 5 billion livres.[130] That would amount to more than 22 billion grams of silver or some 900 grams per capita. We will never have definitive figures here but it is clear that also in France public debts were also high. Debts had always caused big problems for France's government. I have already referred to its frequent defaults.[131] All this apparently did not 'destroy' France's economy. In the first half of the nineteenth century, after more than twenty-five years of war, financial upheaval and paying huge reparations, France still was one of richest and most modern countries in the world. In 1818 its national debt, somewhat surprisingly, was much smaller than that of Britain, the winner of the long wars that had just ended. Per capita it is estimated at 80 francs or 360 grams of silver. In total, that would be about 11 billion grams of silver, less than 50 per cent of GDP.[132] In the United Kingdom at that moment the public debt burden was about 4,600 grams of silver per capita. Part of the explanation of this relatively low debt must have been that, as indicated, the French after the massive domestic confiscations in the beginning of the Revolution, made others pay as much as possible for their wars.[133] France's national debt continued to be less than half its GDP until the 1870s.[134]

The overall goal of this text is to find out what the main differences were between China's state and states in Western Europe. In that respect my conclusion in this chapter can be quite simple: most *Western* states, first and foremost Great Britain, the country that was becoming the richest and most powerful country in the world, knew huge public debts, far higher than Qing China would *ever* know. In fact until the 1850s, China knew no national debt whatsoever. Moreover, almost all Western European countries knew how to deal with debts so that they did not cause *major* structural economic harm. To a certain extent that is even true of Spain. What is just as striking, considering the tradition of claiming that Qing China would have been a despotic state that expropriated its own

---

[126]Bonney, 'The eighteenth century, II', 345.
[127]Bosher, *French Finances*, 22 and 255.
[128]Macdonald, *Free Nation*, 241.
[129]Braudel, *Civilization & Capitalism, III*, 307.
[130]Macdonald, *Free Nation*, 241, note 261 and 312, note 38.
[131]See page 82.
[132]Bonney, 'The eighteenth century. II', 382.
[133]See for Napoleon's dislike of credit page 83.
[134]See for information Dincecco, *Political Transformations*, 142–4 and Ferguson, *Cash nexus*, 130–1 and Piketty, *Capital in the Twenty-First Century*, 132–3.

subjects, is the fact that whereas debasement and government defaults, major instances of expropriation by government, were 'normal' occurrences in the history of most of early modern Western Europe – apart from Great Britain and the Dutch Republic – they were unknown in China at the time.

Over-expenditure was characteristic for *nearly* all governments in Western Europe.[135] Overall, the major exceptions were the tiny republics that together formed 'Switzerland' and that during the entire early modern period continued to spend minimal amounts on defence.[136] There were temporary exceptions like Sweden. In the 1630s, it mobilized an army of some 180,000 soldiers and still managed to incur hardly any debts. During the larger part of the eighteenth century, Prussia also was such an exception: the explanation very probably being that government there was extremely thrifty, used the so-called Canton system to keep in check military costs and collected a substantial income from state domains. Here too, however, in the end big wars and, more in particular, losing them, made the difference. After 1786, the surplus of income over expenditures disappeared. In 1794, the Prussian government had already spent its reserves and started incurring a public debt. When the country became directly involved in the battle against Napoleon, the financial consequences were massive and the disadvantages of the existing system became clear. The country had never developed flexible mechanisms to borrow money and could therefore only afford short wars that it needed to win quickly. Total government income hardly increased, even in the 1790s. Structural reforms were absent. Government began to borrow money but almost all of it came from fairly poor Prussia itself. With the defeat of 1806 it became patently clear things had to change.[137] Whatever may have been the exact amounts extorted by the French, in 1815 Prussia had a public debt of 206 million *thalers*. In another estimate, it was 287 million *thalers*.[138] Per capita that would be some 600 grams of silver. In total it amounted to less than 50 per cent of GDP. From then till 1848 national debt fell sharply as a percentage of GDP. In 1848 it was only 11 per cent.[139]

Military Keynesianism

In the spending and overspending of Europe's fiscal-military states the military played such a prominent role that it will not come as a surprise that several scholars suggest that for the economically more successful ones – first and foremost of course Great Britain, the first industrial nation – military spending should be seen in terms of a Keynesian impulse to the economies involved. Later on in the book, I will briefly discuss the role of violence and war in economic life more in general. Here in this chapter I will only focus

---

[135]See Körner, 'Expenditure' and 'Public credit' and Macdonald, *Free Nation*, 249.
[136]Körner, 'Expenditure', 414.
[137]Wilson, 'Prussia as a fiscal-military state', 121–4.
[138]Bonney, 'The eighteenth century. II', 367.
[139]See Dincecco, *Political Transformations*, 159–60 and Ferguson, *Cash Nexus*, 131.

on possible Keynesian effects of military (over-)spending. In his *Adam Smith in Beijing* the famous Italian scholar Giovanni Arrighi claims that massive military spending had salutary effects on the economy in early modern Europe and refers to this as 'military Keynesianism', a concept that was first coined by William McNeill.[140] He defines it as: 'the practice through which military expenditures boost the incomes of the citizens of the state that has made the expenditure, thereby increasing tax revenues and the capacity to finance new rounds of military expenditures.'[141] I will discuss his views for the case of Great Britain in the very long eighteenth century.[142] For the Chinese case that wouldn't make sense: the military expenses of the Qing were relatively tiny and they never overspent through their army. Let me start my analysis with a comment: although I would not want to turn it that into a major issue, I must say that, personally, I am not convinced the concept 'military Keynesianism' is a very appropriate one in this context. The term 'Keynesianism' suggests 'deficit spending'. In that respect it would have been helpful if Arrighi had also explicitly and systematically referred to government borrowing and/or money creating. As a rule Keynesianism is associated with combating under-consumption and underinvestment, or their opposites. The question then becomes whether military expenditures of Britain's government can be considered as such and how effective they were. To answer that question one in any case has to differentiate between various sources out of which these expenditures were paid. The bulk of regular revenue came from taxes. Over the entire very long eighteenth century, the bulk of Britain's taxes were collected as excises and customs on fairly ordinary consumer goods. I fail to see how taking money from fairly ordinary consumers and then transferring it to the military as such can create a substantial amount of extra demand and growth. Most ordinary taxpayers for most of the time would have had no problem in finding ways to spend it. Taxes paid by 'wealthy' people and transferred to the military may indeed have given a boost to the economy – and in the end to tax revenue. Here we are talking about money that otherwise may *not* have been spent. The effect is of course larger the more the military ploughs money back into the domestic economy, which to a very high extent was the case in Great Britain. In such a scenario taxes can contribute to combating underconsumption and underinvestment. This effect of mobilizing money that otherwise might have been lying idle can of course also exist in the case of government borrowing. Government can try and reach similar macroeconomic effects by, one way or another, increasing the money supply. It is only in cases where government actually increased total consumption and investment that one can speak of a really 'Keynesian' policy.

Considering these qualifications, one might have serious doubts about the Keynesian effects of several ways of paying for war in the case of industrializing Britain. Income

---

[140] McNeill, 'Industrialization of war'.

[141] Arrighi, *Adam Smith in Beijing*, 266. See further, idem, *Long Twentieth Century*, under 'military Keynesianism'.

[142] Arrighi is not the only one here who argues along Keynesian lines. See also McNeill, and the authors referred to when I discuss the 'mobilising' effect of war-related demand on pages 317–18.

tax, on higher income, as existed during the Napoleonic Wars might indeed have boosted total spending. But over the entire period discussed here such taxes were quite exceptional. When it comes to people who lent money to government, they may so have increased the total amount of money in actual circulation and pushed up effective demand. But those people they did not do so for free. They wanted their money back, with a bonus. A quite substantial part of government expenditure therefore always consisted of debt servicing.[143] That was done with tax money that to a large extent was collected on consumption of ordinary goods and in that way actually *diminished* consumption. Such loans to government thus basically boiled down to deferred taxes that as a rule can only be repaid in a growing economy and then in principle have the effect of lowering total consumption/investment.[144]

Increasing the total money supply *in whatever form*, certainly can have Keynesian effects but it can also easily lead to rising prices when a society reaches a situation of full use of its resources. Then much of its effect is an optical illusion. To the extent that it was a reason to enlarge the money supply and actually increase effective demand, military expenditure can certainly have given a boost to Great Britain's economy, in particular, if this occurred in a situation in which its resources were 'under-used'. The question then becomes whether the impact of the military and war in Britain were so big that they led to 'overstretch' and 'crowded out' other economic activities that might have been more productive, or whether they simply mobilized as yet unused resources.[145] Jeffrey Williamson, wondering why economic growth during the Industrial Revolution in Britain was so *slow* – as it indeed was from a current perspective – thinks that can be explained by the fact that during the Napoleonic Wars, Britain indeed suffered from such 'crowding out'. He believes it did not have the resources to quickly industrialize *and* fight very expensive wars at the same time.[146] Usually when economists use the term 'crowding out', they are referring to government spending using up financial and other resources that would otherwise be used by private enterprise. I think Williamson is mistaken here. Actual crowding out would in my view in any case lead to an increase in interest rates for those who want to borrow money. Notwithstanding enormous government borrowing and steeply increasing taxes, money did not become scarce, at least when interest rates are a good indicator. They continued to be quite low. Between 1714 and 1832, the usury laws continued to impose a maximum of 5 per cent interest on commercial loans. Interest rates on government stock were even lower. Industrializing Great

---

[143]See page 186.

[144]See Bonney, 'Introduction' (to the 1995 volume), 14–15.

[145]For the idea of 'overstretch' see Kennedy, *Rise and Fall of the Great Powers*, 'Epilogue'. This would be the essential problem for every great power: 'By going to war, or by devoting a large share of the nation's "manufacturing power" to expenditures upon "unproductive" armaments, one runs the risk of eroding the national economic base.' Ibid., 539. For the concept of 'crowding out' see page 214.

[146]Williamson, *Did British Capitalism Breed Inequality?*, 162.

Britain, even during the Napoleonic Wars, did not suffer from 'an aggregate shortage of savings'.[147] Other resources including labour also do not seem to have been extraordinarily scarce. There certainly were bottlenecks and price rises but no real price explosions with acute scarcities. Over the period 1792–1815, consumer prices, for example, only doubled, whereas commodities prices increased even less.[148] Even at the height of the Napoleonic Wars real per capita income and consumption were not pushed down, nor prices pushed up sharply. Even then Great Britain apparently still had unused or underused resources. I can only endorse this statement by Rodger: 'If taxation and borrowing were such an economic burden, one must … ask why the end of the Napoleonic War was marked by an economic slump rather than a boom.'[149]

To my view there will certainly have been examples of effective Keynesian impulses to Great Britain's economy but I think that we up until now lack is in-depth analyses of them and in particular analyses that show us how to determine the difference between 'bad' overspending and 'good' overspending. There are far too many examples of situations where military deficit spending, in the end, clearly was not good for economic development. When it comes to a strictly empirical, statistical test, I can only refer to the following comment by Ferguson: 'Taking the longest possible view, there appears to be no long-run statistical correlation – negative or positive – between defence expenditure as a percentage of GDP and real growth for either Britain or the United States.'[150] It in any case can only be applauded when scholars would no longer start from 'the implicit assumption … that the money which went to government was simply lost'.[151]

Whatever the actual effect of public debt may have been in early modern economies, people defending a full-blown 'Keynesian' and thus positive interpretation of public debt as a means to combat underinvestment and underconsumption, were exceptional at the time.[152] One can find several examples of people who consider (a certain amount of) public debt as positive, as it can draw idle funds into circulation and so directly fund productive investment and enlarge the stock of liquid money and thus leading to a fall in interest rates. I opened the chapter with a quote by Bishop Berkeley who also wondered in 1735 'Whether such credit be not the principal advantage that England hath over France? I may add, over every other country in Europe?'[153] Hume for a time also was positive in as far as credit lowered interest rates, claiming: 'Interest is the barometer

---

[147]The quotation is from Mathias, 'Financing the Industrial Revolution', 72. See for an extensive analysis along the lines of my text, O'Brien, 'Contributions of warfare', 21–36.

[148]See Graph 4.

[149]Rodger, 'War as an economic activity', 11.

[150]Ferguson, *Cash Nexus*, 403–7. Please notice that after the Napoleonic Wars military spending as a percentage of GDP clearly *decreased*. See page 185.

[151]Rodger, 'War as an economic activity', 10.

[152]For debates about credit and more in particular public debt, see Hont, *Jealousy of Trade*, ch. 4, and Hoppit, 'Attitudes toward credit', ch. 3.

[153]*The Works of George Berkeley* (London 1820) III, 172.

of the state, and its lowness is a sign, almost infallible, of the flourishing of a people.'[154] There were those who did not consider it really risky as long as it was owed to other members of society. Many people regarded public debt simply as a necessary evil to prevent bigger evil:

> The national debt was contracted in defence of our liberties and properties, and for the preservation of our most excellent constitution from popery and slavery. This encouraged the best subjects at the revolution to venture their lives and fortunes in maintaining a long and expensive war.[155]

Although it had important proponents, the argument, however, of those who wanted to pay for wars by increasing current income or drawing on reserves, never made much headway. With the passing of time the idea began to prevail that public debt was becoming too high. Adam Smith, for example, spoke of a 'pernicious system', and for Hume's view I can refer to the opening quotes of this chapter. They both became convinced of the drawbacks of national debt, especially when it was as big as in Britain.[156]

All in all for the case under discussion here the concept 'military Keynesianism' and the supposedly 'self-enforcing', virtuous circle it could start are rather underspecified. To the extent that a thing like 'military Keynesianism' actually existed, which I think was the case in Great Britain, the chances to find examples of it in Great Britain must have been substantial. A more detailed analysis of the money involved, its sources and uses would be needed to determine its exact impact. Studying war also as an economic activity, as, in particular, O'Brien and Rodger suggest, definitely would be a promising and fertile research programme. Arrighi sometimes suggests that the real virtuous circle he is analysing lay in the fact that investments in the military could be an excellent investment that supported trade and empire-building. That may very well be true, but there is nothing much 'Keynesian' about that.

Frugal China

Things could hardly have been more different in Qing China at the time. Official tax rates were quite low there and actual tax levies were even lower. We have already referred to tax exemptions and remittances, grants, tax freezes, and so on. The idea that is so popular in neoclassical and institutionalist literature that all pre-industrial states apart from the Dutch Republic (from its Golden Age onwards) and post-Glorious Revolution Britain would have been 'predatory' states ruled by 'stationary bandits' always on the lookout for money, clearly is incorrect when it comes to early modern China.

---

[154]Hume, *Essays*, 303–4.
[155]Hoppit, 'Attitudes to credit', 316–7. This quotation is from 1733. Hoppit does not indicate whom he quotes.
[156]See for these quotations, Hoppit, 'Checking the Leviathan', 286, and Rothschild, 'English Kopf', 39.

Its rulers were not 'predators' constantly trying to maximize their income. They often were keener on cutting down *expenditure* than on increasing *income*. No Qing emperor in the long eighteenth century had a deficit on its budget. Normally there was money left in the treasury. That of course does not exclude that certain regions received 'Keynesian' impulses via military spending, for example the Sichuan-Tibet region.[157] Under the Kangxi and Yongzheng emperors and for a long time also under the Qianlong emperor the vault of the Board of Revenue accumulated funds. These emperors, who also had substantial reserves in the vaults of the Imperial Household, were in the black and not, as was normal in the West, in the red. In the 1770s, the vault of the Board of Revenue contained some 80 million taels, the highest known reserve of the eighteenth century. In 1796 that surplus was still 70 million taels. This was at a time when the Qianlong emperor had already undertaken more than half of his famous 'ten completed great campaigns'. At the end of the White Lotus Rebellion the surplus had almost entirely disappeared. Thenceforth it was never higher than 33.5 million taels.[158] But even at end of the reign of the Daoguang emperor, in 1850, the treasury of the Board of Revenue still contained 8 million taels[159] Government may have been busy depleting its coffers, but they still were not empty. Even then, government did not have any debts. In the 1840s, according to Man-houng Lin, the Board of Revenue had deficits of 4 per cent of regular revenues. Lin claims that government income would then have been 120 million taels. That would mean that we are talking about a yearly deficit of almost 5 million taels, the silver equivalent of less than £2 million.[160] The way China's government managed to keep its deficits so low, from a European perspective at least, is striking too: it did so by spending less. It felt it had to do so as its revenues tended to decline with increasing tax arrears.[161]

---

[157]See Dai, *Sichuan Frontier and Tibet*, ch. 6.
[158]See for these figures Chang, 'Economic role', 272; Wang, *White Lotus Rebels and South China Pirates*, 201 and Woodside, 'Chi'en-lung reign', 270. For a graph showing the surplus of silver of the Board of Revenue in the Kangxi, Yongzheng and Qianlong reigns, see Lin, 'Shift from East Asia', 94.
[159]Lin, *China Upside Down*, 9 and 10. Westad therefore errs when he claims the Qing coffers would have been emptied already early in the nineteenth century. See his *Restless Empire*, 9.
[160]Lin, *China Upside Down*, 136. After having already finished this manuscript I read Chen, 'Financial strategies' that contains information with regard to the silver reserves in the Qing's Treasury over the period 1709–1850 and with regard to their annual fiscal surpluses over the period 1838–1908. The figures there are somewhat different from those I give in the text but they do not alter the gist of my comments. China's central government under the Qing continued to follow a strategy of 'precautionary saving.'
[161]Lin, *China Upside Down*, 135–6.

CHAPTER 3
FINANCE AND MONEY

FINANCIAL AND MONETARY SYSTEMS

Britain's financial revolution: The emergence of a system of representation and trust?

In Britain central government was able to collect such huge amounts of money in the form of taxes and to maintain such a huge debt because a certain set of institutions – and a certain set of power relations – had emerged whose combined impact is considered to have been so fundamental that in historiography their emergence has come to be known as a 'financial revolution'. This revolution began in the second half of the seventeenth century and accelerated after the Glorious Revolution of 1688, without which it would have been unimaginable. In the context of this text it is not possible and not necessary to go into much detail of *how* exactly things came about. The point is *that* they came about. The main institutional innovations were the creation of a national bank, the creation of a funded national debt, various improvements in the use of bonds and shares, more sophisticated systems of insurance, changes in the functioning of corporate law (e.g. the creation of a New East India Company) and the development of better ways of gathering and using information with regard to country and economy.[1] What actually *happened* has been charted in much detail: what it actually meant for Britain's *economic* history is hotly debated. In the work of scholars like North, Wallis and Weingast, and Acemoglu and Robinson, the Glorious Revolution and the Financial Revolution are tightly intertwined events that firmly set the country on the road to economic development, growth and, in the end, industrialization. From their perspective, these two revolutions created a refined system of well-described and secured property rights and smoothly functioning markets which are the necessary preconditions of and stimuli for permanent economic growth. They did so, moreover, in a state in which people were protected by rule of law and inclusive institutions and therefore willing to look for new economic opportunities instead of focusing on rent seeking.

Many historians are more prudent in their interpretation of what actually happened. Pincus, for example, does not deny the Glorious Revolution was modern and a real revolution. He convincingly claims that institutional changes from the very beginning

---

[1]For a description of what actually happened and changed see, in alphabetical order, Carruthers, *Politics and Markets*; Dickson, *Financial Revolution*; Roseveare, *Financial Revolution*, and Wennerlind, *Casualties of Credit*.

were on the agenda of many revolutionaries. He does point at the fact, however, that this does not mean their victory was permanent. In his view the political climate already began to change again with Sir Robert Walpole, Britain's Prime Minister from 1721 to 1742. Still, according to him, the Tory view on political economy, with its accent on agriculture, landed interest, territorial power and monopolies, would have again gained the upper hand in the 1760s and 1770s.[2] Some, as we already indicated, would claim that there was more continuity with previous developments and that change had already set in earlier.[3] Others may point out that it was not always immediately effective: interest rates on British government issues, for example, only reached the (low) levels of those of the Estates of Holland in the 1720s.[4] The break, moreover, was not as big as often suggested. The Crown, for example, kept more of its power than Whig historiography, which is so fond of zooming in on the contrasts with 'absolutist' France, tends to admit.[5] There are historians who doubt property rights were better protected after 1688.[6] Overall, among historians the idea seems to prevail that the connection between institutional development and economic growth, or rather *modern* economic growth, in Britain after 1688 was much less straightforward and clear than institutionalist economists and social scientists suggest. Whatever the exact importance of institutions for growth in general (that only a minority of scholars would deny), modern or 'Schumpeterian growth', as we know it since the Industrial Revolution, is primarily driven by technological innovation and breakthroughs in the field of energy and technology. How these would be connected to '1688' and all it stands for is anything but obvious. I therefore am rather sceptic about a direct link between specific institutions and the technological breakthroughs of Great Britain's industrialization in a strict sense. But even so it would still be undeniable that the institutional changes that are usually associated with the Glorious and the Financial Revolutions are fundamental when it comes to understanding the strength and flexibility of Britain's state and economy and their *overall* potential for power and plenty. Anyone wanting to discuss that potential thus must pay them attention. I will focus here on developments that directly impinge on Britain's infrastructural power in particular in the fields of (public) finance and money.

Developments like those described under the label 'financial revolution' are only possible in a certain societal setting. In Great Britain after 1688, state and society, in particular 'men of power' and 'men of means' (i.e. government and wealthy subjects), became ever more closely intertwined.[7] Many important political power holders were involved in the establishment of its three major joint-stock companies. In turn, these companies, the Bank of England, the New East India Company and the South

---

[2]Pincus, *1688*, 367–9 and 399.
[3]See the literature under Introduction note 9.
[4]Stasavage, *Public Debt*, 77–82. See also Sussman and Yafeh, 'Institutional reforms'.
[5]For a general toning down of this difference between British 'parliamentarism' and French 'absolutism' see e.g. Henshall, *Myth of Absolutism*.
[6]See Allen, *Global Economic History*, 29, and Hoppit, 'Compulsion, compensation and property rights'.
[7]For more nuance and detail see pages 227–33.

Sea Company, representing moneyed interests, functioned as important sources of money for government when that was short of cash.[8] But actual financial 'support' for government, in particular when it came to lending money to that state, had a broader base: in the middle of the eighteenth century, there were 50,000–60,000 public creditors in Britain. That is not an unimpressive number, but in relation to an electorate of close to 300,000 it still is rather modest. With the massive borrowing of the Napoleonic Wars, the ownership of public debt extended to a point where the creditors constituted a majority of the electorate. By the end of the Napoleonic Wars debt holders numbered around 300,000.[9] The institutions required to manage such a debt had been developed and a kind of shared interest and mutual trust between government and enough of its wealthy subjects had developed.

Apparently investing in government bonds was and continued to be regarded a good and safe investment: not only for the really wealthy, but also for a substantial number of middle class people. Government had established credible government debt. The fact that a substantial part of British national debt was in foreign, mostly Dutch, hands points in the same direction. The financial markets of London and other major financial centres in Western Europe (in particular Amsterdam) had already been integrated in the early eighteenth century. The percentage of foreign holdings of the English government's long-term borrowing, for example, rose from 10 per cent in 1723–4 to 20 per cent in 1750. In 1782, for example, Dutch investment in British funds amounted to 202 million guilders, which is some £20 million.[10] The Bank of England already functioned as an international lender of last resort in Western Europe as early as 1720, more than a century before it played that role for the English domestic economy. Apparently even foreigners trusted Britain's financial institutions, which in this case means they trusted Britain's political system. Their involvement was something of a relief for Britain's capital market. During the Napoleonic Wars London functioned like a magnet for Continental capital and capitalists alike, attracting huge sums of money.[11]

People holding government debts are almost by definition interested in the continuation of the existing political system. They are stakeholders in it. Creditors obviously have an interest that debtors are able to repay. Those who provided loans to Britain's government did so *voluntarily*. That means they must have thought it was not only a safe but also a good investment. Apparently they trusted they would get their money back, *plus* an extra remuneration. The fact that debt payments were 'funded' only strengthened their confidence. The principle of debt funding has been described by Martin Daunton as follows: 'The "funding system" linked the repayment of loans to a specific tax which served as the security or "fund" for each loan, and the limit of borrowing was set by tax revenues which left the government with the delicate task of selecting the tax to back each

---

[8]See for some comments Carruthers, *Politics and Markets*, 'Introduction', 3–26, and 't Hart, 'Mobilising resources'.

[9]Macdonald, *Free Nation*, 227 and 351.

[10]He, *Paths toward the Modern Fiscal State*, 76. Compare 't Hart, 'Mobilising resources', 198–9, and Van Zanden and Van Riel, *Strictures of Inheritance*, 99, where one can find the figure of 202 million guilders.

[11]See Introduction note 18.

loan.'[12] Another 'method' that was experimented with to deal with public debt, was the creating of a so-called 'sinking fund', which was first introduced by Robert Walpole in 1716 and worked quite effectively in the 1720s and early 1730s. In principle, the fund was to receive whatever surplus occurred in the national budget each year.[13] Too often, however, the treasury raided it when it needed money quickly. In the 1780s, it was reintroduced by William Pitt the Younger with better legislation that prevented ministers from raiding it in times of crisis. He increased taxes to ensure that £1 million surplus could be used to reduce the national debt and placed administration in the hands of commissioners. The scheme worked well between 1786 and 1793 with the commissioners receiving £8 million and reinvesting it to reduce the debt by more than £10 million. The fund was abandoned only in the 1820s. Horesh succinctly characterizes the essence of Britain's national debt as 'in the main owed *diffusely* and on a *long-term* basis to *voluntary* bondholders'.[14] During the Napoleonic Wars government needed such enormous amounts of money at such very short notice that it had to resort to introducing an income tax and to raising money via short-term, 'unfunded' obligations that were not secured by earmarked taxes and which it tried to fund over time to make them less costly.[15]

Over the very long eighteenth century there was a lot of improvising and things could easily have gone wrong. But it is very telling in this respect that between 1688 and 1815 interest rates on British government bonds were halved, while taxes and national debt both were high – and inflation substantial – and, what is more, constantly rising.[16] That implied that debt financing, *relatively speaking*, became less of a burden.[17] Interest rates on government debts in Britain were not only decreasing, but, and this of course is very important in a context of various competing states, they also became substantially lower than in other countries, like for example France.[18] Britain's government could borrow more money than its competitors and at lesser costs. One may well, with Epstein, consider the level of these interest rates as a proxy of the degree of trust that people with money to spare have in a government. Certain types of regimes tended to have lower borrowing costs than others.[19] There also existed, still again according to Epstein, a clear correlation between borrowing costs and fiscal efficiency.[20] This idea has been further explored and corroborated by Dincecco, who shows that states gained tax forces through centralization and limitations on the executive power.[21]

---

[12]Daunton, *Progress and Poverty*, 511–7. The definition is on page 511.
[13]See for some comments Soll, *Reckoning*, ch. 7.
[14]Horesh, *Chinese Money*, 70.
[15]Bordo and White, 'Tale of two currencies'.
[16]Daunton, *Trusting Leviathan*, 47.
[17]Macdonald, *Free Nation*, 242.
[18]See page 225.
[19]Epstein, 'Rise of the West', 250. Compare idem, *Freedom and Growth*, and Van Zanden and Prak, 'Towards an economic interpretation', 135. After 1750, the interest rates paid by government in Britain and the Dutch Republic were far below the European average.
[20]Epstein, 'Rise of the West', 251.
[21]See his *Political Transformations*, e.g. 107, where he claims his analysis 'provides powerful support for the argument that fiscal centralization and limited government had major positive effects on public finance'.

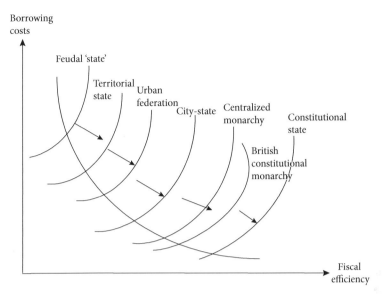

Figure 2 Borrowing costs and fiscal efficiency.

Source: Epstein, 'Rise of the West', 251.

It was the combined presence of a well-functioning bureaucracy, Parliament, the Bank of England and the way in which national debt was funded that enabled Britain's government to get so much credit. The quite peculiar British combination of local self-rule by local elites on the one hand and an efficient, strong and responsive central government on the other would also have been helpful. The system that emerged was not only amazingly efficient in raising money; it also had many intended and unintended societal effects. Ferguson claims its impact can be summoned in the following five points: (1) The need for an efficient tax-gathering bureaucracy implied a need for a system of formal education. (2) The existence of Parliament almost certainly enhanced the quality of legislation in the sphere of private property rights. (3) The development of a sophisticated system of government borrowing through a funded national debt encouraged financial innovation in the private sector. (4) High levels of government bond issuance widened and deepened the capital market. (5) A central bank with a monopoly over note-issue and the government's current account was also capable of developing functions that tended to stabilize the credit system as a whole. He then goes as far as to describe these developments as 'vital institutional preconditions for the industrial revolution'.[22] Each of these claims can probably be contested, but it would be hard to deny the enormous importance for Britain's economy and Britain's power of the emergence and further development of the financial institutions and arrangements that Ferguson is discussing. No state in the world could mobilize so much money at such short notice and for so long.

---

[22]Ferguson, *Cash Nexus*, 16–17.

Britain's financial revolution of the early modern period may have become the most famous one, but in the Dutch Republic, too, we find an advanced financial system. In many respects the British actually built upon foundations that had already been laid there.[23] As a matter of fact, most of them had already been laid or at least experimented with in Italian city-states, like Venice, in the thirteenth century.[24] During most of the seventeenth and eighteenth centuries the steady accumulation of debt in the Dutch Republic was counterbalanced by a decrease in interest rates. In the eighteenth century the return (after taxation) on government bonds during years of peace was 2.5 per cent in Holland and 3 per cent in the other provinces.[25] There apparently was so much capital available that, on top of that, large amounts of Dutch money could be lent to Britain's government and invested abroad. Just like in Britain, principal lenders in the Dutch Republic had an interest in maintaining the financial stability of the state. During the revolt against the Spaniards, among a total population of less than 2 million, some 65,000 investors, mostly from Holland, invested in public loans.[26] For the end of the eighteenth century the number of domestic creditors is estimated at about 100,000. Among them there were many small investors and the role of big institutional investors as compared to Britain was rather small. The total population of what now had become the Dutch Republic had hardly changed in the meantime.

Again, there existed substantial differences between various European countries. Authors like Hoffman, Postel-Vinay and Rosenthal have recently somewhat qualified the very bleak interpretation of France's finances that long dominated historiography.[27] But even they cannot deny that the French state in the end succumbed to a grave financial crisis that led to its demise in the French Revolution.[28] When it comes to public finance I still endorse the position of Cain and Hopkins when they write: 'The suggestion that Britain was about a century ahead of France in evolving modern financial institutions is supported by recent detailed research on public finance and monetary policy.'[29] France *did* fail to develop modern macroeconomic institution.[30] The country lacked a seriously organized banking system and national bank.[31] While taxes and national debt were lower than in Britain, France's pre-revolutionary government nevertheless had bigger problems in finding the money it needed than its British counterpart and it had to pay much more for it. Between 1726 and the French Revolution, France's government on average paid an interest rate of 7.3 per cent on

---

[23]See Tracy, *Financial Revolution*.

[24]Fratianni and Spinelli, 'Italian city-states', and Macdonald, *Free Nation*, ch. 2.

[25]Fritschy, 't Hart and Horlings, 'Long-term trends', 48.

[26]'t Hart, *Making of a Bourgeois State*, 173, and idem, 'Mobilising resources', 199.

[27]See, for example, Hoffman, Postel-Vinay and Rosenthal, *Priceless Markets*.

[28]See for the crisis that was *not* avoided Félix, 'Financial origins', and Norberg, 'French fiscal crisis'.

[29]Cain and Hopkins, *British Imperialism*, 71. See for further background Sonnenscher, *Before the Deluge*.

[30]White, 'France and the failure to modernize macroeconomic institutions'.

[31]Goubert, *Ancien Régime, I*, 55–60. Actually almost all countries lacked a national bank. Sweden got one in 1668, England in 1694, France in 1800, the Netherlands in 1814, Austria in 1817, Belgium in 1850, Germany in 1875 and Italy only in 1893. See Magnusson, *Nation, State and the Industrial Revolution*, 43.

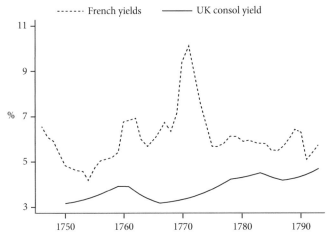

Graph 13 French and British government bond yields, 1746–93.

Source: Stasavage, *Public Debt and the Birth of the Democratic State*, 96. Bonds in Great Britain during the period 1815–1914 tended to yield some 4 to 5 per cent. See note 67 of this chapter.

the money it borrowed, whereas in the case of Britain's government that was only 3.67 per cent.[32]

The absence of a *financial* revolution made the state relatively weak and entailed a *social* revolution.[33] As in the case of China the strength of an economy need not be mirrored in the strength of its state. Pre-revolutionary France presents a good example of the apparent paradox already noticed by Montesquieu and expressed by him in this 'general rule': 'One can raise higher taxes, in proportion to the liberty of the subjects; and one is forced to moderate them to the degree that servitude increases.'[34] In their book on fiscal crises, liberty and representative government in Western Europe in the early modern era, Norberg and Hoffman point at that same apparent paradox: 'In the absolutist states, Spain and France, taxation was relatively light' whereas in the states with strong representative institutions, the Netherlands and eighteenth-century England, 'taxation was extraordinarily heavy'.[35] And they come up with, basically, an identical explanation: 'In the end, liberty was a necessary precondition for the emergence of a strong state, a state of wealth and power.'[36]

Governments like those of 'absolutist' France or 'despotic' China during the early modern era may look impressively powerful because they were not constrained by a system of checks and balances. But they apparently found it much harder to collect

---

[32]Macdonald, *Free Nation*, 242.

[33]See for a comparison of Great Britain and France Bonney, 'Towards a comparative fiscal history', and Daunton, 'Politics of British taxation'.

[34]This quotation is from his *De l'esprit des lois, III*, ch. 7.

[35]Hoffman and Norberg, 'Conclusion', 299. Please note we are talking in terms of averages per capita here.

[36]Hoffman and Norberg, 'Conclusion', 310.

substantial amounts of money or to even overspend without getting in trouble than governments that operated in an institutional setting, where they could somehow be held responsible for their actions, and included more people in their policy making. The more a state is embedded, the more 'infrastructural strength' it can mobilize, whereas a state that is despotically strong, almost by definition, so to say, stands 'opposed' to society, therefore lacks support and in the end is rather 'weak'.[37] Embedded states thank their 'infrastructural' power to the existence of certain channels via which (powerful) members of society can effectively make their voices heard. States with representative governments *can* manage to collect huge amounts of taxes with *relatively* little effort and they can even overspend structurally, because those governments can be checked by their 'power-holding' subjects and are basically trusted by them. It certainly helps when they, like Great Britain, are relatively small and have concentrated moneyed interest. Such a situation can only persist over the long run if certain institutional arrangements exist that protect the rights, including of course the property rights, of those wealthy subjects. In such a setting, to the surprise if not the serious irritation of neoclassical economists, big government need not at all hamper economic growth and welfare.[38]

It has become stock in trade to explain the 'liquidity' of the British fiscal-military state along these lines. Macdonald, in his book with the pregnant title *A Free Nation Deep in Debt. The Financial Roots of Democracy*, claims: 'The most creditworthy states were invariably those in which the people who provided the money also controlled the government.'[39] To underpin it, he points, as first examples, to the Greco-Roman world, then to the Italian city-states, to then pay ample attention to the Dutch Republic and Britain. The thesis that states in which 'the moneyed estates' had leverage in public financial affairs have a stronger public finance than states where those groups were excluded from public decision making runs as a red thread through his book and is at the heart of his comparison of France and Britain in the long eighteenth century. Gorski also points at the strength of the British state and explains it by its 'bureaucratic constitutionalism'. The term 'constitutionalism' stands for the codification of rights, protection and implementation of those rights in institutions and trust. The term 'bureaucratic' refers to the efficiency of the country's bureaucracy. He claims that in post-Glorious Revolution Britain, Parliament had supremacy over legislation and taxation so Britain's high taxes were legitimized and accepted.[40] Dincecco connects financial strength to centralized, limited government and Stasavage, in his book from 2003, to emerging democracy and, in his book of 2011, to the combination of a relatively small size and the presence of urban commercial centres.[41]

---

[37]See Mann, *Sources of Social Power*, passim, and for a comparison of state-formation in Western Europe and China along these lines Weiss and Hobson, *States and Economic Development*, Part One.

[38]See for this thesis e.g. Lindert, *Growing Public*.

[39]See the flap text of Macdonald, *Free Nation*.

[40]Gorski, 'Little Divergence', 184.

[41]Dincecco, 'Fiscal centralization'; idem, *Political Transformations*; Stasavage, *Public Debt*, and idem, *States of Credit*.

It has become fashionable in certain circles to connect the strength of states and economies in terms of their potential for sustained development and growth directly to their 'embeddedness' and the level of trust they generate. Apart from debates on property rights one currently finds many references to 'representation', 'checks and balances', the emergence of the 'rule of law' (formal and equal for all in its application) and to 'inclusive institutions' in literature about economic development.[42] Those are all directly linked to the organization and functioning of the state. So there is every reason to engage with this thesis that I, to already indicate my position, find quite problematic when it comes to explaining Britain's fiscal, financial and general economic history over the very long eighteenth century. I will take a publication by Van Zanden and Prak as point of departure. Their article deals with the connection between citizenship and the financial strength of nations and departs from a similar perspective.[43] It has the advantage that it is more historical, in the sense of concrete and empirical, than the collection of historically rather unspecified and unsubstantiated claims by Acemoglu and Robinson, which I have already dealt extensively with elsewhere, and by North, Wallis and Weingast.[44] Although in the title of their article Prak and Van Zanden only refer to the Dutch Republic, they also regularly comment on the situation in Britain. What counts here are their arguments.

According to them: '[N]ew institutional economics argues that the state should guarantee the system of property rights … supply public goods that help lower transactions costs … and solve market failures. … In return, citizens pay taxes to finance these public goods.'[45] They claim that by creating the conditions for trust and cooperation, citizenship arrangements also lower the transactions cost of the exchange between state and inhabitants. Citizens are prepared to pay relatively high taxes in return for the public goods they desire because they are more or less able to monitor the political process. In such a context, high taxes need not affect economic development negatively but can be transformed into growth-enhancing (public) investments. In that way, states with representative governments can collect more tax revenue *and* be more successful economically than states where tax revenue is lower and representative institutions are less developed. In their words: 'The model of citizenship, pioneered by the city states of Ancient Greece, re-emerged in Western Europe during the Middle Ages … and was redefined on a national scale from the 1770s and 1780s onwards, to become a core institution in nineteenth-century nation states.'[46] Where citizenship existed 'new systems of taxation on wealth and income, that might be considered fairer than, for example, excises and other indirect taxes could be introduced that were individualised … and based on information supplied by the citizens themselves.'[47] According to them, trust is

---

[42] The most recent and influential publications here of course are North, Wallis and Weingast, *Violence and Social Orders*, and Acemoglu and Robinson, *Why Nations Fail*.

[43] Van Zanden and Prak, 'Towards an economic interpretation'.

[44] See my 'Does wealth entirely depend on inclusive institutions and pluralist politics?' For reviews of *Violence and Social Orders* see under Google Scholar.

[45] Van Zanden and Prak, 'Towards an economic interpretation', 113.

[46] Van Zanden and Prak, 'Towards an economic interpretation', 139.

[47] Van Zanden and Prak, 'Towards an economic interpretation', 115.

at the core of the 'civic model': 'The introduction of relatively modern forms of taxation (that is taxes on wealth and income, the latter also being progressive) and the formation of a modern public debt with low interest rates suggests a degree of trust between state and citizens that we argue is typical of the civic model.'[48]

To what extent is their description and analysis, as they clearly claim, helpful and adequate for understanding the situation in Britain in the very long eighteenth century? As such the existence of a positive correlation between a state's 'embedment' – that is, some kind of institutionalized representation of (some of its) its subjects – and its financial strength and resilience is indeed beyond reasonable doubt. But it would be advisable to use concepts like 'citizenship', '(bureaucratic) constitutionalism' and 'representative government', not to mention 'democracy', 'liberty' and 'freedom', with much prudence when referring to countries in the early modern era, including the one we are focusing upon here: Great Britain in the long eighteenth century.[49] That one should avoid a word like 'democracy' is obvious. We are dealing here with a society that does not come anywhere near a modern democracy with all that it implies. Early modern Britain was a society with enormous political – and social and economic – *in*equalities that often were systematically backed up by law, also *after* 1688. In the early modern era concepts like 'freedom' or 'liberty', often actually 'liberties' in the sense of 'privileges', frequently refer to situations – far more, it has to be admitted, on the Continent than in Britain – that by definition imply inequality. To claim that Britain had a constitution from 1688 onwards is also somewhat 'optimist', as is talking about representative government. Gorski's claims that in the post-Glorious Revolution Britain, Parliament had supremacy over legislation and taxation, so that Britain's high taxes were legitimized and accepted taxes, also are rather simplifying and quite optimistic.[50] Legitimized and accepted by whom, I would tend to ask. The concept of 'citizenship' has so many modern, post-French Revolution connotations that using it for earlier periods can easily be misleading.

Even if in eighteenth-century Great Britain every adult male might claim to be a citizen in the sense of falling under the rule of law, formal equality for the law and even the rule of law went hand in hand with a practice in which actual participation in public affairs was confined to a very tiny part of society. Politically the country was quite exclusive. The right to vote and participate in important decision making *de facto* was restricted to a few per cent of the adult male population. In that respect the fact that through the entire nineteenth century far more people, in this context again only meaning *men*, had the vote in France than in Great Britain (or the Netherlands) is something that in the Whig interpretation of British history – a tradition in which I would include the authors discussed here – tends to be simply disregarded.[51] Economic power, too, was very concentrated so in that respect also one might strongly qualify

---

[48]Van Zanden and Prak, 'Towards an economic interpretation', 140.
[49]See for all those terms pages 226–7.
[50]Gorski, 'Little Divergence', 184.
[51]For the spread and the extension of the right to vote in various Western countries see, Chang, *Kicking Away the Ladder*, ch. 3.2.1; Finer, *History of Government, III*, 1637–38, and Van Zanden en Van Riel, *Strictures of Inheritance*, 245.

its inclusiveness. People in the country were very *un*equal when it comes to income, wealth and levels of taxation, *even* as compared to many other societies *at the time*. There continued to exist much exclusion via monopolies, granted and upheld by government. There was a big actual legal inequality between employers and employees and, as we have seen, labour was confronted with lots of coercion. Mercantilist policies, as we will see, were very protectionist and thus exclusive when it came to 'outsiders'. Rule of law indeed became an extremely relevant characteristic of Britain's legal system but only for citizens in the core, not for inhabitants of the rest of the empire who, of course in many other respects also, were much less 'included' than inhabitants of its core isle. As I indicated in my review, Acemoglu and Robinson are over-optimistic in their evaluation of Britain's 'inclusiveness'.[52] In defence of Britain one of course would have to add that in *Ancien Régime* continental Europe inequalities on the basis of *formal* (i.e. juridical) distinctions as a rule were much bigger.

Considering all these comments, the main difference between Britain on the one hand and China on the other hand does not reside so much in the fact that the first country, overall, would be 'more egalitarian', meaning that people there would enjoy more freedom and *de facto* were more actively and successfully engaged in matters of the state than in China. There indeed existed important formal differences in that respect: first and foremost the rule of law and the concept of basic laws that function as a kind of constitution. Here North *cum suis* and Acemoglu and Robinson definitely have a point, and a major one. The main difference, however, that interests us here is that in Britain the people who had money and actually ran the economy also wielded political power and were willing to support the state voluntarily – that is, *when acute need arose* and it was no longer possible to make other people bear the brunt.

The reference to acute necessity is important. We would be well advised to delve somewhat deeper into that positive correlation between 'representation' and 'inclusion', government strength and growth. I will focus here on financial strength where this connection, to my taste, is too often assumed and deduced rather than proven. Did that trade-off between (voluntary) payment of taxes and other contributions by elites to the state, and the provision of public goods to them by the state, that figures so prominently in Prak and Van Zanden's text really exist in Great Britain in the very long eighteenth century? In my view it did only in very specific situations. After 1688, wealthy Britons, as a rule, still only supported the state when they absolutely had to and never unselfishly and enthusiastically. Parliament may indeed have been the place in Britain where government and elites negotiated financial matters. But one should really be wary of

---

[52]See for all my comments on inequality in Great Britain in my 'Does wealth entirely depend on inclusive institutions and pluralist politics?' Very informative when it comes to the stunning inequality in income and especially wealth is Piketty, *Capital in the Twenty First Century*, passim under 'Britain', which was published after I finished that review. It is striking that the two most discussed blockbusters in economics and economic history of the last couple of years, Acemoglu and Robinson, *Why Nations Fail*, and Piketty, *Capital in the Twenty-First Century*, give a completely opposite interpretation of the role of inequality in capitalism. In this, and many other respects, I consider the position of Acemoglu and Robinson historically indefensible.

thinking too much in terms of reciprocity here. The represented elites got much more out of the state than they gave in return. The landed interests, who continued to own the bulk of Britain's wealth during the entire very long eighteenth century,[53] after a brief increase in land taxes during the War of Spanish Succession, were systematically spared, or rather systematically spared themselves: they paid only very little tax on their property, at least until the very end of the eighteenth century.[54] After the end of the Napoleonic Wars, they again were treated relatively leniently and protected by the Corn Laws (1815–46). Basically they themselves decided how much they gave to government. The bulk of tax revenue over the entire period discussed here consisted of customs and excises. Their incidence on the income of the rich was relatively minor. No one would want to call them 'progressive'. Until the definitive introduction in the 1840s of an income tax, levies on forms of income or wealth – apart from the land tax and a couple of minor, assessed taxes – were paid only in periods of utmost necessity, that is, when the British state or the interests of its elites were at serious risk and squeezing the ordinary tax payer no longer sufficed to collect the required amounts of money. In such circumstances, the best example of course being the Revolutionary and Napoleonic Wars with France – but one could also point at the Wars of Spanish Succession – the wealthy *did* agree to pay and collectively donated quite substantial amounts of money.

An income tax, symbol *par excellence* of a progressive tax, indeed was introduced in 1798, as were various other taxes that primarily hit the rich. Between 1799 and 1815 that income tax in total yielded £155 million.[55] But it was abolished as soon as possible, that is, in 1816 – to be reintroduced only in the 1840s. In the meantime 'normal', non-progressive excises and customs again provided the bulk of tax revenue – or rather they became even more important than they had been before in British history. This means that, over the entire period under discussion in this book, a very substantial part of government income in Britain was provided by people who had no clout whatsoever in the country's political system. Those represented in that system, as a rule, contributed relatively speaking little to the state, considering their wealth and income; those not represented, in contrast, relatively speaking contributed a lot. The joke is irresistible: the rich had representation and no taxation, the poor, taxation and no representation. Bargaining in Parliament often, though definitely not always, was *at the cost of* the non-represented.

Moreover, it was not so much 'constitution' and 'representation' *per se* that made the difference but party politics. What mattered in the case of Britain in the very long eighteenth century was the political power of the pressure group(s) representing creditor interests, in this case the moneyed interests among the Whigs. Men who invested in government debt never dominated Parliament numerically. In the period 1690–1710,

---

[53]Piketty, *Capital in the Twenty-First Century*, figure 3.1
[54]In that respect the claim by Acemoglu and Robinson that after 1688 Parliament 'would have moved to start taxing land' is not true. See their *Why Nations Fail*, 195. Their claim, on the same page, that it would have permitted 'the consolidation and elimination of many archaic forms of property and user rights' is very one-sided.
[55]Knight, *Britain Against Napoleon*, 387.

there were thirty-five of them, at best, whereas 257 votes were needed for a majority. Wealthy landowners continued to be very lightly taxed and well protected, as they continued to be by far the biggest group in Parliament over the entire eighteenth century. Between 1803 and 1815, for example, out of a total of 658 MPs, the number of City members of Parliament still 'only' fluctuated between 112 and 124. Approximately half of them were bankers.[56] The vote of moneyed interests among the Whigs was important enough, however, to often make the difference. In the end it was on the Whig party that creditors built their trust.[57] After the Revolution of 1688, Tory gentry and Whigs built a compromise. Macdonald describes it as follows:

> The essence of the eighteenth-century consensus was therefore as follows: the nation's finances would be run by the mercantile interests of London, while the reins of government remained in the hands of the landowners, who were able to ensure that their economic interests prevailed in other matters.[58]

For the small, more 'civic' Dutch Republic, Van Zanden and Prak may very well be right, also with their periodization. Already after 1670, more progressive elements were introduced in its tax system. Elites apparently were willing to tax themselves.[59] But here, too, this was only the case to a limited extend. This 'restricted' willingness in any case did not lead to a substantial increase of total tax income. France on the other hand, to refer to the favourite contrast-case in the literature on Europe, clearly lacked the institutions and the creditor party that were at the heart of the British system. On the eve of its revolution, its budget still was not public; it had no regular parliament to monitor the crown and no experience with systems of servicing debt comparable to those in Britain. Its government had a very bad track record when it came to dealing with debt and creditors. A major part of its wealth was *not* taxed, as most of the wealthy people enjoyed all kinds of exemptions. The government of Revolutionary France that started with a clean slate and could have tried to create more efficient and reliable ways to get funded quite quickly squandered its credibility.[60]

The suggestion that elites in 'inclusive' countries would have been willing to put up with substantial taxes because they got public goods in return, though probably in the end not incorrect, is somewhat rash. When it comes to the public goods provided by government, we have to realize that up until the very last decades of the period we are discussing here, by far the most important one, *when we look at the matter in terms of costs*, was military power. In Great Britain almost all tax money went to central government, which almost entirely spent it, and often more, on financing war. Those scholars who, like Mokyr,[61] consider warfare a net loss for taxpayers and a waste of human lives and

---

[56]Knight, *Britain Against Napoleon*, the note on page 390.
[57]Stasavage, *Public Debt*, passim, in particular 77–82.
[58]Macdonald, *Free Nation*, 230.
[59]See 't Hart, 'United Provinces', and De Vries and Van der Woude, *First Modern Economy*, 112.
[60]Bordo and White, 'Tale of two currencies'.
[61]Mokyr, *Enlightened Economy*, 392.

resources for the world and not a public good, may wonder why Parliament, while having the constitutional right to refuse funds for war, *never* did. For the Dutch Republic, Jan de Vries writes: 'Public goods were hardly ever provided by the central government and rarely by the provincial governments. It was a principle of republican statecraft that infrastructural investments and educational costs be devolved to the lowest possible unit of government and be paid for as much as possible by the direct beneficiaries.'[62]

In any case, for the early modern era and the nineteenth century the relation between the central state and its citizens, in my view, was much less straightforwardly reciprocal than scholars influenced by new institutional economics like to suggest. In that respect the thesis by Van Zanden and Prak that in the nineteenth and twentieth century democratization 'resulted in a strong increase in government spending and taxation' – an effect that they see happening 'in the long run' – may indeed be correct in that long run. But for the largest part of the nineteenth century, spending and taxation by the state as a percentage of GDP clearly *diminished* instead of increased.[63] Prak and Van Zanden, however, also refer to another indicator of the 'commitment' of those represented 'citizens': their willingness to fight for their country. They write: 'Citizens demanded the right to participate in the political process, some measure of democracy and transparency and in return were prepared to defend the national state (*such as through conscription,* [italics added]) and to pay their fair share of taxes.'[64] In the nineteenth century, in any case, most of the voting citizens actually felt very little urge to fight for 'their 'state'. In Britain, universal conscription was only introduced during the First World War. Before that, the bulk of the troops continued to consist of people who were more or less forced to serve: by poverty, lack of alternatives or *literally* where they were pressed. Many men belonging to the economic elite did serve their country in army and navy, but until well into the nineteenth century these tended to come from a quite specific *segment* of that elite, in particular the landed aristocracy. The so-called 'moneyed interests' who are supposed to have been the driving force behind '1688', and on whom institutional economists and their adherents like to focus, kept aloof from military affairs. Overall, elites in Europe *need* not actually serve in army and navy and actually *did* not, even if they lived in a country with 'universal conscription'. There were many exemptions for the wealthy and powerful and they had plenty of possibilities to find replacements. At the end of the nineteenth century, somewhat over half of those who in principle had to serve in the army actually did in so in Germany; somewhat

---

[62]De Vries, 'The Netherlands in the New World', 106–7.
[63]See for the quotes Van Zanden and Prak, 'Towards an economic interpretation', 119 and 140. Magnusson holds a similar view – see his *Nation, State and the Industrial Revolution*, 16: 'Existing evidence … seems to show that during the nineteenth century the public sector share of GDP for most European countries was steadily increasing.' He describes Britain as somewhat of an exception to this general trend but concludes on the same page that, 'the tendency in most other countries is quite different. Here public spending increases both in absolute and relative terms from the 1820s onwards'. To support this claim he refers to Schremmer, 'Taxation and public finance', 178. That text, however, covers pages 314–494 and only deals with the three countries referred to in its title. For the public sector share of GDP in the nineteenth century see Chapter 2 note 24.
[64]Van Zanden and Prak, 'Towards an economic interpretation', 119.

under half in Austria-Hungary; more than three-quarters in France, and less than 30 per cent in Russia.[65]

Up until now we have only been discussing *paying* money to government or *serving* it in the army or navy. When it comes to *lending* money to government, things looked quite different, in any case in Britain. Wealthy Britons, represented in Parliament, were indeed quite willing to shoulder their government's debts. Bonds by and large were in their hands or in those of rich foreigners. They were a safe investment because the people buying them could assure via Parliament that they would get their money back. Creditors were in control, in contrast to the ordinary Britons who had no say whatsoever over the taxes they had to pay. Theirs was a good investment because they could see to it that they would get it back with a bonus. Whether the debt was funded via specific taxes, as normally was the case after some time, or paid out of a 'sinking fund', ordinary Britons had to pay more than their fair share of taxes to enable government to pay off its debts – with a bonus – to their wealthy compatriots who paid less than their fair share in taxes. A large part of government expenditure in Britain was devoted to servicing debts. The actual sums of money involved where huge. Whereas over the period 1700–9 *annual* average debt charges amounted to £1.3 million, this sum had increased to on average almost £30 million annually over the period 1810–49. In terms of silver that is the equivalent of China's total annual official tax income.[66] It would really be too naïve and simplistic to explain the strength of Great Britain's state solely via representation and inclusion. Just as often, if not more often, it was based on non-representation and exclusion. Public debt in particular was a vehicle for redistribution of wealth, making the wealthy even wealthier. To quote Piketty:

> Inflation was virtually zero from 1815 to 1914, and the interest rate on government bonds was generally around four to five per cent; in particular, it was significantly higher than the growth rate. Under such conditions, investing in public debt can be very good business for wealthy people and their heirs.[67]

Some people were motivated primarily by carrots, others primarily, or in any case more, by sticks but, and this is fundamental, the system was institutionally solidly based and held.

China's financial system, or rather its absence

China's system of public finance can only be called quite simple. There was no structure whatsoever to handle national debt. This, as such, of course need not surprise us, as

---

[65]Leonard and Von Hirschhausen, *Empires und Nationalstaaten*, 88. See for further comments Osterhammel, *Verwandlung der Welt*, ch. XI.5.

[66]Mathias, *First Industrial Nation*, 463.

[67]Piketty, *Capital in the Twenty-First Century*, 131. See passim chapter 3. For the pure rate of return on capital in Britain over the period 1770–2010 see ibid., 202, figure 6.3.

there *was* no national debt. Why look for solutions for a non-existent problem? There was no national bank. There were no *formal, institutionalized* ways in which economic elites could be involved in shoring up government finances and the state. None of those institutions and arrangements referred to on pages 219–25, including chartered companies, existed in China. This would cause major difficulties for the country when it had to confront challenges that would have been considered minor in Western Europe at the time. In times of need, China's government could only come up with improvisation. It frequently occurred that elites made 'contributions'. But as a rule that was on an *ad hoc* basis in the form of a gift or support for which they might receive some honour, title or job. Government could also fall back on mobilizing the population to do corvee or assist in big public projects. But that too was *ad hoc*. Overall, as we saw, the importance of irregular, *ad hoc* sources of income, for example, selling titles or offices, and tax farming increase over time. The position and status of merchants, a group of people that was so fundamentally important for public finance in the West, was quite different in China. As compared to their Western counterparts, they were less powerful and held in somewhat lower esteem. They were less well protected against government and government officials. On the one hand, this made it easy and even seductive for officials to bully merchants and to turn them into scapegoats. On the other hand, it made merchants hesitant to fully trust and support government. In my description of the Canton System later in this text, I hope to illustrate briefly how their 'dangerous liaison'[68] – they in the end often did need each other – could work out.

The frugality of China's rulers clearly was a mixed blessing. Their way of running the country's finances worked satisfactorily as long as it was not put to a real test. Neither China's rulers, nor their subjects, ever developed any experience with deficit spending or handling public debt. Deficits in metropolitan or provincial treasuries were simply not allowed to occur. As long as revenues were sufficient, that was not a problem. It, however, could and did become a major problem quite rapidly when government needed much bigger amounts of money, in particular when it needed them on short notice. A tradition of borrowing from one's own population did not exist nor one of borrowing from foreigners. Borrowing from foreigners against substantial interest rates was something unheard of, let alone when those rates were higher than many other countries in the world had to pay.[69] In Britain a complex system had developed with the potential to mobilize enormous sums of money quickly. China completely lacked such a system.

China's rulers clearly thought differently from European rulers when it comes to debt and deficits and they apparently have 'infected' many historians who study China's history to do likewise. Beatrice Bartlett in her book on the history of the Grand Council writes that, on coming to power in 1723, the Yongzheng emperor was confronted with 'arrears in the land tax collections alone [that] came to a *staggering* [italics added] 2.5 million taels'. Those 'staggering arrears' amount to less than £1 million and less than

---

[68]For this expression see Tilly, *Coercion, Capital, and European States*, 58–62. In China the 'liaison' was even more dangerous – for capital, that is.

[69]That was the case in the 1850s. See Stanley, *Late Ch'ing Finance*, 64–72.

1 gram of silver per Chinese. Elsewhere in her book she refers to these 2.5 million taels as 'a very large shortage'.[70] I already mentioned Perdue's calculation of the total costs of the major Qing campaigns between 1747 and 1805. Those were about 300 million taels. If we add regular costs of the military, an estimated 30 million taels a year, that brings the total to some 2,100 million taels. In silver, that is the equivalent of £700 million. On average, we are then talking about the equivalent of less than £12 million *per year* (i.e. over that entire period on average some 6 grams of silver per inhabitant of China). Perdue nevertheless claims the Chinese state came into problems at the end of the eighteenth century because 'military costs rose dramatically'.[71] We find similar comments in Wang's recent book about crisis and reform under the Jiaqing emperor that systematically wants to convey the impression the Qianlong emperor had overstretched the empire and where the author refers to 'the spiralling operational costs of the Qing politics in the late eighteenth century' and claims 'the transactions costs of imperial and central control had reached unacceptable heights'. According to him, 'The cost of sustaining politico-military power in remote peripheries was often unacceptably heavy for a premodern agricultural state'.[72] As a reminder: Great Britain's *total* military expenditure in the period 1793–1815 amounted to some £1,000 million. Per year, that on average is £43 million. That boils down to roughly £3.40 per Briton, the equivalent of over 370 grams of silver.[73]

These differences in thinking about deficits and, especially, in the ability to deal with them became quite glaring in the nineteenth century. I cannot remember having ever read a book on the history of China during that century in which war indemnities and reparations were *not* mentioned among the main reasons why China's state *and* economy faltered. However, when one looks at the actual figures and compares them to figures we have for Europe, one simply has to conclude that, *comparatively speaking*, they were surprisingly low. What caused the problems in China at the time *cannot* have been the amounts of money involved *as such*. They must at least to a large extent have been caused by the incapability of government to tap the country's resources.

In the following paragraphs I will present various figures with regard to war reparations and indemnities, (foreign) debts and the famous 'silver drain' that occurred in the second quarter of the nineteenth century and that also always figures prominently in explanations of China's nineteenth-century predicament. They will all be presented in terms of grams of silver per capita. To get a better sense of order of magnitude: during that second quarter of that century 2 grams of silver more than sufficed for the subsistence of one adult male per day. At the Treaty of Nanking that was ratified after the First Opium War in 1843, it was stipulated that China should pay 'reparations' amounting to $21 million. In silver that is about 1.5 grams per Chinese. Over the entire period between 1842 and 1900, China's war reparations totalled 713 million taels. That

[70]Bartlett, *Monarchs and Ministers*, 27 and 71.
[71]Perdue, 'China's environment', table 1.
[72]See for these quotes Wang, *White Lotus Rebels and South China Pirates*, 33, 191 and 27–8.
[73]See Macdonald, *Free Nation*, 339, plus the explanation Macdonald provides in note 70 on pages 508–10. I here have excluded the Irish from my calculation. *Including* them would reduce the average by one-third to some 250 grams per capita.

boils down to on average some 12 million taels or 1–1.5 grams of silver per capita per year.[74] Government's *foreign* debts at the time also are a topic that has caused huge debates. They have often been considered a major problem at the time and in historiography. For the period 1853–1911, total foreign debt of state and provinces amounted to 227 million taels, less than 20 grams of silver per capita.[75] In the period discussed in this book, the Qing state did not incur any public debts at all. In Europe reparations and (foreign) debts of the magnitudes just referred to would have been considered irrelevant.[76]

Apparently China's public economy could not cope with challenges that would have been considered relatively minor in north-western Europe. That there was something wrong with China's financial system, and, I should add, with its monetary system, on which more will be said later on, also shows in the effects of the famous 'drain' of silver that became apparent from the 1820s onwards and that is always presented as a major cause of the hard times that befell China's economy. That this drain turns out to have been much smaller than has long been claimed, only adds to this view. It in any case was not large on a per capita basis. The extremely high estimates by contemporaries are no longer believed in serious research. Lin Zexu, the commissioner who played such an important role in the outbreak of the First Opium War, thought that several hundred million ounces of silver had left his mother country through the years, in his view all because of opium.[77] In 1837 a censor claimed that the annual drain amounted to in total 60 million taels.[78] With the passage of time estimates have tended to get lower. Morse, late in the nineteenth century, estimated that in the second quarter of the nineteenth century there was a net silver drain from China of over 200 million taels.[79] For the period 1826–40, Dermigny in 1964 estimated it at some 48 million taels.[80] Hao, almost a century after Morse, wrote about a net outflow between 1827 and 1849 of some 95 million taels.[81] A couple of years later Kindleberger came up with an almost identical estimate for that period.[82] In 1990, Lin claimed that for the period 1814–50, the net outflow was in the order of 100 million taels.[83] In her *China Upside Down*, she came up with a new

---

[74]Deng, *China's Political Economy*, 31. The value of the tael fluctuated during this period. Those fluctuations have been taken into account in this calculation.
[75]Deng, *China's Political Economy*, 65.
[76]See for figures about (foreign) debts in north-western Europe and for reparations that several European countries had to pay, Chapter 1 notes 63–9. See for a similar conclusion Chen, 'Financial strategies', chapter 7.5.
[77]Peng, *Monetary History*, 758. I will not discuss the *causes* of this drain, traditionally firmly linked to opium imports. Current explanations are more nuanced and multifaceted. See Lin, *China Upside Down*, ch. 2, and Irigoin, 'Trojan Horse'.
[78]Fairbank, *Trade and Diplomacy*, I, 76. Hamashita, 'Foreign trade finance', 117, gives an estimate, based on contemporary Chinese sources, that between 1821 and 1853 silver at a value of 480 million taels would have left China. That is not credible and in any case overlooks the fact that there were also silver *imports*, in particular of coins, into China.
[79]I found several references to this claim by Morse, for example, in Wang, 'Secular trends', note 34, but could not find the original quotation.
[80]Dermigny, *La Chine et l'Occident*, III, 1341.
[81]Hao, *Commercial Revolution*, 122.
[82]Kindleberger, *Spenders and Hoarders*, 69.
[83]Lin, 'From sweet potato to silver', 321.

estimate: the net outflow of silver from China in the period from 1808 to 1856 would have been some 270 million taels. In this calculation she includes the outflow of silver from China to India of about 11 million taels in the period 1808–14.[84] If we ignore the first ten years of the period for which Lin presents data and focus on the years 1825–56, when the drain on average was much higher, we find an average leakage of about 7 million taels per year. That is less than a gram per year per inhabitant of China. In *terms of value* this is absolutely tiny, less than one-hundredth of a pound sterling, to put it in international perspective, and less than the amount of money an adult Chinese at the time would need for subsistence. It is hard to imagine how such a drain *in terms of value* can have been the cause of a *major* crisis for China's government and for the country.[85] New estimates by, among others, Von Glahn come up with even lower figures. As he points out, the United States for several years sent substantial amounts of silver to China when the inflow from Britain – on which so many researchers always focused – had stopped. Besides, during the period of drain China indeed massively exported *silver* but imported substantial amounts of *silver coins*. On top of that he suggests mistakes have been made in several calculations. For the period 1818–54 he estimates total net outflow at some 94 million taels (i.e. on average some 2.5 million taels per year). That is less than one-third of a gram per Chinese per year.[86] The debate is still going on but its conclusion can in my view not be doubted: in terms of value the silver drain *cannot* have caused the drastic effects commonly ascribed to it.[87]

A comparison with the situation at the time in Britain may, again, be instructive here. Strikingly enough Britain had a trade deficit in its commodity trade that was much *higher* than that of China in the period from the 1820s to the 1850s. Its average annual imports for the period 1834–6 amounted to some £70 million. For the years 1844–6 they had risen to some £91 million. Total exports in these two periods, *including* re-exports, were £46 million and £58 million respectively. That leaves a gap – a drain – of £24 million and £33 million respectively. In taels, that would have been three times as much. Per capita, this is the equivalent of an annual silver drain of at least 150 grams in the first, and about 200 grams in the second, period. Apparently, a healthy economy and a healthy state could deal with this.[88] Actually no such drain occurred. The British made up for this huge deficit in commodity trade by exporting services and capital.[89] This 'solution' shows the enormous importance of the service sector for their economy, an importance that simply cannot be explained without extensive reference to the growth of the fiscal-military state. And it makes one wonder whether it have been possible for the Chinese to try and earn more money by providing services and investment to foreign countries.

---

[84]Lin, *China Upside Down*, 83–5. Please note that I am talking in terms of *net* outflow and turned dollars into taels.

[85]According to Lin, *China Upside Down*, 114, as a proportion of national income, the annual outflow for the period from 1808 to 1856 would have been 0.22 per cent. This is misplaced precision.

[86]Von Glahn, 'Cycles of silver', 50.

[87]Von Glahn, 'Cycles of silver', 51. This article reviews the current debate.

[88]Evans, *Forging of the Modern State*, 415–6.

[89]See pages 388–92.

As such, this of course need not imply that the silver drain was irrelevant for China. Even if the amount of silver that left the country was not impressive in terms of *value*, it may still have been an impressive amount of *money*. That is, the drain may have depleted China of an important means of payment.

Lin's claims that from 2006 that there would have been a net outflow of silver of 270 million taels between 1808 and 1856, would mean that, according to her, 19 per cent of China's silver supply – *not* its total monetary supply – would have left the country. She estimated that this silver supply would have amounted to some 2,000 million dollars/ 1,400 millions taels.[90] The net outflow estimated by Von Glahn would imply a drain of substantially below 10 per cent as compared to a stock of some 1,400 million taels in 1814. His reference to Li suggests a somewhat lower silver stock at the beginning of the drain. Wenkai He accepts an estimate that, because of the drain, China's silver stock would have shrunk between the 1820s and the 1850s by some 40 per cent.[91] He refers to a publication by Wang from 1981, which I could not check. This is the same author who, in 2002, claimed China's silver stock in 1830 amounted to 1,140–1,330 million taels. A 40 per cent drain would then be an outflow of some 500

Table 24 Estimates of Qing China's silver stock (millions of taels)

1750	±500[a]
1800	600–1,100[b]
Pre-1800	615[c]
1814	1,400[d]
1820	350[e]
1830	1,130–1,330[f]
1840	1,330[g]
1850	1,200[h]

Sources:
[a] Liu, *Wrestling for Power*, 60.
[b] According to the Chinese economist He Liping in Von Glahn, 'Cycles of silver', 51.
[c] Deng, 'Miracle or mirage', paragraph 4.1.
[d] Lin, *China Upside Down*, 85.
[e] According to Morse in Lin, *China Upside Down*, 83. I was unable to find the original reference. One finds this very low estimate for the 1820s–1850s also in Chen, *State Economic Policies*, 22, and Pritchard, *Crucial Years*, 103.
[f] Myers and Wang, 'Economic developments', 571. For 1830 Deng, 'Miracle or mirage', paragraph 4.4, also gives the figure of 1,330 million taels.
[g] Myers and Wang, 'Economic developments', 571.
[h] Hamashita, 'Foreign trade finance', 116.

---

[90] Lin, *China Upside Down*, 85.
[91] He, *Paths Toward the Modern Fiscal State*, 34.

million taels. That is really not very plausible. The central question, of course, is can such an outflow of 10 per cent, 20 per cent, maybe even somewhat more of one of its currencies, over several decades, have been the cause of, or a main contributing factor to, China's economic predicament from the 1820s onwards? To me as such it cannot. To really determine the impact of any such drain one would need to know more about what other types and quantities of money were available in China at the time. We will discuss that matter later on.

What does become clear though is that China never had much silver. According to Lin's *high* estimate, China's total silver supply in 1814 would have been about 1,400 million taels. This would mean that at that moment in time, *before* the 'drain' began and *after* many decades of supposedly enormous imports, when the stock must have been bigger than ever during the very long eighteenth century, China still only had a silver supply of at best some 140 grams per capita. As we will see, the silver supply and more in general, and more importantly, the *money* supply in Western European countries per capita was much bigger.[92] If, as all the more specialist literature suggests, silver in fact continued to be quite scarce in China over the entire period it was imported, the question becomes even more pressing why government in China before its drain had not much more seriously and systematically implemented policies to either get more silver into China and/or end China's dependency on imported silver. It also makes one curious about the strategies China's government implemented to do something about the drain – or in any case about its effects – when it actually occurred and why these strategies apparently were not very successful.

Whatever the exact figures may be, it is far from obvious that a drain of the relative size suggested by Lin and Von Glahn would turn China 'up-side down'. It is not mysterious *how* things actually worked out and *how* the 'drain' triggered something more drastic: the fact that silver left the country led to price deflation, which caused hoarding, which in turn made monetary problems more serious. Those in turn were worsened by the fact that the circulation of paper notes sharply decreased, which will not have been unrelated to the shrinking availability of (high-quality) silver and copper.[93] A large part of total tax revenue continued to be collected in a fixed amount of silver, which meant that the real tax burden for ordinary taxpayers increased. An identical amount of silver represented more purchasing power and the exchange rate between copper, the currency in which many of those taxpayers were paid and paid their dues to middlemen, and silver, the currency in which those middlemen paid the government, deteriorated. This will have caused social unrest and tax arrears, which meant less income for government.

But one may well ask whether all this was 'inevitable'. Silver was only one of the (semi-)precious metals that might be used as money: what about those other metals and what about paper money and credit? Silver scarcity was a global problem in the second quarter of the nineteenth century. Why were its effects so disastrous in China, whereas

---

[92]See here pages 240–58.
[93]Wang, 'Evolution of the Chinese monetary system', 442–3.

in many other countries it was not much more than a nuisance? Must not an explanation of China's predicament involve its entire political economy, including the ways in which its rulers dealt with the crisis? In my view China's financial and monetary problems, first and foremost those directly connected to government finance, became so big and unmanageable because of the structure and functioning of its financial and monetary systems. What we are discussing here is not simply a matter of wealth and poverty. It is a matter of the incapability of China's government to mobilize available money and resources. It would lead too far in detail to discuss what solutions have been suggested to deal with China's financial and monetary problems in the first half of the nineteenth century and what measures have actually been taken. Suffice to say here that no effective solutions were found.[94]

Great Britain's monetary system

Fernand Braudel was an extremely perspicuous observer of economic life. He for example made the following claim: 'The character and the state of health of an economy can be guessed almost at first glance from its dominant metal. ... In thriving economies ... silver or gold became prominent.'[95] A sophisticated monetary system as a rule points to a sophisticated economy and a well-organized, sophisticated state. A comparison in this respect can only point to an advantage of Great Britain over China. To systematically and in depth compare the monetary history of both countries would require an entire book. Here I will only briefly refer to some clear and relevant differences.[96]

Let us begin with a survey of the kinds of money in use in Great Britain and some comments regarding a currency that was scarcely used: copper. Whereas in China copper was very important as a currency till the very end of its early modern period in the 1840s, it already in Adam Smith's times was no longer a legal tender in Britain, except in the change of small silver coins.[97] In the second half of the eighteenth century, Britain became a very important copper *exporter*.[98] Between 1800 and 1850 about 40 per cent of global output was produced in British mines in the south-west counties of Cornwall and Devon. It was only in the 1850s that Chile surpassed Britain as a copper producer.[99] In principle, therefore, there *need* not have been a 'problem of small

---

[94]See Chapter 3 note 211.
[95]Braudel, *Civilization & Capitalism,* I, 458.
[96]For general information with regard to the situation in Great Britain see Cameron, 'England 1750–1844'; Capie, 'Origins and development'; idem, 'Money and economic development'; Coppieters, *English Bank Note Circulation;* Dyer and Gaspar, 'Reform'; Feavearyear, *Pound Sterling;* Feinstein, 'Capital formation'; Gayer, Rostow and Schwartz, *Growth and Fluctuation;* Jastram, *Golden Constant;* idem, *Silver;* Lindert, 'English population, wages and prices'; O'Brien, 'Mercantilist institutions', and Quinn, 'Money, finance and capital markets'. General information can be found in Mitchell, *British Historical Statistics.*
[97]Smith, *Inquiry into the Nature and Causes of the Wealth of Nations,* 57. On page 61 of that book Smith writes that copper was not a legal tender for more than the change of a shilling.
[98]For the copper trade see Shimada, *Intra-Asian Trade,* 71–9.
[99]Schmitz, 'Changing structure'.

change'. Just a small fraction of Britain's copper production would have sufficed for coining copper money. As a matter of fact there often were *serious* problems in that respect.[100] From quite early on government was not in favour of the use of copper as an official currency. Taking care that a sufficient supply of it would be available was not high on its agenda. There clearly was a lack of initiative on the part of the treasury. It did not take its responsibilities for providing the country with copper coins very seriously. The upper classes of British society were not concerned about quantity and quality of the regal copper coins. They were not regarded as 'real' money, as Joseph Harris, assay master of the Mint, admitted: 'Copper coins with us are properly not money, but a kind of tokens' – though they were, as he himself admitted, 'very useful in small home traffic.'[101] Not enough of them were issued.[102] There were copper presses for regal base-metal coins from 1672 onwards to keep down issue of private tokens. But the Mint's presses usually stamped blanks which had been prepared by some commercial firm and even in making the dies, sometimes acted just as agent to contractors. The main problem with the official production and provision of small change coin was that it was an exclusive prerogative of protected monopolies so that incentives were lacking for discovering and implementing a sounder system.[103] So-called copper companies produced much of the circulating copper money. Next to that there were many counterfeits and all kinds of token coins. Token coinage was simply too useful, considering the ever-increasing amount of small-scale transactions, to be abandoned. With the passing of time, so much bad money and counterfeit was circulating that something had to be done: an official re-coinage was announced. That occurred in 1797. Matthew Boulton in his mint in Birmingham applied steam power to the machinery for producing the new copper coins. In four years, this mint issued new copper coins worth £275,000. A revised, regularized and much better new copper coinage was introduced.[104]

In stories about Qing China the focus tends to be on silver. In Britain silver coin, as a matter of fact, became rather small change during the eighteenth century. One could refuse payment in silver for sums of over £25. Not much of it was minted and much of the silver that was circulating had seriously deteriorated. Britain was already on a gold standard with gold as the standard of value from 1717 onwards, even though this officially was only the case since 1816. Gold coinage was much more important and much more of it was issued. Over the period 1688–1821 the total valued of gold coinage minted by the Royal Mint was some nine times as high as that of the silver coins it produced.[105] Already in 1730, the Master of the Mint John Conduitt wrote: 'Nine parts in ten, or more, of all payments in England are now made in

---

[100]See for these problems Mathias, 'People's money', and Selgin, 'Institutional roots'. For a broader and more theoretical analysis see Sargent and Velde, *Big Problem of Small Change*.

[101]Davies, *History of Money*, 245.

[102]For copper coin production by the Royal Mint see Challis, 'Appendix I', 691–5.

[103]Selgin, 'Institutional roots'.

[104]Dyer and Gaspar, 'Reform', 444–8.

[105]See Mitchell, *British Historical Statistics*, 653–4.

gold.'[106] According to contemporary estimates, £40 million of gold coins circulated in the United Kingdom in 1798 whereas the amount of silver circulating there – in 1805 – was only £4 million.[107] Adam Smith wrote that in Scotland too more gold would be circulating than silver.[108] Silver nevertheless was quite important for currency. According to the so-called Committee on Coin, in 1790, silver coin was the coin that the poor principally used.[109] It probably was more important than copper in wage payments, although in retail transactions copper probably was the more important metal. Because silver coins were far more practical for everyday transactions than gold coins, the disappearance of silver from the British monetary stock could create problems. It often was in short supply. At times, for example, during the Napoleonic Wars, there might even have existed, as Davies calls it, 'desperate shortage' of silver.[110] One has to realize though that serious shortage of silver coins could and often did co-exist with great wealth in silver plate.[111] The Mint, before 1816, only coined what was offered to it and that was very little. Here too measures, in the end, were taken: between 1811 and 1816 the reformed Royal Mint produced 28 million silver tokens with a value of almost £3.5 million. In 1816 that Mint started coining new silver coins to a value of £1.8 million. It now no longer waited for private individuals to provide silver for coining. Under the new system government could advance money to the Mint so that it could purchase silver when it deemed this necessary.[112]

The reference to gold brings us to another major contrast between China and Britain. China, where gold was mined, did not use it as currency at all. Britain, in contrast, where no gold was mined at all, from 1717 onwards *de facto*, was on a gold standard.[113] After the Great Recoinage of 1696, arbitrage pulled gold into Britain and pushed silver out. Under the bimetallic standard of 1717, gold slowly, over the course of the eighteenth century, displaced silver. Especially after the Treaty of Methuen with Portugal in 1703, gold started to be imported in Britain in large quantities. It would take until 1816, however, before Britain formally adopted the gold standard. Interestingly enough it not only imported huge amounts of gold from Brazil via Portugal,[114] but also a certain amount from China. During the first half of the eighteenth century, gold, in terms of value, represented about one-third of Britain's imports from that country.[115]

---

[106]Dyer and Gaspar, 'Reform', 431.
[107]Coppieters, *English Bank Note Circulation*, 144–5.
[108]Davies, *History of Money*, 280 and 293.
[109]Mathias, 'People's money', 204.
[110]Davies, *History of Money*, 295.
[111]Mayhew, 'Silver in England'.
[112]Dyer and Gaspar, 'Reform', 471, 483 and 484.
[113]Gold, however, then was not exported or melted to turn it into coins. For the introduction of the gold standard in Britain see Feavearyear, *Pound Sterling*, and Goldstram, *Golden Standard*. For the comments on the prohibition of exporting and coining of gold see Capie, 'Emergence of the Bank of England', 297.
[114]Over the eighteenth century, 82 per cent of its gold coins left Portugal, most of them for Britain. See Lains and Ferreira da Silva, *Historia economica de Portugal, I*, 221.
[115]See Deng, 'Miracle or mirage', note 10; Dermigny, *La Chine et l'Occident, I*, 425–6 and 432; Peng, *Monetary History*, 766–7, note 8, and Von Glahn, *Fountain of Fortune*, 119, 129–33, 225, 227 and 255.

Whether we want to focus on copper, silver or gold, it is beyond reasonable doubt that, per capita, Britain's metal monetary stock was much bigger than that of China, even if sometimes it looked insufficient. It moreover increasingly consisted, when it comes to higher values, of good coins. As always in the economic history of early modern Europe there are various, sometimes quite differing estimates. According to Gregory King, in 1688, England's stock of bullion had a value of £28 million.[116] In 1698, Charles Davenant (1656–1714), an 'economist' and 'politician', estimated the value of total money supply of England and Wales at £26.6 million: £5.6 million in silver coins, £6 million in gold coins and the rest in liquid paper.[117] David Hume claimed in 1752 that cash worth £18 million was circulating in England, as against £12 million worth of paper money.[118] We already referred to an estimate that there would have been £40 million of gold coins circulating in the United Kingdom in 1798 and some £4 million worth of silver coins in 1805.[119] It is not exactly clear what to make of these contemporary estimates. Modern research has also produced differing estimates. Rondo Cameron came up with a figure of £20 million worth of circulating specie in England and Wales in 1800.[120] That would boil down to the equivalent of less than 300 grams of silver per capita. Jan de Vries produced an estimate that the metal money supply in 1790 in England alone would be worth £25 million.[121] That would amount to the equivalent of somewhat over 300 grams of silver per capita. Forrest Capie in a recent estimate claims that the metal monetary stock of England alone in 1790 had a value of £44 million. Per capita that would boil down to the equivalent of £5 or over 550 grams of silver.[122]

These are only a few estimates. They clearly are not strictly comparable. What is clear, however, is that, differences notwithstanding, they all come up with a figure that is substantially higher than that for the metal monetary stock – in that case copper cash and silver – of China.[123] According to my own estimates based on an analysis of the relevant literature, the value of the metal monetary stock of Britain (i.e. of actual coins) increased from about £3 to about £4, in the period from 1780 to 1830 – that is, from the equivalent of some 330 to that of more than 440 grams of silver *per capita*. Prices were higher in Great Britain and monetization of the economy more advanced because of, for example, the spread of wage labour, urbanization and high taxes that had to be paid in cash. In that sense indeed more money was needed in Great Britain than in China. For me there is no doubt that the velocity of money circulation will have been higher in Great Britain than in China. In the second half of the eighteenth century, Britain could afford to export huge amounts of bullion, in particular copper but also substantial amounts of silver. Those silver exports regularly led to complaints and definitely were a nuisance. Trade

---

[116]Braudel, *Civilization & Capitalism, III*, 307.
[117]Davies, *History of Money*, 280.
[118]Braudel, *Civilization & Capitalism, I*, 471.
[119]Coppieters, *English Bank Note Circulation*, 144–5.
[120]See Cameron, 'England 1750–1844', 42. The total stock of metals that might be coined of course was bigger.
[121]De Vries, 'Netherlands in the New World', 116.
[122]Capie, 'Money and economic development', 224, table 10.2.
[123]See pages 250–62.

with Asia, the region to which bullion was shipped, was often described as a 'pernicious trade' which 'drains all of Europe of the silver which America brings to it' and all that to satisfy the appetite of the (relatively) well-off people.[124] Or as Carey Reynell put it in the 1680s: 'To the East Indies we carry nothing but ready money, and bring in again nothing worth anything but spices.'[125] But those exports never were a serious problem for the overall functioning of the economy, nor did those complaints lead to fundamental changes of policy. Total monetary supply remained sufficient or at least adequate, as one can see in the declining interest rates.[126]

As yet we have only discussed metal money. One should not overlook the importance of paper money, though, and banks. Part and parcel of Britain's financial revolution was the creation of the Bank of England. Some explanation is in order here. As such it was founded as a private financial institution with a charter that had to be renewed regularly. It was primarily meant to act as an instrument to raise credit for the government, whose main banker it was. Besides it acted as fiscal agent to the Crown. It acquired a monopoly on joint-stock banking in England that lasted till 1826 and that typically enough did not apply to Scotland.[127] Together with the Bank of Scotland, founded in 1695, it was the first enduringly successful note issuer in the West and the ultimate repository of the only true cash. During industrialization Britain had one very large joint-stock bank, the Bank of England, and many scattered small private ones. The Bank of England in several other respects too had a privileged position. Its loans to government were guaranteed. The Exchequer simply had to see to it that they were paid back. It moreover had a full exemption from taxation and was privileged when it comes to notes' issues as compared to other issuers. Counterfeiters of its notes received capital punishment, which puts its notes on a par with the king's coinage. From the 1790s onwards it also printed small notes of £1, £2 and £5, which was very important for a smooth functioning of market transactions. In the 1820s the position of the bank and its role in regulating the money supply was intensely discussed with differing outcomes. Between 1826 and 1844 restrictions on the issuing of notes for other banks were relaxed. From 1834, Bank of England notes were accepted as legal tender. In 1844, it was decided to give the bank the monopoly on paper money issue so that in this respect it became a public institution, with a broad capital base and a large number of shareholders.[128]

---

[124]The quotation is by Anderson, *Historical and Chronological Deduction*. I found it in Berg, 'In pursuit of luxury', 96.

[125]Reynell, *Necessary Companion*, 13–14. I found this quotation in Pincus, *1688*, 371.

[126]Complaints about exports of silver to Asia had always been stock in trade in Western Europe, although, especially in Britain and the Netherlands, they became less frequent in the eighteenth century. For complaints during that century especially with regard to exports to China see Porter, *Ideographia*, ch. 4. For the wider debate see Berg, *Luxury in the Eighteenth Century*, and Piuz, 'Effets du commerce d'outre-mer'. For factual information see Bowen, 'Bullion for trade'.

[127]Scotland had a banking system of its own, with banking assets for the entire nation of £7.46 per capita in 1802. See Devine, *Scottish Nation*, 115.

[128]For the history and functioning of this bank see Capie, 'Emergence of the Bank of England'; Clapham, *Bank of England*; Cottrell, 'Banking and finance'; Daunton, *Poverty and Progress*, ch. 13; Deane, *First Industrial Revolution*, ch. 11, and Mathias, *First Industrial Nation*, ch. 5. I strongly paraphrase Mokyr, *Enlightened Economy*, 225–6.

In the specific context of our discussion of coinage it is not irrelevant to point out that the bank held substantial reserves in coin and in particular in bullion. These reserves fluctuated, sometimes very sharply. In the period from 1816 to 1848, roughly the period that China was confronting its silver drain, their value amounted to £3.6 million at their lowest, in August 1819, and £15.4 million at their highest, in 1844.[129] On average, over that period, they amounted to about £10 million. Such a bank with such reserves did not exist in China, which of cause made it even harder for China's government to have an effective monetary policy.

Talking about banks in this context must also mean to talk about paper money. Banks issuing notes – apart from the Bank of England – had opened all over England already in the eighteenth century.[130] Scholars agree that at the end of that century paper money in form of notes had become a very important part of total money circulation. Estimates, however, of how much of it circulated vary even more widely than in the case of bullion and coins. We already referred to the estimate by Charles Davenant who claimed in 1698 that there was already paper money worth £15 million circulating in Britain and to David Hume who thought that the value of circulating paper money in 1652 amounted to £12 million.[131] John Day, to switch to a modern scholar, regards that as a serious overestimation. He thinks that in 1750 in England, Bank of England notes – he does not refer to other bank notes – amounted to no more than one-tenth of monetary circulation.[132] Glyn Davies, in contrast, is convinced that from the very beginning of the eighteenth century the value of circulating paper money (according to him £15 million) surpassed that of circulating coins in England and Scotland.[133]

Day is right in pointing out that during the entire early modern era most people continued to believe that paper money could only function effectively if it was convertible on demand into gold or silver coin. When it comes to the situation in Britain from the second half of the eighteenth century onwards I think, however, that he exaggerates. The fact that in Britain at the very end of the eighteenth century convertibility was stopped for many years without disastrous consequences shows that its monetary system already was quite advanced. Again, differences between countries in Europe were big. The Bank of Amsterdam, Europe's most celebrated financial institution of the seventeenth and eighteenth centuries, immobilized between 80 and 100 per cent of the funds deposited in its vaults and did not issue notes at all.[134] In France banknote circulation apparently amounted to only 5 per cent of the money stock in 1803.[135]

---

[129]For information with regard to the size of these reserves see Gayer, Rostow and Schwartz, *Growth and Fluctuation*, under the heading 'Finance'. For the period 1817 to 1848 see pages 163, 202, 235, 267, 296 and 329. See for quite similar figures Mitchell, *British Historical Statistics*, 656–7.

[130]Cottrell, 'Banking and finance'.

[131]See page 243.

[132]Day, *Money and Finance*, 2.

[133]Davies, *History of Money*, 281. He does so referring to the estimate by Charles Davenant. See ibid., 280.

[134]Day, *Money and Finance*, 2.

[135]Horesh, *Chinese Money*, 143.

Table 25 Banknote circulation, Bank of England notes, value in million £

1790	8
1870	35

Source: Capie, 'Money and economic development', 224.

Table 26 Banknote circulation, Bank of England notes, value in million £

1750	4.3
1775	8.4
1800	1.5
1811	23.3
1844	20.2

Source: Coppieters, *English Bank Note Circulation*, 149–51.

Table 27 Banknote circulation, Bank of England notes, value in million £, annual averages

1822–6	roughly 20
1826–32	about 20
1832–7	less 20

Source: Gayer, Rostow and Schwartz, *Growth and Fluctuation*, 202, 235 and 267.

Table 28 Country banknotes, value in million £

1792	11
1811	21
1821	8.4
1844	8.2

Source: Coppieters, *English Bank Note Circulation*, 154–5.

Table 29 Total bank notes in million £

1775	10
1800	25
1811	45
1821	32
1831	29
1844	28.5

Source: Cameron, 'England, 1750–1844', 42.

On top of that there, of course, were all sorts of 'money' in the sense of means of payment – for example, private credit in the form of bills of exchange or transferable government bonds.

Let me, in an attempt to give a final synthesis and bring some coherence in my estimates, refer to the estimates by Rondo Cameron (Table 30). Paper money helped to keep Britain's monetary liquidity on an adequate level, although there definitely were moments when silver and copper coins were in very short supply and of quite bad quality. One must be careful not to paint too optimistic a picture of the British situation: just because all ended well, it need not have been well permanently. There were serious problems of small change and there were moments when the financial system functioned badly, in particular, at the end of the eighteenth and the first decades of the nineteenth century.[136] In the late eighteenth century, Britain's gold supplies were severely depleted by wars with America and France. The situation was exacerbated by a commercial crisis, which ruined many business and country banks. There was little choice than to rely increasingly on credit, tokens and paper money. This practical reality was legally enforced in February 1797, when the Bank of England was ordered by the Privy Council to stop redeeming its notes in coin. The policy of cash suspension lasted until 1821. It did *not* lead to a financial breakdown or social revolution. Apparently there was sufficient trust in the system.[137] That is a fact of huge importance: during and just after the Napoleonic Wars, Britain's monetary and financial system did not collapse under a strain that was incomparably bigger than the strain China's monetary and financial systems had to cope with from the second quarter of the nineteenth century onwards. China's monetary and financial systems, however, did *not* stand the test. The last decades of the period we are discussing (i.e. the decades till 1850) saw many lively debates on how to implement the now officially accepted gold standard and devise an effective link between a high-quality gold coinage on the one hand and a controlled yet sufficiently

---

[136]For an overall analysis of Britain's monetary policy see Daunton, *Progress and Poverty*, ch. 13. For a more technical analysis see Gayer, Rostow and Schwartz, *Growth and Fluctuation*, 655–7 and ch. 10.
[137]Eagleton and Williams, *Money*, 218–25.

Table 30 Components of money stocks and means of payment in million £ and percentages, 1688–1855

	Components of money stock and means of payment (£m.)								
	1688–9	1750	1775	1800–1	1811	1821	1831	1844	1855
Specie in circulation	10	15	16	20	15	18	30	36	50
Banknotes	2	5	10	25	45	32	29	28.5	26.7
Deposits		*	*	5†	15†	25†	40	80.5	145
Total money (M1)	12	20	26	50	75	75	99	145	221.7
Other	8	20	37	115†	140†	76	67	75	153
Total means of payment (M2)	20	40	63	165	215	151	166	220	374.7

	Components of money stock (percentages)								
	1688–9	1750	1775	1800–1	1811	1821	1831	1844	1855
Specie in circulation	83.3	75	61.5	40	20	24.0	30.3	25	22.6
Banknotes	16.7	25	38.5	50	60	42.7	29.3	20	12
Deposits		*	*	10†	20†	33.3†	40.4	55	65.4
Total money (M1)	100.0	100.0	100.0	100.0	100.0	100.0	100.0	100.0	100.0

Components of means of payment (percentages)									
	1688–9	1750	1775	1800–1	1811	1821	1831	1844	1855
Specie in circulation	50	37.5	25.4	12.1	7.0	11.9	18.1	16.4	13.3
Banknotes	10	12.5	15.9	15.2	20.9	21.2	17.4	12.9	7.1
Deposits		$\star$	$\star$	3.0	7.0	16.6	24.1	36.6	38.7
Other	40	50	58.7	69.7	65.1	50.3	40.4	34.1	40.9
Total means of payment (M2)	100.0	100.0	100.0	100.0	100.0	100.0	100.0	100.0	100.0

National income (£m.) and velocity of circulation									
	1688–9	1750	1775	1800–1	1811	1821	1831	1844	1855
National income (Y)	50.8	100	135	196.7	255.9	247.4	290.7	403.8	474.5
V1 (= Y/M1)	4.2	5.0	5.2	3.9	3.4	3.3	2.9	2.8	2.1
V2 (= Y/M2)	2.5	2.5	2.1	1.2	1.2	1.6	1.75	1.8	1.3
Per capita income (£)	9.24	16.27	18.17	21.71	24.79	20.50	20.77	24.42	25.2

Sources: Cameron, 'England, 1750–1844', 42, and taken from Mathias, *First Industrial Nation*, 402–3. See there for further comments and explanation in particular of the very speculative figures that are marked here by †.

elastic supply of paper money via a well-functioning bank system on the other hand. There is no need to go into details here. I refer the reader to the literature.[138]

It of course would lead too far to try and give an extensive analysis of the monetary situation in various Western European countries. I will confine myself to some comments on the metal monetary stock of the Dutch Republic and France. In the early modern world that we are discussing here, that probably is the best single indicator of a country's monetary health – as long as most people continued to believe that paper money could only function effectively if it was convertible on demand into gold or silver coin.[139] It will not come as a surprise that the metal monetary stock of the Dutch Republic was big and of high quality. We have estimates of it for various moments in time. Per capita, in terms of grams of silver, it is estimated to have been 576 grams in 1690 and no less than 960 grams in 1790. In 1540, for the totality of the Burgundian Netherlands, per capita, it had only been 95 grams.[140] The monetary system of France during the early modern era has been described as complex and outdated. According to Goubert, for ordinary people money was scarce and its quality mediocre. Only a little of it circulated. But even so, the amount of available precious metal used as money, per capita, was substantially higher than in China. Estimates vary only a little. The circulating metallic money stock is supposed to have been the equivalent of 2,259 tons of silver in 1631. On the eve of the French Revolution, that had increased to 10,000 tons. Per capita that would be the equivalent of 400 grams of silver. France's monetary system basically was bimetallic with a quite important role for gold. On the eve of the French Revolution gold money represented 34 per cent of the money in circulation, silver money 65 per cent and – again quite remarkable in comparison to China – black money of billon or copper barely 1 per cent.[141]

China's monetary system

As regards China, let us also start with the monetary metal that was least important, in this case gold. Substantial amounts of gold were mined in or near China. It, however, was not used as currency. What is even more striking, even though the amounts may not have been staggering, is that, as we already pointed out, gold was often exported. It is

---

[138]Davies, *History of Money*, ch. 7.

[139]I write 'probably', as the British colonies in North America and later on the independent United States managed to have substantial economic development and growth over the very long eighteenth century with a metal monetary stock that was surprisingly small and to a large extent consisted of foreign silver coins. See Irigoin, 'End of a silver era', 230.

[140]De Vries and Van der Woude, *First Modern Economy*, 90, table 4.2.

[141]For estimates with regard to the period just before the French Revolution see, in alphabetical order, Braudel, *Civilization & Capitalism*, I, 466; Day, *Money and Finance*, 8, note 25; McCusker and Riley, 'Money supply', 272–7, and Morineau, 'Frappes monétaires françaises'. De Vries presents an estimate for 1790 of about 350 grams of silver equivalents in his 'Netherlands in the New World', 116. The estimate for 1631 is from Day, *Money and Finance*, 25. The information with regard to the amounts of golden, silver, billon and copper money is from Morineau, 'Frappes monétaires françaises'.

estimated that between 1701 and 1760 the country exported between twenty and forty, and in another estimate even as much as eighty to one hundred, tons of gold to the West, where Britain was the most important importing country.[142] The export of copper and silver was officially prohibited until the first decades of the nineteenth century. Officials often tried to tax silver imports.[143] Government's policy in that respect was quite strict, although in fact from the second half of the eighteenth century onwards some silver did leave the country.[144]

A small excursion is in order here: the fact that gold was often exported from China, whereas silver was massively imported, is not unrelated to the fact that during most of the early modern period, although no longer after the 1770s, silver was cheaper relative to gold in Europe than it was in China. The difference in the silver to gold ratios presented the Europeans with an opportunity to engage in profitable forms of 'arbitrage'. This means that they took silver to China and exchanged it for gold, which *in terms of silver* was much cheaper there. They then took this cheaply acquired gold to Europe where they exchanged it for much more silver than it would have bought them in China. This cheap silver was then taken to China, where it could buy them more gold than at home, and so on. There is proof that Westerners indeed profited from such arbitrage. Traders of the English East India Company had explicit permission to export silver to engage in it.[145] Again, one must be wary to simply talk about 'bullion' in the early modern era. Different metals and metal moneys had different functions and histories.

The main materials that functioned as money in China were copper, silver and paper money or 'credit'. Let us begin our analysis with some comments on silver, which formed the pivot of China's monetary system and has become a central subject in current historiography because of the popularity of the thesis that China would have been 'the silver sink' of the early modern world. Whatever the exact merits of that thesis, silver remained scarce in Qing China in the very long eighteenth century. The estimate of the total silver stock at the beginning of the nineteenth century by Lin, presented earlier in this text, would mean that there has never been more than some 140 grams of silver available per Chinese in our period. As always there are margins and uncertainties but even in my most optimistic estimate, based on studies by experts in monetary history who tend to be far more prudent than the global historians dealing with the topic, the amount of silver available per capita in China in the first decades of the nineteenth century, *after* more than two centuries of silver imports and *before* the famous drain started, certainly was less than 200 grams, in all probability much less.[146]

Whatever the exact figures with regard to imports, exports and production may have been, experts on early modern Chinese history seem to agree that silver was scarce in

---

[142]See the references under Chapter 3 note 115.
[143]See the references under Chapter 3 note 151.
[144]Peng, *Monetary History*, e.g. 672.
[145]See for this thesis e.g. Flynn and Giráldez, 'Arbitrage', and idem, 'Cycles of silver'. See for the example Pritchard, 'Private trade'.
[146]I dealt with this topic in a paper presented at a conference in Les Treilles, France in June 2006. I can send a PDF to those who are interested in reading it.

China already before the famous 'drain' of the second quarter of the nineteenth century. According to Rowe, 'For most of the eighteenth century, the demand for money still increased more rapidly than supply.'[147] Notwithstanding that they may have different opinions about their exact timing and causes, scholars like Fang, Lin and Von Glahn all refer to periods of serious silver shortage in China some time in the eighteenth century.[148] Von Glahn in general writes about a 'persistent scarcity – relative to demand – of monetary media.'[149] Strikingly enough, central government did not do much to change that. It could have stimulated trade with Westerners. That might have brought in more silver. It did nothing of the sort. As compared to most governments in Western Europe, China's central government in this respect was passive at best, if not an active nuisance. There are many examples where it closed silver mines or opposed opening them.[150] It tried to collect duties on silver *imports*. The Qing authorities claimed the right to tax commodities with customs duties. In their view foreign bullion imports were not incoming currency but incoming commodities. They therefore taxed them,[151] insisted that the silver be kept intact after being shipped into China and, in principle, till the second half of the nineteenth century did not officially accept it as legal tender for China's domestic markets. Silver tax payments up until then always had to be made in sycees. The only strategy to combat scarcity seems to have been prohibiting silver exports.

From the perspective of China's rulers there may have been good reasons to not be enthusiastic about stimulating mining or to be careful in dealing with 'the Western barbarians'. My point is that from a strictly *economic* perspective the policies of China's elites do not always strike me as optimal. Central government, for example, did not coin silver to set a standard, which continued to amaze foreigners.[152] Most economists hold the view that governments should set standards for the currency of their countries and guarantee its value. It is only a small minority among them that would claim that banking ought to be 'free' and the money supply 'denationalized' because they doubt that central governments have the will and ability to manipulate the money supply to the best of the public's interest. Examples would be Friedrich Hayek (1899–1992) and other members of the Austrian School of Economics.[153] One may certainly discuss the merits of both points of view as a matter of principle. There are many examples of monetary policies of Western governments that did more harm than good. For example, when governments inflated the money supply too much by debasing the currency, by overspending or printing extra money, or the specific case of eighteenth-century Great

---

[147]Rowe, 'Social stability', 514.

[148]See Fang, 'Conclusions', 398; Lin, 'From sweet potato to silver' and 'Shift from East Asia', and Von Glahn, 'Money use in China'.

[149]Von Glahn, 'Cycles of silver', 59.

[150]See Xu and Wu, *Chinese Capitalism*, 249–53.

[151]See Burger, 'Coin production', 179; Chang, 'Evolution of Chinese thought', 60–1; Deng, 'Miracle or mirage?', part four, and Van Dyke, *Canton Trade*, ch. 7.

[152]In Tibet, that effectively was under Qing rule, a silver coin was minted from 1792 onwards. That was the first imperial coinage of Qing China.

[153]See for further explanation Selgin, *Theory of Free Banking*.

Britain where many of the problems of small change were due to the government's policy of giving the right to coin that change to monopolists. For the specific cases we are discussing here, however, I do think that monetary policies of Great Britain's government in the end had many positive effects whereas for Qing China there is ample evidence in the literature that the lack of a centralized and effective monetary authority – there was neither a national bank nor a national Mint that coined silver – had many disadvantages in this respect. I must admit I am somewhat surprised by Rowe's claim that the 'Qing state showed impressive acumen and vigour' in its 'management of the money supply.'[154] Let me point out several of those disadvantages. The enormous diversity of coins made exchange very complex and one often had to clip or cut moneys to verify their metallic content. That damaged the coins and led to further deterioration. Government knew that many of its subjects preferred to use foreign coins. Still, during the period we are discussing no official Chinese silver coins were ever minted, apart from some experiments that were not regarded a success.[155] Foreign coins simply were better and often were accepted at a premium. When in the 1820s newly devalued coins from Spanish America came to China, there was no monetary authority to coordinate a response.[156] Basically the only policy that government actively, but in vain, tried to implement was to prohibit the export of silver.

The fact that the Qing government did not mint any silver coins meant it could not implement a policy of debasement in the hope to thereby increase the money supply. Nor could it collect seigniorage, as it did on copper coins, although the 'meltage fees' could in practice function as a kind of seigniorage. Under the Qing, they officially could amount to 3 per cent. In practice they could be much higher, especially in the period before the Yongzheng emperor tried to prohibit their excessive collection.[157] Seignorage on small copper cash could of course not amount to much. Here, again, the situation in Britain is peculiar. There, in theory, there was no government seigniorage at all, but as one had to wait weeks, if not months, after bringing one's bullion before receiving one's coins, one in practice paid a duty to the government mint. In France, during the eighteenth century seigniorage officially was no less than 8 per cent.[158] In Europe improving minting technology was important as it gave governments the possibility to differentiate sanctioned currencies from forged or foreign ones. In China there was less pressure and less eagerness to do. European governments apparently cared more about monetary sovereignty. Rulers there always considered coining money a very important 'regal' right of the sovereign, expressed in the fact that coins normally had the sovereign's portrait or a symbol of sovereignty stamped on it; the first portrait of a ruler to appear on a Chinese coin was that of Sun Yat-sen, the first president of China, on dollar coins made in 1912.[159] The potential to collect substantial

---

[154]Rowe, *China's Last Empire*, 37.

[155]See Chapter 3 notes 205–6.

[156]See Burger, 'Coin production', and in particular Irigoin, 'End of a silver era'.

[157]Thornton, *Disciplining the State*, 32.

[158]Smith, *Inquiry into the Nature and Causes of the Wealth of Nations*, 62.

[159]Eagleton and Williams, *Money*, 143.

amounts of seigniorage were much lower there and the government was not very keen on profiting from currency.[160]

China's monetary system, if that is not something of a euphemism considering the huge regional differences and the lack of serious efforts to create a 'national' and 'rational' uniformity, was very complicated.[161] We have started our analysis discussing silver, as in the debates on Chinese currency this metal normally holds centre stage. That does not mean it actually was China's currency. There was no national currency, at least not when it comes to silver or gold: both precious metals were not coined. The silver tael was only a money of account and, what is more, there actually existed numerous, different taels. For everyday small transactions, during the eighteenth and nineteenth centuries, 'copper' or, as others would prefer, 'bronze' was the normal means of payment. Bronze probably is the best description, but as in the literature it has become common to refer to 'copper' and 'copper cash' in this context, I have decided to stick to that usage, as to not create confusion.[162] According to experts, the importance of that metal as a means of payment even increased over the eighteenth century. Scholars like Von Glahn, Vogel and Kuroda on the one hand, and Lin on the other hand, hold differing opinions as to how long this reinforcement of the copper coin system lasted, with Lin in contrast to the other authors claiming that it already ended in the 1770s.[163] According to Von Glahn copper re-emerged as the prevailing monetary standard in the middle and late eighteenth century, most strikingly in the highly commercialized Jiangnan region.[164] When it comes to daily life and ordinary transactions, there can be no doubt that under the Qing copper continued to be the main means of payment and that in this sense it always remained a copper economy. Copper, not silver, was central to China's monetary system. That was even more than normally the case from the 1820s to the 1850s when silver became scarcer. Western observers in the 1850s and 1860s agreed that, even then, 'in China there is no national currency except the copper cash'.[165] As late as 1886 Charles Addis, a Scot working for the Hong Kong and Shanghai Banking Corporation claimed: 'The only money which circulates universally throughout the length and breadth of the land is copper cash. With regard to other kinds, an immense provincialism prevails.'[166]

China had copper mines, especially in Yunnan – where substantial amounts of silver were also mined – and minted its copper coins. The German historian Vogel has made an estimate of the production of the empire's copper mints between 1644 and 1800. He estimates that they produced 330 million strings of 1,000 copper cash each. That, at least

---

[160]Horesh, *Chinese Money*, 240.

[161]See Introduction note 275.

[162]Von Glahn wrote me in an email that I am allowed to quote that he prefers the term 'bronze' although he thinks none of the English translations is ideal. Deng also is in favour of using the term 'bronze'. See note 126 of his 'Miracle or mirage?' Lin, in contrast, prefers the term 'copper'. See Lin, *China Upside Down*, XXIV and XXV.

[163]See for these claims Lin, *China Upside Down*, 29, and Von Glahn, 'Cycles of silver'.

[164]Von Glahn, 'Cycles of silver', 45.

[165]This quotation is from 1868 from Reverend Doolittle. I found it in Horesh, *Chinese Money*, 135.

[166]Horesh, *Chinese Money*, 157.

officially, equals 330 million taels, some 2 million per year.[167] In the second half of the eighteenth century, annual mint output of strings was between 2 and 3 million. According to Peng, copper production during the first hundred years of Qing rule amounted to 10 million catties, which would amount to 3 billion cash or 3 million taels per year. He assumes that this has also been the average for their entire period of rule.[168] The word 'officially' here is very important. In actual fact there were substantial fluctuations in the silver to copper exchange rates and big regional differences. Each province had its mint to produce copper coins. Local authorities had strong incentives to block the outflow of 'their' coin, which of course hampered monetary integration.[169] When discussing these figures one has to realize that coins suffer from wear and tear. At the end of the seventeenth century in Britain, to just give an example, a sack of silver coins with a face value of £100 apparently lost half of its weight in ten years.[170] In case of copper coins, and in particular the bad copper cash one used in China, losses due to wear and tear were extremely high, much higher than those of silver coins.

We are talking about an impressive *and* expensive amount of money, as the cost of minting (i.e. casting copper coin), which was done by hand, on average, was 15 per cent of its value during the beginning of the Qianlong era and there are no indications that it would have become cheaper before the latter half of the nineteenth century.[171] In Europe money already was produced mechanically by striking a die on a solid metal flan. In the late eighteenth century in Britain, as we already indicated, steam power was already being used for coining small change.[172] The first modern minting machinery was only brought to China, from Birmingham, in 1887.[173] The relatively high production costs and the big losses by wear and tear of all the 'small change' used in China were the price one had, and was willing, to pay for using coinage with a low value. For government in China, providing cash for ordinary transactions of ordinary people was a priority, even though supplying small denomination coins inevitably was expensive. According to Kuroda, it is for that very reason that authorities in the Euro-Mediterranean world were inclined to issue precious metal currencies.[174] In Britain government explicitly chose to concentrate on big currencies. Another, connected, disadvantage of primarily using small change is that one needs so much of it: a labourer in London in the beginning of the nineteenth century earned the equivalent of about half a tael of silver per day. According to the official exchange rate in China, that would be some 500 copper cash. With the deterioration of the exchange value of copper to silver – to sometimes 2,500 to 1 – that could become as much as 1,250 copper cash. In China, at the time, daily wages were

---

[167]Vogel, 'Chinese central monetary policy'.

[168]Peng, *Monetary History*, 735 and 775. A catty is some 600 grams.

[169]Deng, 'Miracle or mirage', paragraph 4.2.

[170]See Challis, 'Lord Hasting', 382–3. Systematic and regular recoinage and efforts to improve the quality of coins therefore became were very important in Britain.

[171]Peng, *Monetary History*, 660–1.

[172]See page 241.

[173]Horesh, *Chinese Money*, 110.

[174]See for these comments Kuroda, 'Eurasian silver century'.

much lower. But even if we assume, as we have done in our calculations, that they would hover between 1.5 and, at the very highest, 4 grams of silver per day, we would already be talking about between forty and over a hundred cash at the official rate of 1,000 cash to one tael. This need not have been a problem if there had been something between coins of one cash and the tael, but that was not the case. Payments therefore often were quite laborious. The value of copper cash was too low for substantial transactions whereas that of the tael, over 37 grams of silver, was too high for daily ones. On top of that, according to King the method of casting the copper was 'primitive and less accurate than European methods'.[175] The situation here too, of course, did not improve after the British began to use steam engines in producing their coins.

Production of copper in Yunnan often did not suffice and was not very efficient – partly because of the way in which it was organized, partly because of technical problems.[176] Government was one of the main causes of those organizational problems, in particular, because of its tendency to fix prices at a level that simply was too low. There was an interdiction of private copper smelting and of private mining. At times (e.g. during the first half of the nineteenth century) private mintage of copper coins was forbidden.[177] As copper coining was expensive, many old coins remained in circulation, especially as there was also much counterfeiting that was not systematically and efficiently tackled. Transporting copper from Yunnan to the places where it was most needed was of course expensive. With regard to the nature of the technical problems, it probably is most efficient to simply quote the conclusion of an article by Chen on China's copper production in Yunnan province in China during the eighteenth and the beginning of the nineteenth centuries:

> In the beginning of the nineteenth century, because of the perilous mineshafts that went deeper and deeper, the less rich copper lodes that had been exhausted, the serious flooding of mines, and the fuel shortages for smelting, copper mining became more expensive. To produce 100 catties of copper, 1,400 to 1,500 catties of charcoal were required and soon deforestation occurred in the areas of copper mining, so people must transport charcoal from afar. Copper production in Yunnan declined on account of failure to break through the bottleneck of mining techniques.[178]

---

[175]King, *Money and Monetary Policy*, 45.

[176]For copper production and monetary policy with regard to copper see in alphabetical order He, *Paths toward the Modern Fiscal State*; Horesh, *Chinese Money*; Lin, *China Upside Down*; Shulman, *Copper, Copper Cash and Government Controls*, and Vogel, 'Chinese central monetary policy'. For problems and inefficiencies with regard to the organization and techniques of copper production and distribution see in alphabetical order Chang and Chen, 'Competing monies'; Chen, 'China's copper production'; Dunstan, 'Safely supping'; Fang, 'Copper mining and smelting'; Hirzel and Kim, *Metals, Monies, and Markets*, sections three and four; Horesh, *Chinese Money*; Sun, 'Ch'ing government and the mineral industries', and Xu and Wu, *Chinese Capitalism*, under 'copper', 'copper mines' and 'mining'. For some general information see Balazs, *Chinese Civilization and Bureaucracy*, 44–9.

[177]Lin, *China Upside Down*, 34–5.

[178]Chen, 'China's copper production', 117. For very similar comments see Fang, 'Copper mining and smelting', 285–8.

According to Horesh, 'Yunnan copper mining does not seem to have incorporated water-power devices, horsepower, or mechanized intervention.'[179] Copper output in Yunnan fell to a negligible amount at the same time that copper imports from Japan decreased greatly – from more than a million catties a year in 1790–1817 to an annual average of 543,000 catties in 1840–51.[180]

Government was not actively involved in solving existing technical problems. As this book is about the role of government in the economy, some further comments are in order here. The differences with Britain are striking: in British copper mining in Cornwall and Devonshire the use of Newcomen fire engines and subsequently of Watt's steam engines was frequent and the use of coal as fuel important. Watt and Boulton had actually experimented with their machines in those mines.[181] Britain's government did not play much of a part in developing the steam pump, so it does not seem to make much sense to point the finger at the Chinese rulers for having 'failed' in this respect. It still is striking though that China's government, which interfered so systematically in everything related to the mining, transporting and selling of copper – much *more* than Britain's government – did so little to try and find technical solutions for problems that arose there. In particular since the production and distribution of copper was one of its main tasks.[182] Government was actively, but with varying successes, involved in its extremely complicated and strenuous transport from the mines in south-western China to Peking.[183] In the case of coal, where according to Pomeranz transport problems put China in a less advantaged condition than Britain, it did nothing of the sort.[184]

When discussing decreasing production of copper we should not only, and for certain periods not even primarily, focus on problems in the sphere of production and distribution. Especially at the time of the silver drain, production was often lowered or even stopped on purpose and on instigation of government. This policy was a sharp break with the policies that had existed during the early and mid-eighteenth century when government mints had been reinforced and private investment in copper mining or in copper imports from Japan was allowed and even motivated.[185] Behind this behaviour, which may look somewhat capricious, there often was a clear rationale: to try and control the copper to silver ratio by manipulating supply and demand, in this case the supply of copper. Even if it does not look like a very refined and flexible strategy, it was a strategy nevertheless. It did not work. Policies to prevent silver from leaving the country that were supposed to have the same effect were ineffective too. Silver appreciated almost uninterruptedly against copper from the 1820s to the 1850s.[186]

[179]Horesh, *Chinese Money*, 109.
[180]Wang, 'Evolution of the Chinese monetary system', 442–3.
[181]Shimada, *Intra-Asian Trade*, 71–4, and more in general Weightman, *Industrial Revolutionaries*.
[182]King, *Money and Monetary Policy*, 137: 'The supply of copper was perhaps the most important single factor with which the government had to deal'.
[183]Hirzel and Kim, *Metals, Monies, and Markets*, Section Four.
[184]Pomeranz, *Great Divergence*, 64–7.
[185]Lin, *China Upside Down*, 172–9. For this policy more in general see He, *Paths toward the Modern Fiscal State*, chs 5 and 6.
[186]See page 112.

To be able to determine how successful China's government was in its effort to provide the population with copper, one must know what the production figures that we mentioned earlier might mean for actual money supply, especially from the end of the eighteenth century onwards. We should in any case not look at it in isolation. On the one hand there was an increasing amount of private mints that added to total production, whereas on the other hand, as indicated, copper coins were subject to very high rates of wear and tear and could quickly disappear from circulation. But to at least get an idea: 'officially' (i.e. using the official exchange rate) they would amount to 12,000 tons of silver or about the equivalent of one tael per Chinese, produced over a period of some 160 years, in Vogel's estimate; in Peng's estimate the figure for the entire period of Qing rule will certainly not have been higher, considering the big increase of China's population over time. We do have more specific data. During the Qianlong reign (1736–95) 160 million cash coins were produced and during the Jiaqing reign (1796–1820) 55 million. Per year per capita, that would boil down to 12.5 cash coins during the first reign and less than seven during the second. In the second year of the Yongzheng reign for which we also have data, the figure was eight cash per person.[187] These figures do not exactly point at an ample availability of copper, the common currency, in Qing China either. One would also have to take into account money that was counterfeited. In absolute numbers we again are talking about huge amounts here. According to Deng in 1793 officials gathered some 20 millions catties of fake coins in Hunan, Hubei and Sichuan.[188] In Yunnan alone more than 1 million strings of counterfeit cash coins were withdrawn from circulation during the Jiaqing reign.[189] But even if we were able to exactly determine official, private and counterfeit copper money production, and add that to China's silver stock, we still would have to conclude that the total amount of (semi-)precious metal available for monetary use in Qing China was small. It will definitely have been substantially lower than 200 grams of silver equivalents, with the value of copper (important as it may have been in daily use) amounting to only a fraction of that of silver. Velocity of money use will certainly have been lower here than in Great Britain.

Paper money was not unknown in China. On the contrary: it had been invented there already under the Sung. The first paper money as we know it (i.e. officially issued exchange notes with no date limitation), were the Exchange Certificates issued by the Jin in 1189. There had been previous experiments. After its liberal, inflationary use under the Ming, it had all but disappeared. At the end of the eighteenth century, the role of various paper moneys in general, *not* that of paper money issued by government, as a means of payment had (again) become substantial. Paper money issued by government only reappeared in 1853. But as compared to the situation in Britain, its importance still was fairly minor. Bills of exchange were only used in trade with Westerners at the

---

[187]Burger, 'Coin production', 174 and Appendix.
[188]Deng, *China's Political Economy*, 27. Deng gives more examples there. A catty weighs some 600 grams.
[189]Burger, 'Coin production', 173.

very end of the eighteenth century.[190] According to Wang, for about a century prior to the Opium War, four kinds of 'credit instruments' or 'paper moneys' appeared in China. They all served to remedy, to a greater or lesser extent, the defects of Qing bimetallism. These were silver notes or cash notes, native bank order, draft and a transfer account system known as *kuo-chang*. Private paper notes only appeared on the market very late in the Qianlong reign.[191] In his view the importance of these means of payment increased quickly, although for the period that holds centre stage in our analysis, the end of the eighteenth and the beginning of the nineteenth centuries, we can only guess how important they actually were. In contrast to the time-honoured practice whereby government monopolized the paper notes, in the nineteenth century it was mainly the private, old-style banks and firms that issued silver notes and cash notes for circulation. As pointed out before, government only began to issue paper notes again in 1853.[192] Meanwhile, from the 1830s onwards, opium had begun to function as money in various parts of China.[193] Again, one can only conclude that government was not very helpful.

Reflecting on the question of how important private 'paper money' actually was, Wang comes to the following 'conclusion':

> It is impossible at the present time to make even a rudimentary estimate of the stock of money in eighteenth- and nineteenth-century China. In view of the prevalence of private notes and the proliferation of issuing bodies, however, there is no doubt that paper notes had by the early nineteenth century constituted a substantial portion of the total volume of money in circulation. I would not be surprised if it was a third or even greater.[194]

According to Horesh, whose position I endorse, this would be too optimistic. Horesh claims that private paper money generally was restricted to the immediate region where it was issued and confined to certain regions only. Its use was based on personal and not institutional trust. Private bank note issuance in his view cannot be described as a pillar of the late imperial Chinese monetary system.

> There is no solid foundation on which to assert that money shop scrip (broadly defined) was 'well accepted' in China in the late imperial era. This is because it constituted in all likelihood an insignificant part of China's currency stock prior to 1900 and because the circulation of such scrip was regionally fragmented if not parochial. … On the whole, China's late imperial monetary

---

[190]Burger, 'Coin production', 185.

[191]Wang, 'Evolution of the Chinese monetary system', 436. See also Lin, 'From sweet potato to silver', 310–3, and Peng, *Monetary History*, ch. 8.

[192]Hao, *Commercial Revolution*, 47.

[193]Hao, *Commercial Revolution*, 64–71, and Zheng, *Social Life of Opium*, 150–3.

[194]Wang, 'Evolution of the Chinese monetary system', 436 and 438.

system remained bimetallic in the nineteenth century, as received wisdom would suggest.[195]

He considers it implausible 'that the ratio of all notes as part of the entire Chinese money stock was – even as late as 1900 – much higher than ten per cent' and adds that 'Chinese privately issued notes were *not* considered reliable to the extent that they would compensate for the late imperial relinquishment of monetary reins.'[196]

Qing China lacked a highly developed monetary system. The total per capita monetary stock for China around 1900 has been estimated at 5.2 dollars or the equivalent at the time of 3.77 ounces or some 140 grams of silver. That is very little as compared to developed countries in Europe or the USA.[197] It, moreover, is not only quantities that matter. Let me again quote Wang.[198]

> It is thus evident that under the bimetallic system of Ch'ing China the volume of money depended heavily on the availability of two kinds of metal, silver and copper, over which the monetary authorities exerted no effective control. It was a poor system that lacked the flexibility of adjusting money supply to market demand for circulating media. In addition to the problem of inflexibility, however, other serious defects also existed in the Ch'ing system. The continuing fluctuations in the rate of exchange between the two kinds of money generated unnecessary risks and uncertainty in business transactions. Still worse was its lack of uniformity. Since silver circulated in bullion without standardization, its value was determined by its weight and fineness. It took a professional moneychanger to ascertain the fineness of the white metal. Added to this complexity, was the absence of standard weight in China. The unit of weight called *liang* differed from one place to another and from one trade to another. Accordingly, there appeared literally hundreds of units of account (*tael*) with varying degree of fineness and weight throughout the country. Nor was the cash sector less complicated. The stock of copper cash in circulation consisted of a variety of coins – government authorized, counterfeited and foreign (e.g., those from Japan, Annam). Needless to say, the copper content and weight of these various types differed from one another. This was even true among the officially cast coins, depending upon when and where they were stamped. As a consequence, the monetary world was filled with a multitude of exchange rates between silver and cash, different sorts of cash, and the multiplicity of *taels*, all of which resulted in a chaotic fluctuation of rates. Lastly, both kinds of money,

---

[195]Horesh, *Chinese Money*, 146.
[196]Horesh, *Chinese Money*, 137 and 146. Compare for somewhat differing figures Hao, *Commercial Revolution*, 64–71; Lin, *China Upside Down*, 7, and Peng, *Monetary History*, 780–1.
[197]Horesh, *Chinese Money*, 138 and 143. For comparisons see 143–7.
[198]Wang, 'Evolution of the Chinese monetary system', 335.

copper cash in particular, were too cumbersome to ship over long distances without modern transport facilities and too inconvenient to settle transactions, which involved a large volume of trade.[199]

Later on in the same text Wang points out that 'The problem of inflexibility, complexity, and cumbersomeness inherent in the bimetallic system remained.'[200] The complexity and inefficiency of this system must have pushed up transactions costs.[201] That all was not well with China's money, and that people at the time themselves thought so too, clearly shows in the fact that a foreign currency (i.e. dollars from Latin America) was used in various parts of the country, in particular, those that were involved in overseas trade. Dollars not only functioned as money of account but also as 'real' money. They began to replace un-coined sycee silver as a means of payment there from the 1730s and did so increasingly from the second half of the eighteenth century onwards. As I pointed out earlier, those dollars often were exchanged with a substantial *premium* over their silver value whereas sycee silver was exported in order to acquire silver coins.[202] Many Chinese used foreign coins as they found them convenient to carry and exchange and superior in craftsmanship when it came to shape and design to what the Chinese themselves were able to produce.[203] Rulers in China were aware of this preference of their subjects for foreign coins and often tried to counter it by insisting that foreign coins should be melted and turned into sycees and by prohibiting their domestic production.[204] Towards the end of the eighteenth century, Chinese officials induced some silversmiths to manufacture dollars that in every respect were identical to the Carolus dollar. Those silversmiths, however, did not manage to obtain a similar uniformity in design and weight because numerous artisans working quite independently of each other produced the coins. Moreover, the silversmiths adulterated the money by adding alloy up to 50 per cent. This then led to the prohibition of any further manufacturing of silver dollars in China.[205] Later on we see several renewed (semi-)official efforts to coin good silver coins in China itself. None of them, however, was a success that changed the overall situation.[206] Unsurprisingly not everyone in China could resist the temptation to ignore government regulations and try and unofficially make their own dollars. A further indication, finally, that there was something problematic about

---

[199]Wang, 'Evolution of the Chinese monetary system', 432–3.

[200]Wang, 'Evolution of the Chinese monetary system', 435.

[201]For scholars who, apart from Wang, also consider Qing China's monetary system quite inefficient see Burger, 'Coin production'; Deng, 'Miracle or mirage', and Eastman, *Family, Fields and Ancestors*, 108–12. For somewhat less negative comments see Chapter 3 note 215.

[202]See page 63.

[203]Von Glahn, 'Foreign silver coins'.

[204]Overdijking, *Lin Tse-Hsu*, 32–5.

[205]Kahn, *Currencies of China*, 128–9.

[206]See e.g. Eagleton and Williams, *Money*, 156–7; He, *Paths toward the Modern Fiscal State*, 34; King, *Money and Monetary Policy*, under, 'Silver coinage, Chinese non-dollar'; Peng, *Monetary History*, 675 and 680–1, and Von Glahn, 'Foreign silver coins', 64.

money and the money supply in China would be the persistently high level of Chinese interest rates.[207]

My claim of course is not that one should exclusively lay the blame for all these monetary and financial problems with China's government. But it clearly was not completely 'innocent' in this respect. In a big and very complex society such as Qing China, a good financial and monetary system *in the end* cannot fail to involve the state. The Qing rulers were not as closely involved and interested in financial and monetary affairs as the people who ruled Britain. In this respect a couple of points have to be highlighted. What is really striking is that, as I already mentioned, apart from one irrelevant exception *no* Qing government issued and backed paper money *before* 1853.[208] Peter Perdue, who as a rule is quite positive about the functioning of the Qing state up to the end of the eighteenth century, points out that government efforts to introduce paper money had ended in failure three times before in Chinese history, under the Sung, under the Yuan and under the Ming. Every time China's central government experimented with paper money it led to its over-issue, inflation and debasement, and all the chaos that goes with that. He sees no reason why it would have been otherwise under the Qing. He, rightly I think, points at the importance in these matters of the organization, policy and strength of the state.[209] Paper money is fiduciary money – its use is based on trust, transparency and certain checks and balances. Those were often lacking. During the big silver-drain crisis in the second quarter of the nineteenth century, a major reason to reject all proposals to issue paper notes (and the same goes for big coins with face values that were higher than their intrinsic values) was fear of bureaucratic corruption, fear that people would counterfeit these new moneys and lack of confidence in the state. In that respect the following quote from the governor-general of Jiangsu-Anhui-Jianxi, dating from the period 1849–53, is telling:

> Paper notes have been issued in the past. How can they not be used today? What bank shops issue is also a kind of paper notes. The reason that paper notes can be used among commoners while they cannot be used by the state is not that people do not believe in paper notes; it is because people do not believe in officials. It is not merely because people do not believe in officials; it is officials who do not believe in themselves.[210]

---

[207]For interest rates in China see, in alphabetical order, Horesh, *Chinese Money* under 'interest'; Isett, *State, Peasant, and Merchant*, 271; Pomeranz, *Great Divergence*, 178–9; Yang, *Money and Credit*, 92–103, and Van Zanden, 'Road to the Industrial Revolution', 342–5. For general information on interest rates see Homer and Sylla, *History of Interest Rates*. Rosenthal and Wong in their *Before and Beyond Divergence*, ch. 5, defend the thesis that what we know about the height of Qing China's interest rates need not point at badly functioning credit markets and at scarcity of credit that would hamper growth. I am not convinced by their interpretation and think high interest rates were a serious hindrance to the further development of China's economy.

[208]See, for example, Peng, *Monetary History*, 707–16.

[209]Perdue on page 4 of his review of Latham and Kawakatsu, *Asia-Pacific Dynamism*, on EH.NET March 2002.

[210]For this quotation see Lin, *China Upside Down*, 173.

Readers interested in the debates that were waged and the policies that were tried are referred to the literature. It would take too much space to extensively discuss them, but overall, one must conclude that China's monetary (and financial) problems were not really solved during the nineteenth century and rationalization and modernization of its monetary (and financial) system did not make much headway.[211] We have to realize that, of course, in the meantime in the West the pace of development accelerated, also when it came to paper money. In the early 1800s steel plates and siderography, the process of reproducing steel-engraved designs for printing, had begun to change the world of note printing. Here too China clearly fell behind.[212]

For quite some time, the Qing rulers, overall, did not seem to care very much about China's money. For some two centuries they did not coin any silver money, nor did they print any paper money, though advice was given to do so. Fixation of the silver–copper ratio, immensely important for China's economy, was left almost entirely to the market. When governments intervened in an effort to fix it, they, in vain, tried to do this by prohibiting the export of silver or lowering the production of copper. During the period of the silver drain we see fierce debates and many suggested remedies, but that was in a period of acute crisis and no real solution was found. On top of that, according to experts, those government policies that were tried were not always very adequate. Government was in a quandary. Even if there had been no drain and no political turmoil, it lacked experience in how to deal with the type of situation it was in, and there existed no institutional arrangements that might have facilitated dealing with it. There was no tradition of bargaining with representatives of society, no experience with government borrowing. What would have been complicated enough in normal times became almost infeasible in times of increasing internal unrest and foreign intervention. The 1840s and especially the 1850s and 1860s, with the terrible havoc of the Taiping Rebellion, were a disastrous period in the history of China. China's tax system had always been fragmented. In times of civil war and rebellion that fragmentation only increased. For central government the fact that Peking was not situated in a wealthy part of China became much more of a problem.

Some final comments

In discussing financial and monetary systems we again have to be aware of huge differences between various countries in Western Europe. Britain and the Dutch Republic really were different from, for example, France, Spain or 'Germany'. Great Britain was more of an exception than the rule. According to Richard Bonney, in his introduction

---

[211]See for extended analyses He, *Paths towards the Modern Fiscal State*, ch. 6; Horesh, *Chinese Money*, ch. 4; Hu, *Concise History of Chinese Economic Thought*, ch. 22, Section III; King, *Money and Monetary Policy*, ch. 6; Lin, *China Upside Down*, parts II and III; Peng, *Monetary History*, chs 8.1.3 and 8.1.5, and Zurndorfer, 'Imperialism, globalization and public finance'.
[212]Horesh, *Chinese Money*, 80.

to a book on the rise of the fiscal state in Europe from c. 1200 to 1815, Britain was the only European country that had reached the more advanced stage of what he calls 'a fiscal state' at the time of the Napoleonic Wars. In many financial and monetary matters it was different and more advanced. It is only after the Napoleonic Wars that 'modern' financial and monetary structures were created in most other Western European countries. Overall the modern, bureaucratic state, as we will repeatedly point out in the next chapter, only emerged 'after Napoleon' and it is only then, in the nineteenth century, that we see a Europe-wide convergence of state models. Before that *different* 'states' followed quite *differing* routes.

We must, moreover, be careful not to read history backwards and make Great Britain more advanced than it actually was. Its financial institutions certainly were the most advanced of any *major* state in the world. Its monetary system in the eighteenth century, however, was far from ideal, even for standards of the time. But we see constant efforts – often successful – to improve it and a government that as a rule was concerned and alert. The fact that the country managed to handle its huge national debt does not mean that its government had a brilliant master plan and foresaw the way things would evolve. There was serious doubt about the sustainability of Great Britain's financial and monetary system. Matters could easily have got out of control. Many measures in fact were *ad hoc* and taken not to promote economic development or economic growth but to cope with concrete problems at hand. But the system stood the test and, with adaptations, continued to work even under the enormous stress of the Revolutionary and Napoleonic wars, a massive increase in population, bad harvests and beginning industrialization.

We must, even more, be careful not to paint a too rosy picture of developments in 'the West'. Qing China clearly lacked monetary sovereignty. A country can only really have such sovereignty if it has a central bank and mechanized minting of coin. Before 1850 *only* Great Britain had both of them.[213] Horesh in his comparison of the monetary trajectories of China and Western Europe points out that after 1648 in Western Europe the notion developed of a territorial currency – that is, the idea 'that foreign currency cannot be used at will within another sovereign polity'.[214] That indeed did not exist in Qing China in the period discussed here. Many foreign coins circulated in its economy. But that was also the case in the United States, then the wealthiest country in the world, for the entire first half of the nineteenth century. Many of the problems of the Qing authorities actually were only too familiar to many rulers in *Ancien Régime* Europe.[215]

---

[213]See Von Glahn, 'Cycles of silver', 58, referring to Helleiner, *Making of National Money*.
[214]Horesh, *Chinese Money*, 266–7. On page 84 of that book Horesh points out that 'Throughout the course of the eighteenth century, foreign coins found in England were seen as legitimate only when countermarked'.
[215]For that reason King at times is somewhat less negative about Qing China's monetary system. See his *Money and Monetary Policy*, in particular pages 42–50, where he points out that many of the features of the Chinese system to which foreigners objected were inherent to the nature of metallic money and that the West had only just succeeded itself in solving some of them. He has a point. See also the comments by Horesh, *Chinese Money*, 141, where he compares the situation in China in the late eighteenth century with that in the USA. But that does not change the fact that in this respect too Qing China in the early nineteenth century had become 'backward'.

But whereas industrializing Britain solved them, they continued to haunt China's authorities. Again, my comments are not anachronistic, Eurocentric pedantry. Many people in China at the time knew they needed a better monetary and financial system. But as a rule, change was too little too late. On the other hand, one has to realize, a situation that to us may look inefficient will have created ample opportunities for 'experts' to earn large sums of money, exactly because of its 'complexity' and its 'chaotic' character. This means that certainly not everyone was convinced of the desirability of rationalizing the system.

What is striking in comparison to the Chinese situation is the large number and sophistication of institutions and mechanisms that were or became available to government and society in Britain to actually implement all kinds of financial, monetary and other policies. In that respect China's government at the time simply lacked the means to implement sophisticated, fine-tuned policies. It basically was unprepared and unequipped to deal with the problems it began to face. In comparison with Britain, the means at its disposal can only be called rude and fairly inefficient. That was a major, even fundamental factor in the emergence and deepening of China's economic troubles in the nineteenth century and in its inability to industrialize. Horesh apparently thinks likewise. He emphasizes that subjects like the ones I have dealt with in this chapter cannot be ignored in debates on the Great Divergence. According to him, in the early modern era, mining and metallurgy were much better developed in Europe and its colonies. Better coinage was produced there, which in turn was exchanged in China at a premium. What Asians normally wanted was European *silver coinage* rather than *silver*. Even supposedly advanced non-European monies like those of the Mughal Empire never played a significant role outside India.[216] He concludes that there were several ways in which 'European coin production departed from the rest of the world, beginning as early as the thirteenth century'.[217] In the early modern era, moreover, Europeans acquired 'mastery of global bullion and specie flows'.[218] They were the ones who knew global supply and demand and who profited from arbitrage. His position is diametrically opposed to that of scholars who believe that China's silver imports are proof of its economic superiority. He sees the 'European exchange of Latin American silver for Chinese commodities like silk and tea as essentially a marker of Chinese comparative weakness in the late imperial era rather than as a marker of strength'[219] and claims – I think rather optimistically, as most of what he describes, for the pre-nineteenth-century period (that European sovereigns in the end took over minting, including that of subsidiary coinage; from the end of the Middle ages onwards had recourse to higher-value gold currencies, and then started experimenting with monies and debts that were no longer directly and fully anchored in a metal basis) first and foremost were *British* phenomena.[220] The fact

---

[216]Horesh, *Chinese Money*, 106–7, 112 and 116.

[217]Horesh, *Chinese Money*, 85.

[218]Horesh, *Chinese Money*, 115.

[219]Horesh, *Chinese Money*, 13–14. The quote is on page 14.

[220]This sentence is a paraphrase of Horesh, *Chinese Money*, 117.

that paper moneys in Europe served as a gateway to the modern national debt economy in his view is perhaps 'the most compelling difference' with China's premodern monetary history.[221] In his view the contours of world monetary history 'support … the notion that north-western Europe's departure from the premodern mould long predated 1800' and show a 'Great Money Divergence' already before the Age of Steam. For Great Britain I would certainly agree.[222]

---

[221]Horesh, *Chinese Money*, 69.

[222]For the quotation see Horesh, *Chinese Money*, 84. Chapter 3 of this book is called 'The Great Money Divergence: European and Chinese coinage before the Age of Steam'.

CHAPTER 4
PEOPLE

BUREAUCRATS AND BUREAUCRACY

A fully developed bureaucratic mechanism stands in exactly the same relationship to any other form [of organization] as does the machine to the non-mechanical production of goods. Precision, speed, un-ambiguity, the fact that facts and procedures are documented, continuity, discretion, uniformity, rigid subordination, reduction of friction and material and personal expenses are increased to an optimum ... in a strict bureaucratic administration.

Weber, *Wirtschaft und Gesellschaft*, 561–2
(The translation, not complete, is mine)

The rich have markets, the poor have bureaucrats.

Easterly, *White Man's Burden*, 165

Some comments on the situation in Europe

Talking about the presence and strength of a state implies talking about its personnel: how many people did it actually employ and to what extent could it effectively use these people to promote *its* goals instead of those people using the state to promote *their* goals. Nowadays people working for government are supposed to be officials, employees working in a system that by and large resembles a bureaucracy as Max Weber defined it.[1] According to him, in brief, officials have the following characteristics:

- Officials are free, subject to authority only in their official tasks
- Officials are organized in a clearly defined hierarchy of offices
- Each office has a clearly defined sphere of competence
- Offices are filled by free contract
- Candidates for office are selected according to their qualifications, normally examinations and technical training
- Officials are salaried and granted pensions

---

[1] For this definition *à la* Weber, see Mann, *Sources of Social Power, II*, 444–5. Mann has taken it, in abbreviated form, directly from Weber, *Wirtschaft und Gesellschaft*.

- The office is the sole or primary occupation of the incumbent
- The office constitutes a career involving promotion by seniority or for achievement
- The official is separated from ownership of the means of administration
- The official is subject to systematic discipline and control in official conduct

The first thing we should immediately and emphatically point out before discussing the situation in 'our' era is that a really 'modern', 'Weberian' bureaucracy only appeared very late on the historical stage *anywhere* in the world. In Western Europe by far, the majority of the people rendering services to *central* government in one way or another, at the very least until Napoleonic times, were *not* the kind of officials Weber had in mind and the setting in which they worked was *not* that of a modern bureaucracy. Let us begin with some comments on the general situation in Europe, confining ourselves in this chapter to civilian bureaucracy.

Of the countries we regularly refer to in this text, overall, Prussia probably was the first one to have at least some clear 'bureaucratic' traits in its overall system of government. In this small state already quite early on an offensive started against venality, hereditary offices, tax farming and sinecures, combined with attempts to introduce salaries, the requirement of certain qualifications, a clear hierarchy and strict budget control. But even here it was only in the last decade of the eighteenth century that administration started to resemble a modern bureaucracy, and even then almost all the important positions still were firmly and exclusively in the hands of nobles. As such that can be regarded as an indicator of deficient bureaucratization, but aristocrats of course can *in principle* behave like bureaucrats and in Prussia they were increasingly forced to do so.[2] The Habsburg Empire too was a region where a drift towards more bureaucratic rule occurred already in the eighteenth century.[3] In both these dynastic states the ruling monarchs tried, with some success, to launch a bureaucratic offensive to get a better grip on 'their' country and to strengthen 'their' states.[4] For Prussia's government the number of officials is said to have been 14,000 in the 1780s, which relatively speaking was quite a lot, as the country had only a couple of million inhabitants at the time.[5] The Habsburg Empire is supposed to have had a bureaucracy counting some 15,000 to 16,000 during the rule of Joseph II.[6]

---

[2]For some 'relativizing' of Prussia's fame as a well-organized, centralized, bureaucratic state, see the articles about Prussia in Brewer and Hellmuth, *Rethinking Leviathan*. For an interpretation with specific accents that is more in line with traditional points of view see Gorski, *Disciplinary Revolution*, ch. 3.

[3]See Hochedlinger, 'Habsburg Monarchy', and Plattner, 'Josephinismus und Bürokratie'.

[4]Mann, *Sources of Social Power*, II, 447–52.

[5]Jones, *Emancipation of the Russian Nobility*, 182. As always, much depends on definitions. Brewer and Mann both estimate the number of people forming Prussia's civil service in the early 1750s at about 3,000. But, as Mann indicates, officials working on Prussia's Royal Estates are not included in that number. For the year 1804, for which we have data, those officials alone numbered 27,800. See Brewer, *Sinews of Power*, 127, and Mann, *Sources of Social Power*, II, 390. Considering that Prussia at that time had fewer inhabitants than Great Britain this is a substantial number.

[6]Dickson, 'Monarchy and bureaucracy', 334–9.

For the beginning of the 1790s, I found the estimate of 14,000 bureaucrats.[7] Population of the realm then was over 25 million people.

Both countries probably were more 'bureaucratized' in the eighteenth century than Britain when it comes to the overall set-up of their governmental system. Britain, however, when it comes to the specific but supremely important task of collecting taxes, in particular the excises, had a bureaucracy that was second to none in Europe, in (relative) size as well as in quality. We must be careful not to be too anachronistic and to talk about 'bureaucratic administration' too easily: the total number of 'real', civilian bureaucrats for the whole of Great Britain from a twenty-first-century perspective was tiny. Figures presented by Michael Mann imply there would have been some 20,000 civilian personnel working for central government in Great Britain in the 1760s.[8] According to Harling and Mandler, there would have been 16,267 (civil) public officers in 1797 and 24,598 in 1815. They, however, in their text only refer to Britain.[9] Other estimates are all in about the same order of magnitude. Tax officers formed the great majority of all these officials, overall some 80 per cent.[10] After the Napoleonic Wars there was a general feeling that one must dismantle the fiscal-military state by lowering taxes and debts and reducing the number of people who were paid by the state. Reducing the number of officials working for central government proved not to be easy. The bureaucracy of central government grew in the 1820s and 1830s: in 1827 there were 43 per cent more government employees than in 1797, costing twice as much in real terms.[11] The number of military and civilian officials in all public offices or departments rose from 9,700 in 1782–3 to 24,598 in 1815 and 29,000 in 1849.[12] Civilian officials working for navy, army and ordnance are not included in that figure. In 1815 there were more than 40,000 of them.[13]

Overall, though, bureaucrats and bureaucratic rule still were very exceptional. That also is the case in Europe's overseas colonies. Let me just give two examples: at the end of Queen Anne's reign (1665–1714), the total number of British officials in the American colonies was about 240, while the number of Britons working in civil government in India in 1805 was about 2,000.[14] One has to be very careful not to put too much confidence in numbers, names or titles. In France, often regarded as a formidable example of absolutist rule, at the end of the *Ancien Régime*, of the roughly 300,000 people who held some

---

[7]Beller, *Concise History of Austria*, 103.

[8]Mann, *Sources of Social Power, II*, 393.

[9]Harling and Mandler, 'From "fiscal-military" state to laissez-faire state', 54.

[10]See for Britain Hoppit, 'Checking the Leviathan', 284, where the author claims that in 1770 there were 7,525 fiscal and 1,600 other officers, adding that the last figure is a guess. For 1815 he claims the number of fiscal officers would have been 21,112 and that of all other officers 3,486. From that year to 1829 he sees a slight decrease.

[11]Harling, *Waning of Old Corruption*, 177.

[12]Jupp, *Governing of Britain*, 136. Total salary of those 24,598 officials in 1815 was £3.2 million. For that information see the next note.

[13]Knight, *Britain against Napoleon*, 315–16.

[14]For the first figure see Elliott, *Empires of the Atlantic World*, 452, note 16; for the second one Maddison, *Contours of the World Economy*, 119.

kind of government office, often with an impressive title, only one-fifth at best did so as salaried, removable and working 'commissaires'. The rest consisted of people who had bought or inherited their 'job' and quite often had no professional qualifications.[15] Their lack of competence, fortunately, need not be a serious problem as often their job was a 'sinecure', which means it did not involve any work or only work actually done by someone else. Michael Mann, from whom I took the figures about France in this paragraph, immediately added this important caveat to his calculations: 'But it is only a guess, as nobody knew – which is actually the most significant finding.'[16] Earlier on in the same publication he had already claimed: 'No state knew the number of public officials *until the end of the nineteenth century* [italics added].'[17]

This caution when it comes to numbers, and in particular job descriptions, also applies to Britain. The British state overall was quite efficient in matters related to its income and its logistics. Here indeed it had a quite modern bureaucracy. But even in the first decades of the nineteenth century, after serious reforms, one still could find many sinecurists, for example in the Exchequer. There definitely was no lack of venality, corruption and inefficiency *outside* the Excise Department (e.g. in the Customs Office). When it comes to the rest of administration, we find hardly any of those traits that characterize a modern bureaucracy. Britain was a very strong rationalized state as well as a very weak and 'improvised' one, depending from where and at what one looks. On the local level, for example, we see hardly any professional administrators. There the 'gentleman amateur', who often cultivated his 'studied opposition to the matter-of-fact attitude and business routine', still ruled supreme.[18] So much so that one can find people who, when comparing the mandarins in China and Britain's 'gentlemen rulers', in this specific case after the 1850s, see 'more than a superficial resemblance between the tradition of this Chinese official class and that of the incomparably younger British Civil Service'.[19] We already indicated there were people in Britain in the nineteenth century who thought their civil service should try and copy various aspects of China's 'bureaucratic' system.[20] There indeed were great similarities in the way in which both types of officials were prepared for their job. For both the curriculum gave a large place to classical subjects, leaned heavily on tradition and was very much like what we now know as 'a humanistic education'. Not much attention was paid to vocational training as such. Modern bureaucracy as Weber defines it clearly is a child of the nineteenth century. Before that we see only 'sprouts of bureaucracy'.

---

[15]For required qualifications and the recruitment of government officials see Fischer and Lundgreen, 'Recruitment and training', and Mann, *Sources of Social Power, II*, chs 13 and 14.

[16]Mann, *Sources of Social Power, II*, ch. 13. The figures and the quotation are on page 452.

[17]Mann, *Sources of Social Power, II*, 390. The states he investigates are Britain, France, Prussia-Germany, Austria and the United States.

[18]Mann, *Sources of Social Power, II*, the paragraphs on Britain in chapter 13, and Cain and Hopkins, *British Imperialism*, 38–50. The quotation is from this text, page 39.

[19]Pratt, *China and Britain*, 70–2. The quotation is on pages 71–2.

[20]See under Introduction note 134.

Bureaucrats and bureaucracy in China

As modern bureaucrats really were an oddity *everywhere* on the globe before roughly 1800, China's system of government could look quite professional and rational to contemporaries. During the eighteenth century, many people in Europe regarded it as exemplary. And in various respects China's civil administration indeed was more professional and bureaucratic than that of (most of) Western Europe.[21] It was a professional institution: in the eighteenth century a position as an official, as a rule, was obtained on the basis of qualifications, to wit having passed certain examinations, and not on the basis of status, hereditary rights or purchase. A hereditary aristocracy as existed in Europe played only a very small part in ruling the country. In that respect China, without any doubt, was 'post-feudal', as Woodside would say. One must be careful, however, not to paint too meritocratic a picture of it: not all the important positions were 'achieved', to put it in sociological terms. Although as compared with almost all countries of Europe China's aristocracy was very small, it was not absent. In the entourage of the emperor there were imperial clansmen, direct descendants of Nurhaci, the first Manchu ruler in China. They numbered about 700 from the late sixteenth century through to the end of the nineteenth century. Then there were titular nobles, as a rule civil and military officers who received their title as an honour. They were not an estate or a class by themselves and as a group they had little influence in society, but still their position clearly was 'ascribed'. Finally there were the banner men who held many hereditary military functions. Furthermore, various positions in government were exclusively reserved for Manchus. The system of giving roughly half of the important government jobs to Han and roughly half to Manchus, of course, was very favourable for the Manchus, who were less than 2 per cent of China's total population.[22] So the role of ascription and favouritism definitely was not negligible.

There were no sinecures. Selling official positions – and ranks, titles and chances to get a position – was supposed to be exceptional. It was legal, although it was masked as a reward for the fact that one had given a contribution. It clearly became *more* frequent as time went by.[23] Considering the circumstances, supervision of civil servants was quite strict and systematic.[24] It often took the form of mutual supervision. Government officials, civil and military, were not allowed to work in a region where their family lived or where members of their family were in office. When outside Peking, they were transferred to another district at least once in every three years. This 'rule of avoidance' was applied to prevent them from getting too enmeshed in local politics and becoming pawns of local interests, and in the hope of ensuring that they would continue to be independent servants of the state. Other 'strong' points of the system would be that, at least in theory,

---

[21] I here, as in my European cases, *as a rule* only refer to civilian bureaucrats. The number of military bureaucrats in China was not negligible. Deng claims there were some 2,500 of them. (See his *China's Political Economy*, 25.) Elliott thinks there were more than 10,000. (See Elliott, *Manchu Way*, 134–5.)

[22] Hsü, *Rise of Modern China*, 45–59.

[23] See pages 90–1.

[24] See Kreuzer, *Staat und Wirtschaft* , and Thornton, *Disciplining the State*, chs 1 and 2.

it was identical all over China, as it was run by men with a very similar education and world view. That of course facilitated communication, although provincial officials were not supposed to have direct contact with one another. The system was and was meant to be flexible, adapting to time and place. All in all, it is far from obvious that *at the local level* Chinese mandarins were doomed to be less efficient and less professional than, let us say, British gentlemen – that is, the aristocrats who ran local affairs in their county. On top of that, China's bureaucracy had the unmistakable advantage of being small and cheap. Which brings us to what I regard as the root of most of its problems: it simply was *too* small and *too* cheap.

The number of civil servants employed and paid by the government, compared to (Great) Britain, was surprisingly low. The number of civil 'public servants' in China during the eighteenth century was nearly constant and amounted, depending on the exact definition and on the sources one uses, to between 20,000 and 30,000 people, a number that is *roughly* equal to that of British civil servants at the time.[25] This means that there were, roughly speaking, more than thirty times as many public servants per head of the population in (Great) Britain as there were in China. The numbers we find for China are not just low: they are amazingly low. If we deduct the number of officials that stayed in Peking, we must conclude that no more than some 10,000 to 15,000 officials were supposed to run the country in the provinces. In China Proper in the middle of the nineteenth century, each county magistrate, who was responsible for one of the approximately 1,500 districts, ruled over, on average, some 250,000 people. Eugene Simon estimated that the number of officials in the whole of China in 1885, when he was the French consul there, was still no more than 25,000 to 30,000.[26] Chang, in his book on the income of the Chinese gentry, comes up with a similar figure, claiming that in the 1880s, in total, there were some 27,000 officials in China, counting Han *and* non-Han, civil *and* military officials.[27] That would mean at that time there was one 'real' government official per 14,000 inhabitants. Outside China Proper, bureaucracy also was very thin on the ground. At the end of the eighteenth century, there were 175 Qing officials in Tibet.[28] The following two examples show how different China was in this respect. In Prussia alone, in the 1870s, there were more than 300,000 government employees responsible for their realm of some 24.5 million inhabitants and for helping to run the German *Kaiserreich* that in total had some 40 million inhabitants. Great Britain was much less bureaucratic. We have figures for officials working for central government there for 1850 (40,000) and 1890 (90,000).[29]

The Qing Empire grew enormously in population, size and complexity over the period discussed in this book. The number of government officials, however, hardly increased, if

---

[25]These numbers are not contested. One can find them in many publications. Deng in his *China's Political Economy*, 25, claims, that the Qing Empire had 24,150 civilian officials on its payroll in 1700 and 26,355 in 1850.

[26]Simon, *Paradies der Arbeit*, 16.

[27]Chang, *Income of the Chinese Gentry*, ch. 1.

[28]Dabringhaus, *Qing-Imperium*, 166.

[29]See for these estimates Mann, *Sources of Social Power, II*, 806 and 808.

at all, while the preparation they received for their job continued to be quite inadequate. In principle, only people who had passed at least one exam were qualified for a job as an official. Their number was huge and continued to grow, *as* did the number of those who bought degrees and titles. After the Great Taiping Rebellion (1851–62) there were no less than 1.5 million literati with a degree and about 3 million candidates for the biennial qualifying examinations.[30] Passing exams apparently continued to be considered a major step towards getting a job as an official, the goal of huge numbers of ambitious Chinese. For the overwhelming majority of the aspiring students, however, there was not even a chance to get an *official* job. The same goes for many of the increasing number of people who bought their 'entry-ticket' to officialdom. The fact that the number of people directly buying an office increased so sharply, to at times even becoming the majority, will not have improved quality either. What it very probably did do was increase feelings of frustration by those who had passed exams, even when they ended up earning a good income as official or 'sub-official'. I tend to agree with Ho that the examination system, in which so many people invested so much with an absolutely tiny chance of ever getting a real job, entailed 'wastage of human effort and talent on a scale vaster than can be found in most societies'.[31] In this respect, too, the system was not very efficient to begin with and became increasingly inefficient.

The salaries of those who did get an official job, even when they were supplemented by often quite high honesty-nourishing allowances and, in case of specific officials, with allowances for administrative expenses, were quite low considering the costs involved, but they were only a very tiny part of officials' total incomes. Chang estimates that in the 1880s total *official* income of all officeholders in China, civil as well as military, Han as well as non-Han, amounted to only some 6 million taels per year. Their total *actual* annual income, however, according to him, would have been some 115 million, which would be some 5,000 taels or more than 180,000 grams of silver per official per year.[32] What made getting a position as an official so attractive, apart from the status and its privileges, was not the official salary but the numerous possibilities to collect fees, gifts and bribes and to have other more or less status-related sources of income. The office holders that Chang studied and that he identified with 'the gentry' had income from their office, from so-called gentry functions, teaching, secretarial and educational jobs, but many also from land and mercantile activities. All this can only mean that central government could easily lose grip on 'its' personnel.

In discussing tax collection in Qing China, I already referred to most of the problems that officials had to face in trying to actually do their job and to the 'solutions' they came up with. What applied to taxation, applied to administration in general: there were far too few personnel, their official salaries were far too low and they often were not well prepared. Over time things did not improve. Moreover, in practice, the rule of avoidance resulted in a situation where the official, who came from another region and only had a very small

---

[30]See Elman, *Cultural History of Civil Examinations*, 584.
[31]Ho, *Ladder of Success*, 259.
[32]Chang, *Income of the Chinese Gentry*, ch. 1.

personal staff, became totally dependent, when he wanted to find his way and his aides, on the local 'notables' in 'whose' district he was parachuted. It has long been common to identify these gentry solely with degree holders. That identification is imprecise: 'In different times and localities wealth, pedigree, military power, or religious or technical expertise were far more important than an examination degree in ensuring local power and prestige.'[33] The incoming official was not in a position to pick personnel as he saw fit. He was stuck with the people who presented themselves or were presented to him by local power holders. Local clerks and runners became something of a (semi-)hereditary local network that was either fairly independent or, as a rule, under the protection of the local bosses. It in any case was hardly ever really in the grip of the official. Together, clerks, runners and 'members' of the gentry held the keys to local power, not the official sent by Peking. As he would be gone in at most three years, in all probability, such an official would not be able to create much trust or build a personal power basis. Nor is it very likely that he would feel responsible for any long-term projects. Officials continued to be outsiders. They came and went. The local notables and the clerks and runners whose services they had to use – without being funded to pay them properly – stayed. A system evolved of co-optation, cooperation and complementarity in which officials and local notables merged into a blend that one nowadays tends to call 'the gentry'.[34]

This means that in Qing China 'the state' at the local level in many respects hardly existed, let alone as a formal organization. It was not much more than a very thin administrative superstructure that left day-to-day business, and often much more, to the local elites. Bureaucratic appearances notwithstanding, in China also much if not almost all state rule basically was *indirect* rule.[35] The American historian Morse wrote about the Qing Empire:

> But apart from this [a very occasional contact with criminal justice] and apart from the regular visits of the tax collector, it is doubtful whether the actual existence of a government is brought tangibly to the notice of a tenth, certainly not a fifth of the population.[36]

The many references to China's 'meritocratic' system of selecting its administrators that one finds in texts that sing the praise of China's 'modern' system of rule, moreover, should also be taken with a fair amount of salt. The fact that they were educated and had passed exams should of course not delude us about *what* exactly Chinese officials had learned and *what kind of exams* they had passed. Most of them lacked any specific organizational or technical schooling. What they imbibed during their studies was a certain culture, not certain professional knowledge. What they definitely were all made familiar with was

---

[33]Pines, *Everlasting Empire*, 105.

[34]For information about China's gentry, its training and worldview see Chang, *Chinese Gentry*; Ch'ü, *Local Government*; Elman, *Cultural History*; Ho, *Ladder of Success*; Osterhammel, 'Gesellschaftliche Parameter'; Pines, *Everlasting Empire*; Rowe, *China's Last Empire*, and Smith, *China's Cultural Heritage*.

[35]For the concepts 'direct' and 'indirect rule' see Tilly, *Coercion, Capital, and European States*, ch. 4.

[36]Morse, *Trade and Administration*, 72.

classical learning. Their education was meant to turn them into 'generalist' gentlemen who would rule according to high moral standards, not specialists. The 'Confucianist rejection of the professional expert', of which Weber wrote, certainly existed. Mandarins did not as a rule regard themselves, to quote Confucius, as 'a tool' in an organization and they were wary of specialist competences.[37] The tradition of legalism that emphasized professionalism and legal machinery much more than the moral qualities of the ruler, in the end, lost its struggle with 'Confucianism' when it came to providing an ideological basis to China's system of rule.[38] The fact that there may have been many legalist bureaucratic appearances in Qing China's administrative system should not deceive us into thinking that in practice it actually worked like a bureaucracy or was conceived like one by the people running it. Of course, many of them learned a lot during their careers and some of them acquired quite some specialist expertise, but that, as it were, was more by accident than on purpose. It will *not* have been by accident that officials, as we saw, privately hired thousands of specialists to help them in actually doing their job.[39] We already indicated that one should not be too 'optimist' about the quality, education and integrity of those working for Britain's government either, but there at least in the sphere of tax collecting one could find real professionalism. There is no need to go into much further detail here, as we have already pointed out the weaknesses of China's 'bureaucracy' when we discussed its system of tax collecting. Again, when I refer to problems and weaknesses here, I am not just being anachronistic, using the benefit of hindsight or being Eurocentric, applying 'foreign' standards to Qing China. There were plenty of people who were only too aware of existing problems and there were efforts to remedy them.[40] All that was implemented, in the end, however, were *ad hoc* measures.[41]

The absence of a formal 'rule of law' and of *institutionalized* countervailing powers that could see to its proper functioning, moreover, made the Qing administration vulnerable to 'bad' officials from the bottom to the very top. Lack of funding, lack of qualified personnel, lack of clear rules and the tendency to see any kind of failure by officials as moral failure (i.e. a personal fault) – which also is quite un-bureaucratic – made life hard for all officials and created a situation in which they were almost forced to 'improvize' and then get into trouble.[42] There continued to be a very personal element in the system of rule, in particular at the very top of it. The emperor could clearly make a difference. The rule from 1760 to 1820 of King George III, who, in everyday jargon, can

---

[37]Weber, *Religion of China*, ch. 6.

[38]For a brief introduction to the differences in this respect between 'legalism' and 'Confucianism' see Folsom, *Friends, Guests and Colleagues*, ch. 1. Compare the distinction made by Thornton between a 'bureaucratic' model that in the end lost out and a more 'feudalist' one in Thornton, *Disciplining the State*, 23–4, and ch. 5 in Duara, *Rescuing History*, where an analysis is provided of that so-called 'fengjiang' or 'feudal' tradition.

[39]See Chapter 1 note 336.

[40]See for examples Kuhn, *Origins of the Modern Chinese State*, and Mann Jones, *Hung Liang-Chi*.

[41]See for efforts to reform and rationalize China's administration Will, 'Chine moderne et sinologie' and 'Développement quantitatif'. For the specific efforts by the Yongzheng emperor see Thornton, *Disciplining the State*. For efforts to reform the tax system see Zelin, *Magistrate's Tael*.

[42]Thornton, *Disciplining the State*, chs 1 and 2, provides some good examples.

only be described as 'mad', did not prevent Britain from waging and winning a global war and beginning its take off.[43] The fact that the Qianlong Emperor in his old age increasingly left the actual ruling to others had very wide-ranging and negative effects for his entire empire. However, one should be careful for the Chinese case and distinguish theory from practice. Pines rightly claims that: 'Few if any monarchs in human history could rival the theoretical power of their Chinese counterparts.' Chinese emperors were 'in theory all but divine'. In practice, however, 'the emperors' weakness rather than excessive authoritarianism was the rule'. Pines characterizes their usual position as one of 'impotent omnipotence'.[44] Most emperors were overwhelmed by the magnitude of their power. Overall, there were many weak emperors in China's history. From the perspective of officials a weak emperor was preferable because they then, as often was the case, could do the actual ruling. The succession of three very strong emperors under the Qing, the Kangxi, Yongzheng and Qianlong emperors was exceptional.

THE OVERWHELMING IMPORTANCE OF THE MILITARY

Some comments on the situation in Europe

In the previous paragraphs we have been discussing civilian personnel. From our current perspective they are the typical government employees. At the time, however, the number of military men dwarfed that of civilian personnel in all the countries discussed in this text. The typical government 'employee', to again use an anachronistic term, in the early modern era was a soldier. In this case, too, it is hard to come up with trustworthy and comparable figures that enable us to make salient comparisons over time and between countries. Let me refer to just two problems. The first one is the difference between the number of soldiers 'on paper' and that of people who were actually mobilized. In China, to give just one example, many thousands of people were classified as banner men who in reality could not be considered soldiers at all. The second problem is the difference between periods of war and periods of peace. That difference could be enormous. Nevertheless, one conclusion can be drawn without any hesitation: Western Europe in the early modern era was heavily militarized, far more than Qing China.

Although it certainly existed, one must be careful to not exaggerate the militarization of Western European society during the early modern era. Basically in this period what Azar Gat calls an iron rule throughout history, 'that no more than one per cent of a state's population (and normally less) could be sustained economically on a regular basis as fully professional troops', was not disproved.[45] Countries that 'violated' it did so in very specific circumstances and normally paid a price for it. Maximum army size did tend to increase, but so did, be it less substantially, population. Troops, apart from that increasing

---

[43]See Colley, *Britons*, ch. 5.
[44]For the quotations see Pines, *Everlasting Empire*, 45, 64 and 72–3.
[45]Gat, *War in Human Civilization*, 364 for the quotation and 474 for the claim that this rule continued to apply in early modern Western Europe.

part that became a standing army, as a rule were quickly demobilized. To a certain extent, their increasing size and rising costs were an optical illusion as central governments on purpose chose to no longer fall back on their 'barons' to provide them with troops, build fortifications and organize all kinds of corvee. The policy of centralization and the rise of direct rule inevitably implied centralization of command and recruitment, and centralization of costs. The fact that in many countries, in particular the countries that Charles Tilly would describe as 'coercion-intensive',[46] using conscripts became increasingly normal and important also complicates the picture. They could be much cheaper than mercenaries and often were expected to take care of at least part of their own income. In the end, though, developments boiled down to a situation where more troops had to be more fully provided for by the state over a longer period of time.

According to Tilly the period from roughly 1400 to 1700 can in important parts of Europe be characterized as one of 'brokerage' in which 'mercenary forces recruited by contractors predominated in military activity, and rulers relied heavily on formally independent capitalists for loans, for management of revenue-producing enterprises, and for installation and collection of taxes'.[47] This period, again according to Tilly, was succeeded by one of 'nationalization', which ran from roughly 1700 to 1850 in much of Europe. In this period 'states created mass armies and navies drawn increasingly from their own national populations, while sovereigns absorbed armed forces directly into the state's administrative structure, and similarly took over the direct operation of the fiscal apparatus, drastically curtailing the involvement of independent contractors'.[48] The actual periodization appears to have been less clear-cut, with the process of 'nationalization' often only really beginning to take off with the French Revolution. As recent research has shown, the so-called 'contractor state' in which private and public enterprise were closely intertwined persisted over the entire eighteenth century.[49] In Britain, to give but one example, the Royal Navy had docks of its own, but between 1803 and 1815 private shipyards that contracted their job built 84 per cent of warships or 72 per cent by tonnage. Contractors in that period were even far more important than they had been in the eighteenth century.[50] But as a rough first characterization and indication of overall trends of development Tilly's concepts are certainly useful.

Let me begin by looking at things from a purely quantitative perspective and present a couple of estimates to show *how* heavily early modern Europe, overall, was militarized.[51]

---

[46]Tilly, *Coercion, Capital, and European States*. See in particular, 16–20.

[47]Tilly, *Coercion, Capital, and European States*, 29.

[48]Tilly, *Coercion, Capital, and European States*, 29.

[49]See Chapter 1 note 299 for Britain and the contractor state. For serious and convincing critique of Tilly's periodization and the assumptions behind it, see Fynn-Paul, *War, Entrepreneurs and the State*.

[50]Knight, *Britain against Napoleon*, ch. 12. The reference to shipbuilding is on page 359.

[51]See for, sometimes widely differing, estimates with regard to the size of various armies in early modern Europe, Black, *A Military Revolution*, 6 and 7; Karaman and Pamuk, 'Ottoman state finances', 612 (with several figures that to me seem not very probable); Landers, *The Field and the Forge*, ch. 13.2; Lucassen and Lucassen, 'Mobility transition in Europe revisited. Sources and methods', the internet version, 65–102; Porter, *War and the Rise of the State*, 67, table 3.1, and Tilly, *Coercion, Capital, and European States*, 79. All my figures are from these texts, unless indicated otherwise. The best and most detailed source is the text by Lucassen and Lucassen.

The British case, as before, will be dealt with in more detail separately. Prussia has always been 'famous' for its militarism. In 1740 it had more than 80,000 military men on a total population of 2.2 million inhabitants.[52] This figure would increase even further: at the death of Frederick the Great in 1786, Prussia's army, consisting of mercenaries and an increasing number of conscripts, numbered almost 200,000 men. Prussia's population then was less than 6 million. It was without any doubt a heavily militarized *state*, but not necessarily a heavily militarized *society*: 'only' 81,000 of these soldiers were native-born Prussians.[53] In 1813, its armed forces had increased yet further to 280,000 troops.[54] Prussia was much less of a special case than people tend to think. It has been calculated that in 1780 what we would now call 'Germany', roughly the Holy Roman Empire of those days without Austria, in total had an army of 320,000 soldiers. That means its armed forces amounted to 2 per cent of the total population.[55] The army of the Austrian Empire during the Seven Years War (1756–63) numbered 200,000 men from a population of about 18 million. For 1789, when total population had increased to about 25 million people, the nominal strength of its regular infantry and cavalry troops is estimated at 315,000. Including artillery, the contingent of the so-called Military Border, plus militia, the military apparatus may have reached 500,000 troops in 1790.[56]

The Dutch Republic still acted as a major power in Europe in the seventeenth century. That means that it must have had a substantial army: it did. In 1670 its entire army may have amounted to 110,000 troops; during the Wars of Spanish Succession (1702–13), its strength never was less than 100,000. As its population at that time was only about 2 million people that means that in periods of serious conflicts it had an army that, relatively speaking, was even bigger than that of Prussia in the eighteenth century. In 1700, the army of France, a country with about 20 million inhabitants at that time and Europe's super-power, counted 400,000 people, a number that would only be surpassed in the 1790s. One could give many more examples of heavily militarized countries. In 1700, Sweden had a population of less than 1.3 million people and yet its army counted 100,000 soldiers. During the Thirty Years War (1618–48) it, at times, had been as big as 180,000 troops. No less than about four-fifths were foreign mercenaries. At the time of the death of Gustavus Adolphus in 1632, less than 10 per cent of Sweden's army was Swedish; the remainder mostly was German.[57] To all intents and purposes, war was a very international affair.[58] One could find foreigners not just among ordinary soldiers, but also among commanders.

---

[52]Gorski, *Disciplinary Revolution*, 80.

[53]Clark, *Iron Kingdom*, 215. Compare, however, Wilson, 'Prussia as a fiscal-military state', note 68, where it is claimed that many troops already counted as foreigners when they had been recruited outside their home canton.

[54]Lynn, 'Nations in arms', 207.

[55]Stier and Von Hippel, 'War, economy and society', 244.

[56]Hochedlinger, 'Habsburg Monarchy', 88.

[57]Thomson, *Mercenaries, Pirates & Sovereigns*, 30.

[58]See, for example, Bell, *First Total War*, ch. 1.

Table 31 Foreigners in eighteenth-century armies

Country	Year	Foreign component (percentage)
Prussia	1713–40	34
	1743	66
	1768	56
	1786	50
Britain	1695	24
	1701	54
	1760s	38
	1778	32
France	1756–63	25
	1789	22
	Pre-Revolution	33
Spain	1751	25
	1799	14

Source: Thomson, *Mercenaries, Pirates & Sovereigns*, 29.

It is not much use discussing country after country. Estimates exist of the total number of military personnel in Europe in the period discussed here. According to Parker, in 1710 in total about 1.3 million troops were simultaneously on foot in Europe.[59] Luh claims that over the eighteenth century this number increased even further and that 2 million men were in military service on the eve of the French Revolution.[60] After the Revolutionary and Napoleonic Wars the size of armies tended to reduce.

To get an impression of how many people were actually involved, one has to consider the fact that between 1500 and 1850 armies lost some 10 to 15 per cent of their troops annually in peacetime and 15 to 40 per cent in wartime. Overall average 'wastage', due to death, invalidity, desertion or enlistment elsewhere, will certainly not have been below 20 per cent.[61] Table 33 gives the total number of people that at any time during a fifty-year period served in the armies of several European countries. We have to realize that service in the army tended to be a matter of several years. In France conscripts enlisted for six years during the period 1793–1815, at times even for seven or eight years. Most of Britain's professional soldiers up until 1847 had a lifetime enlistment of, in practice, normally twenty-one years.[62]

---

[59]Parker, *Military Revolution*, 46.

[60]Luh, *Ancien régime Warfare*, 13.

[61]Parker, *Military Revolution*, 46 and 53–8. For the cost of war in terms of mortality and population loss see Landers, *The Field and the Forge*, ch. 14.

[62]Lucassen and Lucassen, 'Mobility transition in Europe revisited. Sources and methods', the internet version, 67–9. See page 69 for more examples of very long periods of duty, twenty-five years in Russia in the period between 1793 and 1834.

Table 32 Military personnel as percentage of total population, 1760–1850

Year	Great Britain	Austria-Hungary	France	Prussia-Germany
1760	2.36	1.66	1.78	4.14
1770	0.58	1.17	0.82	
1780	2.76	1.41	0.89	3.76
1790	0.97	1.52	0.85	3.42
1800	4.91	1.35	2.93	3.73
1810	5.30	2.38	3.66	3.88
1820	1.02			1.33
1830	1.01	1.38	1.23	1.15
1840	1.10	1.56	1.02	1.05
1850	1.20	1.56	1.09	1.04

Source: Mann, *Sources of Social Power, II*, 393.

Table 33 Total numbers of people that served in the army over periods of fifty years each, in several European countries, in thousands

	UK	NL	FRA	GER	SP/POR	ITA	AUS/ HUN	TOTAL
1651–1700	500	595	2,000	1,000	1,200	200	650	6,145
1701–50	1,000	810	1,620	2,000	700	750	1,500	8,380
1751–1800	1,000	500	1,990	2,200	800	750	2,500	9,740
1801–50	1,250	100	3,860	2,500	1,430	800	2,000	11,940
1851–1900	1,340	100	1,000	2,000	1,500	420	1,200	7,560

Source: Based on Lucassen and Lucassen, 'Mobility transition in Europe revisited. Sources and methods', web version, 102.

That number would increase even further if we were to include soldiers that were not officially employed by government. At home, governments often could fall back on reserve armies, and European chartered companies overseas also had troops, in army and navy – some of them mercenaries from the mother country; others from other European countries, and the bulk of them non-Europeans. In our analysis of the British case, we find that in total here too we are talking about many tens of thousands of people. On top of that, there were a huge number of camp followers, the so-called army 'train', consisting of servants, wives, children, prostitutes, victuallers and others. Their average number for the early modern period has been estimated at some 50 per cent of the size of the armies they were following at war strength. At times it was much higher. Over time, these army trains became smaller, until their complete disappearance during the nineteenth century.[63]

Apart from the armies there of course were the navies. In the seventeenth century, the Dutch Republic on various occasions managed to mobilize a war fleet with more than 20,000 sailors. At that time, that still sufficed to enable a country to act as a naval superpower in Europe. But here too we see a big increase in size and scale. In the 1790s, for example, both France and Russia had a war fleet with about 65,000 men.[64] At that time, however, even fleets of that size no longer sufficed to rule the waves. A further extension of the French fleet, that had become a serious rival to that of Britain, in particular when in the 1770s it could be combined with the fleet of France's ally Spain, had simply proved too burdensome for the French treasury.[65] At the end of the eighteenth century, the waves were firmly ruled by Britain's Royal Navy, whose size, as we will see later on, was even larger. Most of the sailors serving on men-of-war worked on merchants' ships when off duty. In European countries bordering the Atlantic alone, in that way, at the end of the eighteenth century, a stock of some 300,000 to 400,000 trained sailors had been created; for the British Isles some 100,000 to 150,000; in France, Spain and the Netherlands each some 60,000, and in Denmark-Norway some 40,000. 'Wastage' of manpower on men-of-war was enormous.[66] Here too many of the serving troops were foreigners.

Considering what has been said above, it will not come as a surprise that actual warfare increasingly became a massive affair. I will again give a couple of telling examples.[67] Here, too, one can never be sure about exact numbers. Differences between official numbers (i.e. 'paper strength') and reality could be immense. But the trend is beyond any reasonable doubt. When in 1494 Charles VIII of France invaded Italy, he did so with 18,000 troops. In 1552, no less than 55,000 Habsburg troops laid siege to the French city of Metz, without, for that matter, in the end conquering it. Albrecht von Wallenstein, the Bohemian military entrepreneur who worked for the 'German' emperor during the Thirty Years War (1618–48), raised an effective army of 125,000 men in 1628. In 1708, during the Spanish War of Succession (1702–13), there at times were more than 300,000 people involved in one campaign. With the principle of the *levée en masse*, or 'general mobilisation', that was introduced in France during the Revolutionary Wars, we enter a new era. In that system, all adult males of a certain age living in a certain country became potential soldiers. In that sense, Revolutionary and Napoleonic France indeed waged the first total wars.[68] In September 1794, the army of

---

[63]Lucassen and Lucassen, 'Mobility transition in Europe revisited. Sources and methods', the internet version, 74–5.

[64]Harding, *Seapower and Naval Warfare*, 140.

[65]Baugh, 'Naval power'.

[66]Frykman, 'Seeleute', 57. For more and more detailed information see Lucassen and Lucassen, 'Mobility transition in Europe revisited. Sources and methods', the internet version, 41–64. See for some examples of 'wastage' 285–6.

[67]I took the examples that follow from Tallett, *War and Society*, 4–13. The reference to the siege of Metz is in Parker, *Military Revolution*, 24.

[68]Bell, *First Total War*.

the newly created Republic of France numbered, at least in theory, no less than 1,169,000 men. In reality, the number probably was 'only' 730,000. In 1798, the new system of conscription was formalized by law and officially introduced in all parts of the French Empire. Many countries in Europe that were fighting Napoleon had to follow suit and at least experiment with forms of mass conscription. Prussia did so most radically whereas Great Britain was a striking exception. In 1810, Napoleon had 370,000 soldiers in Spain. The army with which he invaded Russia counted *at least* 600,000 men. Some 200,000 of them were French; 100,000 came from annexed departments, and the rest were allied troops.[69] Between 1800 and 1815, the French state drafted at least 2 million people. These were not all French. They came from all over France's European empire. At its peak in 1809–12, that empire had 44 million inhabitants. The increase in scale showed on the battlefield: in 1813 more than 500,000 soldiers fought the Battle of Leipzig. Of them 150,000 were killed or wounded.[70] Here, too, one must not simply think in terms of a straightforward development: over most of the eighteenth century, the size of armies indeed increased, but actually there was less and less fierce fighting than in the previous century with, among others, the acrimonious and devastating religious wars. Warfare in the eighteenth century by and large was more limited, with commanders trying to not endanger their troops. The best example here probably is Prussia, which was very keen on *not* really engaging the enemy in big battles. The Revolutionary and Napoleonic Wars were an extremely violent interlude.

After the Napoleonic Wars, there was a substantial demobilization. Much of the military history of the rest of the nineteenth century would be characterized by efforts to somehow incorporate broader layers of the national population via conscription or recruitment without stunting the further professionalization of the army and more specifically its officer corps. During the Napoleonic Wars this development of professionalization, especially of the officer corps, had been combined, in a rather uneasy union, with massification. Among officers professionalism now prevailed, reinforcing bureaucracy. On the other hand there was enormous growth of the numbers of rank and file, consisting of volunteers, people who were pressed and, in many countries, increasingly conscripts.[71] The use of conscripts could have the effect of increasing efficiency, as they had a quite differentiated societal background and came from many walks of life, whereas the mercenaries who were so important in the armies of the *Ancien Régime* often were, or at least were considered to be, 'the dregs of society'.[72]

Considering the fact that in most countries the disappearance of Napoleon was accompanied by a political restoration, putting one's trust in the chauvinism and military fervour of the masses probably was no longer a very promising strategy. That is, if it had ever been one, which must be severely doubted. It is not by accident that the bulk of

---

[69]Parker, *Military Revolution*, 151–3, and Black, *European Warfare*, 158.

[70]Bell, *First Total War*, 7.

[71]This paragraph strongly paraphrases Black, *European Warfare*, ch. 12, and Mann, *Sources of Social Power, II*, 402–43.

[72]For a more nuanced view see Way, 'Klassenkrieg', 95–104.

the ordinary soldiers from then onwards tended to become recruited among specific 'trustworthy' parts of the population. The *levée en masse* clearly was not a panacea and it was not tried as such. Fear of 'the masses' never fully disappeared. General conscription, for example, was only introduced in Italy in 1862, in the German Empire in 1871 and in Britain during the First World War.[73] What is more, even if one could mobilize masses of enthusiast fighters, what in the end counted in the modern armies that took shape was training, discipline and skills, much more than 'the right mentality'. The main challenge had now become how to find the right mix between quality and quantity. According to most experts it would take till the 1860s before the Prussians came up with an adequate solution in setting up armies consisting of a standing nucleus of highly trained officers and shifting troops of soldiers who all had to go through a three-year military service and were mobilized in case of need.

These comments have already taken us from the strictly quantitative to the organizational. The first thing that strikes one in studying military affairs in early modern Western Europe is that for so long, just like in civil administration, 'indirect rule' prevailed. At the beginning of the eighteenth century, there still was no European central government that possessed the bureaucratic or financial capability to fully administer its own army. In the context of the military, too, the word 'bureaucratic' should be used with utmost care when discussing Europe in the early modern period. It is only at the end of the eighteenth century, for example, that in Britain and Prussia, two frontrunners in military bureaucratization, that army officers were state employees rather than state agents.[74] An amazing variety of private contractors, financiers, recruiters – in brief *private* entrepreneurs – continued to be important in taking care, on behalf of government, and, not to forget, themselves, of finding people, provisions and money for armies and navies.[75] Every study of the armed forces in early modern Europe stresses the extent of private involvement *in* or even private management *of* public affairs. This mix continued to exist in many countries up into the nineteenth century. As in civilian matters, where high-handed, 'autonomous' aristocrats, tax farmers, holders of venal offices and so on wielded power that we would nowadays regard as public, in military affairs too central government often had to confine itself to ruling indirectly and trying to control from afar. From the second half of the seventeenth century onward, however, we see the slow emergence of more (direct) government control and 'bureaucratization', of which the 'professionalization' we referred to of course is a part. Here also one should be careful not to exaggerate and see too many 'sprouts of modernity' too early. On the eve of the Revolutionary and Napoleonic Wars, for many aristocrats war still was a matter of honour and display more than a serious profession. The military and military men were not as separated from the rest of society and other occupations as they would become.[76]

---

[73]Moran and Waldron, *People in Arms*.
[74]Childs, 'Army and the state', 61.
[75]See Parrott, *Business of War*, and Tallett, *War and Society*.
[76]Bell, *First Total War*, ch.1.

There continued to be quite some amateurism. Being an aristocrat often still sufficed to be regarded as a competent military. Even in the Dutch Republic over 60 per cent of colonelcies in the eighteenth century were in the hands of members of the nobility. This social context of warfare was only challenged in the late eighteenth century, with its increasing emphasis on formalized professionalism based on formal education. We already referred to the widespread sale of offices in France. That also occurred in the French army. By 1787, the number of officers in it had swollen to 36,000, only a third of which were in active service whereas all were drawing pay. There were 1,171 general officers, compared with just over 80 in Prussia's army and Austria's 350. Officers' pay consumed at least half of the French army's budget.[77] In many countries, including to some extent in Britain, it continued to be possible, for a very long time, to buy military offices.[78] But whatever the social background or position of military men, the degree of administrative sophistication required to sustain the large-scale Western military systems of the period was considerable and only increased with the passing of time. We see an accelerated development in both qualitative and quantitative terms from the late seventeenth century, particularly in Austria, Britain, France, Prussia and Russia. According to Michael Mann, during the eighteenth century military administration became 'relatively centralized, routinized, disciplined, homogenous and bureaucratic'. Salaries became normal and sailors and soldiers became paid employees. He claims that the military can be regarded as 'by far the most modern eighteenth-century power organization'.[79] In his view, bureaucratization enabled armies to grow. It won out simply because informal, 'looser' military organization perished on the battlefield.

Great Britain as a military superpower

Let us again look at the British case somewhat more in depth and then compare it with China. Great Britain undoubtedly became a heavily militarized country.[80] During the Nine Years War (1689–97), its government on average paid 116,000 people to do service in army and navy. During the War of Spanish Succession (1702–13), that number had increased to, on average, 136,000. During the Seven Years War (1756–63), it was 167,000. During the American Wars (1776–84), the number had again increased, now to 191,000. With the Revolutionary and Napoleonic Wars, a new phase in British military history was entered. In 1809, Britain's army alone had 234,177 effective rank-and-file soldiers, to which some 30,000 officers, NCOs and suchlike must be added. In 1813,

---

[77]See Gat, *War in Human Civilization*, 489, and Félix and Tallett, 'French experience', 158. Felix and Tallett there also point out that by 1750 in the French army there were as many pensioned officers as officers on active commission.

[78]For an analysis meant to show that this actually also had quite positive effects see Allen, *Institutional Revolution*, ch. 6.

[79]Mann, *Sources of Social Power, II*, 424.

[80]See for basic information Brewer, *Sinews of Power*, 30; Evans, *Forging of the Modern State*, under 'army size' and 'navy strength'; Harding, *Seapower and Naval Warfare*, 139, and Rodger, *Command of the Ocean*, 636–9.

Table 34 Number of sailors approved by Parliament in Great Britain

1760–3	70,000
1783	110,000
1790s	110,000–120,000
1804	100,000
1810–13	145,000

Source: Hall, *British Strategy*, 11.

the number of regular British and foreign soldiers in Britain's army was over 250,000. Casualties were immense: during the Napoleonic Wars, there never were fewer than 16,000 of them per year. In 1809 there were more than 24,000. It will not come as a surprise that among those thousands of troops there were many foreigners. The last time that Britain's government resorted to mercenaries was during the Crimean War (1853–6), when it hired over 16,000 Germans, Italians and Swiss. During the Napoleonic Wars, between one-sixth and one-seventh of its troops came from abroad.[81] Strikingly enough, in 1819 government already passed the Foreign Enlistment Act under which it was forbidden for 'any natural-born subject of the British Crown' to enlist in 'the army of any foreign entity'.[82]

In normal situations Britain's army actually was kept quite small. That certainly was not the case with its navy. That was kept on the alert even in times of peace. The numbers of sailors voted by Parliament (Table 34) are impressive. The actual numbers almost always fell short of these levies by some 3,000 to 16,000. This means that next to the roughly 260,000 soldiers just referred to, Britain's government, at the height of the Napoleonic Wars, also mobilized some 150,000 naval personnel. The navy was a real 'men-eater'. From 1776 to 1783, to just give one example, it alone recruited between 230,000 and 235,000 men.[83] Finding such numbers of sailors could easily become a major problem, as not everyone was up to the rather complicated tasks that could face seamen on big men-of-war and one of course had to be careful not to inflate wages of seamen in the merchant navy.[84] Many foreigners were recruited: in the 1790s on British men-of-war it was quite normal that 25 to 30 per cent of the crew consisted of Irish sailors who had been pressed into service.[85] Problems were only augmented by the fact that so many sailors died while serving: between 1774 and 1780

---

[81]Hall, *British Strategy*, 1–3.
[82]Thomson, *Mercenaries, Pirates & Sovereigns*, 58.
[83]Rodger, *Command of the Ocean*, 396.
[84]The role of skilled and experienced labour diminished over the eighteenth century. In the Royal Navy at the end of the century it was considered sufficient when one in four sailors could be regarded as such. See Frykman, 'Seeleute', 63.
[85]Rodger, 'Shipboard life in the old navy', 30.

alone some 20,000.[86] During the Revolutionary and Napoleonic Wars, the number of casualties of course rose: they cost the lives of almost 90,000 seamen of the Royal Navy. In the Caribbean alone, 24,000 died between 1793 and 1801. The total number of army, navy and transport casualties in Caribbean operations in that period of time was between 64,000 and 69,000.[87] Being on an ocean-going ship wasn't good for your health anyhow: on slave ships usually 20 to 25 per cent of the *crew* died during one trip.[88]

Some figures can illustrate how big Britain's war fleet was and how much, with the passing of time, it increased in size. I will only refer to war ships here, although these were not always completely distinct from 'ordinary' ships, so the total number of vessels used during war could be much higher. We already saw that, according to Knight, in 1809 the effective size of the Royal Navy would have reached its maximum with 709 ships in commission.[89] Hall, for exactly the same year, estimates the Royal Navy at in total some 1,000 vessels, including smaller warships.[90] Over the eighteenth century, Britain's war fleet became by far the biggest in Europe.

Table 35 The strengths of the European navies, 1775–1815 (tonnage of sailing vessels above 500 tons in thousands of displacement tons)

	1775	1785	1795	1805	1815
Britain	327.3	433.2	511.5	571.5	609.3
France	190.1	259.6	284.4	182.2	228.3
Spain	188.8	198.4	264.0	138.7	59.9
Russia*	77.9	127.3	181.7	131.9	167.3
Netherlands	67.5	85.0	76.4	43.5	71.4
Denmark/Norway	80.9	84.4	83.6	63.2	7.8
Sweden	50.0	66.4	38.9	36.7	36.5
Portugal	39.3	33.7	49.8	54.1	44.4
Naples	4.4	7.6	27.6	12.5	14.9
Venice	17.4	20.4	20.9	–	–

Source: Duffy, 'Worldwide-war', 185 and 204.

*Including the Black Sea till 1785.

[86]Kemp, *British Sailor*, 139.
[87]See for these figures Pope, *Life in Nelson's Navy*, 131, and Duffy, *Soldiers, Sugar and Seapower*, 334.
[88]Christopher, *Slave Ship Sailors*, 183–4, and Rediker, *Slave Ship*, 244.
[89]See Chapter 5 note 121.
[90]Hall, *British Strategy*, 1.

Britain's navy was not only much bigger than that of its competitors: it was also very well equipped and more efficient.[91] All in all, at the height of the conflict with Napoleon, the British state had no less than 400,000 professional people in arms, on land and at sea. These people were fighting all over the globe. In the last decades of the eighteenth and the beginning of the nineteenth centuries the British army and the British navy engaged in battle in a staggering number of places in Europe, Africa, Asia and the Americas. Even in operations far from home the number of people could be quite high. To just give one example, the number of British troops and European troops in British pay sent to the Caribbean from 1793 to 1801 alone, when Britain was also involved in fierce fighting in many other regions, was almost 90,000.[92] Britain's armed forces, however, were not confined to the military and naval personnel in direct government service. Apart from them there were the armed forces of the East India Company. In 1793, the number of *European* troops there was 18,768; in 1815, some 31,611. The number of Indian troops in those years was 69,661 and 195,572 respectively. They were entirely paid for by 'the natives' they were supposed to keep in check.[93] Whereas the number of soldiers in the British army was reduced after the Napoleonic Wars, the number of military personnel in India increased even further. Just before the Mutiny of 1857, there were 100,000 European soldiers – in another estimate I found a number of 45,000 – and 250,000 from India.[94] Violence in India had been outsourced by Britain's government to the East India Company from the very beginning. The same goes for the activities of privateers. Their number and their impact were far from negligible. Although they were private 'entrepreneurs', they were actively supported by the British state. In 1708, for example, a prize act was passed that officially allowed privateers to retain all their prizes and stated that they were to be paid a bounty based on the number of prisoners they took. In 1744, the king granted pardons to all criminals who would serve as privateers. Britain's government in this respect went further than that of most other countries: British privateers were allowed to also attack neutral commerce. They acted as an auxiliary to the Royal Navy.[95] We are not dealing with a marginal phenomenon. Between 1793 and 1815, the Admiralty issued 4,000 Letters of Marque to privateers.[96] During the period from 1803 to 1806 alone, 47,000 men were given protection from impressment because they served on such vessels.[97] So many privateers and semi-privateers were active during

---

[91]See for explanation of this high efficiency Chapter 5 note 41.

[92]Duffy, *Soldiers, Sugar, and Seapower*, 330.

[93]Duffy, 'World-wide war', 202, table 9.2.

[94]See Duffy, 'World-wide war', 202, and Moore, 'Imperial India', 427. Dalziel, *Penguin Historical Atlas of the British Empire*, 78, gives the figure of 45,000 European soldiers at the time.

[95]Thomson, *Mercenaries, Pirates & Sovereigns*, 22–6.

[96]Hall, *British Strategy*, 11. Knight gives the following definition of a Letter of Marque: a licence issued by the Admiralty allowing a privately owned ship to attack the shipping of a hostile nation named in the document. He specifically refers to the British situation but the principle is identical in other European nations. Knight, *Britain against Napoleon*, 537.

[97]Hall, *British Strategy*, 11. The importance of these volunteers is strongly qualified by Knight, as is their number, in his *Britain against Napoleon*, 76.

the Napoleonic Wars that government could not keep them under control, if it had wanted to. Even though I have presented only fairly anecdotic evidence, it must have become clear that privateering was a non-negligible contribution to the total array of armed forces that government in Britain could mobilize against its enemies. After the Napoleonic Wars, both Britain and France stopped issuing Letters of Marque and therewith actually ended the practice of privateering. It was banned under international law, under British pressure, in 1856.

As if all this were not enough, there also were a couple of hundred thousand men in Britain, at the height of its conflict with France, who in part-time and volunteer units were expected to defend the home front. Patriotic feeling was successfully mobilized against Napoleon. The chief tasks of defence always fell to the professional soldiers but these additional forces were not unimportant. Britain did not experiment with forms of mass conscription but it did mobilize a huge home defence by means of militiamen who enlisted for a limited period and only for service in Britain. This militia as a rule was some 20 per cent of the army's total force. The number of its volunteers reached as high as 414,000 in 1803. In the period 1804 to 1806, there still were some 300,000. Then a steep decline set in. They numbered fewer than 70,000 in 1812. Over the period 1804–1813, on average there were some 80,000 volunteer soldiers who served five years in Britain. Their training was a mere twelve or twenty-four days a year. Next to this militia, there also was an Army of the Reserve that at times numbered some 30,000. The so-called Sea Fencibles were the equivalent for the navy of the volunteering home defence. Their number at times reached 25,000.[98]

The population of Great Britain was just under 11 million in 1801 and just over 12 million in 1811. The population of Ireland at the time was between 5 and 6 million. According to the figures I have just presented, certainly more than 1 million of them had, in one way or another and at one time or another, taken up arms against the French threat. This figure is not improbable: Patrick Colquhoun in 1815 calculated that the total military and naval strength of the British Empire was over 1 million men, an estimate that in his case included the East India Company's armed forces.[99] Without any doubt, Linda Colley is right when she speaks of 'a nation in arms'.[100] At no time during the height of the Napoleonic Wars were there fewer than some 500,000 men in arms – that is not including those serving in the Royal Navy. Actually, Britain's war effort was bigger than even all these figures suggest: the country had developed a tradition of supporting its allies on the Continent with money. The sums involved were huge. In total £66 million was paid in support of overseas allies against the French.[101] In the years 1812 to 1815, Britain paid between one-fifth and a quarter of its war expenditure to allies, sustaining about 500,000 allied troops, mostly Russian, Prussian and Austrian. If we

---

[98]All these figures are from Hall, *British Strategy*, ch. 1.

[99]Colquhoun, *Treatise on the Wealth, Power and Resources*, 7.

[100]Colley, *Britons*, 285. Compare Cookson, *British Armed Nation*, who points out that local power and local elites still played a key role in mobilizing war resources, including sentimental and ideological support.

[101]Knight, *Britain against Napoleon*, 388–9.

include these in the British Armed Forces, we would have to conclude that these might have numbered some 1.5 million people at that specific moment in time. The numbers are huge, even in comparison with other European countries. There is an estimate that during the Napoleonic Wars 'Britain raised armed forces which amounted to between eleven and fifteen per cent of adult male population, or about three times the "military participation ratio" of France.'[102] If we look at Britain's armies and fleets and at all it took to make them operational worldwide, one must conclude that as a country with less inhabitants and a smaller surface than many of the provinces of China, it had logistic capacities that simply had *no* parallel in any state anywhere on the globe.[103] The importance of being willing and able to develop this kind of *infrastructural* power and its implications for economic development tend to be underestimated by all parties who discuss 'the rise of the West'.

For British society 'the business of war' entailed all sorts of institutional rationalization and innovation but much less militarization than might be expected. Notwithstanding the enormous growth of the military and its importance over the entire eighteenth century and until Napoleon was defeated, Britain's army and navy were not actual state-builders as, according to Tilly, early modern armed forces normally were.[104] Britain's armed forces stood much more outside and beyond political and social institutions than, for example, those of Prussia.[105] Its *standing* army, on purpose, actually was quite small and based in Ireland. The navy, which of course was quite big and capital intensive but permanently at seas, enjoyed priority. The majority of the troops were deployed *outside* Britain, in Ireland and the colonies, which had to help in their provisioning. The army and navy of course were big consumers of British products but not as much as Prussia's army, for example. There were always many 'foreigners' among the troops. They, in particular, came from Ireland and Scotland but Great Britain was also a major customer of Germany, at the time a main exporter of mercenaries. During the War of American Independence, for example, there were 19,000 Hessians in British service.

For a long time, the army continued to be dominated by the relatively small landowning class. Statistics based on the backgrounds of officers receiving commissions suggest that this dominance *increased* during the period 1780–1830. That of course does not mean there was no professionalization. In the Royal Artillery and Royal Engineers jobs could not be purchased. Here technical proficiency was the criterion for entry and advancement. Officers in other sectors of the army, however, or their families or patrons, paid for commissions and promotion to the rank of lieutenant-colonel according to an official scale calculated by rank and prestige of the regiment. During the Peninsular War (1808–14), 70 per cent of officers owed their position to promotion by seniority or merit, 20 per cent to purchase and the rest to family or political string pulling. In the navy, shipboard instruction and examinations ensured technical expertise, but the

---

[102]Rodger, 'War as an economic activity', 5.
[103]See Duffy, 'World-wide war'.
[104]Tilly, *Coercion, Capital, and European States*, ch. 3.
[105]Childs, 'Army and the state'.

pace of an officer's promotion largely depended on one's kinfolk's social and political connections.[106]

Just as in its fiscal history, the Napoleonic Wars were a kind of apogee and turning point in Britain's military history. The nation was only kept in arms as long as was strictly necessary. No national system of conscription was implemented or even planned. Over the nineteenth century the importance of countryside aristocrats in the military diminished, as did the so-called 'amateur military tradition'. But we see nothing like the militarization that took place in Continental Europe where countries prepared for 'national' or 'people's' wars. Britain's wars predominantly were small imperial wars fought in faraway places. As in so many respects of state-building, in terms of military affairs too, Britain during the nineteenth century took a different road from most Continental states and to a certain extent can be said to have lost in strength and infrastructural power as compared to them. It definitely was not a trendsetter any more after it had beaten Napoleon.[107]

China's military

The differences with China really were big. If China's central government had mobilized as many people as Great Britain/the United Kingdom at the time of the Napoleonic Wars – that is, if it would have mobilized the equivalent of one out of every eighteen people living in the country to serve in army and navy – its armed forces would have counted about *eighteen million* people! If we include the 500,000 allied troops paid for by Britain and in that way fix the total number of men employed in Britain's armed forces at 1.5 million, an equally militarized China's would have had an army of *twenty-seven* million people.

It never came anywhere near that number – far from it. According to European standards, China's army was small. Figures with regard to its exact size vary, not least because figures regarding Manchu strength in principle were secret in Qing times. So we have to deal with estimates and reconstructions. At the end of the eighteenth century, excluding local militia, whose numbers were not significant, the army's official 'paper' size was less than a million people.[108] Basically Qing China's army consisted of two separate parts. The so-called Banner troops were, in principle twenty-four banners, one-third Manchu, one-third Mongol and one-third Han. In practice they increasingly consisted of just Manchus. These banner troops came closest to what one in the West would call an army – that is, a military entity that could be used in offensives.[109] Apart from that,

---

[106]James, *Warrior Race*, 327–34.
[107]See e.g. Chapter 5 note 27.
[108]See, however, the estimate by Lord Macartney on page 188.
[109]See Elliott, *Manchu Way*, 95 for the location of these troops. They quite often were not near any border.

Table 36 Officially allotted number of Green Standard troops

1662–1722	590,000
1764	630,000
1785	590,000
1812	660,000
1825	618,000
1850	585,000

Source: Powell, *Rise of Chinese Military Power*, ch. 1. All these figures are based on Wade, 'Army of the Chinese empire'. See for very similar figures McKeown, 'Different transition', 296. See there for the original source. In some of the Green Standard Units only a sixth to a half of the enlisted personnel actually existed. For estimates in the same order of magnitude see: Hsü, *Rise of Modern China*, 62; Mote, *Imperial China*, 860–1; Van der Ven, 'Onrush of modern globalization', 179, with an estimate of between 600,000 and 750,000 troops, and Woodside, 'Ch'ien-lung reign', 268–9.

there were the so-called Green Standard troops, which were more like a police force and mainly consisted of Han Chinese, spread in sometimes surprisingly small contingents over the entire country. The Banner Armies are supposed to have numbered 200,000 to 250,000 and in a very high estimate 300,000 soldiers.[110] Here there is the problem that it is not always clear who actually belongs to them. For the Green Standard Army, the estimates are presented in Table 36.

The total number of troops will have been some 800,000 to 900,000.[111] What is striking as compared to the situation in Europe and considering the big increase in the total population of China is that apparently the size of the army was quite stable. At the end of the rebellion of the Three Feudatories in the 1680s, Green Standard forces numbered about 900,000 troops and banner forces between 200,000 and 350,000. After hostilities stopped, the Green Standard forces were reduced to about 600,000.[112] During the first half of the nineteenth century nothing much changed as compared to the previous century in terms of overall army size. A calculation was made in 1821 that official troops, Chinese, Manchu and Mongol, amounted to 740,900.[113] According to an estimate in 1825 the Banner troops consisted of 10,529 officers, 236,014 non-commissioned officers and privates, 41,422 supernumeraries and 5,327 craftsmen and retainers. They were spread

[110]See Hsü, *Rise of Modern China*, 62; McKeown, 'Different transition', 294, where he mentions the number of 180,000 to 300,000 soldiers; Mote, *Imperial China*, 860–86; Van der Ven, 'Onrush of modern globalization', 179; Woodside, 'Ch'ien-lung reign', 268–9.
[111]See Lin, *China Upside Down*, 130. The period she refers to is 'during the Qing dynasty'. According to Pomeranz in the 1780s the Qing in total had some 900,000 people in arms. Pomeranz, 'Weather, war, and welfare', note 15.
[112]Kessler, *K'ang-Hsi*, 108.
[113]Huc, *L'empire Chinois*, 254.

all over the country with a heavy concentration in Peking and strong contingents in Manchuria. Régis-Évariste Huc, to whom we referred earlier, writes in the 1840s that, at least officially, China had 1,232,000 imperial troops and only 31,000 marine.[114] Again, one can also find quite different estimates. According to the *Chinese Repository* in an article published in 1843, the Qing Empire's army would consist of officially 250,000 Manchus and 600,000 Han.[115] In my view that indeed still was the order of magnitude. The size of the army apparently was not regarded as problematic. According to an estimate by the French consul Eugene Simon, in the last decades of the nineteenth century China's *standing* army still counted no more than 100,000 troops.[116] In that respect it is striking that in the middle of the sixteenth century, under the Ming, China's army had numbered about 845,000 men and in 1040, under the Song, even about 1.2 million men. In the middle of the sixteenth century China's total population was certainly much less than 200 million, in 1040 certainly less than 100 million.[117]

Whatever figure they take as point of departure, all experts would agree that in reality China's army was smaller, at times even substantially smaller, than official figures suggest. What really counts in a conflict is the actual strength of an army, not its paper strength – although of course when you have to pay for your 'paper' soldiers, they, in that respect, are quite real. Adshead thinks that at the very end of the eighteenth century its real strength was closer to half a million and claims that it is 'doubtful whether more than 100,000 men were ever put into the field at once'.[118] Huc himself wrote that only one-third of the official number of soldiers could be considered professional, effective military men.[119] There were large numbers of rusticated or even completely idle banner men who could not be called 'soldiers' in anything but name. According to Deng, the Green Standard army in 1851 ran at only half its capacity.[120] What is very important and a big contrast with what we see in most of Europe is that China's army knew no conscription and that the army did not function as 'school of the nation'.

The number of soldiers mobilized during military campaigns also was small as compared to what was becoming standard in Europe. When the Qing army in its conflict with Russia in the Amur region laid a second siege to the fortress of Albazin in 1686, some 2,000 to 10,000 Manchus faced some 350 Russians; that is, according to one estimate. According to another one, the numbers were 5,000 against 800. Whatever the exact numbers, considering that this apparently was an important event, these are very small armies indeed.[121] When the Kangxi emperor was on campaign in the 1690s against Galdan, the leader of the Zunghars in Central Eurasia, he had an army of in total some

---

[114]Huc, *L'empire Chinois*, 254.

[115]*Chinese Repository* XII 1843. The *Chinese Repository* was a periodical published in Canton from 1832 to 1851 for the use of Protestant missionaries working in Southeast Asia. I found this reference in Latourette, *The Chinese, their History and Culture*, I, 49–50.

[116]Simon, *Paradies der Arbeit*, 48.

[117]See Huang, *Taxation and Government Finance*, 290, and Elvin, *Pattern of the Chinese Past*, 84.

[118]Adshead, *China in World History*, 246.

[119]Huc, *L'empire Chinois*, 254–5.

[120]Deng, *China's Political Economy*, 30.

[121]Black, *War and the World*, 72, note 20.

70,000 men. In 1754, the Qianlong emperor sent two armies, each of 25,000 troops, to intervene in internal Zunghar affairs and grasp power. The big campaigns of the Qing in Central Asia in the middle of the eighteenth century that Peter Perdue discusses in an effort to show the (to him, apparently considerable) logistic capabilities of the Qing Empire, in total involved three main armies of 50,000 men each. They stayed on each campaign for one or two years. That would mean that in total 150,000 troops would have been in the field.[122] I could present more figures and refer to the 100,000 troops that were used on Taiwan in 1788 to quell the rising by Triade leader Lin Shuangwen.[123] But that would not change the overall picture. The biggest number of people that I came across involved in one, in this case very brief, campaign is that of 300,000 troops, a combination of Qing troops and Khoshot Mongols, who invaded Tibet in 1720 and occupied Lhasa.[124] As compared to what we see of mobilizations in Europe's small countries such numbers are low. Chinese armies too, of course, had their train of followers and people they employed. By the late eighteenth century, for example, at times several hundreds of thousands of men were hired in local labour markets to join expeditions into western Sichuan and Tibet as labourers, which on a local scale could certainly give a boost to economic development there.[125]

In this respect, too, the number of people involved did not show a clear tendency to increase like in Western Europe. On the contrary, one is tempted to say: in 1644 the Manchus had conquered Peking with almost 120,000 soldiers of their own and 60,000 Mongols.[126] In the nineteenth century, however, enormous masses could be mobilized in rebellions against government that forced government to mobilize bigger forces too. During the Taiping Rebellion, for example, no less than 750,000 rebels tried to conquer Nanking. The Taiping themselves claimed to have 1,300,000 men in their land and water forces.[127] As always it is hard to know what to make of such figures. According to Deng their standing army numbered some 600,000 people and that of the Nian Rebels who were active at the same time some 200,000.[128] Here too there are differing claims. McKeown, for example, writes about 850,000 Taiping troops, but that does not undermine the gist of my claims.[129]

---

[122]The figures for the Kangxi campaign of the 1690s and the Qianlong campaign of 1754 are from Perdue, *China Marches West*, 181 and 272. For the information regarding the campaigns in Central Asia see Perdue, 'Military mobilisation', 776.

[123]Dabringhaus, *Qing-Imperium*, 41.

[124]Perdue, *China Marches West*, 235.

[125]For some figures see Dai, *Sichuan Frontier and Tibet*, 180–2. For the economic impact of the military there see ibid., ch. 6.

[126]Wakeman, *Great Enterprise*, I, 310.

[127]Powell, *Rise of Chinese Military Power*, 21.

[128]Deng, *China's Political Economy*, 39.

[129]McKeown, 'Different transition', 296.

CHAPTER 5
THE MILITARY AND THE ECONOMY

From military to economic revolution and/or the other way around?

The Great Divergence as we discuss it here manifested itself in terms of the emergence of big differences in *wealth* between various parts of the world. But the very long eighteenth century that we are analysing here also ended as a period of huge imbalances in terms of political and military *power*. The question simply forces itself on any serious observer whether it was 'by accident' that the world's economic hegemon in the nineteenth century also was its military and political hegemon, in particular of course when, as is the case in this text, one wants to focus on the role of the state in the Great Divergence. Does causality go from 'the economic' to 'the military' and 'the political', or the other way around? Are they all expressions of an underlying strength of, in this case, a couple of Western societies, first and foremost Britain? Or is there no connection at all? Actually answering that question may be impossible but one can at least make some comments about the chronological connections between 'industry' and 'empire' in the West, more in particular Britain, that help in thinking about possible answers to that question. 'Industry' here is shorthand for the emergence of modern economic growth in the nineteenth century, as a rule symbolized by industry, and 'empire' for the forceful territorial extension of political power. The relevance of the next paragraphs in this text lies in the attempt to indicate that Western global power and advantage resided not only in its economy as such but also and to a large extent in the characteristics of its states. I would go even further and claim that without those characteristics not only its politico-military but also its economic dominance would be very hard to imagine.

Let us start with the thesis that 'the West' conquered the globe *thanks to* industrialization and its technological breakthroughs. It has respected adherents. Paul Kennedy in a book about the rise of British naval mastery from the 1980s is quite explicit:

> [The Industrial Revolution] was to provide the foundation for the country's continuing and increasing growth, making it into a new sort of state – the only real world power at the time. Industrialization not only furthered the British supremacy in commerce and finance and shipping, it also underpinned its own naval supremacy with a previously unheard-of economic potential.[1]

---

[1]Kennedy, *Rise and Fall of British Naval Mastery*, 150–1.

Further on in the same book he adds:

> 'Britain enjoyed effortless naval supremacy in the years following 1815' in part
> because its competitors 'possessed an industrial strength that was infantile by
> comparison'.[2]

The late Paul Bairoch also was quite outspoken: 'During the eighteenth and nineteenth
centuries colonialism was primarily a result of industrial development and not vice
versa.'[3] More than twenty years later Jack Goldstone was just as explicit:

> It was not colonialism and conquest that made possible the rise of the West, but
> the reverse – it was the rise of the West [in terms of technology] and the decline of
> the rest that made possible the full extension of European power across the globe.[4]

These are just quotes of some influential scholars among many others like Michael Adas,
Robert Marks and Stephen Morillo, and to a certain extent Clive Ponting.[5] The claim that
it would be just the other way around, that 'empire' one way or another would have caused
'industry', has been endorsed by many scholars over the years and has always been at the
core of Wallerstein's world-systems analysis. Let me immediately put my critique on the
table: in my view the first claim *under*-estimates Western expansion that had already
taken place before modern economic growth emerged with industrialization, as shown
in the figures of Tables 39 and 40, and *over*-estimates the impact of industrialization in
Western Europe in the first half of the nineteenth century. The Wallersteinian claim,
in any case, when it is supposed to apply to the whole of Western Europe is far too
undifferentiated. There are simply too many examples of 'industry' without 'empire', and
of 'empire' without 'industry'.[6]

One can, of course, in principle also deny the existence of any connection between
political development and economic development defined as 'the capability to get things
done' in the case of the emergence of modern economic growth in Great Britain. That
is the position of Gregory Clark, who claims that Britain's dominance in the nineteenth
century basically was just an extension of its position in the previous century and that only
now Britain's population had grown much larger: 'Thus it seems that Britain's rise to world
dominance was a product more of the bedroom labours of British workers than of their
factory toil.'[7] In his view empire is not caused by industry, nor is there any connection the
other way around. His explanation of Britain's industrialization is entirely endogenous.[8]

---

[2]Kennedy, *Rise and Fall of British Naval Mastery*, 157. I wonder what Kennedy means by 'effortless'.
[3]Bairoch, *Economics and World History*, 82. See also in the same book page 85.
[4]Goldstone, *Why Europe?*, 69.
[5]See Adas, 'Imperialism and colonialism', 387; Marks, *Origins of the Modern World*, 11; Morillo, 'Guns and
government', 79, and Ponting, *World History*, 677–9.
[6]The same goes for the claim that modern growth can only continue when one acquires an empire. I here refer
to my analysis in *Escaping Poverty*.
[7]Clark, 'What made Britannia Great?', 51.
[8]See Clark, *Farewell to Alms*.

And finally, there is the possibility to suggest that both 'industry' and 'empire' as economic and politico-military primacy were the result of underlying phenomena like the rise of modernity, rationalization or capitalism (the last an example of rationalization) and that they mutually reinforce each other. This thesis of course has an impressive pedigree. Max Weber is certainly its most famous classic proponent; in recent scholarship I guess that would be Michael Mann. His view boils down to the claim that primacy will be acquired by societies that have more infrastructural power (politically, ideologically, economically and militarily) than other societies. Without making any broad sociological statements, John Darwin seems to share this view when he claims that the Industrial Revolution was 'not the only or sufficient explanation of European expansion. The Eurasian Revolution was in fact three revolutions: in geopolitics, in culture and in economics'.[9] According to him the immediate cause of the revolutionary change in Europe's relations with the rest of Eurasia indeed cannot have been the increase of economic efficiency we associate with the Industrial Revolution. Industrialization had barely set in before the turn of the eighteenth to the nineteenth century. Even in 1850, only Great Britain was firmly heading to become a steam- and coal-based economy: the rest of Europe became industrialized even later.[10] This means there must have been something peculiar about the power of Britain as a fiscal-military state and as a nation before it was an industrial nation. According to Darwin, Britain was the first modern society in the world – that is, if we accept his definition of modernity:

> The best test of modernity might be the extent to which, in any given society, resources and people could be mobilized for a task, and redeployed continuously as new needs arose and new pressures were felt. In principle, many different societies possessed this ability. In practice, and for reasons that we are far from understanding fully, for almost two centuries after 1750 it was North West European societies (and their transatlantic offspring) that mobilized fastest and also coped best with the social and political strains that being mobile imposed.[11]

I fully endorse this view in which the emphasis is on *infrastructural power* in a broad range of aspects, not just the economy. Notwithstanding his broad definition of modernity it sometimes looks as if Darwin in the end wants to give primacy to the politico-military factor – for example when he writes: 'Perhaps it was not Europe's modernity that triumphed, but its superior capacity for organized violence' or 'Europe's sudden acquisition of a Eurasian pre-eminence was the result ... of a series of forced entries or

---

[9] By the 'Eurasian Revolution' Darwin means the geopolitical, cultural and economic changes in the period from the 1750s to the 1830s in which the long equilibrium of Eurasian cultures and continents was swept away by Europe's rise to a commanding lead. See his *After Tamerlane*, 160.

[10] Darwin, *After Tamerlane*, 161 and 196.

[11] Darwin, *After Tamerlane*, 27.

forcible overthrows.'[12] I do not see a contrast here and regard this 'superior capacity' as one of several expressions of the region's thorough rationalization.

The position one wants to take in this debate on the connection between the Great Divergence as the emergence of Western *economic* global primacy and western *politico-military* global primacy, of course, depends on how one defines the Great Divergence. For me the Great Divergence is the direct outcome of the emergence of modern economic growth in Great Britain and later on in several parts of the West as opposed to the rest of the world. That modern economic growth was the result of a cluster of innovations in the sphere of energy use and technology, *facilitated* and *supported* by institutional changes. The breakthroughs in the sphere of energy and technology are quintessential: without them it would simply have been impossible to break through the Malthusian ceiling.[13] This has consequences for 'dating' the Industrial Revolution and Great Divergence. As late as 1830, steam power was still fairly unimportant as a source of *power*, in comparison to the 'traditional' energy sources that were still in use at the time as well as in comparison to the amounts consumed later on. Von Tunzelmann estimates that around 1800 only one-tenth of all coal consumed in Britain was used for producing steam power. For 1830, that would have increased to about one-sixth.[14] According to him in that year the power of stationary steam engines and steam engines on ships combined amounted to about 200,000 horsepower. The use of steam engines on trains in 1830 still was very much in its infancy.[15] Minchington, who only refers to stationary engines, thinks that in 1830 these had 165,000 horsepower.[16] Although certainly not negligible as such, these figures pale compared to what was to come. In 1840 the total amount of steam-power available in Britain had grown to 620,000 horsepower, in 1870 to 4 million horsepower and in 1896 to over 13 million horsepower, or the equivalent of the amount of labour power of over 390 million adult men.[17] Admittedly, coal, had already become fairly important as a source of *heat* by 1830.[18] As such – for example, in iron production – it clearly had already begun to make a difference. In 1700, Great Britain produced only about 23,000 tons of raw iron; in 1830 that had increased to about 1 million tons. But here, too, we are only at the very beginning of a steep and steady increase. Twenty years later, production was 3 million tons, just before the First World War almost 10 million.[19] This increased production will no doubt have had its impact on Britain's military strength.

---

[12] Darwin, *After Tamerlane*. The quotations are on pages 27 and 162.

[13] See my *Escaping Poverty*, chs 1, 6 and 7 for further explanation.

[14] Von Tunzelmann, *Steam Power*, under 'coal consumption'.

[15] Von Tunzelmann, *Steam Power*, 29–30.

[16] Minchington, 'Energy basis', 356.

[17] See for these figures Landes, *Unbound Prometheus*, 292 and 104.

[18] For the production and consumption of coal in industrializing Britain see, in alphabetical order, Daunton, *Progress and Poverty*, 585; Mathias, *First Industrial Nation*, 481; Minchington, 'Energy basis'; Sieferle, *Subterranean Forest*, 88, and Von Tunzelmann, *Steam Power*. From 1700 to 1830 British coal production increased from about 3 million to about 30 million tons. By 1900 it had again increased tenfold to about 300 million tons. Till the 1850s, exports of coal were only a couple of per cents of total production.

[19] Matthias, 'Economic expansion', 10, and idem, *First Industrial Nation*, 483–4.

But it would be exaggerated to claim that Britain's actual warfare by the 1830s had already somehow become 'industrialized' – not only because mechanized arms production still was non-existent. Just as, if not more, important is that in overseas warfare neither transport nor communication had gone through fundamental technological changes. Trains as yet played no role in warfare: neither did steamships, apart from a couple of experiments in the 1820s. We can only conclude that substantial imperial expansion had already taken place *before* Britain's industrialization had any technological impact on its military.[20] The following quote of Washbrook refers to the British conquest of India. What is said here also applies to a great number of other examples of British expansion:

By convention, the conquest [of India] began with the Battle of Plassey in 1757: but 1757 was before Britain had acquired very much of the technological superiority and industrial modernity which were later to mark its world dominance. The 'conquering' British in India were very few in number (only 30,000 as late as 1805), sailed in wooden ships and carried muzzle-loading muskets, which were frequently fired back at them … the roots of the conquest need to be sought in early modern – rather than modern – time.[21]

The British forces, commanded by Robert Clive in the Battle of Plassey, were outnumbered thirty to one. Even the fact that the British had bribed one of the opposing generals to do nothing only reduced the odds to about thirteen to one. The British had eight cannon while their opponents had fifty-three. The famous Royal Navy played an absolutely pivotal role in the making of Britain's empire. It purchased its first iron ship only in 1845.[22] To quote Gregory Clark:

Naval power remained based on sailing ships until surprisingly late in the Industrial Revolution. The first steam-powered ocean-going warship, the French *Le Napoléon*, did not enter service until 1852. This was still a wooden ship. The modern iron-hulled armoured battleship came only with the British *Warrior*, which entered service in 1861. So until 1850 naval ships would have looked very similar with no Industrial Revolution.[23]

---

[20]See for timing Etemad, *Possessing the World*. Dalziel, *Penguin Historical Atlas of the British Empire*, nicely shows how the British Empire grew step by step.

[21]Washbrook, 'India in the early modern world economy', 89.

[22]For a brief discussion of 'steam at sea', see Black, *War and the World*, 166–8; Headrick, *Tentacles of Progress*, 23–5, and idem, *Tools of Empire*, chs 1 and 2 – where on page 36 the comment is made with regard to iron ships and the Royal Navy – and Pacey, *Technology in World Civilization*, 142–5. For a general overview of the role of technology in Western imperialism see Headrick, *Tools of Empire*. The *Nemesis*, the first British ocean-going iron warship that was so important in the First Opium War, actually was owned by the East India Company and had received a Letter of Marque from the Admiralty.

[23]Clark, 'What made Britannia Great?', 47–8.

The West already had a clear military advantage *before* its industrialization. Experts in military history now tend to agree that the impact of (beginning) industrialization on the military remained minor for quite some time. It was not until the Crimean War (1853–6) that warfare really began to be 'industrialised' with cataclysmic consequences.[24] The revolution in telecommunication that was to have major consequences for warfare also basically was a phenomenon of the second half of the nineteenth century.[25] In military terms Western countries were more effective than the rest of the world already *before* they industrialized.[26] Surprisingly enough Great Britain's lead as compared to the rest of Europe in this respect actually was bigger *before* it industrialized than when it had taken off.[27]

It is not irrelevant to point out that Britain's expansion during the period from 1780 to 1830 was largely at the expense of regions in Asia. From the second half of the eighteenth century onwards, the balance of power between the fiscal-military states of the West and the big 'Eastern' empires was beginning to shift so clearly that, even without the additional advantages of industrialization, the West was already making huge inroads into what we would now call 'India', the Ottoman Empire – where especially the role of Russia tends to be neglected – and finally, from the 1830s onwards, China, where one, again, should not overlook Russia's encroachments. Consensus is emerging that 'the rise of the West' in this respect clearly was made easier by the fact that it was accompanied, or even preceded, by 'a decline of the East'. When 'East' and 'West' entered on a collision course from the second half of the eighteenth century onwards, various regions in the East were already facing serious domestic problems.[28] Think of the Mughal Empire, that in fact only continued to exist on paper, the Safavid Empire and the Ottoman Empire. For China and Japan at the time there, as yet, were no signs that their future would be strikingly different from their past. What *should* have troubled rulers all over the globe was Western mastery at sea: that had already become uncontested.[29] This 'decline of the East' though was not a fully autonomous development: the West definitely played a part in it.

In discussing new sources of energy and new technologies, we have not exhausted the ways in which industrialization might have helped Britain to its military successes before the 1830s. The economic transformation that Britain was going through may

---

[24]See e.g. Black, *European Warfare*, 203; Boot, *War Made New*, 114–15; Lynn, 'Nations in arms', 212; McNeill, *Pursuit of Power*, 225–7 and 233–6, and Murray, 'Industrialization of war'.

[25]See Headrick, *Invisible Weapon*.

[26]For Western military supremacy *before* industrialization see in alphabetical order: Black, *A Military Revolution?*; idem, *War and the World*; idem, *War in the Early Modern World*; idem, *Military Power*; Chase, *Firearms*; Hanson, *Why the West has Won*; Headrick, *Power over People* and *Tools of Empire*; Hoffman, 'Prices, the Military Revolution, and Western Europe's comparative advantage', and idem, 'Why was it Europeans who conquered the World?'; Lynn, *Battle*; McNeill, *Pursuit of Power*; Parker, *Military Revolution*, and idem, *Cambridge Illustrated History of Warfare*; Rogers, *Military Revolution Debate*, and Thompson, 'Military superiority thesis'.

[27]See for this claim the Master's thesis by Maciej Hacaga, *The British Global Hegemony 1763–1914 and Energy. The Intricate Nexus*. I can send a PDF to the interested reader.

[28]See Bayly, *Imperial Meridian*.

[29]Black, *European Warfare*, ch. 12.

Table 37 Average annual rates of growth of British national income per capita in real terms

1700–60	0.30
1760–1800	0.17
1800–30	0.52
1830–70	1.98

Source: Mokyr, 'Accounting for the Industrial Revolution', 4, Table 1.

already have influenced the course of the wars it was involved in from the second half of the eighteenth century onwards by the simple fact of adding to its coffers.[30] One might indeed expect that the economic transformations that Britain was undergoing at the time and the growing 'sprouts of industrialisation' would have positive effects on its *wealth* which in turn would enhance its power. However, most economic historians nowadays agree that Britain indeed had entered a period of fundamental *economic transformation* from the 1750s onwards, but at the same time deny that *economic growth* during this first phase of its industrialization, let us say from the 1780s to roughly as late as 1850(!), was substantial. On the contrary, most economic historians claim that it was quite small and will not have surpassed about 0.5 per cent per capita per annum.[31] Most of the growth over the period 1830–70 dates from the last two decades. In particular the 1840s were not exactly a period of boom. The fact that Britain conquered so much of the world at the time therefore cannot be simply explained by an increase of its wealth. Britain's population, as pointed out by Clark, did grow, but as compared to that of many Asian states like 'India', and course China, it continued to be quite small.

In 1830, Britain had already doubled the size of its empire as against seventy years before and had thus become by far the most important colonial power on the globe. Only some 12 per cent of the inhabitants of the British Empire then lived in the United Kingdom, which in surface amounted to less than 5 per cent of the British Empire in its entirety. Again, this is *before* Britain had evolved into an *industrial* superpower. There must have been something special about Britain and its state *before* it became a country of coal, steam and iron that enabled it to conquer so much land outside Europe, often not only defeating the original rulers but *also* its European imperialist competitors, including France, which was much bigger and had many more inhabitants. Would it be too far-fetched to claim that this peculiarity was its fiscal-militarism? It is obvious, though, that the fiscal-military states in Western Europe as a rule were 'expensive' states: only fairly rich economies could afford to spend such enormous amounts of money on strengthening their state apparatus. This means that, as so often in history, we are facing

---

[30]See for this claim e.g. Lynn, 'Nations in arms'.
[31]In this respect in particular the work of Crafts and Harley is important. See for some 'results' Daunton, *Progress and Poverty*, 125–36, and Mokyr, 'Accounting for the Industrial Revolution', 4, Table 1.

complex causal chains with feedbacks. But to me it is clear that from a geopolitical and geo-economical perspective having a fiscal-military state made a difference and paid. It had made tiny Britain the most powerful country in the world even before it actually was its first industrial nation.

Fundamental changes in Great Britain's military?

Brute force in terms of sheer manpower obviously counted for much in warfare in the early modern era, but it has never been the only factor that determines the effectiveness of an army. That depends on a whole range of factors. According to Geoffrey Parker the West had already developed a distinctly 'Western' way of war *before* the early modern era, characterized by (1) heavy reliance on technology, (2) discipline as a way of enhancing efficiency, (3) an aggressive military approach, (4) the ability to change as well as conserve military practices and (5) the power, organizational strength and will to finance, change and expand war.[32] In the early modern period so many radical changes were implemented that various distinguished military historians, among them Parker himself, have begun to write about a 'Military Revolution', a concept that as so often in historiography did not go uncontested.[33] But even authors who contest specific aspects of the concept as it was first introduced, and who are reluctant to use the word 'revolution' for a process that took centuries to run its course, cannot and do not deny that very fundamental and consequential changes did occur in Western warfare during the early modern period, *apart* from the immense increase in scale and costs that we already referred to.

I will mention only some very striking developments. When it comes to technology, first and foremost, there is the increasing role and importance of firearms in warfare on land as well as at sea, which would prove to be extremely important for Western Europe's rise to global primacy. This increased use of firearms was one of the main reasons for changes in tactics and strategy. These, in turn, could only be implemented by an army with a strong infantry and artillery that was much more professional and, which is very important, much more disciplined than had been the case with most medieval armies. In that respect we clearly see a 'downgrading [of] the centrality of technology'[34] in recent literature, whereas the role of training and discipline now is often highlighted. Many scholars now consider Western successes as inconceivable without the superior discipline that is epitomized by its trained and drilled soldiers fighting in organized units. Or as Kenneth Chase succinctly puts it: 'What set the Europeans apart were training and discipline' and 'there was more to European military superiority than just hardware'.[35]

---

[32]See for a short explanation Parker, 'Introduction'.
[33]The concept was coined by Michael Roberts in 1955, in a lecture called 'The military revolution, 1550–1660'. See, for a revised version, Rogers, *Military Revolution Debate*. See for further literature Chapter 5 note 26.
[34]Black, *European Warfare*, 196.
[35]Chase, *Firearms*, 200 and 206.

The Western approach to war is considered to be characterized by its aggressiveness centred on winning a decisive victory and annihilating, not merely defeating, the enemy's forces. Destroying them always counted as the dominant consideration. This is an approach to battle that had been evolving since the time of the ancient Greeks and that involved applying maximum discipline and violence at the point of engagement. Some authors, like Victor Hanson, want to extend this focus on a 'Western way of war' by arguing that Western success on the battlefield is a cultural phenomenon, not just the result of good fortune in the allocation of resources or the serendipity of technology. According to him free nations produce leaders and soldiers who take the initiative. Citizens who are protected by law against arbitrary action feel free to 'audit' battles and criticize soldiers, leading to improved strategy and tactics. Western military command structures of course were and are hierarchical, but not unduly so: they adapt well to changing circumstances.[36] In this context William Thompson has correctly directed the attention at a related point that in the context of this book is quite relevant: the ability of Europeans to cultivate local allies and manipulate the weaknesses and vulnerabilities of indigenous political structures against their non-European opponents. Besides, they for some time avoided really strong opponents and controlled intercontinental long-distance trade and the seas.[37]

When it comes to the ability to change as well as conserve practices, it is clear that Western military organization and command became more impersonal and increasingly subject to the application of science and reason. The fact that troops tended to become 'standing' armies will surely have helped in this respect. Army officers in particular became increasingly professional. Again, the Napoleonic Wars accelerated developments. Important organizational changes were implemented while at the same time there was a huge increase in size of the armies that were mobilized. They of course also were important in that they 'nationalized' warfare and so increased the role of patriotism and subsequently nationalism.[38] Substantial technological breakthroughs occurred only later on, already far into the nineteenth century.[39] With increasing scale, complexity and costs, waging war and running a 'Western' army became a very complex logistical undertaking. Staggering amounts of people, resources and money were involved. The fact that in the West soldiers were paid in money and their material was bought on the market also turned it into big business, requiring complicated and huge transactions. For a long period of time this provided a separate role for military entrepreneurs. In the end, however, governments took matters fully in their own hands, not in the sense that the 'business of war', in the widest sense of the word, would be 'nationalized' – many private businessmen continued to be involved – but in the sense that private business when involved had to operate according to strict rules in which government no longer transferred any sovereign rights to private entrepreneurs. The permanent warfare that

---

[36]Hanson, *Why the West Has Won*. See for a critical 'response' Lynn, *Battle*.
[37]Thompson, 'Military superiority thesis'.
[38]See Black, *Western Warfare*, and Wawro, *Warfare and Society*.
[39]For the moment technology really started to matter see Chapter 5 note 24.

was so typical for early modern Western Europe gave excellent training facilities, to put it cynically, and it forced all the parties involved to permanently 'rationalize' and 'improve' their armies. All these quantitative and qualitative changes made those armies ever more formidable and tended to give the West an increasing lead over 'the rest'.

One can certainly debate whether Great Britain went through a real military revolution and all that would imply according to those who defend and further develop that concept, but I do not think it can be doubted that in many respects Great Britain clearly was part and parcel of a wider European trend towards rationalization and professionalization of the military, in particular when it came to its navy.[40] That became by far the strongest of the entire world. This was not only a matter of money, although the steady financial support of government and the fact that the Royal Navy was a national priority clearly helped. Nor was it only a matter of size: at times the French fleet, especially when it was combined with fleets of its allies, was as big as that of Britain. It clearly also was a matter of organization. As far as possible, Britain's fleet was kept in active service at sea and maintained at wartime strength. Its ships received good maintenance in British docks in- and outside Britain, which of course helped to keep them active and their seamen, including the officers, on duty. Foreign seamen were allowed to sign on but when and where possible able-bodied Britons were trained. In that way, the navy managed to have sufficient personnel. Ships and seamen were exchanged between the merchant fleet and the Royal Navy in case of need and merchant yards were used to build ships for that navy. There was a centralized admiralty that took care of coordination.[41] In all these respects the British Royal Navy was more efficient than its French counterpart. Discipline was extremely harsh, but that was normal in all Western navies.[42]

Stasis in China?

China of course was not completely static in these respects.[43] Nor was it patently 'backward'. We already referred to Jeremy Black's claim that during the eighteenth

---

[40]For the claim that Great Britain had its 'military revolution' see Wheeler, *Making of a World Power*. For the claim it did not see Rodger, 'War as an economic activity', and idem, 'From the 'military revolution' to the 'fiscal-naval state'.

[41]See for these and other points that turned the Royal Navy into the world's most efficient naval war machine Allen, *Institutional Revolution*, ch. 5; Baugh, 'Naval power', and Morriss, *Foundations of British Maritime Ascendancy*. For the exchange of personnel between Royal Navy and merchant marine that led to a situation where naval service became quite common in the career of the typical merchant seaman see Earle, *Sailors*, ch. 12.

[42]See Frykman, 'Seeleute auf den europäischen Kriegsschiffen', 65–72.

[43]For information on China's military under the Qing see, in alphabetical order, Di Cosmo, *Military Culture*; idem, 'European technology and Manchu power', and idem, 'Did guns matter?'; Elleman, *Modern Chinese Warfare*; Elliott, *Manchu Way*; Fung, 'Testing the self-strengthening'; Graff and Higham, *Military History*, in particular the contributions by Lococo, 'Qing Empire', and Horowitz, 'Beyond the marble boat'; Kuhn, *Rebellion and Its Enemies*; Lorge, 'War and warfare'; idem, *War, Politics and Society*; idem, *Asian Military Revolution*; Powell, *Rise of Chinese Military Power*; Van der Ven, *Warfare in Chinese History*; idem, 'Military mobilization'; Waley-Cohen, *Culture of War*, and Wang, *Anglo-Chinese Encounters*. See also the special issue of *Modern Asian Studies* 30, 4 (1996) on war in modern China.

century Qing China had been 'the most dynamic state and the most successful military power in the world, on land'.[44] In one of his numerous other publications he wrote: 'Seventeenth-century China was a militarily capable, expansionist, non-European power.'[45] He does so referring to the fact that the Qing managed to stop the Russian expansion in the direction of the Amur River and had some success in Mongolia, where in the end they conquered Outer Mongolia. But he overstates his case: I have already indicated how few people were involved in that Sino-Russian conflict and would want to point out that the Russians at the time still were far removed from being a great military power. The Mongols may well have been fierce opponents, but their armies were not big and they were not heavily armed. In short, we are not talking about major wars of the type we see in Western Europe at the time but rather about 'skirmishes'. In the eighteenth century, Chinese armies indeed won many victories and made large conquests in their march towards 'the West', to paraphrase Peter Perdue. After all, this was a century in which Qing China more than *doubled* its size. Who would not regard this as a signal that all was well? Nevertheless claims such as those by Black are rather far-fetched. China's successes tell us more about the *weakness* of its adversaries than about the *strength* of China. Beating the Zunghars apparently counts as the main military feat of the Qing in the eighteenth century. But what does that really mean when, as Perdue himself writes, the total Zunghar population has been estimated at some 600,000 people at the moment when the Qianlong Emperor won his struggle against them?[46] Overall, the forays into Central Eurasia (i.e. what was to become the Ili protectorate, the Tarim Basin and Eastern Turkestan, and Tibet) may have been impressive in terms of territorial conquest and very important in securing the supply of warhorses. From a strictly military perspective, though, they really did not mean that much. The fact that the military campaigns under the Qianlong emperor into Burma and Vietnam – as compared to China very tiny states with quite small armies – resulted in anything but resounding victories also does not exactly suggest that Qing China at the time would have been a military superpower.[47]

China clearly booked some military successes in the eighteenth century and one must be careful not to paint too bleak a picture of its military strength, even for the rather disastrous nineteenth century. In the so-called Ili crisis of 1881, Russia was forced to make concessions. In the Sino-French war of 1884–5, Chinese armies beat the French a couple of times. At the very outbreak of the war between China and Japan, there still lingered an afterglow of admiration for China as a venerable society and there still were people who felt impressed by 'the only Asiatic state that really commands the

---

[44]Black, *Warfare in the Eighteenth Century*, 31.

[45]Black, *War and the World*, 72.

[46]Perdue, *China Marches West*, 285. That makes one Zunghar against more than 400 Chinese. There are other somewhat higher estimates but orders of magnitude are similar.

[47]See for these campaigns Elliott, *Emperor Qianlong*. For the campaign into Burma of 1765–70 see Dai, 'Disguised defeat'. Dai describes it as the most disastrous frontier war the Qing ever waged. The Qing won the Sino-Nepalese War of 1788–93. But in strictly military terms their victory was anything but impressive.

respect of the great powers of the world'. They did so as they felt that the country had seen some impressive military reforms. With the loss of the war against Japan, this perception changed rapidly and the image turned very bleak.[48] But whatever exact impression one wants to convey of the strength of China's army, one has to realize that all the successes that the country booked during the eighteenth century were booked in Asia on land and none of them against a 'substantial' enemy and none involving a navy. In contrast, the range, variety and extent of British military activities at the time were really striking: it counted big and strong countries among its opponents during its many wars and its navy at the end of the eighteenth century was really without an equal in the world.

The point is not that China in contrast to Europe would have been a peace-loving society with a 'Confucianist' elite that did not like fighting. Hans van der Ven writes: 'Leaving aside the issue of what a Chinese cultural essence might be or if such a thing exists, it is plain that China's history is at least as violent as Europe's.'[49] That may be exaggerated. But it is a fact Qing China was not exactly a nonviolent and non-bellicose society. One can refer to many conflicts like rebellions and cases of severe repression and even genocide, as in the case of the Zunghars, and to several wars.[50] But whatever other images they may have liked to propagate of themselves, the ruling Manchu elite clearly (also) regarded itself as a group of warriors. The point here simply is that the Chinese state and the Chinese military were not operating in a multipolar state-system like the states in Western Europe. They could 'confine' themselves to fighting on a much smaller scale and with a much lower intensity, for the simple reason that they had less challenging and less dangerous neighbours which had important implications – for example, for their weaponry. Military historians have long tended to focus heavily on firearms. In and for 'the West' these indeed were enormously important, if not decisive. For that reason, much has been made of the fact that in developing them China lagged behind Europe, which I think it clearly did. The solution of the main military problems that *eighteenth-century* China faced, however (i.e. those of the steppe border), had little to do with better firearms. So why would the Manchus bother?[51] In the nineteenth century when the Qing ought to have bothered, their response was too slow.

However this may be, overall, as compared to Western Europe, China undoubtedly was falling behind in military affairs. All revisionism notwithstanding, I am still entirely unconvinced that in the very long eighteenth century there would have been a 'revolution' going on there similar to that in Western Europe – not in the army, and definitely not in the navy. Especially when it comes to discipline, training and standardization, the massive use of advanced firearms, the application of 'science' and the 'nationalization' of the army, changes of a scale, scope and impact comparable to what was happening in Western Europe were absent in China. It is one of the many ironies of history that Qing

---

[48]I paraphrase Paine, *Sino-Japanese War*, 14–15, from where I also took the quotation.
[49]Van der Ven, 'War in the making of modern China', 737.
[50]See e.g. Elvin, 'Historian as haruspex', 105.
[51]See for further background Chase, *Firearms*, under 'China'.

rule as such in all probability was *saved* by the superior armed force of the West, in the sense that in the 1850s and 1860s Qing rulers were supported by Western powers – for example by direct interventions on their behalf, by the provision of modern arms and training, and by a supply of officers for military contingents like the Ever Victorious Army. Thanks to these interventions the Qing could keep China more or less together and themselves on the throne.[52] The fact that they managed to substantially increase their revenue in the last half-century of their rule, to some extent also was due to Western support. The Maritime Customs Office that was founded in 1858 and that developed into an efficient collector of revenue for them, stood under Western supervision.[53] Western powers, in the end, were not interested in breaking up China. The British had always preferred trade over land and the United States, whose word quickly began to count for much, were in favour of an 'open-door' policy. In political and military terms, China had much more to fear from Russia and Japan.

Even if one does not explicitly compare China's army during the very long eighteenth century with armies in Western Europe, one does come across some obvious weaknesses that tended to become more glaring with the passing of time.[54] To begin with, there were what I would call 'organizational' weaknesses. The Manchus' fear of strong local military leaders led them to create a quite decentralized military structure. Military commanders were always entangled in webs of checks and balances that made it impossible for them to amass much personal power over troops in more than one province. Even in their 'own' provinces, they never really reigned supreme and alone. The number of soldiers under their direct command was small, often surprisingly so. Up until the end of the rule of the Qianlong Emperor, this indeed prevented the emergence of any strong warlords that could ignore or even challenge Peking. However, there was a price to pay: it was not easy to efficiently mobilize a strong, unified 'national' army in case of need. With the weakening of the hold of central government, we see a rise of warlords who created their own powerbase in one or a couple of provinces and who more or less ignored Peking in day-to-day affairs.

The fact that the army consisted of forces that were either Manchu (or Mongol) or overwhelmingly Han, and that both had their own specific organization and command structure, did not help maximizing efficiency either, nor did the fact that, in both the Banner troops and the Green Standard forces, heredity played a big part in the recruitment of soldiers.[55] The lack of trust of the Manchu elite in their military commanders, especially when they were not Manchu, made them opt for a system in

---

[52]See for further information Kuhn, 'Taiping Rebellion'.

[53]It actually had a predecessor founded in 1854, the Shanghai Customs House, that originated in an agreement that the Chinese Superintendent of Customs would employ foreign nationals nominated by the consuls of Britain, France and the United States. See Lyons, *China Maritime Customs*, 7. Sir Robert Hart was its Inspector General from 1863 to 1911. This fact qualifies Wong's comments that *the Qing* were successful in collecting taxes in the second half of the nineteenth century.

[54]I have distilled these weaknesses from the literature I refer to in the notes. Particularly helpful was Powell, *Rise of Chinese Military Power*.

[55]For this 'provincialization' see Kuhn, *Rebellion and Its Enemies*.

which, just like in civilian administration, military officials rotated. This, again, was to prevent strong ties of loyalty developing between them and their troops. From a strictly military perspective that probably was not a clever strategy. The fact that in the Chinese system of administration as it was taken over by the Manchus the status of military personnel as compared to that of civilian officials continued to be quite low was not helpful either. With the passing of time, differences and divisions between officers and troops, between various ethnic groups like Manchus, Mongols and Han, between people from various provinces or simply between different troops increasingly began to effect efficiency negatively. As we will see on pages 410–12, China effectively did *not* have a national army in the nineteenth century.

A second fundamental weakness concerned funding. Just like in civil administration, this simply was inadequate. Government expenditure was not even sufficient to cover current, 'normal' cost of the relatively small armed forces of China, let alone allow a substantial increase or modernization of those forces. I have already indicated that many soldiers had to try and take care of their own livelihood and that of their dependents and that the pay they received was insufficient; that is, *if* they received any payment at all. If they were paid in silver – which was anything but normal – they suffered from the fact that their wages were not corrected for inflation, which over the period from 1750 to at least the 1820s was quite substantial. If, as was normally the case, their pay consisted of copper cash, they, from the late 1810s onwards, also faced the problem that the value of copper decreased sharply as compared to that of silver. Quite a lot of soldiers, from the late eighteenth century onwards, simply were impoverished.[56] That will not have been good for their morale nor for their preparedness for war. Problems connected to funding tended to increase.

That brings us to a next set of 'weaknesses'. If we are to believe contemporary commentators, the efficiency of the Manchu banner troops, who had been the backbone of the Qing armed forces, was decreasing. To a somewhat lesser extent this also applied to the Green Standard forces. The training of the Banner troops, if they were actually trained, was quite traditional and their discipline deficient. When it came to the use of firearms, there was hardly any practice, let alone actual combat experience.[57] The long period of peace, or rather the absence of wars, that set in after the big campaigns of the Qianlong era made the troops less war hardened. One clearly sees elements of complacency and saturation. Coming conflicts with Western powers could have been foreseen if only government circles had been keen on gathering information about those powers. That clearly was not the case. If they prepared for war at all, it was for a war like those in the past. It was noticed that military success on land was only relative whereas performance at sea was painfully inadequate. The Qing court was never committed to developing a strong navy and continued to underestimate the British.[58] In that respect Macartney, head of the British embassy to China at the end of the eighteenth century,

---

[56]See Crossley, *Orphan Warriors*.
[57]See Crossley, *Orphan Warriors*, passim, and Elliott, *Manchu Way*, 175–91.
[58]See Wang, *Anglo-Chinese Encounters*, ch. 2.

was indeed a good observer when he wondered how the rulers of the Chinese Empire at the Court of Peking could be

> ignorant that a couple of English frigates would be an overmatch for the whole naval force of the empire, that in half a summer they could totally destroy all the navigation of their coasts and reduce the inhabitants of the maritime provinces, who subsist chiefly on fish, to absolute famine.[59]

In 1809, the Qing had to call upon 'barbarians', in this case the British and the Portuguese, to help them in their efforts to suppress pirates in the Southern China Seas. Yet, nothing much was done to improve the situation and to seriously start building a fleet.[60] China's marine forces were simply unable to wipe out the pirates and thus had to come to a compromise in 1810 by proclaiming a great amnesty. This piracy was not a minor affair. In 1809 the number of men involved was estimated at almost 70,000.[61]

During the British–American War in 1812 the Jiaqing Emperor commented:

> When two small countries have petty quarrels overseas, the Celestial Empire is not concerned with them. … [If they would bring their wars to China] then not only shall we destroy their warships, but we shall also suspend their trade.[62]

His successor the Daoguang Emperor did not invest extra money in modernizing his naval forces and coastal defences continued to be severely inadequate. When in 1834 two British ships intruded into Chinese waters the emperor himself complained:

> How laughable and deplorable is it that we cannot even repel two barbarian ships. Our military had decayed so much. No wonder the barbarians are looking down on us.[63]

We already pointed out that in 1831 the Chinese navy still only counted 31,000 men. Basically, China was unprepared militarily and unaware of any danger. It suffered from a self-imposed blindness. Commissioner Lin, one of the best informed Chinese at the time when it comes to foreign affairs, was sure, just before the outbreak of the First Opium War, that the West would be no match for China when it came to a military confrontation. Or rather, he was convinced that Westerners would not dare to let it come that far. He thought the British troops would not be able to move because of their puttees and assumed the British could not survive without tea and rhubarb anyhow.[64]

---

[59]See for this quote Cranmer-Byng, *Embassy to China*, 170.
[60]For some further information on China's maritime forces see, in alphabetical order, Andrade, 'Company's Chinese pirates'; Antony, 'State, community, and pirate suppression'; Murray, 'Piracy and China's maritime transition', and Wang, *Anglo-Chinese Encounters* and the book by Wang referred to in the next note.
[61]See Wang, *White Lotus Rebels and South China Pirates*, ch. 3.
[62]Westad, *Restless Empire*, 38. The reference in that text is somewhat confusing.
[63]Sng, 'Size and dynastic decline'.
[64]Overdijking, *Lin Tse-Hsu*, Appendix six.

Ch'i-ying, the Tartar-general of Canton, claimed the barbarians would not be able to see well in the dark.[65]

Finally, there is the factor of technology. Even if in current historiography technology and weaponry figure less prominently than they did in traditional explanations of why China in many respects was reduced to the status of a semi-colony, it would be pushing things too far to deny their importance. During the First Opium War the Chinese army still included swordsmen and archers, its guns were much less efficient than those of the British and it had no gunboats.[66] Lord John William Napier, appointed as Superintendent of British trade in China in 1833, in a letter to Earl Grey of India in 1834 wondered: 'What can an army of bows, and arrows, and pikes, and shields do against a handful of veterans.'[67]

If by some mysterious mechanism the best eighteenth-century Chinese army would have been placed on a European battlefield it would have been routed, whereas the best European army, if by that same mechanism it would have found itself placed in China, would surely have been victorious. The fact that for a long time for Westerners it was logistically impossible to transfer a big, well-equipped army to China – let alone for the Chinese to transfer a big, well-equipped army of theirs to Europe – of course brings us into the realm of the counterfactual here. The huge problems, however, which tiny military forces from the West could cause for China from the First Opium War onwards, to me, are a clear indicator that my counterfactual is solid. It would not have been by accident that from the eighteenth century onwards, new ideas and techniques in the field of the military without exception went from West to East.[68] In military matters Macartney, whose comments on China's fleet I just quoted, very probably was right, again, when in 1793 he compared China to

> an old, crazy, First rate man of war, which a fortunate succession of able and vigilant officers had contrived to keep afloat for these 150 years past, and to overawe their neighbours merely by her bulk and appearance, but whenever an insufficient man happens to have the command upon deck, adieu to the discipline and safety of the ship. She may perhaps not sink outright; she may drift some time as a wreck and will then be dashed to pieces on the shore: but she can never be rebuilt on the old bottom.[69]

What actually happened during the First Opium War is telling. The British sent 16 men-of-war, with 540 pieces of artillery, 4 armed steamboats and 30 ships on which 4,000 troops were transported. They did so to fight many thousands of miles away from home

---

[65]Hsü, *Rise of Modern China*, 192.
[66]Headrick, *Tools of Empire*, 90–1.
[67]Hsü, *Rise of Modern China*, 175.
[68]Ralston, *Importing the European Army*.
[69]See for this quotation Cranmer-Byng, *Embassy to China*, 212–13.

in a country with over 400 million inhabitants and the advantage of fighting in its own waters and on its own land. That hugely populous and, according to the California School, highly developed country proved to be no match for this tiny army and signed a humiliating peace treaty after what can hardly be called more than some skirmishes. China could have been whipped off the map in the second half of the nineteenth century. Sun Yat-sen (1866–1925) thought Britain and France would be able to colonize China within 45–50 days.[70] That China did not become a real colony is because its imperialist opponents were not united and not willing to accept that one of them became too powerful.

WAR, THE MILITARY AND ECONOMIC INNOVATION

> Homo economicus … does not go to war, and rather too many economic historians prefer to avert their eyes from the real world in which things are different.
>
> Rodger, 'War as an economic activity', 9

> War and taxation in the eighteenth century may, in the long run, have been what made Britain great.
>
> Beckett and Turner, 'Taxation and economic growth', 401

> The Industrial Revolution 'occurred precisely during and because of the Napoleonic Wars.'
>
> Neal, *Rise of Financial Capitalism,* 218

The main business of all the governments we deal with in this book was war. Their expenditures, in any case, overwhelmingly were related to it. It therefore need not come as a surprise that scholars have been pondering the relation between 'war', 'the military' and 'the economy', in particular for the Western world where war and preparation for war were quite normal and military expenditures very high and that (nevertheless?) became the richest part of the world. Recently Rafael Torres Sánchez, editor of a volume on the fiscal-military state, indicated he would want to explain 'how this relationship between state, war, and development could evolve', taking it as a fact that 'Europeans managed to grow not so much by accreting years of peace and *despite* war but rather *with* war.'[71]

Most mercantilists were convinced that there was a positive connection between power and, as they called it, 'plenty',[72] and that for power one needs armed forces. It was quite obvious to them that economic interests *could* and in case of need *should*

---

[70]I found this remark in Deng, *China's Political Economy,* 31.
[71]Torres Sánchez, 'Triumph of the fiscal-military state', 14, and the flap text of the book in which this article is published.
[72]See for these concepts Viner, 'Power versus plenty'.

be supported by the use of the military. Even people who did not share the standard mercantilist views, like the Dutch free trader Pieter de la Court, nevertheless considered it naïve to act as if the world was a safe and peaceful place.

> If we consider the uncertainty of this world, especially in Europe, and that we by traffick and navigation have occasion to deal with all nations, we ought to hold for a firm and general maxim, that an assured peace is, in relation to Holland, a mere chimera, a dream, a fiction, used only by those, who like syrens or mermaids, endeavour by their melodious singing of a pleasant and firm peace, to delude the credulous Hollanders, till they split upon the rocks.[73]

It can hardly be a coincidence that in countries that wanted to catch up 'modernizers' later on, without exception, were convinced that wealth and power presuppose each other and that they (e.g. in China and Japan after their 'opening' by the West) explicitly called for a 'rich country and a strong army'.

War and, more broadly, violence has always been a fact of life with major economic impact. According to Marx: 'Force is the midwife of every old society which is pregnant with a new one. It itself is an economic power.'[74] About a century ago, Sombart wrote on war and capitalism linking war – and thus the state – profits and capital accumulation.[75] Many scholars were to follow.[76] I already referred to Findlay and O'Rourke's *Power and Plenty*. In various places in their book they come quite close to Rapp's thesis that 'the state, not the individual firm was the relevant unit of competition in early modern international competition'.[77] We have already seen that they attribute mercantilism and all the violence that often entailed a central role in the Britain's industrialization, although they continue to assume that a policy of *laissez-faire* and free trade would have led to even better results. In the end, as so often with mainstream economists, they prefer a fine theory over a messy reality.[78] In 2009, Arrighi in his *Adam Smith in Beijing* discussed the positive effects of what he called 'military Keynesianism' and the armaments race. In 2014, Morris in his *War. What Is It Good For?* claimed that war has 'over the long run made humanity safer and richer' and that 'by creating larger societies, stronger governments and greater security, war has enriched the world'. This logic works out 'with the passage of time – maybe decades, maybe centuries.' One can summarize this thesis in the claim that war can be productive by making governments that make peace that leads to wealth.[79] For the specific case of Great Britain, as we will see,

---

[73]De la Court, *True Interest and Political Maxims*, 242.

[74]Marx, *Capital, I*, 916.

[75]Sombart, *Krieg und Kapitalismus*.

[76]I just refer, in chronological order, to Nef, *War and Human Progress*; Lane, *Profits from Power*; McNeill, *Pursuit of Power*; Sen, *Military Origins of Industrialization*; Tilly, *Coercion, Capital, and European States*; Porter, *War and the Rise of the State*; Weiss and Hobson, *States and Economic Development*, and Cooper and Ruttan, *Is War Necessary for Growth?*

[77]Rapp, 'Unmaking of the Mediterranean trade hegemony', 515.

[78]See the review by Reinert in *Journal of Global History*.

[79]See for the direct quotations Morris, *War*, 7.

several scholars have emphasized war and preparation for war are not necessarily bad for economic development.[80]

It is easy to imagine all kinds of positive effects of the use of brute force. The winner of a conflict, although of course there sometimes were staggering prices to pay, by definition also wins something: booty, payments from the loser(s), territory, a weakened competitor and so on. A successful show of force may pay off in the sense that it could be used to back up economic policies. Think of the actual protection of trade and traders, blue-water policy and, of course, empire-building. Some people obviously could and did indeed gain by war. Nor can one deny that people often *thought* war in the end would pay, and therefore more or less enthusiastically were willing to pay for it. If we look at the situation in Europe itself, everyone can think of wars that turned out as planned and may well have paid. If we look at it from the perspective of the world, it is evident that Europeans turned their ample experience in wielding violence to economic use in other continents by plunder in its purest form or by building real or trade empires.

But it of course is just as easy to point out enormous costs. Think of the enormous sums of money it cost to win a war, or even worse the enormous sums of money it could cost to, in the end, still lose it. What about the enormous destruction and interruption of economic life caused by it? Even if, one way or another, investing in the military in the end would turn out to have been profitable, could not the same or far better results have been booked more easily and against less cost in a more peaceful world? To prove that war and preparing for war pays, one would have to determine all of its societal costs and benefits and compare those to a counterfactual situation without war and war preparations. We will never be able to do that. Even if we would only consider direct monetary costs and revenue 'the prospects for striking anything other than a conjectural balance sheet look entirely remote'.[81] Making such a balance sheet would, moreover, bring us in a realm of speculation that would not have made sense to people in early modern Europe. To behave like a stubborn pacifist – or a staunch free trader – simply was not an option in the war-prone and highly combative environment in which European states in the early modern era operated. Warfare, violence, aggression and unfair competition were simple facts of life that one had to accept as such. Losing a war often simply was not an option. Violence often had *no* economic rationale whatsoever. Wars often were about the dynasty or 'the state' and those who decided to wage them almost as a rule were not primarily concerned about the economy. Over time economic factors did begin to play an important role in the considerations of various European governments. But that as such does not guarantee their wars would make economic sense. Even if a war seemed to 'make sense' economically when it began, things might look quite differently at its end, in particular, in case one lost. The connection between war and the economy, or more in general between power and profit, was also fiercely debated in early modern Europe,

---

[80] See the quotes on page 311 and Chapter 5 note 95.
[81] O'Brien, 'Contributions of warfare', 36.

with most people tending to endorse the idea that violence and force were facts of life and that only strong nations could have strong economies.

Besides in the early modern world trade was considered as one of the main sources of economic strength, if not, as mercantilists thought, its main source. And trade indeed to a large extent did depend on power. Contemporaries knew that and said so without any inhibition. Industrialization was already at quite an advanced stage when Britain could finally try and rule the waves without shows of military strength and by simply relying on its economic supremacy. Which even then, it did not. The many expensive wars that Britain waged were quite helpful in giving it global oceanic supremacy. In that way, they can be considered an 'investment' in Britain's economy. We will never be able to determine whether they were a 'good' investment in strict balance sheet terms. We do know for certain that wars were enormously expensive. The sum total of British military expenditure between 1680 and 1815 was not very different from the sum total of British domestic exports in this same period.[82] But again, what would have happened if Britain had stayed clear of all the wars it eventually was involved in? We do not know. What is striking is that even notorious losers of wars like Austria, France and Germany became and continued to be highly developed and quite rich countries. Is being part of the warring states system and thus participating in cut-throat competition what really matters, rather than winning?

The economic impact of war: The British case

Even if no definitive answer can be provided in balance sheet terms as we already indicated in our discussion of military Keynesianism and even if to some extent it is anachronistic, the question of the economic impact of war cannot be simply ignored. Let us therefore try and deal with it in some detail in the specific case of Great Britain in our period. The impact of war on China's economy was so marginal in comparison with that of Britain that it is not much use to try and discuss any potential positive connections between war and economic development in its case. Before we go more into detail, a couple of comments are in order with regard to Rafael Torres Sánchez's statement[83] on a possible connection between warfare and the rise of the fiscal-military state on the one hand and economic development and economic growth on the other. The period between the 1680s and the 1820s undoubtedly saw an accelerating build-up of fiscal-military states all over Europe. That, however, does not mean that, at least up until the Revolutionary and Napoleonic Wars, which in many respects were quite extraordinary, this build-up would have been directly linked to incessant and escalating warfare in Europe. After the War of Spanish Succession (1702–13), there were *relatively* few major wars in Europe in which *all* big European powers participated. Spending on armies and navies increased, as did

---

[82]For a comparison of British war expenditure and the value of British trade see Harley, 'Reassessing the Industrial Revolution', 218, and Mitchell, *British Historical Statistics*, 448–52.
[83]See page 311.

their sizes, but rulers were quite careful not to see them destroyed and their investments vanish. In brief: preparation for war certainly increased; actual warfare did not. When on the other hand we look at the economic side of the equation, we have to conclude that the eighteenth century, including the period of the Revolutionary and Napoleonic Wars, was *not* a period of impressive economic growth, far from. This means that, *in any case for the eighteenth century*, Torres may well have started from false premises when he edited his volume. These general comments also apply to Britain. Up until the end of the Napoleonic Wars, it indeed increased the size of army and navy – and its expenditure on them – without, however, necessarily entirely using them. When it comes to growth most economic historians would now agree that up until a couple of decades into the nineteenth century the country went through a phase of economic build-up and development, but not yet of substantial growth in terms of an increase of GDP per capita in real terms. It was only a couple of decades into the nineteenth century that real income in Britain began to really grow – that is, at a time when tax pressure (tax revenue as percentage of GDP) *de*creased, government no longer had budget deficits and major warfare was quite sporadic. The period between Waterloo and Sarajevo when Western Europe took off was very peaceful – for European standards and in Europe.

Furthermore, there again are peculiarities of Great Britain. To begin with it fought none of its many wars in the eighteenth century – but it was no different in the nineteenth century – on its own territory. From the Second Jacobite Rising (1745–6) onwards, the country was also spared major explosions of domestic violence. What is also exceptional is the importance of its navy as compared to its army, one of the reasons its connection between state-formation and the military was different from states with a huge standing army at home.[84] What of course is of utmost importance is the fact that, apart from the American War of Independence, it did not lose any significant conflict from the 1750s to the end of the period under discussion here.[85] Even during the Napoleonic Wars it did not introduce a *levée en masse*. After those wars it quickly demobilized and focused on its empire, where its wars, as compared to what was normal in Europe, were rather small.

To 'measure' the economic impact of war, one might focus on its direct costs and benefits and try and represent them on a neat balance sheet. Although I am convinced the outcome would be quite negative, I consider it impossible to actually come up with such a sheet. That, however, is not what really matters here. I hope to have shown elsewhere that modern economic growth is not primarily a matter of accumulation but of innovation.[86] I therefore want to focus on whether war gave fundamental impulses to innovation. Arrighi in his *Adam Smith in Beijing* not only discusses military Keynesianism but also develops a somewhat differing line of reasoning that focuses more on innovation. For him, 'the synergy between capitalism, industrialism, and militarism, driven by interstate competition, did engender a virtuous [*sic*] circle of enrichment and empowerment

---

[84]See for the difference such an absence can make Downing, *Military Revolution.*
[85]Strikingly enough this conflict, over time, was not in any significant way detrimental to Anglo-British trade.
[86]That is the main thesis of my *Escaping Poverty.*

for the peoples of European descent'.[87] According to him, it was the expansion of England's entrepôt trade and massive governmental expenditure during the Napoleonic Wars that turned British industrial capacities into an effective instrument of national aggrandizement.[88] In contrast to China, in Western Europe war had not only become a fully commercialized activity but it had also taken the form of an incessant armament race. He regards that race as 'the primary source of the endless stream of innovations' that in my view characterizes modern economic growth.[89] For him the industrial revolution, or at least the revolution in capital-goods manufacture, was 'largely a by-product of the European armament race'.[90] Authors like Weiss and Hobson agree and refer to various examples of what they regard as highly important technological spin-offs that spread from the military sector over the rest of the economy during Britain's early industrialization.[91] Examples of such spin-offs clearly exist.[92] But do they really turn the armament race into 'the primary source of the endless stream of innovations' and the engine of modern economic growth? At least for the period from the 1850s onwards, it would be hard to find a scholar in the field who would deny that the 'military-industrial complex' was a major source of innovations. I agree, though, with Elvin that calling it 'the primary source' is certainly quite exaggerated and half true, at the very best.[93] Apart from the fact that 'necessity is the mother of innovation-explanations', as such, they are much less straightforward than they seem,[94] there simply are too many exceptions where the primary source of technological advance was science, or I would claim 'technological tinkering'. When it comes to timing in the context of the case we are dealing with, the industrial innovation of war in many respects *followed* the industrial innovation of civil society instead of preceding it. Two further additional comments are also in order. First, why is it that the effects of war and preparation for war could be so different for different countries? Second, there is the comment I already made that one may wonder whether war-instigated innovations were not enormously costly. I doubt anyone would be willing to defend the claim that the staggering amounts of money spent in the arms race that characterized the world of early modern Europe was the most efficient way to produce the inventions and innovations that (may have) resulted from it. What might be defended, however, is the claim that without the extreme challenges provided by war many innovations simply would not have occurred at all because they were the result not of any kind of rational economic calculation but of the absolute necessity not to lose the war. That necessity urges efforts that otherwise would have been lacking. War

---

[87] Arrighi, *Adam Smith in Beijing*, 95.

[88] Arrighi, *Adam Smith in Beijing*, 243.

[89] Arrighi, *Adam Smith in Beijing*, 272.

[90] Arrighi, *Adam Smith in Beijing*, 268. Arrighi bases himself here on ideas of William McNeill.

[91] Weiss and Hobson, *States and Economic Development*, 78–81. Mumford too sees a clear connection here. See his *Technics and Civilisation*, 163, where he claims that in general 'bloodshed kept pace with iron production.'

[92] See e.g. Knight, *Britain against Napoleon*, ch. 12.

[93] See Elvin, 'Historian as haruspex', 102.

[94] In the case of acute warfare, for example, the extreme pressure on production and productivity need not at all have a positive impact on innovation, to the extent that it can have a quite negative effect on the funding of R&D, in general and, of fundamental, theoretical research.

or the threat of war without any doubt are terrible means to create changes and increase efficiency – the same goes for mercantilism – but it is not easy to see how at least certain 'great leaps forward' might have been made in times of peace and fair competition.

Intense militarization certainly had what one might call 'mobilizing effects'. War or the threat of war leads to a situation in which the available resources of an economy are used as intensely as possible and production and productivity are pushed to their limits in a context where costs are far less of a direct concern than during times of peace and tranquillity. This means that resources that may have been underemployed, and there in all probability always were many of those in a pre-industrial economy, get 'activated'. Some scholars claim this is what happened in Britain during the Napoleonic Wars and regard that as basically positive for its economy, in particular, since the country was spared the destruction of these wars that were fought some place else.[95] The domestic economy of Britain did not do badly during those wars in terms of production and productivity. Cotton production increased three times between the mid-1790s and 1813. Iron and steel manufacturing output increased fourfold in that same period. Investment in infrastructure was huge.[96] Incomes of British farmers are estimated to have increased continuously by 1 or 2 per cent per year during the Napoleonic Wars.[97] At the end of the Napoleonic Wars Great Britain's economy was booming. Peace brought a slump. History provides many examples of explosive growth during war. A large part of the Golden Age of the Dutch economy coincided with the Eighty Years War between the Dutch and Spain. Over the entire twentieth century, the US economy went through its biggest boom during the Second World War. It of course helps when one wins. For the French economy the Revolutionary and Napoleonic Wars were detrimental.[98] They marked a (further) divergence of France and Great Britain.[99]

Military demand could be so massive that meeting it provided a real challenge for producers. Several authors find it, for example, hard to imagine the stormy growth in the production of steam engines, iron railways and iron ships, and the many innovations in their production, without the impetus of war.[100] The massive demand for standardized goods like arms and uniforms, to mention another example, created economies of scale and therewith stimulated the concentration of production. In transport and communication, military considerations had always been very important. In the large-scale modernization of these sectors, that, however, only set in after 1850 and that

---

[95]See e.g. Davis, *Industrial Revolution and British Overseas Trade*, 74; Deane, 'War and industrialisation', 97; O'Brien 'Contributions of warfare', and Rodger, 'War as an economic activity', passim. In particular O'Brien makes it very plausible that even during that war Great Britain could continue to tap underused resources in its economy. See also my comments on 'crowding out' on pages 214–15.

[96]Knight, *Britain against Napoleon*, 352–3 and 392–3.

[97]O'Brien, 'Triumph and denouement', 197.

[98]For the economic impact of the Napoleonic Wars in several countries see Aerts and Crouzet, 'Economic effects'; O'Brien, 'Impact of the Revolutionary and Napoleonic wars', and O'Rourke, 'Worldwide economic impact'. For some more anecdotal comments on their impact in Great Britain and France see Knight, *Britain against Napoleon*, ch. 12.

[99]Verley, *L'échelle du monde*, 459–516.

[100]See for this claim Arrighi, *Adam Smith in Beijing*, 268. He refers to McNeill, *Pursuit of Power*, 211–12.

often came close to a militarization, they were predominant.[101] Even though the actual 'industrialization' of warfare itself only began in the 1840s, with the Crimean War as a turning point,[102] the economic impact of wars in terms of concentrated demand already was enormous. The Napoleonic Wars basically still were pre-industrial wars in which man and horsepower were decisive and in which the relevant innovations were in the field of organizational, strategic and logistical 'software' rather than in technological 'hardware'. But the demands they made on resources were staggering and the pressure they put on the productive capacity of the countries involved was immense. In Great Britain they certainly accelerated 'rationalization',[103] and not just in the obvious sectors. Rodger points out that one single organization, the navy, was buying a fifth of all the products traded on the national agricultural market. That must have had an impact on that sector.[104]

It would be mistaken to only focus on direct technological or economic effects of war. Its impact on institutional development, first and foremost state-formation, in Europe is obvious and very probably even more consequential. Tilly's most famous quote, 'War made states and states made war', certainly applies to the period in European history we are dealing with here. It would be quite a challenge to find any institution we associate with the modern state that is *not* somehow connected to war. One can only agree with Francis Fukuyama: 'The most important effects of war may not be who wins, loses or suffers. Rather, war's deeper consequences concern its long-term impact on the very type of society we live in.'[105] Here Tilly's *Coercion and Capital* and, more detailed in this respect, Porter's *War and the Rise of the State* are fundamental and, in my view, convincing reading. Morris in his *War. What Is It Good For?* in the end argues along similar lines but with much less analytical skill and historical depth and strikingly enough without any reference to these two books. War has often functioned as a motor for institutional innovation with major consequences for the infrastructural power of states. In the case of Great Britain one can indeed see many positive spin-offs in terms of rationalization of governance that are directly or indirectly linked to the sinews of power and to war. The rise of the infrastructurally strong British state with all its 'mercantilist' institutions, organizations and policies and its enormous power to mobilize resources is very hard to imagine without them. Acute crises often accelerated processes of 'rationalization', as clearly shown, for example, in the fight against 'old corruption' and other inefficiencies during the Revolutionary and Napoleonic Wars.[106] War and its preparation became a matter of utmost national concern and in Western Europe they tended to involve increasingly institutionalized, nationwide bargaining in which subjects slowly became citizens.[107] For Great Britain it is clear that the rationale behind many of the institutional changes and innovations that made up its 'Financial

---

[101]That militarization was much more prominent in several countries on the Continent than in Great Britain.
[102]See Chapter 5 note 24.
[103]I just refer to Bell, *First Total War*; Knight, *Fighting against Napoleon*, and my comments on pages 137–8.
[104]Rodger, 'War as an economic activity', 14.
[105]See Fukuyama on the back flap of Porter, *War and the Rise of the State*.
[106]Knight, *Britain against Napoleon*, ch. 11.
[107]For the concept of bargaining see Tilly, *Coercion, Capital, and European States*, under 'bargaining'.

Revolution' in the widest sense of the term – that is fundamental in understanding how Britain could rise to the status of world power – was to find ways to finance wars and deal with the public debts they created.[108] Here there clearly is a link between (financial) innovation and warfare. Once again has to be careful, however: for many other countries warfare, in the field of finances and otherwise, only led to improvisation, increased coercion or big problems and chaos. The 'positive link' was absent or in any case much less clear in, for example, France and Spain during the early modern era. It was also absent for quite some time in a country like Prussia that, to make things even more complicated, in the end became a far more formidable military power than the Dutch Republic that for quite some time had about the same number of inhabitants and in the seventeenth century was the wealthiest and financially the most sophisticated country of Europe. It, to give a last example, was absent in the Ottoman Empire, which was not exactly short of wars. Again, Great Britain actually was fairly exceptional and once again it shows one has to be careful with 'necessity-is-the-mother-of-invention' and 'competition-propels-progress' explanations. One may in any case wonder whether permanent warfare was actually *needed* to come up with these innovations. I would guess such warfare and the need for funds it generates certainly are not sufficient and probably not even necessary conditions for financial innovation. Fact is that those often *did* actually emerge in response to situations of war.

Mancur Olson in his work focuses on a quite specific connection between war and institutional change when he argues that wars and their aftermaths often destroy 'sclerotic' societal structures and institutions and eliminate vested interests that oppose innovation.[109] In doing so, they enable societies to make a new start with a new, clean slate. One could also refer here to Thomas Piketty, who points at the enormous impact of the First and Second World Wars on the economies of several Western countries, in particular in destroying accumulated wealth.[110] Countries that lost wars, as long as they continued to have sufficient human capital, often knew strong development and growth after their defeat. Rosenthal and Wong in their *Before and Beyond Divergence* also come up with a more indirect and maybe somewhat unexpected link between war and economic growth in claiming that permanent wars made manufacturing production in Western Europe unsafe outside cities. It was therefore concentrated in cities where wage costs were higher which stimulated innovation and so triggered the technological breakthroughs that led to 'industrialization'. For the case of Great Britain, the first and, for decades, dominant industrial nation, that explanation simply does not make sense. I have already discussed their claim in my *Escaping Poverty* and refer the reader to that text.[111]

The links discussed above are somehow indirect. There are also more direct ones, in the sense that war tended to be an enormous undertaking that as such required a major

---

[108]Scholars explicitly making this connection are e.g. Arrighi, *Long Twentieth Century*, pages 13 and 17 and ch. 3; Ferguson, *Cash Nexus*, passim, and Weiss and Hobson, *States and Economic Development*, 79–92 and 112–39.
[109]Olson, *Rise and Decline*.
[110]Piketty, *Capital in the Twenty-First Century*, under 'World Wars I and II' and under 'Shocks'.
[111]Vries, *Escaping Poverty*, 184–6.

organizational and institutional infrastructure. In the West, armies and navies became the biggest, most costly and most sophisticated enterprises at the time. War increasingly evolved in the direction of a modern, 'rationalized' business, run by professionals. In this respect, too, war may have functioned and often indeed did as 'mother of invention'. Marx already indicated that the military in many respects prefigured the capitalist mode of production with its use of wage labour and machinery, its division of labour and all the logistical and managerial arrangements that large-scale enterprise require.[112] He also, just like Max Weber, pointed at the importance and role of discipline in the military as well as the factory.[113]

Let us again delve somewhat deeper into the British case. In Chapter 2 we presented figures with regard to Britain's government expenditure, including its military expenditure, in relative and absolute terms. Those figures were huge. So were the numbers of people involved. Let us here, to get a more concrete image of the organization and business of war and its economic impact in the broadest sense, only focus on Britain's navy. The Royal Navy became the largest single employer of civilians in the country. In 1700, the staff of its logistical departments totalled 6,500. In 1814, it stood at 17,300.[114] A first class naval vessel at the end of the eighteenth century had a crew of 900. Building ships of the size used in Britain and provisioning them involved enormous amounts of people, money and resources.[115] It was definitely more complicated, from an organizational perspective, to build and maintain a first class navy at the time than to mobilize a large land army. Not only was the Royal Navy a big enterprise, its production was concentrated and modern. To quote James:

> Its vast complexes contained the first modern factories where ropes and wooden pulleys were mass-produced using the most up-to-date industrial technology. The steam-driven pump introduced for draining a Portsmouth dry-dock in 1799 was the first of many, and between 1802 and 1812, steam engines were introduced to drive sawmills and the machine tools that turned out 130,000 pulleys per year.[116]

Huge amounts of money and know-how were involved in its investments. Brewer's comparison with industrial investments is quite enlightening here.

> The capital assets of a large business in the early eighteenth century rarely exceeded £10,000. Ambrose Crowley's iron works, regarded as the wonder of their age, had a fixed capital of £12,000. A substantial multi-storey cotton spinning mill built at the end of the century cost a mere £5,000. By comparison naval vessels cost a small fortune. In the late seventeenth century the navy spent between £33,000 and

---

[112]See for these comments Arrighi, *Adam Smith in Beijing*, 265.

[113]See page 421.

[114]James, *Warrior Race*, 274.

[115]The English East India Company, in contrast to the Dutch East India Company, did not build its ships itself.

[116]James, *Warrior Race*, 274. See also, for many examples, Knight, *Britain against Napoleon*, ch. 12.

£39,000 to build a first-rate ship, between £24,000 and £27,000 to build a second-rate, and between £15,000 and £17,000 to construct a third-rate vessel. By the second half of the eighteenth century the cost of constructing the largest ships had nearly doubled. In 1765 the 100-gun first-rate Victory cost £63,174 to build. Even the smaller royal naval vessels were more expensive than most industrial plant.[117]

A new seventy-four gun ship, fully outfitted, might typically cost almost £50,000 in the 1780s.[118] In terms of money, the business of war completely dwarfed all other businesses. To again quote John Brewer:

> In the first half of the eighteenth century the British Navy boasted twenty ships of the first and second rates, approximately forty vessels of the third rate, as well as an additional 120 smaller vessels of the fourth, fifth and sixth rate. If we assume that the costs of ship construction had not risen since the late seventeenth century, then the entire fleet amounted to a capital investment of nearly £2.25 million whose replacement cost was approximately four per cent of national income This can be compared with the total fixed capital in the 243 mills in the West Riding woollen industry in 1800, which has been estimated at £402,651 with an average of £1657 per textile mill. The fixed capital in one of the largest sectors of the nation's most important industry was therefore a mere eighteen per cent of the fixed capital required to launch the British navy.[119]

I take a final example from Peter Mathias. He refers to a very highly capitalized, large-scale London brewery, Truman, Hanbury and Buxton, that was considered a vast manufacturing plant for its time. In 1800 its total gross assets were £334,000. Of this total, beer stocks were £100,000, raw material stocks £75,000, trade debts (i.e. beer delivered but not yet paid for, together with loans) £100,000. 'Fixed stock', public-house leases and casks together totalled only £50,000, of which the actual brewery and its plant, excluding casks, came to only £26,000.[120]

Over time the number of ships increased. The effective size of the Royal Navy reached its maximum in 1809 when 709 ships measuring 469,227 tons were in commission. Between 1803 and 1815, no less than 515 warships were built in British dockyards. The price of building them, moreover, rose: in 1815 a 100-gun ship was launched at Plymouth Dockyard costing £110,000.[121] All those ships moreover needed maintenance.

---

[117]Brewer, *Sinews of Power*, 34.

[118]Baugh, 'Naval power', 238.

[119]Brewer, *Sinews of Power*, 34–5. Using rather low estimates of just construction costs, Brewer suggests that the British navy in the first half of the eighteenth century amounted to an investment worth about 4 per cent of national income.

[120]Mathias, 'Financing the Industrial Revolution', 76.

[121]Knight, *Britain against Napoleon*, 315, 368 and 359. See also for example Rodger, 'War as an economic activity', 10: 'A seventy-four gun ship of the line about 1805, fitted, rigged and armed, cost about £80,000, or the price of sixteen cotton mills'

The navy spent £13,000 every six months simply to keep a first-rate battleship shipshape and seaworthy.[122]

And then of course there were the crews that had to be provided for. Mid-eighteenth century average shipboard population was 40,000.[123] In the period from 1805 to the end of the Napoleonic Wars there often were over 100,000 seamen and marines on board ships of the Royal Navy. The upkeep of navies was expensive and required lots of cash, specialized equipment and many months' supply of food, drink and replacement stores at the outset of each undertaking. The total amounts of provisions they required can only be guessed at: every seaman at the time was entitled to a weekly diet of seven pounds of biscuit, six pounds of meat, seven gallons of beer, two pints of pease and three pints of oatmeal, plus smaller quantities of butter, cheese and vinegar. When supplies were available, they were also issued fresh meat and vegetables. At times as much as 100,000 tons of shipping was used to provide for army and navy.[124] The navy was less of a drain on the bullion reserves, as one might have expected, as crews were paid only at the ports where their vessels were commissioned (i.e. in Britain). That meant that, as virtual prisoners on board ship, they often went for years on end without being paid.

These references were only to the navy. When we look at the armed forces in their entirety, figures become even more staggering. To quote Peter Mathias:

> Consider the single statistic that the total military costs of the French wars for Britain between 1793 and 1815 amounted to approximately £1,000 million, with over £500 million in mobilized savings produced for government loans by way of the long-term capital market, spread over twenty-two years, whereas the total accumulated capital in the canal system, from 1750 to 1820 was about £20 million. Moreover, transport investment was one of the 'lumpiest' forms of productive investment to be undertaken. In 1809–1810 it was reckoned that the annual investment in fixed capital in the entire cotton industry was £0.4 million. That was less than one per cent of the military budget of £45 million, spent during that year.[125]

I can only endorse the following two comments by Brewer: 'As an organization, the fiscal-military state dwarfed any civilian enterprise'[126] and 'If we are interested in the history of organizations, and not merely the history of production, then it is to military rather than civilian enterprise that we should turn.'[127] In size and complexity nothing was comparable to the logistics of war. Financing the Industrial Revolution was 'small beer' compared to the costs of waging war.[128]

---

[122]Brewer, *Sinews of Power*, 35.
[123]Baugh, *British Naval Administration*, 246.
[124]Hall, *British Strategy*, 37 and 43.
[125]Mathias, 'Financing the Industrial Revolution', 72. Compare for this estimate of costs tables 17–18.
[126]Brewer, *Sinews of Power*, 34.
[127]Brewer, *Sinews of Power*, 37.
[128]Rule, *Vital Century*, 276.

In this context one must refer to the East India Company, half private and half public, half firm and half sovereign, that also counted as an enormous enterprise in its day. In 1815, the political economist Patrick Colquhoun calculated that the company offered direct employment to over 48,000 British subjects. The number of Britons who for their livelihood were, one way or another, dependent on the company, at home, abroad or on sea, can be taken to have been about double.[129] I have already referred to its huge armies.[130] By comparison, the Dutch East India Company in 1753, at its height, in total (i.e. in the Dutch Republic, Asia and on its ships) employed over 38,000 people.[131]

---

[129]Bowen, *Business of Empire*, 271.
[130]See page 287.
[131]Gaastra, *Dutch East India Company*, ch. 3.

CHAPTER 6
ECONOMIC POLICIES

THE PRACTICE OF MERCANTILISM IN WESTERN EUROPE

Trade is the basis of finance, and finance is the sinews of war.

Jean-Baptiste Colbert (1619–83)
France's Minister of Finance

Whenever we look closely into the nature of British free trade, monopoly is pretty generally found to lie at the bottom of its 'freedom'.

Karl Marx, 'Free trade and monopoly',
New York Daily Tribune, 25 September 1858

What Adam Smith famously described as the human propensity to 'truck, barter and exchange' has always coexisted uneasily with a rival temptation to take, bully, and extort.

Seabright, *Company of Strangers*, 233

If I were forced to characterize the economic policy of European governments in the early modern era with one word, that word would be 'mercantilist'. That is not without its risks. Talking about mercantilism as a 'European' economic policy can easily suggest much more uniformity and 'system' than in fact existed. The word only came into existence after the fact and many measures actually were taken *ad hoc* and not as part and parcel of some big master plan. There was much improvisation. Often things worked out unexpectedly or, according to place and time, differently. But that does not exclude the existence of a 'core' of assumptions and principles that *were* adhered to by most European rulers most of the time. Unfortunately, that core of ideas tends to be misrepresented in two ways: either as a single-minded, if not simple-minded, obsession with trade and trade balances that mistakes bullion for wealth or, more recently, as a system of nothing but rent seeking.[1]

The way to best describe the underlying principles and goals of many, if not most, economic policies adopted by rulers in Europe in the early modern era is to follow in the footsteps of the German economist Gustav von Schmoller and the Swedish economic

---

[1] The still dominant idea that mercantilists would be obsessed with trade balances and bullion originated with Adam Smith. For a brief introduction into 'mercantilist' thinking about trade balances and free trade see Irwin, *Against the Tide*, part one. The interpretation of mercantilism as a form of rent seeking has been propagated in particular by Ekelund and Tollison in *Mercantilism as a Rent-Seeking Society* and *Politicized Economics*.

historian Eli Heckscher.[2] They, with various other authors, regarded mercantilism as a form of 'economic nationalism'. Governments in Europe were constantly benchmarking and emulating the most successful economies in the European states-system and regarded it as their task to create a *competitive* advantage for the economies of their own countries instead of, to put it in modern terms, simply accepting whatever static, largely resource-based *comparative* advantage those economies may have had.[3] This means that they differentiated between 'good' production and 'bad' production, as well as between 'good' trade and 'bad' trade. What they wanted their countries to produce were (manufactured) goods or services with high added value and substantial spin-offs. They promoted the substitution of the import of such goods by goods produced in their own country and hoped to create export surpluses. Mercantilism therefore implied all kinds of policies of promoting manufacturing. That sector was widely regarded as having more potential for creating wealth than agriculture. This creation of wealth was primarily understood in terms of the state and its government, not the nation: at the heart of concerns lay state finances and state strength rather than national income and public welfare.[4] This connection with state strength also explains whence the name mercantilism comes. Most 'mercantilists' regarded trade as the best means of strengthening the state. The main goal of manufacturing was to sell the manufactured goods abroad. That would not only enable the government of the exporting state to collect more taxes but would also impoverish the country that has to pay for its imports because it has to pay for them in hard cash. In that way government there can collect less taxes. This effect of course is optimal when the actual importing and exporting of goods, especially in the case of shipping, was taken care of as much as possible by fellow countrymen.[5] Measures were taken, like the famous Navigation Acts in Britain, to see to it that this was the case. The following quote made by a certain William Carter in Britain in 1685 synthesizes it all succinctly and clearly:

> If it be from our manufactures alone that the riches of this nation comes, and if it be from our manufacturing chiefly that our shipping is employed, and our mariners bred, if it be from our trading alone, and from the riches which our trading brings in, that his Majesty's customs are raised, and that our fleets have been hitherto built and maintained, and the dominion of the seas hath been preserved, then it is and must be from our manufacture only that our bullion hath been brought in,

---

[2] I just refer to two of their (translated) works: Schmoller, *The Mercantile System*, and Heckscher, *Mercantilism*. For critical comments (in several respects deservedly so) see: Coleman, *Revisions in Mercantilism*; idem, 'Mercantilism revisited', and for nuanced and up-to-date analyses Stern and Wennerlind, *Mercantilism Reimagined*.

[3] For (literature on) the concepts 'competitive advantage' and 'comparative advantage' see Wikipedia.

[4] For mercantilism and state finances see Bonney, 'Early modern theories of state finance'.

[5] For different varieties of mercantilist thinking in which its attention to production and competition clearly comes to the fore see Magnusson, *Mercantilism. The Shaping of an Economic Language*, and idem, *Mercantilism. Critical Concepts in the History of Economics*; Erik Reinert, 'Role of the state' and *How Rich Countries Got Rich*; Sophus Reinert, *Translating Empire*, and Stern and Wennerlind, *Mercantilism Reimagined*. For further information see Chapter 6 notes 9–11.

and that the rents of our nobility and gentry doth depend and are sustained. And therefore it must be granted me, that there is no higher interest in the nation.[6]

In implementing policies like these, state-building went hand in hand with the construction of a national economy. 'Mercantilism' was a double-faced phenomenon: it functioned as a unifying system that 'nationalized' the economic activities in a country by tearing down all barriers to internal, *domestic* trade. It, in the words of Heckscher, 'opposed everything that bound down economic life to a particular place and obstructed trade within the boundaries of a state.'[7] In *foreign* trade, in contrast, it erected many barriers. Underlying this mercantilist development policy, Reinert distinguishes two major principles that, expressed in modern terms, can be described as, first, specializing in sectors of production (of commodities as well as services) with high added value where one can create *increasing returns* and, second, trying to create a setting of *imperfect competition* so that one can influence the market.[8] Here again it is evident that mercantilism is not just a trade policy. It implies a wide range of measures to support production as well. 'Mercantilists' strove for 'improvement' and in that sense assumed that what we now call economic growth would be possible but always in an extremely 'comparative' and thus competitive setting of 'jealousy of trade' where the gains of the one very easily turned into the losses of the other.

As such, mercantilism was a broad European movement, carried by a broad consensus.[9] To keep things manageable, we will focus on the *actual economic policies* of Britain, the country that, probably to the surprise of many readers who tend to associate mercantilism with the France of Colbert or the Prussia of Frederick the Great, happened to be the place where mercantilism originated and the most successful example of its application in practice.[10] With regard to other European countries I only

---

[6]Carter, *The Reply of W.C.*, 49. I found the quotation in Pincus, *1688*, 371.

[7]Heckscher, *Mercantilism, II*, 273.

[8]Reinert, *How Rich Countries Got Rich*, in particular chs 1 to 3 and the Appendices.

[9]There nevertheless were significant differences between various countries, even in Western Europe. France in many respects clearly was a mercantilist country when we look at the policies of its government. But the position of its 'moneyed interests' as compared to the political elite was much weaker there than in Britain. For, in particular, intellectual debates see Terjanian, *Commerce and Its Discontents*. For a comparison of the situation in Great Britain with that in the Dutch Republic, see Ormrod, *Rise of Commercial Empires*. In Central Europe a variety of economic policy by government that often is called 'cameralism' became quite popular. For 'theory' see Tribe, 'Cameralism and the science of government'; idem, *Governing the Economy*, and Wakefield, 'Cameralism'. For the not always very successful 'practice' see Hackl, 'Staatliche Wirtschaftspolitik'; Munch, 'Growth of the modern state', 207–14; Sandgruber, *Österreichische Geschichte*, 87–157, and Wakefield, *Disordered Police State*.

[10]In my text I focus on actual policies; they are what matters for my research questions, not theoretical debates. For an encyclopaedic synthesis of 'British mercantilism' see Magnusson, *Mercantilist Theory and Practice*. For a succinct sketch of mercantilist measures taken by the British government, see Ashworth, *Customs and Excise*; Chang, *Kicking Away the Ladder*, 19–24; O'Brien, 'Mercantilism and imperialism', and Ormrod, *Rise of Commercial Empires*. For recent debates see Stern and Wennerlind, *Mercantilism Reimagined* and *The William and Mary Quarterly* 69, 1 (2012): 3–70. For a brief overview of British mercantilist *trade* policies, see Howe, 'Restoring free trade'; Morgan, 'Mercantilism and the British Empire', and Ormrod, *Rise of Commercial Empires*. For general analyses of the role of the state in economic development in industrializing Britain, see Daunton, *Progress and Poverty*, part five; Harris, 'Government and the economy', and O'Brien, 'Political preconditions'.

want to point out that the Dutch Republic, that other success story when it comes to economic development in Western Europe in the early modern era, also was much more mercantilist than neoclassical economists who equate economic development with the presence of a market economy would want to accept.[11]

What the historian Brisco wrote in 1907 to characterize the economic policy of Robert Walpole (1676–1745), Great Britain's first minister under George I (1714–27), in fact applies to Great Britain's economic policy during the entire period we are discussing here: '(Manufactures) had to be protected at home from competition with foreign finished goods; free exportation of finished articles had to be secured and, where possible, encouragement had to be given by bounty and allowance.'[12] Walpole himself stated: 'It is evident that nothing so much contributes to promote the public well-being as the exportation of manufactured goods and the importation of foreign raw materials.'[13] Mercantilist thinking as a form of economic nationalism was quite popular among the elite: or rather it basically was regarded as self-evident. Whigs as well as Tories, to use these not unproblematic terms, whatever their differences of opinion, after 1688 were convinced that the state had a role to play in economic life and should try and promote prosperity.[14] It was obvious to anyone that in this context prosperity came with power. Daniel Baugh correctly claims that between 1650 and 1750:

> Everyone then responsible for public policy thought that English wealth could not long be sustained without power to defend both trade and the realm, and also thought that England's power to defend could not be long sustained without trade and wealth. The evidence is ubiquitous and consistent. The first place to look is to the opening words of the 1651 and 1660 Navigation Acts. Moreover, in the decades after *The wealth of nations* was published, no one shared Smith's outlook on this question. Power and prosperity could not be separated.[15]

As we have seen before, not even Adam Smith himself endorsed the ideas that Baugh ascribes to him. He too thought that political economy was about wealth and power of the state and he too was in favour of the Navigation Acts.[16] Lord Heldernesse in 1757 in a letter assumed that all would agree with him in the principle:

> We must be merchants, while we are soldiers: that our trade depends upon a proper exertion of our maritime strength – that trade and maritime force depend on each other – and that the riches which are the true resources of this country, depend chiefly upon its commerce.[17]

---

[11]See Davids, 'From de la Court to Vreede', and Klein, 'A new look'. O'Brien considers the Dutch Republic as a successful mercantilist state for at least some hundred to hundred and thirty years. See his 'Study of contrasts', 20.
[12]Brisco, *Economic Policy of Robert Walpole*, 129. I found this quotation in Chang, *Kicking Away the Ladder*, 22.
[13]Chang, *Kicking Away the Ladder*, 21.
[14]See Pincus, *1688*, ch. 12.
[15]Baugh, 'Maritime strength', 188.
[16]See Introduction note 23 and more in general chapters IV ii and IV iii of his magnum opus.
[17]I found this quote in Rodger, 'War as an economic activity', 7.

Things certainly did not change in the following decades. In a memorandum for the consideration of his majesty's ministers, of 31 March 1800, it reads:

> It is obvious that the present strength and pre-eminence of this country is owing to the extent of its resources arising from its commerce and its naval power, which are inseparably connected.[18]

In 1825 political commentator David Robinson claimed that free-trade policies would be a disaster for Britain and sang the following song of praise of protectionism.

> The greatest improvements have been made in our manufactures when they have been the most free from such [foreign] competition. Our cotton manufacturers have made the greatest varieties in their articles, and the greatest reductions in their prices, when it has been perfectly unknown. Our iron and several other articles, which a few years since were greatly inferior to those provided in other countries, have been brought to equal and in some cases to surpass those of all other parts, entirely without such competition. Under a system which studiously prevented such competition, which jealously excluded the foreigner from our home market, we have far outstripped all other nations in manufactures ... we have rendered ourselves the first manufacturing nation in the universe.[19]

Mercantilist policies have only really been dismantled in Britain in the 1840s and 1850s. That the British, and other mercantilist powers, were serious about this *inseparable* connection between power and profit shows in the fact that they did not hesitate to use violence and even wage major wars to protect or further their commerce. We will expand on that further on in this chapter.

Let me first expand some more on the underlying principles of mercantilist policies. As indicated, mercantilism was not just a simple-minded obsession with precious metals. Those scholars who present it as nothing but 'bullionism' are not fair to the mercantilists. Not just because that 'obsession', considering the fundamental importance of bullion for the economies we are discussing here, was not so simple-minded after all, as there existed very good reasons to worry about bullion, but also because mercantilists actually held a much broader view on wealth and its creation. Erik Reinert presents a long list of ways in which a government can support the economy and help in generating wealth. He begins by distinguishing between three roles central government can play, to wit acting as provider of institutions, acting as an institution that takes care of income distribution and, third, acting as promoter of economic growth. He then becomes more specific with regard to that third role by claiming that government might try and do the following: get the nation into the right business, create a comparative advantage in the right business,

---

[18]O'Brien and Engerman, 'Exports and the growth of the British economy', 177. The memorandum was written by Henry Dundas, President of the Board of Control of the East India Company.
[19]Ashworth, *Customs and Excise*, 374–5.

supply infrastructure, set standards, provide skilled labour and entrepreneurship, create demand (especially high-quality demand), lay an emphasis on knowledge and education, provide a legal system and finally act as an entrepreneur and capitalist of the last resort.[20] European 'policy-makers' in the early modern era used almost all of these strategies.

Nor was mercantilism in practice simply rent seeking. It is one-sided, and in various respects simply wrong, to look at the protective measures that were taken in 'the age of mercantilism' as nothing but means to facilitate rent seeking via collusion between central government and various monopolists, with all parties involved only acting for their own benefit. Of course, there were patent examples of rent seeking – for example, in the selling of certain monopolies. But government was not simply, as Marx and Engels claimed:, 'a committee for managing the common affairs of the whole bourgeoisie' – if only because there were not many such 'common' affairs.[21] The interests of the agrarian elites in the countryside, the financial capitalists in the City of London, the rising industrial entrepreneurs and the chartered trading companies, for example, could be very different and even conflicting. The same goes for the interests of the woollen sector and the cotton sector, of industries producing for the domestic market and industries producing for export, old industries and new industries, chartered companies and private traders, the port of London and other ports. Moreover, and very importantly: the state also had interests of its *own* that quite often were defined primarily in terms of power rather than profit.

Ormrod has convincingly shown that in Britain's government policy, at least for the period he covers, there occurred a shift from supporting specific interest groups in various monopolistic organizations to trying to support 'Britain incorporated' and to do things in the interest of the national economy and the nation.[22] What indeed is striking in the British case are the permanent references by all sorts of people in all sorts of debates to 'the nation', 'the commonwealth', 'the state', 'the common good', 'the national interest' and the like that are considered as 'conceptually distinct from the summation of the private interests of England's population'.[23] Of course, it was never easy to decide what exactly that interest would be and how to successfully promote it. Of course, there were differences of opinion, conflicts and changes over time, as a rule described in terms of an opposition between 'Tories' and 'Whigs'. In highly simplified terms one might say that Tories tended to be 'landed interests', more prone to regarding military prowess as the basis of economic strength, more interested in empire and dominion, less opposed to Crown and Church, absolutism and monopoly, and overall more 'mercantilist'. For Whigs, who more often were moneyed interests, wealth in the end did not so much reside in having land but in labour as productive capacity and in trade. They valued industry and trade as motors of prosperity over land and dominions and tended to

---

[20]Reinert, 'Role of the state'. Reinert also refers to the fact that government would have to look to it that real wages were high. As he himself correctly points out, this particular goal appeared on the state's agenda only quite late.

[21]Marx and Engels, *Communist Manifesto*, 82.

[22]Ormrod, *Rise of Commercial Empires*.

[23]See Pincus, *1688*, ch. 12, in particular 396–9.

think less in terms of zero-sum games, in which growth for all was impossible and a very strong and militarily active state quintessential.[24] These differences of opinion and emphasis certainly existed but we should not make too much of them when it comes to the questions that interest us here: it was obvious to all that government should protect the national economy.

With the Napoleonic Wars, patriotic Tory militarism certainly received a boost but more 'liberal' Whigs continued to challenge the idea of Britain as a military nation and even began to do so increasingly, praising inventors and discoverers more than military heroes. For them the economy was at the basis of Britain's strength, not military prowess. In 1793 James Currie, Fellow of Royal Society, claimed that Britain had prospered '*in spite* [italics added] of the wretched politics of its rulers.'[25] In the eyes of liberal Whigs, Britain would never have been able to spend as much as it did in its fights against Napoleon without additional income thanks to industry and commerce.[26] In their opinion it was machinery and mechanical invention 'which more than any other cause, had raised this kingdom to its high rank among the commercial nations of the world.'[27] In 1834 Lord Macaulay, a Whig historian par excellence, would write that the industry of individuals had made the country 'richer and richer' *despite* four decades of Tory 'mismanagement' since the 1790s.[28] In the context of such debates, the question whether free trade and free enterprise or protectionism would be best for Great Britain became more topical.[29]

All the talk about 'the national economy' and 'the nation' that one comes across in discussions about the nation's political economy must not be interpreted as if the views of the ordinary people prevailed or were seriously taken into account. Post-1688 Great Britain continued to be far too much of an elitist, undemocratic society for that. But what its government stood for, and was expected to stand for, often was *more* than just very specific private interests. Specific interest groups of course were quite influential but economic policies primarily were about strengthening 'the economy' in a quite specific sense: the strengthening of that economy should in any case also strengthen the *state*. Mercantilism here was *not* per se a policy of creating economic growth, nor was it a policy aimed at industrializing the country, at least not in the modern meaning of that word. The concept of (modern) economic growth as it is defined nowadays (i.e. as the sustained and substantial increase of real income per capita in a certain society) was not, as is often claimed, unknown, at least in principle, but such growth definitely was not regarded as something normal. Whatever views one may have had on the *sources of* and *possibilities for* growth, in the sphere of international competition the idea that one could only increase one's wealth over the back of one's competitors *in practice* almost always prevailed. Or to put it in contemporary terms: 'the increase and wealth of all states, is

---

[24]See Pincus, *1688*, ch. 12 for debates in the seventeenth and the beginning of the eighteenth centuries, and Macleod, *Heroes of Invention*, passim, for debates since the 1750s.

[25]I found this quotation in MacLeod, *Heroes of Invention*, 69–70.

[26]MacLeod, *Heroes of Invention*, 95.

[27]MacLeod, *Heroes of Invention*, 102.

[28]I found this quotation in MacLeod, *Heroes of Invention*, 138.

[29]MacLeod, *Heroes of Invention*, 137–8.

evermore made upon the foreigner'.[30] Industry in the modern sense of the word of course was unknown but elaborating mercantilist policies did in practice imply numerous measures to support manufacturing, as we will see later on.

Neither were mercantilist policies as such about enriching *the people*. In many cases one feels tempted to say: 'On the contrary'. When certain social arrangements based on the concept of a 'moral economy' got in the way of the ideal of strengthening the state and the economy, they were ignored and often even attacked by ruling elites.[31] Think in the case of Britain, for example, of the enclosures or the liberalizing of the grain trade that allowed merchants to buy and sell at times and places as they pleased. Mercantilist policies were not meant to protect regional or local interests: national considerations, that is, *raison d'état* prevailed. Mercantilist states were warfare states rather than welfare states. Nor was they meant to protect labour. With the passing of time, government became less opposing and even 'neutral' or 'positive', when it came to the introduction of implements or methods of production that might deprive ordinary people of work.[32] On top of that it always put a lot of emphasis on disciplining the labour force, as a rule choosing the side of capital in case of conflicts between 'capital' and 'labour'.

The 'mercantile system' was *not* meant to provide for 'security and wealth' or 'the livelihood' of the 'ordinary populace', a goal that was very high on the agenda of Qing rulers. Reading British mercantilist thinkers one can find telling quotes like this one by Arthur Young from 1771: 'Everyone but an idiot knows that the lower classes must be kept poor or they will never be industrious', or this one by Bernard Mandeville, who in 1714 claimed that in order that society might be happy 'it is a requisite that great numbers of them [i.e. the labouring classes] be poor'.[33] William Temple (1628–99) was even more explicit: 'The only way to make the poor industrious is to lay them under the necessity of labouring all the time they can spare from meals and sleep in order to procure the necessities of life'. He claimed that the typical labourer when given 'high wages and plenty' would live on 'great heaps of fat beer or bacon, and eat perhaps till he spewed; and then having gorged and gotten dead drunk, lie down like a pig, and snore till he was fresh'.[34] During the eighteenth century we see gradual changes in these respects. More people started thinking about wages in terms of the carrot of incentives instead of the stick of necessities.[35] Moreover there developed a more positive enlightened view on free labour in the sense that it would be a fundamental right of every person to exercise his labour power completely at his own discretion.[36]

---

[30] Pincus, *1688*, 375.

[31] For the concept 'moral economy', see Thompson, 'Moral economy'.

[32] See for this gradual switch, Berg, *Machinery Question* and MacLeod, *Inventing the Industrial Revolution*, chs 9 and 11.

[33] See for these quotations, Furniss, *Position of the Labourer*, 118. See also Lis and Soly, *Worthy Efforts*, ch. 7.

[34] For these quotations see Ashworth, *Customs and Excise*, 61, where one can also find the original references.

[35] See Coats, 'Economic thought'; idem, 'Changing attitudes'; De Vries, 'Industrial Revolution and the Industrious Revolution'; Hatcher, 'Labour, leisure and economic thought'; Lis and Soly, *Worthy Efforts*, ch. 7, and Wiles, 'Theory of wages'.

[36] See for this 'enlightened' view Lis and Soly, *Worthy Efforts*, 494–509. Considering my comments on unfree labour in Great Britain in the following paragraphs, these ideas apparently did not have much impact on actual labour relations.

Considering the often very harsh policies in dealing with 'ordinary working people', it is striking that Britain went through some really major upheavals, like its industrialization and various major and long wars, without a social revolution that eclipsed its establishment. Apparently there was sufficient national cohesion in Britain's society – and sufficient 'hard' *and* 'soft' power in the hands of government – to weather even quite serious storms. The systematic effort by government to see to it that there was a system of poor relief would not have been without effect in this respect.

Some comments on mercantilism and labour in Great Britain

What kind of measures did British governments take to strengthen their country with respect to other countries? Let me begin with some comments on the domestic situation, in particular with regard to labour. For a country to be internationally competitive its labour costs must not become too high. In Britain, nominal wages were very high but apparently they were not internationally uncompetitive. Increasingly 'the market' was supposed to take care of that competitiveness. That fitted in perfectly with the general tendency to indeed turn Britain into a free-market economy when it comes to *domestic*, internal exchange. But even at home government did not refrain from intervening in, especially, what in modern terms one might call the 'labour market' when it thought there were good, 'national' reasons to do so.

In the grand narrative with regard to the rise of the West that I am trying to counter in this text the emergence of Western capitalism and industrialization are often almost automatically identified with the creation of 'free labour'. Some figures to show how important *un*-free labour was *in* and *for* Great Britain, that 'cradle of capitalism' and the world's first industrial nation, might therefore be very informative.[37] I will give them in the coming paragraphs without pretending to be exhaustive. I just want to give an impression of orders of magnitude to bring home my point that even there a *surprisingly large* part of labour was unfree. On a global scale, un-free labour definitely was the rule, not the exception. According to Arthur Young, in 1772, only 4 per cent of the earth's labour force was free. The remaining 96 per cent, in his words, laboured as slaves, serfs, indentured servants, or vassals.[38] Looked at from a global perspective, there are good reasons to assume that the importance of un-free labour *increased* rather than *decreased* over the entire early modern period. Overall, however, it is striking how important un-free labour was in 'Enlightened' Europe and even in Britain in the eighteenth century.

The law, overall, in Britain was quite friendly to 'employers' and quite harsh to 'employees'. One must not forget that even though the idea that all Englishmen – and that indeed meant all English *men* – were 'free-born', may have been quite popular, free labour in the modern sense of the word still was far from normal. The terms of many contracts were quite one-sided. Even labour that was regarded as 'free' at the time, as a

---

[37]For the expression 'cradle of capitalism' see Macfarlane, 'Cradle of capitalism'.
[38]Young, *Political Essays*, 20–1.

rule had to deal with all kinds of restrictions that nowadays in the Western world would be considered unacceptable in labour relations. Steinfeld in his book on the invention of free labour in English and American law focuses on the nineteenth century, as he thinks that it was only during that century that free labour as we define it emerged.[39] In my view he is right. Let me first refer to some countrywide *general* regulations that had their constraining effects on the 'free' functioning of the labour market. An actual labour *market* implies a mobile labour force. But in the early modern era such mobility was hard to square with the age-old principle that people had to be settled and belong to a certain place and group. It was only all too often associated with vagrancy, poverty and crime. The so-called 'laws of settlement', that continued to be applied in one way or another till the first decades of the nineteenth century, could be a serious impediment to free migration. Originally they were meant to prevent people who were 'likely to be chargeable', i.e. people who for one reason or another might someday need relief, from settling or staying somewhere else than in their 'own' parish. That proved to be too strict. So after some time in practice only those who actually needed support could be sent back and then only to their parish of origin, which meant people who were on the road needed a certificate that proved where they in the end belonged. In special cases exemptions were provided, as was the possibility to transfer money instead of forcing people to go back. Barriers against labour mobility thus were certainly weakened with the passing of time and in the end they were not effective. But they existed and for paupers, it long continued to be difficult to move to another place.[40]

When looking at forms of more direct intervention in labour *relationships* there is the so-called Statute of Artificers, which dated from 1563 and dealt with, among other things, apprenticeship clauses and public control over the movement of labour. It was only officially repealed in 1814. Under that Statute in so-called enumerated trades young people were held in apprenticeship for several years and treated as children, when they clearly had become adults. The 1814 reform, usually presented as a sign that the labour market was now much more 'liberalized', in fact had no effect on the contractual aspects of labour relationships. On the whole, work-related criminal sanctions were *reinforced* between 1720 and 1850. Several laws were adopted to strengthen criminal sanctions in the event of breach of contract. Penalties were also stipulated for those who refused a job. Wage earners were considered as domestics and were, above all, supposed to provide a service. The term 'servant', from the sixteenth century onwards, was increasingly used as indication for *any* sort of wage earner, including journeymen, artificers and other workmen. The labour of such servants was usually conceived as a master's property.[41] The number of domestic servants, in the strict sense of the term, overwhelmingly female, was huge. In 1851 there were some 900,000 of them, and for the very beginning of the nineteenth century we have an estimate by Patrick Colquhoun

---

[39]See Stanziani, 'Legal status'; Steinfeld, *Invention of Free Labour* and idem, *Coercion, Contract and Free Labour*.
[40]For information on background and practice of 'the principle of settlement', that was put into an Act in 1662, see Daunton, *Progress and Poverty*, 459–63.
[41]In all my comments on the position of labour in Britain I am strongly paraphrasing Stanziani, 'Legal status'.

there would have been some 800,000. That certainly is too high but if we were to count all the women doing waged domestic work, it may not have been too far off the mark.[42] Their position too, although they worked for wages and on the basis of a contract, was not that of free labour in the current sense of the word.[43] That basically was the case for almost all people working for others.

The modern concept of a contract as a way of expressing reciprocal obligations on a voluntary basis was very exceptional before 1880. Despite the existence of contracts, even 'free' labour for a long time continued to be considered the property of the employer. When employers claimed breach of contract many forms of 'free labour' actually continued to be or even increasingly became subject to criminal law. In such a case jail could ensue for workers but *not* for masters. A similar inequality also shows in the Combination Acts that were in force till 1824, and even then were only slightly relaxed. They prohibited labour to 'combine' in order to raise its wages, whereas 'combining' for employers in any case in practice was very easy. Industrialization in Great Britain in its early stages certainly was *not* characterized by a growing predominance of free labour. Great Britain did *not* industrialize earlier than the rest of Western Europe because of its 'free labour'. The opposite might even be true: 'Nowhere else (than in England) was national labour legislation enforced so consistently and for so long.'[44] It would take till the 1870s and 1880s before the rights of labour were seriously and structurally improved.

Factory workers, the embodiment *par excellence* of the Industrial Revolution and of the new 'free labour', were only a very small fraction of all working people in Great Britain.[45] Moreover, a very large part of the people working for wages in Britain's factories, before and in the beginning of industrialization, consisted of women and children. Their position, especially as members of a household, by definition was one of restricted freedom. Out of a factory workforce of 344,000 in Britain in 1832, only 26 per cent were males over eighteen. Females over eighteen comprised 30 per cent, while males and females under eighteen made up the remaining 44 per cent[46] Of the total workforce in cotton and wool factories over the period 1835–70, only between 31 and 35 per cent were adult males.[47] Actually, wage labour was long more common in the countryside than in towns.

I have already mentioned that, in the eyes of a modern observer, the freedom even of labour that was regarded as free at the time and that had a formal contract left much to be desired. Very often – for example in the case of orphans in care of the state, people working in so-called 'poor houses' or in so-called 'bridewells' or houses of correction, pauper apprentices, collier serfs, men pressed into service with the Royal Navy or

---

[42]See Mathias, *First Industrial Nation*, 260 and for Colquhoun's estimate and its (im-)plausibility, Steedman, *Labours Lost*, 37–8.

[43]See Steedman, *Labours Lost*.

[44]Lis and Soly, *Worthy Efforts*, 444.

[45]See e.g. Mathias, *First Industrial Nation*, 260–1.

[46]Caton, *Politics of Progress*, 537.

[47]Evans, *Forging of the Modern State*, 423. See for further information, in chronological order, Berg, 'What difference did women's work make'; Humphries, 'Lure of aggregates', and Allen, 'High wage economy'.

convicts who were simply put to work – one cannot even speak of a contract, in the sense of a voluntary agreement between two free parties, at all. The number of people put away in workhouses or poor houses amounted to 90,000 in 1776 and 123,000 in 1850. There can be no doubt that many of them, if not the majority, were *not*, as originally had been intended, able-bodied, full-time employed adults. But these places nevertheless housed a substantial labour force.[48] Several thousands of people – in the 1770s some 9,000 to 13,000 per year – were put to work in bridewells.[49] In the first decades of industrialization, thousands of orphans or children from workhouses worked as pauper apprentices for mill owners who practically owned them. They were bound by contract to work at their mills until they became adults. By the late 1790s, for example, about a third of the workers in the cotton industry were pauper apprentices.[50] In Scottish pits, until the last quarter of the eighteenth century, one could find so-called 'collier serfs', tied to the pits for life.[51]

People who joined the army or the navy quite often also did not do so voluntarily.[52] We already pointed at that in general terms.[53] In Britain the conditions could vary: undoubtedly some people joined the services because of lust for adventure. Many, however, were driven by poverty and then often seduced or simply misled and many, in particular in the navy, were actually forced to serve. Poverty and lack of alternatives had always been and continued to be the most important reasons to 'voluntarily' choose for the military. In 1846, two-thirds of the army's recruits in Britain enlisted because they were destitute. Not by accident, many soldiers came from Ireland. The majority of those who did enlist did so in an alcoholic haze. The number of people needed by the armed forces was immense and was only increased further by the large number of casualties and desertions. Therefore every form of inducement and coercion was seen fit to provide a steady flow of men to compensate for the huge losses that were normal in army and especially navy. The bounty paid by the army to recruiting officers was much higher than that paid by the navy. The Royal Navy would not have been able to find enough sailors without impressment: the forcible recruitment of seamen and all males between the ages of 18 and 55 who 'used the sea' to man its fleets in wartime. This policy was only abolished in 1833. Let me again give some figures. During the Seven Years War (1756–63) roughly 185,000 men were enlisted at least once on one of its ships. That is 9 per cent of all adult males: probably half of them were impressed. That would be some 90,000 men.[54] In the period from 1776 to 1783, about one-third of the people serving in the Royal Navy, some 80,000 people, had been pressed into

---

[48]Many poor houses took care of the elderly and the young who were *not* able to look after themselves, see Daunton, *Progress and Poverty*, 454–5.

[49]Patriquin, *Agrarian Capitalism*, 109.

[50]See e.g. Humphries, *Childhood and Child Labour*.

[51]Daunton, *Progress and Poverty*, 225.

[52]For the information with regard to the British Army in the following paragraphs see Higgs, *Information State*, 134–44; James, *Warrior Race*, 292–316, and Way, 'Klassenkrieg'. For information with regard to the Royal Navy, see Earle, *Sailors*, ch. 12; Frykman, 'Seeleute'; Rodger, *Command of the Ocean*, and Rogers, *Press Gang*.

[53]See pages 77–8.

[54]Rogers, 'Vagrancy', 107–8.

their job.[55] The policy had staunch supporters. According to one of them, it would free the nation of 'idle and reprobate vermin by converting them into a body of the most industrious people, and even, becoming the very nerves of our state'.[56] The number of people needed was such that there were bound to be problems in finding enough sailors for the Royal Navy as well as for the merchant fleet. In times of crisis and acute shortages, the merchant fleet could offer wages that were substantially higher than the wages of sailors on men-of-war and it tried, often successfully, to exempt its sailors in order to protect commerce. This often drove recruiters to look for recruits among casual workers and the unemployed, felons, criminals, convicts and former rebels. Foreign birth did not disqualify a sailor from impressment. According to the government of the United States, there were still some 6,000 of its citizens in Britain's navy in 1807. It claimed they had all been impressed to serve.[57] The British Army also could be desperate for men. That shows in the fact that it bought 10 per cent of all slaves imported into the British West Indies. Many people not only did not join the services voluntarily: they also found out it was almost impossible to leave. Most recruits were induced to pledge themselves to an unlimited service, which until 1829 usually meant twenty-one years in the infantry and twenty-four years in the cavalry. In the navy in principle service also was unlimited. An attempt in 1806 to introduce a limited service for only seven years did not work in practice.[58] Whoever entered the world of the military became subject to very harsh discipline and was completely at the mercy of his superiors. It was up to these superiors to decide whether one might leave the forces. They tended to do so at the end of war when many soldiers and sailors were discharged and sent home.

Britain's armed forces were a major productive force. They functioned as a collective of 'military workers' who defended and expanded Britain's economy. Overseas they, moreover, also often performed more than military tasks and were used to build roads, fortresses and so on. Colonial governments all over Europe, if and when possible, used soldiers as a cheap, docile and *un-free* labour force. It has been estimated that more than 6 million European soldiers were involved in empire-building in the period from 1815 to 1900. A substantial number of them stayed behind in the colonies. More than 2 million Russian soldiers crossed the Ural. What of course specifically interests us here is that the number of British soldiers that at one time or another during this period was active overseas amounted to more than a million.[59] It would be a major mistake to not regard military labour as *productive* labour. That major mistake is often made.[60] Analysing and understanding the strength of Britain's economy in the very long eighteenth century without systematic reference to the military simply is not feasible.

The many thousands of indentured labourers working in various parts of the British Empire, according to modern standards, can hardly count as 'free labour' either. Of

---

[55]Rodger, *Command of the Ocean*, 396.
[56]Rogers, 'Vagrancy', 108. The original quotation is in Philonauta, *The Sailor's Happiness* (London 1751), 19–20.
[57]Thomson, *Mercenaries, Pirates & Sovereigns*, 31.
[58]Hall, *British Strategy*, 4.
[59]Bosma, 'European colonial soldiers', table 1.
[60]For a general, global introduction see Zürcher, *Fighting for a Living*.

the total number of Europeans that immigrated between 1700 and 1775 to the thirteen colonies that were to become the United States, 104,000 were indentured servants, 52,000 convicts and prisoners, and only 152,000 free people.[61] Between one-half and two-thirds of *all* white immigrants to the American colonies after the 1630s came under indenture. Of the people who settled in Virginia in the seventeenth century 75 per cent or more were servants.[62] The status of indentured labour often was not far removed from that of serfs. There were many of them. According to Stanziani, for the whole of Europe till the 1830s, some 300,000 people could be considered as such.[63] Then there were convicts who were forced to provide labour. Nearly one thousand convicts a year left Britain in the half-century after 1718.[64] The British exported some 50,000 convicts, in particular from Ireland, to their North American colonies. When that was no longer possible, Australia became the favourite destination for their deported convicts. Between 1788 and 1868, no fewer than 165,000 were sent to Australia to perform hard labour. Often convicts were transported from one part of the empire to another. Between 1787 and 1825 some 4,000 to 6,000 of them were sent from India to Bengkulen and in the period between 1790 and 1860 some 15,000 from India to the Strait Settlements.[65] We already referred to the policy of banishing people. That expression has a 'political' connotation. It often simply meant sending poor and unemployed people abroad, preferably to colonies. That policy also existed in Britain, although with the passing of time it became much less popular.[66]

And then of course, as the full opposite of free labour, there is slavery. There also were some people *in* Great Britain that one might call 'slaves'. In the early seventeenth century, many Indians who had been forcibly conscripted in the Royal Navy entered England. Many others were simply given to Britons to serve in their families. In the eighteenth century their condition became quite similar to that of chattel slaves in Africa. They worked without wages, could be resold and there was hardly any chance they would ever become free again. When Britain's Parliament tried to better control the East India Company, new regulations were enforced that obliged the company to take care of the maintenance of these slaves and provide them with a safe passage back to India. Michael Fisher estimates that around 10,000 servants/slaves were shipped back to India between 1800 and 1813 on the expense of the East India

---

[61]Fogleman, 'From slaves, convicts, and servants to free passengers', 71, table A.3.
[62]These figures are based on an estimate by Galenson, *White Servitude*, 3–4. For more general information see Emmer, *Colonialism and Migration*, and more recently Christopher, Pybus and Rediker, *Many Middle Passages*. For figures with regard to the end of the period under discussion, and later, see Northrup, *Indentured Labour*.
[63]Stanziani, 'Legal status', 381.
[64]Eltis, 'Cultural roots', 26.
[65]See for information Bosma, 'European colonial soldiers'; Meredith and Oxley, 'Condemned to the colonies', and Yang, 'Indian convict workers'. The British were not the only Europeans putting convicts or surplus labour to work somewhere in their empire. Bosma claims the number of convicts who were sent from Europe overseas or across the Ural during the nineteenth century would have been over 1 million. See page 319 of his article. Compare, however, his note 6 on that page.
[66]See Morgan and Rushton, *Banishment in the early Atlantic World*, and Swingen, 'Labor: employment, colonial servitude, and slavery'. In Russia more than 750,000 people were exiled to Siberia between 1832 and 1887. See Bosma, 'European colonial soldiers', note 6.

Company.[67] But as a rule and rightly so, talking about slaves in this context means talking about the Atlantic. This of course is not the place to discuss the functioning and importance of Atlantic slavery. For such discussion I refer the reader to the literature.[68] I here only want to add two comments. The first one being that one should not forget that Africa and Asia also had huge numbers of slave labour from which the British economy might profit, as it certainly did in the Indian case.[69] The second is that, apart from these 'real' slaves, Indian labour was directly exploited by the East India Company under conditions that resembled those of slaves or serfs far more than those of free labour. With the disappearance of that company, labour conditions did not necessarily improve. The situation on many of the new tea plantations in parts of India like Assam was appalling. Tens of thousands of coolies were working there in conditions that in practice were almost undistinguishable from a very harsh form of slavery, a situation that for many persisted until the beginning of the twentieth century.[70] Even this cursory overview shows that un-free labour was of fundamental importance to the economy of Great Britain at the time of its take-off. 'Capitalist' Britain profited directly or indirectly from an enormous amount of un-free labour, at home, on sea and abroad. Freedom and unfreedom as described here are legal conditions and therefore also 'matters of the state' and deserve to be discussed here.

British trade: Prohibitions, tariffs and support

In the last instance, mercantilists wanted to promote the production of goods that could be sold abroad. Measures meant to concretely and directly promote certain kinds of production and trade are too numerous to mention, but I will refer to a couple of very telling examples. Famous, or if you want notorious, are the various so-called Navigation Acts. These in fact were British acts, as Scotland before 1707 and Ireland, for most of the time, were not profiting from them. The most important ones were enacted in 1651, 1660, 1663 and 1673, basically to thwart the Dutch. They were only repealed in 1849.[71] In the course of time, they included, among others, regulations like the following. The coastal trade (of Britain) was limited to English-owned ships. Imports from Europe of so-called 'enumerated' articles such as flax and wine had to be carried in ships owned in England or the producing country. There was a ban on the import of goods such as timber and tobacco through Holland or Germany, and long-distance import trades from Asia, Africa and America were confined to English ships which came directly from the country of growth or port of shipment. The trade

---

[67]Fisher, *Counterflows to Colonialism*, and idem, 'Bound for Britain'.
[68]See for references my *Escaping Poverty*, 253–62.
[69]See e.g. Major, *Slavery, Abolitionism and Empire*.
[70]See Moxham, *Tea. Addiction, Exploitation and Empire*, chs 3 and 4, and Macfarlane and Macfarlane, *Green Gold*, chs 10 and 11.
[71]See Harper, *English Navigation Acts*. The term 'Navigation Acts' in fact is used to refer to a whole set of acts. Therefore one can also come across references to Acts of, for example, 1662 or 1696.

of the colonies was limited to English shipping and exports of an ever expanding list of enumerated colonial products had to be sent to England before they were re-exported to Europe.[72]

There were many other laws interfering with foreign trade or at least regulating it. Some imports were completely prohibited. For example, there were laws prohibiting colonies to produce manufactured goods that might compete with manufactures produced in Britain. Here one might think of regulations that prohibited the export of woollen products from the colonies into Britain. I have already referred to the way in which Irish production of woollens and their export was thwarted. Similar measures were taken with regard to the American colonies. In 1700, a ban was issued on the import of dyed and printed calicoes and silks from Asia; in 1721 a total ban was granted on the importing of Indian calicoes for sale in Britain itself. This stimulated re-exports and the production of fustians – a cloth that is a mix of linen and cotton – and of cotton cloth in Britain.[73] Interestingly enough in the context of this book, porcelain imports from China were not prohibited. They were, however, subject to a tax that helped in building up production of domestic alternatives.

We did discuss taxes, including customs, quite extensively in a previous chapter. But we did so first and foremost in terms of the amounts of money involved. That is too narrow an approach. Taxation, overall, can be a powerful economic tool. It can redistribute wealth by targeting specific groups of producers, consumers or distributors. It can influence the price of products or activities, sometimes by making them so expensive as to almost banish them completely, just as it can subsidize or at least support other products or activities. It can redefine taste when it is collected on consumption – it is not by accident that there always were fierce debates in Britain about whether certain kinds of goods should be taxed or not and in particular whether government should tax 'necessities'. At the level of production, it can specify and police a commodity's ingredients and manufacturing process. It can be a major factor in setting all kinds of standards for, for example, quality, measures, packing and so on. It can influence scale and concentration of productive activities.

In mercantilist Britain, fiscal policy indeed became part and parcel of a much broader economic policy. It was constantly debated, assessed and changed in broad public debates.[74] Britain's custom duties, for example, originally were collected for fiscal rather than protective reasons. But with the passing of time they increasingly were used to also manipulate trade to the advantage of Britain – that is, as a means to support and promote (certain) domestic industries.[75] High customs could, for example, protect and nurture domestic infant industries and discourage imports. The levying of customs duties increasingly became part and parcel of the mercantilist project of protecting and supporting 'Britain Incorporated'.[76] Britain's policy – again – was somewhat exceptional.

---

[72]See for these and many other examples Daunton, *Progress and Poverty*, ch. 20.

[73]O'Brien, Griffiths and Hunt, 'Political components'.

[74]In this paragraph I heavily draw on Ashworth, *Customs and Excise*.

[75]See for this change Davis, 'Rise of protection'.

[76]More will be said on that later on. See pages 343–4.

Bosher, for example, when comparing France's policies with those of Britain writes that France 'valued the customs for their financial yields. It treated them primarily as a tax rather than an instrument of economic policy.'[77] This must not be taken to imply Britain's government would not have been interested in the income it collected via customs and excises. It of course was and had to be, as the sums of money involved were huge.

This kind of protectionism too was not confined to what many would like to describe as the bad old days of mercantilism *before* Adam Smith. In the 1820s, for example, the average tariff rate for imported manufactured goods was between 45 and 55 per cent.[78] It was only after 1850, and even then only quite temporarily, that Britain really became a free-trading nation. Overall, its tariffs in the first half of the nineteenth century were so high – *higher* for example than in France – and continued to be high for so long that any explanation of the first industrial revolution by reference to the existence or emergence of a free-trade economy is extremely improbable.[79] When Britain's economy took off, the country definitely was not a free trader in matters of international trade. There can be no doubt that many producers and traders profited from protectionism. More in general, protectionism need not be a bad thing for economic development. There is sufficient proof that its effects depend on the circumstances and the kind and duration of protective measures.[80]

Let me give a couple of specific examples of how the customs were used in a policy to protect certain interests. Sometimes their use was clearly political. Overall, for example, tariffs on French wines were virtually prohibitive from the last quarter of the seventeenth century onwards. They were all but banned from British markets, as Britain's

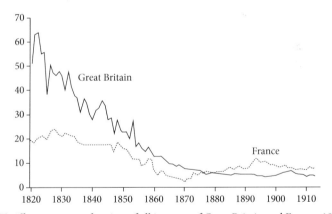

Graph 14 Tariff revenues as a fraction of all imports of Great Britain and France, 1820–1914.

Source: Nye, *War, Wine, and Taxes,* 4.

---

[77]Bosher, *Single Duty Project,* 95.
[78]Bairoch, *Economics and World History,* 40, table 3.3.
[79]For a general overview of British tariffs and other forms of interference in foreign trade and a comparison with the situation in France see Nye, *War, Wine, and Taxes,* ch. 1.
[80]There apparently is 'bad' and 'good' protectionism. See for further explanation my *Escaping Poverty,* 288.

government was not keen on supporting its archenemy's economy. Port wines from Britain's semi-colony Portugal were treated much more leniently.[81] The tariff weapon was used quite discriminately. The tax income collected on regulated Asian trade goods, for example, for the period 1765–1812, described by Javier Cuenca-Esteban, was much bigger than might be expected considering the amounts and total values involved. The trade in those goods seldom employed more than 3 per cent of British tonnage. But it brought 17 per cent of total tax revenue on imports retained for home consumption and 24 per cent of net customs and excise revenues on worldwide imports.[82]

There were policies that were clearly in favour of certain interest groups, at home or abroad. Owners of sugar plantations in the British West Indies in that respect are a notorious example: in the 1750s, sugar was 50 per cent *more* expensive in Britain than on the Continent because of preferential treatment for West Indian landlords.[83] Actually between 1768 and 1782 all imports from the British West Indies – except ginger! – were sold in Britain at prices that were above the world market price because of preferential treatment for West Indian landlords[84] In the 1820s and 1830s, the fact that West Indian sugar planters and refiners received preferential treatment over their East Indian colleagues still was cause for heated debates.[85] Till 1845, colonial sugar paid 25s. 3d. per hundredweight, foreign free labour sugar 35s. 9d. In 1845, these taxes were cut to 14s. and 23s. 4d., at a loss to the Exchequer of £1,330,000 a year.[86] The tea trade of the East India Company also profited from protection, at the expense of Britain's tea drinkers. Taxes on tea, to which we already referred earlier, were notorious. In the 1770s, average tea prices (i.e. sales prices of the East India Companies in England and the Dutch Republic) were all but identical. In the 1820s, Dutch prices had decreased by two-thirds, English prices by only one-quarter. According to John Crawfurd, a famous Scottish Orientalist, over the period from 1819 to 1829 British subjects had been paying nearly twice as much for their tea as those who had purchased it on the American market. In 1830, in a report of the Select Committee on the Affairs of the East India Company and the trade between Great Britain, the East Indies and China, experts claimed that the East India Company monopoly on the tea trade with China led to between £1 million and £2.6 million in extra costs for the public.[87] The end of its monopoly did not immediately, as might be expected, lower overall prices.

Monopolies of course are a very patent form of protection of a specific group of economic agents against competitors. They did not all but disappear in Great Britain as institutionalists like Acemoglu and Robinson like to suggest but never actually show.[88]

---

[81]For Britain's policies with regard to French wines see Nye, *War, Wine, and Taxes*, ch. 3.

[82]Cuenca-Esteban, 'Fiscal dimensions'.

[83]Thomas and McCloskey, 'Overseas trade and empire', 98.

[84]Thomas and McCloskey, 'Overseas trade and empire', 98.

[85]Kumagai, *Breaking into the Monopoly*, 207.

[86]Burnett, *Plenty and Want*, 23–4.

[87]For these data see Kumagai, *Breaking into the Monopoly*, 139, 150 note 112 and 208–9. For Crawfurd's calculation see Crawfurd, *Chinese Monopoly Examined*, 87. Crawfurd was a fierce opponent of the East India Company.

[88]See their *Why Nations Fail*, ch. 7.

They of course will often have implied extra costs for consumers and may have hampered improving efficiency. Tariff policies were sometimes used with the same goal of protecting specific economic agents. The interests assembled in the East India Company that wanted to protect their tea, and those of the owners of sugar plantations in the Caribbean that were not in favour of seeing coffee planters using more of the scarce land for growing coffee, managed to influence tax policy, at least during the eighteenth century, in such a way that it was more favourable for them than for coffee growers.[89] Whether one would drink tea or coffee thus also was influenced by politics. As was the choice of what coffee one might drink. In the nineteenth century colonial coffee was taxed less than foreign coffee. In 1842 the tax rate was fixed at 4d. per pound for colonial coffee and 8d., lowered two years later to 6d., for foreign coffee.[90] By the first quarter of the nineteenth century, the British government imposed duties of approximately 100 per cent on all foreign timber while colonial timber was accepted at nominal rates. The prices of timber from the Baltic and Scandinavia were artificially raised to such an extent that in every year from 1816 to 1846, Canadian timber accounted for at least 60 per cent and in most years for over 75 per cent of all un-sawn timber imports into Britain despite the far longer distance in shipping required to transport timber from Upper and Lower Canada than from Scandinavia or the Baltic states.[91]

And then of course there is protection of interests at home. We already saw how wool interests were protected against foreign competition. That may well have enabled the rise of a domestic British cotton industry, but it of course made life more expensive and restricted choices for British consumers. This policy too lasted longer than is often thought. In 1830, for example, an excise on printed calicoes was still in existence.[92] Tariffs on imported iron increased no less than fivefold between 1688 and 1759.[93] How effective the Corn Laws from 1815, meant to prevent the import of cheap grain into Britain, have actually been has always been hotly debated. They in any case were only officially repealed in 1846. The fact that in 1722 all export duties on British goods were abolished does not mean that exports were not interfered with. There was a long tradition of giving export bounties and drawbacks to encourage exports and re-exports.[94] Such re-exports were very important for Britain's economy.[95] Certain exports were simply prohibited. The prohibition of exporting textile machines and some other devices was only lifted in 1843. Between 1719 and 1825 emigration of artisans and artificers was officially forbidden. To give one example of taxes on exports: while total output of all coalmines could even have doubled between 1790 and 1815, and its real prices in Britain, except London, were falling, taxes on coal exports were jacked up by 70 per cent.[96]

---

[89]Smith, 'Accounting for taste'.

[90]Burnett, *Plenty and Want*, 24.

[91]Potter, 'British timber duties'.

[92]Kumagai, *Breaking into the Monopoly*, 256.

[93]Parthasarathi, *Why Europe Grew Rich*, 168–70.

[94]A drawback is a return payment on certain taxed imports and home-produced goods that were subsequently exported. See Ashworth, *Customs and Excise*, 42, and Hoppit, 'Bounties, the economy and the state'. In case of exports to the colonies, these drawbacks were abolished after a while.

[95]See Mitchell, *British Historical Statistics*, 448–52.

[96]O'Brien, 'Contributions of warfare', 53.

Adding up all those interventions, we may not be discussing a full-blown, systematically applied industrial policy, but it would not be too far-fetched to talk of a recognized, actively pursued and ultimately successful strategy to strengthen national manufacturing and trade. From William Pitt the Younger, who was what we would now call Prime Minister from 1783 to 1801 and from 1804 to 1806, onwards, there was a calculated policy to tax the new export-oriented industries, pottery, iron, cotton, and wool, either lightly or not at all. British iron production was greatly aided by heavy protectionist import duties upon superior Swedish and Russian iron. The time of nurturing predominantly non-exporting industries was clearly over then. They rather began to be squeezed. Industries that produced largely for export began to surge forward and to look for foreign markets. They began to favour policies of open trade.[97] Considering that there was an emerging 'industrial policy', it need not come as a surprise that there also existed what one might, somewhat anachronistically, call 'industrial lobbying'.[98] What is more, that lobbying could have an impact. In the 1780s, excising cotton cloth was proposed. Various big cotton manufacturers threatened to go to Ireland if that were to happen. Pitt then told the Commons that the excise on plain cottons and fustians would be repealed. There were permanent and lively public and parliamentary debates about economic policies, exchanges of information and changes in policy over time.

Government could even go as far as to directly interfere in production. In 1797, the opium monopoly in India, which from 1773 onwards had been held by the East India Company, was taken over by a government agency. This meant that opium *production* in fact became a government monopoly. The actual *trade* in opium was now in the hands of private traders. That enabled Britain's government to claim it was not involved in it.[99] Interestingly enough this monopoly on the production of opium in India continued to exist even after the end of the company. It survived three attempts by royal commissions, the last one in 1892, to examine whether it should be abolished.[100] That only happened in the beginning of the twentieth century.

Protected trade, the use of violence and territorial power

That a country had to protect its economy was self-evident to any mercantilist. We already referred to all sorts of strategies to do so in previous paragraphs. In the context of trade, the idea of 'protecting' often had to be taken quite literally. In the early modern era on the open seas there usually was only a very thin line separating trade, privateering and piracy. This means that the use of force was a fairly normal ingredient of the business of trade for all parties involved, not just as protection against others but also as a means of increasing one's own profits. In 1614 Jan Pieterszoon Coen (1587–1629), one of the

---

[97]See Ashworth, 'Revenue'; Berg and Clifford, 'Luxury', and O'Brien, 'Triumph and denouement'.
[98]See Dietz, *Before the Age of Capital*, and MacLeod, *Heroes of Invention*.
[99]Trocki, *Opium, Empire and the Global Political Economy*, 62–3.
[100]Wong, *Deadly Dreams*, 426.

founders of Dutch power in what we nowadays call Indonesia, famously wrote: 'Trade cannot be maintained without war, nor war without trade.'[101] Sir Josiah Child (1630–99), English merchant, economist and governor of the East India Company, pointed out in 1669 that 'all trade [is] a kind of warfare.'[102] According to historian John Elliott, in the Caribbean, to refer to another important trading region, things were not really different: 'Trade and piracy were liable to be synonymous in this lawless Caribbean world of the later seventeenth and early eighteenth centuries.'[103] For the Dutch West India Company in the 1620s and 1630s, the costs of and income from war and privateering far exceeded those of actual trade.[104] The costs of protection could be enormous. For the entire period of 1613–1792, military expenditure in the East by the Dutch East India Company was about 30 per cent of all the company's overseas investments.[105]

The neat distinction that is nowadays made – often also quite optimistically! – between peaceful trade on the one hand and the power-play of politics and war on the other overall was quite blurred during the early modern era. Mercantilism meant rivalry, 'jealousy of trade', 'trade wars' and, at times, real wars.[106] As pointed out earlier, the distinction between the public and the private was just as 'porous'. The Dutch West India Company was established for the purpose of doing Spain and Portugal as much damage as possible. Privateering was one of its main activities.[107] In Britain Sir Walter Raleigh (1552–1618), a contemporary of Coen, had claimed that: 'Whosoever commands the sea, commands the trade of the world, commands the riches of the world, commands the world itself.'[108] Centuries later not much had changed and people had no compunction about admitting it. In Britain during the very long eighteenth century the connection between power and plenty was obvious to anyone. The Secretary for the State of War, Henry Dundas, told the Commons in 1801 that Britain's overall aim that year, as it had been in previous wars, was 'the destruction of the commerce and colonial possessions of the enemy'.[109] This tight connection between power and plenty continued to be a simple fact of life, even after the heydays of official mercantilism were over. Britain continued to be prepared to go to war to protect or promote her economic interests. The First Opium War (1839–42), a very interesting example in the context of this book, was to a very large extent an 'economic' war, masterminded in detail by William Jardine, a merchant with interests in China. The same is true for the Second Opium War, known as the Arrow War (1856–60), the diplomatic smokescreens notwithstanding. The British waged it to get direct access to China's tea-producing areas and to be able to monopolize the Chinese opium market.

---

[101]I found this quotation in Parker, 'Introduction', 9.

[102]Pincus, *1688*, 595.

[103]Elliott, *Empires of the Atlantic World*, 224.

[104]See Brandon, *Mars and Mercury*, table 2.5.

[105]Gaastra, '"Sware continuerende lasten en groten ommeslagh"', 87–8.

[106]For the extent to which 'trade wars' could lead to 'real' wars see Reinert, 'Rivalry', and Shovlin, 'War and peace'.

[107]Enthoven and Postma, *Riches from Atlantic Commerce*.

[108]James, *Warrior Race*, 269.

[109]James, *Warrior Race*, 273. For Dundas see also Chapter 6 note 18.

The *Manchester Guardian* of 11 March 1857 did not beat about the bush: 'Like many of the wars in which England has engaged, this is a merchant's war.'[110]

Two fundamental institutions of British society at the time clearly show the fundamental importance of power for the economy, to wit the Royal Navy and the East India Company. Much of the activities of the Royal Navy boiled down to literally protecting Britain's economic interests by means of its 'blue water policy'. Its ships protected British vessels, cleared the seas for British traders, defeated enemies or at least kept them at bay and helped in 'conquering' markets.[111] It, moreover, guaranteed a relatively uninterrupted delivery of goods by British ships in times of 'peace' and saw to it that the British had fewer shipping losses than competitors in time of war. All this certainly lowered costs for merchants and made their trade easier.[112] Having control of the seas, moreover, as was the case for Britain in the early nineteenth century, proved far more useful in terms of waging economic war than having one's basis in land power as Napoleonic France had.[113] The navy in that way too certainly provided a public good. Nowhere is that inseparable connection between power and profit epitomized better than in that typically European, mercantilist institution of the chartered company: a private enterprise that received a monopoly of trade *and* various sovereign rights from central government in exchange for certain services and payments. Western chartered companies and private traders in the early modern era clearly were not averse to using violence. We have seen that they had huge armies.[114] As a rule, they preferred to conquer new and 'privileged' *markets* while incurring as few fixed military and political overhead costs as possible. The best strategy to realize that, normally, was to occupy strategic places, show that one could be really violent if need be, bribe or 'persuade' the right people and for the rest try and simply trade. With the passing of time, though, the temptation, or necessity, to conquer land simply became too big, just as the temptation to use one's comparative advantage in wielding violence. In using it on their own behalf and on behalf of other parties, the companies more and more became enmeshed in local power struggles. After the battle of Plassey in 1757, the English East India Company *de facto* began to take control in Bengal. From then on it would be hard to deny that it had become a territorial power. Just as a reminder: Bengal at the time is estimated to have had some 30 million inhabitants, more than four times as many as England and Wales together.[115] The Dutch East India Company from the very beginning expanded in Asia. It basically already became a colonial territorial power, especially in what is now called Indonesia, during the eighteenth century.[116] While this was not a planned development,

---

[110]See Wong, *Deadly Dreams*, 'Conclusion'. The claim that William Jardine masterminded the First Opium War is on page 210; the quotation from the *Manchester Guardian* on page 458.
[111]Baugh, 'Maritime strength'.
[112]See Menard, 'Transport costs'.
[113]O'Brien, 'Hanoverian state'.
[114]See page 287.
[115]For the expansion of the British in India see Dalziel, *Penguin Historical Atlas of the British Empire*, 36–7, 58–9 and 78–9.
[116]For Dutch expansion on Java and more in general in Southeast Asia between 1646 and the beginning of the nineteenth century see Barraclough, *Times Atlas of World History*, 176–7, and the maps in Jacobs, *Merchant in Asia*.

it was not a total break with the past either. Both chartered companies continued to be *companies*, and 'policies of commerce' continued to be of the utmost importance for them. These 'policies of conquest' were not necessarily successful in the sense of being profitable enough to keep the companies as such afloat. Practically all the European chartered companies were failures, as Steensgaard rightly reminds us.[117] The Dutch East India Company turned into a debt-ridden multinational that went bankrupt at the end of the eighteenth century. Its English counterpart lasted longer and overall fared better, but it also often had huge debts whereas its income and profitability increasingly were derived more from territorial empire-building than from trading.

Chinese economic policy: Agrarian paternalism at home and when it comes to foreign trade

The Qing state in the long eighteenth century clearly was not mercantilist – in all probability for the very simple reason that it did not have to be. States in Europe, being parts of a highly competitive states system, had to constantly be 'fit' in order to 'survive'. They therefore needed ever-increasing amounts of money. Until it was 'opened' by Westerners in the 1840s, Qing China, as a mega-power surrounded by much weaker neighbours, did not face *similar* challenges. Of course, there had been challenges from its peripheries and in the first decades of Qing rule from supporters of the Ming who had ruled China before the Manchu invasion. But basically in the second half of the eighteenth century those challenges had been adequately dealt with. As compared to the permanent, life-threatening challenges that states had to put up with in early modern Europe, the threat to Qing rule in the period from the 1680s to the 1840s never again became substantial. With the defeat of the remnants of Ming resistance and the successful offensive actions by the Yongzheng and Qianlong emperors, and, what often tends to be forgotten, with the effective negotiations with Russia that after the treaties of Nerchinsk in 1689 and Kiakhta in 1727 secured the northern borders, the Qing empire had become, at least, twice as big and, in 'Bismarckian' terms, 'satisfied'.

Central government during the mid-Qing could and indeed did function according to a different logic and rationality from that of its mercantilist counterparts in Western Europe. It is always risky, as with mercantilism in the Western European case, to try and define that policy with one concept, but if forced to do so I would, following Wong, choose 'agrarian paternalism'.[118] Agriculture was regarded as the fundament of economy *and* society. Rulers regarded it as their duty to look, like a father, after 'people's livelihood' – that is, to provide for the security and wealth of their subjects. They had to be restrained and interpret the state's mandate as one of managing and stabilizing

---

[117]See his comment in Cavaciocchi, *Prodotti e techniche d'oltremare*, 717.
[118]For a general reference to literature on this topic see Introduction note 108. In this and the next paragraph I, in particular, use and paraphrase the introduction of Antony and Leonard, *Dragons, Tigers and Dogs*, 1–26, and Wong, *China Transformed*.

wealth rather than controlling and extracting it. Good rulers were supposed to tax lightly and not interfere at the local level.

What is relevant in the context of this book, of course, is what kind of economic policies central government implemented during the very long eighteenth century and with what concrete goals? In general terms, these questions can be answered fairly easily. Its main goal was to promote a prosperous agrarian economy and it did what it deemed necessary to reach that goal: maintaining, repairing and expanding waterworks, spreading all kinds of technological knowledge with regard to not only agriculture but also handicrafts and water-management, influencing and occasionally regulating the distribution of certain goods like seeds and grain, running a system of ever-normal granaries, opening new land, encouraging and facilitating migration to new settlements and providing free land there, providing disaster relief and so on. Although it stressed grain production, it also supported the production of textiles and, very importantly, aided trade by taxing minimally. Quite often the state confined itself to monitoring. But at times it took a more activist and interventionist stance. It clearly though was not a developmental state in which fiscal, monetary and financial policies were part and parcel of an overall strategy of trying to fundamentally change and 'upgrade' the economy. Let us go somewhat more in detail and distinguish between domestic economic policy and policies related to foreign (economic) affairs.

In Western historiography the conviction has long prevailed that China's rulers distrusted merchants, permanently kept them under watch and ward and squeezed them when they saw fit. According to many historians this view must be revised. I have already quoted Wong as saying that the Chinese state, in contrast to states in Western Europe, did little to impede either domestic or foreign trade and referred to his claim that 'the Chinese state's policies towards long-distance trade, both domestic and foreign, promoted Smithian growth in ways that exceeded contemporary European practices'. We saw that he even goes as far as to suggest that merchants in the West may have been more heavily taxed and preyed upon than their Chinese counterparts. Wong's views in this respect also really are too rosy, in particular when it comes to foreign trade. There were good reasons to modify accepted views, but I think this is one of the many examples when it comes to the historiography of early modern China of revisionism gone *too* far. So let us first discuss the policies of the Qing with regard to the domestic economy and then have a look at their foreign economic policies.

Policies with regard to trade overall fitted in nicely with the general objectives of Qing rule. In official 'Confucianist' theory the merchant was not normally held in high esteem. In practice, however, he and his role were clearly accepted and even appreciated. It was obvious that a big country like China could not do without trade and traders. Commercial exchange therefore *as a rule* was accepted and supported and, which is very significant, *as such* it was left almost completely untaxed. Internal tariffs, until the second half of the nineteenth century, did not amount to much. They were absent in Britain, but when one compares the situation in China with that in France, for example, one can only conclude that domestic trade was much more interfered with in that European country than in the Middle Kingdom. I guess most merchants would prefer being somewhat despised but untaxed over being respected but squeezed by the tax man. There were many examples of rich and, one may say, 'successful' traders in Qing China. I will refer to some of them on pages 356–8. In brief, there can be little doubt that government was aware of the importance of commerce for China's agrarian society.

The 'livelihood of the people', however, was considered too important to leave it *entirely* to merchants and the market. Domestic exchange was left to its own devices *as long as* trade and traders were regarded as enhancing the common wealth. That meant that Qing rulers could easily become quite suspicious and intervene when it came to *certain kinds* of trade and *certain kinds* of traders. They clearly did not look favourably upon merchants whose profits were *too* high and who therefore 'must' have been making deals at the expense of 'the ordinary people'. Nor did they like concentrations of merchant power and capital to become *too* big. It is not unimportant to point out that it was entirely up to the government to decide when this was supposedly the case. The reaction of China's bureaucracy to commercial activity always tended to be ambiguous, or as some might prefer, hesitant. It tended to assess the effects of trade from several points of view. The pull of 'dirigisme' was particularly strong in the direction of putting a brake on exports. Interestingly enough, sending goods to other provinces might already be regarded as a form of exporting them, which tells us something about the way in which at least some people conceived of the empire.[119]

With regard to internal, domestic trade there was a tendency to 'correct' the market. The Qing state was not a disinterested *laissez-faire* state but rather a very interested *physiocratic* one. The objective of its policies, in the words of William Rowe, was 'less one of *letting* the market accomplish its task than of *making* it do so'.[120] That should not be confounded with a staunch policy of interventionism. Though, apparently, even the occasional interventions by the mandarins that did take place sufficed to frighten away several merchants from the grain trade.[121] State granaries were used to influence prices in times of dearth and to provide the poorest people with cheap grain. Land might be (re-)distributed in times of crisis. All kinds of contributions could be 'asked' from the rich in times of need. Government considered these types of intervention legitimate and just and, what of course in the end counts most, there was no one who could stop it from intervening. The rule, however, was that, to put it in modern terms, the market should take care of itself. A caveat is in order here too: in discussing the relative aloofness of central government, one has, as always in discussing China in this period of time, to realize that at the local or regional level all kinds of very 'annoying' interference may have existed of which central government had no knowledge and which it even might have opposed. In that respect, as in many others, the mountains indeed were high and Peking far away, as the old proverb has it.

---

[119]These are paraphrases of claims made by Will in his *Bureaucracy and Famine*, 211, 215 and 217.
[120]See for this quotation that has the italics in the original Rowe, *Saving the World*, 162. For the comparison of Qing policies with those of the French physiocrats see Isett, *State, Peasant, and Merchant*, 241, 252–3 and 255.
[121]See for examples Dunstan, *Conflicting Counsels*, ch. 6.

There were other forms of state intervention in the market or, more broadly, the economy. For the sale of a couple of basic commodities like salt and iron, groups of merchants were granted monopolies. Their activities, however, were strictly regulated and supervised, like in the case of the Hong merchants in Canton, on whom more will be said later. It would be a serious mistake to regard these merchant groups as a kind of Chinese counterpart to the chartered companies that were so important in the history of Western Europe. As a rule, monopolists in China simply took care of the distribution of certain sources of (government) revenue because this was regarded as 'too cumbersome' for the state officials. In the context of copper production and distribution, for example, government tended to favour a policy of 'recruiting investors' (i.e. merchants of substantial means) who were then to cater to its needs under specified conditions with specified obligations. This meant that in the last instance they basically were government servants.[122] In the tea trade between Sichuan and Tibet, government sold licences to traders trying to keep a hold on it. Imperial government held some lucrative monopolies to itself, for example, ginseng and jade (till the death of the Qianlong emperor), gold and fur in Manchuria. It had domain lands and banner lands, whose size as a percentage of total acreage, however, was very small. There were specific government workshops producing directly for the court. There was heavy government meddling in the production *and* sale of copper. Government kept a close watch over all types of mining.[123]

As a rule labour was free in China. Slavery was not unknown but of marginal importance. The idea inherent to oriental despotism, that basically every Chinese was a slave of the government, lacks any basis. The state, though, could 'ask' people for all kinds of corvee, participation in all kinds of 'campaigns' and the handing over of all kinds of 'contributions'. There were a decreasing number of serfs working for banner men in Manchuria and there were convicts doing forced labour in Xinjiang and Manchuria. But their numbers were really small as a percentage of the total labour force. In Northern China one could find peasants whose taxes were paid by their landlords and who basically were in the position of peons. But their number was relatively low and they were, in any case, not in any way slaves or serfs of the state.[124] Income from government properties and monopolies as a whole was only tiny as compared to total GDP. In brief, government intervention in the domestic economy, though clearly not unimportant and in various respects indeed a serious nuisance, in all probability was too rare rather than too frequent.

---

[122]See for this policy of 'recruiting investors' Sun, 'Ch'ing government and the mineral industries', 844–5. Compare Balazs, *Chinese Civilization and Bureaucracy*, 49.

[123]For examples in China Proper see Xu and Wu, *Chinese Capitalism*, under 'copper', 'copper mines', 'coal', 'coal mining', 'silver' and 'gold extraction', and volumes 9 and 10 of the *Cambridge History of China* under 'mining' and 'mines'. As indicated, government, at least in the case of copper mining, sometimes also had other, more 'economic' reasons for interfering. See pages 256–8. For examples with regard to Xinjiang and Tibet see page 401. For comments with regard to the situation in Manchuria see pages 403–5.

[124]See e.g. Bernhardt, *Rents, Taxes, and Peasant Resistance*, 28.

The Qing and foreign trade

When it came to foreign trade, *especially* trade with Western 'barbarians', things clearly were different. This kind of exchange was watched systematically and closely. The point of course is not *that* China's rulers were quite interventionist in this respect: so were mercantilist rulers in the West. Western mercantilism probably more than anything else was about interference in and manipulation of foreign trade. The point is *how* and *to what purpose* rulers interfered. In Western Europe – and most clearly in Britain and the Dutch Republic – we see something of a symbiosis and a mutual re-enforcement of 'power' and 'profit' (i.e. of officialdom and merchants), with both parties, not necessarily for the same reasons, sharing the conviction that foreign trade was of the utmost importance and must be stimulated. In China, on the contrary, rulers were quite sceptical of the positive effects of foreign trade and, in particular, the contacts with foreigners such trade implied. They were much less obsessed by it, and, what is very important, they did not feel the urge to support it for financial reasons. In contrast to Western rulers, they were not permanently forced to wage extremely expensive wars or at least to be prepared for them.

In discussing customs revenue of China's government I have already briefly referred to China's foreign trade. As a percentage of GDP, it was really minor; in absolute terms we are still talking about huge amounts of goods. With a different government policy, however, foreign trade might not only have been substantially bigger. It might also have been taxed more heavily. A huge economy like that of China, almost by definition, is fairly closed in statistical terms. Its imports as well as its exports will, as a rule, be relatively minor as compared to its GDP, in particular in a pre-industrial setting where transportation is so cumbersome, slow and expensive. Even a quite different foreign trade policy could never have effects similar to those of mercantilism in Britain. But political decisions *did* make a difference. Adam Smith's comments in this long quote are still valid:

> The great extent of the empire of China, the vast multitude of its inhabitants, the variety of climate, and consequently of productions in its different provinces, and the easy communication by means of water carriage between the greater part of them, render the home market of that country of so great extent, as to be alone sufficient to support very great manufactures, and to admit of very considerable subdivisions of labour. The home market of China is, perhaps, in extent, not much inferior to the market of all the different countries of Europe put together. A more extensive foreign trade, however, which to this home market added the foreign market of all the rest of the world; especially if any considerable part of this trade was carried on in Chinese ships; could scarcely fail to increase very much the manufactures of China, and to improve very much the productive powers of its manufacturing industry. By a more extensive navigation, the Chinese would naturally learn the art of using and constructing themselves

all the different machines made use of in other countries, as well as the other improvements of arts and industry which are practised in all the different parts of the world.[125]

After China had been forced to open its economy to trade with Westerners, its volume of foreign trade *did* grow and we also see a substantial increase in production of, for example, tea for export. That could be regarded as an indicator that Smith was right in his comment on China's foreign trade.[126]

As it was, customs were low and the bulk of them were collected on internal trade. There were tariffs and there clearly was interference. No central government in the world has ever been totally abstinent in that respect. Export of silver and copper was often prohibited.[127] But we see nothing even remotely similar to Western mercantilist policies. As a source of income, taxes on foreign trade were next to irrelevant for government. Taxes on internal trade yielded more than those on external trade, but even when they were added up they amounted to next to nothing as compared to land taxes, let alone GDP. Interference in foreign trade was not guided by mercantilist considerations of maximizing surpluses on the balance of trade but by political or strictly fiscal considerations. Two phenomena strike me as particularly interesting in the context of this book. The first is the existence of an *export* duty on tea, to which we already referred. This was collected by China's government at the time of the First Opium War (1839–42) and continued to exist after it.[128] The second is the fact that members of China's ruling elite, in this case more specifically the so-called *Hoppos* (superintendents), repeatedly tried to tax silver when it was *im*ported into China.[129]

Government officials had the right and the power to intervene in economic affairs and they were not hesitant to use that power – more often and more intensively than current revisionism suggests – even if that might be to the direct disadvantage of merchants and producers. *If* there was such a thing as a partnership between rulers and merchants, it was never in doubt who were the minor, 'junior' partners. *Raison d'état* always prevailed. In this respect it certainly is of more than just symbolic significance that Peking continued to be the political capital of China whereas the economic heart of the country clearly had long moved southward. In Britain, in contrast, London was not only the political capital but also by far the most important economic centre. Political and economic power were intertwined, mixed and physically concentrated on a couple of square miles in London's centre. The Manchu elite that ruled China clearly did not live in a mercantile environment and it did not look at the world like merchants or entrepreneurs would. The same goes for the Han courtiers and the officials who were with them in Peking or

---

[125]Smith, *Inquiry into the Nature and Causes of the Wealth of Nations*, 680–1.
[126]See Chapter 1 note 467 for information on the substantial growth of exports after China's opening. Relatively speaking, however, exports continued to be quite unsubstantial.
[127]Which as such would be hard to square with Frank's thesis that China was a major exporter of copper during the eighteenth century. See page 365.
[128]Wong, *Deadly Dreams*, 343.
[129]See Chapter 3 note 151.

Chengde. The interest of government in trade as such was very small. It simply did not regard overseas trade as very important. Maritime China remained a small segment of a larger system of defence, diplomacy and trade. In their confrontation with Britain, China's rulers could not imagine that this country would go to war for trade – that is, for the sake of merchants. It took them and many Chinese merchants a long time before they realized that a supportive state was necessary to enable merchants to compete at all.[130] China's rulers often, quite understandably, I again want to add, had different priorities to those in the Western world.

In literally every textbook on China's history during the very long eighteenth century, and more in general during the early modern period, one can easily find numerous examples of government rulings that were hampering, if not downright banning, foreign trade and that were hostile to emigration by Chinese as well as immigration by foreigners. One need not be a champion of mainstream free-market economics to suspect that such measures must have had some negative effects on China's economy and will not always have been enthusiastically welcomed by its merchants and producers.[131] China's rulers were not very keen, to put it mildly, on 'opening' China for foreign trade and foreign traders and saw no need for 'international relations'. The Macartney Embassy that is referred to in each and every book on Qing China was not the only mission that turned out to be a fiasco. Macartney himself refers to six previous embassies.[132] An embassy from the Netherlands, sent in the 1790s, achieved no results either.[133] The Amherst Mission sent by Britain in 1816, also was a failure. When the Russians sent an embassy from Irkutsk in the beginning of the nineteenth century to negotiate either an opening of Chinese ports to Russian shipping or permission for overland caravans to enter the interior of China, it did not even succeed in reaching Peking.[134] There simply is no equivalent of *this kind of* interference in the history of Britain. Moreover, I would want to add, even if China's government had interfered 'sporadically', it is not so much the frequency of interference that matters in the end as the simple fact that government might interfere any time it saw fit. This must have created an atmosphere of insecurity, risk aversion, hoarding and caution among Chinese merchants and 'entrepreneurs'.

What China's rulers in particular frowned upon, and therefore wanted to concentrate, control and if need be prohibit, were intense contacts between their subjects and Western 'barbarians'. Whereas in the principles of the old tribute system one could already see 'the primacy of politics', this became even more prominent and obvious in the so-called 'Canton system' that to a large extent may be regarded as an outgrowth of a tributary mentality. That system was created with the purpose of keeping a close eye on Westerners

---

[130]Wang, *Anglo-Chinese Encounters*, ch. 3.
[131]See, for all sorts of intervention, for example Chang, 'Evolution of Chinese thought'; Eastman, *Family, Fields and Ancestors*, 123–35; Fang, 'Retarded development', 395–9; Hsü, *Rise of Modern China*, ch. 7; Lee, 'Trade and economy'; Van Dyke, *Canton Trade* and *Merchants of Canton and Macao*; Wakeman, 'Voyages'; Will, *Bureaucracy and Famine*, ch. 9; Wills, 'Maritime Asia'.
[132]Cranmer-Byng, *Embassy to China*, 353.
[133]Duyvendak, 'Last Dutch embassy'.
[134]Findlay and O'Rourke, *Power and Plenty*, 300.

and their trade by forcing them to concentrate their activities in Canton and, for a major part at least, only deal with specific, selected trade partners.[135] Of course, in practice things were much less clear-cut than in theory. There was extensive smuggling, evasion, corruption, collusion and compromise, and even after 1757 Canton actually was *not* the only place where Sino-Western trade took place. There also were legally permitted trade contacts between Westerners (in these cases Portuguese and Spaniards) and Chinese, via Macao and Xiamen, and, what should not be forgotten, there was intensive trade between Westerners and Chinese *outside* China (e.g. in Manila or Batavia). There was trade with Russia over land. But still, I challenge all my revisionist colleagues to construct a convincing argument that the Canton system would have been a scheme *to promote* China's foreign trade like the Navigation Acts were in the case of Britain.

The idea of concentrating trade in one harbour as such of course was not unknown in Europe either. Just think of the efforts of the Spanish and Portuguese rulers to make all trade with other continents pass via the harbours of Seville and later Cadiz in the case of Spain, or Lisbon in the case of Portugal. Considering that the main export product from China to the West quite soon was to become tea, most of it from Fujian, the choice of Canton, however, was not exactly an obvious one. It would have been much more practical to export tea from another harbour, for example Fuzhou, that had a much better connection to the tea-producing areas. Choosing Canton had quite negative effects for the economy of the south-east coast that had also, during the first decades of actual Qing rule, suffered from government policies that made overseas trade all but impossible. Government, however, was not willing to change its policy. The Daoguang emperor personally opposed opening Fuzhou to Western commerce and an evident understanding existed among local officials to discourage exports.[136] It was only allowed to transport tea from the inland regions where it was grown to Canton overland, which was far more expensive than by sea. Samuel Ball, who stayed in China from 1804 to 1826 and wrote extensively about tea manufacture and trade, thought this overland transport was almost ten times as expensive as transport by sea.[137] According to Robert Fortune in 1848 the transport costs of tea from the hinterland to Shanghai were on average 50 per cent of the total costs at that point, whereas for Canton that was 70 per cent. A shift to Shanghai did not immediately occur because, among other reasons, government officials did their utmost to prevent that from happening.[138]

For silk, similar restrictions applied for basically similar reasons. It could be transported only from Canton and the trade had to be intermediated by a small group of merchants. These restrictions were only abolished by the Nanking Treaty in 1842 and even after that government for quite some time levied transit duties on silk *as if* it had

---

[135]The so-called Hong merchants are normally described as members of a monopolistic guild. Actually they did not have a real monopoly. See this chapter note 141.

[136]Gardella, *Harvesting Mountains*, 50.

[137]Zhuang, *Tea, Silver, Opium and War*, 8–9.

[138]I take this information from Chang, *Income of the Chinese Gentry*, 167, where the reader can find the original references.

been sent to Canton, whatever the actual port it had been shipped to.[139] On top of that, silk exports from China had even been banned from 1759 to 1764 at the request of the Imperial Manufactures, as it was feared that exports could jeopardize their supply of raw material and push up prices. The government was afraid of missing tax income and losing 'control' of these goods when they would be transported overseas. Up until 1848, tax payments in rice, so-called 'stipend rice', were shipped via four internal waterways from eight provinces at enormous cost. From then on it was transported by sea. That reduced costs by 65 per cent.[140] Overall, government was more occupied with preventing contacts with foreigners from getting too intense and too 'free' than with stimulating them. The difference between the approach of China's central government and that of a mercantilist country like Britain can be nicely illustrated when we compare the status of British merchants and their trading companies involved in 'the China trade' with that of their Chinese counterparts who were their official trade partners in Canton. It, admittedly, is Eurocentric to solely focus on Sino-Western relations here. In strictly quantitative terms they will have been less important than China's contacts with other regions in Asia, although one has to realize that some of that trade (e.g. with India) to a large extent was in British hands. A substantial and increasing amount of the trade between Westerners and Chinese, moreover, was in the hands of the East India Company and the Hong merchants, two parties that tend to be described as 'monopolists'.[141] On the other hand, even though the fear of bad, 'barbarian' influences was particularly strong in the case of contacts with Westerners, the way in which Westerners and Western trade were dealt with nevertheless gives a good indication of where Peking's priorities lay. Many of its restrictive measures, moreover, targeted *all* foreign trade and it intervened in restrictive ways in all foreign trades of the country that I know of. Hampering immigration as well as emigration to, for example, Manchuria and Taiwan also would not have been very helpful in that respect.[142]

But let us focus on the comparison between traders working for, or under the cloak of, Western chartered companies and their Chinese trade partners.[143] To begin with,

---

[139]Federico, *Economic History of the Silk Industry*, 34–5, and Chang, *Income of the Chinese Gentry*, 167, where the reader can also find the original source for this claim.

[140]Deng, *China's Political Economy*, 29.

[141]I have put the term 'monopolists' in quotes as both parties never had a real monopoly. In the case of the *Hong* this was because the *Hoppos* (customs superintendents) did not want them to monopolize trade in a cartel, the so-called *Cohong*. From 1771 the Hoppos definitively prohibited price-fixing and forced the Hong merchants to make their deals separately. Moreover, there always were certain goods in which trade was free, and even of the so-called 'enumerated goods' it as a rule was allowed to trade a certain percentage on a free market. In the case of the British East India Company there increasingly was competition of so-called 'private' or 'country' trade. See Van Dyke, *Canton Trade*, under 'monopoly and monopolise', and Greenberg, *British trade*. Van Dyke also gives information with regard to the size of Western trade with China in Canton, in this case in particular British trade, which was *not* in the hands of a chartered company.

[142]See pages 394–6.

[143]For the working of the Canton system see Van Dyke, *Canton Trade*, and, with a somewhat changed interpretation in which the Hong merchants look less dependent on the whims of bureaucrats, idem, *Merchants of Canton and Macao*. For further information see Greenberg, *British Trade*; Hao, *Commercial Revolution*, ch. 2; Hsü, *Rise of Modern China*, ch. 7, and Morse, *Gilds of China*, 57–85.

Western merchants who worked with one of the chartered companies, because of their charter, were much less at the mercy of the state *in their daily operations* than the Chinese 'Hong' merchants. Chartered companies, moreover, had access to external finance via emerging capital markets, whereas Hong merchants had to borrow money from Westerners or people from India, who, considering the high interest rates in China, were quite willing to 'help' their trade partners.[144] And finally, as compared to the highly integrated bureaucratic apparatuses of the English and the Dutch East India Companies, Chinese Hong merchants were part of an organization that was only weakly integrated. They were not *partners* of the various government officials they had to deal with, but *subordinates*, as they often found out the hard way. *Hong* merchants basically were little better than government servants, squeezed between central government and the Westerners they traded with. Chartered companies, as collectives and for their members, had all sorts of means and rights that Hong merchants could only dream of.[145]

Belying the old cliché of the rapacious, despotic state that had no respect whatsoever for property, let alone for mercantile profit, merchants in China, whether they were active in international trade or otherwise, could become immensely rich. Between 1738 and 1804, the so-called 'factory merchants' and 'transport merchants', who held the monopoly of producing, transporting and selling salt from the Liang-Huai salt district, had to pay nearly 40 million taels as official exactions to the imperial treasure. That looks impressive; considering, however, the fact that their *yearly* profits have been estimated at between 6 million and 7 million taels, this burden must have been quite bearable and the merchants quite rich.[146] We know of individuals in China during the eighteenth century who had a personal capital of more than 10 million taels, mostly earned in trading salt.[147] The aggregated profits of the salt merchants of Yang-chow in the second half of the eighteenth century have been estimated at some 250 million taels.[148] To put things in perspective: the total sum of taxes that was levied at the time annually for central government, including so-called surcharges, has been estimated at between 50 million and 80 million taels. Or to make another comparison: the total value of Chinese goods exported via the English East India Company from China between 1720 and 1833 never exceeded 6.5 million taels per annum.[149] In the nineteenth century, too, one could still make a fortune as a 'merchant'. Chang in his book on the income of the Chinese gentry in the late nineteenth century comes up with many examples of extremely wealthy gentry merchants.[150] Chinese rulers were aware of the positive effects of trade on China's

---

[144]See for just some examples of Chinese merchants borowing from Westerners Greenberg, *British Trade*, ch. 4, and Van Dyke, *Canton Trade*, under 'interest rates'. Apparently Western interest rates were (much) lower than was normal in China.

[145]Zhuang, *Tea, Silver, Opium and War*, ch. 1.

[146]Feuerwerker, *China's early Industrialization*, 50–1.

[147]Osterhammel, *China und die Weltgemeinschaft*, 75.

[148]Ho, 'Salt merchants', 149.

[149]Zhuang, *Tea, Silver, Opium and War*, 158–9.

[150]Chang, *Income of the Chinese Gentry*, ch. 6.

economy and they definitely were not systematically intent on making life complicated for traders.

The merchants' position overall, however, was often precarious and the many rulings and interventions by officials made things very complicated and often unpredictable for Western traders as well as their Chinese counterparts. This shows, very probably in an extreme way, and here we return to Canton and the Sino-Western trade, in the careers of most Chinese merchants who had the often dubious privilege of being member of the Hong 'guild'; a 'privilege' for which, by the way, they had to pay 200,000 taels to government officials.[151] Being a member of the Hong was normally regarded a burden rather than a privilege. The Hong, in the words of Frederick Wakeman Jr, played an 'unwilling role ... as security merchants'.[152] They had to put up with extortion by officials who could demand huge contributions and any member of the Hong in the end could be held accountable for the debts of any other member. An overall judgement of their position though is not easy. Morse refers to many contributions that were forced upon members of the Cohong, including, as indicated, as much as 200,000 taels for admission to the 'guild', and claims that one of its members in total paid more than 2 million taels in contributions. But on the other hand he points to the huge fortune of a certain Howqua who in 1834 had amassed some 26 million silver dollars (i.e. some £6 million). That, according to contemporaries, probably made him the owner of the largest mercantile fortune on earth. According to Morse, 'The Chinese [i.e. the Hong merchants] were quite content.'[153] Hsü overall also is not outspokenly negative, but reading his work it is plain that state interference could become quite a nuisance.[154] Hao, in his book on the commercial revolution in nineteenth-century China, concludes: 'The Hong merchants' foreign indebtedness was such a common phenomenon that in 1829 the number of entirely solvent firms was reduced to three.'[155] Zhuang, in the conclusion of his chapter on the Canton system, writes:

> The Chinese merchants were the only victims of the Canton System, the normal Chinese merchants were excluded from foreign trade in Canton and the Hong

---

[151]Morse, *Gilds of China*, 81.

[152]Wakeman, *Strangers at the Gate*, 44.

[153]Morse, *International Relations of the Chinese Empire, I*, 86.

[154]See for concrete examples of interference Hsü, *Rise of Modern China*, ch. 7, and for 'merciless exploitation' ibid., 146. According to Hsü, between 1773 and 1832, Hong merchants contributed nearly 4 million taels to various government projects. According to Zhuang, *Tea, Silver, Opium and War*, 41 and 42, it would have been 7 million. Hsü adds that this was not all that was asked of them. His overall interpretation of their position though is not really negative, as he writes: 'On the whole, however, they fared quite well, and a number of them succeeded in amassing great wealth' (ibid., 146). One of the examples he gives again is Howqua. This wealthy merchant, however, got involved in a conflict with government and in the end was squeezed and regarded as a traitor. See Wakeman, *Strangers at the Gate*, under 'Howqua'. Interesting from our perspective is that Wakeman, like Hsü, writes that the *recorded* contributions of the Hong merchants were some 4 million taels between 1773 and 1832, but indicates that one family alone, the Wu family, may actually have given more than 10 million taels. See his *Strangers at the Gate*, 48. Deng, *Chinese Maritime Activities*, 111, refers to Hong merchant Pan Youdu (1755–1820) who alone over the course of his lifetime 'donated' at least 800,000 taels.

[155]Hao, *Commercial Revolution*, 307.

merchants mostly went bankrupt since they had to bear such heavy exactions from the government and exploitation by Westerners.[156]

Earlier on in that book he had already claimed: 'The destiny of most Hong merchants was eventual bankruptcy.'[157] These two scholars apparently do not hold a very rosy view of the Hong's position. Deng, however, refers to a certain Pan Youdu (1755–1820), who clearly was a successful Hong merchant: in 1820 he had accumulated a family fortune of 10 million Mexican dollars. Twenty years later that fortune is supposed to have doubled.[158] As indicated, Van Dyke in his recent *Merchants of Canton and Macao* seems to have become less negative about the Hong's position.

Whatever the exact position of the Hong merchants may have been, in all the texts I have read about the Canton system – or indeed about any other example of Chinese foreign trade – I have not been able to find anything that I could interpret as an example of government actively 'promoting Smithian growth', as Wong calls it. Overall, there clearly was a tendency for officials to check up on 'businessmen', to exert pressure on them and to remind them of their low social status and their moral duties. Whatever one may think of this in moral or social terms, *from a strictly economic perspective* the Chinese primacy of politics, officialdom and reproducing the social and moral order, especially when combined with widespread extortion, corruption, incompetence and lack of interest in economic matters among many officials, was not positive for the development of trade, especially trade with Westerners. This is confirmed in what happened later on with the efforts at self-strengthening and the experiments with creating 'official supervision and merchant management' as ways of promoting economic modernization.[159] Overall, in Qing China, the structure of government and the ways in which it intervened in economic affairs were as often part of the problem as they were part of the solution.

In this respect it is striking that Chinese merchants operating outside China received hardly any support from China's (i.e. 'their') government. This is in stark contrast to what happened in the West, where such merchants often were regarded as outposts of empire.[160] With regard to the slaughter of more than 10,000 Chinese by the Spaniards in Manila in 1603, the historian Schurz writes:

After the famous insurrection of 1603, the Spaniards were amazed at the apparent callousness and lack of interest at the sanguinary reprisals that had been taken on the Sangley population [i.e. the Chinese] of the islands. When the viceroy of one of

---

[156]Zhuang, *Tea, Silver, Opium and War*, 51.

[157]Zhuang, *Tea, Silver, Opium and War*, 19. On pages 47 and 48 of that book, there is a long list of Hongs who went bankrupt.

[158]Deng, *Chinese Maritime Activities*, 111. See also Chapter 6 note 154.

[159]See, for example, Feuerwerker, *China's Early Industrialization*, and his description of the problematic functioning of the system of 'official supervision and merchant management', and Perkins, 'Government as an obstacle'.

[160]For the attitude of China's central government with regard to Chinese merchants overseas and the way these merchants operated in 'foreign' territories, see Deng, *Chinese Maritime Activities*; idem, *Maritime Sector*; Pomeranz, *Great Divergence*, 201–6, and Wang, 'Merchants without empire'.

the coast provinces urged the emperor to avenge the slaughter of so many Chinese, there was no response to his appeal. Two years had already passed.[161]

In 1639–40, again large numbers of Chinese were massacred there and again China's government did not react.[162] In 1742, when the Dutch colonial government of the Dutch Indies apologized to the Qing Imperial court for the massacre in 1740 of thousands of Chinese in Batavia, the Qianlong emperor is reported to have said that 'those who leave their ancestors' tombs to make profits overseas are outcasts of China, and no longer have anything to do with the Court, no matter what happens to them'.[163] The historian Purcell estimates that in the year 1763 – during Britain's occupation of Manila – Spanish loyalists massacred 6,000 ethnic Chinese for siding with the Filipinos in a conspiracy to oust the Spanish regime. Again, the Qing government did not react.[164] Interestingly enough, all these massacres did not deter Chinese from continuing to come to Manila and Batavia. Whatever may have been the reasons for government's abstinence, one thing is clear: from the perspective of the merchant active in international trade, there was much more to expect and much less to fear from central government in Western Europe, especially Britain and the Dutch Republic, than in China.

The effects of 'isolationism'

Compared to mercantilist governments in the West, China's rulers can only be described as fairly uninterested in international trade and international relations. When they took interest in them, it was hardly ever to strengthen China's economic position as opposed to that of other countries. China's contacts with the outside world certainly were more frequent and often also more 'open' than has long been suggested by authors who like to think of early modern Qing China as a 'closed' empire. But as compared to what went on in Western Europe, China at the time nevertheless can only be regarded as much more 'autarkic', in a material *as well as* in an immaterial sense. As a country it exchanged fewer goods, people and ideas and less capital with other continents than Western European countries, first and foremost Britain and the Dutch Republic, did. Overall, as compared to their counterparts in Western countries, China's rulers were not exactly well informed about matters that lay outside their own orbit. Whereas in London and Amsterdam one could collect information about all quarters of the globe quite easily, in Peking or any other Chinese town one would have a very hard time to find *any* up-to-date and trustworthy information whatsoever about what went on in other continents. China's court was uninformed about Europe and many other parts

---

[161]Schurz, *Manila Galleon*, 93.

[162]Brook, *Vermeer's Hat*, 178–81.

[163]The exact number of victims is unclear. Deng, *Maritime Sector*, 134, claims that 100,000 Chinese were massacred. That must be an error. I found many different estimates under 'Chinese massacre' and 'Batavia massacre', almost all referring to between 5,000 and 10,000 and sometimes 'several tens of thousands' victims.

[164]I could not obtain the original publication in which Purcell makes that claim, so I refer to Borschberg, 'Chinese merchants', 370.

of the world, not only in economic but also in political and military matters. It was quite ignorant of civilizations in other parts of the globe. Scores of anecdotes[165] and Chinese maps clearly illustrate that.[166] Government policies made China at the time much less open to external influences than societies in the West.[167] The anecdote is even told, though there is no independent proof that it is true, that the Qianlong emperor had to be informed about the size and population of India and about who was ruling there.[168] When talking to Macartney, he inquired how far England was from Russia and whether Italy and Portugal were not near England and tributary to it.[169]

Looking at it from a *comparative* perspective, Waley-Cohen's claim that 'from the late sixteenth to the late eighteenth century. … Chinese were extremely interested in Europe and all it had to offer' is rather weird.[170] Whatever indicator one might think of to measure interest in other continents – the number of people going there, the number of people coming from there, the number of texts written and read about them,[171] the number of people learning languages that were spoken there, the number and variety of goods imported from them and so on – China would time and again score very badly, in any case much worse than Western Europe. If the Chinese had always been so open to the rest of the world, why did they still have to learn so much about it after the West forcefully intruded into their country in the middle of the nineteenth century?[172] In economic affairs, government's ignorance of the outside world, and especially the world outside Asia, was pronounced. In military affairs it was shocking and irresponsible. Even simple contact between Chinese and foreigners in China was quite complicated considering the differences between Chinese and western languages and because it was forbidden for Chinese to teach their language to foreigners.[173]

Permanently benchmarking and emulating other countries and competing with them was the essence of Western mercantilism. What happened elsewhere clearly did *not* play

---

[165]I just refer for a couple of such anecdotes to Teng and Fairbank, *China's Response to the West*, 17–21. See further Introduction notes 119–21.

[166]For Chinese maps and the way in which they charted the rest of the world, see Smith, *Chinese Maps*. In comparison to the number, range and quality of the maps made and collected in North Western Europe, in particular in the Dutch Republic, China's cartography – when it comes to charting *other* continents – can only be called very underdeveloped. See for general comments Black, *Power of Knowledge*, under 'cartography'.

[167]See, for example, Gregory, *The West and China*; Gunn, *First Globalization*, and Mungello, *Great Encounter*.

[168]Teltscher, *High Road to China*, 2–3 and 219–20.

[169]Elliott, *Emperor Qianlong*, ch. 8. Elliott claims that to a large extent we are dealing here with feigned ignorance that moreover is to be excused because there was no need for China's elite to know much about the rest of the world. Westad, *Restless Empire*, 31–2, holds a similar view.

[170]Waley-Cohen, *Sextants of Beijing*, 128.

[171]No one will ever be able to write a Chinese equivalent (*Europe in Chinese Encyclopaedias*) of Lehner, *China in European Encyclopaedias*.

[172]For efforts by Chinese to tell other Chinese about the rest of the world, and especially 'the West', see Drake, *China Charts the World*; Leonard, *Wei Yuan*, and *Renditions. Chinese Impressions of the West*. For the ways in which the Chinese did or did not take over Western knowledge in the early modern period, see Elman, *On their Own Terms*. Schell and Delury, *Wealth and Power*, is full of quotations showing how much Chinese reformers over the last two centuries have been aware of their country's ignorance when it came to the rest of the world and of the negative effects of that ignorance.

[173]Black, *Power of Knowledge*, gives many examples of negative consequences of the fact that China did not engage with overseas foreign civilizations outside its orbit.

an important role in thinking about or organizing China's 'national' economy. Peking, for example, hardly knew what went on in Canton in Sino-Western trade, let alone what was going on in Western economies. It also was ignorant of what went on in Western economic thinking.[174] Being less informed than your competitor puts you at a serious disadvantage. That is one of the reasons that in Canton, appearances notwithstanding, in the end it was Western traders who pulled the strings and not their Chinese counterparts.[175] As Adshead succinctly and correctly puts it: 'If Europe came to dominate the world, it was possibly because Europe first perceived there was a world to dominate.'[176] The Italian writer Tommaso Campanella (1568–1639) as early as 1599 wrote in his *La monarchia di Spagna*: 'Knowing the world is already half possessing it.'[177] In Western Europe enormous amounts of information were gathered about other parts of the world. Early modern Europeans were well aware of the 'Baconian' connection between knowledge and power, as is amply illustrated by Jeremy Black in his *The Power of Knowledge* to which I refer the reader. *As compared to* Western Europe and its global information gathering, China was self-enclosed and uninterested. What Headrick claims for the nineteenth century was already correct earlier on: 'In every part of the world, Europeans were more knowledgeable about events on other continents than indigenous people about their neighbours.'[178] The combined effort to 'explore, control and utilize' that was so characteristic of Western dealings with people in its colonies and other parts of the world in general, for better and for worse, was almost entirely lacking in the Middle Kingdom.[179]

As an increasing number of scholars realizes, quite close links existed between intercontinental trade, exchange and empire on the one hand and the rise of 'science', or, if that is too big a word, the accumulation of useful and reliable knowledge on the other. Although (semi-)private initiatives certainly played a big role, the importance of the state in this respect can hardly be overlooked.[180] Private persons as well as governments were extremely interested in collecting information of whatever kind.[181] Europe's state system facilitated the growth of knowledge in the sense that no state

---

[174]Lin, *China Upside Down*, 180–3. See also Hu, *Concise History of Chinese Economic Thought*, chs 22 and 23.
[175]See for the lack of interest of China's government in Sino-Western trade – and its lack of knowledge of it – Van Dyke, *Canton Trade*, 'Conclusion', and Wong, *Deadly Dreams*, 373–4.
[176]Adshead, *Central Asia in World History*, 77.
[177]See for this quotation Gruzinski, *Quatre parties du monde*, 157.
[178]Headrick, *Tools of Empire*, 208.
[179]See for that combined effort Abernethy, *Dynamics of Global Dominance*.
[180]For the connection between knowledge and empire in the early modern world in general see Black, *Power of Knowledge*. For early modern Britain see Drayton, *Nature's Government* and 'Knowledge and empire'; for the Dutch Republic, Cook, *Matters of Exchange* and Huigen, De Jong and Kolfin, *Dutch Trading Companies*, and for France, McClellan and Regourd, *Colonial Machine*.
[181]For general information on the importance of 'information' in the Western world see Black, *Power of Knowledge*, and Dudley, *Information Revolutions*. Headrick, *When Information Came of Age*, is focused on the long eighteenth century and especially on the technologies of gathering, processing and presenting knowledge. For the economic importance of information in the mercantile economies of Britain and the Dutch Republic, and for the role of the state in its gathering and spreading, see Rothschild, 'English Kopf', and the texts referred to in Chapter 8 notes 29–30 for Britain, and Lesger, *Rise of the Amsterdam Market*, for the Dutch case. For the gathering of information by governments about their own countries and their own populations see pages 416–20.

could really stop it. Europe consisted of a large number of independent, competing 'laboratories' in each of which ideas could emerge, be borrowed and tested. That definitely was an advantage. According to Mokyr, 'Europe differed in that the seeds of innovation sprouted and flourished' as an effect of political competition.[182] People propagating new ideas in his view

> were able to play different political units, as well as spiritual and temporal authorities against each other. Multicentrism made it possible for original thinkers to move between different regions and spheres of influence, to seek and change protectors. When some centres were destroyed by political events, the centre of gravity shifted elsewhere.[183]

Admittedly, China consisted of millions of different, competing individuals and many different regions. So there is no reason to believe that as such it would generate less dynamism. But even those millions of people in China simply did *not* cover 'all under heaven'. The overwhelming majority of them, as Han, shared many ideas and interests. People living in the Qing Empire were not living in a world that was as 'diverse' as that of many Western Europeans living in their parcellized small continent with its many overseas connections and colonies. The fact that China was governed in a secluded, secretive and not very transparent way was not exactly helpful in furthering the exchange of ideas and thereby stimulating all sorts of innovation either.

Europe's state system, in contrast, also actually *promoted* the growth of knowledge, as its competitive structure put a premium on it. In comparing Britain with China in this respect, we have to realize that for China's government and even for China's society at large there, as yet, may not have been a *necessity* to be well informed about what was going on elsewhere on the globe until the First Opium War. In a competitive setting like that of the European states system, information, *ceteris paribus*, is more important than in a hegemonic setting like that of the Middle Kingdom with its satellites. On the other hand, when the First Opium War broke out, China's government had already had the opportunity to collect information on its British adversaries for more than a century. It never seriously did. That is a very serious form of neglect for a government that claims its main ambition is to take care of the security and wealth of its subjects.

As far as it was 'xenophobic' and closed, Qing China was not in a good position to become what Amy Chua calls 'a hyperpower', an example of those 'remarkably few societies – barely more than a handful in history – that amassed such extraordinary military and economic might that they essentially dominated the world'. According to her, each of the hyper-powers in world history was 'at least by the standards of its time, extraordinarily pluralistic and tolerant'. Each of them, so she claims, 'succeeded by harnessing the skills and energies of individuals from very different backgrounds, and by attracting and exploiting highly talented groups that were excluded in

---

[182]Mokyr, 'Intellectual origins of modern economic growth', 340.
[183]Mokyr, 'Intellectual origins of modern economic growth', 342.

other societies'. Although Chua's thesis is somewhat over the top and its empirical underpinning not impressive, its main thrust that, whatever the potential advantages, a country definitely also pays a price for keeping the foreign and the foreigner out sounds highly plausible.[184] The father of modern world history, William McNeill, would in any case agree: 'The principle factor promoting historically significant change is contact with strangers possessing new and unfamiliar skills.'[185] The role of knowledge and information in societal development is crucial and the advantages in this respect of 'open' competing societies over 'closed' isolated ones seems fairly obvious.[186] The rulers of Qing China apparently did not consider themselves to be confronted with competitors that actually seemed to provide a viable or maybe even better alternative for the existing imperial order. External threats were either successfully dealt with or, in case of the West, seriously underestimated. Strikingly enough rebels in the country itself, until the Taiping Rebellion, apparently had no alternatives to offer either. They rebelled but were not revolutionary and either tended to think in terms of breaking away or, as a rule, 'restore the old order' and 'go back to the good old days'. In the period under discussion here, Qing China's institutional set-up as such was never fundamentally challenged or systematically compared to alternatives. Western Europe faced bigger institutional challenges and considered a broader range of alternatives to learn and choose from – also overseas. It tried to make the best of that situation. If one compares the level and intensity of *institutional* innovation in Great Britain and in China in the early modern period, the *topos* of Qing China as 'immobile empire' is much less of a mistaken cliché than is claimed by current revisionism. When it comes to institutional innovation, China clearly was a laggard as compared to Great Britain, which at the time copied and experimented with entirely new solutions as it saw fit. In China in the period under discussion no alternative has ever been suggested for the existing system of centralized imperial rule. Its 'successful' institutional arrangements turned into fetters of development, which enabled the restless Europeans to in the end leave the over-confident Chinese behind.[187] In defence, so to say, of the Qing one has to add that it is very hard to imagine what viable alternative they could realistically have come up with for their system of rule in the international and national constellation of the nineteenth century.

Considering their 'let's leave well alone' philosophy, for Chinese elites there indeed may not have existed an urgent need to learn things from Europe or other parts of the world. But this of course is not identical to claiming, as Hobson does in his rather wild and unbalanced book on the Eastern origins of Western civilization, that China to all intents and purposes was 'superior' to Europe, that, in his words, from 1492 to the 1850s

---

[184]See for these quotations page XXI and the flap-text of Chua, *Day of Empire*. For a more extensive definition see pages XXI–XXII.

[185]McNeill, *Rise of the West*, XVI.

[186]See for two recent and eloquent books that defend this thesis Ridley, *Rational Optimist*, and Wright, *Nonzero*.

[187]For an analysis of how China's 'successful' institutional arrangements turned into fetters of development see Pines, *Everlasting Empire*.

it was just a 'late-developer'.[188] There can be no doubt that in various respects China was more advanced than Europe, but neither can it be doubted that in other respects it was the other way around. China's rulers could have profited from taking Western and other 'barbarians' more seriously. In a broad range of matters, towards the end of the eighteenth century, the Chinese simply and clearly were not, or no longer, superior.

China's rulers were not constantly benchmarking their empire. They could have asked themselves whether everything was really well with their realm as compared to other realms. Their soldiers over the eighteenth century won many victories and conquered great territories. But they could and should have known that, militarily, they wouldn't be a match for Western countries. They, however, chose to ignore that or in any case they did nothing to change that situation. When it came to the functioning of their polity, the impact of population pressure and the ecological situation provided clear signs that things were not going well already at the end of the eighteenth century. When it comes to the economy there seems to be a consensus among revisionists that all actually was quite well until, with opium imports and the so-called 'silver drain' from the beginning of the nineteenth century onwards, a process started that culminated in the Opium Wars and in which the economic situation too started deteriorating. In my view, revisionists in this respect also are far too optimistic.

Was China's economy up until the silver drain in the nineteenth century really as advanced as revisionists want us to believe? Or, what is wrong with the thesis that China was the global silver sink

A substantial number of scholars no longer want to endorse the view that economically – and in various other respects – Qing China was fairly closed to the outside world. Several of them now even go as far as to claim that China would have been the 'centre' of the emerging global economy of the early modern era. In certain circles this has even become an uncontested truth that tends to be regarded as a sign of Qing China's economic primacy. That is supposed to have manifested itself in the fact that in its trade with the West, the only other serious candidate for being the centre of the global economy, it would primarily have sold all sorts of manufactures, and Westerners almost exclusively paid for those Chinese manufactures with silver. As we are dealing here with the 'age of mercantilism' in European economic history, it does not look far-fetched to assume that if there had been an alternative Europeans would have preferred it over exporting a precious metal like silver. Thus, so the argument goes, the drain of silver can only be regarded as a sign of weakness and desperation and of China's economic power and success, which in turn implies that government cannot have been a serious hindrance to China's foreign trade.

The existence of huge flows of silver to China over much of the early modern era, as such, has always been a well-known fact. The opinion that specifically China

---

[188]Hobson, *Eastern Origins of Western Civilisation*.

would be the place where the bulk of American silver ended was already often voiced in the early modern era. The 'sink metaphor', which is used to indicate that China would be a place on the globe where the bulk of silver bullion was heading to stay, is not an invention of modern historians.[189] Contemporaries widely discussed the phenomenon, which occurred in two cycles: from the 1540s to the 1640s and, after the major troubles of the Ming–Qing transition, again from roughly 1700 to the 1750s. In their many publications Flynn and Giráldez have turned this phenomenon into the cornerstone of their effort to 'reOrient' the economic history of the early modern era, to put it in Frank's terms. They present various estimates of the amount of silver they think ended up in China.[190] In their view China would have absorbed two-thirds or even three-quarters of *all* silver produced in Latin America – plus huge amounts from Japan. Considering that it, including Annam and Burma, also produced substantial amounts of silver itself[191] and officially did not export any silver, the country must, during many decades, have functioned as the place where most of the world's silver came to rest. It was only in the nineteenth century that this situation is supposed to have changed.

The silver-sink thesis gained wide support. Arrighi apparently thinks three-fourths of New World silver found its way into China.[192] Pomeranz and Topik write: 'New World gold and silver were shipped in huge quantities to Asia – perhaps fifty per cent of these metals found their way to China alone.'[193] Hobson, William and John McNeill, and Ponting in their 'textbooks' endorse it too.[194] Flynn and Giráldez in their analysis tend to put a certain emphasis on the arbitrage profits that traders could make because of the different silver-to-gold ratios in China and Western Europe. Those different ratios would explain why silver went to China and why gold left the country. Several scholars, however, hold the view that the silver exports from the West to China are an indicator of Western economic weakness and Chinese economic strength. With characteristic vigour, Gunder Frank defended this thesis:

China's even greater [i.e. than India's], indeed the world economy's greatest, productivity, competitiveness, and centrality were reflected in its most favourable balance of trade. That was based primarily on its world economic export leadership in silks and ceramics and its exports also of gold, copper-cash, and later of tea. These exports in turn made China the 'ultimate sink' of the world's silver, which flowed there to balance China's almost perpetual export surplus. Of course, China was only able to satisfy its insatiable 'demand' for silver because it had an

---

[189]For several telling quotes see Chuang, 'Trade between China, the Philippines and the Americas'.

[190]See the Bibliography for their relevant publications. A good introduction can be found in their 'Cycles of silver' and 'Arbitrage'.

[191]According to Lin, probably about a third originated from domestic or semi-domestic (i.e. Annamese or Burmese) production. See Lin, *China Upside Down*, 70.

[192]Arrighi, *Adam Smith in Beijing*, 336.

[193]Pomeranz and Topic, *World that Trade Created*, 103.

[194]Hobson, *Eastern Origins*; McNeill and McNeill, *Human Web*, and Ponting, *World History*.

inexhaustible supply of exports, which were in perpetual demand elsewhere in the world economy.[195]

Frank regards global trade in the early modern era as a game with winners and losers and defines this game in quite 'bullionist' terms: the winners being those countries that ended up with the biggest supply of silver. He is convinced that those winners lived in Asia – to be more precise in China. That country, in his view, had become the major power in 'the global trade carrousel' and the winner in 'the global casino' of trade.[196] Europe, so he claims, as late as 1750, remained a marginal player in the world economy.[197] Marks agrees and goes even further. In his view Europe should be regarded as little more than 'a peripheral, marginal player trying desperately to gain access to the sources of wealth generated in the East'.[198] Chase-Dunn and Hall, to mention just two more authors of a surprisingly large group, claim that Europe's 'long-distance trade with China was one of unequal exchange in which the Chinese were gaining greater returns'.[199]

All this, still according to revisionist interpretations, can only mean that the policies of China's governments with regard to international trade cannot have been as 'bad' as has usually been claimed. On the contrary, they must have been quite sensible and efficient. This thesis of course has to be addressed in a book that deals with the role of the state in the economic development of Britain and China. At first sight, one may indeed be tempted to think in terms of highly productive Chinese, quietly staying at home and collecting huge amounts of silver, versus desperate, underdeveloped Europeans, who crossed various oceans, hoping to receive some crumbs from China's well-served table. It does not take much reflection, and only some empirical knowledge, to realize, however, that this 'silver-sink thesis' and all that it stands for – among other things that China's government did a good job and was not hindering foreign trade – is not exactly plausible.

Before we briefly discuss this topic, we have to first get some facts straight. The first one would be that recent literature has shown that revisionists have been too optimistic when it comes to Qing China's wealth. Apparently Qing China was poorer than Great Britain at the time when that country took off. There, moreover, are indications that all sorts of trouble were already breeding in the country before Western impact became clearly negative. But let us here focus on the silver-sink thesis as a thesis about trade and productivity. To begin with, there is the fact that this net silver import surplus of China in its trade with the West cannot have been as big as many revisionists claim. Sino-Western trade only really took off a couple of decades into the eighteenth century. Before that it was tiny. The impressive increase in this trade that so often is referred to in

---

[195]See for example Frank, *ReOrient*, 75, 117, 127–8, 148, 175, 177–8 and 185. The quotation is on pages 127–8.
[196]See for these expressions Frank, *ReOrient*, chs 2 and 3.
[197]Frank, *ReOrient*, e.g. 75, 100–1, 179–85, 193, 195–7 and 270–1. This of course is a weird claim, that moreover is hard to square with Frank's own claim that the Europeans would import enormous amounts of goods from China in exchange for silver.
[198]Marks, *Origins of the Modern World*, 43.
[199]Chase-Dunn and Hall, *Rise and Demise*, 191.

the literature can to a large extent be explained by its strikingly low point of departure in the beginning of the eighteenth century. As percentages of their GDPs, the commercial exchanges between China and Britain, overall by far the biggest European trade partner of China, in the very long eighteenth century were very small.[200] This implies that the amounts of silver that ended up in China over the entire early modern period *must* have been much smaller than has been claimed in various recent publications by global historians. Trade with Japan, which had been very important and had indeed supplied China with huge amounts of silver, was severely reduced during the eighteenth century. Trade over the Pacific between Acapulco and Manila and from there to China, just like Sino-Japanese trade, has been neglected by historians for too long. It is now no longer doubted that it was substantial. But still, it certainly was less sizeable than Sinocentrists like Flynn and Giráldez suggest and it too had begun to decline by the end of the eighteenth century. Overland imports never became substantial.[201] During the eighteenth century for all major Western trading nations – except the Dutch Republic – the Atlantic was much more important than Asia. The combined trade of Britain, France and the Dutch Republic with the Western hemisphere, for example, was three times as big as that with Asia.[202] China certainly did 'collect' substantial amounts of silver during the last decades of the eighteenth century and into the second decade of the nineteenth century. But the point is that many serious scholars, in particular specialists in the economic history of China, have come up with estimates that are much lower than those suggested by various global historians but are systematically ignored by them. The matter at hand is very complicated. My reading of the literature convinced me that over the period 1500–1820, China, even in an *extremely optimistic* estimate, definitely did not collect more than 30 per cent of all silver produced and marketed in Latin America. That is a lot but, considering its huge population, not striking.[203] The Europeans kept more, in total and per capita. They on top of that collected the bulk of Latin American *gold*, whose major importance for various European economies is completely ignored by proponents of the silver-sink thesis.[204] If there are good reasons to be much less optimistic about the size of Chinese silver imports, there are also – and this is the point I want to make – good reasons to be less optimistic about how well China was doing in international trade. When it comes to the British side, the drain of silver from Britain to China did cause

---

[200]See Chapter 1 notes 460–6.

[201]For a quantitative analysis of trade connections between Europe and Asia that is not, as the title suggests, confined to Cape-route trade but also includes information on trade over the Pacific, trade via land routes, and Sino-Japanese trade, and that provides information about silver flows, see De Vries, 'Connecting Europe and Asia'.

[202]De Vries, 'Connecting Europe and Asia', 93, table 2.15. For the Iberian Peninsula too, trade relations with the West were more important than those with the East.

[203]De Vries, 'Connecting Europe and Asia', 81. See also my Les Treilles paper cited in Chapter 3 note 146.

[204]For various estimates of silver and gold production in the Americas – roughly 80 per cent of total world production in the period from 1500 to 1800 – and for export from there to Europe see Barrett, 'World bullion flows'. In terms of value, gold would have amounted to about one-fourth of the combined silver and gold *production* as well as of silver and gold *exports* from the Americas to Europe. In the eighteenth century, the importance of gold in total bullion exports from the Americas was bigger, at times some 30 per cent. None of this gold ended up in China; a large part went to Britain.

problems for the East India Company and could be quite a nuisance, but it never caused any major overall trouble for Britain's economy.

Already in the 1810s, substantial amounts of silver began to *leave* China, in particular in exchange for Indian opium, and China's overall silver balance of trade slowly started to incur a net deficit, the famous drain we already referred to.[205] From the beginning of the nineteenth century onwards, the British stopped shipping *silver* from Britain to China. In strictly *bilateral* terms, though, Britain, the biggest Western trade partner of China at that time, *as a country*, continued to have a trade balance deficit with the Middle Kingdom. That was the case for quite some time even *after* the First Opium War. This deficit caused much excitement in Britain and it undoubtedly was one of the reasons, or I would rather say pretences, for the First Opium War. One should, however, keep in mind that the (British) East India Company and British private traders, who did the actual trading, had a *surplus* in their exchanges with China. From the 1820s onwards, China bought far more from British traders (whether they acted as employees of the company or as 'private traders') than it sold to them. Western traders, very prominently among them traders from Britain, carried large amounts of goods from other countries in their ships to China, to begin with cotton and later on of course opium, both from India, and they earned lots of money in doing so. They also earned by selling goods they had bought in China at home or in other countries.[206] In *multilateral* terms and looked at from the perspective of the East India Company or private *traders*, the China trade had always been quite profitable, which of course need not surprise anyone: why else would they have continued trading?

This is highly relevant for my analysis and therefore some further clarification might be in order. Proponents of the silver-sink thesis focus on *commodity trade* and *bilateral* (i.e. country-to-country) exchanges. They thereby overlook two main facts: to begin with, that services can also create income. One definitely can, for example, earn money by trading commodities produced by other people. In the setting we are discussing here, this may very well have been a *more* profitable and *more* productive activity in terms of value added than actually producing them. In this respect it is telling that Great Britain, even during the nineteenth century when it counted as 'the first industrial nation' and was widely considered to be 'the workshop of the world', as a rule had a *negative* balance of trade when it came to commodities and more than made up for this deficit by its surplus on the exchange of services and capital.[207] Secondly, proponents of the silver-sink thesis, and more in general those who claim that the West 'lost' in its exchanges with China, apparently ignore that one always has to consider trade flows in the *totality* of foreign exchange relations and in the *entire* balance of payments of a country. Britain paid for an increasing amount of the goods it bought in

---

[205]See Bowen, *Business of Empire*, 225, figure 8.1 that shows that silver exports by the East India Company from the turn of the century increasingly went to India instead of China. This switch from surplus to drain was not in any way connected to the fact that Britain was industrializing at the time. This would again be an argument to not assume too tight a connection between industrialization and Western supremacy.
[206]Wong, *Deadly Dreams*, 369–74.
[207]See for further comments pages 237 and 391–2.

China with goods it had bought elsewhere. It took care of all the transporting involved and often re-exported them, in certain cases after having processed them. As we will see, it was the British who did the bulk of the value adding, not the Chinese.

The comments made so far refer to matters of quantity. Just as important, if not more so, is the fact that proponents of the silver-sink thesis systematically give a wrong characterization of the goods that were exchanged between China and the West. They persistently refer to huge amounts of *manufactured goods* that would have been involved and regard their (presumed) predominance in China's exports as proof of China's superior productive capacities. An analysis of China's trade from the 1750s onwards, however, shows that the role of various manufactures in its exports – that was not big anyhow – *diminished* quite quickly. It did so to such an extent that at end of the eighteenth century it had become almost non-existent. Thinking of Chinese manufactures, porcelain is one of the first products that come to mind. China's porcelain production indeed was impressive in terms of quantity as well as quality. We are talking here about a very 'sophisticated', one might even say 'industrially' produced, commodity. For a long time the Europeans, while trying fanatically, simply did not know how to produce it. The amounts imported by Westerners were so substantial that porcelain quickly lost its status as a 'luxury' product and became so cheap, that it began to be used as ballast in trading ships. From 1709 onwards, however, the secret of its production was unravelled and after a couple of decades Europe already made substantial amounts of it. In the second half of the eighteenth century, it was surpassed as a commodity of mass consumption by European substitutes. Imports from China, that *in terms of money* never had amounted to very much anyhow, began to trickle.[208] In 1791, the English East India Company stopped importing it in bulk.[209] It, or rather private traders, from then on only bought small amounts of very specific and expensive luxury porcelain of superb quality and complexity.

Another manufactured product from China that immediately comes to mind would be silk. Again, we are talking about a highly sophisticated commodity. The last thing that I would want to do here is belittle the craftsmanship of Chinese producers. But the silk that was exported by China increasingly was *raw* silk, not silk clothing. A closer look at China's exports to the West in the late eighteenth century shows that, overall, exports of silk increased over the eighteenth century. Compared to total domestic production they never became massive. The exports of silken *fabrics*, however, actually declined.[210] These

---

[208]For detailed information with regard to the amounts of porcelain exported from China to Western Europe, its price and total value, see, in alphabetical order, Berg, 'Manufacturing the Orient'; Dermigny, *La Chine et L'Occident*, I, 388–92; Findlay, 'Pilgrim art', 168–9, and Jörg, *Porcelain and the Dutch China Trade*. The importance of porcelain in intercontinental trade in terms of money can easily be overrated. According to Findlay after 1717 it amounted to only about 2 per cent of the value of all Asian imports of the British East India Company. Of all Dutch East Indian shipments from Asia between the beginning of the seventeenth and the end of the eighteenth centuries, porcelain amounted to some 5 per cent, admittedly yielding annual profits of between 80 and 100 per cent. China's domestic consumption of porcelain had always dwarfed its exports. Its exports to Europe were relatively small also, when compared to total foreign trade: that was overwhelmingly with other Asians.
[209]Hobhouse, *Seeds of Change*, 134–9. Berg and Clifford, 'Luxury', 1107, refer to high tariffs and to price setting by an oligopoly of dealers in Britain to keep porcelain prices down.
[210]Dermigny, *La Chine et L'Occident*, I, 403.

exports did not generate fundamental changes in China's textile sector as a whole, nor did they become a threat to the silk industry in Europe. This of course need not surprise us considering European protectionism.[211] When it comes to other textiles, China did export cotton textiles, so-called *nankeens*. At the end of the eighteenth century these became quite popular in the West. From then onwards, however, they increasingly had to compete with machine-produced textiles from Britain, which was not easy. Cotton production for export never really took off.[212] Interestingly the Chinese produced an enormous amount of raw cotton at home. On top of that, they imported huge amounts from India and other parts of Asia, in the last decades of the eighteenth century, partly to make up for decreases in their own production. Apparently the sheer availability of cheap raw cotton is not a sufficient condition for developing a booming cotton industry as Californians, in particular Pomeranz, so emphatically suggest for the British case. When mentioning China's exports, Gunder Frank also refers to gold and copper. That is odd: both are *not* manufactured commodities, and if one wants to claim they are, then so is silver. Moreover, why exporting silver would be a sign of weakness (i.e. for Europe) and exporting gold a sign of strength (i.e. for China) escapes me. With regard to copper, I can only say that China never exported much copper in the eighteenth century or later on. It rather was a copper-importing country.[213]

China's export position, overall, in the final decades of the eighteenth century was already weakened. When it comes to the export of medicinal rhubarb, this suffered from the fact that from 1777 it began to be commercially grown in Oxfordshire.[214] A similar story can be told with regard to ginseng, the sale of which in principle was a lucrative government monopoly. From the last decades of the eighteenth century China began to import a variety of ginseng from North America, transported by ships from the United States.[215] Exports to Western countries, here including Russia and the United States – from the late eighteenth century onwards a very important but often overlooked trade partner for China – during the second half of the eighteenth century increasingly, and in the case of Britain even almost *exclusively*, began to consist of tea, the other main items being *raw* silk, rhubarb, various metals and drugs. For Britain, the importance of tea rapidly became overwhelming. According to Zhuang it was tea that drew European vessels to China.[216] Earl W. Pritchard put things even more explicitly when he wrote in the 1930s that in the second half of the eighteenth century tea was in fact becoming 'the god to which everything else was sacrificed'.[217] Its increasing

---

[211]China's role in the international silk trade was relatively minor until the 1850s, began before declining again rapidly from the beginning of the twentieth century onwards. See Federico, *Economic History of the Silk Industry*, 196, Table AI, and 200, Table AIII. By far the biggest exporter until the 1850s was Italy.

[212]For cotton production, i.e., the production of raw cotton, yarn and cloth, and its imports and exports see Chao, 'Production textile'; Chao *Development of Cotton Textile Production*, and Pomeranz, *Great Divergence*, Appendix F (for raw cotton production).

[213]See e.g. Shimada, *Intra-Asian Trade*.

[214]See Wood, *Silk Road*, 14. Lin Zexu (see page 373) apparently did not know that.

[215]See Dolin, *When America First Met China*, under 'Ginseng'.

[216]Zhuang, *Tea, Silver, Opium and War*, 59.

[217]Pritchard, *Crucial Years*, 163.

importance in the China trade dates already from the early eighteenth century. Up to the 1760s the Dutch were just as important in that trade as the English, even though the English were the biggest *consumers* of tea from the very beginning. Tea continued to be by far the most important product in the Dutch China trade till the dissolution of the Dutch East India Company in the 1790s. After that dissolution, tea imports by the Dutch never really recovered.[218] After the Commutation Act of 1784, the British became the most important tea *traders* too, followed by the Americans and then the Russians, who at first only imported Chinese tea over land. Over the period 1760–95, tea represented no less than 81 per cent of the exports of the English East India Company via Canton and it provided no less than 90 per cent of the profits that company made in its China trade. At end of its monopoly in 1834, tea was the only product the company imported from China.[219] In Sino-Russian trade, as indicated, developments were similar. Whereas in the period 1760–85, tea was 15 per cent of Russia's imports from China, in 1825 that had become 87 per cent and in 1850 no less than 95 per cent. In Sino-American trade the preponderance of tea was less pronounced, but still, in 1822 tea comprised 36 per cent of Chinese exports to the United States, increasing to 65 per cent in 1837.[220]

Tea at the time was much more of a processed good than many people might think – and it still is. It required highly varied, complex procedures to convert the raw vegetable matter of the leaves into a consumable commodity. Chinese tea, moreover, was not a homogeneous commodity. It took professional tea tasters and buyers from the West a minimum of five to six years to acquire basic credentials. Differences between various teas in China were as big as those between wines in Europe's viniculture.[221] Tea *literally* was a 'manu-factured' product (i.e. a hand-made product), the production of which required extensive expertise and experience but in which 'advanced technology', in the form of complex implements or 'machines' of any kind, played no role. China's excellent export position was not so much caused by the sophistication of its productive technology – although tea-growing and -producing is anything but easy – as by the fact that at the time China had all but a monopoly on growing tea plants. The other tea-producing country in Asia, Japan, had stopped producing for export. China's monopoly lasted until 1839, when the Assam Company started a commercial tea venture in Assam. That, ironically enough, happened at almost exactly the same moment the British began their war against China to guarantee they would find the wherewithal to pay for Chinese tea via the sale of opium from India. Traders of the East India Company with its monopoly on the China trade understandably had never been enthusiastic about plans to try and grow tea plants some place else. Their monopoly, however, no longer existed from 1834 onwards.

---

[218]Zhuang, *Tea, Silver, Opium and War*, 104–21.
[219]See for these figures Osterhammel, *China und die Weltgemeinschaft*, 118, and Zhuang, *Tea, Silver, Opium and War*, 141.
[220]Hao, *Commercial Revolution*, 14 and 16.
[221]Gardella, *Harvesting Mountains*, 8–12.

Digesting all this information with regard to the composition of China's exports, one can only conclude that, basically, China had already become an exporter of tea, semi-manufactured goods and raw materials decades *before* the First Opium War.[222] Its downgrading from an industrial producer to a producer of primary goods had been almost entirely completed *before* that war and *before* Britain had become a major exporter of industrial products. In strictly economical terms, China had already become peripheral *before* the country suffered from formal imperialism by Western powers, Russia and Japan – at least, *as far as* it was integrated in a global division of labour, which to an overwhelming extent it was not. When we look at Britain and its exports over the period from roughly the 1780s to the 1850s, we can draw two conclusions that make the silver-sink thesis even less convincing. The first is that never in that entire period was the value of manufactured goods in its total exports less than 80 per cent.[223] The second is that, over that entire period, the importance of China in Britain's total intercontinental trade was and continued to be relatively small, especially as compared to its trade with the United States, the West Indies and Canada.[224]

The logic of mercantile capitalism

As such, the information in the previous paragraphs would already be enough to discard the silver-sink thesis: the amounts of silver were much smaller than proponents of the thesis suggest; we are only talking about a fairly brief period; British traders with China did not have an overall deficit on their trade – a deficit existed only in their bilateral trade with that country; overall, they were adding lots of value and earning good profits – and finally China's export consisted only to a small and decreasing extent of manufactured goods. I would, however, like to make a couple of extra comments that I think are relevant in the context of our analysis of differences in the political economy of Qing China and Western Europe, in particular Britain. To begin with, I harbour serious doubts whether in the case of early modern Sino-Western exchange it is correct to equate – as is quintessential in the silver-sink thesis – the party that exchanges silver with the 'buying' and 'losing' party, and the party that exchanges 'ordinary' commodities for silver with the 'selling' and 'winning' party. The fact that Westerners continued to export silver to China for a couple of decades already suffices to make such an interpretation highly unlikely. Why on earth would Europeans have done that if they were constantly short-changed? To claim that they simply could not live without tea is not convincing. In this respect too modern revisionists tend to, probably unwittingly, copy ideas that were cherished in China at the time, having the same highly unrealistic interpretation of the importance of China's export products for Britain as, for example,

---

[222]See Deng, *Chinese Maritime Activities*, the chapter 'Markets and trade patterns'.

[223]Evans, *Forging of the Modern State*, 417.

[224]See the previous note and, for more detailed information, Wong, *Deadly Dreams*, ch. 14, which deals with the period from the late 1820s onwards.

Lin Zexu (1785–1850). This Chinese commissioner wrote in a letter to Queen Victoria in January 1840:

> Of all that China exports to foreign countries, there is not a single thing, which is not beneficial when eaten, or of benefit when used, or of benefit when resold: all are beneficial. Is there a single article from China, which has done any harm to foreign countries? Take tea and rhubarb, for example; the foreign countries cannot get along for a single day without them. If China cuts off these benefits with no sympathy for those who are to suffer, then what can the barbarians rely upon to keep themselves alive?[225]

Chou Hsu, Censor of Jiangnan, claimed in a memorial of 1838 that the foreign barbarians would become blind if they were no longer able to buy Chinese tea and rhubarb. They would get constipated and might even die. Lin Zexu first shared this view and indeed believed that by no longer exporting these products China could decide on the life and death of the British. Later on he developed doubts, though.[226] This of course is all wildly exaggerated: The British could have done without *any* of China's export products. They had done so for ages. There can only be one answer to the question why British and other traders persisted in going to China to exchange silver, and some commodities, for Chinese goods: they did so because, one way or another, that was a good bargain for them and, as I will show in the case of tea, not just for them but also for many of their compatriots and consumers all over the world. The reason that it was lucrative for British traders, apart from arbitrage profits made in exchanging silver and gold, must have been that in the end consumers somewhere in the world were willing and able to pay so much for their Asian products that it was worthwhile to go there and buy them.

I will not again discuss the arbitrage profits made in exchanging silver for gold that made it a very lucrative and 'rational' strategy for Western *traders*[227] to export silver to China – even though in many concrete instances their existence forces one to see the silver exports and 'deficits' of Westerners in a completely different light. Let me instead illustrate my point with reference to tea. The first thing that strikes in a comparison of the amounts of money that Chinese producers and traders received for 'their' tea with the amounts paid for it by consumers in Britain, or in the countries where the British shipped it, is that the differences were so big. In brief, most of the 'added value' was 'added' (i.e. earned) by people who were *not* Chinese. A very substantial part of the consumer price was pocketed by British merchants who brought the tea to Britain and sold it there or – which, considering the importance of re-exports of tea, is not entirely irrelevant – some place else. We lack the exact data to give a neat balance sheet indicating

---

[225]'Lin Tse-hsü's moral advice to Queen Victoria', 25.

[226]See for this information Overdijking, *Lin Tse-Hsu*, 79–81.

[227]I here explicitly refer to *traders*. For *governments* things could be different. For them the export of silver or more in general bullion might indeed be problematic as the military normally wanted to be paid in hard coins.

who exactly earned what in the commodity chain of tea production. Tea leaves had to undergo processing before they were exported. The exact value of tea as it left China is often unknown. There were many varieties of tea, each with their own price. Often it simply is not possible to trace how much was exported of each variety, and so on.[228] That does not mean it would be impossible to support my claim that it was the British and *not* the Chinese who were the real beneficiaries of the tea trade.

Let me just present one 'stylized' example. Fujian was the area that produced most of the tea that was exported from China to 'the West'. In the first decades of the nineteenth century, tea was sold there for 12 taels per picul of roughly 60 kg to local traders. Hong merchants, buying the tea from those merchants, as a rule paid about 20 taels for a picul and sold it for about 27 taels to English traders. The East India Company in turn sold that same tea in England for a price of about 60 taels per picul.[229] We are talking about some 17 grams of silver per pound. That already is more than double the price for which the Hong had sold it. Whereas for the Hong the difference between purchase and sale was 7 taels per picul, for the East India Company that was 33 taels. This difference is not the result of high costs of transportation from China to Britain: in the first half of the nineteenth century, those amounted to 'only' some 30 to 40 per cent of prime costs at the moment.[230] Strikingly enough, according to English traders, the role of the Chinese in the tea trade still was too big.[231] They wanted to get closer to the 'source' themselves, eliminate middlemen, get hold of bigger supplies and deal with bigger suppliers.[232]

The price of 60 taels that we just referred to is not the price consumers in Britain or elsewhere had to pay. That not only included remunerations for the producers and traders in China and for the British traders but also a (large) transfer of money, in the form of a tax duty, to Britain's government, and of course a certain amount of money to the British retailers who actually sold them their tea. We already referred, earlier on, to the existence of very high duties on tea. Till 1784, government in Britain levied a custom tax on tea that, on average, roughly was 100 per cent. That caused so much smuggling that it was decided to lower it to a little over 12 per cent. During the Napoleonic Wars it was again raised to some 100 per cent – though not for all varieties – and by and large stayed at that level till the end of the period we discuss here. The amounts of money involved were anything but negligible. Between 1711 and 1810 no less than £77 million, or the equivalent of over 230 million taels, ended up in government coffers as tea duties.[233] That is roughly the equivalent of China's ordinary land tax revenue over more than four years in the eighteenth century. Over the period 1835–62, per year an average of £5.2 million (i.e. some 20 per cent) of total customs income of Great Britain

---

[228]Wong, *Deadly Dreams*, 362.

[229]Zhuang, *Tea, Silver, Opium and War*, 40 and 89, and Gardella, *Harvesting Mountains*, 36–9.

[230]Mui and Mui, *Management of Monopoly*, 61–5, and Gardella, *Harvesting Mountains*, 39.

[231]For a concrete example of the payments to the Chinese that English traders regarded as costs to undercut see Macfarlane and Macfarlane, *Green Gold*, 109.

[232]See e.g. Wong, *Deadly Dreams*, 355–60.

[233]Macfarlane and Macfarlane, *Green Gold*, 99.

consisted of tea duties.[234] To get an idea of orders of magnitude: over the period 1835–1857 the income government collected via the tea duty on average was about two-thirds of the Royal Navy's expenditure.[235] The contrast with China is again striking: the Qianlong emperor later in his reign received 865,000 taels annually from tea duties in his private purse and that was considered a lot.[236]

The figures presented above with regard to price differences between tea as raw material in China and as end product before taxation in Britain are anecdotic. These are just examples. To make an exact and representative calculation of the various mark-ups between primary producer and final consumer would be far from easy if not impossible. This, moreover, is not the place to try and make very detailed calculations. A very rough, 'stylized' general approximation, though, can be produced to give at least an idea. It would look as follows. During the first decades of the nineteenth century, the price of ordinary tea – let me remind the reader again that there are many varieties and qualities of tea and therefore many tea prices – doubled between the moment it left the farm

Table 38 Ratio of sales prices in Europe to purchase prices in Asia of the Dutch (VOC), English and French (C de I) East India Companies, 1641–1828

Period	VOC	VOC China trade	EIC	EIC tea trade	C de I
1641–50	3.97				
1651–60	3.43				
1661–70	3.32		2.71		
1671–80	2.89		2.40		
1681–90	2.59		2.08		
1691–1700	2.77		3.35		
1701–10	2.63		2.73		
1711–20	2.66		2.75		
1721–30	2.25		2.60		2.16
1731–40	2.44		1.96		1.90
1741–50	2.46	2.07	2.26		1.76
1751–60	2.19	1.88			1.80
1761–70	2.37	1.51			1.80
1788–96				1.86	
1814–28				2.03	

Source: De Vries, 'Limits of globalization', 723.

[234] Wong, *Deadly Dreams*, 344–9.
[235] See for this claim Wong, *Deadly Dreams*, 350–5.
[236] Elliott, *Emperor Qianlong*, 134.

somewhere in China and the moment it was shipped in Canton, then again between leaving Canton and the moment when the tax man came to tax it in Britain, and then again because of the duty that was collected on it before it could actually be sold. And then the retailer of course still had to take his share.[237]

The *added value* generated in the entire production- and distribution-chain of tea is of course not identical to the *profits* made in that process by the various parties involved. We have some indications of the profits the East India Company made on its tea trade. We are referring here to net profits as a percentage of total costs, including charges, insurance and interest payments. Over the period 1788–96, they on average were 15.85 per cent; over the period 1793–1811, 26.18 per cent, and over the period 1814–28, 25.14 per cent. In the period from 1815 to 1834, the East India Company on average made a yearly profit of more than £1 million. More than 90 per cent of that profit was made on tea.[238] For private merchants we only have anecdotal information. We, for example, know that over the period 1840–50 a private merchant called Melrose made an average profit on his tea trade of 13 per cent.[239] All this does not exactly look like bad business run by desperate traders. The markups we have constructed here for tea transported by British traders and sold in Europe are not exceptional. In long-distance trade in the early modern era, traders as a rule created much more added value, and normally had much higher profits, than the actual producers of the commodities that were traded. According to Kirti Chaudhuri, back home, European traders often sold what they had bought in Asia for 200 to 400 per cent above the Asian price.[240] Kent Deng holds the view that European merchants normally sold their Chinese imports at three to four times the price they had paid for them in China.[241] Sucheta Mazumdar, referring though to the sixteenth century, writes that Spanish-American merchants would quadruple or quintuple their investments in the China–Mexico trade.[242]

In the pre-industrial world we are discussing here, it was only rarely the producers and (small) local traders who made big profits. Where those were most common was in long-distance trade. In that trade merchants could buy quite cheap in one place and then sell dear someplace else and so make substantial profits, in particular of course when they could trade on a large scale and manage to keep competition to a minimum. Qing rulers could have profited substantially from reading the analysis of the logic of this large-scale, mercantile capitalism that Braudel presents in *Civilization & Capitalism*, under the apt title 'Capitalism on home ground'.[243] To him capitalists are the people at the pinnacle of trading activity; the ones who hold 'the commanding heights'. They are

---

[237]I constructed this estimate on the basis of information in: Gardella, *Harvesting Mountains*; Hobhouse, *Seeds of Change*; Macfarlane and Macfarlane, *Green Gold*; Mui and Mui, *Management of Monopoly*; Wong, *Deadly Dreams*, and Zhuang, *Tea, Silver, Opium and War*.

[238]Zhuang, *Tea, Silver, Opium and War*, 159–60.

[239]See for these figures Mui and Mui, *Management of Monopoly*, 152 and 133.

[240]Chaudhuri, 'Circuits monétaires internationaux', 64.

[241]Deng, 'Consumer goods for silver reserves'.

[242]Mazumdar, *Sugar and Society*, 77.

[243]Braudel, *Civilization & Capitalism, II*, ch. 4.

well-enough informed and materially able to select in what sectors and places they want to be active. They earn their profits thanks to the lack of transparency of the markets in which they operate and that they to a large extent manipulate and try to monopolize. Support from the state is essential in those efforts. He claims that long-distance trade, where one has to operate on very different and distant markets and where information, capital and 'connections' are of the utmost importance, is the setting *par excellence* where capitalists feel at home and can earn superior profits: 'Long-distance trading was not everything, but it was the only doorway to a superior profit level.'[244] In all probability that is an exaggeration of the real profitability of long-distance trade. But I would think that the following claim, also made by him in that same volume, is correct: 'In the eighteenth century, one can undoubtedly say that *almost* everywhere in Europe, *large-scale* profits from trade were superior to *large-scale* profits from industry or agriculture'[245] (italics in the original). One can already find this point of view in the work of Karl Marx who wrote about the stage preceding modern industrial capitalism, which we now usually describe as mercantile capitalism: 'It is already evident here how in all spheres of social life the lion's share falls to the middleman. In the economic domain, for example, financiers, stock-exchange speculators, merchants and shopkeepers skim the cream.'[246] The Chinese state, by its interference in various sectors of China's long-distance trade and by its relative lack of support for it as compared to Western mercantilist governments, definitely bears responsibility for the fact that trade volumes, added values and profits in those sectors for the Chinese were smaller than they might have been.

Mercantile capitalists could increase their profits even more when they not only bought their trade goods some place cheaply to sell them for a much higher price elsewhere, but also were able to directly or indirectly manipulate the production of those goods so as to make them even cheaper and easier to collect. Although mercantile capitalists, as Braudel emphasizes – probably too strongly – indeed were reticent to lock up their capital in the sphere of production and tried to keep their options open, they actually almost always did interfere in production, if only by coordinating it. In the history of Western mercantile capitalism one finds various examples of such interventions. The most radical example in the early modern era was the creation of plantation economies where slaves provided labour. But one might also think of the (re-)introduction of forms of serfdom in which the people who provided still had some means of subsistence but were no longer formally free. Then there was a second option of absorbing surplus labour of free people, who as a rule still had at least some means of subsistence, via 'putting out'. Finally, there was the possibility to use seasonable labour or the labour of immigrants. In all these strategies, the merchant-entrepreneur could profit from the fact that the labour he used need not be rewarded at total reproduction costs, as it either still had some means of reproduction of its own or could, in the case

---

[244]Braudel, *Civilization & Capitalism, II*, 601.
[245]Braudel, *Civilization & Capitalism, II*, 428.
[246]Marx, *Capital, I*, 907.

of migration or the import of slaves, be incorporated from outside the system, or both. In the first strategy of using direct coercion, the connection with political leverage is obvious. That element of leverage, however, is not entirely lacking in putting-out either, as this mode of producing can only emerge in societies where rulers accept a situation in which a substantial part of the population, in particular in the countryside, can no longer fully provide for its subsistence, either via their own farm or their main job. The first two of these strategies, strikingly enough, were *all but entirely absent* in early modern China. Great Britain was the core of an economic system where these strategies were all quite common; see, for example, British behaviour in the Caribbean and later in India. The efforts of the British to 'open' China basically boiled down to an attempt to also manipulate the *production* of tea, make it more efficient, more geared to British demand and of course cheaper.[247]

Chinese producers and traders, evidently, did make money in the tea trade, as in other intercontinental trades. But by staying at home and 'only' producing certain goods and then, at best, bringing them to the coast, they earned much less than they might have had they themselves controlled the entire chain from production to (foreign) consumption.[248] They did know that the British made big profits in selling goods from China. In his famous letter to Queen Victoria, Commissioner Lin wrote:

> The goods from China carried away by your country not only supply your own consumption and use, but also can be divided up and sold to other countries, producing a threefold profit.[249]

In stimulating *and* taxing foreign trade, China's government also might have earned more than it did. In these respects – and that is the reason for discussing the silver-sink thesis in the first place – all was *not* well, let alone optimal, when it came to China's foreign trade. I would claim that government was at least partially to blame for that.[250] British traders as well as British governments earned lots of money because of the tea trade. That fact in no way affected *total* tea consumption negatively: that continued to increase steeply. Would not Chinese traders have been able to earn a lot more if they had taken more of long-distance, transcontinental exports, and imports, in their own hands? Would not China's government have been able to earn more by stimulating and then taxing trade more? The 10 per cent taxes it did collect on exports do not strike me as a very efficient way to tap trade. Again, all this of course does not mean that a mercantilist China might have profited from international trade as much as Britain did. The enormous size of its domestic market simply ruled that out. But as it was, a

---

[247]For Western European mercantile capitalism I refer, next to Braudel, to Van Zanden, *Rise and Decline*. My description is based on his analysis and strongly paraphrases him.

[248]It is striking that in Manchuria, too, it was foreigners who controlled large-scale export trade. See Reardon-Anderson, *Reluctant Pioneers*, 169–70, and ch. 7.

[249]'Lin Tse-hsü's moral advice to Queen Victoria', 26.

[250]As always in this text I look at matters from a strictly *economic* perspective. China's government may have had excellent (other) reasons to act the way it did.

disproportionate amount of profits, added value and employment went to British subjects or the British state.

The impact of the policy of China's rulers on potential earnings for Chinese producers but especially for Chinese traders who lived in China when it comes to foreign trade was not positive, in any case not when one looks at it in terms of economic maximization. Chinese traders living *outside* China may well have earned a lot of money. But for China's economy at the time that was fairly irrelevant: they were not in any systematic way actually part of it. China's rulers controlled trade with Westerners, restricted it to certain places and did not stimulate Chinese merchants to participate more actively in that trade – if they did not actually make it impossible for them to do so – by, for example, trying to bring tea to Western Europe or wherever it may have been in demand *themselves*, or to go and look for silver some place in the world *themselves*. If those merchants had been allowed to freely go abroad and return and *if* they had been supported by their state, like their Western counterparts, not only *higher* profits and *higher* tax revenues might have been possible: Chinese merchants might also have been able to build *global* networks and acquire *global* expertise. By not fully opening up their economy China's governing elites created a situation in which their country did not optimally profit from what modern economists call 'the gains from trade'.

The positive effects of having an open economy can also be more indirect. To the extent that an economy, for whatever reason, is less open, it will be less challenged and chances will be smaller that it will profit from so-called 'spin-off' effects. China's foreign trade was not only, relatively speaking, smaller than that of Western European countries, it was also less diverse. We have seen that its exports, already long before the First Opium War, had become restricted to a small number of goods, most of them (semi-) raw materials, the production of which did not have many spin-off effects. When we look at imports, the situation was different from that in Western Europe too. Whereas in Britain, for example, imports from Asia, like porcelain and textiles, cotton or silk, triggered a process that for the sake of convenience we can call 'import substitution', nothing of the sort happened in China.[251] Its imports from other Asian countries in the very long eighteenth century for the largest part consisted of basic foodstuffs. Neither in quantitative nor in qualitative sense did these have substantial spin-offs. By far the most important good it imported from the West was silver. That will definitely have had positive effects in, for example, easing China's monetization and all that goes with it. One may, however, also point at possible negative effects and suggest that these imports turned China into a silver junkie that became far too dependent on imports for the functioning of its monetary and financial system. Or one may point out that all the labour and resources used for producing goods that then were exchanged for silver could

---

[251]The term 'import substitution' has been put in quotes. I agree with Maxine Berg that in this context it is not entirely satisfactory as it 'does not adequately capture the process of market development, both internal and internal, and the dynamic interaction of product development and technological change' that was taking place in eighteenth-century Britain and elsewhere in Europe when producers tried to respond to the Asian challenge. See Berg, 'In pursuit of luxury', 102.

have been used to more effect had China created a monetary system that hinged less on silver and more on paper money. That, however, would have required the existence of a different, more robust state.[252]

What I wanted to show in my extended excursion on the China-silver-sink thesis is that there are good reasons to (a) be less elated about China's foreign trade relations and about its economic 'primacy' and to (b) take the negative implications of the trade policies of its government more seriously. In the end the ones who profited most from Sino-Western trade, even during the days of persistent silver exports from the West to China, were *Western* traders, *Western* governments, who taxed the imported goods, and *Western* consumers, who purchased the luxuries they wanted to purchase. *Comparatively speaking*, China's economy and government gained little. To regard people who, like the British, could afford to buy their favourite drink at the other side of the globe, notwithstanding enormous markups – mainly due to the activities of *British* middlemen and the *British* Excise – as desperate and poor, as various defenders of the silver-sink thesis do, of course is ludicrous. The same of course applies to imports of products like spices, textiles or coffee from Asia.

---

[252]Flynn and Giráldez, the authors who are most outspoken in claiming that China was the globe's silver sink, are also quite explicit in claiming that in the end this was *not* favourable for China's economy. See their 'Money and growth'. Frank holds the view that the sustained import of silver into China led to economic growth that lay at the basis of the sharp increase of its population in the eighteenth century, which, according to him, in turn lay at the basis of the emergence of a 'high-level equilibrium trap'. See Frank, *ReOrient*, 298–314. See further Li, 'Paradoxical effect of silver'.

CHAPTER 7
EMPIRE AND ECONOMY

EMPIRE-BUILDING IN THE WEST: THE LOGIC BEHIND IT

I would annex the planets if I could.

Cecil Rhodes in his Last Will and Testament of 1902

Britain, as with most other Western European countries, became the centre of an empire. Its mercantilist leanings certainly were not innocent to that. Mercantilists by definition are always on the lookout for markets. Conquering markets in Europe was anything but easy. It was not easy in the economic sense of finding new, foreign customers: almost all European countries had mercantilist rulers who tried to maximize exports and minimize imports. Nor was it easy in the sense of actually conquering tracts of land and forcing their inhabitants to become subservient trade partners. All nations in Europe were heavily militarized and differences in military efficiency were never very big for long. So there were good reasons to try one's luck elsewhere, hoping one could profit from the ample experience one had gathered in economic and real warfare at home. As various European powers thought this was a sensible strategy, the competitiveness of the European state system simply spread over the rest over the globe. The zero-sum-game approach so typical of mercantilism implied that if one did not control a certain place oneself, someone else would, with all the negative consequences that, by definition, was supposed to have. In that vein Sir Francis Baring (1740–1810) claimed in 1795, with reference to the importance of the Cape that Britain had just acquired, that it 'consists more from the detriment which would result to us were it in the hands of France, than from any advantage we can possibly derive from it as a colony'. Examples like this can easily be multiplied. This 'logic' led to efforts to control and conquer markets all over the world. State-building, mercantilism and empire-building, or in any case territorial expansion, in fact became inseparably connected for all bigger European powers, with the difference that some tried to build their empire overseas and others tried to extend their grip over land.

One therefore simply cannot write a book on the role of the state in Western economic development in the early modern era without dedicating a chapter to empire-building. Again, one must be careful not to generalize too easily. The focus here will be on overseas expansion as Britain became the core of a huge overseas empire, but Europe of course also had its continental empires; just think of the Russian, Habsburg and Ottoman Empires. Even when only discussing Western European overseas empires it is quite dangerous to generalize. The Spanish and Portuguese seaborne empires, while not exactly identical, were quite distinct from those of the Dutch and the British. Apart from that, there were differences over time. The empires of the British and the Dutch, for example, as we already pointed out in discussing their 'Indian' chartered companies, tended to increasingly transform from 'empires of trade' into 'territorial empires'. Finally there were enormous differences related to where one was active and what kind of societies one had to deal with. It evidently matters whether one's counterpart is a 'defenceless' American tribe or the mighty Middle Kingdom, to just give two extremes.[1]

The fact that the state sooner or later in one way or another always got involved in expansionists' overseas projects, does not mean that empire-building was solely or even primarily a matter of state policy: far from it. Quite often, the state followed rather than led. Differences in this respect between various Western European countries and between those countries and China in some cases were substantial, as could be differences in who actually conquered and governed the overseas realms – government officials, private persons or a combination of both. Think, for example, of the different ways in which Western countries like Britain and the Netherlands operated in the Americas, where private enterprise played a big role, and in parts of Asia, where chartered companies for a long time were the most important agents. But whatever the exact mix between private and public, *in the end* central government always became heavily involved. To this generalization I would immediately, at the very beginning of this chapter, like to add a second one: whatever may have been the costs of empire for government, in principle in Western countries empire was expected to, at the very least, pay for itself.

Imperialism is normally associated with conquest and territorial expansion or, to quote John Darwin, 'the attempt to impose one's state predominance over other societies by assimilating them to its political and cultural and economic system'.[2] In that sense British mercantilism, to again focus on Britain, clearly has *not* been imperialist per se, *not* from the very beginning and *not* permanently. On the contrary: just like in the case of the Dutch Republic, its 'overseas expansion', if that indeed would be a correct term, for a long time was more driven by the wish to profit via conquering *markets* than by the 'normal' logic of empire-building that in the end is characterized by the wish to conquer *land*. What prevailed for a long time during the early modern period in mercantile nations like Britain and the Dutch Republic was, to put it in Arrighi's terms, 'the logic of capital' not 'the logic of territory',[3] a distinction that reminds us of that between 'empire of commerce' and 'empire of conquest' that Lang made in the 1970s.[4] Reality of course always tends to be more complex, but as such this distinction undoubtedly has its value.

What has been said in the previous paragraph applies to the situation in Africa and Asia. What happened in the Americas basically was quite distinct and a kind of

---

[1] For a description and analysis of the logic of European colonialism see Abernethy, *Dynamics of Global Dominance*.

[2] Darwin, *After Tamerlane*, 416.

[3] Arrighi, *Long Twentieth Century*. See under 'capitalism, logic of power' and 'territorialism, logic of power' in the index.

[4] Lang, *Conquest and Commerce*.

'windfall' – that is, for the conquerors. Because of the very specific conditions in which the clash between the Old and the New Worlds took place, a relatively tiny 'investment' in people, resources and time sufficed to get free reign in an immense continent. For the British, North America quickly developed into a real colony – that is, a place where people settle to make a living, like their first colony Ireland. After losing Brazil, the Dutch no longer had any 'grand designs' in the Western hemisphere and no longer made any effort to create an institutional unification of their 'colonies' there. In Asia, the situation was quite different. Here the role of chartered companies was much bigger and much more lasting. We have already shown how they increasingly became territorial powers.

Empire-building in the West: Land and people

Imperialism was a broad European phenomenon. So let us, before we focus on Britain, first give some broader information. When people talk about the age of (Western) imperialism, they normally refer to the period from roughly the 1870s to 1914. That is not surprising. Between 1878 and 1914 alone, Western states acquired some 25 million km² of land. According to Parker, in 1914 in total 84 per cent of the globe was in the hands of Western powers or settlers who originally had come from Europe. In 1800, again according to Parker, that had been 'only' (my quotes) 35 per cent.[5] Which, and that is the point I want to make here, of course is still amazing, considering how small Western Europe itself is.

Conquering land implied subjecting people. According to Shammas, in 1775 already about one in seven people in the world lived under European rule.[6] In total, rulers of

Table 39 Western European empires: approximate square mile distribution by geographical area c. 1775 (in percentage of square miles)

| | Empires | | | | | |
Areas	Spanish	Portuguese	Dutch	British	French	Danish
Europe	3.9	0.9	2.5	11.3	81.8	99.1
Atlantic Isles	0.1	0.1	–	3.9	–	–
Coastal Africa	0.0	9.1	38.0	2.7	0.7	–
Americas	93.7	89.6	22.5	59.3	17.4	0.9
SE Asia	2.4	0.2	37.0	22.8	–	–
Total (km²)	4,937,994	3,666,777	651,533	788,846	259,627	15,580

Source: Shammas, 'Revolutionary impact of European demand', 167.

---

[5]Parker, 'Introduction', 9, and idem, Military Revolution, 5.
[6]Shammas, 'Revolutionary impact', 167–8 and 184–5.

Table 40 Great Britain's overseas empire in thousands of km^2 and thousands of people

		1760	1830	1880
Size		3,153	7,416	22,741
	Dominions	3,116	3,919	18,016
	Colonies	37	3,497	4,725
Population		2,791	189,090	271,023
	Dominions	1,692	1,260	8,936
	Colonies	1,099	187,830	262,087

Source: Etemad, *Possessing the World*, tables 8.1, 8.2, 9.1 and 9.2.

Western Europe in 1775 had some 110 million subjects: some 50 million at home, in the mother countries, and some 60 million elsewhere. That of course is already substantial. Even more so when one realizes that various countries in Western Europe had no overseas extensions at all, or only tiny ones.

Whereas Shammas presents her figures more or less in passing, Bouda Etemad presents a very extensive, quantitative analysis of Western empire building from the eighteenth century onwards.[7] From his book I took the information shown in Table 40 with regard to Great Britain. As that table shows in 1880 more than 22 million km^2 and some 271 million people outside the British Isles were under British rule. Great Britain's empire became about double the size of the whole of China.[8] Even so, however, its population still was 'only' about three-quarters of that of China. Again, in all these calculations 'informal' empire is not taken into consideration.

It is important to realize that not only do these figures refer to a huge *extension* but also behind them there lays a big *change*. Between 1760 and 1830, Britain lost its colonies in what we now call the 'United States', whereas it acquired big parts of Asia, in particular in India. The meaning of the fact that the United States of America became an independent successor state of what till the 1770s used to be British colonies is not always fully appreciated in books dealing with global history. Pomeranz, for example, attaches enormous importance to what he calls Britain's 'Atlantic periphery', in which he clearly continues to include the United States. When Britain started to seriously industrialize, however, the USA had become an independent state. The Spanish and Portuguese colonies in America became independent in the beginning of the nineteenth century. If the 'ghost acreage' of the Americas was so ideally suited to easing domestic pressure on land, as according to Pomeranz it did for Britain and more in general for

---

[7]Etemad, *Possessing the World*.
[8]For a systematic comparison of size and duration of empires see Taagepera, 'Size and duration', and Turchin, 'Theory for formation of large empires'.

Western Europe, then why did not others, for example the Chinese, or earlier the Portuguese, the Spaniards or the Dutch, (also) profit from it? In principle there was an enormous bonanza of 'ghost acreage' available in the Americas for *any* contender, not just the British or the Europeans.[9] I agree with Pomeranz that imagining the Chinese profiting from this bonanza would require some radical rethinking. It would have meant that the Chinese no longer, for example, went to Java to trade but to Acapulco. Before the development of the steam ship that would not have been easy and it would have taken radical changes in China's political economy.[10] But in the end such comments are only a convincing refutation of the possibility of China exploiting the Americas in case one thinks that exploiting America had been a fairly easy, cheap and natural thing to do for the British: it definitely wasn't. The costs in resources and to a lesser extent people were enormous, as was the effort it took. Beware, I am not just referring to the actual 'costs' made in conquering the periphery, but also to what it took to combat other Europeans, in and outside Europe, in order to be able to get and keep it.

We have now briefly discussed empire in terms of additions of land and people to the mother country: but what about empire as a place where 'superfluous' people from the mother country could go? Overall, the importance of empire as a kind of demographical safety valve was not yet very high for Western Europe before the nineteenth century.[11] *Overall* this also applies to Britain. I use the caveat 'overall', as there were not only substantial *differences* between the four 'nations' that from the beginning of the nineteenth century formed the United Kingdom of Great Britain and Ireland, but also big *changes* over time. In total, during the seventeenth century about 1 million people left the British Isles, the main destination being the American colonies. That is a very substantial amount of people, as total population of all four 'nations' (i.e. England, Wales, Scotland and Ireland) together in 1700 still was not higher than some 10 million. In this migration, England and Wales were much more prominent than Scotland and Ireland. Net English emigration alone was over 700,000. America was the favourite destination. During the seventeenth century it alone was the destination of some 377,000 to 397,000 people from the British Isles. About 350,000 of them were from England and Wales. Never during the entire period from 1600 to 1800 was English net emigration higher than in the troubled years of the Civil War and the Commonwealth.[12] I already referred to the substantial exodus from England, Wales and Scotland in the seventeenth century to Ireland, when Ireland's status was that of a simple overseas British colony. In the period from 1700 to 1780 the total number of

---

[9]The term 'ghost acres' was introduced by Borgström in his *Hungry Planet*. He defined it as 'the amount of land needed by a nation to produce the equivalent amount of food it procures by trade and sea'. Pomeranz uses the concept in a broader sense, also including the amount of land a nation needs to produce the equivalent of the energy it procures from fossil fuels and the equivalent of land it needs to produce the equivalent of the amount of textiles it procures via trade. I also use this broader definition. In the context of the specific questions raised in this book, Jones introduced it in his *European Miracle*, ch. 4.

[10]Pomeranz, 'Without coal?', 251–2.

[11]See for an overview of migratory movements in Europe including migration to other continents, Lucassen and Lucassen, 'Mobility transition revisited'.

[12]Ferguson, *Empire*, 74–5, and Horn, 'British Diaspora'.

British migrants to America was some 270,000. The share of England and Wales was much smaller, about one-third (i.e. only some 80,000). The rest went from Scotland and even more from Ireland. Emigration to regions other than America was negligible. Between 1780 and 1815 we see a sharp rise in the number of Irish people leaving for the Americas: their number may have exceeded 100,000 to 150,000. The number of English, Welsh and Scottish emigrants was much more modest at the time. Britain's army and navy had begun to absorb enormous amounts of people and therefore, until after the French Wars, Britain's government was inclined to *discourage* emigration, certainly of people with 'useful knowledge'.[13]

After the Napoleonic Wars, things again changed substantially. Between 1820 and 1850 almost 2.4 million people left the United Kingdom to settle in countries outside Europe. In particular the United States received many of them. About 80 per cent of the 600,000 emigrants who left England, Wales and Scotland between 1815 and 1850 headed for 'the land of unlimited possibilities'. Among Irish migrants, the biggest contingent of migrants, the United States were just as popular, if not more so. The 'mainland' of industrializing Britain, though, also attracted many of them. It has been estimated that in 1841 there were 830,000 'effective' Irish in Britain, of whom 450,000 were Irish-born and the rest descendents of Irish emigrants.[14] Starting in the 1840s, a disastrous decade, especially in Ireland, we see a formidable number of people leaving the British Isles. In the sixty-four years from mid-century to the beginning of the First World War, no less than 13 million people left, again most of them for the United States and *not* for countries that were part of the British Empire.[15] But that of course is largely outside the period under discussion in this book.

What this brief overview shows is that, during the very long eighteenth century that we focus upon in this book, not many people left Britain to settle somewhere else in the British Empire: most of those who left settled in the 'United States', before and even more after their independence. More in general, until the beginning of the nineteenth century overseas colonies, and even more broadly overseas countries in general, were *not* important population outlets for almost all other imperialist countries in Western Europe. Although in this case too, one has to be careful not to generalize too easily. From 1492 to 1760 there was a net immigration to the Americas of 678,000 people from Spain, 523,000 people from Portugal, 100,000 people from France and 20,000 people from the Netherlands.[16] In 1820, the total number of

---

[13]Horn, 'British Diaspora', 30–5.

[14]Mokyr, 'Editor's introduction', 95.

[15]See for this information Ferguson, *Empire*, 113, and Matthias, *First Industrial Nation*, 248 and 452. I came across even higher estimates of total migration from the British Isles. Marjory Harpers claims that 22.6 million individuals left the British Isles between 1815 and 1914. See her 'British migration', 75. She, however, does not provide any source for this figure. Dalziel, *Penguin Historical Atlas of the British Empire*, to give just one last source, estimates that between 1821 and 1911 about 17 million people left the British Isles. For the period 1815–1924, he gives a figure of about 21 million. See pages 61 and 68 of the book. Here too references are lacking.

[16]Eltis, 'Slavery and freedom', 28, table I. According to Eltis in this period 746,000 people left Great Britain for the Americas. The figure differs from the one given by Horn (see note 13) but so does the period Eltis covers.

Europeans that had moved to the New World after its discovery is estimated at some 2.6 million, which is not exactly an impressive number.[17] At the height of this transatlantic migration in the early modern era, some 15,000 people left Europe for the New World annually. The annual average for the period from 1500 to 1800 definitely was less than 10,000 of a population that in 1800 had reached some 100 million for Western Europe alone. Again, what we see, even in Western Europe – and the number of people migrating overseas from the rest of the continent was really negligible – are huge differences.

Western European migration to Africa was even less substantial. The number of Europeans who left their continent to settle there in fact was negligible. In 1750, the number of Europeans actually living in Africa lay between 15,000 (according to Bairoch) and 26,000 (according to Etemad), about half of them residents of the Cape Colony.[18] The importance of Asia for European migration was quite small too. In the 300 years between 1500 and 1800, not more than some 2 million Europeans left for Asia.[19] They were like 'flies upon the wall' in this huge continent during the early modern period. There are various estimates of the number of Westerners living there at specific moments during the eighteenth century. Steensgaard, who coined the phrase 'flies upon the wall', estimates their number at probably no more than 10,000 in the middle of the eighteenth century.[20] Estimates by Bairoch and Etemad are in the same order of magnitude.[21] The Dutch historian Els Jacobs claims that in 1750 the Dutch East India Company alone employed some 25,000 Europeans in Asia. That seems to imply that the total number of Europeans must have been higher than is suggested by Bairoch, Etemad and Steensgaard. But many of those 'Europeans' in fact were descendants of company servants born in Asia, Eurasians of mixed blood or Asians. After 1750, moreover, the number of European personnel apparently decreased.[22] At that time some 5,000 new personnel arrived annually, in part to take over the positions of the many employees who did not survive their stay in the tropics. There were many such cases. Between 1733 and 1795 at least 85,000 employees of the company died in Asia because of malaria.[23] Holden Furber, to present my last estimate, comes up with yet another figure: 'All things considered, it is most unlikely that in any year between 1600 and 1740 more than fifty thousand Europeans were living in Asia: the total may have reached

---

[17]Eltis, 'Free and coerced migrations', 62. Eltis' estimates from 1999 (see the previous note) differ from those presented in 2002.

[18]Bairoch, *Victoires et déboires*, II, 570; Etemad, *Possessing the World*, 21.

[19]De Vries, 'Connecting Europe and Asia', 72. De Vries refers to the total number of *Europeans* that went to Asia on board ships owned by one of the European companies that traded with Asia at the time. We are talking about, on average, less than 7,000 people per year, half of whom sailed on ships of the Dutch East India Company. Of the 1 million people who left the Dutch Republic this way – many of them, by the way, *not* Dutch – only one-third returned.

[20]Steensgaard, 'Asia'. The quotation is on page 86.

[21]Bairoch thinks there were some 15,000. See Bairoch, *Victoires et déboires*, II, 570. Etemad estimates the number of Westerners living in Asia in 1760 at 18,000. See his *Possessing the World*, 21.

[22]Gaastra, *Dutch East India Company*, ch. 3.

[23]Jacobs, *Merchant in Asia*, 9.

seventy-five thousand by 1800.'[24] But whatever may have been the exact number of Europeans leaving for Asia and living there at any particular moment, it clearly was a matter of a couple of tens of thousands, at the very best, not more. At the very end of the eighteenth century there still were no more than some 30,000 Britons in India. Overall, one can only conclude that emigration from Western Europe to other continents during the early modern era was insubstantial. With the 1840s, a new era began: literally tens of millions of Europeans were to leave the continent in the period to the First World War, especially for the New World.

The importance of empire and ghost acreage for the economy of Great Britain

That fact that empire in many respects *preceded* modern economic growth and industrialization to my view does not mean it somehow *caused* them – in any case not in the sense that it would have provided the necessary money or resources for it. The thesis that the periphery provided *the* or at least *a* major source of accumulation, which in turn would provide the means to pay for the take off, in my view is no longer defensible. Among economic historians one can hardly find anyone still defending it. The view has come to prevail that *innovation* is the motor of modern economic growth not *accumulation* and that things were no different in the case of the first industrial nation. Analyses tend to focus on institutions that stimulate and sustain innovation. As I discussed this thesis extensively elsewhere I will not do that again here.[25] What I will briefly discuss here is the specific turn that Pomeranz has given to the debate on the 'contribution of the periphery' by focusing on what he calls 'ghost acreage' and on the importance of 'empire' for the development of the service sector.

The Wallersteinian approach to studying the relations between core and periphery in the modern world-system or, for that matter, in 'ordinary' empires, where the core is supposed to feed itself on tribute from the periphery, basically focuses on yields and profits in *monetary* terms. In this respect, there clearly were differences between Britain and China. In his comparison of 'China' and 'Europe', Pomeranz, has given a specific twist to that Wallersteinian approach by suggesting that the importance of at least some of the Western colonies or dependencies primarily lay in the 'ghost acreage' they provided for the core and not in direct material 'profit' as a result of exploitation. He goes as far as to suggest that the exploitation of its Atlantic, circum-Caribbean periphery and the *non-consensual*[26] trade with that periphery were crucial for Britain's economic development in the very long eighteenth century and 'probably roughly as important to … [its] economic transformation as its epochal turn

---

[24]Furber, *Rival Empires of Trade*, 300.
[25]See my *Escaping Poverty*, passim under 'innovation'.
[26]For explicit references to the non-consensual character of the trade between Britain and its circum-Caribbean periphery, and to exploitation and coercion, see pages 4, 18, 20, 23–5, 193 and 207 of his *Great Divergence*.

to fossil fuels'.[27] The fundamental importance, according to him, of that periphery lay in the fact that it provided Britain with land-intensive goods, in that way easing the pressure on its land and, less prominently but definitely not irrelevantly, in the fact that it acted, largely involuntarily, as a consumer of British exports. Let us, considering the popularity of Pomeranz's views and his explicit claim that the availability of this specific ghost acreage would constitute a fundamental *difference* between early modern Britain and China, delve somewhat deeper into the role of ghost acreages – and the importance of the state in acquiring them – in the history of both countries in the early modern era.

Let me start with some comments on the British side of the equation. I will be brief, as I have dealt with the exact relationship between Great Divergence and ghost acreage for the case of industrializing Great Britain extensively in my *Escaping Poverty* and I would like to focus on China here. I would in any case like to strongly qualify the importance of ghost acreage in *causing*[28] the Great Divergence. History of course never is that simple, but if I were forced to choose between two simple alternatives – to wit: Britain's ghost acreage *caused* its industrial revolution; or Britain's industrial revolution *created* its ghost acreage – I would endorse the second claim. Industrializing Britain did what all 'core' states have done in global economic history: 'leave' the production of raw materials and basic commodities to the periphery – or force it upon that periphery – and specialize in what really pays. Money to pay for the import of raw materials and foodstuffs was earned in industry and services, where a comparative advantage was acquired. Overseas investment and migration *turned* land into ghost acreages that could actually export to 'the core' what that 'core' needed. Ghost acreage only emerged in the context of an emerging global division of labour *created* by developments (in the field of technology, economy and power politics) started and concentrated in the British 'core region' that gave it comparative advantages, also over regions over which it had no political leverage, for example, the independent United States, Central and Eastern Europe or the Netherlands, or a region that actually was part of the United Kingdom itself like Ireland.

When it comes to demand from the ghost acreage regions, I will only make some brief comments. The parts of the Atlantic world where the British indeed had and kept

---

[27]Pomeranz, *Great Divergence*, 23. See for three further examples the flap text: 'Together coal and the New World allowed Europe to grow along resource-intensive, labour-saving paths'; page 7: 'the British story is unimaginable … without two crucial discontinuities – one created by coal and one by the colonies', and page 23: 'Europe's overseas extraction deserves to be compared with England's turn to coal as crucial factors leading *out* of a world of Malthusian constraints.' Please note the casual (and confusing) switching between Europe, Britain and England. I fail to see why coal and colonies would be crucial *discontinuities* in Britain's history of the eighteenth century. Coal was already part of Britain's energy history for centuries and its importance already was about equal to that of *all* other energy suppliers, including human and animal energy, combined in 1700. See Warde, *Energy Consumption*, 69, Table 4. Britain's colonial activities also were not something that came out of the blue. The two major discontinuities in that respect are the enormous increase in leverage the British established in India and the independence of the United States. These strikingly enough are hardly if at all discussed by Pomeranz.

[28]That Britain's industrialization could not have been sustained without the imports of certain resources and the export of certain finished products is obvious and no point of discussion.

political leverage were fairly small and did not have many inhabitants. Slaves formed by far the biggest part of the population of the British Caribbean Islands. On Jamaica, for example, in 1800 they accounted for about 90 per cent. The total number of slave inhabitants of the British Caribbean in 1790, at the height of sugar production by slaves, was 480,000. That is substantial. But can purchases on their behalf really have had the consequences Pomeranz attaches to them?[29] Only half or even fewer of those slaves in the British Caribbean were engaged on sugar plantations. The rest worked on secondary crops, livestock or gardening pens. Exports played a much smaller role in the economies in the Caribbean than has often been suggested. According to Eltis in those colonies the majority of production was focused on reproducing the colony itself and not on exports.[30] Contrary to Pomeranz's assertion, we know that slaves in the South of the United States also produced some subsistence goods like grain, vegetables, meat, potatoes and clothes for their own consumption.[31]

All my comments here and more extensively in *Escaping Poverty* are of course not meant to suggest that empire and ghost acreage would have been irrelevant for Great Britain's growth. What I want to do is deny they would be somehow its cause or motor. But on the other hand I also want to emphasize that their relevance is not confined to direct exchange and accumulation. At the centre of its empire Great Britain became a truly *global* player that was in permanent contact with different places all over the world: it exchanged goods, services, information, ideas and people with a huge number of often very different civilizations and in many different ways profited from that. It was a hub of global exchange of every kind. That certainly gave a boost to its dynamism. As part of a global empire it often had to heed (potential) competitors from all over the globe. The fact that it was a global *overseas* empire, moreover, entailed very specific challenges and possibilities that also cannot have failed to elicit many specific responses. The total 'impact' of empire directly and more indirectly as a 'dynamizing factor' must have been much bigger in the case of Great Britain – even if many Britons may have been absent-minded imperialists – than in that of China Proper and this impact in my view was very important for development.

I think not only about all sorts of import substitution effects but also, very importantly, of effects on Britain's service sector. During the nineteenth century, the period it was the first industrial nation, that sector was immensely important for Britain's economy. Even in 1850, when the country was widely regarded as the workshop of the world, less than half of Britain's total labour force was working in manufacturing in the widest sense of the word. The number of people working in *modern* industry was only a small fragment of them.[32] More than a quarter of Britain's labour force was working in services. This sector had been very important for Britain's economy over the

---

[29]Blackburn, *Making of New World Slavery*, 404. This number was lower than that of the French Caribbean, where there were 675,000 slaves.
[30]Eltis, 'Slave economies'. See also Engerman, 'Atlantic economy', 150.
[31]Fogel, *Without Consent or Contract*, 44–5.
[32]See Matthias, *First Industrial Nation*, 260–1.

entire period that is covered in this book. In terms of money its importance probably was even bigger than in terms of employment. An analysis of the group of very wealthy persons in Great Britain during the period 1860–79, in any case, shows that, of the non-landed fortunes at death of £500,000 or more, no less than 56 per cent was in the hands of people working in finance or commerce.[33] It is hard to imagine this booming commercial and financial sector without empire, and empire, I would add, without a certain type of state.

Overall, industrializing Britain during the period that is classically seen as when the Industrial Revolution took place (i.e. roughly from the 1760s to the 1830s) was much less of an industrial country than the traditional focus on coal, steam and factories suggests. In the 'industrial' northeast of England, the share of the secondary sector in total labour force in that period *de*creased rather than *in*creased. That percentage had already been very high during the early modern era. Increases took place elsewhere. Seen over the entire country the secondary sector's relative importance grew more between 1500 and 1750 than it did between 1750 and 1850. From the end of the eighteenth century onwards it was the service sector that knew a strong and sustained growth in terms of employment, in particular in transport. The heydays of industrial Britain when 'Lancashire' prevailed over 'London' were only a brief interlude. With Rubinstein, one could defend the provocative thesis that Britain's was *never* fundamentally an industrial and manufacturing economy. In his view it *always*, even at the height of the Industrial Revolution, essentially was a commercial, financial and service-based economy whose comparative advantage lay with commerce and finance.[34] Cain and Hopkins in their brilliant *British Imperialism* basically defend the same thesis in their exposé about 'gentlemanly capitalism', which I, as such, would endorse. But whatever the exact merits of this thesis, Great Britain became the dominant player in the emerging global economy, not so much by its industry, although that of course was very important, as by its services. In certain industrial sectors it indeed was and continued to be a giant. In 1913 it still was the biggest and most efficient producer of cotton and wool in the world. It still had more than half of the cotton spindlage of Europe in that year 1913.[35] In 1870 the United Kingdom still produced half of the world's pig iron and it still had more than 20 per cent of the entire world's horse power when it comes to steam engines.[36] But things changed fast. In 1913, Germany produced more than double as much iron and steel and the United States four times as much. When it comes to total energy consumption Great Britain was almost overhauled by Germany in that year, whereas the United States consumed almost three times as much.[37] The service sector

---

[33]Cain and Hopkins, *British Imperialism*, 115. What is striking is that the number of very wealthy landowners at the time still was four times as high as that of very wealthy financiers and merchants combined.

[34]Rubinstein, *Capitalism, Culture and Decline*. For a brief but very helpful text that clearly illustrates the enormous importance of the service sector for Britain's economy see Eisenberg, *Rise of Market Society in England*.

[35]Landes, *Unbound Prometheus*, 214–15.

[36]Landes, *Unbound Prometheus*, 219–21 and 291–3.

[37]Kennedy, *Rise and Fall of the Great Powers*, 200–1. Actually Kennedy refers to Britain in his tables, but I assume he means Great Britain.

now in Great Britain clearly grew at the expense of manufacturing, which became less of a leading sector.[38]

It was in the service sector that Great Britain's global primacy was striking. Let me give some figures with regard to the period just before the First World War to illustrate this claim.[39] Great Britain then owned more ships than the rest of the world put together. It had some 40 per cent of all national registered tonnage at the time. Its ships undertook over half of the world's overseas trade and it produced almost 60 per cent of steamship tonnage worldwide. Two-thirds of its fleet were sold second hand to other fleets. Some 50 per cent of all foreign investment on the globe was British. The country was the greatest capital exporter in the world as well as its greatest market. Its foreign investment was much higher than in Germany and the United States. It also was predominant in the new field of telecommunication: in 1892 Britain's government and British companies owned two-thirds of all cables in the world. In 1908 they owned 60 per cent of all submarine cables. The country played a key role in the emergence of a multilateral trade system and in managing the Gold Standard.

Great Britain's global economic primacy is simply inexplicable without its industrial revolution but also without its financial and commercial sectors, which are inseparably connected to empire *and* the state. I therefore fully endorse the claim by Cain and Hopkins 'that the story can no longer be told as if all routes led into or out of industrialization, and that the assumption that services derived from or were parasitic on manufacturing has to be demonstrated and not simply taken as given'.[40] That implies that the role of the state in the emergence of Great Britain's modern economy and its modern growth must also have been quite substantial.

China and empire

How about China's empire-building? Can we really, as various authors claim, discern some (striking) parallels with imperialism as we have seen emerging in the West?[41] To be able to judge, one first has to determine who exactly in the context of China's empire did the conquering and colonizing and who was conquered and colonized. I bring this point up because the thesis might be defended that the Qing were a group of conquerors who, from their Manchu lands in the North, first conquered China Proper and then various other territories so that Manchuria (or as one currently prefers in China, the 'Three North-eastern Provinces') has to be regarded as the actual 'core' of the empire, whereas China Proper, and all other regions that were conquered by the Manchus, were nothing but subjected parts of a basically *Manchurian* empire. I don't think, in the end, this makes much sense.

---

[38]Landes, *Unbound Prometheus*, ch. 5, in particular 326–58.

[39]All the information in this paragraph, unless indicated otherwise, comes from David M. Williams and John Armstrong, 'Technological advances in the maritime sector and some of their implications for trade, modernisation and the process of globalisation in the nineteenth century.' Paper presented at the XV World Economic History Conference in Utrecht, 3–7 August 2009.

[40]Cain and Hopkins, *British Imperialism*, 8.

[41]See pages 25–6.

The Qing Empire indeed first and foremost was a project of the Manchus. There are various clear indicators for that, for example, the way in which the most important positions in China's civilian and military administration were allocated. Also quite telling is the fact that in the *Li-fan yüan*, let us say China's 'Colonial Office', no position of any importance was ever held by a Han. This central government institution was entirely a Qing creation with no Ming precedent and its president was directly responsible to the emperor. It had been created already in 1636 as 'the Mongolian Office' and in the end became responsible for all matters dealing with Mongolia, Tibet, Xinjiang and Manchuria, and for that matter Russia.[42] The Manchu rulers behaved like privileged conquerors that in various ways profited from subduing other people, with whom, all assimilation notwithstanding, they never fully merged and whose civilization they never fully adopted. Manchus, moreover, had much better chances to get government jobs than others. The banner men and their dependents were heavily subsidized and paid less taxes. The Qing conquest elites never abandoned their Manchu identity and never ruled fully in Chinese style. They monopolized certain sectors of government like finances. At best, they opted for a hybrid constitution that departed from both Manchu and Han traditions. Their ideological and political imperatives did not always line up with the concerns and interests of the civil bureaucracy and with Han officialdom in general. This, for example, shows in the fact that, in contrast to many of these Han officials, they, from the 1680s onwards, resolutely opposed migration of Han into their homeland. This, by the way, did not stop them from sending large numbers of convicts there. Manchuria was regarded as the cradle of the Manchu people and the place to keep alive their martial traditions. After 1680, this policy of protecting the Manchu homeland from Han settlers to secure Qing patrimony even became a central pillar of the Qing imperial edifice, although the Qianlong emperor sometimes changed policy.

But all this does not change the fact that China Proper was the Qing's power basis and the very core of the empire, not its periphery. The Manchu Qing *did* accommodate themselves in many ways to the culture and institutions existing in China Proper. Peking was the capital, not any Manchurian town, although Mukden served as an auxiliary, purely nominal, capital. Manchuria's position in the Qing Empire simply was incomparable to that of Britain in its empire. In various respects it looked more like a dependency of China than its 'core'. Notwithstanding the fact that, as indicated, some resources from China Proper did flow there and various monopolies were kept by people from there, Manchuria was *not* the place where money and resources from the empire were accumulated and *not* its power base. Let me quote James Reardon-Anderson:

> The Manchus recognized that China Proper was the core of their empire and the main source of its wealth and power, while Manchuria was part of a periphery that must serve the function of protecting and preserving this core.[43]

---

[42]Dabringhaus, *Qing-Imperium*, 23–8, and Hsü, *Rise of Modern China*, 53.
[43]Reardon-Anderson, *Reluctant Pioneers*, 87.

Many Manchus inside as well as outside Manchuria were surprisingly poor. Manchuria itself was and continued to be a quite empty land where Manchu rulers retreated every now and then. The number of Manchus living there permanently was not big. These are the most recent estimates of total population of the region: 1.1 million in 1750; 2 million in 1800; and 5.3 million in 1850.[44] Many people went there as seasonal migrants. If they settled, they did so illegally. In brief: the Manchus may have been ruling the empire, but China Proper was its heartland.

Now that this point is settled, how much land and how many people did the Qing add to China Proper and their own homeland? We have established that the size of the land that was subject to British rule increased more than twentyfold between 1688 and 1830. Things were quite different in the Qing Empire; China Proper always continued to be a very substantial part of the entire realm. As a reminder: Qing China in its entirety was never bigger than some 14 million km². 'China Proper', depending on the exact definition, is about 3.5 million to 4 million km². If we would include Manchuria, that at the time measured about 1.2 million km² and evidently was part of the Qing Empire from the very beginning, relatively speaking, China's territorial expansion would be even smaller, from roughly 5 million to at most somewhat less than 15 million km². Even if we were to include China's tribute states, which would really be stretching the concept 'empire' too far, 'China Proper' never was less than a fifth of the Qing Empire in its entirety.[45] We of course have to realize that Qing China was such a big country that it simply *could not* increase its size twentyfold as Britain had done via its empire in roughly the 120 years between 1760 and 1880. Nor could it, like Britain, increase its population eightfold by building an empire in that same period of time. The population of China Proper in 1760 will have amounted to some 250 million. To increase that eightfold, China would have had to add some 1,750 million people to its realm. That is more than the population of the entire world, which in 1870 still was only some 1,270 million.

When it comes to population, we see an overwhelming and continuing predominance of China Proper: easily 90 per cent of the inhabitants of the empire lived there.[46] As indicated, by far the majority of the people in China, some 90 per cent, were and continued to be Han. Looked at from that angle, the enormous increase in attention for the non-Han in current historiography is something of an overreaction. Millions of migrants left the very densely populated regions of 'old' China to move more inland, especially to Hubei, Hunan, Guangdong, Guanxi, Guizhou, Sichuan and Yunnan. China, so to say, was filled up. Especially after the 1750s, the part of total population living in the new settler regions increased substantially.[47] Overall, government supported migration to the

---

[44]Isett, *State, Peasant, and Merchant*, 310–12.

[45]Including tribute states in the case of China would oblige us to include 'informal empire' in the case of Britain.

[46]See, for example, the population figures for the various regions of Greater China in 1787 in Ho, *Studies on the Population*, Appendix II, 283, and for 1843, Naquin and Rawski, *Chinese Society*, 213.

[47]Pomeranz, 'Re-thinking the late-imperial Chinese economy'. Compare the information in Ho, *Studies on the Population*, 283. For internal migration in China see Deng, 'Unveiling China's true population statistics'; Kolb, 'About figures and aggregates', and Pomeranz and Topik, *World that Trade Created*, 59–62. For a map indicating the major population movements during the eighteenth century, see Myers and Wang, 'Economic developments', 567.

less densely populated hinterlands in China Proper, although normally it did resist Han settlement in Manchuria's frontier provinces. What is striking in the Chinese situation in this respect is that most migrants move from relatively rich but crowded places to relatively poor but less densely populated ones.[48] The number of people going to regions *outside* the eighteen provinces of China Proper continued to be very small in the period we discuss here. *In principle*, the Qing may have been in favour of adding new land to their empire with all the possibilities that opened. But they also were well aware of the costs involved and of the increasing chances that conflicts would break out between new settlers and original inhabitants. James Reardon-Anderson speaks of a policy of stop and go and points at differences in approach when it comes to different regions. In the end, political considerations always were paramount.[49]

The enormously extended regions of Xinjiang, what now is called Qinghai, and Tibet remained almost empty; the island that is now called Taiwan also was not very densely settled.[50] The population of Xinjiang continued to be counted in the hundreds of thousands. Qing authorities for a long time were ambivalent about allowing Han immigration there. From 1760 to 1830 they prohibited Chinese from settling permanently in the Tarim Basin. Most Chinese settlers that did go 'West' concentrated in Urumchi and Zungharia. In 1830, the total Chinese population (including Chinese Muslims) in Xinjiang still was only around 155,000. After 1831, it was allowed and even encouraged to migrate to the Tarim Basin, which started a bigger inflow.[51] Qinghai had even fewer inhabitants. The number of Tibetans directly subject to the government in Lhasa was and continued to be small. In 1800 it was still well under 4 million. The number of Chinese living in the region was negligible. The policy of the Qing with regard to Han immigration into Taiwan, a region that was only conquered by the Qing in the 1680s, also was ambivalent.[52] During the eighteenth century, for example, colonization was prohibited outright. Whatever may have been official policy, over time the population did increase and immigration did play a role in that. In 1684, the population of Qing-controlled Taiwan was approximately between 100,000 and 150,000. Fifty years later, notwithstanding severely restricted official immigration into the island, this number had nearly tripled to 415,000. Halfway through the nineteenth century, the population had again increased substantially, but the island certainly did not have more than 2 million inhabitants, in all probability much less. The total number of Mongolian-speaking people in the entire empire, excluding the Mongolian banner men, in the beginning decades of the nineteenth century was less than 3.5 million, 700,000 of them in Outer Mongolia and 2.6 million in Inner Mongolia. The Qing government opposed Han

---

[48]Pomeranz, 'Institutions and economic development'.

[49]Reardon-Anderson, *Reluctant Pioneers*, 161–2. See also Isett, *State, Peasant, and Merchant*, 320, and Umeno, 'Han Chinese immigrants in Manchuria'.

[50]See for information on the population size of these regions Fletcher, 'Ch'ing Inner Asia' and 'Heyday of the Ch'ing order'; Millward, *Beyond the Pass*, 51 and 271–2, note 21, and ch. 7, and Naquin and Rawski, *Chinese Society*, 213.

[51]Millward, *Eurasian Crossroads*, 104–5.

[52]See for figures on Taiwan's population and on migration to the island Chang, 'Chinese migration', and Shepherd, 'Some demographic characteristics'.

settlement in most of Mongolia. It was only Southern Mongolia, the region of the 'great bend' of the Yellow River, which attracted Chinese. If we look at the total number of inhabitants, we only see relatively minor shifts.

I have already indicated that in 1851 the total population of Manchuria, a region of more than 1.2 million km^2, still numbered only a little over 5 million. That was much more than in the beginning of the seventeenth century and the actual number of inhabitants at any moment in time will have been even larger because of the seasonal labour force that went there without permanently settling. But even when taking that in consideration, the region continued to be quite empty. The Manchu emperors long preferred a Manchuria untrammelled by Han settlers and only officially opened the borders in the northeast in 1860. Even then it was not wholeheartedly but because in the end they preferred 'Sinicisation' to Russian colonization. Between roughly 1890 and 1937, about 25 million Chinese went to Manchuria, of whom two-thirds returned.[53] This shows how much of the potential of their empire was *not* used by the Qing. Going to Xinjiang, most parts of Mongolia or, for that matter, Tibet was not a very alluring prospect for most Han Chinese who wanted to live from the land. Not only were these regions, overall, not very fertile: they also were 'foreign' to them. They would probably have felt even less at ease there than in south-western China, where so many did go – or Manchuria, where relatively few went. In brief, there were not many people to exploit in the regions that were added to China Proper, nor were there many Chinese settling there. The military presence of the Qing in their newly acquired regions as a rule was not very impressive. In Xinjiang, for example, immediately after its conquest, some 40,000 Chinese military troops were stationed. Their number increased to 50,000 by the mid-nineteenth century.[54] The number of Sino-Tibetan troops who had to oversee the situation in Tibet on behalf of the Qing rulers was only a couple of thousand, at best.[55] All the regions outside China Proper might have had the advantage that densely populated China Proper could try and discharge surplus population there. In the period we discuss here, this scarcely happened.

The figures presented so far with regard to extra land and population acquired by the rulers of various Western European countries and those of China point to huge differences in scale between Western empire-building and empire-building by the Qing. When we look at the newly acquired territories from the perspective of their functioning as population outlets, the differences, admittedly, are less pronounced, though not absent. But to me the differences found so far would already be sufficient reason to not regard it as very sensible to speak of 'striking resemblances' in this respect. But this is not all: there were more, quite significant, differences. Think, for example, of the enormous effort it took Britain in terms of money, resources, time and people to create and maintain its

---

[53]Gottschang and Larry, *Swallows and Settlers*, 2 and 38.

[54]Millward, *Eurasian Crossroads*, 99.

[55]Dabringhaus, *Qing-Imperium*, 184–8. After the rule of the Qianlong emperor, who at the end of his reign intervened in Tibet with a substantial armed force to expel the Gurkha invaders from Nepal, basically the country was left unprotected by the Chinese government. Qing authority shrank. When in 1854 the Gurkhas again invaded the country, the Qing did nothing and Tibet had to sign a treaty in which it promised to pay reparations and declared it would accept Nepalese protection.

empire. I only have to refer to my comments in previous chapters on the height of its taxes and its public debt and on its military and naval apparatus. *Compared* to that, China got its empire very cheap. Again, we are talking about completely different orders of magnitude.[56]

When it comes to the benefits of empire in economic terms there clearly were differences too. Talking about *the* benefits, or *the* costs, of empire obviously is fairly simplistic. One has to be more specific and can, for example, distinguish between the benefits and costs for private persons, for government and for society as a whole, in that last case expressing them in terms of the positive or negative contribution to GDP. On top of that there is the distinct possibility that per category there might be differing outcomes. The balance sheets for government, society or various individuals or companies could turn out to be quite different. Think for example of the possibility that there might be private gains but governmental and social losses. Depending on the research question, it may make sense to differentiate between the short term and the long term. The results of an enquiry may differ with differing moments. Moreover, it may make sense, as we already suggested and did, to distinguish between monetary costs and benefits and costs and benefits in non-monetary terms. From these various angles the question whether the empire paid has been and still is hotly debated in British and, more in general, European historiography.[57] What cannot be doubted, however, is that at least various groups in British society made enormous profits. Nor can it be denied that the role of economic considerations was quite different in British as compared to Chinese imperialism. Let me expand a little on that.

Chinese 'imperialism' first and foremost was a matter of territorial safety. Until the reign of the Qianlong emperor, it was almost entirely defence driven – that means searching for protection against the nomads of the steppe. Under that emperor it clearly was more expansionist, but basically it still was defensive. But whatever may have been the exact reasons for the various policies as they were implemented, China's expansion under the Qing was *not* driven by economic considerations and as a rule it was *not* a matter of private enterprise. I do not think it would be far-fetched to claim that the first characteristic to a large extent can be explained by the second. The Qing were in charge and they were not in it for the money: 'No great revenues flowed to Peking from Inner Asian dependencies. Indeed there was nothing the Qing wanted from them but peace.'[58] These words, by one of the most prominent specialists in the history of Central Asia, in fact apply to the way the Qing, as a rule, dealt with *all* their subjected neighbours. Roy Bin Wong comments that the Chinese state was more likely to invest in peripheries than to extract resources

---

[56]Two important comments are in order here: first, the bulk of the costs involved for Britain were incurred in fighting other Western states in Europe and, increasingly, overseas. Second, the British undertook systematic efforts to, at least in certain regions, make empire pay for itself. Think, for example, of the system of recruiting Indians for the 'British army' in India and of making Indians pay, via taxes, for the costs the British incurred in ruling them, and more.

[57]The amount of literature is staggering. I refer to Introduction note 80 for authors who think that for Britain empire paid. For a nuanced and cautious view that also pays attention to later periods see O'Brien, 'Imperialism'. For a European-wide analysis in which the British case is extensively discussed see Etemad, *De l'utilité des empires*, and O'Brien and Prados de la Escosura, *Costs and Benefits*.

[58]Fletcher, 'Ch'ing Inner Asia', 106.

from them.[59] Comparing the motives for Qing imperialism with the driving forces behind European expansion, Sabine Dabringhaus also points at fundamental differences. About Qing imperialism she writes: 'The search for wealth, for gains in trade or the wish to convert unbelievers did not play any role.'[60] It was initiated, and to a very large extent implemented, by a state that had its own 'raisons d'état'. If David Abernethy is right in claiming, as I think he is, that Western European empire-building was driven and characterized by an urge to explore, control and utilize and by a triple assault on the power of the public sector, the profits in the private sector and the sphere of religion and culture of the people it colonized, I think we have to conclude that Qing China was *not* imperialist.[61] That would also be true if we would use Darwin's definition of imperialism as 'the attempt to impose one's state predominance over other societies by assimilating them to its political and cultural and economic system'.[62] Western rule as it extended overseas functioned according to different logics, even in an empire like that of Spain, a country where, next to profit and religion, territorial extension had always been an important consideration. In particular between 1770 and 1840, to focus on an extremely important period for our analysis, we see a conscious, focused attempt on the part of Britain, on its way to becoming the biggest colonial power in the West, to exploit her overseas dependencies for economic purposes. In contrast to what happened in Qing China, in the West, in particular in Britain and the Dutch Republic, the role of private enterprise – that obviously was looking for profit – in creating as well as running the empire always was very big, if not decisive; its collaboration with the state almost always intense.

The regions that the Qing absorbed into their empire were not (turned into) cash cows. In the case of Tibet the tiny costs for the Qing of controlling the region were borne by the region itself, but nothing was taken out of the region.[63] With regard to Xinjiang, Peter Perdue writes: 'Xinjiang never became self-sufficient, so it was a drain on the treasury', adding that 'it also never became truly integrated with the interior by private trade'.[64] According to Fletcher, by 1800 something like 1.2 million silver taels had to come each year from China Proper for Xinjiang to meet its expenses.[65] State farms had been founded, in particular near Urumchi, on which criminals, people who had been banned to this outpost of the empire and Han soldiers who were stationed there worked the land. As such, these farms were successful: they produced enough to feed those troops. But as indicated, overall, costs of the occupation were higher than its yields. When unrest broke out in the region in the nineteenth century, this drain of course only got bigger. For regions like Mongolia and modern-day Qinghai the story will not have been fundamentally different. Manchuria too, for that matter, cost the government money that had to come

---

[59]Wong, *China Transformed*, 148.

[60]Dabringhaus, *Qing-Imperium*, 235. The translation is mine.

[61]Abernethy, *Dynamics of Global Dominance*.

[62]Darwin, *After Tamerlane*, 416.

[63]Dabringhaus, *Qing-Imperium*, 212.

[64]Perdue, *China Marches West*, 397.

[65]Fletcher, 'Ch'ing Inner Asia', 61. Compare Millward, *Beyond the Pass*, 58–61, and idem, *Eurasian Crossroads*, 102–5.

from China Proper. The bulk of the funds needed to pay for the administration of the so-called north-eastern Provinces in any case came from China Proper. In essence the peasants of China subsidized the dynasty's strategic and patrimonial interests in its homeland.[66] Sichuan too very often depended on outside financial support.[67] The same goes for Taiwan, which was never turned into a 'Wallersteinian' periphery. The difference between the way the Qing dealt with the island and the way the Japanese did when it had become their colony is striking.[68] One need not enter into the debate about whether and in what respects Japan's colonization was a success, for whom and at what costs, to admit that Japan did manage to alter Taiwan's economy and gear it to that of the motherland.[69]

These comments naturally lead to some more general reflections on China's international relations as compared to those of states in Western Europe. In those reflections I will base myself upon – and paraphrase – the enlightening and helpful brief analysis of Giovanni Arrighi in his *Adam Smith in Beijing*.[70] Arrighi relativizes the 'traditional' view that states and their organization in an interstate system were something typically European. In the early modern era, so he claims, there also was a China-centred state system. Both systems were similar enough to make a comparison of them analytically meaningful. There are major differences, though. The dynamic of the European system was characterized by an incessant competition among its national components and by a tendency towards the geographical expansion both of the system and of its shifting centre. What is crucial in this respect is the absence of any tendency among East Asian states to build *overseas* empires and to engage in an armament race on a scale comparable to what occurred in Europe. Qing expansion, at least till the 1760s, was meant to change borders that were hard to defend into a pacified periphery and a buffer against raiders and conquerors from Inner Asia. In the West we see a ceaseless and limitless expansionism. There is no Chinese equivalent of Cecil Rhodes' quote with which I started this chapter. China was the clear and undisputed centre of an East Asian states system, but those states that paid tribute to it were not colonies, nor were they peripheries of a Chinese core. In Western Europe there was more of a balance of power with various contenders for hegemony. Arrighi, I think correctly, claims that the extraversion of the European power struggle was a major determinant of the peculiar combination of capitalism, militarism and territorialism that propelled the globalization of the European system. Western Europe was much more interested in long-distance trade and, in general the importance of that trade was bigger there than it was in the

---

[66]For this information see Isett, *State, Peasant, and Merchant*, ch. 1. Compare Reardon-Anderson, *Reluctant Pioneers*, 58–9 and 72. Both Jilin and Heilongjiang were 'deficit' provinces that received annual silver transfers from the 'surplus' provinces in the more richly endowed China Proper. Eighty per cent of the budget of the first province and almost the entire budget of the second one were paid for by such subsidies. During the first half of the nineteenth century, annual deficits of these provinces amounted to over 1 million taels.

[67]Dai, *Sichuan Frontier and Tibet*, provides numerous examples. See, for example, ch. 6.

[68]See Shepherd, *Statecraft and Political Economy*, for the period from the 1680s to 1800 and Mazumdar, *Sugar and Society*, ch. 7, for differences in policy between China and Japan later on.

[69]See for a first introduction to that debate the *Cambridge History of Japan*, Volumes 5 and 6, under 'Taiwan'.

[70]Arrighi, *Adam Smith in Beijing*, 309–44.

East. In the East Asian system we see an opposite dynamic, which is understandable in light of the success of Asia's development as the largest market economy at the time. For China, control of trade routes was much less important than peaceful relations with neighbouring states. Foreign trade was often discouraged rather than encouraged. The European dynamic led to a sequence of ever more powerful states that identified themselves with capital and capitalists. There is no parallel in East Asia for that. It also led to the development of superior military force that was to become the key to the subjection of East Asia to the West.

That overseas expansion of the West, with all the huge differences between various countries and over time, always implied a strong element of exploitation and an effort to create peripheries in the 'Wallersteinian' sense of the word. Westerners as a rule tried to create relations of exploitation and unequal exchange in which the economies of their overseas possessions were actually transformed and manipulated, if needs be by brute force, to serve the interests of the 'core' region that had incorporated them. They always tried to create a division of labour in which the 'core' specialized in producing goods with high added value and the peripheral regions were *made to* specialize in the production of raw materials or basic products, added little value and earned the *un-free* labourers only low wages. Western 'core' states used their military and economic power to back up the functioning of this division of labour and to channel profits in their direction. A very clear example in the British case – only one among many – would be Britain's possessions in the Caribbean. Their entire mode of production was changed and geared to Britain's economy: their labour force (i.e. slave labour) to a very large extent was actually imported by the British; their products, predominantly sugar, and much of the profits earned in producing them, were exported to Britain; while most of the goods that were not produced locally were imported from or via Britain.

The relation between China Proper, Manchuria and their various new territorial acquisitions was quite different. It clearly was not one between 'core' and 'periphery' like that described by Wallerstein. New territories like Taiwan, Mongolia, Tibet and Xinjiang were not 'forced' in one way or another to make their economies serve that of China. No fundamental changes in their mode of production were instigated by their new relationship with Qing China, nor did their overlords in China put them under pressure to introduce such changes. The migrants or sojourners who went to China's frontier, inside or outside China Proper, replicated the China they came from. The modes of production, trade, transportation and finance inherited from China Proper were reproduced or passed on with little or no change.[71] We do not see the emergence of any plantations where sugar, tea, tobacco, silk or cotton were grown: not in the newly conquered regions, nor in the internal periphery and nor, for that matter, in China Proper itself.[72] Possibilities to profit from the new lands as they presented themselves often were not utilized. As we already indicated, government, for example, often was reticent to let

---

[71]See, for example, for the situation in Manchuria Reardon-Anderson, *Reluctant Pioneers*, 170. Compare Wong's comments on the 'fractal' quality of China's societal structure in Wong, *China Transformed*, 121–2.
[72]See for that observation, for sugar, Mazumdar, *Sugar and Society*, 'Conclusion', and for tea Gardella, *Harvesting Mountains*, chs 2 and 4, and Vries, *Zur politischen Ökonomie des Tees*, 97–126.

Han Chinese settle in peripheral zones. It did not exactly promote trade in or with its new territories. There are various examples of government discouraging or even prohibiting the mining of precious metals and minerals in Xinjiang, or the starting of various projects that might help in developing the region.[73] Tibet was known, in any case in the West, to be rich in minerals. This explains Western (i.e. British) interest in the region. The Qing state did not take it upon itself to exploit them, nor did it encourage or help others to do so.[74] During the eighteenth century it not only tried to strictly regulate migration to Taiwan: it also frequently restricted its trade.[75] The case of Manchuria, which is especially interesting in this respect, will be discussed more extensively later (pages 403–5). Nor did the Qing as rulers – and their country – systematically profit from the activities of the millions of overseas Chinese. Those were not regarded as 'parts' of the empire. It will not come as a surprise that the structures and institutions of mercantile capitalism that evolved in Western Europe in the wake of its overseas expansion, and the building of its fiscal-military imperialist states, were all lacking in China.

China and ghost acreage

When it comes to the new regions over which in one way or another it extended its rule, China (i.e. first and foremost the government and to a lesser extent the mercantile and agricultural elites) clearly could have done more to open them up and turn them into areas that could supply China Proper with all kinds of resources. Whether that would have been of much avail in really 'escaping' from Malthus may be doubted. But it definitely could have helped to keep him at bay for much longer. Taiwan clearly could have been of more use to China, as could Mongolia, Qinghai and Xingjian, though even now these last three regions are still quite empty and underdeveloped. That is not true for Taiwan, but that in the end is rather small. So probably we have to conclude that, in pre-industrial circumstances, exploiting them to the full, or even exploiting them more fully, would have been quite complicated. To keep things manageable, I will not go into highly speculative scenarios in which China colonizes parts of Asia or even parts of other continents, even though the *fact* that Britain became the 'core' of a global 'empire' is much more 'far-fetched' than the *fiction* that China would have done so. Let us focus on what *realistic* possibilities were open to the Qing to ease Malthusian constraints for the densely populated, if not already over-populated, heartlands of China Proper in the period of time that Britain 'prepared' its take off.

We may leave aside the possibility for China to import land-intensive goods from other countries in such amounts that it would really make a difference *for the entire nation*. China's population is simply too big for that. But I fail to see why such imports could not have had a big impact in certain regions. An example that comes to mind is

[73]See, for examples, Dabringhaus, *Qing-Imperium*, 77 and 79, and Fletcher, 'Ch'ing Inner Asia', 66.
[74]See, for examples, Dabringhaus, *Qing-Imperium*, 111–12, and Teltscher, *High Road to China*.
[75]Chang, 'Chinese migration to Taiwan', 112.

the enormous amount of cotton that China imported from India at the time of Britain's industrialization. This has been brought up in debates on Pomeranz's thesis and it is very apt as it refers to the symbol *par excellence* of Britain's industrialization and the main import product for its factories. Mark Elvin claims that, between 1785 and 1833, the single province of Guangdong imported, on average, each year six times as much raw cotton from India as the whole of Britain used annually at the time of Arkwright's first water frame.[76] According to H. V. Bowen, in 1805, 55.3 million pounds of cotton were shipped from British India into Canton. That cotton was and continued to be substantially cheaper than Chinese cotton. At that time, the retained imports of wool-cotton into Great Britain stood at 58.9 million pounds.[77] According to Prasannan Parthasarathi, to give a last example, in 1815, the amount of Indian cotton that China imported via Canton roughly equalled Britain's cotton imports at the time.[78] In terms of silver that cotton from India will no doubt have been much cheaper than that from America. It in any case was substantially cheaper than that from China itself.[79] On top of that, China produced enormous amounts of very cheap cotton at home. Why exactly did that massive availability of land-intensive raw material not turn Guangdong into a Chinese Lancashire of sorts? If the explanation has to be that Guangdong had no coal, then why did it not at least lead to the development of large-scale concentrated production in manufactures, that is, the kind of factories without steam engines?

Let us concentrate on Qing China's 'internal peripheries' and their role in the development of the country and ask the following question: if land-intensive goods indeed would have been so fundamental for Britain, then what about the exports of such goods from China's frontier regions to its heartland? Provided we do *not* take the terms in their very specific 'Wallersteinian' meaning, China, and I here mean China Proper, did have core regions and peripheries *inside* its own polity. Very densely populated and highly developed regions of the country like Lingnan, the region of the Lower Yangtze or the southeast coast did import huge amounts of land-intensive goods from less densely populated, less developed parts of China's hinterland, including Manchuria.[80] Those regions thereby performed the function that 'peripheries' are supposed to perform for 'cores'. Taken as a block, developed China was more or less permanently short of food. In his book on agricultural development in Jiangnan, Bozhong Li devotes an entire chapter, called 'The externalisation of agriculture', to the importance for the economy of that region of imports of grain and bean cake from other parts of China.[81] When discussing the economy of the Pearl River Delta, Robert Marks comments: 'The system

---

[76]Elvin, *Pattern of the Chinese Past*, 312–13. That water frame was patented in the 1760s.
[77]See Bowen, 'British exports of raw cotton', 115–16.
[78]Parthasarathi, 'Review article', 283–4.
[79]In the year 1793–4, raw cotton from India cost 10 to 12 taels per picul. Raw cotton produced in China cost 3 to 5 taels more. According to two sources from 1804 and 1813, Indian raw cotton still remained cheaper than Jiangnan cotton by around one picul per tael. See for this information and references Bowen, 'British exports of raw cotton', 124–5.
[80]For a map showing interregional grain transfers in Qing China see Myers and Wang, 'Economic developments', 613.
[81]Li, *Agricultural Development*, ch. 6.

as a whole was not sustainable without greater and greater inputs from outside.'[82] If we are to believe the figures presented in their publications and, by the way, also in Pomeranz's *Great Divergence*, China's heartland in fact was *more* dependent on its 'internal periphery' than Great Britain was on its overseas periphery, in any case for the period we are discussing here.[83]

What in Pomeranz's view, however, marks the fundamental difference is exactly the fact that the frontier regions in China were *not* Wallersteinian peripheries and that their relationship with China Proper never turned into one of periphery and core as Wallerstein understands these terms – the main reason being that the mode of production in China's periphery was so similar to that in China Proper with a labour force that, unlike in a Wallersteinian periphery, was free. The more developed regions of China, moreover, being part of the same state as the peripheral regions, did not exert any leverage, politically or otherwise, over the actual functioning of the economy of their 'peripheral' trade partners. This will indeed have, as Pomeranz suggests, played a part in the gradual disappearance, from the middle of the eighteenth century onwards, of the 'frontier' situation that had initially characterized China's 'internal periphery'. Almost by definition the opening up of new territories at first resulted in surplus production. In the course of the eighteenth century it was Sichuan that produced the most remarkable and durable surpluses of foodstuffs.[84] With the filling up of the various 'peripheral' regions in China with peasants who increasingly produced for their own consumption, however, those regions lost their ability to function as providers of basics resources to China's core, whereas they, at the same time, also began to import less from that core. Relations between heartland and frontier tended to become *less* instead of more intense with the passing of time.[85] The impact of inputs from peripheral regions decreased and, anyhow, they apparently never provided the relief that Pomeranz claims Britain's Atlantic periphery provided for Britain. But that of course still does not provide a good reason to (1) so very emphatically point at the importance for Britain's development of its imports of basic goods from an external periphery and (2) only somewhat in passing refer to the imports from the periphery for China's core. The amounts of land-intensive products imported into the centre of China were huge, as Pomeranz and other Californians themselves indicate. They lasted for quite some decades. Why would they, and in particular the cotton imports into Guangdong, have to be less important and less consequential than the imports from its Atlantic periphery for Britain?

In this respect, it is highly interesting what happened in Manchuria, or rather what did *not* happen there. We see some 'filling up' here too. The 'frontier' moved somewhat

---

[82]Marks, 'Commercialization without capitalism', 76.

[83]For some figures in Pomeranz's work with regard to imports of China's core regions from their peripheries see, for example, his 'Beyond the East-West binary', 583–4, where he refers to bean-cake imports into Jiangnan from Manchuria.

[84]See, for examples and further explanation, in alphabetical order, Isett, *State, Peasant, and Merchant*, 212, 214, 243, 274, 366–7; Pomeranz, *Great Divergence*, ch. 6; idem, 'Rethinking the late imperial Chinese economy', and Will, *Bureaucracy and Famine*, ch. 13.

[85]For a description of this filling-up process and an analysis of its causes and effects, see the previous note.

northward and the region became more or less a developed province, although it never needed to *im*port grain. But considering what happened there after the 1850s, it all was too little too late. According to Yong Xue, Manchuria could have functioned as a huge reservoir of ghost acreage – and also as a provider of coal – for China Proper during the very long eighteenth century.[86] One can only agree with him when he writes: 'The vast virgin lands in Manchuria offered a real windfall, representing a piece of geographical luck for Jiangnan.'[87] Manchuria enjoyed extraordinary natural endowments. The breath of its farmland was enormous. I want to remind the reader that Qing Manchuria in its entirety, till the Russians took over part of it in the 1850s, measured about 1.2 million km². That is a tract of land roughly twice as big as contemporary France. At the end of the nineteenth century a traveller still characterized it as a region that was agriculturally rich beyond the dreams of avarice. Whereas many forests in China Proper had been stripped bare by the end of the eighteenth century, the Manchurian lands remained cloaked in what appeared to be endless woodlands. The region had plenty of fur-bearing animals, fish and oysters. Its soil contained gold and, as discovered late in the nineteenth century, copper, lead and tin. It was famous for its ginseng.[88] But the Qing elite did not really care.

It would of course be incorrect to suggest that nothing happened. The virgin lands in Manchuria did provide China Proper with soybean. But they could have done so much more and much earlier: that would have meant more fertilizer and more pig food. Pomeranz and Li Bozhong do refer to its soybean production and to substantial exports of soybeans to China Proper. According to Xue, however, their estimates of exports are too high. He thinks Manchurian bean-cake exports to Jiangnan were at best 10 per cent of Pomeranz's estimate and only 4 per cent of that by Li Bozhong, which in the end Pomeranz regards as more likely than his own. So Manchuria according to him (i.e. Xue) did much less to relieve pressure in China Proper than these two experts suggest. He also shows, and that in this context is more important, that even if their estimates were correct, production still was much lower than what the region might have produced if it had been opened and if it had been systematically exploited. That becomes only too apparent after the 'opening' of Manchuria, when the region was turned into the biggest soybean producer in the world, producing more than 5 million tons or almost 60 million shi per year, which is three times as much as Li Bozhong's over-optimistic estimate for Manchuria's exports roughly a century earlier.[89]

Manchuria could have become a major grain supplier for the capital too. That claim is not an anachronistic assumption. Manchuria had potential: it had excellent soil and enough water for farming. Grain prices there were only half what they were in China

---

[86]Xue, 'A "fertiliser revolution"?', passim.
[87]Xue, 'A "fertiliser revolution"?', 219.
[88]See for these descriptions Reardon-Anderson, *Reluctant Pioneers*, 9 and 103–4.
[89]Xue, 'A "fertiliser revolution"?', 196–7 and 218–19. In the context of my research it is quite striking that the Qing government only in 1772 definitely abolished all restrictions – that were meant to protect Manchurian consumers – on transporting soybeans and bean cakes by sea out of their 'homeland'. See Xue, 'A "fertiliser revolution"?', 202 and 209.

Proper. People at the time knew this and made suggestions about how to use the region's potential. He Qizhong, an imperial censor, for example, did so in the middle of the eighteenth century. Let me again quote Xue:

> If the Qing government had coordinated a series of agricultural projects in Manchuria instead of prohibiting immigration into the region, if commercial institutions in China had been effective enough to channel the large amount of capital needed to develop the frontiers and establish large plantations as the British did in North America, then a large amount of Manchurian grain could have flowed into Beijing.[90]

For the nineteenth century, talking about industrialization means talking about coal. That was yet another resource that Manchuria could have supplied to parts of China Proper. He Qizhong, the imperial censor to whom we just referred, in 1745 reported abundant coal resources in Fengtian (modern Liaoning), which were located fairly close to seaports. He urged that this natural bounty be exploited to relieve the shortage of firewood in the region.[91] Nothing of the sort happened. One cannot therefore, with Yong Xue, escape the conclusion that the opportunities provided by Manchuria, which indeed could fittingly be labelled 'China's geographical luck', were squandered. With him one can point at various reasons for that, like tensions between Han and Manchus or internal institutional defects of the Ming and Qing states. Fundamental for the subject of this book is the fact that government was unwilling to grasp those opportunities itself or give private entrepreneurs the possibility to do so.

If we are to believe Pomeranz, 'coal' and 'colonies' were the two main reasons that Britain could industrialize and leave China behind. My thesis would be that China, in a way, also had its 'coal' and its colonies, but that government was a serious hindrance in making the most of them. When it comes to coal mining, the Qing often prohibited opening mines in the first place or wanted those already opened closed down. Initiatives by government itself to open mines or to 'modernize' them are absent. When it comes to the exploitation of newly incorporated territories or of Manchuria, we can only conclude that many chances were not utilized, or rather not even considered. A policy of colonization like that seen in the West was never tried. Chinese merchants who were active overseas were not supported either. If only for these reasons, one simply cannot discuss the causes of the diverging developments of China's and Britain's economy without extensively dealing with the role of China's government. In this respect, as in various others, that role was not positive, which of course does not mean that the outcome would have been positive if Qing China had started to act on the global stage in ways similar to that of imperial Britain.

We pointed earlier on to the Western tendency to exploit and subject their peripheries. This will not have been unrelated to the fact that, overall, in Western imperialism there

---

[90]Xue, 'A "fertiliser revolution"?', 220.
[91]Xue, 'A "fertiliser revolution"?', 219.

was a strong tendency to emphasize the differences in, for example, religion, level of development or – to put it in rather 'anachronistic', modern terms – race or nation between colonizing and colonized people. Here too, one should be wary not to generalize too easily: the behaviour of the Spaniards in their American colonies, for example, was quite distinct from that of the British.[92] But in general one may say that newly acquired lands and people tended to be less rejected by China's rulers than was the case when European imperialists encountered their colonial subjects. This difference in attitude must have had economic consequences. We have already referred to the tendency of the Manchu Qing to accommodate in our discussion of their behaviour in China Proper. Outside China Proper, as a rule, the Qing were satisfied with exerting some kind of indirect rule and they often did accept local law. There was intermarriage between the Manchus and other peoples in the empire. China's empire-building basically boiled down to a 'normal' extension of its rule overland to incorporate, if that is not too strong a term, civilizations of a kind that it had already known for a long time and that did not present much of a challenge and stimulus to its economy and society. We, of course, are discussing differences of 'emphasis': in the West and Western colonies in the early modern era one also finds examples of accommodation and indirect rule.

One must, of course, not exaggerate the 'mild' character of Qing imperialism like Hobson does when he claims that China chose to eschew imperialism and that China's identity was more of a defensive construct.[93] In their frontier wars the Qing could be very hard and cruel. They clearly did not only rely on 'soft' power. Perdue does not hesitate to call the massive killing of Zunghars at the end of the Qing campaign against them 'a deliberate use of massacre'.[94] When the Qing, during the eighteenth century began to exercise political and social control over the areas of Hunan, Hubei, Guangdong, Guangxi, Guizhou, Sichuan and Yunnan that were also inhabited by non-Han people, their approach was not always 'accommodating'. Many Han went there and drove the original inhabitants uphill and away from fertile land. In, for example, Guizhou and Hunan there was harsh pressure on indigenous people – often, it has to be added, but clearly not always, against instructions of central government.[95] On Taiwan and in Tibet the behaviour of the Qing also could be quite harsh every now and then. It will not have been by accident that many of the rebellions that started to plague the empire in the late eighteenth century, and that often were brutally crushed, broke out in regions where Han and non-Han lived in a troublesome coexistence.

The Manchus did adopt certain Han features and liked to make appeals to 'universal values' and 'similarity', but they did so selectively and while maintaining their separateness through their privileges, religious ceremonies, the banner system and compulsory exercises in horsemanship and military drills. Their homeland continued to be a key

[92]Elliott, *Empires of the Atlantic World*, ch. 3.
[93]Hobson, *Eastern Origins of Western Civilisation*, 69–70 and 308.
[94]See Perdue, *China Marches West*, 284, for the quotation. See for the way the Zunghars were dealt with ch. 7.
[95]See Richards, *Unending Frontier*, 131–7. For brutal Chinese imperialism in Guizhou see e.g. Blunden and Elvin, *Cultural Atlas of China*, 38, and Jenks, *Insurgency and Social Disorder*. For general comments see the texts by Perdue referred to in the Bibliography.

element in their identity, even though most Manchus never lived there. They and the Han Chinese over whom and with whom they ruled, moreover, were not uniform in their behaviour towards 'the other' at their various frontiers. The situation in the northeast, the northwest, the southwest and at the maritime frontiers, including Taiwan, simply was too different. Their view on the residents of these frontiers varied from 'culturalism' to 'racism', not of course in the modern, biological sense of the word but more in terms of a kind of geographic determinism. The Han as settled agriculturalists tended to always feel superior over non-sedentary people like pastoralists. 'Culturalists' among Manchus and Han claimed that the 'uncivilized' frontier's people could be civilized. 'Racists' in that respect were much more hesitant and basically preferred to keep the 'uncivilized' outside 'real' civilization. They preferred exclusion and isolation over efforts at integration.

When it comes to migration by Han people to one of the frontiers, we have already noticed that this led to mixed feelings and differing policies. On the one hand, incorporating extra land in the empire meant more production and more 'civilization'. On the other hand, it almost inevitably led to conflicts with the people who were the original settlers. From the second half of eighteenth century, according to Perdue, the ruling Manchus tended to lean towards the more racialist ideology described in the previous paragraph. Population pressure in China Proper and the ensuing increase in migration and trade tended to make the situation at the frontiers tenser. According to him, intelligent policies could have prevented frictions, but the Qing had lost the ability or will to wage a differentiating policy and so provoked more resistance.[96]

But even so, as compared to Western empire-building overseas, the Qing Empire was rather something of an 'informal empire', exerting quasi-colonial rule.[97] To all intents and purposes it was a classic 'frontier empire'. It is true that both Western European states and China acquired new lands over which they exerted their rule and that in that sense both were 'imperialist'. But that is as far as 'striking resemblances' in this respect go. Again, differences were much more salient than similarities.

---

[96] This paragraph is paraphrasing Perdue, 'Nature and nurture'. I refer the reader also to his 'Erasing the empire'.
[97] See for these terms and this interpretation Osterhammel, *Colonialism*, 20.

CHAPTER 8
STATE-BUILDING, NATION-BUILDING AND 'LEGIBILITY'

STATE AND NATION IN GREAT BRITAIN AND CHINA

To begin with, Britain had the advantage of being a nation.

Landes, *Wealth and Poverty*, 219

Too much liberty without any unity …

Sun Yat-sen about the Chinese[1]

Mercantilism, interpreted as a form of economic nationalism, could very easily entail *empire*-building. With its focus on the national economy, it almost inevitably entailed *nation*-building of some kind, although it fell short of creating 'modern' nations. As long as there were differing estates and as long as rulers only ruled *over* their subjects and not in one way or another *in their name*, it would be incorrect to speak about their realms in terms of modern nations. Such nations are characterized by an element of inclusiveness: all partake in it and 'the people', in the end, are sovereign. Mercantilist rulers are not known for their enthusiasm about popular sovereignty and in that sense clearly were not keen on creating a modern nation state. But their policies of strengthening the state almost by definition implied creating more uniformity among their subjects, restricting the powers of various estates, if and when possible, and trying to mobilize as many people as possible in support of the state. This actually, sometimes quite unintentionally, led to nation-building, which in turn could, in various ways, affect the strength of states.

Being a nation could in several respects have its advantages. A sense of belonging and cohesion of its inhabitants clearly can strengthen a state. Think for example of administrative and military affairs. Being able to rally 'the masses' for 'the common cause' that is supposed to be embodied in their nation and its state undoubtedly helps in waging war, especially when one is confronted with an opponent that cannot count on the support of the bulk of the populace.[2] A government that can motivate and mobilize the masses to fight for 'their' imagined community and whose people give their first and overarching loyalty to the state clearly has an advantage over a government whose people

---

[1]I found this quotation in Schell and Delury, *Wealth and Power*, 133.
[2]For the role of factors like 'national solidarity' or 'citizenship' in the development of military power I refer back to the literature in Introduction notes 232–3 and 281–4. I have put the words 'national solidarity' and 'citizenship' in quotes because these terms are too modern and therefore anachronistic for the phenomena I refer to.

feel they have other obligations and sympathies that they value higher than the nation with its impersonal bonds. Patriotism can be a very potent force in case of conflicts. Britain would never have been able to wage its prolonged battle against France without a healthy, and often unhealthy, dose of chauvinism that, especially during the major wars against Bonaparte, began to consist of a compound of xenophobia, 'racial' superiority and the conviction that God favoured a godly people. It is not by accident that the French revolutionary concept of the *levée en masse* and the idea of mass conscription and indoctrination found support in government circles in various countries. Though, interestingly enough, not in Britain, which is widely regarded as the first modern nation state in Europe but only introduced conscription during the First World War.[3]

We must of course be wary not to exaggerate the 'patriotic' enthusiasm of conscripts at the time of the Revolutionary and Napoleonic Wars. Nor should we underestimate the pitfalls of mobilizing huge numbers of people who had no military experience or training whatsoever. But, on the other hand, for many, joining the army now opened career paths, which had hardly been the case for those men who had been conscripted in European armies, especially in Central and Eastern Europe, earlier. Mass conscription, moreover, had the advantage that people from all walks of life entered the army. This may have improved the quality of human resources. Whatever may have been the exact ratio of advantages to disadvantages, the enthusiasm of many professionals and of many what we would now call more 'conservative' and 'right-wing' politicians about 'mobilizing the masses' – if it had ever existed – tended to subside in the period of European history that is normally described as the Restoration (1815–48). In the end drills, training and very harsh discipline, as a rule, were far more important, and reliable, in providing and explaining efficiency and coherence than feelings of common identity. As indicated earlier, what as a rule came out was a kind of compromise between on 'professionalization' on the one hand and on the other hand 'massification'. With the exception of Britain, European powers sought to maintain a substantial standing army composed of conscripts and professionals, as well as an ever larger array of reservists who could be mobilized and deployed quickly enough to decide the outcome of the war at hand. In that respect the models for the armies of the twentieth century were the armies of 1866 and 1870, not the revolutionary armies of 1793–4.[4]

One always has to be careful not to be seduced into making too stark a contrast. Nevertheless there clearly was a difference in the level of patriotic enthusiasm and the potential for mass-mobilization between Britain and China. In the following quote Jeremy Black is explicitly referring to warfare, but his statement can surely be given a much broader meaning: 'Although the Chinese army certainly lagged behind western forces in technology, this gap was not large enough to explain the tremendous victories the western powers won. Instead, a failure of leaders to unite the country behind them was crucial.'[5] One can find many such quotes: 'Within the Imperial Army there was no

---

[3]See, for example, James, *Warrior Race*, under 'conscription'.
[4]I here almost literally paraphrase Sheehan, 'What it means to be a state', 14.
[5]Black, *War and the World*, 181.

sense of loyalty or cooperation between the troops and their commanders or between the commanders of the various units. The army lacked any sense of cohesion and purpose.'[6] There often was mistrust between Manchus and Han. Manchus were afraid that Han troops would not support them in battle.[7] There were deep-seated differences between them. Provincial autonomy, moreover, was quite substantial. 'Barbarian affairs' were not national affairs but resorted under the provincial governments. A Chinese nationalism, if it were to emerge, almost by necessity could only be anti-Manchu. People in practice more often than not were loyal to their province or village. That became painfully clear in the nineteenth century in various conflicts in which central government was involved and that parts of the country simply did not regard as their business. We see that happening during the First Opium War, when most provinces that were not directly involved simply stayed out of the conflict, and, again, during the war between France and China in 1884–5, when large parts of China did not participate in the war effort.[8] During the Sino-Japanese War of 1894–5, one fleet, that of the Northern Seas, and troops from one army, the Huai Army that almost entirely was recruited in Anhui province, did all the fighting. They did so under command of Li Hung-chang, the famous leading spirit of the Self-strengthening Movement. Li had no command over the rest of the army and navy: those remained passive, with many leaders from the South gloating over Li's misfortune.[9] When comparing the Japanese and Chinese in 1894, a commentator of the *London Times* wrote: 'Another essential difference between the people is their exhibition of patriotism. The Japanese are saturated with it, while the Chinese have none.'[10] Many inhabitants of China, and their regional bosses, felt that central government failed them in the nineteenth century. It had the obligation to keep the foreigners out and to look after their livelihood: in these respects it simply no longer did a good job. It is not easy to disentangle cause and effect here. It was the weakness of the Qing state that made its rulers rather unsuccessful in keeping out the Westerners. That in turn weakened their authority and therewith their strength. The fact that the Qing at various occasions fell back upon Western support to prop up their position did not help either. Deng in his recent book provides many examples for the nineteenth century that show to what extent China in (the second half of) that century no longer was a national territorial state under central rule.[11] It is not by accident that all reformers in the nineteenth and twentieth centuries wanted the Chinese to become a nation. According to Liang Qichao (1873–1929), the source of their country's backwardness was the Chinese lack of 'national consciousness'. China needed 'new citizens'. Sun Yat-sen, as we have seen, held the view that the Chinese

---

[6]Folsom, *Friends, Guests and Colleagues*, 61. Folsom here refers to government troops confronting the Taiping.

[7]See for this claim, for example, Crossley, *Orphan Warriors*, 54–5.

[8]Overdijking, *Lin Tse-Hsu*, 100, note 1.

[9]See e.g. Hsü, *Rise of Modern China*, ch. 14.

[10]I found this quotation in Paine, *Sino-Japanese War*, 237. The comment is in the *London Times*, 26 December 1894, page 4, but there is no reason to assume that things would have been different earlier on during the nineteenth century.

[11]Deng, *China's Political Economy*, ch. 5.

had 'too much liberty without any unity' and were 'a sheet of loose sand' that needed more 'discipline'.[12]

It is often overlooked that the emergence and cultivation of a strong sense of national identity – or if one wants 'nationalism', even though that term might be too strong and not entirely adequate in this context – and of national institutions is of immense importance for what one might call 'economic mobilization'. Differentiating between 'the military' and 'the economic' in this context would not have made much sense to many people, inside as well as outside Europe, at the time we are discussing in this book. Just think of the 'Fukoku kyōhei' motto, meaning 'rich country and strong army', that was so popular during Meiji rule in Japan. China's reformers also wanted 'a rich country with a powerful army'.[13] One may discuss how important they exactly were, but it would be hard to attribute no role to Japan's 'strong' state and its nationalism in explaining its economic success.[14] A systematic policy of trying to strengthen the economy of a state obviously has more chances of success when that state is strong and large parts of the population support that goal, identify with that state and think it represents 'their' nation. The big upheavals that are part and parcel of economic modernization and international competition can be weathered much better by people who feel they are unified in a nation than by a polity whose population lacks a clear sense of cohesion, identity and purpose. In Britain apparently that sense had developed. We have already indicated that the integration of the Scots in Great Britain looked quite successful. As far as I have been able to find out, in Wales there have never been serious problems about being in one polity with England. Many more Irish were involved in British empire-building than one might think.

Considering the way in which the discipline originally developed and considering the collectivist connotation of many of its central concepts, one can only be surprised about the extent to which current mainstream economics ignores the importance of collectives as 'states' and 'nation' and tries to, directly or indirectly, reduce all economic phenomena to rational choices by individuals. Even when we look at the history of economics in Great Britain – a country fond of its individualistic tradition – we come across concepts like 'moral economy', 'political economy', 'the wealth and poverty of nations', 'Gross Domestic Product', 'national income', 'national debt', 'growth' and so on: all concepts, like the concept 'economy' meaning 'household management' itself, that refer to collectives and not individuals. Looking at the history of the discipline on the European Continent, references to collectives are even more prominent. Rostow in his *Stages of Economic Growth* pointed at the fundamental role of nationalism as a precondition for a society to take off and at the very important role of nationalist responses to threats by more advanced nations.[15] Gerschenkron in his *Economic Backwardness in Historical Perspective* emphasized the importance of a belief in a new era and a new world for

---

[12]See for these quotations Schell and Delury, *Wealth and Power*, 92, 101 and 133.
[13]Pines, *Everlasting Empire*, 164.
[14]For that role I refer to Greenfeld, *Spirit of Capitalism*, ch. 3, and Norman, *Japan's Emergence*.
[15]See his *Stages of Economic Growth* under 'nationalism'.

societies that want to catch up. In his view industrialization, and more in general economic modernization, as a rule require a kind of 'national mobilization'.[16] At the moment, however, economists seem to all but completely ignore international rivalry as a motor of growth. Helpman in his excellent analysis of economic growth, *Mystery of Economic Growth*, does not even discuss concepts like 'international competition', 'nationalism', 'catching up' and 'hegemony'. Krugman claims that it would be a weird idea to think that states compete when it comes to their economies.[17] Even if the idea would indeed be weird (which it certainly is not), economic rivalry between states simply is a major fact in global history. To deny that or to simply say it ought not to be the case is not exactly helpful in a discipline that is supposed to be a social and empirical science. How could there be comparative advantage – a concept Krugman loves – let alone competitive advantage if there were no states? In that respect mercantilists – not by accident mostly businessmen and/or politicians, not academics – understood much better how real economies work. Development is not something that simply occurs but something that one has to pursue. Interstate competition often provided the *stimulus* if not the sheer *necessity* to develop. Any historian can easily come up with many examples of 'the will to develop'. The fact that Qing China did not feel seriously threatened by any external force as late as the 1840s may well have contributed to the fact that it lacked this will for so long.[18]

Historians overall seem to be far less reticent to admit the economic importance of nationalism. I can refer to the quote by Landes at the beginning of this chapter. According to Liah Greenfeld, Britain was not just a nation: it was the first nation in the world.[19] Like Landes, she regards that as anything but irrelevant in economic history. After her book on the origins of modern nationalism, she wrote one dealing with 'the spirit of capitalism'. In it she sets out to show, by analysing the cases of Britain, the Dutch Republic, France, Germany, Japan and the United States of America, that mobilizing nationalism, or if that would be too modern a term, 'patriotic sentiments', is fundamental in a strategy of creating economic growth, in mercantilist times as well as in times when *laissez-faire* had made more headway.[20] According to her, nationalism is the factor responsible for the reorientation of economic activity towards growth. The inclusive nature of nationalism and its core principles of fundamental equality of membership and popular sovereignty would give people with a national identity a sense of dignity. That lies at the basis of patriotism and commitment to national causes. That commitment will of necessity include the economy among the areas of competition with other nations and thus a commitment to constant growth. The sustained growth characteristic of modern economies is not *self*-sustained: it is stimulated and sustained by nationalism.

---

[16]See Gerschenkron, *Economic Backwardness*, 22–6.
[17]See Krugman, *Pop Internationalism*.
[18]Weiss and Hobson, *States and Economic Development*, 184 and 'Conclusion'.
[19]Greenfeld, *Nationalism*. Compare Colley, *Britons*.
[20]Greenfeld, *Spirit of Capitalism*. The rest of this paragraph paraphrases fragments of this book on pages 1, 3 and 23.

Considering the apparent importance of 'nationalism', some comments on its absence or at least weakness in Qing China are in order. In China, nationalism as the political principle that nation and state must be congruent could hardly be anything else than weak.[21] Here, in a way, China paid a price for being ruled so 'lightly'. The foundations for modern nationalism that in many Western states had been laid before the French Revolution, by and large, were lacking in the Middle Kingdom. Its system of light government, with low taxes, a very small state bureaucracy and a large amount of local autonomy and self-rule, resulted in a condition where the state was not embedded *in* society but at best a thin layer lying *over* it. In many respects China first and foremost was a collection of regions or rather provinces. Its administration actually was decentralized, as the provincial governors were almost independent in the exercise of their powers. As we have seen, the state scarcely penetrated below the level of the district. As such, China's rulers almost entirely lacked *institutional, China-wide* structures or resources that might have helped them in building a Chinese nation, whereas, on the other hand, their subjects almost entirely lacked *institutional, China-wide* structures and resources that might have enabled them to look at China as a state that was 'theirs' and in which they could actively participate. Unlike in Western Europe, there was no tradition of institutionalized bargaining – especially over taxes and warfare – between central government and representatives of various societal groups that were acknowledged as such and could claim rights and privileges. That made it hard to mobilize 'the people' or 'the elites' for a national cause.

Nationalism is a complex and multifaceted phenomenon with many varieties. An interesting analytical distinction – reality of course is not that neat – is that between top-down state-makes-nation nationalism and a more bottom-up nation-makes-state nationalism.[22] Both of these varieties of nation- and state-building were very weak, if not entirely absent, in Qing China in the period discussed here. We have seen that representatives of central government were few and far between and not really integrated in society. They lacked infrastructural power. State officials could not and overall did not *want* to create active citizens. There was no direct and massive mobilization of the people by and for the state. For bottom-up nationalism conditions were not very favourable either. There was no entrenched aristocracy with a local base that, like in many parts of Europe, might serve as a rallying point or point of departure in a process of state-building, or for that matter, as its opponent. Nor was there an ongoing process in which the existing elites and their 'supporters' actively participated in state- and nation-building and became integral parts of an emerging national state. When it comes to the involvement of people with the state, we see much apathy and lethargy.

---

[21]For Chinese nationalism under the Qing see Dikötter, *Discourse of Race*; Dittmer and Kim, *China's Quest*; Duara, *Rescuing History*; Esherick, 'How the Qing became China'; Schell and Delury, *Wealth and Power*, and Zhao, *Nation State by Construction*.

[22]For 'classical' texts on characteristics, origins and varieties of nationalism and its connection to state-formation, I refer to Gellner, *Nations and Nationalism*; Hobsbawm, *Nations and Nationalism*, and various publications by Hutchinson and Smith e.g. *Nationalism*. For an effort to analyse the differences in this respect between 'China' and 'Europe' see Wong, *China Transformed*.

Perspicuous people at the time were aware of that. Some even suggested creating a kind of feudal system with local magnates in order to involve 'the local' in the 'national'.[23] True as all these comments may be, they must of course not be exaggerated: even as a multicultural empire, the enormous Qing Empire continued to exist for over one and a half centuries and basically still exists in the twenty-first century. Mechanisms must have been at work that differed from the ones regarded as the 'normal' ingredients of nation-building in the West.

Nationalism normally feeds on competition with other nations; there will not have been a fertile basis for that in a country that regarded itself as the Middle Kingdom and 'all under Heaven' and that, to a large extent, could get away with behaving accordingly. In contrast to the condition of rather intermittent, 'peripheral' war in China that hardly impacted on the daily life of people in China Proper, the condition of almost permanent war and mass mobilization in Western Europe kept patriotism awake. Europeans were provided with ample opportunity to hate one's neighbours and indulge in self-exaltation. In Europe, to put it in William James's words, war up until his days had been 'the gory nurse that trained societies into cohesiveness'.[24] Scholars who emphasize that the state in China first and foremost was a moral order do have a point but it would be hard to deny that a state that is *not* militarily strong and unified can easily lose its 'mandate from heaven' when it encounters a state that because of war has become strong and unified and presents clear alternatives. There were other factors 'inhibiting' a domestic development of Chinese nationalism under Qing rule. I have already pointed out that the Manchus were a small elite of foreign conquerors. Even when they did their best to be 'benevolent' and act as 'pure Chinese', as they often did, their position could very easily become disputed and it increasingly was. Then there were the differences between north and south China; those between Han Chinese and other peoples living inside China Proper, and increasingly, with the growth of empire, in the newly conquered regions. China did become ethnically more diverse, which as a rule does not make the project of nation-building easier. Many problems indeed occurred in regions that were recently added to the realm where non-Han were the majority of the population. Maybe China had simply become too big. All this undoubtedly posed problems for the emergence of a strong national identity, although one may doubt whether *these* problems actually were bigger than in many a European country. Qing China was much more of a nation state in terms of having one predominant *ethnie* than the big empires in Europe. Even after the big extension of its realm in the eighteenth century, still some 90 per cent of its population was Han. In the Habsburg Empire at the end of the nineteenth century only about a quarter of the population was German, in the sense of speaking German. In the Ottoman Empire, halfway through the nineteenth century, half of the population was not Muslim. Russians clearly were the biggest single group in the European part of

---

[23]See e.g. Duara, *Rescuing History*, ch. 5, where an analysis is provided of this so-called 'fengjiang' or 'feudal' tradition with its limited central control and an expanded role for lineage and kinship organizations.

[24]James, 'Moral equivalent of war', 1283. On page 1293 he adds: 'War has been the only force that can discipline a whole community.' I found these quotes in Sheehan, 'What it means to be a state', 13.

the Russian Empire at the end of the nineteenth century, with over 55 per cent. But still, Ukrainians accounted for over 20 per cent and Poles for about 10. On the other hand, none of these empires, including that of the Hohenzollern, which was much less multi-ethnic than the ones mentioned before, survived the turmoil of the First World War, whereas more unified national states such as Britain and France did.

In a previous paragraph I pointed out that nationalism – or in any case a developed sense of national consciousness and cohesion – may have a positive impact on economic development, and more broadly on modernization. Things of course can also work the other way around – modernization and the kind of economic development that goes with it can cause an upsurge of nationalism. In fact, this connection is made much more often than the one I referred to. As Ernest Gellner shows in his brilliant and classic analysis, there are excellent reasons to interpret nationalism as an *effect* of modernity and one of its most important corollaries, modern economic growth.[25] This growth can only be *sustained* when there is a substratum of a shared culture and, in turn, it is *facilitated* by more efficient means of communication and transport, more and better education and increasing urbanization. As so often in history, causality actually was reciprocal. In this respect, Qing China was in a very awkward position: it lacked a clear sense of collective destiny that might help in creating economic growth and it lacked the economic growth that might have helped in providing the infrastructure needed to be able to create a sense of collective destiny. This sense of belonging to a nation and of wanting to partake in it is not something that comes naturally. The question whether nations and nationalism are 'primordial' or 'constructed' is one of the most hotly debated topics in Western historiography. But it is not disputed that in Britain, as in most of the older 'states' in the West, nations to a large extent were built (i.e. 'made') by their rulers. Many strategies were used to make people think and act in terms of 'the national interest'.

'Governmentality', knowledge and discipline

Governments in Western Europe increasingly cared about whom their subjects were and what they were doing and thinking, and they increasingly *had* to. So they started to systematically collect information about them and to monitor and police them. With the increasing need for tax money and conscripts, to mention only the most obvious reasons, it became increasingly relevant for rulers to know exactly how many subjects they had, where they lived, what they did, possessed, earned, thought and so on. To find that out, governments – and this is a phenomenon we see all over Europe – had to make the societies over which they ruled, or in any case wanted to rule, 'legible'. It was James Scott who introduced this concept in social science. This is what he means by it:

> To make a society legible, to arrange the population in ways that simplified the classic state functions of taxation, conscription and prevention of rebellion.

---

[25]Gellner, *Nations and Nationalism*.

I began to see legibility as a central problem in statecraft. The pre-modern state was, in many crucial respects, partially blind. It knew precious little about its subjects, their wealth, their landholdings and yields, their location, their very identity. It lacked anything like a detailed 'map' of its terrain and people. It lacked, for the most part, a measure, a metric, that would allow it to 'translate' what it knew into a common standard necessary for a synoptic view. As a result its interventions were often crude and self-defeating.[26]

State officials created standard grids whereby they could centrally record and monitor often exceptionally complex, 'illegible' local social practices. As examples, Scott refers to the creation of permanent last names, the standardization of weights and measures, the establishment of cadastral surveys and population registers, the invention of freehold tenure, the standardization of language and legal discourse, the design of cities and the organization of transportation. Governments all over Europe increasingly 'X-rayed' their societies to make them 'governable', as Foucault would say,[27] via measures calculated to make the terrain, its products and its workforce more legible – and hence easier to deal with – from above and from the centre. I do not see an equivalent of equal intensity of such policies in China. Government there need not bother so much, as it did not need to – and preferably did not *want* to – mobilize resources and people in its competition with the government of other states. This competition in the end was the main driving force behind European governments' addiction to collecting information. That was often gathered to find out how strong – or weak – one was economically, militarily, and also in the field of science, as compared to others and to look for ways of improving one's country's international position. It will not have been by accident that the enlightened idea of promoting 'progress' via the collecting *and* applying of useful and reliable knowledge became uniquely popular in government circles of Europe that already in the eighteenth century wanted to rationalize their states and societies.

Science and scientists were given an increasingly important role in that process. This had already started in the early modern era when scientific societies, whose members knew that science as such does not know borders, were often expected to serve the national interest and seen as pawns in an international competition. The Dutch Society of Science, for example, founded in 1752, was explicitly devoted to the promotion of Dutch 'national' interest. The English Royal Society, founded in 1662, professed to strive for 'the knowledge of natural things and useful arts to the glory of God the creator and for application to the good of mankind', but, in practice, it too was not free from national self-interest. With the passing of time the role of knowledge and the men of knowledge in public life only increased. Information, increasingly in quantitative form, became regarded as extremely important for governing. In Great Britain, to again focus

---

[26]Scott, *Seeing Like a State*, 2.
[27]See Foucault's many lectures dealing with 'governmentality' at the Collège de France in the 1970s and 1980s that have been published by Palgrave Macmillan in the series *Michel Foucault, Lectures at the Collège de France*.

on that country, government, whatever its actual social leanings, was very interested in 'improvement', 'reason' and 'progress'.[28] It moreover tended to think that 'science', including the sciences of 'political economy' and 'political arithmetic', could promote its goals.[29] In comparing the Chinese situation to that in Great Britain, it is striking to what extent a scientist like Newton and an inventor–engineer like Watt could become widely honoured, national heroes in their country.

European governments became increasingly fascinated by collecting and using data, not by accident called 'statistics', for a wide range of purposes and actively stimulated activities that they thought might bring about the kind of society and economy that a strong state needed.[30] A clear example would be the development of censuses and population registers. Mapping of course also fits in this effort to make society legible. The number of maps available in society reached an absolutely unprecedented level and they became ordinary objects. I here refer to my comments on pages 40–1. In this context one must not forget to point out the developing of ways to calculate probability and risk and their use in, for example, insurance, in which government also played a part.[31] We are dealing with a broad European phenomenon in which Great Britain clearly did not always lead the way. We already saw it was very slow in developing a national cadastre. It also was not a frontrunner when it came to introducing censuses and population registers. The United Kingdom conducted its first regular national census only in 1801. Ireland was not yet included; that was only the case from 1821 onwards. Cadastre and census were less important for Great Britain's rulers as the main taxes were not on land but on consumer goods and – as is particularly relevant for the census – the country did not introduce mass conscription in the period discussed here. In standardization the country also was somewhat of a laggard. The metric system was introduced in Revolutionary France in 1794. The definitive metre was fixed in 1799. That was not unproblematic. After 1812, pre-metric units were again permitted. It was only in 1837 that the metric system again became obligatory. The legacy of revolutionary and, in particular, Napoleonic France when it comes to 'rationalizing' the system of rule in France and all the regions the French conquered can hardly be overestimated. When it comes to the metric system, Britain, as is well known, did not adopt it. In standardizing time, though, the British did take the lead. The British Post Office gave the initial push

---

[28]See for 'improvement', 'reason' and 'progress' in Great Britain, Borsay, 'Culture of improvement'; Caton, *Politics of Progress*; Macleod, *Heroes of Invention*; Mokyr, *Enlightened Economy*; Porter, *Enlightenment*, and Spadafora, *Idea of Progress*.

[29]See for the promotion of science and technology by the state, for example, Gascoigne, 'Royal Society'; MacLeod, *Heroes of Invention*, and Shapin, 'Image of the man of science'. See for the development of political arithmetic and political economy, for example, Hoppit, 'Political arithmetic', and Poovey, *History of the Modern Fact*.

[30]See for the case of Great Britain Higgs, *Information State*, and for an overview of statistical information collected at the time Palmer, *Economic Arithmetic*. In this respect the increasing importance of all sorts of accounting and accountability and of the idea that reality is measurable should be mentioned. See e.g. Soll, *Reckoning*, chs 7 and 8. For an analysis with broader geographical coverage see Headrick, *When Information Came of Age*, and Heilbron, 'Measure of Enlightenment'. Finally I of course want to refer to Black, *Power of Knowledge*, and Dudley, *Information Revolutions*.

[31]Bernstein, *Against the Gods*.

when it started to run all its mail coaches throughout Great Britain in accordance with a uniform standard of time. With the expansion of the railway network the urge to have a uniform time in the entire country only increased. So-called 'railway time' became Greenwich Mean Time. In 1855, 98 per cent of all public clocks in Britain were indicating that time.[32] Standardizations of this kind had a scientific and technical side as well as a political and legislative side. What is striking in that respect is that scientists independently tended to push for more standards and increasingly the central state regarded it as part and parcel of its task to implement and guarantee them. Modern economic life is unimaginable without abundant flows of information and without standardization: the production and maintenance of both of these are mainly provided and enforced by the modern state and its bureaucratic apparatus. The effect of their existence in terms of lowering transactions costs must have been very substantial. The importance of the fact that, as a rule, it has been the state that collected, provided and standardized this information is all too often still underestimated, as is the importance of the fact that, in this respect too, Qing China was and continued to be a 'weak' state with a very weak statistical 'basis'.

What has enabled modern economic growth to be sustained is a permanent flow of innovations, which fed on inventions, which in turn would have been unimaginable without the development of big science. Nowadays, research and development and science play a fundamental role in technological innovation. The most advanced economies have become knowledge economies. During 'take-off' the role of science was less predominant though certainly not negligible. Several excellent books have recently been published about the role of all sorts of useful and reliable knowledge in the emergence of the first industrial economy.[33] It is no use repeating their content here or trying to compress them in a couple of sentences. So-called new growth theory tends to attribute a central role to the state in the production of such knowledge.[34] Those books, however, all show – and this is what matters in the specific context of this book – that *direct* involvement of the British state in the development of science, technology and the spreading of their results through education during take off was rather small. They all show that we must not exaggerate the proactive, developmental role of the British state here. That very probably was bigger in France, with less success. Government in any case did not itself have any research and development programmes nor did it massively support private research or education. That industrializing Great Britain was a knowledge economy was not an intended direct result of government policies. The role of Great Britain's government, however, though normally indirect, nevertheless was fundamental in creating institutional and material infrastructures where inventions could be made and turned into economically relevant innovations. It endorsed a scientific worldview.

---

[32]Zerubavel, 'Standardization of time'.

[33]The books I have in mind are Jacob, *First Knowledge Economy*; Leonard, *Mothers of Innovation*, and Mokyr, *Enlightened Economy*.

[34]See my *Escaping Poverty* under, 'economic growth, theories of economic growth, new'. After I finished that book Mazzucato, *Entrepreneurial State*, was published in which the state figures as a major provider of funds for innovations and as an entrepreneur in its own right that makes high-risk bold investments. See its flap text.

It did not oppose research and, what is more important, increasingly also did not oppose inventions and innovations that could have major and at times disturbing social impact. It respected scientists, inventors and entrepreneurs, often stimulated them, gave them prizes and honoured them. All this certainly was not unimportant and stood in striking contrast to the world *outside* Europe. Differences with China, where government did not do those things, were very substantial. In a European context, Great Britain's government was not really exceptional.

My claim in this book is that Great Britain became a state with far more infrastructural power than Qing China. That power, of course, to a large extent depends on the actual presence of institutional and material infrastructures. Institutional changes have already been referred to often so let us here comment briefly upon material infrastructure. The importance of transport is fundamental in this respect.[35] In the period 1700–1830 efficiency in road transport in Great Britain more or less tripled due to technological and institutional changes. Government's role was mainly confined to establishing turnpike trusts by Acts of Parliament. During that same period, the capacity of British canals almost tripled, which was fundamental in enabling coal use inland. The introduction of the steamship, of course, was a sensational innovation. In overseas trade, however, it only really took off in the second half of the nineteenth century. But there had already been a substantial lowering of costs of that trade before: mainly because of 'smoother markets and safer seas' thanks to protection by the Royal Navy.[36] Less sensational but hugely important was the coastal trade, in particular the transporting of coal from the north to London. That amounted to about half a million tons annually in the first half of the nineteenth century. Here too efficiency increased and here too the state played a role. When it comes to building railroads, central government in Great Britain was quite reluctant to assume too big a role but it, of course, could not simply leave everything to the market. The same goes for the development of good postal services. In all these respects, the contribution of the state in Great Britain was quite substantial and as a rule positive, whereas in China government, as in so many other respects, certainly from the end of the reign of the Qianlong emperor onwards, was less prominently active and less helpful.[37] Again differences became more striking than resemblances and more to the disadvantage of China.

We already pointed out the importance of the collection of information for rulers. Government policies, however, were not confined to simply gathering information in the hope to then be able to know and manipulate things: they also, if not even more so, aimed at knowing and *changing* behaviour. As Scott shows in his *Seeing Like a State*, there is a clear link between knowledge, especially knowing 'your' people, and administration. Habsburg Emperor Joseph II made no secret of that: 'If one is to rule countries well, one must first know them exactly.'[38] Which brings us to an important

---

[35]In my comments I follow Mokyr, *Enlightenment Economy*, ch. 10.
[36]See Menard, 'Transport costs'. The quotation is on page 275.
[37]See Kim, 'Transport in China'.
[38]I found this quotation in Kain and Baigent, *Cadastral Map*, 195.

aspect of the role of the state in promoting economic development – to wit the ways in which and the extent to which governments have tried to turn their subjects into what they regarded as decent, civilized, law-abiding and, what is very important in the context of this text, hard-working people: in brief, the kind of people who are willing to shoulder the efforts of their rulers to increase the wealth of the state and to fight its wars. What we see in all of Western and Central Europe, from the beginning of the early modern era onwards, is an effort to discipline the populace into 'correct', 'predictable' or, as it increasingly came to be considered, 'normal' behaviour. That process of 'disciplining' or 'civilizing' without any doubt is one of the main features of the social history of early modern Europe. The amount of literature devoted to this effort to create 'modern man' is staggering.[39] At times it was pushed forward by central or local government; at times by the Protestant and Catholic 'clergies'; at times by employers, and often by those members of 'the bourgeoisie' who regarded themselves as 'civilized'. As a rule, all these 'elites' worked together as, overall, whatever may have been the exact reasons for their efforts, they in the end wanted to create a fairly similar new kind of 'reliable persons' and 'docile bodies'. Most of the 'disciplining' could only persist and hope to be effective – which quite often it was *not* – when central government at least condoned it. As a rule it was its main supporter or even instigator. A disciplinary society emerged with many disciplining institutions like the army, the bureaucracy, poor houses and workhouses, asylums, (manu-)factories and schools.

We already hinted at the crucial importance of training and discipline in the military revolution that involved millions of soldiers. People in the military increasingly were expected to behave like professionals in a tightly coordinated way.[40] They were expected to perform in a clear and logical chain of command, not as individual, let alone individualistic, fighters. War and battle were no longer supposed to be occasions to show individual initiative and bravery. They were becoming matters of collective, coordinated endeavour and they were supposed to proceed according to plans and strategies. It is not by accident that it has become popular to talk about the army as a 'war machine'. Nor is it by accident that Max Weber refers to army discipline as the 'Mutterschoss' (i.e. the womb) of all discipline.[41] Discipline on men-of-war, and on merchant ships, was very harsh and the work organized as in a floating

---

[39]I did not by accident refer to modern 'man'. There also was a huge effort of disciplining women but that was far less concerned with *changing* their public behaviour than with *reducing* it and giving them a specific, confined role in private life. There is a long tradition of studying these topics, with the work of Weber, Elias and Foucault as major sources of inspiration. I just refer to the following, somewhat older syntheses: Burke, *Popular Culture*; Muchembled, *Popular Culture and Elite Culture*, and Spierenburg, *Broken Spell*, and the article by Raeff, 'Well-ordered police state'. More recent is Gorski, *Disciplinary Revolution*. Rowe, writing about China in the eighteenth century, claims that many if not most Chinese bureaucrats offered a Chinese parallel to the quest for a 'well-ordered police state' that Raeff sees as a distinctive project of political leaders in the early modern West. See Rowe, *Saving the World*, 333. This may well be true in general but *not* to my view when it comes to disciplining *labour*.

[40]The amount of literature about the development of military discipline is huge. Let me give just one example for Britain: James, *Warrior Race*, Part Four.

[41]Weber, *Wirtschaft und Gesellschaft*, 686.

factory.[42] We see the same principles emerging in the new bureaucracies. People working for government increasingly were expected to act according to rules and in a disciplined manner. Everywhere in Western Europe governments set out to create a 'rationalized' system of direct rule, trying to eliminate the 'intermediate rule' of 'unruly' aristocrats, holders of hereditary offices and tax farmers and to get rid of venality, sinecures and so on. Where possible, intermediate, 'indirect' rulers were supplanted by 'real' bureaucrats who worked for the government and for nobody else and who had to follow its rules, which increasingly were written rules, and nobody else's. Again, one must be careful not to predate these processes and regard them as quite straightforward. Success was often quite limited. Professional bureaucracies, even more than professional armies, overall, are children of the nineteenth century. But it was already clear earlier on in which direction developments were heading.

This disciplinary revolution began to extend over the entire population. For one reason or another, 'the elites' began to resent and combat what they were now beginning to regard as 'uncivilized', 'unruly' or 'indolent' behaviour by 'the masses'. If we are to believe William Temple and Adam Smith, even taxes were used as a way of manipulating the morality of the labouring ranks.[43] Especially interesting from the perspective of the economic historian are the numerous initiatives to create a disciplined labour force. Those efforts became ever more pressing as people increasingly began to work for wages on behalf of other people who were *not* family. Concepts of work, leisure and poverty (were) changed. The idea began to prevail that work was a job, maybe even a calling, but in any case a duty. Workhouses, poor houses, prisons and the like were created all over Europe to 'reform' those who did not voluntarily comply. They were forced to work in an effort to create, in Foucault's terms, 'docile bodies'.[44] Begging and vagabondage became punishable offences. Not to work was now considered a crime. Penal workhouses proliferated throughout Northern Europe. They became quite numerous in the Netherlands, Germany and Austria, where they were called *tuchthuizen* (in the Netherlands) and *Zuchthäuser* (in Germany and Austria), both to be translated as 'houses of discipline'. In England, by 1750, almost every market town and industrialized parish had its own workhouse. We have already seen how many people they put up. European states were very active when it came to moral and social disciplining and instigating 'a reformation of manners'. These policies, poverty and at times new patterns of consumption led to an increase in the number of people who worked, the number of hours they worked and the intensity of their work. Over time these all rose in early modern Europe in what has been called an 'industrious revolution'.[45] This revolution was not something that stopped with the beginning of industrialization. Some scholars would even claim that it then only intensified. According to the economic historian

---

[42]Frykman, 'Seeleute'.
[43]Ashworth, *Customs and Excise*, 334–5.
[44]See Foucault, *Discipline and Punish*, Part 3.1, 135–70.
[45]See De Vries, *Industrious Revolution*, ch. 3. See for critical comments on the specific interpretation De Vries gives of this phenomenon e.g. Allen and Weisdorf, 'Industrious revolution', and Malanima, *Pre-Modern Economy*, 238.

Voth, the number of hours worked by Britain's labour force increased by at least 20 per cent over the period from 1750 to 1830.[46] The intensity of their work became more supervised and its tempo, which often came to depend on machines, increased. This 'industrious revolution' was definitely *not* a uniquely European phenomenon. The concept actually was first introduced in an analysis of developments in Tokugawa Japan.[47] It also is applicable to China in the early modern era.[48] But the settings in which people in China and in Europe worked often differed substantially. I will discuss those differences briefly on pages **.

With the coming of factories, having disciplined labour, not by accident often simply called 'factory *hands*', became even more urgent and systematic.[49] One cannot imagine a factory without discipline. There is a substantial amount of literature in which the importance of a disciplined labour force in modern industry is highlighted. A scholar like Stephen Marglin would go as far as to claim that the primary reason to build factories was to ensure that 'bosses' could really control the production process and thus discipline their labour force. What is especially interesting in the context of this book is the question to what extent there were fundamental differences in this respect between, on the hand, Western countries (and Japan) and, on the other hand, China and many other underdeveloped countries. Gregory Clark has claimed that differences in discipline would explain the very fact that certain countries are rich whereas others are not. According to him, poor countries suffer from low labour quality. Labour there lacks discipline, is very frequently absent and factories employ far too many personnel.[50] Even if that would be pushing things quite far, or, I would rather say, way too far, everyone acquainted with literature on the industrialization of Western Europe knows that factory discipline was a very important concern for employers and labourers.

These disciplinary efforts aiming at the minds, hearts and, in particular, bodies of the population of Western Europe were so massive that one can only wonder how Wong in his *China Transformed* can claim that: 'Early modern European states did not share the Chinese state's view that shaping society's moral sensibilities was basic to the logic of rule.'[51] He may have a point with regard to parts of the population living in the countryside. But we have to realize that the advanced regions of Western Europe

---

[46]Voth, *Time and Work*, 130 and 270–1.

[47]Hayami, 'Great transformation', and Hayami, Saito and Toby, *Emergence of Economic Society*, in particular 'Introduction'.

[48]See e.g. Pomeranz, *Great Divergence*, under 'industrious revolution'.

[49]For introductory literature on the disciplining of labour in general and the specific problems related to disciplining factory labour see, in alphabetical order, Furniss, *Position of the Laborer*; Lis and Soly, *Poverty and Capitalism* and *Worthy Efforts*; Marglin, 'What do bosses do?'; Pollard, *Genesis of Modern Management*; Rule, *Experience of Labour*; Steinfeld, *Invention of Free Labour*; Thompson, *Making of the English Working Class* and 'Time, work-discipline and industrial capitalism', and Vogt, *Time and Work*.

[50]See Clark, *Farewell to Alms*, chs 16 and 17. On page 357 it reads: 'It becomes apparent that the nature of the labour force was the key issue limiting efficiency in low-wage economies.'

[51]Wong, *China Transformed*, 97. For a similar claim ('The ambit of Chinese imperial authority and power stretched far beyond those of European states in spatial scale and substantive variety') and the suggestion that in Europe states lacked a 'deep concern with elite and popular education and morality … and … [an] invasive curiosity about and anxiety over potentially subversive behaviour' see Wong, *China Transformed*, 103 and 101.

where mercantilism was most successful were highly urbanized, much more so than China. People in early modern European towns undoubtedly would be surprised to hear that government did not care about their morals. Part of the explanation for Wong's idiosyncratic interpretation of the social history of early modern Europe might be that he thinks that, to the extent that something like a programme of 'moral reform' did exist in Europe, it was mainly driven by the Church and not by the state. According to him, 'The Chinese effort to reach the minds and hearts of peasants contrasts strongly with European states, which left such matters to religious authorities.'[52] By putting it like this, Wong creates a distinction between worldly and religious authorities and between 'the public' sphere on the one hand and 'the moral' and 'the religious' spheres on the other hand, which is artificial and anachronistic for post-Reformation Western Europe. A Dutch expert on the history of religion during the early modern era does not hesitate to claim that 'the increase of the power of the secular authorities over the churches was a constant during the early modern period.'[53] The so-called confessional states produced by the Reformation identified the interests of the dominant church with those of the political community.[54] This certainly applies to countries where Protestantism had prevailed. But it is also true for Catholic countries. Salmon claims that in France in the sixteenth century every village pastor 'also was a government agent', a situation that actually became formalized during the French Revolution; and Dorn, in a text about Protestant Prussia in the eighteenth century writes: 'Each protestant pastor was a government servant.'[55] Let me also quote from an article on the growth of the modern state in Germany at the time in which one clearly sees how what we would nowadays call 'politics', 'ethics' and 'religion' were 'blended'.

> Territorial lords' growing claims to exercise all-encompassing regulation of all aspects of life was reflected especially clearly in the theory and practice of Policey (polity or regulation). ... Policey referred not only to a polity, but also generally to the condition of good order and the ways and means of establishing it. ... In modern terms, they [i.e. Police-ordinances] dealt with questions of private or civil law, from the regulation of marriage, the family, guardianship and inheritance, to regulation of property, work, and credit. However, they also covered problems of religion, morality sociability and general security and thus encompassed the 'public' sphere as well. ... In the period after the Thirty Years War (1618–1648) and during the eighteenth century Policey regulation was enormously expanded and the Church became to be simply conceived as part of the state administration. The conception of the office of German princes continued to be coloured by religion until long into the eighteenth century. This conception portrayed princes

---

[52]Wong, *China Transformed*, 97.

[53]Van Rooden, 'Kerk en religie', 394.

[54]A confessional state is a state which officially practises a particular religion and at least encourages its citizens to do likewise.

[55]See Salmon, *Society in Crisis*, 79, and further, and Dorn, 'Prussian bureaucracy', 409.

as devoted *Landesväter* (fathers of the country) tirelessly active for the well-being of the *Landeskinder* (children of the country) or subjects.[56]

Church and state actually worked very closely together in Western Europe in their common project of disciplining the population. There is a huge literature on what in German is called *Sozialdisziplinierung*, in which the combined efforts of state and church to discipline the population during the early modern era is discussed.[57] There were some differences between Catholic and Protestant regions, the Protestant 'reformed' churches by and large being more 'thorough' in their disciplining. Very important for the economic historian, because their effect is so obvious, are the successful attempts, especially in Protestant countries, to reform the calendar and eliminate as many saints' days and religious holidays as possible and therewith significantly increase the number of working days per year.[58] In Britain, to return to the country that is central to our entire comparative analysis, there was a state with a single confession of faith established by law. There was an official religion and an official church, the Church of England. Its members were privileged; so-called dissenters were discriminated against until 1832. A serious and fierce debate has been waged regarding whether actually it too during the period 1688–1832 was not a 'confessional state'.[59] I have already pointed out that in implementing the Poor Laws religious and secular authorities were hand in glove. I do not think it is much use going into further detail.

For anyone reading the relevant literature, two conclusions are inescapable. First, there were massive efforts to reform manners in Catholic as well as – and very probably even more so – in Protestant countries in early modern Europe. The history of Western Europe in the early modern era is fundamentally shaped by the Reformation and the Counterreformation, the Inquisition, the ferocious Wars of Religion, the Great Witch Hunt, the Great Confinement and so on. In all regions of Christian Europe sovereignty was in the hands of the state, *not* the church. The Inquisition, for example, fell under secular rule; secular authorities burned (or hanged) witches. Second, these efforts almost always were a *common* endeavour of secular and religious authorities. Of course, with the passing of time, there may have been changes in what interested the authorities, in the relative importance of what we would now call 'the secular' and 'the religious' and in the impact and the severity of measures taken. But any student of that history can only read the claims by Wong about the lack of interest of secular authorities in the morale of their subjects and about the distinction between and separation of state and church with amazement. For what we would now regard

---

[56]Munch, 'Growth of the modern state', 208–11. For the ways in which the secular and the religious were intertwined in early modern Germany see Von Greyerz, 'Confession', and the article referred to in the next note.

[57]Behrens, 'Sozialdisziplinierung'. This social disciplining often is *directly* connected to *Konfesssionalisierung*.

[58]See Gorski, 'Little Divergence', 175–7, and De Vries, *Industrious Revolution*, 87–92.

[59]See Clarke, *English Society* and 'England's Ancien Régime'. For the debate see Google under 'England confessional state'. For the specific position of Catholics and dissenters see Colley, *Britons*, 324–34, and Daunton, *Progress and Poverty*, 478–9 and 481–2.

as a 'separation' of church and state, one has to wait until into the nineteenth century, and even then the ties between politics, religion and ethics were not severed in many European countries.

It of course is all but impossible to really prove such a claim, but as far as I can see the state in Western Europe was *more* rather than less actively involved in, and much keener on, disciplining bureaucrats, soldiers and especially wage labour than was the case in China. Chinese bureaucrats were closely watched – as far as possible, that is. Discipline in the Chinese military was regarded as rather slack and wage labour was all but absent in Qing China at the time. I especially want to point at the efforts in the West to create a docile labour force that might function as a simple 'factor of production', working for wages in a setting entirely outside of or in any case broader than just the household. Even if the Chinese state had been more active than states in the West in disciplining and instructing its people, I still think that, from an economic perspective, the disciplining and instructing of Western states was more important because, apart from anything else it may have intended, it had a very clear focus on *efficiency* whereas, to put it somewhat simplistically, the Chinese focus was much more on *decency*. China's government certainly showed interest in the behaviour of its labour force. That labour force, however, in its overwhelming majority was rural and worked in the setting of a household economy. Administration of discipline was not lacking there. But it was done by the (male) head of the household who *by law* had an almost unrestricted freedom to do as he saw fit, not by some unacquainted stranger or by an abstract state.[60] In Britain working with or for non-family was quite normal. In China it certainly was not. Proletarian wage labour, which in Britain already in the eighteenth century had become a substantial part of the entire labour force, was next to absent in Qing China. For its rural households, China's rulers systematically promoted the canonical gender division of labour between spinning and weaving as women's work and cultivating the land as men's work.[61] Irrespective of whether this met with much success, I would regard such advice much less an expression of concern with economic efficiency than with decency and tradition.

---

[60]See, for example, De Moor and Van Zanden, 'Girlpower', and Wolf, 'Europe and China'.
[61]For the thesis that there was a strong cultural pressure to keep women at home see, Goldstone, 'Gender, work and culture'; Huang, *Peasant Family and Rural Development*, under 'women', and Mann, *Precious Records*, ch. 6. These authors think this pressure had negative effects on the economy. For a less negative interpretation that stresses that women did more than their share of production see Bray, *Technology and Gender*, and Pomeranz, 'Women's work, family and economic development'. Gardella points at the widespread existence of female wage labour in the production of tea. See his *Harvesting Mountains*, 172–3. It is in any case clear that in practice the admonitions of the rulers often were not heeded.

CONCLUDING REMARKS

Ultimately the best case to be made for mercantile policy is a weak one: The creation of a large and fiscally voracious state bureaucracy did not impede Britain's transformation into the first modern industrial economy. But it still remains to be determined whether Britain grew because of, or in spite of, mercantilist policy.

Nye, *War, Wine and Taxes,* 24

The mercantile system ... was the crutch with which capitalism learned to walk.

Norman, *Japan's Emergence as a Modern State,* 110

The fact that mercantilism is at the root of all successful capitalism is not considered.

Reinert, 'How rich nations got rich', 13.

The Chinese government was an almost unbelievably weak instrument [for promoting economic development]

Perkins, 'Government as an obstacle to industrialization', 492

Our comparative analysis of the importance, role and function of the state in the economies of (Great) Britain and China during the very long eighteenth century has revealed major differences. For scholars who are familiar with the relevant literature in the field, this cannot have come as a major surprise. Many quite confident claims about 'surprising resemblances' or, for that matter, less often, 'surprising differences' between 'Europe' and 'China' that recently have popped up in monographs and textbooks could quite easily have been avoided by checking the relevant, recent literature and by using a systematically comparative approach.

Taking into consideration differences in population, the revenue that Great Britain's central government collected was many times larger than that of its Chinese counterpart. The same applies to its expenditures. In (Great) Britain these were so high that government incurred huge debts that it, however, always managed to honour. In China government until halfway into the nineteenth century never spent more than it received. The amount of money Great Britain's government handled per capita was huge in nominal terms (i.e. expressed in silver equivalents) *as well as* in real terms (i.e. expressed in terms of domestic purchasing power or in terms of labour days). It added up to a very substantial part of Great Britain's GDP. In comparison to it, the income of China's central government per capita paled, in absolute as well as in real terms, and it amounted to a substantially smaller part of GDP. China's central government collected far less money from its subjects and far fewer labour days than was the case in Britain. Whereas in Great Britain the role of indirect taxes was very prominent, in China land taxes continued to provide the bulk, by far, of government revenue. In Great Britain the collection of government revenue was more centralized and uniform, regionally as well as when it comes to social groups, than it was in China. All substantial payments to government in Great Britain had to be made in silver, gold or paper money. In China substantial amounts of taxes continued to be paid in kind or in copper, the least valuable of the precious metals. Looking at the way in which revenue was collected, Great Britain clearly was more efficient and less corrupt than China, where people quite often had to pay much more to (semi-)officials than was officially due and where a smaller percentage of official revenue came at the disposal of government. In both countries war was the main expenditure. When it comes to welfare spending fixed by central government – regardless of who actually implemented it – Great Britain spent a higher percentage of GDP on it than China. Great Britain's tax system was permanently discussed and often changed. That of China was surprisingly immobile. Revenues and expenditures of Great Britain's government per capita, moreover, steeply increased – nominally and in real terms – until the end of the Napoleonic Wars to then more or less become stable in real terms. Again, the situation in China was quite different. Government income and expenditure there per capita in nominal terms was more or less stable but almost certainly declined substantially in real terms between the beginning of the seventeenth century and 1850.

The fact that it collected so much money enabled Great Britain's government to, again, relatively speaking, have a much larger 'bureaucracy' and employ many more soldiers and navy personnel than the Qing rulers. When we talk about Britain's bureaucracy in this book, we basically are discussing its 'fiscal bureaucracy'. In *other sectors* of civil administration, Great Britain until long into the nineteenth century continued to be run by 'amateur gentlemen'. At the local level, British society clearly was left to its own devices and at that level the cherished image of Britain as a 'self-ruling gentlemanly society' indeed reflected an actual situation. The bureaucrats that Britain did have operated in a professional, well-trained and well-paid bureaucracy at the level of central government and were more than anything else concerned with collecting as much tax money as possible for the state. That is more than can be said of their Chinese counterparts who, relatively speaking, only formed a tiny group and, as a rule, were underpaid, severely understaffed and not professionally trained for their jobs. Britain's soldiers and sailors operated in an army and navy which were much better equipped, much better organized and much more disciplined (i.e. simply much stronger) than their Chinese counterparts. Whereas in Great Britain the number of civilian and military personnel as a percentage of total population stayed about the same over the period 1750–1850, it sharply decreased in China. Considering what has been said before, it will not come as a surprise that Great Britain's system of public finances was much more sophisticated than that of China and enabled government to borrow *and* pay back enormous amounts of money. Its monetary system was more closely watched by government, more uniform, less inefficient and less complicated than China's. The economy of Great Britain could dispose of more and better money, in the form of coins as well as in the form of private or official paper money. Its interest rates were also lower.

Whereas government efficiency and infrastructural power increased in Great Britain, the opposite occurred in China after the heydays of the Qing. To describe the situation in Great Britain in terms of state-*de*formation as Victoria Tin-bor Hui does for the whole of early modern Europe is completely erroneous. All the information I have collected points at massively *rising* tax revenues for government, hugely *increasing* armies, *bigger* bureaucracies, *consolidation and extension* and so on. State-formation is the evident trend. It is Qing China that from the 1780s onwards might be described in terms of state-*de*formation. Even at its height it was a weak state when it came to its infrastructural power. Let me, to make clear what I mean by that claim, briefly repeat what is meant by infrastructural state power and by the three elements of which it consists. Infrastructural power has been defined as 'the capacity of rulers to actually penetrate civil society and to implement political decisions logistically throughout the realm' – that is, their capacity to get things done – consists of three elements: penetrative power, extractive power and negotiated power. I consider Qing China as weak – and weakening over time – in terms of its penetrative power. Its capacity to reach into and directly interact with the population actually was minimal and decreased. Its extractive power also was relatively small. As compared to Great Britain it only extracted few resources, financial, material and human, from society and in this respect too things did not improve. For such 'extractive power' to be stable, routinized, enduring and substantial, it presupposes negotiation with the main social power groupings. That was lacking in Qing China, again in contrast to Great Britain. We see no such process of negotiating and no nationwide network of autonomous groupings with which government *could* have negotiated in an 'institutionalized', regular setting. Qing China thus also was quite weak as compared to Great Britain when it comes to the negotiated aspect of infrastructural power: a form of power that implies a rudimentary reciprocity between political and economic power actors. A strategy to coordinate the economy and to *structurally* change it or to even set it on a path of growth was lacking and would have become[1] increasingly unrealistic to the extent that the empire became larger, more populous and more diverse. Qing China certainly was *not* a developmental state. Its governments wanted security and a certain 'traditional' welfare, but not structural changes and innovations, the essential precondition and essence of modern economic growth.

One should, however, not lose sight of the very important fact that in various respects China's rulers simply were far less keen on having and wielding such infrastructural power than their British counterparts. I never came across a firm government intention to maximally penetrate society and maximally extract resources from it, nor one to negotiate with 'representatives' of the population. What undoubtedly is highly important

---

[1] I write 'would' because such a strategy actually was *never* even discussed, let alone tried, during the period discussed in this book.

here, apart from basic ideological differences and the immense problems of implementing infrastructural power in a huge pre-industrial empire, is the national and international political context in which the two governments were operating. The Qing were foreigners who ruled over a huge empire that to them basically looked secure until a couple of decades into the nineteenth century. So they could afford to focus on the livelihood of the people and had to in order to safeguard their mandate from heaven. They should have seen the looming threat but, considering that they didn't, their behaviour as such was not irrational. Britain's government first and foremost worried about survival in a fiercely competitive international context and acted accordingly. No doubt the fact that public life went through far more institutional innovation in Great Britain than in China can be attributed to a large extent to that 'anxiety'.

As already pointed out, in contrast to what happened in the West, the infrastructural power of China's state, which was weak to begin with, decreased even further during the last third of the very long eighteenth century. Considering the amazingly small number of officials that worked for central government, the immense empire can never have been ruled directly from Peking in a very effective way. In practice there must have been an enormous amount of local autonomy, with, at best, indirect guidance from the capital. One can only be impressed that imperial rule nevertheless functioned so well for so long and can in all probability explain this by the pragmatism of the rulers, their flexibility, the social policies they implemented and by the moral and ideological status of mandarin rule. The Qing Empire had been an extremely successful ideological and moral construct but it began to lose effectiveness from the end of the eighteenth century onwards. Central government increasingly had to cope with a crisis of legitimacy. The appearance of the Westerners and the disappearance of silver only aggravated domestic troubles. Symptoms of a real crisis became apparent. Empires almost by definition are prone to disintegration, even if they are fairly homogenous like the Qing Empire. The fact that it had expanded its realm over regions with ethnically differing populations only added to its problems from the later eighteenth century onward. Even for China Proper the chance that disintegration might occur, along provincial lines, was never absent. The fact that central government in Beijing had so successfully built on co-opting the local gentry, who were allowed broad autonomy, turned into a disadvantage as it hampered reform and supported centripetal developments. Increasingly during the nineteenth century, with accelerations of the process especially after the 1850s, central rule by the Qing became, to repeat the apt phrase by Patricia Crone, too weak to make things happen but still strong enough to prevent them from happening.[2]

Government in Great Britain, considering the norms of the time, not only was a big spender and an important employer, but also played a quite prominent role in trying to actively steer the economy in a certain direction. It was quite interventionist, first and foremost in matters of international economic relations. Its economic policy was mercantilist with all that implies and which means that government showed two faces.

---

[2]Crone, *Pre-Industrial Societies*, 57.

In matters related to the *internal* market, apart I would say from some aspects of the labour market, it clearly and increasingly promoted *laissez-faire*. In matters directly related to international competition and 'national interest' it did not and continued to be quite interventionist up until several decades into the nineteenth century. Great Britain's large international trade (in absolute terms and as a percentage of GDP) became an important source of government income. Government systematically tried via every possible means – taxation, subsidies, tariffs, bans and so forth – to support and promote sectors of production and trade that it regarded as important for the national economy. It 'negotiated' with entrepreneurs and traders, often supported them and was even willing to go to war to help them. Government policies in China were very different, focused as they were on the preservation of the existing economic order and on 'people's livelihood'. Government did not hesitate to intervene in order to *preserve* that order but hardly ever did anything to *change* it. This also extended to the field of politics, social relations, morals, 'science' or technology. Government literally was conservative. When it comes to foreign trade, it was fairly sceptic and overall not really supportive.

At its height China under the Qing was about double the size it was under the Ming. The first three Qing emperors certainly were successful empire-builders. Great Britain, however, nevertheless was much more of an imperialist country than China. Its expansion in terms of extra land and extra population was far more impressive and its rulers did their utmost to profit from empire. In the process of building its empire their country became the centre of a diverse conglomerate of countries that it turned into peripheries that had to serve its purposes to a much higher extent than China did, and it profited much more from them. We have already pointed at the fact that Great Britain's government was much more nationalist than China's when it came to the economy. More in general one can conclude that it tried to create a 'British state' and a 'British nation'. It put substantial effort into making its society legible – although certainly *less* than several other European countries – participated in creating a dense material and institutional infrastructure and put a lot of effort into turning its subjects into a disciplined, hard-working and obedient labour force. Overall, it did so quite successfully. Chinese rulers, as far as they tried, were less successful in all these respects. At the very end of the period discussed here China still lacked a strong nationalist ideology. China's government undoubtedly did try to discipline its subjects too, but the focus was much less on economic efficiency.

What differences did differences make?

There can be no doubt whatsoever that the British state was as different as could be from the Chinese state. Western European states in general were, although it is important to realize that in many, and often very fundamental, respects Great Britain was *not* simply like the rest of Western Europe. What of course is cardinal for my research is to what extent the differences we have found mattered for economic development and (modern) economic growth in both countries. In many respects their impact is quite obvious but certainly not in all, so some comments certainly are in order.

It has become usual in analysing the Great Divergence to differentiate between Smithian growth, the main form of pre-industrial growth, which is driven by specialization and market extension, and Schumpeterian growth, which is driven by permanent innovation and is considered characteristic for the industrial era.[3] As far as the Qing state facilitated market exchange and specialization it certainly created a favourable environment for Smithian growth. Qing China's economy no doubt was commercialized. But even in its heyday the Qing state did not try to push China's economy towards any fundamental change or innovation. It at best strove for static efficiency – that is, 'spreading the best techniques available across a vast area'.[4] One may really doubt whether it has ever been strong enough to accomplish *more*; that is, *if* it had wanted to. It never seemed eager to push forward fundamental changes itself and as a rule was unwilling to support private initiatives that might disturb the existing order.[5] From the last decades of the eighteenth century onwards Qing rulers found it increasingly difficult to uphold even the basic elements of good governance. Their contribution to economic growth now became neutral at best if not clearly negative. Nothing in the structure of their state or their policies was geared towards economic innovation so their intentional contribution to the emergence of Schumpeterian growth clearly was nil. It in many respects was too weak to support a process of 'industrialization', even if that that would have 'spontaneously' occurred in the private economy.

The British state was far stronger than that of the Qing and therewith in a much better position to support and adjust the major structural changes involved in the emergence of modern economic growth. Great Britain's economy developed and grew in the early modern era. Already in the eighteenth century, before modern industry had made any substantial impact on its economy, the country had become one of the richest in the world. It did so having a fiscal-military, mercantilist state. Then it became the place where the first industrial revolution occurred, the birthplace of modern economic growth. During the period in which it was transformed into an industrial nation (i.e. between roughly 1750 and 1850), it *continued* to be quite fiscal-military, till at least the 1820s, and in many respects mercantilist till at least the 1840s. The popular suggestion that Great Britain, following Adam Smith's advice, abolished 'the mercantile system' and *then* industrialized gets the timing wrong. There can be no doubt that over the second half of the very long eighteenth century Great Britain in several respects developed in the direction of a *laissez-faire* economy, domestically and in its foreign economic relations, and that in the 1850s it indeed was the free-trade nation *par excellence*, but scholars agree that by then it was a full-blown industrial nation. The take off into self-sustained growth and the development of a modern industrial society overwhelmingly took place in a fiscal-military, mercantilist setting. One can only be surprised about the continuing popularity of the classic liberal narrative of Great Britain's industrialization

---

[3]For further explanation of those concepts see my *Escaping Poverty*, under 'economic growth'.
[4]For this quote see Wong, *China Transformed*, 280.
[5]Actually, there were not many of such initiatives.

that so systematically ignores Great Britain's persistent interventionist and militarist tradition.[6]

Mercantilism has always had a bad name among mainstream economists, starting of course with Adam Smith who constructed the 'mercantile system' to then take it apart. Economists, and many economic historians, as a rule have tended to regard mercantilism as an unsound economic policy that simply *cannot* have contributed positively to the emergence of modern economic growth in Great Britain. Experts at the time, in contrast, almost all were convinced that at least many aspects[7] of current mercantilist practice were sound or in any case provided the only realistic strategy to increase the wealth of the nation. An increasing number of scholars find it rather improbable that all those contemporaries were completely mistaken – which it is.

To begin with, it was all but inevitable to behave like a mercantilist. What alternative would governments have had in the context of the cutthroat interstate competition that existed in early modern Europe? To claim, as mainstream economists do, that it would have been better for their economies if countries would *not* have been mercantilist but had played things according to the rules of international free trade and fair competition is to completely ignore the reality of the early modern era in Western Europe. For any single country in early modern Western Europe it would have been economic masochism, if not simply economic suicide, to act according to what has become known as the 'Washington consensus'.[8] Not one of the major players in Europe's state system showed a principled willingness to *voluntarily* play the international trade game according to the rules of the market, and not one of them was powerful enough to *force* other major players to do so. Transnational organizations that might have enforced free and fair trade were non-existent. States that did not develop a big and strong military apparatus were doomed politically as well as economically. Claiming like McCloskey, Mokyr or Nye that mercantilism and fiscal-militarism were 'inefficient' *historically* does not make much sense.[9] Here too it seems that Adam Smith had more common sense than many of his followers when he wrote that 'defence' is more important than 'opulence'.[10] I would not be studying the causes of the Industrial Revolution in Great Britain if that country had lost the Napoleonic Wars against France.

But the fact that something is 'inevitable' of course need not mean it is good. The overwhelming majority of modern economists will have no problem whatsoever to prove

---

[6]It is not only have many economists and economic historians that forgotten how systematically and for how long Great Britain's policies were mercantilist. To again quote Ashworth: 'So successful had been the former combination of protection and nurturing domestic industries that the fact that many of these manufactures would not have existed if it had not been for high tariffs was fairly much ignored by leading politicians.' Ashworth, *Customs and Excise*, 379. Many Britons began to think about their nation as a free-trade nation. See Trentmann, *Free Trade Nation*.

[7]The support for monopolies was frequently contested, especially of course by those excluded, as was simple bullionism.

[8]For an excellent description of that 'paradigm' by someone who personally does not endorse it see the Foreword by Robert H. Wade to Chang and Grabel, *Reclaiming Development*.

[9]See pages 10–12.

[10]See Introduction note 23.

on their blackboards and behind their computers that mercantilism, the fiscal-military state and probably even imperialism all must have been very bad for Britain's economy. And indeed, it is not a major challenge to come up with examples and arguments that show how they can have had negative effects. But central government and its (economic) policies were so prominently present in the economy over the entire period we discuss here that to me – just like for Reinert in the quote on page 427 or for Rodger in a recent article[11] – it is stretching credibility to claim that Great Britain, the most mercantilist country in the world, first became so wealthy and then on top of that industrialized *in spite of them*. The burden of proving that industrialization takes place under the aegis of 'the rise of the market' now clearly is with mainstream economists. What Sophus Reinert says about his book also goes for mine:

> This book maintains that the historical evidence now is so heavily in favour of industrial and military policies successfully encouraging long-term economic development in England, admittedly through far more complex means than simply setting tariffs to encourage domestic manufactures, that the burden of proof falls on neoclassical economics, not on the historic record.[12]

My book was primarily meant to determine and show *what* the differences were between China and Great Britain in the early modern era with respect to the importance, role, and function of their state apparatus and policies. As said before, in many respects the economic advantages and disadvantages of the way the two polities were set up and functioned in terms of its efficient infrastructural power and dynamism, including of course its military strength that enabled Great Britain to tell China what to do instead of the other way around, and its monetary, financial and institutional sophistication are fairly obvious. When it comes to the role of war and to the exact advantages and disadvantages of various forms of protectionism, the challenge ahead is to indicate in detail *how* exactly the differences we found impinged on the economies of both countries and on their development. What has become evident is that the state matters in ways that are not adequately dealt with by most economists, whether it is neoclassical economists who claim that it should only facilitate the market and get the prices right; neo-institutionalists like North, Wallis and Weingast or Acemoglu, Simon and Robinson who claim it should just take care of inclusive institutions; Keynesianists who primarily focus on expenditures, or neo-Marxists who like to treat the state as just a representative of certain societal classes. The history of economically successful states like industrializing Great Britain does not so much falsify these claims as show that such states as a rule during their take off were agents who certainly facilitated markets, competition and spending but *also* manipulated and directed them towards specific goals. In doing so they show that intervention, protection and monopoly need not necessarily have negative effects on development, even though they often do. We must be careful not to exaggerate

---

[11]Rodger, 'War as an economic activity', 18.
[12]Reinert, *Translating Empire*, 7.

contrasts or let current and future analyses be based on caricatures. When it comes to the domestic situation, mercantilism as economic nationalism overall clearly was *pro-market*. Mercantilists favoured the creation of free and fair, smoothly functioning national markets and their policies were instrumental in extending and liberating the market economy. Considering the overwhelming importance for all major European economies of their domestic market this of course is far from irrelevant.

What in any case has to be studied more in depth are the consequences of the fact that mercantilism actually was much more than just a fascination with bullion and/or a strategy of collusion of government and monopolists. It also, and I would say in practice *primarily*, was a policy of strengthening the national economy with a focus on strengthening manufacturing and trade to so strengthen the nation and the state. It would be misleading to call it an *industrialization* policy: before Great Britain actually industrialized no one knew what modern industry was. But I would want to call it developmental: it certainly consisted of measures that, often successfully, aimed at *developing*, that means on producing goods with high(er) added value, that were (more) knowledge and capital intensive and that were better than those of foreign competitors so that they could be sold abroad for a good price. Concepts that immediately come to mind are 'benchmarking', 'protectionism', 'export orientation', 'import substitution' and 'conquering markets'. Mercantilism clearly favoured producers and traders over consumers. Many of Great Britain's producers and merchants often successfully negotiated with the country's rulers, in contrast to their Chinese counterparts. Many of the country's important 'industries' and 'trades' have been helped by government policies and in many cases their rise – whatever the costs, which at times certainly were huge – is hard to imagine without those policies. In a mercantilist world the best way for a government to support its economy was to be an outstanding mercantilist. In the very long eighteenth century mercantilism was the game that was played: the British excelled in it. Next to several other 'advantages', that is what brought them the Industrial Revolution. My final comments in this context concern British 'exceptionalism' and the question of timing: what in any case should not be lost sight of is that to a very large extent Britain indeed was a peculiar state, which may have given its mercantilism a particular effectiveness, and that the policies of that state changed over time. It is important to realize that at the height of its industrial primacy, let us say from the 1850s to the 1870s, Great Britain indeed *was* a champion of free trade and not a mercantilist country. More in general one can claim that as a rule economic superpowers tend to be heavily protectionist during their rise to become free traders when they have become economic hegemons.[13]

Great Britain's state and its policies obviously were not ideal for promoting or supporting economic growth and development but they in many respects certainly had favourable effects. What is particular to *modern* economic growth is the fact that it is sustained. It can be because of a permanent flow of innovations that feeds on inventions based on the application of science. It is knowledge driven. So-called new growth theory tends to attribute a central role to the state in the production of

---

[13]See for this thesis and examples Chang, *Kicking Away the Ladder*.

knowledge.[14] In the First Industrial Revolution in Great Britain, that initiated the Great Divergence, however, the role of the state *in this respect* was rather small. Government in any case did not itself have any research and development programmes, nor did it massively support private research or education. Its role was mainly indirect. It endorsed a scientific worldview. It did not oppose research and, more importantly, increasingly also did not oppose inventions and innovations, even if they might have major and at times disturbing social impact. It respected scientists, inventors and entrepreneurs, and often stimulated them, gave them prizes and honoured them. All this certainly was not unimportant and stood in striking contrast to the world *outside* Europe. In a European context, though, Britain's government was not really exceptional in these respects. That industrializing Great Britain was a knowledge economy was not an intended, direct result of government policies.

On the other hand though, the role of government was extremely important in sectors of the economy whose contribution to Great Britain's take off can hardly be overestimated. In analyses of the Great Divergence the focus always – and rightly so – tends to be on industry and the major technological and energetic changes that took place there. In bringing about those changes as such the role of government was fairly marginal. But even if growth would have been entirely confined to the industrial sector, one still has to realize that Great Britain's industrial development would not have been sustainable without certain imports and exports and that at least part of those imports and exports would not have developed the way they did without all sorts of mercantilist manipulation. Actually, however, Great Britain's modern economic growth was *not* only generated in modern industry but also in agriculture and, even more, the service sector. In both of these sectors, in particular of course in the service sector, government policies had a substantial impact. Mercantilism, to use that shorthand, without any doubt contributed to and facilitated the emergence of Great Britain's modern economy in which after 1850 the service sector with its shipping, banking, insurance, foreign investment and, more in general, services creating 'invisible' exports was the most important sector of the economy. These activities already were a very substantial source of income in Britain *before* the Industrial Revolution and had always been tightly connected to the fiscal-military, mercantilist state. Great Britain's service sector certainly was not a simple offshoot of what went on in industry or agriculture. It had its own dynamics and it is hard to imagine how those could ever have originated without Britain's history of mercantilist and imperialist policies backed by its fiscal-military state. Without those policies and that state Great Britain would not have become the world's most developed, most wealthy and most powerful nation. Mercantilism and the fiscal-military or rather fiscal-naval state, in my view, did not cause modern economic growth in Great Britain in the sense that they would be a sufficient condition for it, but considering the specific conjuncture in which Great Britain took off, I would certainly consider them a necessary condition for the emergence of the first modern industrializing economy.

---

[14]See my *Escaping Poverty* under 'economic growth, theories of economic growth, new'. After I finished that book Mazzucato, *Entrepreneurial State*, was published in which the state figures as a major provider of funds for innovations and as an entrepreneur in its own right that makes high-risk bold investments. See its flap text.

APPENDICES

APPENDIX A

Literature dealing with the question to which extent Great Britain was different from/similar to other (Western) European countries

For a brief outline of the classical British 'Whig' view on Britain's 'exceptional path' see Brewer and Hellmuth, *Rethinking Leviathan*; Macfarlane, *Riddle of the Modern World*; idem, *Invention of the Modern World*, and Winch, 'Introduction'. The reader who wants to find out for himself in what respects Britain indeed may have been peculiar when it comes to topics that are discussed in this book is referred, for a first introduction, to Ertman, 'Sinews of power'; Brewer, 'Eighteenth-century British state', and Wood, *Pristine Culture of Capitalism*, for peculiarities of the British state; to O'Brien, 'Fiscal exceptionalism', and Daunton, 'Trusting Leviathan' for peculiarities of the British tax system; to Macdonald, *Free Nation Deep in Debt*, chapters 4–8, for the peculiarities of British finance; to Innes, 'The state and the poor'; Lindert, 'Poor relief before the welfare state', and Patriquin, 'Agrarian capitalism' for peculiarities of the British system of poor relief; to Rodger, *Command of the Ocean*, for peculiarities of the British Royal Navy; to James, *Warrior Race*, for peculiarities of the British army; to Colley, *Britons*, and, although it deals with an earlier period, Greenfeld, *Nationalism*, for peculiarities of British nationalism; to Cain and Hopkins, *British Imperialism*, for peculiarities of British imperialism and Britain's 'gentlemanly capitalism'; to Etemad, 'Colonial and European domestic trade', for some peculiarities of Britain's economic relations with its empire during the eighteenth and nineteenth centuries; to Porter, *Enlightenment*, for peculiarities of Britain's Enlightenment; to Allen, *British Industrial Revolution*; Wrigley, 'The divergence of England' and 'The great commerce of every civilized society', for peculiarities of Britain's economy and urbanization; to Warde, *Energy Consumption in England and Wales*, for peculiarities of Britain's energy system; to Allen, 'Great divergence', for peculiarities of wages in Britain and, finally, for Britain's peculiar industrialization to Berend, *Economic History of Nineteenth-Century Europe*; O'Brien, 'Do we have a typology for the study of European industrialization'; Verley, *L'échelle du monde*, chapter three, and my *Escaping Poverty*, 18–33. The reader interested to find out in what respects foreigners at the time thought that Britain was peculiar is referred to Rothschild, 'English Kopf'.

APPENDIX B

Estimates of official regular (tax) revenue/income of central government in Qing China[1]

Deng claims that the fixed revenue of the Qing state, at least till 1850, was never more than 80 million taels plus the grain tribute of 4 million shi. Deng, *Political Economy of China*, 17.

He claims that till the 1840s the annual income of Qing central government always amounted to some 40 million taels and that in the 1880s annual tax revenue had risen to 80 million. He, *Paths Towards the Modern Fiscal State*, 131 and 153.

---

[1] My sources use different terms and indicators, which can be quite confusing. I here use their original wording.

Appendices

Lee estimates that total revenue of the Qing government till the First Opium War hovered at between 60 million and 80 million taels. Lee, *Political Economy of a Frontier*, table 1.6. Elliott, Will and Wong refer to this estimate and apparently accept it. They clearly have only taxes – and surcharges on taxes – in mind. Elliott, *Manchu Way*, 489, and Will, Wong and Lee, *Nourish the People*, 494.

Liu gives an estimate of tax revenue of 56 million taels in 1770 and 88 million taels in 1880. Liu, *Wrestling for Power*, 104.

Ma estimates annual average revenue of Qing central government at 35 million taels for the period 1700–49, at 33 million taels for the period 1750–1800 and at 37 million taels for the period 1800–50. Ma, 'Rock, scissors, paper', 28. I calculated these figures on the basis of Ma's data in terms of tons of silver and his claim that a tael would be 37 grams of silver.

Sng claims central government's tax revenue in Qing China never amounted to more than 80 million taels. Sng, 'Size and dynastic decline', 34–5.

Wang estimates total tax revenue, including so-called surcharges, for 1753 at almost 74 million taels and for 1908 as almost four times as much. Wang, *Land Taxation*, 72 and 80.

Chang estimates that annual government revenue as recorded by central government in the 1880s was some 80 million taels. Chang, *Income of the Chinese Gentry*, 328.

Figures in the order of magnitude given above are current in survey texts dealing with the Qing state. See e.g. Hsü, *Rise of Modern China*, 59–65; Rawski, 'Qing formation', 213–8; Rowe, *China's Last Empire*, under 'taxation'.

BIBLIOGRAPHY

Abernethy, David, *The Dynamics of Global Dominance. European Overseas Empires, 1415-1980* (New Haven and London 2000).

Abramovitz, Moses A., 'Catching up, forging ahead and falling behind'. *The Journal of Economic History* 46 (1986): 385–406.

Acemoglu, Daron and James A. Robinson, *Why Nations Fail. The Origins of Power, Prosperity and Poverty* (London 2012).

Adas, Michael, 'Imperialism and colonialism in comparative perspective'. *The International History Review* 20, 2 (1998): 371–88.

Adshead, S. A. M., *Central Asia in World History* (Houndmills and London 1993).

—, *China in World History*, third edition (New York 2000).

Aerts, Eric and F. Crouzet (eds), *Economic Effects of the French Revolutionary and Napoleonic Wars. Proceedings of the Tenth International Economic History Congress* (Leuven 1990).

Allen, Douglas W., *The Institutional Revolution. Measurement and the Economic Emergence of the Modern World* (Chicago and London 2012).

Allen, Robert C., 'The great divergence in European wages and prices from the Middle Ages to the First World War'. *Explorations in Economic History* 38 (2001): 411–47.

—, 'Real wages in Europe and Asia: a first look at the long-term patterns', in Robert C. Allen, Tommy Bengtsson and Martin Dribe (eds), *Living Standards in the Past. New Perspectives on Well-Being in Asia and Europe* (Oxford and New York 2005), 111–30.

—, 'Agricultural productivity and rural incomes in England and the Yangtze Delta, c. 1620-c. 1820'. *The Economic History Review* 62, 3 (2009): 525–50.

—, *The British Industrial Revolution in Global Perspective* (Cambridge 2009).

—, *Global Economic History. A Very Short Introduction* (Oxford 2011).

—, 'The high-wage economy and the Industrial Revolution. A restatement'. *Discussion Papers in Economic and Social History,* 115, June 2013, on Allen's website.

Allen, Robert C. and Jacob Weisdorf, 'Was there an "industrious revolution" before the industrial revolution? An empirical exercise for England, c. 1300-1830'. *The Economic History Review* 64, 3 (2011): 715–29.

Allen, Robert C., Tommy Bengtsson and Martin Dribe (eds), *Living Standards in the Past. New Perspectives on Well-Being in Asia and Europe* (Oxford and New York 2005).

Allen, Robert C., Jean-Pascal Bassino, Debin Ma, Christine Moll-Murata and Jan Luiten van Zanden, 'Wages, prices, and living standards in China, 1738-1925: in comparison with Europe, Japan and India'. *The Economic History Review* 64, 1 (2011): 8–38.

Amsden, Alice H., *The Rise of the 'rest'. Challenges to the West from Late-Industrializing Economies* (Oxford 2001).

Anderson, Adam, *An Historical and Chronological Deduction of the Origins of Commerce, from the earliest Accounts to the Present Time* (London 1764).

Anderson, Perry, *Passages from Antiquity to Feudalism* (London 1978; originally 1974).

Andrade, Tonio, 'The Company's Chinese pirates'. *Journal of World History* 15 (2005): 415–44.

Antony, Robert, 'State, community, and pirate suppression in Guangdong province, 1809-1810'. *Late Imperial China* 27 (2006): 1–30.

Antony, Robert J. and Jane K. Leonard, 'Dragons, tigers and dogs: an introduction', in idem, *Dragons, Tigers, and Dogs. Qing Crisis Management and the Boundaries of State Power in late Imperial China* (Ithaca, New York 2003), 1–26.

Bibliography

—(eds), *Dragons, Tigers, and Dogs. Qing Crisis Management and the Boundaries of State Power in late Imperial China* (Ithaca, New York 2003).

Arrighi, Giovanni, *The Long Twentieth Century. Money, Power, and the Origins of Our Time* (London 1994).

—, *Adam Smith in Beijing. Lineages of the Twenty-First Century* (London and New York 2007).

Arrighi, Giovanni, Takeshi Hamashita and Mark Selden, 'Introduction: the rise of East Asia in regional and world historical perspective', in Giovanni Arrighi, Takeshi Hamashita and Mark Selden (eds), *The Resurgence of East Asia. 500, 150 and 50 years Perspectives* (London and New York 2003), 3–16.

—(eds), *The Resurgence of East Asia. 500, 150 and 50 years Perspectives* (London and New York 2003).

Ashworth, William J., *Customs and Excise. Trade, Production and Consumption in England, 1640-1845* (Oxford 2003).

—, 'Revenue, production and the early modern English/British fiscal-state', in Simonetta Cavaciocchi (ed.), *La fiscalità nell'economia europea secc. XIII-XVIII = Fiscal Systems in the European Economy from the 13th to the 18th Centuries* (Florence 2008), 1045–54.

Asselain, Jean-Charles., *Histoire économique de la France du XVIIIe siècle à nos jours. 1. De l'Ancien Régime à la Première Guerre mondiale* (Paris 1984).

Austin, Gareth and Kaoru Sugihara (eds), *Labour-Intensive Industrialization in Global History* (London 2013).

Avery, Martha, *The Tea Road. China and Russia Meet Across the Steppe* (Beijing 2003).

Baechler, Jean, *The Origins of Capitalism* (London 1976; originally, in French, Paris 1971).

Baechler, Jean, John A. Hall and Michael Mann (eds), *Europe and the Rise of Capitalism* (Oxford 1988).

Bairoch, Paul, *Révolution industrielle et sous-développement,* fourth edition (The Hague 1974).

—, *Economics and World History. Myths and Paradoxes* (Brighton 1993).

—, *Victoires et déboires. Histoire économique et sociale du monde du XVIe siècle à nos jours* (Paris 1997).

Balazs, Etienne, *Chinese Civilization and Bureaucracy. Variations on a Theme* (New Haven and London 1964). The book is edited, with an introduction, by Arthur F. Wright and translated by H. M. Wright.

—, 'China as a permanently bureaucratic society', in idem, *Chinese Civilization and Bureaucracy. Variations on a Theme* (New Haven and London 1964), 13–27.

—, 'The birth of capitalism in China', in idem, *Chinese Civilization and Bureaucracy. Variations on a Theme* (New Haven and London 1964), 34–54.

—, *Political Theory and Administrative Reality in Traditional China* (London 1965).

Bannerman, Gordon E., *Merchants and the Military in Eighteenth-Century Britain. British Army Contracts and Domestic Supply, 1739-1763* (London 2008).

Barbour, Violet, *Capitalism in Amsterdam in the Seventeenth Century* (Ann Arbor 1963).

Barraclough, Geoffrey (ed.), *The Times Atlas of World History* (London 1979).

Barrett, Ward, 'World bullion flows, 1450-1800', in James D. Tracy (ed.), *The Rise of Merchant Empires. Long-Distance Trade in the early Modern World 1350-1750* (Cambridge 1990), 224–54.

Barrow, John, *Travels in China* (London 1804). I use the General Books LLC Publication of 2009.

Bartlett, Beatrice S., *Monarchs and Ministers. The Grand Council in mid-Ch'ing China, 1723-1820* (Berkeley 1991).

Bastid, Marianne, 'The structure of financial institutions of the state in the late Qing', in Stuart R. Schram (ed.), *The Scope of State Power in China* (London and Hong Kong 1985), 51–80.

Bateman, Victoria N., *Markets and Growth in early Modern Europe* (London and Brookfield 2012).

Baugh, Daniel A., *British Naval Administration in the Age of Walpole* (Princeton 1965).

—, 'Maritime strength and Atlantic commerce. The use of 'a grand marine empire', in Lawrence Stone (ed.), *An Imperial State at War* (London 1994), 185–223.

—, 'Naval power: what gave the British navy superiority?', in Leandro Prados de la Escosura (ed.), *Exceptionalism and Industrialisation. Britain and its European Rivals, 1688-1815* (Cambridge 2004), 235–60.

Bayly, C. A., *Imperial Meridian. The British Empire and the World, 1780-1830* (London 1989).

Béaur, Gérard, Pillipp Schofield, Jean-Michel Chevet and Maria-Teresa Perez-Picaso (ed.), *Property Rights, Land Markets and Economic Growth in the European Countryside (Thirteenth-Twentieth Centuries)* (Turnhout 2013).

Beckett, J. V., 'Land tax or excise: the levying of taxation in seventeenth- and eighteenth-century England'. *English Historical Review* 100 (1985): 285–308.

Beckett, J. V. and M. Turner, 'Taxation and economic growth in eighteenth-century England'. *The Economic History Review*, second series XLIII (1990): 377–402.

Beerbühl, Margrit Schulte, 'Supplying the belligerent countries: Transnational trading networks during the Napoleonic Wars', in Richard Harding and Sergio Solbes Ferri (eds), *The Contractor State and its Implications, 1659-1815* (Las Palmas 2012), 21–34.

Behrens, Ulrich, '"Sozialdisziplinierung" als Konzeption der Frühneuzeitforschung. Genese, Weiterentwicklung und Kritik'. *Historische Mitteilungen* 12 (1999): 35–68.

Bell, David A., *The First Total War. Napoleon's Europe and the Birth of Modern Warfare* (London 2007).

Beller, Steven, *A Concise History of Austria* (Cambridge 2006).

Benewick, Robert and Stephanie Donald, *The State of China Atlas* (Harmondsworth 1999).

Berg, Maxine, *The Machinery Question and the Making of Political Economy, 1815-1848* (Cambridge 1980).

—, 'What difference did women's work make to the industrial revolution?'. *History Workshop Journal* 35, 1 (1993): 22–44.

—, 'Manufacturing the Orient. Asian commodities and European industry (1500-1800)', in Simonetta Cavaciocchi (ed.), *Prodotti e techniche d'oltremare nelle economie Europee secc. XIII-XVIII* (Prato 1998), 385–419.

—, *Luxury in the Eighteenth Century: Debates, Desires, and Delectable Goods* (Basingstoke 2003).

—, 'Consumption in eighteenth- and early nineteenth-century Britain', in Roderick Floud and Paul Johnson (eds), *The Cambridge Economic History of Modern Britain, Volume I, Industrialisation, 1700-1860* (Cambridge 2004), 357–87.

—, 'In pursuit of luxury: global history and British consumer goods in the eighteenth century'. *Past and Present* 182 (2004): 82–142.

—, *Luxury and Pleasure in Eighteenth-Century Britain* (Oxford and New York 2005).

Berg, Maxine and Helen Clifford, 'Luxury, consumer goods and British taxation in the eighteenth century', in Simonetta Cavaciocchi (ed.), *La fiscalità nell'economia europea secc. XIII-XVIII = Fiscal Systems in the European Economy from the 13th to the 18th Centuries* (Florence 2008), 1101–14.

Bernhardt, Kathryn, *Rents, Taxes, and Peasant Resistance. The Lower Yangzi Region, 1840-1950* (Stanford 1992).

Bernhardt, Kathryn and Philip Huang, *Civil Law in Qing and Republican China* (Stanford 1999).

Bernstein, Peter L. *Against the Gods. The Remarkable Story of Risk* (New York 1996).

Bernstein, William J., *The Birth of Plenty. How the Prosperity of the Modern World was Created* (New York 2004).

Biernacki, Richard, *The Fabrication of Labour. Germany and Britain, 1640-1914* (Berkeley 1995).

Black, Jeremy, *A Military Revolution? Military Change and European Society 1550-1800. Studies in European History* (Houndmills and London 1991).

Bibliography

—, *War and the World. Military Power and the Fate of Continents 1450-2000* (New Haven and London 1998).

—, *Warfare in the Eighteenth Century* (London 2002; originally 1999).

—, *Western Warfare, 1775-1882* (Bloomington 2001).

—, *Kings, Nobles & Commoners. States & Societies in early Modern Europe. A Revisionist History* (London and New York 2004).

—, *European Warfare in a Global Context, 1660-1815* (London and New York 2007).

—, *The Power of Knowledge. How Information and Technology Made the Modern World* (New Haven 2014).

—(ed.), *War in the early Modern World, 1450-1815* (London 1999).

Blackburn, Robin, *The Making of New World Slavery. From the Baroque to the Modern 1492-1800* (London and New York 1997).

Blaut, Jim, *The Colonizer's Model of the World. Geographical Diffusionism and Eurocentric History* (New York 1993).

Blockmans, Willem P., *A History of Power in Europe* (New York 1997).

Blue, Gregory, 'China and Western social thought in the modern period', in Timothy Brook and Gregory Blue (eds), *China and Historical Capitalism. Genealogies of Sinological Knowledge* (Cambridge 1999), 57–109.

Blunden, Caroline and Mark Elvin, *Cultural Atlas of China* (New York: revised edition 1998).

Blussé, Leonard, *Visible Cities. Canton, Nagasaki, and Batavia and the Coming of the Americans* (Cambridge, MA 2008).

Bodde, Derek and Clarence Morris, *Law in Imperial China* (University of Pennsylvania Press 1973).

Bödecker, Ehrhardt, *Preussen und die Marktwirtschaft* (Munich 2007).

Bonney, Richard, 'Introduction', in Richard Bonney (ed.), *Economic Systems and State Finance* (Oxford 1995), 1–21.

—, 'Early-modern theories of state finance', in Richard Bonney (ed.), *Economic Systems and State Finance* (Oxford 1995), 163–230.

—, 'The eighteenth century. II. The struggle for great power status and the end of the old fiscal regime', in Richard Bonney (ed.), *Economic Systems and State Finance* (Oxford 1995), 315–90.

—, 'Revenues', in Richard Bonney (ed.), *Economic Systems and State Finance* (Oxford 1995), 423–505.

—, 'Introduction', in Richard Bonney (ed.), *The Rise of the Fiscal State in Europe c.1200-1815* (Oxford 1999), 1–17.

—, 'France 1494-1815', in Richard Bonney (ed.), *The Rise of the Fiscal State in Europe c.1200-1815* (Oxford 1999), 123–76.

—, 'Towards the comparative fiscal history of Britain and France during the "long" eighteenth century', in Leandro Prados de la Escosura (ed.), *Exceptionalism and Industrialisation. Britain and its European Rivals, 1688-1815* (Cambridge 2004), 191–215.

—, 'The apogee and fall of the French *rentier* regime, 1801-1914', in José Luís Cardoso and Pedro Lains (eds), *Paying for the Liberal State. The Rise of Public Finance in Nineteenth-Century Europe* (Cambridge 2010), 81–102.

—, 'The rise of the fiscal state in France, 1500-1914', in Bartolomé Yun-Casalilla and Patrick K. O'Brien (eds), *The Rise of Fiscal States. A Global History, 1500-1914* (Cambridge 2012), 93–110.

—(ed.), *Economic Systems and State Finance* (Oxford 1995).

—, *The Rise of the Fiscal State in Europe c.1200-1815* (Oxford 1999).

Boot, Max, *War Made New: Technology, Warfare, and the Course of History, 1500 to Today* (London 2006).

Bordo, Michael D. and Roberto Cortés-Conde (eds), *Transferring Wealth and Power from the Old to the New World: Monetary and Fiscal Institutions in the 17th through the 19th Centuries* (Cambridge 2001).

Bordo, Michael D. and E. N. White, 'A tale of two currencies: British and French finance during the Napoleonic War'. *The Journal of Economic History* 51 (1991): 303–16.

Borgström, Georg, *The Hungry Planet. The Modern World at the Edge of Famine,* first edition (New York 1965).

Borsay, Peter, 'The culture of improvement', in Paul Langford (ed.), *The Eighteenth Century, 1688-1815* (Oxford 2002) 183–212.

Borschberg, Peter, 'Chinese merchants, catholic clerics and Spanish colonists in British-occupied Manila, 1762-1764', in Gungwu Wang and Ng Chin-Keong (eds), *Maritime China in Transition 1750-1850* (Wiesbaden 2004), 355–71.

Bosher, J. F., *The Single Duty Project. A Study of the Movement for a French Customs Union in the Eighteenth Century* (London 1964).

—, 'French administration and public finance in their European setting', in A. Goodwin (ed.), *The New Cambridge Modern History. Volume VIII. The American and French Revolutions, 1763-93* (Cambridge 1965), 565–91.

—, *French Finances 1770-1795* (Cambridge 1970).

Bosma, Ulbe, 'European colonial soldiers in the nineteenth century: their role in white global migration and patterns of colonial settlement'. *Journal of Global History* 4, 2 (2009): 317–36.

Bowen, H. V., *The Business of Empire. The East India Company and Imperial Britain, 1756-1833* (Cambridge 2006).

—, 'British exports of raw cotton from India to China', in Giorgio Riello and Tirthankar Roy (eds), *How India Clothed the World. The World of South Asian Textiles, 1500-1850* (Leiden and Boston 2009), 115–37.

—, 'Bullion for trade, war, and debt relief: British movements of silver, to, around, and from Asia, 1760–1833'. *Modern Asian Studies* 14, 3 (2010): 445–75.

Bowen, H. V. and A. González Enciso (eds), *Mobilising Resources for War. Britain and Spain at Work during the early Modern Period* (Pamplona 2006).

Bown, Stephen R., *Merchant Kings: When Companies Ruled the World, 1600-1900* (New York 2010).

Braddick, Michael J., *The Nerves of the State. Taxation and the Financing of the English State, 1558-1714* (Manchester 1996).

—, 'The early modern English state and the question of social differentiation, from 1550 to 1750'. *Comparative Studies in Society and History* 38, 1 (1996): 92–111.

Bradford De Long, J., 'Overstrong against thyself: war, the state and growth in Europe on the eve of the Industrial Revolution', in Mancur Olson and Satu Kähkönen (eds), *A Not-So-Dismal Science. A Broader View of Economies and Societies* (Oxford 2000), 138–67.

Branch, Jordan, *The Cartographic State. Maps, Territory, and the Origins of Sovereignty* (Cambridge 2013).

Brandon, Pepijn, *Mars and Mercury. War, State, and Capital in the Dutch Cycle of Accumulation (1600-1795)* (Leiden and Boston 2015).

—, 'Finding solid ground for soldiers' payment. 'Military soliciting' as brokerage practice in the Dutch Republic (c.1600-1795)', in Stephen Conway and Rafael Torres Sánchez (eds), *The Spending of States. Military Expenditure during the Long Eighteenth Century: Patterns, Organisation, and Consequences, 1650-1815* (Saarbrücken 2011), 51–82.

Brandt, Loren, Debin Ma and Thomas G. Rawski, 'From divergence to convergence. Re-evaluating the history behind China's economic boom'. *Journal of Economic Literature* 52, 1 (2014): 45–123.

Braudel, Fernand, *Afterthoughts on Material Civilization and Capitalism* (Baltimore 1977).

—, *Civilization & Capitalism, 15th-18th Century. Volume One. The Structures of Everyday Life* (London 1979); *Volume Two. The Wheels of Commerce* (London 1982); *Volume III. The Perspectives of the World* (London 1984).

—, *L'identité de la France. Seconde partie. Les hommes et les choses* (Paris 1986).

Bibliography

—, *A History of Civilizations* (Harmondsworth 1995). This book was first published in French in Paris in a collective volume in 1963. It was published, also in Paris, as a separate volume in 1987, with the title *Grammaire des civilisations*.

—, 'À propos des origines sociales du capitalisme', in R. de Ayala and P. Braudel (eds), *Les écrits de Fernand Braudel II. Les ambitions de l'histoire* (Paris 1997), 359–71.

Braudel, Fernand and Frank C. Spooner, 'Prices in Europe from 1450 to 1750', in E. E. Rich and C. H. Wilson (eds), *The Cambridge Economic History of Europe. Volume 4. The Economy of Expanding Europe in the Sixteenth and Seventeenth Centuries* (Cambridge 1967), 375–486.

Bray, Francesca, *Technology and Gender. Fabrics of Power in Late Imperial China* (Berkeley, Los Angeles and London 1997).

Brenner, Robert and Christopher Mills Isett, 'England's divergence from China's Yangzi Delta: property relations, microeconomics and patterns of development'. *Journal of Asian Studies* 61 (2002): 609–62.

Brewer, John, *The Sinews of Power. War, Money, and the English State, 1688-1783* (London 1988).

—, 'The eighteenth-century British state. Contexts and issues', in Lawrence Stone (ed.), *An Imperial State at War* (London 1994), 52–71.

—, 'Servants of the public - servants of the crown: officialdom of eighteenth-century English central government', in John Brewer and Eckhart Hellmuth (eds), *Rethinking Leviathan. The Eighteenth-Century State in Britain and Germany* (Oxford 1999), 127–48.

Brewer, John and Eckhart Hellmuth, 'Introduction: Rethinking Leviathan', in John Brewer and Eckhart Hellmuth (eds), *Rethinking Leviathan. The Eighteenth-Century State in Britain and Germany* (Oxford 1999), 1–21.

—(eds), *Rethinking Leviathan. The Eighteenth-Century State in Britain and Germany* (Oxford 1999).

Brezis, Elise S., 'Mercantilism', in Joel Mokyr (ed.), *The Oxford Encyclopaedia of Economic History. Volume 3* (Oxford 2003) 482–5.

Brisco, Norris Arthur, *The Economic Policy of Robert Walpole* (New York 1907).

Broadberry, Stephen and Bishnupriya Gupta, 'The early modern Great Divergence: wages, prices and economic development in Europe and Asia, 1500-1800'. *The Economic History Review* 59 (2006): 2–31.

Broadberry, Stephen, Hanhui Guan and David Daokui Li, 'China, Europe and the Great divergence: a study in historical national accounting, 980-1850', http://eh.net/eha/wp-content/uploads/2014/05/Broadberry.pdf.

Brook, Timothy (ed.), *The Asiatic Mode of Production in China* (New York 2001).

—, *Vermeer's Hat. The Seventeenth Century and the Dawn of the Global World* (New York 2008).

Brook, Timothy and Gregory Blue (eds), *China and Historical Capitalism. Genealogies of Sinological Knowledge* (Cambridge 1999).

Bryant, Joseph M., 'The West and the Rest revisited: debating capitalist origins, European colonialism, and the advent of modernity'. *Canadian Journal of Sociology/Cahiers Canadiens de Sociologie* 31, 4 (2006): 403–44.

Buck, John Lossing, *Land Utilization in China* (Oxford and London 1937).

Buisseret, David (ed.), *Monarchs, Ministers, and Maps. The Emergence of Cartography as a Tool of Government in early Modern Europe* (Chicago 1992).

Buoye, Thomas M., *Manslaughter, Markets, and Moral Economy. Violent Disputes over Property Rights in Eighteenth-Century China* (Cambridge 2000).

Burbank Jane and Frederick Cooper, *Empires in World History. Power and the Politics of Difference* (Princeton and Oxford 2010).

Burger, Werner, 'Coin production during the Qianlong and Jiaqing reigns (1736-1820): Issues in cash and silver supply', in Thomas Hirzel and Nanny Kim (eds), *Metals, Monies, and Markets in early Modern Societies: East Asian and Global Perspectives* (Berlin 2008), 171–90.

Burke, Peter, *Popular Culture in early Modern Europe* (New York 1978).

Burnett, John, *Plenty and Want. A Social History of Diet in England from 1815 to the Present Day* (London and New York 1966).

—, *Liquid Pleasures. A Social History of Drinks in Modern Britain* (London 1999).

Bush, Barbara, *Imperialism and Postcolonialism* (Harlow 2006).

Butterfield, Herbert, *The Whig Interpretation of History* (Harmondsworth 1931).

Cain, P. J. and A. G. Hopkins, *British Imperialism, 1688-2000,* second edition (Harlow and London 2001).

Cameron, Rondo E., 'England 1750-1844', in Rondo E. Cameron, Olga Crisp, Hugh T. Patrick and Richard Tilly (eds), *Banking in the early Stages of Industrialization: A Study in Comparative Economic History* (New York 1967), 15–59.

Canadian Journal of Sociology/Cahiers Canadiens de Sociologie 33, 1 (2008) a debate on Bryant, 'The West and the Rest revisited', with contributions by Jack Goldstone, Rosaire Langlois, Joseph M. Bryant and Mark Elvin.

Canny, Nicolas, 'English migration into and across the Atlantic during the seventeenth and eighteenth centuries', in Nicolas Canny (ed.), *Europeans on the Move. Studies on European Migration, 1500-1800* (Oxford 1994), 39–75.

Capie, Forrest, 'The origins and development of stable fiscal and monetary institutions in England', in Michael D. Bordo and Roberto Cortés-Conde (eds), *Transferring Wealth and Power from the Old to the New World: Monetary and Fiscal Institutions in the 17th through the 19th Centuries* (Cambridge 2001), 19–58.

—, 'The emergence of the Bank of England as a mature central bank', in Donald Winch and Patrick K. O'Brien (eds), *The Political Economy of British Historical Experience, 1688-1914* (Oxford 2002), 295–318.

—, 'Money and economic development in eighteenth-century England', in Leandro Prados de la Escosura (ed.), *Exceptionalism and Industrialisation. Britain and its European Rivals, 1688-1815* (Cambridge 2004), 216–34.

Capra, Carlo, 'The eighteenth century. I. The finances of the Austrian monarchy and the Italian states', in Richard Bonney (ed.), *Economic Systems and State Finance* (Oxford 1995), 295–314.

Cardoso, José Luís and Pedro Lains, 'Introduction: paying for the liberal state', in José Luís Cardoso and Pedro Lains (eds), *Paying for the Liberal State. The Rise of Public Finance in Nineteenth-Century Europe* (Cambridge 2010), 1–26.

—(eds), *Paying for the Liberal State. The Rise of Public Finance in Nineteenth-Century Europe* (Cambridge 2010).

Carruthers, Bruce G., *Politics and Markets in the English Financial Revolution* (Princeton 1996).

Carter, William, *The Reply of W. C.* (London 1685).

Cassis, Youssef, *Capitals of Capital. The Rise and Fall of International Financial Centres, 1780-2009,* second edition (Cambridge 2013).

Caton, Haron, *The Politics of Progress. The Origins and Development of the Commercial Republic, 1600-1835* (Gainesville 1988).

Cavaciocchi, Simonetta (ed.), *Prodotti e techniche d'oltremare nelle economie Europee secc. XIII-XVIII* (Prato 1998).

—(ed.), *La fiscalità nell'economia europea secc. XIII-XVIII = Fiscal Systems in the European Economy from the 13th to the 18th Centuries* (Florence 2008).

Cecchitti, S. G., M. S. Mohanty and F. Zampolli, 'The real effects of debt', Bank for International Settlements Working Papers No. 352, September 2011, http://www.bis.org/publ/work352.pdf

Ch'ü, T'ung-tsu, *Local Government under the Ch'ing* (Cambridge, MA 1962).

Challis, C. E., 'Lord Hasting to the Great Silver Recoinage', in C. E. Challis (ed.), *A New History of the Royal Mint* (Cambridge 1992), 179–397.

—, 'Appendix I, Mint Output, 1220-1985', in C. E. Challis (ed.), *A New History of the Royal Mint* (Cambridge 1992), 673–98.

—(ed.), *A New History of the Royal Mint* (Cambridge 1992).

Bibliography

Chang, Chung-li, *The Chinese Gentry. Their Role in Nineteenth-Century Chinese Society* (Seattle and London 1955).

—, *The Income of the Chinese Gentry. A Sequel to the Chinese Gentry: Studies on their Role in Nineteenth Century Society* (Seattle 1962).

Chang, Ha-Joon, *Kicking away the Ladder. Development Strategy in Historical Perspective* (London 2002).

—, *Rethinking Development Economics* (Anthem 2003).

Chang, Ha-joon and Ilene Grabel, *Reclaiming Development. An Alternative Economic Policy Manual. With a Foreword by Robert H. Wade* (London and New York 2014).

Chang, Hsin-pao, *Commissioner Lin and the Opium War* (New York 1964).

Chang, Pin-tsun, 'The evolution of Chinese thought on maritime foreign trade from the sixteenth to the eighteenth century'. *International Journal of Maritime History* 1 (1989): 51–64.

—, 'Chinese migration to Taiwan in the eighteenth century: a paradox', in Gungwu Wang and Ng Chin-Keong (eds), *Maritime China in Transition 1750-1850* (Wiesbaden 2004), 97–114.

Chang, Pin-tsun and Chau-nan Chen, 'Competing monies in Chinese history from the fifteenth to the nineteenth century', in Van Cauwenberghe (ed.), *Money, Coins, and Commerce: Essays in Monetary History of Asia and Europe (From Antiquity to Modern Times)* (Leuven 1991), 375–84.

Chang, Te-ch'ang, 'The economic role of the imperial household in the Ch'ing dynasty'. *Journal of Asian Studies* 31 (1972): 243–73.

Chang, Y. Z., 'China and English Civil Service reform'. *The American Historical Review* 47 (1942): 539–44.

Chao, Kang, *The Development of Cotton Textile Production in China* (Cambridge, MA 1977).

—, 'La production textile dans la Chine traditionelle'. *Annales. Économies, Sociétés, Civilisations* 39 (1984): 957–76.

Chapman, Stanley, *Merchant Enterprise in Britain. From the Industrial Revolution to World War I* (Cambridge 1992).

Chase-Dunn, Christopher and Thomas Hall, *Rise and Demise: Comparing World Systems* (Boulder 1997).

Chase, Kenneth, *Firearms. A Global History to 1700* (Cambridge 2003).

Chaudhuri, Kirti N., 'Circuits monétaires internationaux, prix comparés et spécialisation économique, 1500-1750', in John Day (ed.), *Études d'histoire monétaire* (Lille 1984), 49–67.

Chen, Jerome, *State Economic Policies of the Ch'ing Government, 1840-1895* (New York 1980).

Chen, Li, 'Legal specialists and judicial administration in Late Imperial China, 1651–1911'. *Late Imperial China* 33, 1 (2012): 1–54.

Chen, Qiang, 'The Needham Puzzle reconsidered. The protection of industrial and commercial property rights'. *Economic History of Developing Countries* 27, 1 (2012): 38–66.

Chen, Shao-Kwan, *The System of Taxation in China in the Tsing Dynasty, 1644-1911* (New York 1914).

Chen, Tsu-yu, 'China's copper production in Yunnan province 1700-1800', in Van Cauwenberghe (ed.), *Money, Coins, and Commerce: Essays in Monetary History of Asia and Europe (From Antiquity to Modern Times)* (Leuven 1991), 95–118.

Chen, Zhiwu, 'Financial strategies for nation building', http://www.nber.org/chapters/c12070.pdf.

Cheung, Sui-wai, 'Copper, silver, and tea. The question of eighteenth-century inflation in the Lower Yangzi Delta', in Billy K. L. So (ed.), *The Economy of Lower Yangzi Delta in late Imperial China. Connecting Money, Markets, and Institutions* (London 2012), 118–32.

Childs, John, 'The army and the state in Britain and Germany during the eighteenth century', in John Brewer and Eckhart Hellmuth (eds), *Rethinking Leviathan. The Eighteenth-Century State in Britain and Germany* (Oxford 1999), 53–70.

Christian, David, *History of Russia, Central Asia and Mongolia* (London 2007).

Christopher, Emma, *Slave Ship Sailors and their Captive Cargoes, 1730-1807* (New York 2000).

Christopher, Emma, Cassandra Pybus and Markus Rediker (eds), *Many Middle Passages. Forced Migration and the Making of the Modern World* (Berkeley, Los Angeles and London 2007).

Chua, Amy, *Day of Empire. How Hyperpowers Rise to Global Dominance – and Why They Fall* (New York 2007).

Chuan, Hang Sheng, 'Trade between China, the Philippines and the Americas during the sixteenth and seventeenth centuries', in Dennis O. Flynn and Arturo Giráldez (eds), *Metals and Moneys in an Emerging Global Economy* (Aldershot 1997), 281–6.

Chun, Hae-Jong, 'Sino-Korean tributary relations in the Ch'ing period', in John K. Fairbank (ed.), *The Chinese World Order* (Cambridge, MA 1968), 90–111.

Clapham, J. H., *The Bank of England. A History* (Cambridge 1944).

Clark, Christopher, *Iron Kingdom. The Rise and Downfall of Prussia, 1600-1947* (London 2006).

Clark, Gregory, 'What made Britannia Great? How much of the rise of Britain to world dominance by 1850 does the Industrial Revolution explain?', in Timothy J. Hatton, Kevin O'Rourke and Alan M. Taylor (eds), *The New Comparative Economic History. Essays in Honor of Jeffrey G. Williamson* (Cambridge, MA and London 2007), 33–58.

—, *A Farewell to Alms. A Brief Economic History of the World* (Princeton and Oxford 2007).

Clarke, J. C. D., *English Society, 1688-1832: Ideology, Social Structure and Political Practice during the Ancien Regime* (Cambridge 1985).

—, 'England's Ancien Regime as a confessional state'. *Albion. A Quarterly Journal Concerned with British Studies* 21, 3 (1989): 450–74.

Coats, A. W., 'Changing attitudes towards labour in the mid-eighteenth century'. *Economic History Review,* 2nd series, 11 (1958): 35–51.

—, 'Economic thought and Poor Law policy in the eighteenth century'. *Economic History Review* 13 (1960): 39–51.

Cohen, H. Floris, 'The rise of modern science as a fundamental pre-condition for the Industrial Revolution'. *Österreichische Zeitschrift für Geschichtswissenschaften* 20, 2 (2009): 107–32.

—, *How Modern Science Came into the World. Four Civilizations, one 17th-century Breakthrough* (Amsterdam 2011).

Coleman, David, 'Mercantilism revisited'. *Historical Journal* 23 (1980): 773–91.

—(ed.), *Revisions in Mercantilism* (London 1969).

Colley, Linda, *Britons. Forging the Nation, 1707-1837* (New Haven and London 1992).

—, 'The reach of the state, the appeal of the nation. Mass arming and political culture in the Napoleonic Wars', in Lawrence Stone (ed.), *An Imperial State at War* (London 1994), 165–84.

Colli, Andrea, *The History of Family Business, 1850-2000* (Cambridge 2003).

Colquhoun, Patrick, *A Treatise on Indigence* (London 1806).

—, *A Treatise on the Wealth, Power and Resources of the British Empire in every Quarter of the World* (London 1815).

Conchon, Anne, 'Resources fiscales et financement des infrastructures en France au XVIIIe siècle', in Simonetta Cavaciocchi (ed.), *La fiscalità nell'economia europea secc. XIII-XVIII = Fiscal Systems in the European Economy from the 13th to the 18th Centuries* (Florence 2008), 1055–64.

Conway, Stephen, *The British Isles and the War of American Independence* (Oxford 2000).

—, 'Checking and controlling British military expenditure, 1739-1783', in Torres Sánchez (ed.), *War, State and Development. Fiscal-Military States in the Eighteenth Century* (Pamplona 2007), 45–68.

Conway, Stephen and Rafael Torres Sánchez (eds), *The Spending of States. Military Expenditure during the Long Eighteenth Century: Patterns, Organisation, and Consequences, 1650-1815* (Saarbrücken 2011).

Cook, Harold J., *Matters of Exchange: Commerce, Medicine and Science in the Dutch Golden Age* (New Haven 2007).

Bibliography

Cookson, J. E., 'Political arithmetic and war in Britain, 1789-1815'. *War and Society* 1 (1983): 37–60.

—, *The British Armed Nation, 1793-1815* (Oxford 1997).

Cooper, R. N. and V. W. Ruttan, *Is War Necessary for Economic Growth? Military Procurement and Technology Development* (Oxford 2006).

Cooter, Robert D. and Hans-Bernd Schäfer, *Solomon's Knot. How Law can End the Poverty of Nations* (Princeton 2012).

Coppieters, Emmanuel, *English Bank Note Circulation, 1694-1954* (Leuven 1955).

Cotterell, Roger, 'The development of capitalism and the formation of contract law', in Bob Fryer, Alan Hunt, Doreen McBarnet and Bert Moorhouse (eds), *Law, State and Society* (London 1981), 54–69.

Cottrell, P. L., 'Banking and finance', in J. Langton and R. J. Morris (eds), *Atlas of Industrializing Britain, 1780-1914* (London and New York 1986), 144–55.

Cranmer-Byng, J. L. (ed.), *An Embassy to China. Being the Journal Kept by Lord Macartney during his Embassy to the Emperor Ch'ien-lung 1793-1794* (London 1962).

Crone, Patricia, *Pre-Industrial Societies* (Oxford and Cambridge, MA 1989).

Crossley, Pamela Kyle, *Orphan Warriors. Three Manchu Generations and the End of the Qing World* (Princeton 1990).

—, *The Wobbling Pivot. China since 1800* (Malden 2010).

Crossley, Pamela Kyle, Helen Siu and Donald Sutton (eds), *Empire at the Margins. Culture, Ethnicity, and Frontier in early Modern China* (Berkeley 2006).

Cuenca-Esteban, Javier, 'The British balance of payments, 1772-1820: India transfers and war finance'. *The Economic History Review* 54 (2001): 58–86.

—, 'Comparative patterns of colonial trade: Britain and its rivals', in Leandro Prados de la Escosura (ed.), *Exceptionalism and Industrialisation. Britain and its European Rivals, 1688-1815* (Cambridge 2004), 35–68.

—, 'Fiscal dimensions of Britain's regulated trade with Asia, 1765-1812', in Torres Sánchez (ed.), *War, State and Development. Fiscal-Military States in the Eighteenth Century* (Pamplona 2007), 69–86.

Cullen, L. M., 'Merchant communities overseas: the Navigation Acts and Irish and Scottish responses', in L. M. Cullen and T. C. Smout (eds), *Comparative Aspects of Scottish and Irish Economic and Social History* (Edinburgh n.d. c. 1976), 165–76.

—, *A History of Japan. Internal and External Worlds, 1582-1941* (Cambridge 2003).

Cushman, Jennifer, *Fields from the Sea. Chinese Junk Trade with Siam during the late Eighteenth and early Nineteenth Centuries* (Ithaca 1993).

Dabringhaus, Sabine, *Das Qing-Imperium als Vision und Wirklichkeit. Tibet in Laufbahn und Schriften des Song Yun* (1752-1835) (Stuttgart 1994).

Dai, Yingcong, 'A disguised defeat: the Myanmar campaign of the Qing Dynasty'. *Modern Asian Studies* 38, 1 (2004): 145–89.

—, 'Yingyung Shengxi: Military entrepreneurship in the High Qing'. *Late Imperial China* 26, 2 (2005): 1–69.

—, *The Sichuan Frontier and Tibet. Imperial Strategy in the early Qing* (Seattle and London 2009).

—, 'Military finance of the high Qing period: an overview', in Nicola Di Cosmo (ed.), *Military Culture in Imperial China* (Cambridge, MA 2009), 296–316.

Dalziel, Nigel, with an introduction by John Mackenzie, *The Penguin Historical Atlas of the British Empire* (London 2006).

Darwin, John, *After Tamerlane. The Global History of Empire* (London and New York 2007).

—, *The Empire Project. The Rise and Fall of the British World-System 1830-1970* (Cambridge 2009).

—, *Unfinished Empire. The Global Expansion of Britain* (London 2012).

Daunton, Martin, *Progress and Poverty. An Economic and Social History of Britain 1700-1850* (Oxford 1995).

—, *Trusting Leviathan. The Politics of Taxation in Britain, 1799-1914* (Cambridge 2001).

—, 'Trusting Leviathan: the politics of taxation, 1815-1914', in Donald Winch and Patrick K. O'Brien (eds), *The Political Economy of British Historical Experience, 1688-1914* (Oxford 2002), 319–50.

—, 'Creating legitimacy: administering taxation in Britain, 1815-1914', in José Luís Cardoso and Pedro Lains (eds), *Paying for the Liberal State. The Rise of Public Finance in Nineteenth-Century Europe* (Cambridge 2010), 27–56.

—, 'The politics of British taxation, from the Glorious Revolution to the Great War', in Bartolomé Yun-Casalilla and Patrick K. O'Brien (eds), *The Rise of Fiscal States. A Global History, 1500-1914* (Cambridge 2012), 111–42.

Davids, Karel, 'From de la Court to Vreede. Regulation and self-regulation in Dutch economic discourse from c. 1660 to the Napoleonic era'. *Journal of European Economic History* 30, 2 (2001): 245–89.

Davies, Glyn, *History of Money. From Ancient Times to the Present Day,* third edition with revisions (Cardiff 2002).

Davis, Mike, *Late Victorian Holocausts. El Niño Famines and the Making of the Third World* (London and New York 2001).

Davis, Ralph, 'The rise of protection in England, 1689-1786'. *Economic History Review* 19 (1966): 306–17.

—, *The Industrial Revolution and British Overseas Trade* (Leicester 1979).

Day, John, *Money and Finance in the Age of Merchant Capitalism* (Malden, MA 1999).

—(ed.), *Études d'histoire monétaire* (Lille 1984).

De la Court, Pieter, *The True Interest and Political Maxims of Holland and West-Friesland* (London 1702; originally 1662).

De Moor, Tine and Jan Luiten van Zanden, 'Girlpower. The European marriage pattern (EMP) and labour markets in the North Sea region in the late medieval and early modern period'. *Economic History Review* 63, 1 (2009): 1–33.

De Vito, Christian G. and Alexander Lichtenstein, 'Writing a global history of convict labour'. *International Review of Social History* 58, 2 (2013): 285–325.

De Vries, Jan, 'The Industrial Revolution and the Industrious Revolution'. *The Journal of Economic History* 54 (1994): 249–70.

—, 'The Netherlands in the New World: the legacy of European fiscal, monetary, and trading institutions for New World development from the seventeenth to the nineteenth centuries', in Michael D. Bordo and Roberto Cortés-Conde (eds), *Transferring Wealth and Power from the Old to the New World: Monetary and Fiscal Institutions in the 17th through the 19th Centuries* (Cambridge 2001), 100–39.

—, 'Connecting Europe and Asia: a quantitative analysis of the Cape-route trade', in Dennis O. Flynn, Arturo Giráldez and Richard von Glahn (eds), *Global Connections and Monetary History, 1470-1800* (Aldershot and Burlington 2003), 35–106.

—, 'The industrious revolution and economic growth', in Paul A. David and Mark Thomas (eds), *The Economic Future in Historical Perspective* (Oxford 2003), 43–72.

—, *The Industrious Revolution. Consumer Behaviour and the Household Economy, 1650 to the Present* (Cambridge and New York 2008).

—, 'Limits of globalization in the early modern world'. *Economic History Review* 63 (2010): 710–33.

De Vries, Jan and Ad van der Woude, *The First Modern Economy. Success, Failure, and Perseverance of the Dutch Economy from 1500 to 1815* (Cambridge 1997).

Deane, Phyllis, *The First Industrial Revolution* (Cambridge 1965).

—, 'War and industrialisation', in J. M. Winter (ed.), *War and Economic Development. Essays in the Memory of David Joslin* (Cambridge 1975), 91–102.

Deane, Phyllis and W. A. Cole, *British Economic Growth, 1688-1959,* second edition (Cambridge 1959).

Bibliography

Deng, Gang, *Chinese Maritime Activities & Socioeconomic Development; c. 2100 B.C. -1900 A.D* (Westport 1997).

—, 'The foreign staple trade of China in the pre-modern era'. *The International History Review* XIX (1997): 253–304.

—, *Maritime Sector, Institutions and Sea Power of Premodern China* (Westport 1999).

—, *The Premodern Chinese Economy. Structural Equilibrium and Capitalist Sterility* (London and New York 1999).

Deng, Kent G., 'A critical survey of recent research in Chinese economic history'. *Economic History Review* 53, 1 (2000): 1–28.

—, 'Unveiling China's true population statistics for the pre-modern era with official census data'. *Population Review* 43, 2 (2004): 1–38.

—, 'Consumer goods for silver reserves and silver reserves for consumer goods. International trade and material life in Ming-Qing China'. Paper presented at the London School of Economics and Political Science, December 2004. Unpublished.

—, 'Why the Chinese failed to develop a steam engine'. *History of Technology* 25 (2004): 151–71.

—, 'Sweet and sour Confucianism'. Paper presented at the Tenth Global Economic History Conference September 2006 Washington. Unpublished.

—, 'Miracle or mirage? Foreign silver, China's economy and globalization from the sixteenth to the eighteenth centuries'. *Pacific Economic Review* 13, 3 (2008): 320–58.

—, 'The continuation and efficiency of the Chinese fiscal state, 700 BC-AD 1911', in Bartolomé Yun-Casalilla and Patrick K. O'Brien (eds), *The Rise of Fiscal States. A Global History, 1500-1914* (Cambridge 2012), 335–52.

—, *China's Political Economy in Modern Times. Changes and Economic Consequences, 1800-2000* (London and New York 2012).

—, 'Demystifying growth and development in North Song China, 960–1127'. Working Paper 178, 2013 in The Economic History Working Papers Series of the Department of Economic History of the London School of Economics and Political Science. The paper can be downloaded from the website of the Department.

Dermigny, Louis, *La Chine et l'Occident: commerce à Canton au XVIIIe siècle* (Paris 1964).

Devine, T. M., 'Scotland', in Roderick Floud and Paul Johnson (eds), *The Cambridge Economic History of Modern Britain, Volume I, Industrialisation, 1700-1860* (Cambridge 2004), 388–416.

—, *The Scottish Nation 1700-2007* (reissued, with new material; London 2006).

Di Cosmo, Nicola, 'European technology and Manchu power: reflections on the military revolution in seventeenth-century China', in Solvi Sogner (ed.), *Making Sense of Global History. The XIXth International Congress of the Historical Sciences, Oslo 2000. Commemorative Volume* (Oslo 2001), 119–39.

—, 'Did guns matter? Firearms and Qing formation', in Lynn A. Struve (ed.), *The Qing Formation in World-Historical Time* (Cambridge, MA and London 2004), 121–66.

—(ed.), *Military Culture in Imperial China* (Cambridge, MA 2009).

Dickson, P. G. M., *The Financial Revolution in England* (London 1967).

—, *Finance and Government under Maria Theresa, 1740-1780. Volume I. Society and Government* (Oxford 1987).

—, *Finance and Government under Maria Theresa, 1740-1780. Volume II. Finance and Credit* (Oxford 1987).

—, 'Monarchy and bureaucracy in late-eighteenth century Austria'. *English Historical Review* 110 (1995): 323–67.

—, 'Count von Zinzendorfs 'New Accountancy'. The structure of Austrian government finance in peace and war'. *International History Review* 29 (2007): 22–56.

Dietz, V. E., *Before the Age of Capital. Manufacturing Interests and the British State, 1780-1800* (Stanford University 1991). Unpublished.

Dikötter, Frank, *The Discourse of Race in Modern China* (Stanford 1994).

Dincecco, Mark, 'Fiscal centralization, limited government, and public revenues in Europe, 1650-1913'. *The Journal of Economic History* 69, 1 (2009): 48–103.

—, *Political Transformations and Public Finances. Europe, 1650-1913* (Cambridge 2011).

Dirlik, Arif, 'Chinese historians and the Marxist concept of capitalism: A critical examination'. *Modern China* 8, 1 (1982): 105–32.

Dittmer, Lowell and Samuel S. Kim (eds), *China's Quest for National Identity* (Ithaca 1993).

Dodgen, Randall A., *Controlling the Dragon. Confucian Engineers and the Yellow River in Late Imperial China* (Honolulu 2001).

Dolin, Eric Jay, *When America First Met China. An Exotic History of Tea, Drugs, and Money in the Age of Sail* (New York 2012).

Donnelly, James S. Jr., *The Great Irish Potato Famine* (Stroud 2001).

Dorn, Walter L. 'The Prussian bureaucracy'. *Political Science Quarterly* 46, 3 (1931): 402–23; 47, 1 (1932): 75–94.

Downing, Brian M., *The Military Revolution and Political Change. Origins of Democracy and Autocracy in early Modern Europe* (Princeton 1992).

Drake, Fred W., *China Charts the World. Hsu Chi-yü and his Geography of 1848* (Cambridge, MA and London 1975).

Drayton, Richard, 'Knowledge and empire', in P. J. Marshall (ed.), *The Oxford History of the British Empire. The Eighteenth Century* (Oxford and New York 1998), 231–52.

—, *Nature's Government: Science, Imperial Britain, and the 'improvement' of the World* (Yale 2000).

—, 'The collaboration of labour: slaves, empires and globalizations in the Atlantic world, c. 1600-1850', in A. G. Hopkins (ed.), *Globalization in World History* (London 2002), 98–114.

Duara, Prasenjit, *Rescuing History from the Nation. Questioning Narratives of Modern China* (Chicago 1995).

Duchesne, Ricardo, 'On the rise of the West: researching Kenneth Pomeranz's *Great Divergence*'. *Review of Radical Political Economics* 36 (2004): 52–81.

Dudley, Leonard, *Information Revolutions in the History of the West* (Cheltenham 2008).

—, *Mothers of Innovation: How Expanding Social Networks gave Birth to the Industrial Revolution* (Cambridge 2012).

Duffy, Michael, *Soldiers, Sugar and Seapower. The British Expeditions to the West Indies and the War against Revolutionary France* (Oxford 1987).

—, 'World-wide war and British expansion, 1793-1815', in P. J. Marshall (ed.), *The Oxford History of the British Empire. The Eighteenth Century* (Oxford and New York 1998), 184–207.

Dunstan, Helen, 'Safely supping with the devil: The Qing state and its merchant suppliers of copper'. *Late Imperial China* 13, 2 (1992): 42–81.

—, *Conflicting Counsels to Confuse the Age. A Documentary Study of Political Economy in Qing China, 1644-1840* (Ann Arbor 1996).

—, *State and Merchant. Political Economy and Political Process in 1740s China* (Cambridge, MA 2006).

Dupeux, Georges, *French Society, 1789-1970* (London 1976; originally Paris 1972).

Duyvendak, J. L., 'The last Dutch embassy to the Chinese court, 1794-1795'. *T'oung Pao* 34 (1938): 1–137.

Dyer, G. P. and P. P. Gaspar, 'Reform, the new technology and Tower Hill, 1700-1966', in C. E. Challis (ed.), *New History of the Royal Mint* (Cambridge 1992), 398–606.

Eagleton, Catherine and Jonathan Williams, with Joe Cribb and Elizabeth Errington, *Money. A History*, second edition (London 2007).

Earle, Peter, *Sailors. English Merchant Seamen 1650-1775* (London 2007).

Eastman, Lloyd, *Family, Fields and Ancestors. Constancy and Change in China's Social and Economic History, 1550-1949* (New York 1988).

Bibliography

Ebrey, Patricia Buckley, *Cambridge Illustrated History of China* (Cambridge 1996).

Eisenberg, Christiane, *The Rise of Market Society in England, 1066-1800* (Oxford and New York 2013).

Ekelund, Robert P. and Robert D. Tollison, *Mercantilism as a Rent-Seeking Society. Economic Regulation in Historical Perspective* (College Station Texas 1981).

—, *Politicized Economics. Monarchy, Monopoly and Mercantilism* (College Station Texas 1997).

Elleman, Bruce A., *Modern Chinese Warfare, 1795-1989* (London and New York 2001).

Elliott, John H., 'A Europe of composite monarchies'. *Past and Present* 137 (1992): 48–71.

—, *Empires of the Atlantic World. Britain and Spain in America 1492-1830* (New Haven and London 2006).

Elliott, Mark C., *The Manchu Way. The Eight Banners and Ethnic Identity in late Imperial China* (Stanford 2001).

—, *Emperor Qianlong. Son of Heaven, Man of the World* (New York 2009).

Elman, Benjamin A., *A Cultural History of Civil Examinations in late Imperial China* (Berkeley, Los Angeles and London 2000).

—, *On their Own Terms. Science in China, 1550-1900* (Cambridge, MA and London 2005).

Eltis, David, 'The slave economies of the Caribbean: Structure, performance, evolution and significance', in Franklin W. Knight (ed.), *The Slave Societies of the Caribbean. Volume III of General History of the Caribbean* (London 1997), 105–37.

—, 'Slavery and freedom in the early modern world', in Stanley L. Engerman (ed.), *Terms of Labor: Slavery, Serfdom and Free Labor* (Stanford 1999) 25–49.

—, 'Free and coerced migrations from the Old World to the New', in David Eltis (ed.), *Coerced and Free Migration. Global Perspectives* (Stanford 2002), 33–74.

—, 'The cultural roots of African slavery', in David Northrup (ed.), *Atlantic Slave Trade*, second edition (Boston and New York 2002), 23–30.

Elvin, Mark, *The Pattern of the Chinese Past* (Stanford 1973).

—, 'The technology of farming in late-traditional China', in Randolph Barker and Radha Sinha (eds), *The Chinese Agricultural Economy* (Boulder 1982), 13–31.

—, 'Three thousand years of unsustainable growth: China's environment from archaic times to the present'. *East Asian History* 6 (1993): 7–46.

—, *Another History. Essays on China from a European Perspective* (Canberra 1996).

—, 'Skills and resources in late traditional China', in Mark Elvin (ed.), *Another History. Essays on China from a European Perspective* (Canberra 1996), 64–100.

—, 'Braudel and China', in John Marino (ed.), *History and the Social Sciences in Braudel's Mediterranean: Sixteenth-Century Essays and Studies. Sixteenth Century Journal* (Truman State University Press 2002), 225–53.

—, *The Retreat of the Elephants. An Environmental History of China* (New Haven 2004)

—, 'The historian as haruspex'. *New Left Review* 52 (2008): 83–109.

—, 'Why intensify? The outline of a theory of the institutional causes driving long-term changes in Chinese farming and the consequent modifications to the environment', in Sverker Sörlin and Paul Warde (eds), *Nature's End. History and Environment* (London 2009), 273–303.

—, 'The environmental impasse in Late Imperial China', in Brantley Womack (ed.), *China's Rise in Historical Perspective* (Lanham 2010), 152–69.

Elvin, Mark and Josephine Fox, 'Marriages, births, and deaths in the Lower Yangzi Valley during the later eighteenth century', in Clara Wing-chung Ho (ed.), *Windows on the Chinese World* (Lanham 2009), 67–111. Accompanied by a website containing the quantified data and basic computer programs (in PERL) in free downloadable form: http://gis.sinica.edu.tw/QingDemography

Elvin, Mark and Tsui-jung Liu (eds), *Sediments of Time. Environment and Society in Chinese History* (Cambridge 1998).

Emmer, P. C. (ed.), *Colonialism and Migration: Indentured Labour before and after Slavery* (The Hague 1986).

Engerman, Stanley L., 'The Atlantic economy of the eighteenth century'. *The Journal of European Economic History* 24 (1995): 145–76.

Enthoven, V. and J. Postma (eds), *Riches from Atlantic Commerce. Dutch Transatlantic Trade and Shipping 1585-1817* (Leiden 2003).

Epstein, Stephan R., *Freedom and Growth. The Rise of States and Markets in Western Europe, 1300-1750* (London 2000).

—, 'The rise of the West', in John A. Hall and Ralph Schroeder (eds), *Anatomy of Power. The Social Theory of Michael Mann* (Cambridge 2006), 233–59.

Epstein, Stephan R. and Maarten Prak (eds), *Guilds, Innovation and the European Economy* (London 2008).

Ertman, Thomas, *Birth of the Leviathan. Building States and Regimes in Medieval and early Modern Europe* (Cambridge 1997).

Esherick, Joseph E., 'How the Qing became China', in Joseph Esherick, Hasan Kayali and Eric van Young (eds), *Empire to Nation. Historical Perspectives on the Making of the Modern World* (Lanham 2006), 229–59.

Etemad, Bouda, *Possessing the World. Taking the Measurements of Colonisation from the Eighteenth to the Twentieth Century* (New York 2007). The book was originally published in French as *La possession du monde. Poids et mesures de la colonisation, XVIIIe-XXe siècles* (Brussels 2000).

—, *De l'utilité des empires. Colonisation et prosperité de l'Europe* (Paris 2005).

Evans, Eric J., *The Forging of the Modern State. Early Industrial Britain, 1783-1870* (Harlow 1983).

Evans, Peter B., Dietrich Rueschemeyer and Theda Skocpol (eds), *Bringing the State Back in* (Cambridge, MA 1985).

Everest-Phillips, Max, 'The myth of "secure property rights". Good economics as bad history and its impact on international development'. May 2008, Strategic Policy Impact and Research Unit Working Paper, No. 23, online at http://www.odi.org.uk/sites/odi.org.uk/files/odi-assets/publications-opinion-files/4251.pdf

Fairbank, John K., *Trade and Diplomacy on the China Coast. The Opening of the Treaty Ports, 1842-1854* (Cambridge, MA 1953).

—(ed.), *The Cambridge History of China. Volume 10. Late Ch'ing, 1800-1911, Part One* (Cambridge 1978).

Fairbank, John K., Martha Henderson Coolidge and Richard J. Smith, *H.B. Morse, Customs Commissioner and Historian of China* (The University of Kentucky Press 1995).

Fairbank, John K. and Ssu-yü Teng, 'On the Ch'ing tributary system'. *Harvard Journal of Asiatic Studies* 6 (1941): 135–246.

Fang, Xing, 'The retarded development of capitalism', in Xu Dixin and Wu Chengmin (eds), *Chinese Capitalism, 1522-1840* (Houndmills, London and New York 2000), 375–401.

—, 'Conclusions', in Xu Dixin and Wu Chengmin (eds), *Chinese Capitalism, 1522-1840* (Houndmills, London and New York 2000), 375–429.

Fang, Xing, Shi Qi, Jian Rui and Wang Shixin, 'The growth of commodity circulation and the rise of merchant organisations', in Xu Dixin and Wu Chengmin (eds), *Chinese Capitalism, 1522-1840* (Houndmills, London and New York 2000), 165–83.

Fang, Zhuofen, Hu Tiewen, Jian Rui and Fang Xing, 'Copper mining and smelting in Yunnan', in Xu Dixin and Wu Chengmin (eds), *Chinese Capitalism, 1522-1840* (Houndmills, London and New York 2000), 265–88.

Feavearyear, Sir Albert, *The Pound Sterling. A History of English Money* (Oxford 1963).

Federico, Giovanni, *An Economic History of the Silk Industry, 1830-1930* (Cambridge 1977).

Bibliography

Fei, Xiaotong, *From the Soil. The Foundations of Chinese Society. With an Introduction and Epilogue by Gary G. Hamilton and Wang Zheng* (Berkeley, Los Angeles and London 1992). The book is a translation of Xiangtu Zhongguo, a set of essays written by the author shortly after the Second World War.

Feinstein, Charles H., 'Capital formation in Great Britain', in Peter Mathias and Michael M. Postan (eds), *Cambridge Economic History of Europe*. Volume VII. Part One (Cambridge 1978), 28–96.

—, 'Pessimism perpetuated: real wages and the standard of living in Britain during and after the Industrial Revolution'. *The Journal of Economic History* 58, 3 (1998): 625–58.

Félix, Joël, 'The financial origins of the French Revolution', in Peter R. Campbell (ed.), *The Origins of the French Revolution* (Basingstoke 2006), 35–62.

Félix, Joël and Frank Tallett, 'The French experience, 1681-1815', in Christopher Storrs (ed.), *Fiscal-Military State in Eighteenth-Century Europe. Essays in Honour of P.G.M. Dickson* (Farnham, UK and Burlington, US 2009), 147–66.

Ferguson, Niall, *Empire. How Britain Made the Modern World* (London 2003).

—, *Civilization. The West and the Rest* (London 2011).

—, *The Great Degeneration. How Institutions Decay and Economies Die* (Harmondsworth 2012).

Fernandez, Paloma and Andrea Colli (eds), *The Endurance of Family Business. A Global Overview* (Cambridge 2013).

Ferrarese, Andrea, 'Il problema della decima e i suoi effeti sull settore primario nell'Europa mediterranea', in Simonetta Cavaciocchi (ed.), *La fiscalità nell'economia europea secc. XIII-XVIII = Fiscal Systems in the European Economy from the 13th to the 18th Centuries* (Florence 2008), 925–56.

Feuerwerker, Albert, *China's early Industrialization. Sheng Hsuan-Huai (1844-1916) and Mandarin Enterprise* (Cambridge, MA 1958).

—, *The Chinese Economy, ca. 1870-1911* (Ann Arbor 1969).

—, *State and Society in Eighteenth-Century China. The Ch'ing Empire in its Glory* (Ann Arbor 1992; reprint, originally 1976).

—, 'The state and the economy in late imperial China', in idem, *Studies in the Economic History of late Imperial China. Handicraft, Modern Industry and the State* (Ann Arbor 1995), 13–45.

—, *Studies in the Economic History of late Imperial China. Handicraft, Modern Industry and the State* (Ann Arbor 1995).

—, *The Chinese Economy, 1870-1949* (Ann Arbor 1996).

Findlay, Robert, 'The pilgrim art: the culture of porcelain in world history'. *Journal of World History* 9, 2 (1998): 141–87.

—, 'China, the West, and world history in Joseph Needham's *Science and civilisation in China*'. *Journal of World History* 11 (2000): 265–303.

Findlay, Ronald and Kevin H. O'Rourke, *Power and Plenty. Trade, War, and the World Economy in the Second Millennium* (Princeton and Oxford 2007).

Fine, S. E., *Production and Excise in England 1643-1825* (unpublished PhD thesis Harvard 1937).

Finer, S. E., *The History of Government* (Oxford and New York 1997).

Fink, Leon, *Sweatshops at Sea. Merchant Seamen in the World's first Globalized Industry, from 1812 to the Present* (Chapel Hill 2011).

Fischer, David Hackett, *Historians' Fallacies. Toward a Logic of Historical Thought* (New York 1970).

Fischer, Wolfram and Peter Lundgreen, 'The recruitment and training of administrative and technical personnel', in Charles Tilly (ed.), *The Formation of National States in Western Europe* (Princeton 1975), 456–561.

Fisher, Michael H., *Counterflows to Colonialism. Indian Travellers and Settlers in Britain, 1600-1857* (Delhi 2004).

—, 'Bound for Britain: Changing conditions of servitude, 1600-1857', in Indrani Chatterjee and Richard M. Eaton (eds), *Slavery and South Asian history* (Delhi 2006), 187–209.

Fitzpatrick, David, 'Ireland and the empire', in Andrew Porter (ed.), *The Oxford History of the British Empire. The Nineteenth Century* (Oxford and New York 1999), 421–95.

Fletcher, Joseph, 'Ch'ing Inner Asia c.1800', in John K. Fairbank (ed.), *The Cambridge History of China. Volume 10. Late Ch'ing, 1800-1911, Part One* (Cambridge 1978), 35–106.

—, 'Sino-Russian relations, 1800-1862', in John K. Fairbank (ed.), *The Cambridge History of China. Volume 10. Late Ch'ing, 1800-1911, Part One* (Cambridge 1978), 318–50.

—, 'The heyday of the Ch'ing order in Mongolia, Sinkiang and Tibet', in John K. Fairbank (ed.), *The Cambridge History of China. Volume 10. Late Ch'ing, 1800-1911, Part One* (Cambridge 1978), 351–408.

Floud, Roderick and Deirdre McCloskey (eds), *The Economic History of Britain since 1700. Volume 1, 1700-1860,* second edition (Cambridge 1994).

Floud, Roderick and Paul Johnson (eds), *The Cambridge Economic History of Modern Britain, Volume I, Industrialisation, 1700-1860* (Cambridge 2004).

Flynn, Dennis O. and Arturo Giráldez, *China and the Birth of Globalization in the Sixteenth Century* (Farnham and Burlington 2010).

—, 'Arbitrage, China, and world trade in the early modern period'. *Journal of the Economic and Social History of the Orient* 38, 4 (1995): 429–48.

—, 'Money and growth without development: The case of Ming China', in A. J. H. Latham and Heita Kawakatsu (eds), *Asian-Pacific Dynamism, 1550-2000* (London 2000), 199–215.

—, 'Cycles of silver: global unity through the mid-eighteenth century'. *Journal of World History* 13, 2 (2002): 391–428.

—, 'Globalization began in 1571', in Barry K. Gills and William R. Thompson (eds), *Globalization and Global History* (London and New York 2006), 232–47.

Flynn, Dennis O., Arturo Giráldez and Richard von Glahn (eds), *Global Connections and Monetary History, 1470-1800* (Aldershot and Burlington 2003).

Fogel, Robert W., *Without Consent or Contract. The Rise and Fall of American Slavery* (New York 1994).

Fogleman, Aaron S., 'From slaves, convicts, and servants to free passengers. The transformation of immigration in the era of the American Revolution'. *Journal of American History* 85 (1998): 66–76.

Folsom, Kenneth E., *Friends, Guests and Colleagues: The Mu-fu System in the late Ch'ing Period* (Berkeley 1968).

Fortune, Robert, *The Tea Districts of China and India* (London 1853).

Foucault, Michel, *Discipline and Punish* (Harmondsworth 1977; originally Paris 1975).

—, *Lectures at the Collège de France*. A series of books published by Palgrave and Macmillan 2003–14.

Frank, Andre Gunder, *ReOrient. Global Economy in the Asian Age* (Berkeley, Los Angeles and London 1998).

Fritschy, Wantje, 'Taxation in Britain, France and the Netherlands in the eighteenth century'. *Economic and Social History in the Netherlands* 2 (1990): 56–79.

Fritschy, Wantje, Marjolein 't Hart, and Edwin Horlings, 'Long-term trends in the fiscal history of the Netherlands, 1515-1913', in Bartolomé Yun-Casalilla and Patrick K. O'Brien (eds), *The Rise of Fiscal States. A Global History, 1500-1914* (Cambridge 2012), 39–66.

Frykman, Niklas, 'Seeleute auf den europäischen Kriegsschiffen des späten 18. Jahrhunderts', in Marcel Van der Linden and Karl Heinz Roth (eds), *Über Marx hinaus. Arbeitsgeschichte und Arbeitsbegriff in der Konfrontation mit den globalen Arbeitsverhältnissen des 21. Jahrhunderts* (Berlin and Hamburg 2009), 55–84.

Fung, Allen, 'Testing the self-strengthening: the Chinese army in the Sino-Japanese War of 1894-1895'. *Modern Asian Studies* 4 (1996): 1007–31.

Furber, Holden, *Rival Empires of Trade in the Orient, 1600-1800* (Minneapolis 1976).

Furniss, Edgar S., *The Position of the Laborer in a System of Nationalism. A Study of the Labor Theories of the Later English Mercantilists* (Boston 1920).

Bibliography

Fynn-Paul, Jeff (ed.), *War, Entrepreneurs, and the State in Europe and the Mediterranean, 1300-1800* (Leiden 2014).

Gaastra, Femme, '"Sware continuerende lasten en groten ommeslagh". Kosten van de oorlogsvoering van de Verenigde Oost-Indische Compagnie', in Gerrit Knaap and Ger Teitler (eds), *De Verenigde Oost-Indische Compagnie tussen oorlog en diplomatie* (Leiden 2002), 81–104.

—, *The Dutch East India Company. Expansion and Decline* (Zutphen 2003).

Galenson, David W., *White Servitude in Colonial America: An Economic Analysis* (Cambridge 1981).

Gamble, Sidney D., 'Daily wages of unskilled Chinese labourers, 1807-1902'. *The Far Eastern Quarterly* 3 (1943): 41–73.

Gardella, Robert, *Harvesting Mountains. Fujian and the China Tea Trade, 1757-1937* (Berkeley, Los Angeles and London 1994).

Gascoigne, John, 'The Royal Society and the emergence of science as an instrument of state policy'. *British Journal for the History of Science* 32 (1999): 171–84.

Gat, Azar, *War in Human Civilization* (Oxford and New York 2006).

Gates, Hill, *China's Motor. A Thousand Years of Petty Capitalism* (Ithaca and London 1996).

Gauci, Perry (ed.), *Regulating the British Economy, 1660-1850* (Farnham and Burlington 2011).

Gayer, Arthur D., Walt W. Rostow and Anna Jacobson Schwartz, *The Growth and Fluctuation of the British Economy, 1790-1850* (originally London 1953; new edition 1975).

Gellner, Ernest, *Nations and Nationalism* (Oxford 1983).

—, *Plough, Sword and Book. The Structure of Human History* (London 1988).

Gerlach, Christian, 'Wu-wei in Europe. A study of Eurasian economic thought', London School of Economics, Department of Economic History. Working Paper no 12/05, 2005.

Gernet, Jacques, *A History of Chinese Civilization* (Cambridge 1982).

Gerschenkron, Alexander, *Economic Backwardness in Historical Perspective. A Book of Essays* (Cambridge, MA 1966).

Getzer, Joshua, 'Theories of property and economic development'. *Journal of Interdisciplinary History* 26, 4 (1996): 639–69.

Giersch, C. Patterson., *Asian Borderlands. The Transformation of Qing China's Yunnan Frontier* (Cambridge, MA 2006).

Glaeser, Edward L. and Andrei Shleifer, 'Legal origins'. *Quarterly Journal of Economics* 117 (2002): 1193–229.

Glete, Jan, *Navies and Nations. Warships, Navies and State Building in Europe and America, 1500-1860* (Stockholm 1993).

Golas, Peter J., *Science and Civilisation in China. Part V, Volume Thirteen* (Cambridge 1999).

Goldstone, Jack A., *Revolution and Rebellion in the early Modern World* (Berkeley, Los Angeles and Oxford 1991).

—, 'Gender, work and culture. Why the industrial revolution came early to England and late to China'. *Sociological Perspectives* 39 (1996): 1–21.

—, 'Efflorescences and economic growth in world history. Rethinking "the rise of the West" and "the Industrial Revolution"'. *Journal of World History* 13 (2002): 323–89.

—, *Why Europe? The Rise of the West in World History, 1500-1850* (New York 2008).

Goldscheid, Rudolf, *Staatssozialismus oder Staatskapitalismus* (Vienna 1917).

Gommans, Jos, 'Warhorse and post-nomadic empire in Asia, c.1000-1800'. *Journal of Global History* 2, 1 (2007): 1–23.

Goody, Jack, *The East in the West* (Cambridge 1996).

—, *Capitalism and Modernity: The Great Debate* (Cambridge 2004).

—, *The Theft of History* (Cambridge 2006).

—, *Renaissances. The One or the Many?* (Cambridge 2010).

—, *The Eurasian Miracle* (Cambridge 2010).

Gorski, Philip S., *The Disciplinary Revolution. Calvinism and the Rise of the State in early Modern Europe* (Chicago and London 2003).

—, 'The Little Divergence: the Protestant Reformation and economic hegemony in early modern Europe', in William H. Satos Jr. and Lutz Kaelber (eds), *The Protestant Ethic Turns 100. Essays on the Centenary of the Weber Thesis* (Boulder and London 2006), 165–90.

Gottschang, Thomas and Diana Lary, *Swallows and Settlers. The Great Migration from North China to Manchuria* (Ann Arbor 2000).

Goubert, Pierre, *L'Ancien Régime* (Paris 1969 and 1973).

Grafe, Regina, 'Polycentric states: The Spanish reigns and the "failures" of mercantilism', in Philip J. Stern and Carl Wennerlind (eds), *Mercantilism Reimagined. Political Economy in early Modern Britain and its Empire* (Oxford and New York 2013), 241–62.

Graff, D. A. and R. Higham (eds), *A Military History of China* (Boulder 2002).

Greenberg, Michael, *British Trade and the Opening of China 1800-1842* (New York and London 1951).

Greenfeld, Liah, *Nationalism. Five Roads to Modernity* (Cambridge, MA and London 1992).

—, *The Spirit of Capitalism. Nationalism and Economic Growth* (Cambridge, MA and London 2001).

Gregory, John S., *The West and China since 1500* (Houndmills 2003).

Gross, Jean-Pierre, 'Progressive taxation and social justice in eighteenth-century France'. *Past and Present* 140 (1993): 79–126.

Grove, Linda and Mark Selden (eds), *Takeshi Hamashita. China, East Asia and the Global Economy. Regional and Historical Perspectives* (Abingdon and New York 2008).

Gruzinski, Serge, *Les quatre parties du monde. Histoire d'une mondialisation* (Paris 2004).

Guldi, Jo, *Roads to Power. Britain Invents the Infrastructure State* (Cambridge, MA and London 2012).

Gunn, Geoffrey, *First Globalization. The Eurasian Exchange, 1500-1800* (Oxford 2003).

Gupta, Bishnupriya and Debin Ma, 'Europe in an Asian Mirror: The Great Divergence', in Stephen Broadberry and Kevin O'Rourke (eds), *The Cambridge Economic History of Modern Europe. Volume I, 1700-1870* (Cambridge 2010), 264–85.

Guy, R. Kent, 'Who were the Manchus? A review essay'. *Journal of Asian Studies* 61 (2002): 151–64.

—, *Qing Governors and their Provinces. The Evolution of Territorial Administration in China, 1644-1796* (Seattle and London 2010).

Habakkuk, H. J., 'The market for monastic property'. *The Economic History Review* 10 (1958): 362–80.

—, 'Public finance and the sale of confiscated property during the Interregnum'. *The Journal of Economic History* 23, 1 (1963): 77–87.

Hacking, Ian, *The Taming of Chance* (Cambridge 1990).

Hackl, Bernhard, 'Die staatliche Wirtschaftspolitik zwischen 1740 und 1792: Reform versus Stagnation', in Helmut Reinalter (ed.), *Josephinismus als Aufgeklärter Absolutismus* (Vienna, Cologne and Weimar 2008), 191–272.

Hall, Christopher D., *British Strategy in the Napoleonic War, 1803-1815* (Manchester 1992).

Hall, John A., *Powers & Liberties. The Causes and Consequences of the Rise of the West* (Harmondsworth 1985).

—, 'States and economic development: reflections on Adam Smith', in idem (ed.), *States in History* (Oxford 1986), 154–76.

Hall, John A. and Ralph Schroeder (eds), *An Anatomy of Power. The Social Theory of Michael Mann* (Cambridge 2006).

Hamashita, Takeshi, 'The tribute trade system and modern Asia', in A. J. H. Latham and Heita Kawakatsu (eds), *Japanese Industrialization and the Asian Economy* (London and New York 1994), 91–107.

—, 'Tribute and treaties: maritime Asia and the treaty ports networks in the era of negotiation', in Giovanni Arrighi, Takeshi Hamashita and Mark Selden (eds), *The Resurgence of East Asia. 500, 150 and 50 Years Perspectives* (London and New York 2003), 17–50.

—, 'Foreign trade finance in China: silver, opium and world market incorporation, 1820s to 1850s', in Linda Grove and Mark Selden (eds), *Takeshi Hamashita. China, East Asia and the Global Economy. Regional and Historical Perspectives* (Abingdon and New York 2008), 114–44.

Hanson, Victor Davis, *Why the West has Won. Carnage and Culture from Salamis to Vietnam* (London 2002).

Hao, Yen-p'ing, *The Commercial Revolution in Nineteenth-Century China. The Rise of Sino-Western Mercantile Capitalism* (Berkeley, Los Angeles, London 1986).

Harding, Richard, *Seapower and Naval Warfare, 1630-1830* (London 1999).

—, 'Parliament and the British fiscal-military state: ideology, consent and state expenditure, 1739-1748', in Stephen Conway and Rafael Torres Sánchez (eds), *The Spending of States. Military Expenditure during the Long Eighteenth Century: Patterns, Organisation, and Consequences, 1650-1815* (Saarbrücken 2011), 31–51.

Harding, Richard and Sergio Solbes Ferri (eds), *The Contractor State and its Implications, 1659-1815* (Las Palmas 2012).

Harley, C. Knick, 'Reassessing the industrial revolution: A macro view', in Joel Mokyr (ed.), *The British Industrial Revolution. An Economic Perspective* (Boulder 1993), 171–226.

—, 'Trade: discovery, mercantilism and technology', in Roderick Floud and Paul Johnson (eds), *The Cambridge Economic History of Modern Britain, Volume I, Industrialisation, 1700-1860* (Cambridge 2004), 175–203.

Harling, Philip, *The Waning of 'old corruption'. The Politics of Economical Reform in Britain, 1779-1846* (Oxford 1996).

Harling, Philip and Peter Mandler, 'From "fiscal-military" state to laissez-faire state, 1760-1850'. *Journal of British Studies* 32 (1993): 44–70.

Harper, Lawrence A., *The English Navigation Acts: A Seventeenth-Century Experiment in Social Engineering* (New York, 1939; reprinted 1964).

Harris, Jose, 'From poor law to welfare state? A European perspective', in Donald Winch and Patrick K. O'Brien (eds), *The Political Economy of British Historical Experience, 1688-1914* (Oxford 2002), 409–38.

Harris, Ron, 'Government and the economy, 1688-1850', in Roderick Floud and Paul Johnson (eds), *The Cambridge Economic History of Modern Britain, Volume I, Industrialisation, 1700-1860* (Cambridge 2004), 204–37.

't Hart, Marjolein, *The Making of a Bourgeois State. War, Politics and Finance during the Dutch Revolt* (Manchester 1993).

—, 'The United Provinces, 1579-1806', in Richard Bonney (ed.), *Rise of the Fiscal State in Europe c.1200-1815* (Oxford 1999), 309–25.

—, 'Mobilising resources for war. The Dutch and British financial revolutions compared', in Torres Sánchez (ed.), *War, State and Development. Fiscal-Military States in the Eighteenth Century* (Pamplona 2007), 179–200.

Hartley, Janet, 'Russia as a fiscal-military state, 1689-1815', in Christopher Storrs (ed.), *The Fiscal-Military State in Eighteenth-Century Europe. Essays in Honour of P.G.M. Dickson* (Farnham, UK and Burlington, US 2009), 125–46.

Hartmann, Peter Claus, *Das Steuersystem der europäischen Staaten am Ende des Ancien Regime* (Munich 1979).

Hatcher, John, 'Labour, leisure and economic thought before the nineteenth century'. *Past and Present* 160 (1998): 64–115.

Hayami, Akira, 'A great transformation. Social and economic change in sixteenth- and seventeenth-century Japan'. *Bonner Zeitschrift für Japanologie* 8 (1986): 3–13.

Hayami, Akira, Osama Saito and Ronald P. Toby (eds), *Emergence of Economic Society in Japan 1600-1859. The Economic History of Japan 1600-1990. Volume One* (Oxford 2004).

He, Wenkai, *Paths toward the Modern Fiscal State: England, Japan, and China* (Cambridge, MA and London 2013).

Headrick, Daniel R., *The Tools of Empire. Technology and European Imperialism in the Nineteenth Century* (New York 1981).

—, *The Tentacles of Progress. Technology Transfer in the Age of Imperialism, 1850-1940* (New York and Oxford 1988).

—, *The Invisible Weapon. Telecommunications and International Politics, 1851-1945* (New York and Oxford 1991).

—, *When Information Came of Age. Technologies of Knowledge in the Age of Reason and Revolution 1700-1850* (Oxford 2000).

—, *Power Over Peoples. Technology, Environments, and Western Imperialism, 1400 to the Present* (Princeton and Oxford 2010).

Hechter, Michael, *Internal Colonialism. The Celtic Fringe in British National Development, 1536-1966* (London 1975).

Heckscher, Eli F., *Mercantilism* (second English edition; London 1962, revised and edited by E. F. Söderlund). The text was originally published in Swedish in 1931.

—, *An Economic History of Sweden* (Cambridge, MA 1954).

Heijdra, Martin, 'The socio-economic development of rural China during the Ming', in Denis Twitchett and Frederick W. Mote (eds), *The Cambridge History of China. Volume 8. The Ming Dynasty, 1368-1644. Part Two* (Cambridge 1998), 417–578.

Heilbron, John L, 'The measure of Enlightenment', in Tore Frängsmyr, John L. Heilbron and Robin E. Rider (eds), *The Quantifying Spirit in the Eighteenth Century* (Berkeley, Los Angeles and Oxford 1990), 207–42.

Heinrich, Mathias, 'Welfare and public philanthropy in Qing China'. *Chinese History and Society. Berliner China Hefte* 33 (2008): 123–34.

Helleiner, Eric, *The Making of National Money. Territorial Currencies in Historical Perspective* (Ithaca 2003).

Helpman, Elhanan, *The Mystery of Economic Growth* (Cambridge, MA and London 2004).

—(ed.), *Institutions and Economic Performance* (Cambridge, MA 2008).

Henderson, W. O., *Studies in the Economic Policy of Frederick the Great* (London 1963).

Henshall, Nicolas, *The Myth of Absolutism. Change and Continuity in early Modern European Monarchy* (Harlow 1992).

Herlihy, Patricia, 'Revenue and revelry on tap. The Russian tavern', in Mack P. Holt (ed.), *Alcohol. A Social and Cultural History* (Oxford and New York 2006), 185–202.

Herman, Arthur, *How the Scots Invented the Modern World. The True Story of How Western Europe's Poorest Nation Created Our World & Everything in it* (New York 2004).

Herman, John E., *Amid the Clouds and Mist. China's Colonization of Guizhou, 1200-1700* (Cambridge, MA and London 2007).

Herrmann, Albert, *An Historical Atlas of China* (Amsterdam 1966).

Herndom, T., M. I. Ash and R. Pollin, 'Does high public debt consistently stifle economic growth? A critique of Reinhart and Rogoff'. This text is on the website of the Political Economy Research Institute of the University of Massachusetts.

Hewitt, Rachel, *Map of a Nation. A Biography of the Ordnance Survey* (London 2010).

Hibbert, Christopher, *The Dragon Wakes. China and the West, 1793-1911* (London 1970).

Higgs, Edward, *The Information State in England* (Houndmills 2004).

Hill, Richard, *The Prizes of War. The Naval Prize System in the Napoleonic Wars, 1793-1815* (Stroud 1998).

Hinton, Harold C., *The Grain Tribute of China, 1845-1911* (Cambridge, MA 1956).

Bibliography

Hirzel, Thomas and Nanny Kim (eds), *Metals, Monies, and Markets in early Modern Societies: East Asian and Global Perspectives* (Berlin 2008).

Ho, Ping-ti, 'The salt merchants of Yang-chou: A study of commercial capitalism in eighteenth-century China'. *Harvard Journal of Asiatic Studies* 17, 1 and 2 (1954): 130–68.

—, *Studies on the Population of China, 1368-1953* (Cambridge, MA 1959).

—, *The Ladder of Success in late Imperial China. Aspects of Social Mobility, 1368-1911* (New York and London 1971; originally 1962).

Hobhouse, Henry, *Seeds of Change: Five Plants that Transformed Mankind* (London and Basingstoke 1999).

Hobsbawm, Eric J., *Industry and Empire* (London 1968).

—, *Nations and Nationalism since 1780. Programme, Myth, Reality* (Cambridge 1990).

Hobson, John M., *The Eastern Origins of Western Civilisation* (Cambridge 2004).

Hochedlinger, Michael, 'The Habsburg Monarchy; from "military-fiscal state" to "militarization"', in Christopher Storrs (ed.), *Fiscal-Military State in Eighteenth-Century Europe. Essays in Honour of P.G.M. Dickson* (Farnham, UK and Burlington, US 2009), 55–94.

Hoffman, Philip T., 'Early modern France, 1450-1700', in Philip T. Hoffman and Kathryn Norberg (eds), *Fiscal Crises, Liberty and Representative Government, 1450-1789* (Stanford 1994), 226–53.

—, 'Prices, the Military Revolution, and Western Europe's comparative advantage in violence'. *The Economic History Review* 64, 1 (2011): 39–59.

—, 'Why was it Europeans who conquered the world?'. *The Journal of Economic History* 72, 3 (2012): 601–33.

Hoffman, Philip T. and Jean-Laurent Rosenthal, 'The political economy of warfare and taxation in early modern Europe: historical lessons for economic development', in John N. Drobak and John V. C. Nye (eds), *The Frontiers of the New Institutional Economics* (San Diego 1997), 31–55.

Hoffman, Philip T. and Kathryn Norberg (eds), *Fiscal Crises, Liberty and Representative Government, 1450-1789* (Stanford 1994).

Hoffman, Philip T. and Kathryn Norberg, 'Conclusion', in Philip T. Hoffman and Kathryn Norberg (eds), *Fiscal Crises, Liberty and Representative Government, 1450-1789* (Stanford 1994), 299–312.

Hoffman, Philip T., David Jacks, Patricia A. Levin and Peter H. Lindert, 'Real inequality in Western Europe since 1500', *The Journal of Economic History* 62, 2 (June 2002): 322–55.

Hoffman, Philip T., Gilles Postel-Vinay and Jean-Laurent Rosenthal, *Priceless Markets: The Political Economy of Credit in Paris, 1660-1870* (Chicago 2001).

—, *Surviving Large Losses. Financial Crises, the Middle Class, and the Development of Capital Markets* (Cambridge, MA and London 2007).

Homer, Sidney and Richard Sylla, *A History of Interest Rates,* third edition (New Brunswick, New York 1996).

Hont, Istvan, *Jealousy of Trade. International Competition and the Nation State in Historical Perspective* (Cambridge, MA 2005).

Hopkins, A. G. (ed.), *Globalization in World History* (London 2002).

Hoppenbrouwers, Peter, 'Mapping an unexplored field. The Brenner debate and the case of Holland', in Peter Hoppenbrouwers and Jan Luiten van Zanden (eds), *Peasants into Farmers. The Transformation of Rural Economy and Society in the Low Countries (Middle Ages-19th Century) in Light of the Brenner Debate* (Turnhout Belgium 2001), 41–66.

Hoppit, Julian, 'Attitudes to credit in Britain, 1680-1790'. *Historical Journal* 33 (1990): 305–22.

—, 'Reforming Britain's weights and measures'. *The English Historical Review* 108 (1993): 82–104.

—, 'Political arithmetic in eighteenth-century England'. *The Economic History Review* 49 (1996): 516–40.

—, 'Checking the Leviathan, 1688-1832', in Donald Winch and Patrick K. O'Brien (eds), *The Political Economy of British Historical Experience, 1688-1914* (Oxford 2002), 267–94.

—, 'Compulsion, compensation and property rights in Britain, 1660-1833'. *Past and Present* 210 (2011): 93–128.

—, 'The nation, the state, and the First Industrial Revolution'. *Journal of British Studies* 50, 2 (2011): 307–31.

—, 'Bounties, the economy and the state in Britain, 1689-1800', in Perry Gauci (ed.), *Regulating the British Economy, 1660-1850* (Farnham and Burlington 2011), 139–60.

Horesh, Niv, *Chinese Money in Global Context. Historic Junctures between 600 BCE and 2012* (Stanford 2014).

Horn, James, 'British Diaspora. Emigration from Britain, 1680-1815', in P. J. Marshall (ed.), *The Oxford History of the British Empire. The Eighteenth Century* (Oxford and New York 1998), 27–52.

Horowitz, Richard S., 'Beyond the marble boat: the transformation of the Chinese military, 1850-1911', in D. A. Graff and R. Higham (eds), *Military History of China* (Boulder 2002), 153–74.

Horrell, Sara, and Jane Humphries, 'Old questions, new data and alternative perspectives: families' living standards in the Industrial Revolution'. *The Journal of Economic History* 52, 4 (1992): 849–80.

Horstman, Allen, '"Taxation in the Zenith": taxes and classes in the United Kingdom, 1816-1842'. *The Journal of European Economic History* 32 (2003): 111–37.

Hostetler, Laura, *Qing Colonial Enterprise. Ethnography and Cartography in early Modern China* (Chicago and London 2001).

Howe, Anthony, 'Restoring free trade: the British experience, 1776-1873', in Donald Winch and Patrick K. O'Brien (eds), *The Political Economy of British Historical Experience, 1688-1914* (Oxford 2002), 193–214.

Hsiao, Kung-Chuan, *Rural China. Imperial Control in the Nineteenth Century* (Seattle 1960).

Hsü, Immanuel C. Y., *The Rise of Modern China,* sixth edition (Oxford and London 2000).

Hu, Jichuang, *A Concise History of Chinese Economic Thought* (Beijing 1988).

Huang, Guosheng, 'The Chinese maritime customs in transition, 1750-1850', in Gungwu Wang and Ng Chin-keong (eds), *Maritime China in Transition 1750-1850* (Wiesbaden 2004), 169–90.

Huang, Philip C. C., *The Peasant Economy and Social Change in North China* (Stanford 1985).

—, *The Peasant Family and Rural Development in the Yangzi Delta, 1350-1988* (Stanford 1990).

—, *Code, Custom and Legal Practice in China: The Qing and the Republic Compared* (Stanford 2001).

Huang, Ray, *Taxation and Governmental Finance in Sixteenth-Century Ming China* (Cambridge 1974).

—, *Broadening the Horizons of Chinese History* (New York 1999).

Hubatsch, Walther, *Frederick the Great. Absolutism and Administration* (London 1973).

Huc, Régis-Évariste, *L'empire Chinois. Faisant suite à l'ouvrage intitulé Souvenirs d'un voyage dans la Tartarie et le Tibet* (edited by Du Rocher; Monaco 1980; originally 1854). There are various editions of this book in English under the title *The Chinese Empire: Forming a Sequel to the Work entitled 'Recollections of a Journey through Tartary and Tibet'*, and *A Journey through the Chinese Empire*.

Hui, Victoria Tin-bor, *War and State Formation in Ancient China and early Modern Europe* (New York 2005).

Huigen, Siegfried, Jan L. de Jong and Elmer Kolfin (eds), *Dutch Trading Companies as Knowledge Networks* (Leiden 2010).

Humphries, Jane, 'Household economy', in Roderick Floud and Paul Johnson (eds), *The Cambridge Economic History of Modern Britain, Volume I, Industrialisation, 1700-1860* (Cambridge 2004), 238–67.

Bibliography

—, *Childhood and Child Labour in the British Industrial Revolution* (Cambridge 2010).

—, 'Rent seeking or skill creating? Apprenticeship in early industrial England', in Perry Gauci (ed.), *Regulating the British Economy, 1660-1850* (Farnham and Burlington 2011), 235–58.

—, 'The lure of aggregates and the pitfalls of the patriarchal perspective: a critique of the high wage economy interpretation of the British industrial revolution'. *The Economic History Review* 66, 3 (2013): 693–714.

Hung, Ho-fung, 'Imperial China and capitalist Europe in the eighteenth century'. *Review* 24 (2001): 473–514.

—, 'Orientalist knowledge and social theories: China and European conceptions of East-West differences from 1600-1900'. *Sociological Theory* 21 (2003): 254–80.

—, 'Contentious peasants, paternalist state, and arrested capitalism in China's long eighteenth century', in Christopher Chase-Dunn and Eugene N. Anderson (eds), *The Historical Evolution of World-Systems* (New York 2005), 155–73.

—, 'Agricultural revolution and elite reproduction in Qing China: the transition to capitalism debate revisited'. *American Sociological Review* 73 (2008): 569–88.

Hutchinson, John and Anthony D. Smith (eds), *Nationalism* (Oxford and New York 1994).

Inikori, Joseph E., *Africans and the Industrial Revolution in England. A Study in International Trade and Economic Development* (Cambridge 2002).

Innes, Joanna, 'The state and the poor: eighteenth-century England in European perspective', in John Brewer and Eckhart Hellmuth (eds), *Rethinking Leviathan. The Eighteenth-Century State in Britain and Germany* (Oxford 1999), 225–80.

—, 'The distinctiveness of the English Poor Laws, 1750-1850', in Donald Winch and Patrick K. O'Brien (eds), *The Political Economy of British Historical Experience, 1688-1914* (Oxford 2002), 381–408.

Irigoin, Alejandra, 'The end of a silver era. The consequences of the breakdown of the Spanish peso standard in China and the United States, 1780-1850s'. *Journal of World History* 20, 2 (2009): 207–43.

—, 'A Trojan Horse in Daoguang China? Explaining the flows of silver in and out of China'. Working Paper 173, 2013 in The Economic History Working Papers Series of the Department of Economic History of the London School of Economics and Political Science. The paper can be downloaded from the website of the Department.

Irwin, Douglas A., *Against the Tide. An Intellectual History of Free Trade* (Princeton 1996).

Isett, Christopher Mills, *State, Peasant, and Merchant in Qing Manchuria, 1644-1862* (Stanford 2007).

Jacob, Margaret C., *Scientific Culture and the Making of the Industrial West* (New York and Oxford 1997).

—, *The First Knowledge Economy. Human Capital and the European Economy* (Cambridge 2013).

Jacobs, Els M., *Merchant in Asia. The Trade of the Dutch East India Company during the Eighteenth Century*, the paperback edition (Leiden 2014).

Jacobsen, Stefan Gaarsmand, 'Chinese influences or images? Fluctuating histories of how Enlightenment Europe read China'. *Journal of World History* 24, 3 (2013): 623–60.

Jacques, Martin, *When China Rules the World. The Rise of the Middle Kingdom and the End of the Western World* (London 2009).

James, Lawrence, *Warrior Race. A History of the British at War* (London 2001).

James, W., 'The moral equivalent of war', in idem, *Writings 1902-1910* (New York 1987). The text is available on internet.

Jastram, Roy W., *The Golden Constant. The English and American Experience, 1560-1976* (New York 1977).

—, *Silver. The Restless Metal* (New York 1981).

Jay, Peter, *Road to Riches or the Wealth of Man* (London 2000).

Jenks, David, *Insurgency and Social Disorder in Guizhou. The "Miao" Rebellion, 1854-1873* (Honolulu 1994).

Johnson, Chalmers, *Japan: Who Governs? The Rise of the Developmental State* (New York and London 1995).

Johnson, David, *Napoleon's Cavalry and Its Leaders* (London 1978).

Jones, Eric L., *Growth Recurring. Economic Change in World History* (Cambridge 1988).

—, *The European Miracle. Environments, Economies and Geopolitics in the History of Europe and Asia* (second edition; Cambridge 1987; third edition; Cambridge 2003).

—, 'Economics without history: objections to the rights hypothesis'. *Continuity and Change* 12, 3 (2013): 323–46.

Jones, R. E., *The Emancipation of the Russian Nobility, 1762-1785* (Princeton 1973).

Jörg, C. J. A., *Porcelain and the Dutch China Trade* (The Hague 1982).

Journal of Asian Studies, 61, 2 (2002) a special issue dedicated to Pomeranz, *Great Divergence*.

Jupp, Peter, *The Governing of Britain 1688-1848* (London 2006).

Jutte, Robert, *Poverty and Deviance in early Modern Europe* (Cambridge 2006).

Kahn, Eduard, *The Currencies of China: An Investigation of Gold and Silver Transactions Afflicting China, with a Section on Copper* (unknown binding, published by S. J. Durst 1978).

Kahn, Robert A., *A History of the Habsburg Empire* (Berkeley, Los Angeles and London 1974).

Kain, Roger J. P. and Elizabeth Baigent, *The Cadastral Map in the Service of the State. A History of Property Mapping* (Chicago 1992).

Kang, David C., *East Asia before the West: Five Centuries of Trade and Tribute* (New York and Chichester 2010).

Karaman, K. Kıvanç and Sevket Pamuk, 'Ottoman state finances in European perspective, 1500-1914'. *The Journal of Economic History* 70 (2010): 593–627.

Kaske, Elisabeth, 'The price of an office: Venality, the individual and the state in 19th-century China', in Thomas Hirzel and Nanny Kim (eds), *Metals, Monies, and Markets in early Modern Societies: East Asian and Global Perspectives* (Berlin 2008), 281–308.

Kearney, Huge, *The British Isles. A History of Four Nations* (Cambridge 2006).

Keith, G. S., *Different Methods of Establishing a Uniformity of Weights and Measures Stated and Compared* (London 1817).

Keller, Wolfgang, Ben Li and Carol H. Shiue, 'The evolution of domestic trade flows. When foreign trade is liberalized: Evidence from the Chinese Maritime Customs Service', in Masahiko Aoki, Timur Kuran and Gérard Roland (eds), *Institutions and Comparative Economic Development* (New York 2012), 152–72.

Kemp, Peter, *The British Sailor. A Social History of the Lower Deck* (London 1970).

Kennedy, Paul, *The Rise and Fall of British Naval Mastery* (London 1983).

—, *The Rise and Fall of the Great Powers* (New York 1987).

Kenny, Kevin (ed.), *Ireland and the British Empire* (Oxford 2004).

Kessler, Lawrence D., *K'ang-Hsi and the Consolidation of Ch'ing Rule, 1661-1684* (Chicago 1976).

Kim, Nanny, 'Transport in China in der Späten Kaiserzeit, 1500-1900: eine Bestandaufnahme', in Rolf Peter Sieferle (ed.), *Transportgeschichte. Der Europäische Sonderweg. Band 1* (Berlin 2008), 209–92.

Kindleberger, Charles P., *Spenders and Hoarders. The World Distribution of Spanish American Silver 1550-1750* (Singapore 1989).

King, Frank H. H., *Money and Monetary Policy in China, 1845-1895* (Cambridge, MA 1965).

King, Steven, 'Poor relief and English economic development reappraised'. *The Economic History Review* 50 (1997): 360–68.

Kiser, Edgar and Joshua Kane, 'Revolution and state structure: the bureaucratization of tax administration in early modern England and France'. *American Journal of Sociology* 107 (2001): 183–223.

Kiser, Edgar and Xiaoxi Tong, 'Determinants of the amount and type of corruption in state fiscal bureaucracies. An analysis of Late Imperial China'. *Comparative Political Studies* 25 (1992): 300–31.

Kishimoto, Mio, 'New studies on statecraft in Mid- and Late-Qing China: Qing intellectuals and their debates on economic policies', *International Journal of Asian Studies* 6, 1 (2009) 87–102.

—, 'Property rights, land and law in Imperial China', in Debin Ma and Jan Luiten van Zanden (eds), *Law and Long-Term Economic Change. A Eurasian Perspective* (Stanford 2011), 68–90.

Klein, P. W., 'A new look at an old subject: Dutch trade policies in the age of mercantilism', in S. Groenveld and M. Wintle (eds), *State and Trade. Government and the Economy in Britain and the Netherlands since the Middle Ages* (Zutphen 1992), 39–49.

Knight, Roger, *Britain against Napoleon. The Organization of Victory, 1793-1815* (London 2013).

Knight, Roger and Martin Wilcox, *Sustaining the Fleet, 1793-1815. War, the British Navy and the Contractor State* (Woolbridge 2010).

Knowles, David, *The Religious Orders in England, Vol. III, The Tudor Age* (Cambridge 1959).

Koenigsberger, Helmut G., *Politicians and Virtuosi. Essays in early Modern History* (London 1986).

—, 'Dominium regale or dominium politicum et regale. Monarchies and parliaments in early modern Europe', in Helmut G. Koenigsberger (ed.), *Politicians and Virtuosi. Essays in early Modern History* (London 1986), 1–25.

—, 'The crisis of the seventeenth century: a farewell?', in Helmut G. Koenigsberger (ed.), *Politicians and Virtuosi. Essays in early Modern History* (London 1986), 149–68.

Körner, Martin, 'Expenditure', in Richard Bonney (ed.), *Economic Systems and State Finance* (Oxford 1995), 393–422.

—, 'Public credit', in Richard Bonney (ed.), *Economic Systems and State Finance* (Oxford 1995), 507–38.

Kolb, Raimund, 'About figures and aggregates: some arguments for a more scrupulous evaluation of quantitative data in the history of population and agriculture in China 1644-1949', in Rolf Peter Sieferle and Helga Breuninger (eds), *Agriculture, Population and Economic Development in China and Europe* (Stuttgart 2003), 200–75.

Kozub, Robert M., 'Evolution of taxation in England, 1700-1850: a period of war and industrialization'. *The Journal of European Economic History* 32 (2003): 363–87.

Kreuzer, Peter, *Staat und Wirtschaft in China. Die kulturelle Grundlage politischer Steuerung: Verwaltungskultur und Verwaltungsstil der Qing Administration* (Frankfurt am Main 1998).

Krug, Leopold, *Betrachtungen über den Nationalreichtum des preußischen Staates und über den Wohlstand seiner Bewohner* (Aalen 1970).

Krugman, Paul, *Pop internationalism* (Cambridge, MA 1996).

Kuhn, Philip A., *Rebellion and Its Enemies in late Imperial China. Militarization and Social Structure, 1796-1864* (Cambridge 1970).

—, 'The Taiping Rebellion', in John K. Fairbank (ed.), *The Cambridge History of China. Volume 10. Late Ch'ing, 1800-1911. Part One* (Cambridge 1978), 264–317.

—, *Soulstealers: The Chinese Sorcery Scare of 1768* (Cambridge, MA 1990).

—, *Origins of the Modern Chinese State* (Stanford 2002).

Kumagai, Yukihisa, *Breaking into the Monopoly. Provincial Merchants and Manufacturers' Campaigns for Access to the Asian Market, 1790-1833* (Leiden and Boston 2012).

Kuroda, Akinobu, 'The collapse of the Chinese imperial monetary system', in Kaoru Sugihara (ed.), *Japan, China and the Growth of the Asian International Economy, 1850-1949* (New York 2005), 103–26.

—, 'The Eurasian silver century, 1276-1359: commensurability and multiplicity'. *Journal of Global History* 4, 2 (2009): 245–69.

La Porta, Rafael, Florencio Lopez-de-Silanes, Andrei Shleifer and Robert W. Vishny, 'Law and finance'. *Journal of Political Economy* 106 (1998): 1113–55.

Lach, Donald F., *Asia in the Making of Europe. Three Volumes* (Chicago 1976, 1978, and 1998).

Lai, Hui-min, 'The economic significance of the Imperial Household Department in the Qianlong period', http://ahes.ier.hit-u.ac.jp/ahec_tokyo/papers/S1C-2_Lai.pdf.

Lains, Pedro and Alvaro Ferreira da Silva, *Historia economica de Portugal 1700-2000. Volume One. O seculo XVIII* (Lisbon 2005).

Landers, John, *The Field and the Forge. Population, Production, and Power in the Pre-Industrial West* (Oxford 2003).

Landes, David S., *The Wealth and Poverty of Nations. Why Some are so Rich and Some so Poor* (New York and London 1998).

—, 'Reply to Peer Vries and Om Prakash'. *Itinerario. European Journal of Overseas History* 23, 1 (1999): 8–15.

—, *The Unbound Prometheus. Technological Change and Industrial Development in Western Europe from 1750 to the Present,* second edition (Cambridge 2003).

Lane, Frederic C., *Profits from Power. Readings in Protection Rent and Violence-Controlling Enterprises* (New York 1979).

Lang, James, *Conquest and Commerce. Spain and England in the Americas* (New York 1975).

Larsen Kirk W, *Tradition, Treaties and Trade. Qing Imperialism and Choson Korea, 1850-1910* (Cambridge, MA 2008).

Latham, A. J. H. and Heita Kawakatsu (eds), *Asian-Pacific Dynamism, 1550-2000* (London 2000).

Latourette, Kenneth S., *The Chinese, their History and Culture, I and II* (New York 1934).

Lavely, William and Roy Bin Wong, 'Revising the Malthusian narrative: the comparative study of population dynamics in late imperial China'. *The Journal of Asian Studies* 57 (1998): 714–48.

Lawson, Philip, *The East India Company. A History* (third impression; London and New York 1997).

Lee, Chul-sung, 'Re-evaluation of the Choson Dynasty's trade relationship with the Ch'ing Dynasty'. *International Journal of Korean History* 3 (2002): 95–122.

Lee, James, 'Trade and economy in pre-industrial Asia, c.1500–1800: East Asia in the age of global integration'. *The Journal of Asian Studies* 58 (1998): 2–26.

—, *The Political Economy of a Frontier. South West China, 1250-1850* (Cambridge, MA 2002).

Lee, James and Wang Feng, *One Quarter of Humanity. Malthusian Mythology and Chinese Realities, 1700-2000* (Cambridge, MA and London 1999).

Legarda, Benito J. Jr., *After the Galleons. Foreign Trade, Economic Change and Entrepreneurship in the Nineteenth-Century Philippines* (Madison, WI 1999).

Lehner, Georg, *China in European Encyclopaedias, 1700-1850* (Leiden and Boston 2011).

Leonard, Jane K., *Wei Yuan and China's Rediscovery of the Maritime World* (Cambridge, MA and London 1984).

—, *Controlling from Afar. The Daoguang Emperor's Management of the Grand Canal Crisis, 1824-1826* (Ann Arbor 1996).

Leonard, Jane K. and John R. Watt (eds), *To Achieve Security and Wealth. The Qing Imperial State and the Economy, 1644-1911* (Ithaca, NY 1992).

Leonard, Jörn, 'Imperial projections and piecemeal realities. Multiethnic empires and the experience of failure in the nineteenth century', in Maurus Reinkowski and Gregor Thum (eds), *Helpless Imperialists. Imperial Failure, Fear and Radicalization* (Göttingen 2012), 21–46.

Leonard, Jörn and Ulrike von Hirschhausen, *Empires und Nationalstaaten im 19. Jahrhundert* (Göttingen 2009).

Lesger, Clé, *The Rise of the Amsterdam Market and Information Exchange: Merchants, Commercial Expansion and Change in the Spatial Economy of the Low Countries, c.1550–1630* (Aldershot 2006).

Levi, Margaret *Of Rule and Revenue* (Berkeley 1988).

Li, Bozhong, *Agricultural Development in Jiangnan, 1620-1850* (Basingstoke and London 1998).

Li, Jianan, Daniel M. Bernhofen, Markus Eberhardt and Stephen Morgan, 'Market integration and disintegration in Qing Dynasty China: evidence from time-series and panel time-series methods'. http://www.etsg.org/ETSG2013/Papers/060.pdf.

Li, Lillian M., *China's Silk Trade: Traditional Industry in the Modern World 1842-1937* (Cambridge, MA 1981).

Bibliography

—, 'Grain prices in Zhili Province, 1736-1922: a preliminary study', in Thomas G. Rawski and Lillian M. Li (eds), *Chinese History in Economic Perspective* (Berkeley, Los Angeles and Oxford 1992), 69–99.

—, 'Integration and disintegration in North China's grain markets, 1738-1911'. *The Journal of Economic History* 60 (2000): 665–99.

—, *Fighting Famine in North China. State, Market and Environmental Decline, 1690s-1990s* (Stanford 2007).

Li, Xiantang, 'The paradoxical effect of silver in the economies of Ming and Qing China. On the new myth created by the "global economic view" of Andre Gunder Frank and Kenneth Pomeranz', in Q. E. Wang, *The California School in China*, special issue of *Chinese Studies in History* 45 (2011): 88–99.

Lieberman, Victor, *Strange Parallels. Southeast Asia in Global Context, c. 800-1830. Volume I: Integration on the Mainland* (Cambridge, MA 2003).

—, *Strange Parallels. Southeast Asia in Global Context, c. 800-1830. Volume II: Mainland Mirrors: Europe, Japan, China, South Asia, and the Islands* (Cambridge, MA 2009).

—(ed.), *Beyond Binary Histories. Re-imagining Eurasia to c. 1830* (Ann Arbor 1997).

Lin, Man-houng, 'From sweet potato to silver: the New World and eighteenth-century China as reflected in Wang Hui-Tsu's passage about the grain prices', in Hans Pohl (ed.), *The European Discovery of the World and its Economic Effects on Pre-industrial Society, 1500-1800: Papers of the Tenth International Economic History Congress* (Stuttgart 1990), 304–27.

—, 'The shift from East Asia to the world. The role of maritime silver in China's economy in the seventeenth to late eighteenth centuries', in Gungwu Wang and Ng Chin-keong (ed.), *Maritime China in Transition 1750-1850* (Wiesbaden 2004), 77–96.

—, *China Upside Down. Currency, Society, and Ideologies, 1808-1856* (Cambridge, MA and London 2006).

'Lin Tse-hsü's moral advice to Queen Victoria', in Ssu-Yü Teng and John K. Fairbank (eds), *China's Response to the West. A Documentary Survey, 1839-1923* (New York 1966), 24–8.

Lindert, Peter H., 'English population, wages and prices, 1541-1913'. *Journal of Interdisciplinary History* 15, 4 (1985): 609–35.

—, 'Poor relief before the welfare state: Britain versus the Continent, 1780-1880'. *European Review of Economic History* 2 (1998): 101–41.

—, *Growing Public. Social Spending and Economic Growth since the Eighteenth Century* (Cambridge 2004).

—, 'De bonnes idées en quête de nombres. Response à Gilles Postel-Vinay et R. Bin Wong'. *Annales. Histoire, Sciences Sociales* 62, 6 (2007): 1417–23.

Lindert, Peter H. and Jeffrey G. Williamson, 'Revising England's social tables, 1688-1812'. *Explorations in Economic History* 19 (1982): 385–408.

Linklater, Andro, *Owning the Earth. The Transforming History of Landownership* (London 2013).

Lis, Catharina and Hugo Soly, *Poverty and Capitalism in Pre-Industrial Europe, 1450-1850* (Brighton 1979).

—, *Worthy Efforts. Attitudes to Work and Workers in Pre-Industrial Europe* (Leiden and Boston 2012).

List, Friedrich, *Das nationale System der politischen Ökonomie*, edited and introduced by Artur Sommer (Basel-Tübingen; 1959; originally 1841).

Liu, Guanglin William, *Wrestling for Power. The State and the Economy in later Imperial China, 1000-1700* (Cambridge, MA 2005).

Liu, T., 'An estimation of China's GDP from 1600 to 1840'. *Economic Research Journal* 10 (2009): 144–55.

Liu, Ts'ui-jung, 'Rice culture in South China, 1500-1800. Adjustment and limitation in historical perspective', in A. Hayami and Y. Tsubouchi (eds), *Economic and Demographic Development in Rice Producing Societies. Some Aspects of East Asian Economic History, 1500-1900* (Leuven 1989), 119–41.

Liu, Yong, *The Dutch East India Company's Tea Trade with China 1757-1781* (Leiden and Boston 2007).

Livi Bacci, Massimo, *Population of Europe* (Oxford 2000; originally 1998).

Lococo, Paul Jr., 'The Qing Empire', in D. A. Graff and R. Higham (eds), *Military History of China* (Boulder 2002), 115–33.

Lorenzetti, Luigi, Michela Barbot and Luca Mocarelli (eds), *Property Rights and their Violations/ La propriété violée: Expropriations and Confiscations, 16th-20th Centuries/Expropriations et confiscations, XVIe-XXe siècles* (Bern 2012).

Lorge, Peter, 'War and warfare in China, 1450-1815', in Jeremy Black (ed.), *War in the early Modern World, 1450-1815* (London 1999), 87–104.

—, *War, Politics and Society in early Modern China, 900-1795* (London and New York 2005).

Lorge, Peter, *The Asian Military Revolution. From Gunpowder to the Bomb* (Cambridge 2008).

Lu, Feng and Peng Kaixiang, 'A research on China's long-term rice prices (1644-2000)'. *Frontiers of Economics in China* 1 (2006): 465–520.

Lucassen, Jan and Leo Lucassen, 'The mobility transition revisited, 1500-1900. Sources and methods', http://socialhistory.org/sites/default/files/docs/publications/respap46.pdf. This is a text from 2010 providing further background for iidem: 'The mobility transition revisited, 1500-1900. What the case of Europe can offer to global history'. *Journal of Global History* 4 (2009): 347–77. I use both versions and indicate in my notes, which one is used.

—(eds), *Globalising Migration History. The Eurasian Experience (16th-21st Centuries)* (Leiden 2014).

Luh, Jürgen, *Ancien régime Warfare and the Military Revolution. A Study* (Groningen 2000).

Lynn, John A., 'Nations in arms, 1763-1815', in Geoffrey Parker (ed.), *Cambridge Illustrated History of Warfare. The Triumph of the West* (Cambridge 1995), 186–213.

—, *Battle: A History of Combat and Culture* (Boulder 2003).

Lyons, Thomas P., *China Maritime Customs and China's Trade Statistics, 1859-1948* (New York 2003).

Ma, Debin, 'Economic growth in the Lower Yangzi region of China in 1911–1937: A quantitative and historical analysis'. *The Journal of Economic History* 68, 2 (2008): 355–92.

—, 'Law and economic change in traditional China: A "legal origin" perspective on the Great Divergence', in Debin Ma and Jan Luiten van Zanden (eds), *Law and Long-Term Economic Change. A Eurasian Perspective.* (Stanford 2011), 46–67.

—, 'Rock, scissors, paper: the problem of incentives and information in traditional Chinese state and the origin of the Great Divergence'. Working Paper 152, 2011 in The Economic History Working Papers Series of the Department of Economic History of the London School of Economics and Political Science. The paper can be downloaded from the website of the Department.

—, 'Chinese money and monetary system, 1800-2000', in Gerard Caprio (ed.), *Handbook of Key Global Financial Markets, Institutions and Infrastructure I* (London 2013), 57–64.

Ma, Debin and Jan Luiten van Zanden (eds), *Law and Long-Term Economic Change. A Eurasian Perspective* (Stanford 2011).

Ma, Ye, Herman de Jong and Tianshu Chu, 'Living standards in China between 1840 and 1912: A new estimate of gross domestic product per capita', http://ggdc.eldoc.ub.rug.nl/FILES/root/WorkPap/2014/GD-147/gd147.pdf.

Macauley, M., 'A world made simple: law and property in the Ottoman and Qing Empires'. *Journal of Early Modern History* 5 (2001): 331–52.

Macdonald, James, *A Free Nation Deep in Debt. The Financial Roots of Democracy* (Princeton and Oxford 2006).

Macfarlane, Alan, 'The cradle of capitalism: The case of England', in Jean Baechler, John A. Hall and Michael Mann (eds), *Europe and the Rise of Capitalism* (Oxford 1988), 185–203.

—, *The Riddle of the Modern World. Of Liberty, Wealth and Equality* (Houndmills 2000).

—, *The Invention of the Modern World* (Les Brouzils 2014).

Bibliography

Macfarlane, Alan and Iris Macfarlane, *Green Gold. The Empire of Tea* (London 2003).

MacLeod, Christine, *Inventing the Industrial Revolution: The English Patent System 1660-1800* (Cambridge 1988).

—, *Heroes of Invention. Technology, Liberalism and British Identity, 1750-1914* (Cambridge 2007).

Maddison, Angus, *Chinese Economic Performance in the Long Run* (Paris 1998).

—, *The World Economy. A Millennial Perspective* (Paris 2001).

—, *Contours of the World Economy, 1-2030 AD. Essays in Macro-Economic History* (Oxford 2007).

Magnusson, Lars, *Mercantilism. The Shaping of an Economic Language* (London and New York 1994).

—, *Mercantilism. Critical Concepts in the History of Economics* (London 1996).

—, *Nation, State and the Industrial Revolution. The Visible Hand* (London and New York 2009).

—(ed.), *Mercantilist Theory and Practice. The History of British Mercantilism* (London 2008).

Major, Andrea, *Slavery, Abolitionism and Empire in India, 1772-1843* (London 2012).

Malanima, Paulo, *Pre-Modern European Economy. One Thousand Years (10th-19th Centuries)* (Leiden and Boston 2009).

Mancall, M., 'The Kiakhta trade', in C. D. Cowan (ed.), *Economic Development of China and Japan. Studies in Economic History and Political Economy* (London 1964), 19–48.

Mann Jones, Susan, *Hung Liang-Chi (1746-1809). The Perception and Articulation of Political Problems in late Eighteenth-Century China* (Michigan 1972).

Mann Jones, Susan and Philip A. Kuhn, 'Dynastic decline and the roots of rebellion', in John K. Fairbank (ed.), *The Cambridge History of China. Volume 10, Late Ch'ing, 1800-1911, Part One* (Cambridge 1978), 107–62.

Mann, Michael, 'The autonomous power of the state: its origins, mechanisms and results', in John Hall (ed.), *States in History* (Oxford and Cambridge, MA 1986), 109–36.

—, *The Sources of Social Power. Volume I. A History of Power from the Beginning to A.D. 1760* (Cambridge 1986).

—, *State, War and Capitalism. Studies in Political Sociology* (Oxford 1988).

—, *The Sources of Social Power. Volume II. The Rise of Classes and Nation States, 1760-1914* (Cambridge 1993).

—, 'Response', in John A. Hall and Ralph Schroeder (eds), *Anatomy of Power. The Social Theory of Michael Mann* (Cambridge 2006), 343–96.

—, *The Sources of Social Power. Volume IV. Globalizations, 1945-2011* (Cambridge 2012).

—, *The Sources of Social Power. Volume III. Global Empires and Revolution, 1890-1945* (Cambridge 2012).

Mann, Susan, *Local Merchants and the Chinese Bureaucracy, 1750-1950* (Stanford 1987).

—, 'Liturgical governance and the merchant class', in idem, *Local Merchants and the Chinese Bureaucracy, 1750-1950* (Stanford 1987), 12–28.

—, *Precious Records. Women in China's Long Eighteenth Century* (Stanford 1997).

Marglin, Steven A., 'What do bosses do?', *Review of Radical Political Economy* 6 (1974): 60–112.

Marks, Robert B., 'Commercialization without capitalism. Processes of environmental change in South China 1550-1850'. *Environmental History* 1 (1996): 56–82.

—, *Tigers, Rice Silks & Silt. Environment and Economy in Late Imperial South China* (Cambridge 1998).

—, *The Origins of the Modern World. A Global and Ecological Narrative* (Lanham 2002).

—, *China. Its Environment and History* (Lanham 2012).

Marshall, P. J. (ed.), *The Oxford History of the British Empire. The Eighteenth Century* (Oxford and New York 1998).

Marx, Karl, *Capital. A Critique of Political Economy.* (Harmondsworth 1976). Introduced by Ernest Mandel and translated by Ben Fowkes.

Marx, Karl and Friedrich Engels, *The Communist Manifesto* (Harmondsworth 1967).

—, *Marx Engels Werke* (Berlin 1990).

Mathias, Peter, *The First Industrial Nation. An Economic History of Britain, 1700-1914* (London 1969).

—, *The Transformation of England. Essays in the Economic and Social History of England in the Eighteenth Century* (London 1979).

—, 'Taxation and industrialization in Britain, 1700-1870', in Peter Mathias (ed.), *The Transformation of England. Essays in the Economic and Social History of England in the Eighteenth Century* (London 1979), 116–30.

—, 'The people's money in the eighteenth century: the Royal Mint, trade tokens and the economy', in Peter Mathias (ed.), *The Transformation of England. Essays in the Economic and Social History of England in the Eighteenth Century* (London 1979), 190–210.

—, 'Financing the Industrial revolution', in Peter Matthias and John A. Davis (eds), *The First Industrial Revolutions* (Oxford and Cambridge, MA 1989), 69–85.

—, 'Economic expansion, energy resources, and technical change in the eighteenth century: a new dynamic in Britain'. Paper presented at the Conference Economia e Energia, Secc. XIII-XVIII, Prato, 15-17 April 2002. Unpublished.

Mathias, Peter and Patrick K. O'Brien, 'Taxation in Britain and France, 1715-1810. A comparison of the social and economic incidence of taxes collected for central government'. *Journal of European Economic History* 5 (1976): 601–50.

Maverick, Lewis, *China. A Model for Europe* (San Antonio 1946).

Mayhew, Nicolas J. 'Silver in England, 1600–1800. Coinage outputs and bullion exports from the records of the London Tower Mint and the London Company of Goldsmiths', in John H. Munro (ed.), *Money in the Pre-Industrial World. Bullion, Debasements and Coin Substitutes* (London 2012), chapter six.

Mazumdar, Sucheta, 'Chinese Hong merchants and American partners: International networks in a new age of global commerce, ca.1750-1850'. *Journal of World History*, forthcoming.

—, *Sugar and Society in China. Peasants, Technology and the World Market* (Cambridge, MA and London 1998).

Mazzucato, Mariana, *The Entrepreneurial State. Debunking Public Versus Private Sector Myths* (London 2013).

McCants, Anne E. C., 'Exotic goods, popular consumption, and the standard of living; thinking about globalization in the early modern world'. *Journal of World History* 18, 4 (2007): 433–64.

McClellan, James E. III and François Regourd, *The Colonial Machine. French Science and Overseas Expansion in the Old Regime* (Turnhout 2011).

McCloskey, Deirdre. N., *Bourgeois Dignity. Why Economics can't Explain the Modern World* (Chicago 2010).

McCusker, John J., *Money and Exchange in Europe and America, 1660-1775. A Handbook* (Williamsburg 1978).

McCusker, John J. and James Riley, 'Money supply, economic growth, and the quantity theory of money: France, 1650-1788', in Eddy van Cauwenberghe and Franz Irsiger (eds), *Munzprägung, Geldumlauf und Wechselkurse/Minting, monetary circulation and exchange rates. Akten des 8th International History Congress Section C7* (Budapest 1982), 255–90.

McKeown, Adam, 'A different transition: Human mobility in China, 1600-1900', in Jan Lucassen and Leo Lucassen (eds), *Globalising Migration History. The Eurasian Experience (16th-21st Centuries)* (Leiden 2014), 279–306.

McNeill J. R. and William H. McNeill, *The Human Web: A Bird's-Eye View of World History* (New York 2003).

McNeill, William H., *The Pursuit of Power. Technology, Armed Force and Society since A.D. 1000* (Chicago 1982).

—, 'The industrialization of war'. *Review of International Studies* 8, 3 (1982): 203–13.

—, *The Rise of the West. A History of the Human Community. With a Retrospective Essay* (Chicago 1990).

—, *The Global Condition. Conquerors, Catastrophes, and Community* (Princeton 1992).

McNicholas, Mark, 'Scamming the purchase-of-rank system in Qing China'. *Late Imperial China* 34, 1 (2013): 108–36.

Menard, Russell R., 'Transport costs and long-range trade, 1300-1800. Was there a European transport revolution in the early modern era?', in James D. Tracy (ed.), *The Political Economy of Merchant Empires. State Power and World Trade, 1350-1750* (Cambridge 1991), 228–75.

Meredith, David and Deborah Oxley, 'Condemned to the colonies. Penal transportation as the solution to Britain's law and order problem'. *Leidschrift* 22, 1 (2007): 19–40.

Metzger, Thomas, 'T'ao Chu's reform of the Huaipei Salt Monopoly, *Papers on China* vol. 16 mimeographed (Cambridge, MA 1962), 1–39.

Millar, A. E., 'Revisting the Sinophilia/Sinophobia dichotomy in the European Enlightenment through Adam Smith's "Duties of government"'. *Asian Journal of Social Science* 38, 5 (2010): 716–37.

Miller, Judith A., *Mastering the Market. The State and the Grain Trade in Northern France, 1700-1860* (Cambridge 1999).

Millward, James A., *Beyond the Pass. Economy, Ethnicity and Empire in Qing Central Asia, 1759-1864* (Stanford 1998).

—, *Eurasian Crossroads. A History of Xinjiang* (London 2007).

Minchington, W., 'The energy basis of the British Industrial Revolution', in G. Bayerl (ed.), *Wind- und Wasserkraft. Die Nützung regenerierbarer Energiequellen in der Geschichte* (Düsseldorf 1989), 342–62.

Mitchell, B. R., *British Historical Statistics* (Cambridge 1988).

Modern Asian Studies 30, 4 (1996) a special issue on war in modern China.

Moe, Espen, *Governance, Growth and Leadership. The Role of the State in Technological Progress, 1750-2000* (Farnham 2007).

Moers, Colin, *The Making of Bourgeois Europe* (London and New York 1991).

Mokyr, Joel, 'Is there still life in the pessimist case? Consumption during the Industrial Revolution, 1790-1850'. *The Journal of Economic History* 48, 1 (1988): 69–92.

—, 'Editor's introduction: the New Economic History and the Industrial Revolution', in idem, *The British Industrial Revolution. An Economic Perspective* (Boulder 1993), 1–131.

—, 'Accounting for the Industrial Revolution', in Roderick Floud and Paul Johnson (eds), *The Cambridge Economic History of Modern Britain, Volume I, Industrialisation, 1700-1860* (Cambridge 2004), 1–27.

—, 'The intellectual origins of modern economic growth'. *The Journal of Economic History* 65 (2005): 285–351.

—, 'Intellectual property rights, the Industrial Revolution and the beginnings of modern economic growth'. *American Economic Review Papers and Proceedings*, May 2009, 349–55. This text is available on Mokyr's website.

—, *The Enlightened Economy. An Economic History of Britain 1700-1850* (New Haven and London 2009).

—(ed.), *The British Industrial Revolution. An Economic Perspective* (Boulder 1993).

Moore, Robin J., 'Imperial India, 1858-1914', in Andrew Porter (ed.), *The Oxford History of the British Empire. The Nineteenth Century* (Oxford and New York 1999), 422–46.

Moran, Daniel and Arthur Waldron (eds), *The People in Arms. Military Myth and National Mobilization since the French Revolution* (Cambridge 2003).

Morgan, Gwenda and Peter Rushton, *Banishment in the early Atlantic World. Convicts, Rebels and Slaves* (London 2013).

Morgan, Kenneth, *Slavery, Atlantic Trade and the British Economy, 1660-1800* (Cambridge 2000).

—, 'Mercantilism and the British Empire, 1688-1815', in Donald Winch and Patrick K. O'Brien (eds), *The Political Economy of British Historical Experience, 1688-1914* (Oxford 2002), 165–92.

Morillo, Stephen, 'Guns and government: a comparative study of Europe and Japan'. *Journal of World History* 6, 1 (1995): 75–106.

Morineau, Michel, 'Budget de l'état et gestion des finances royales'. *Revue Historique* 264 (1980): 289–336.

—, 'Les frappes monétaires françaises 1726 à 1793. Premières considérations', in John Day (ed.), *Etudes d'histoire monétaire* (Lille 1984), 69–142.

Morris, Ian, *War. What is it Good for? The Role of Conflict in Civilisation, from Primates to Robots* (London 2014).

Morriss, Roger, *The Foundations of British Maritime Ascendancy. Resources, Logistics and the State, 1755-1815* (Cambridge 2011).

Morse, Hosea Ballou, *The Gilds of China* (London 1909).

—, *The International Relations of the Chinese Empire. Volume One. The Period of Conflict, 1834-1860* (London 1910).

—, *The International Relations of the Chinese Empire. Volume Two. The Period of Submission, 1861-1893* (London 1918).

—, *The Trade and Administration of China*, third revised edition (London 1921).

—, *The Chronicles of the East India Company Trading to China, 1635-1834*. Five Volumes (Oxford 1926–29).

Mote, Frederick W., *Imperial China 900-1800* (Cambridge, MA 1999).

Moxham, Roy, *Tea. Addiction, Exploitation and Empire* (New York 2003).

Muchembled, Robert, *Popular Culture and Elite Culture in France, 1400-1750* (Louisiana State University Press 1985).

Mui, Hoh-cheung and Loma H. Mui, *The Management of Monopoly. A Study of the East India Company's Conduct of its Tea Trade 1784-1833* (Vancouver 1984).

Mumford, Lewis, *Technics and Civilization* (London 1934).

Münch, Paul. 'The growth of the modern state', in Sheilagh Ogilvie (ed.), *Germany. A New Social and Economic History. Volume II* (London 1996), 196–232.

Mungello, D. E., *The Great Encounter of China and the West, 1500-1800* (Lanham 1999).

Murphey, Rhoads, *The Outsiders. The Western Experience in India and China* (Ann Arbor 1977).

Murray, Dian, 'Piracy and China's maritime transition 1750-1850', in Gungwu Wang and Ng Chin-keong (eds), *Maritime China in Transition 1750-1850* (Wiesbaden 2004), 43–60.

Murray, Williamson A., 'The industrialization of war, 1815-1871', in Geoffrey Parker (ed.), *Cambridge Illustrated History of Warfare. The Triumph of the West* (Cambridge 1995), 216–41.

Myers, Ramon H. and Yeh-chien Wang, 'Economic developments, 1644-1800', in Willard J. Peterson (ed.), *Cambridge History of China. Volume 9. Part One. The Ch'ing Dynasty to 1800* (Cambridge 2002), 563–645.

Naquin, Susan, *Millenarian Rebellion in China. The Eight Trigrams Uprising of 1813* (New Haven and London 1977).

Naquin, Susan and Evelyn S. Rawski, *Chinese Society in the Eighteenth Century* (New Haven and London 1987).

Neal, Larry, *The Rise of Financial Capitalism. International Capital Markets in the Age of Reason* (Cambridge 1990).

Nee, Victor and Richard Swedberg (eds), *The Economic Sociology of Capitalism* (Princeton 2005).

Needham, Joseph, *The Grand Titration: Science and Society in East and West* (London 1969).

Nef, John, *War and Human Progress* (Cambridge, MA 1950).

Bibliography

Nexon, Daniel H., *The Struggle for Power in early Modern Europe. Religious Conflict, Dynastic Empires and International Change* (Princeton 2009).

Ni, Shawn and Pham Hoang Van, 'High corruption income in Ming and Qing China'. *Journal of Development Economics* 81, 2 (2006): 316–36.

Nivison, David S., 'Ho-shen and his accusers: ideology and political behaviour in the eighteenth century', in David S. Nivison and Arthur F. Wright (eds), *Confucianism in Action* (Stanford 1959), 209–43.

Nivison, David S. and Arthur F. Wright (eds), *Confucianism in Action* (Stanford 1959).

Norberg, Kathryn, 'The French fiscal crisis of 1788 and the financial origins of the revolution of 1789', in Philip T. Hoffman and Kathryn Norberg (eds), *Fiscal Crises, Liberty and Representative Government, 1450-1789* (Stanford 1994), 253–98.

Norman, E. Herbert, *Japan's Emergence as a Modern State. Political and Economic Problems of the Meiji Period* (New York 1946).

North, Douglass C., *Structure and Change in Economic History* (New York 1981).

—, *Institutions, Institutional Change and Economic Performance* (Cambridge 1990).

—, 'Institutions and credible commitment'. *Journal of Institutional Economics* 149 (1993): 11–24.

—, *Understanding the Process of Economic Change* (Princeton 2005).

North, Douglass C. and Robert P. Thomas, *The Rise of the Western World. A New Economic History* (Cambridge 1973).

North, Douglass C., John Joseph Wallis and Barry R. Weingast, *Violence and Social orders. A Conceptual Framework for Interpreting Recorded Human History* (Cambridge 2009).

—, 'Violence and the rise of open-access orders'. *Journal of Democracy* 20, 1 (2009): 55–68.

North, Douglass C. and Barry R. Weingast, 'Constitutions and commitment: the evolution of institutions governing public choice in seventeenth-century England'. *The Journal of Economic History* 49 (1989): 803–32.

North, Michael, *Geschichte der Niederlande* (Munich 1997).

—, 'Finances and power in the German state system', in Bartolomé Yun-Casalilla and Patrick K. O'Brien (eds), *The Rise of Fiscal States. A Global History, 1500-1914* (Cambridge 2012), 145–63.

Northrup, David, *Indentured Labor in the Age of Imperialism, 1834-1922* (Cambridge 1995).

—, *The Atlantic Slave Trade*, second edition (Boston and New York 2002).

Nye, John V. C., *War, Wine, and Taxes. The Political Economy of Anglo-French Trade, 1689-1900* (Princeton and Oxford 2007).

Ó Gráda, Cormac, Richard Paping and Eric Vanhaute (eds), *When the Potato Failed. Causes and Effects of the last European Subsistence Crisis, 1845-1850* (Turnhout Belgium 2007).

O'Brien, Patrick, 'European economic development. The contribution of the periphery'. *Economic History Review* 35, 1 (1982): 1–18.

—, 'The costs and benefits of British imperialism, 1846-1914'. *Past and Present* 120 (1988): 163–200.

—, 'The political economy of British taxation, 1660-1815'. *Economic History Review*, 2nd series 41 (1988): 1–32.

—, 'The impact of the Revolutionary and Napoleonic Wars, 1793-1815, on the long-run growth of the British economy'. *Review (Fernand Braudel Center)* 12, 3 (1989): 335–95.

—, 'Political preconditions for the Industrial Revolution', in Patrick K. O'Brien and Ronald Quinault (eds), *The Industrial Revolution and British Society* (Cambridge 1993), 124–55.

—, 'The study of contrasts across Europe. An interview with Patrick O'Brien by Peer Vries'. *Itinerario. European Journal of Overseas History* 23, 3/4 (1999): 3–24.

—, 'Imperialism and the rise and decline of the British economy, 1688-1989'. *New Left Review* 238 (1999): 48–80.

—, 'Mercantilism and imperialism in the rise and decline of the Dutch and British economies 1585-1815'. *De Economist* 148, 4 (2000): 469–501.

—, 'Fiscal exceptionalism. Great Britain and its European rivals from Civil War to triumph at Trafalgar and Waterloo', in Donald Winch and Patrick K. O'Brien (eds), *The Political Economy of British Historical Experience, 1688-1914* (Oxford 2002), 245–66.

—, 'Fiscal and financial preconditions for the rise of British naval hegemony, 1485-1815. Working Papers in Economic History. Number: 91/05. November 2005. London School of Economics and Political Science.

—, 'The Hanoverian state and the defeat of the Continental System: a conversation with Eli Heckscher', in Ronald Findlay, Rolf G. H. Hendriksson, Hakan Lindgren and Mats Lundahl (eds), *Eli Heckscher, International Trade and Economic History* (Boston 2006), 373–408.

—, 'Contentions of the purse between England and its European rivals from Henry V to George IV: A conversation with Michael Mann'. *Journal of Historical Sociology* 19, 4 (2006): 341–63.

—, 'Taxation for British mercantilism from the Treaty of Utrecht (1713) to the Peace of Paris (1783)', in Torres Sánchez (ed.), *War, State and Development. Fiscal-Military States in the Eighteenth Century* (Pamplona 2007), 295–356.

—, The history, nature and economic significance of an exceptional fiscal state for the growth of the British economy, 1453-1815. Working papers in Economic History Number 109/08 October 2008 London School of Economic and Political Science.

—, 'The triumph and denouement of the British fiscal state: taxation for the wars against Revolutionary and Napoleonic France, 1793-1815', in Christopher Storrs (ed.), *The Fiscal-Military State in Eighteenth-Century Europe. Essays in Honour of P.G.M. Dickson* (Farnham, UK and Burlington, US 2009), 167–200.

—, 'Contributions of warfare with Revolutionary and Napoleonic France to the consolidation and progress of the British Industrial Revolution'. Working Paper 150, 2011 in The Economic History Working Papers Series of the Department of Economic History of the London School of Economics and Political Science. The paper can be downloaded from the website of the Department.

—, 'Mercantilist institutions for a first but precocious industrial revolution: The Bank of England, the Treasury and the money supply, 1694-1797'. Working Paper 156, 2011 in The Economic History Working Papers Series of the Department of Economic History of the London School of Economics and Political Science. The paper can be downloaded from the website of the Department.

O'Brien, Patrick K. and Stanley L. Engerman, 'Exports and the growth of the British economy from the Glorious Revolution to the peace of Amiens', in Barbara L. Solow (ed.), *Slavery and the Rise of the Atlantic System* (Cambridge 1991), 177–209.

O'Brien, Patrick K., Trevor Griffiths and Philip Hunt, 'Political components of the Industrial Revolution: Parliament and the English cotton textile industry, 1660-1774'. *Economic History Review* 44 (1991): 395–423.

O'Brien, Patrick K. and Philip A. Hunt, 'England 1485-1815', in Richard Bonney (ed.), *Rise of the Fiscal State in Europe c.1200-1815* (Oxford 1999), 53–100.

O'Brien, Patrick K. and Leandro Prados de la Escosura (eds), *The Costs and Benefits of European Imperialism from the Conquest of Ceuta, 1415, to the Treaty of Lusaka, 1974. Proceedings of the Twelfth Economic History Congress Madrid 1998.* Published as *Revista de Historia Económica* 16, first issue of 1998.

O'Rourke, Kevin, 'The worldwide economic impact of the French Revolutionary and Napoleonic Wars, 1793-1815'. *Journal of Global History* 1, 1 (2006): 123–50.

Ogilvie, Sheilagh, *Institutions and European Trade: Merchant Guilds, 1000-1800* (Cambridge 2011).

—(ed.), *Germany. A New Social and Economic History. Volume II* (London 1996).

Bibliography

Olson, Mancur, *The Rise and Decline of Nations. Economic Growth, Stagflation, and Social Rigidities* (New Haven 1982).

—, 'Dictatorship, democracy, and development', in Mancur Olson and Satu Kähkönen (eds), *A Not-So-Dismal Science. A Broader View of Economies and Societies* (Oxford 2000), 119–37.

—, *Power and Prosperity. Outgrowing Communist and Capitalist Dictatorships* (New York 2000).

Olson, Mancur and Satu Kähkönen (eds), *A Not-So-Dismal Science. A Broader View of Economies and Societies* (Oxford 2000).

Oppenheim, Walter, *Europe and the Enlightened Despots* (London 1990).

Ormrod, David, *The Rise of Commercial Empires. England and the Netherlands in the Age of Mercantilism, 1650-1770* (Cambridge 2003).

Osborn, Anne, 'Property, taxes and state protection of rights', in Madeleine Zelin, Jonathan K. Ocko and Robert Gardella (eds), *Contract and Property in early Modern China* (Stanford 2004), 120–59.

Osterhammel, Jürgen, *China und die Weltgemeinschaft. Vom 18. Jahrhundert bis in unsere Zeit* (Munich 1989).

—, *Colonialism. A Theoretical Overview* (Princeton 1997).

—, 'Gesellschaftliche Parameter chinesischer Modernität'. *Geschichte und Gesellschaft* 28 (2002): 71–108.

—, *Die Verwandlung der Welt. Eine Geschichte des 19. Jahrhunderts* (Munich 2009).

Otruba, Gustav, 'Staatshaushalt und Staatsschuld unter Maria Theresia und Joseph II', in Richard Georg Plaschka and Grete Klingenstein (eds) *Österreich im Zeitalter der Aufklärung. Kontinuität und Zäsur in Europa zur Zeit Maria Theresias und Josephs II.* (Vienna 1985) 197–249.

Otruba, Gustav and Markus Weiss (eds), *Beiträge zur Finanzgeschichte Österreichs (Staatshaushalt und Steuern, 1740-1840)* (Linz 1986).

Overdijking, G. W., *Lin Tse-Hsu. Een biografische schets* (Leiden 1938).

Overton, Mark, *Agricultural Revolution in England. The Transformation of the Agrarian Economy, 1500-1850* (Cambridge 1996).

Pacey, Arnold, *Technology in World Civilization* (Cambridge, MA 1996).

Paine, S. C. M., *The Sino-Japanese War of 1894-1895. Perceptions, Power, and Primacy* (New York 2003).

Palmer, S. H., *Economic Arithmetic. A Guide to the Statistical Sources of English Commerce, Industry and Finance 1700-1850* (New York 1977).

Park, Nancy E., 'Corruption in eighteenth-century China'. *The Journal of Asian Studies* 56 (1997): 967–1005.

Parker, Geoffrey, *The Military Revolution. Military Innovation and the Rise of the West, 1500-1800* (revised second edition; Cambridge 1999, the first edition dates from 1990).

—, 'Introduction: the Western way of war', in Geoffrey Parker (ed.), *Cambridge Illustrated History of Warfare. The Triumph of the West* (Cambridge 1995), 2–12.

—(ed.), *Cambridge Illustrated History of Warfare. The Triumph of the West* (Cambridge 1995).

Parrott, David, *The Business of War. Military Enterprise and Military Revolution in early Modern Europe* (Cambridge 2012).

Parthasarathi, Prasannan, 'Review article: the Great Divergence'. *Past and Present* 177 (2002): 275–93.

—, *Why Europe Grew Rich and Asia did not. Global Economic Divergence, 1600-1850* (Cambridge 2011).

Patriquin, Larry, *Agrarian Capitalism and Poor Relief in England 1500-1860. Rethinking the Origins of the Welfare State* (Houndmills 2007).

Paul, Helen Julia, 'Joint-stock companies as the sinews of war. The South Sea and Royal African Companies', in Torres Sánchez (ed.), *War, State and Development. Fiscal-Military States in the Eighteenth Century* (Pamplona 2007), 277–94.

Paul, Jeff-Fynn (ed.), *War, Entrepreneurs, and the State in Europe and the Mediterranean, 1300-1800* (Leiden 2014).

Pearson, M. N., 'Merchants and states', in James D. Tracy (ed.), *The Political Economy of Merchant Empires. State Power and World Trade, 1350-1750* (Cambridge 1991), 41–116.

Peden, G. C., 'From cheap government to efficient government: the political economy of public expenditure in the United Kingdom, 1832-1914', in Donald Winch and Patrick K. O'Brien (eds), *The Political Economy of British Historical Experience, 1688-1914* (Oxford 2002), 267–94.

Peng, Xinwei, *A Monetary History of China. Two Volumes* (Bellingham Washington 1994) translated by Edward H. Kaplan.

Perdue, Peter C., 'Military mobilization in seventeenth- and eighteenth-century China, Russia and Mongolia'. *Modern Asian Studies* 30 (1996): 757–93.

—, 'Empire and nation in comparative perspective: frontier administration in eighteenth-century China'. *Journal of Early Modern History* 5, 4 (2001): 282–304.

—, *China marches West. The Qing Conquest of Central Eurasia* (Cambridge, MA and London 2005).

—, 'China's environment, 1500-2000: is there something new under the sun? Paper presented at the conference Toward the twentieth century in Asia: Comparative perspectives on politics, economy and society in China and India. May 19-22-2005, Durham, Duke University. Unpublished.

—, 'Erasing the empire, reracing the nation: racism and culturalism in Imperial China', in Carole McGranaghan, Ann Stoler and Peter C. Perdue (eds), *Imperial Formations* (Santa Fe 2007), 141–72.

—, 'Review of Hui, *War and state formation in Ancient China and early modern Europe*'. *Journal of Global History* 2, 1 (2007): 120–1.

—, 'Nature and nurture on imperial China's frontiers'. *Modern Asian Studies* 43, 1 (2009): 245–67.

Perkin, H. J., *The Origins of Modern English Society, 1780-1880* (London 1969).

Perkins, Dwight H., 'Government as an obstacle to industrialization: the case of nineteenth-century China'. *The Journal of Economic History* 27 (1967): 478–92.

—, *Agricultural Development in China, 1368-1968* (Chicago 1969).

Peterson, Willard J. (ed.), *The Cambridge History of China. Volume 9. Part One. The Ch'ing Dynasty to 1800* (Cambridge 2002).

Peyrefitte, Alain, *L'empire immobile ou le choc des mondes* (Paris 1989). There is a new English edition *The Immobile Empire* (New York and Toronto 2013).

Pfeil, Tom, *'Tot redding van het vaderland'. Het primaat van de Nederlandse overheidsfinanciën in de Bataafs-Franse tijd, 1795-1810* (Amsterdam 1998).

Phipps, J., *A Practical Treatise on the China and Eastern Trade* (London 1836).

Pieper, Renate, 'Financing an empire: the Austrian composite monarchy, 1650-1848', in Bartolomé Yun-Casalilla and Patrick K. O'Brien (eds), *The Rise of Fiscal States. A Global History, 1500-1914* (Cambridge 2012), 164–90.

Pierenkemper, Toni and Richard Tilly, *The German Economy during the Nineteenth Century* (New York and Oxford 2004).

Piketty, Thomas, *Capital in the Twenty-First Century* (Cambridge and London 2014; originally Paris 2013).

Pincus, Steve, *1688. The First Modern Revolution* (New Haven 2009).

—, 'Rethinking mercantilism: Political economy, the British Empire, and the Atlantic world in the seventeenth and eighteenth centuries'. *The William and Mary Quarterly*, 69, 1 (2012): 3–34. Reactions by Cathy Matson, Christian J. Koot, Susan D. Amussen, Trevor Burnard, Margaret Ellen Newell and a reply by Steve Pincus, 35–70.

Bibliography

Pines, Yuri, *The Everlasting Empire. The Political Culture of Ancient China and its Imperial Legacy* (Princeton and Oxford 2012).

Piuz, Anne-Marie, 'Les effets du commerce d'outre-mer sur la pensée économique (XVIe-XVIIIe siècles)', in Simonetta Cavaciocchi (ed.), *Prodotti e techniche d'oltremare nelle economie Europee secc. XIII-XVIII* (Prato 1998), 927–49.

Plattner, Irmgard, 'Josephinismus und Bürokratie', in Helmut Reinalter (ed.), *Josephinismus als Aufgeklärter Absolutismus* (Vienna, Cologne and Weimar 2008), 53–96.

Poggi, Gianfranco, *The Development of the Modern State: A Sociological Introduction* (Stanford 1978).

Polanyi, Karl, *The Great Transformation. The political and economic origins of our time* (New York 1944).

Pollard, Sidney, *The Genesis of Modern Management. A Study of the Industrial Revolution in Great Britain* (London 1965).

Pomeranz, Kenneth, *The Making of a Hinterland. State, Society, and Economy in Inland North China, 1853-1937* (Berkeley, Los Angeles and Oxford 1993).

—, 'Rethinking the late imperial Chinese economy: development, disaggregation and decline, c. 1730-1930'. *Itinerario. European Journal of Overseas History* 24, 3 and 4 (2000): 29–74.

—, *The Great Divergence. China, Europe, and the Making of the Modern World Economy* (Princeton 2000).

—, 'Beyond the East-West binary: resituating development paths in the eighteenth-century world'. *Journal of Asian Studies* 61, 2 (2002): 539–90.

—, 'Women's work, family and economic development in Europe and East Asia: long-term trajectories and contemporary comparisons', in Giovanni Arrighi, Takeshi Hamashita and Mark Selden (eds), *The Resurgence of East Asia. 500, 150 and 50 years Perspectives* (London and New York 2003), 124–72.

—, 'Standards of living in eighteenth-century China: regional differences, temporal trends and incomplete evidence', in Robert C. Allen, Tommy Bengtsson and Martin Dribe (eds), *Living Standards in the Past. New Perspectives on Well-Being in Asia and Europe* (Oxford and New York 2005), 23–54.

—, 'Without coal? Colonies? Calculus? Counterfactuals & industrialization in Europe & China', in Philip Tetlock, Richard Ned Lebow and Geoffrey Parker (eds), *Unmaking the West: 'What-if' Scenarios that Re-Write World History* (Ann Arbor 2006), 241–76.

—, Institutions and economic development in Qing China Paper presented at the XV World Economic History Conference in Utrecht 3-7 August 2009. Unpublished.

—, Ten years after: Responses and reconsideration'. *Historically Speaking* 12, 4 (2011): 20–5.

—, 'Weather, war, and welfare'. *Historically Speaking* 14, 5 (2013): 30–3.

Pomeranz, Kenneth and Steven Topik, *The World that Trade Created. Society, Culture and the World Economy, 1400 to the Present* (New York and London 1999).

Ponting, Clive, *World History. A New Perspective* (London 2001).

Poovey, Mary, *A History of the Modern Fact. Problems of Knowledge in the Sciences of Wealth and Society* (Chicago and London 1998).

Pope, Dudley, *Life in Nelson's Navy* (London 1981).

Porter, Andrew (ed.), *The Oxford History of the British Empire. The Nineteenth Century* (Oxford and New York 1999).

Porter, Bruce D., *War and the Rise of the State. The Military Foundations of Modern Politics* (New York 1994).

Porter, David, *Ideographia. The Chinese Cipher in early Modern Europe* (Stanford 2001).

Porter, Michael E., *The Competitive Advantage of Nations* (London and Basingstoke 1990).

Porter, Roy, *English Society in the Eighteenth Century* (London 1982).

—, *Enlightenment. Britain and the Creation of the Modern World* (London 2000).

Powell, Ralph L., *The Rise of Chinese Military Power, 1895-1911* (Princeton 1955).

Powelson, John P., *Centuries of Economic Endeavor. Parallel Paths in Japan and Europe and their Contrast with the Third World* (Ann Arbor 1994).

Prados de la Escosura, Leandro (ed.), *Exceptionalism and Industrialisation. Britain and its European Rivals, 1688-1815* (Cambridge 2004).

Pratt, Sir John, *China and Britain* (London 1940).

Pritchard, Earl H., *The Crucial Years of early Anglo-Chinese Relations, 1750-1800* (Washington 1937).

—, 'Private trade between England and China in the eighteenth century, 1680-1833'. *Journal of the Economic and Social History of the Orient* 1 (1958): 108–37 and 221–56.

Quinn, Stephen, 'The Glorious Revolution's effect on English private finance: a micro-history'. *The Journal of Economic History* 61 (2001): 593–615.

—, 'Money, finance and capital markets', in Roderick Floud and Paul Johnson (eds), *The Cambridge Economic History of Modern Britain, Volume I, Industrialisation, 1700-1860* (Cambridge 2004), 147–74.

Raeff, Mark, 'The well-ordered police state and the development of modernity in seventeenth- and eighteenth-century Europe: an attempt at a comparative approach'. *American Historical Review* 80 (1975): 1221–43.

Ralston, David B., *Importing the European Army. The Introduction of European Military Techniques and Institutions into the Extra-European World, 1600-1914* (Chicago 1990).

Rankin, Mary B. and Joseph E. Esherick (eds), *Chinese Local Elites and Patterns of Dominance* (Berkeley 1990).

Rapp, Richard T., 'The unmaking of the Mediterranean trade hegemony'. *The Journal of Economic History* 35 (1975): 499–525.

Rauscher, Peter, Andrea Serles and Thomas Winkelbauer (eds), *Das "Blut des Staatskörpers". Forschungen zur Finanzgeschichte der Frühen Neuzeit. Historische Zeitschrift. Beiheft* 56 (Munich 2012).

Rawski, Evelyn S., *The Last Emperors. A Social History of the Qing Imperial Institutions* (Los Angeles, Berkeley and London 2001).

—, 'The Qing formation and the early-modern period', in Lynn A. Struve (ed.), *The Qing Formation in World-Historical Time* (Cambridge, MA and London 2004), 207–40.

Rawski, Thomas G. and Lillian M. Li (eds), *Chinese History in Economic Perspective* (Berkeley, Los Angeles and Oxford 1992).

Reardon-Anderson, James, *Reluctant Pioneers. China's Expansion Northward, 1644-1937* (Stanford 2005).

Rediker, Markus, *The Slave Ship: A Human History* (London 2007).

Redlich, Fritz, *The German Military Enterpriser and his Work Force: A Study in European Economic and Social History* (Wiesbaden 1964–65).

Reed, Bradly W., *Talons and Teeth. County Clerks and Runners in the Qing Dynasty* (Stanford 2001).

Reinalter, Helmut (ed.), *Josephinismus als Aufgeklärter Absolutismus* (Vienna, Cologne and Weimar 2008).

Reinert, Erik S., 'The role of the state in economic growth'. *Journal of Economic Studies* 26, 4/5 (1999): 268–326.

—, *How Rich Countries Got Rich . . . and Why Poor Countries Stay Poor* (New York 2007).

—, 'Review of Findlay and O'Rourke, *Power and plenty*'. *Journal of Global History* 4, 3 (2009): 512–4.

Reinert, Sophus A., *Translating Empire. Emulation and the Origins of Political Economy* (Cambridge 2011).

—, 'Rivalry: greatness in early modern political economy', in Philip J. Stern and Carl Wennerlind (eds), *Mercantilism Reimagined. Political Economy in early Modern Britain and its Empire* (Oxford and New York 2013), 348–70.

Bibliography

Reinhart, Carmen M. and Kenneth S. Rogoff, *This Time is Different. Eight Centuries of Financial Folly* (Princeton and Oxford 2009).

—, Growth in a time of debt, http://scholar.harvard.edu/files/rogoff/files/growth_in_time_debt_aer.pdf *American Economic Review: Papers & Proceedings* 100 (May 2010): 573–8.

Renditions. A Chinese-English Translation Magazine. Special Issue 53-54 (2000) *Chinese Impressions of the West.*

Reynell, Carey, *A Necessary Companion, or the English Interest Discovered and Promoted* (London 1685).

Rhoads, E. J., *Manchus and Han. Ethnic Relations and Political Power in late Qing and early Republican China, 1861-1928* (Washington 2001).

Richards, John F., *The Unending Frontier. An Environmental History of the early Modern World* (Berkeley, Los Angeles and London 2003).

—, 'Fiscal states in Mughal and British India', in Bartolomé Yun-Casalilla and Patrick K. O'Brien (eds), *The Rise of Fiscal States. A Global History, 1500-1914* (Cambridge 2012), 410–41.

Ridley, Matt, *The Rational Optimist. How Prosperity Evolves* (London 2011).

Riedel, Adolph F., *Der Brandenburgisch-preußische Staatshaushalt in den beiden letzten Jahrhunderten* (Berlin 1866).

Riello, Giorgio, *Cotton. The Fabric that Made the Modern World* (Cambridge 2013).

Riello, Giorgio and Tirthankar Roy (eds), with the collaboration of Om Prakash and Kaoru Sugihara, *How India Clothed the World. The World of South Asian Textiles, 1500-1850* (Leiden and Boston 2009).

Riley, James, *The Seven Years War and the Old Regime: The Economic and Financial Toll* (Princeton 1986).

Ringmar, Erik, *Why Europe was First. Social Change and Economic Growth in Europe and East Asia, 1500-2050* (London and New York 2007).

Robins, Nick, *The Corporation that Changed the World. How the East India Company Shaped the Modern Multinational*, second edition (London 2002).

Rodger, N. A. M., *The Command of the Ocean* (London 2004).

—, 'War as an economic activity in the "long" eighteenth century'. *International Journal of Maritime History* 22, 2 (2010): 1–18.

—, 'From the "military revolution" to the "fiscal-naval state"'. *Journal of Maritime Research* 13, 2 (2011): 119–28.

Rodrik, Dani, Arvid Subramanian and Francesco Trebbi, 'Institutions rule. The primacy of institutions over geography and integration in economic development'. *Journal of Economic Growth* 9 (2004): 131–65.

Rogers, Clifford J. (ed.), *The Military Revolution Debate. Readings on the Military Transformation of early Modern Europe* (Boulder 1995).

Rogers, Nicholas, 'Vagrancy, impressment and the regulation of labour in eighteenth-century Britain'. *Slavery and Abolition* 15, 2 (1994): 102–13.

—, *The Press Gang. Naval Impressment and Its Opponents in Georgian Britain* (New York and London 2008).

Rosenberg, Nathan and Luther E. Birdzell, *How the West Grew Rich. The Economic Transformation of the Industrial World* (New York 1986).

Rosenthal, Jean-Laurent and Roy Bin Wong, *Before and Beyond Divergence. The Politics of Economic Change in China and Europe* (Cambridge, MA and London 2011).

Roseveare, Henri, *The Financial Revolution, 1660-1760* (London and New York 1991).

Rostow, Walt W., *The Stages of Economic Growth* (London 1960).

Rothschild, Emma, 'The English Kopf', in Donald Winch and Patrick K. O'Brien (eds), *The Political Economy of British Historical Experience, 1688-1914* (Oxford 2002), 31–60.

Rotwein, E. (ed.), *David Hume, Writings on Economics* (Edinburgh 1955).

Rowe, William T., *Saving the World. Chen Hongmou and Elite Consciousness in Eighteenth-Century China* (Stanford 2001).

—, 'Social stability and social change', in Willard J. Peterson (ed.), *The Cambridge History of China. Volume 9. Part One. The Ch'ing Dynasty to 1800* (Cambridge 2002), 473–562.

—, 'Provincial monetary practice in eighteenth-century China. Chen Hongmu in Jiangxi and Shaanxi', in Christine Moll-Murata, Song Jianze and Hans Ulrich Vogel (eds), *Chinese Handicraft Regulations of the Qing Dynasty* (Munich 2005), 347–71.

—, *China's Last Empire. The Great Qing* (Cambridge, MA and London 2009).

—, 'Money, economy, and polity in the Daoguang-era paper currency debates'. *Late Imperial China* 31, 2 (2010): 69–96.

—, 'Introduction: The significance of the Qianlong-Jiaqing transition in Qing history'. *Late Imperial China* 32, 2 (2011): 74–88.

Rubinstein, W. D., *Capitalism, Culture and Decline in Britain 1750-1990* (London 1993).

Rubiés, Joan-Pao, 'Oriental despotism and European Orientalism: Botero to Montesquieu'. *Journal of Early Modern History* 9, 2 (2005): 109–80.

Rule, John, *The Experience of Labour in Eighteenth-Century Industry* (London 1981).

—, *The Vital Century. England's Developing Economy, 1714-1815* (Harlow 1992).

Salmon, J. H. M., *Society in Crisis. France in the Sixteenth Century* (London 1979).

Sandgruber, Roman, *Österreichische Geschichte. Ökonomie und Politik. Österreichische Wirtschaftsgeschichte vom Mittelalter bis zur Gegenwart* (Vienna 1995).

Sargent, T. J. and F. R. Velde, *The Big Problem of Small Change* (Princeton 2002).

Schell, Orville and John Delury, *Wealth and Power. China's Long March to the Twenty-First Century* (New York 2013).

Schell, William Jr., 'Silver symbiosis: ReOrienting Mexican economic history'. *Hispanic American Historical Journal* 81, 1 (2001): 89–133.

Schluchter, Wolfgang (ed.), *Max Webers Studie über Konfuzianismus und Taoismus. Interpretation und Kritik* (Frankfurt am Main 1983).

Schlüter, André, *Institutions and Small Settler Economies: A Comparative Study of New Zealand and Uruguay 1870-2008* (New York: Palgrave Macmillan, forthcoming).

Schmidt, Peer, 'Tabacco - its use, and consumption in early modern Europe', in Simonetta Cavaciocchi (ed.), *Prodotti e techniche d'oltremare nelle economie Europee secc. XIII-XVIII* (Prato 1998), 591–616.

Schmitz, Christopher J., 'The changing structure of the world copper market, 1870-1939'. *Journal of European Economic History*, 26, 2 (1997): 295–330.

Schmoller, Gustav von, *The Mercantile System and Its Historical Significance* (New York 1967).

Schmoller, Gustav von and Wilhelm Naudé, *Die Getreidehandelspolitik und Kriegsmagazin-verwaltung Brandenburg-Preussens bis 1740* (Berlin 1901).

Schneider, Jürgen, 'Die neuen Getränke: Schokolade, Kaffee und Tee (16.-18.Jahrhundert)', in Simonetta Cavaciocchi (ed.), *Prodotti e techniche d'oltremare nelle economie Europee secc. XIII-XVIII* (Prato 1998), 541–90.

Schremmer, D. Eckart, 'Taxation and public finance: Britain, France and Germany', in Peter Mathias and Sidney Pollard (eds), *The Cambridge Economic History of Europe. Volume VIII. The Industrial Economies: The Development of Economic and Social Policies* (Cambridge 1969), 314–494.

Schurman, F. H., 'Traditional property concepts in China'. *Far Eastern Quarterly* 15 (1956): 507–16.

Schurz, William L., *The Manila Galleon. The Romantic History of the Spanish Galleons Trading between Manila and Acapulco* (New York 1939).

Schwartz, Herman M., *States versus Markets. The Emergence of a Global Economy,* second edition (Houndmills 2000).

Bibliography

Scott, Hamish, 'The fiscal-military state and international rivalry during the long eighteenth century', in Christopher Storrs (ed.), *The Fiscal-Military State in Eighteenth-Century Europe. Essays in Honour of P.G.M. Dickson* (Farnham, UK and Burlington, US 2009), 23–54.

Scott, James A., *Seeing like a State. How certain Schemes to Improve the Human Condition have Failed* (New Haven and London 1998).

Seabright, Paul, *The Company of Strangers. The Natural History of Economic Life* (Princeton 2010).

Selgin, George, *The Theory of Free Banking* (Lanham 1988).

—, 'The institutional roots of Great Britain's "Big problem of small change"'. *European Review of Economic History* 14, 2 (1 2010): 305–34.

Sen, Gautam, *The Military Origins of Industrialisation and International Trade Rivalry* (London 1984).

Shammas, Carole, *The pre-industrial consumer in England and America* (Oxford 1990).

—, 'The revolutionary impact of European demand for tropical goods', in John J. McCusker and Kenneth Morgan (eds), *The Early Modern Atlantic Economy* (Cambridge 2000), 163–86.

Shapin, Steven, 'The image of the man of science', in Roy Porter (ed.), *The Cambridge History of Science. Volume IV. Eighteenth-Century Science* (Cambridge 2003), 159–83.

Sheehan, James, 'What it means to be a state: states and violence in twentieth-century Europe'. *Journal of Modern European History* 1, 1 (2003): 11–23.

Sheils, William, 'Modernity, taxation and the clergy: the disappearance of clerical taxation in early modern England', in Simonetta Cavaciocchi (ed.), *La fiscalità nell'economia europea secc. XIII-XVIII = Fiscal Systems in the European Economy from the 13th to the 18th Centuries* (Florence 2008), 745–56.

Shepherd, John R., *Statecraft and Political Economy on the Taiwan Frontier, 1600-1800* (Stanford 1993).

—, 'Some demographic characteristics of Chinese immigrant populations. Lessons for the study of Taiwan's population history', in Gungwu Wang and Ng Chin-Keong (eds), *Maritime China in Transition 1750-1850* (Wiesbaden 2004), 115–38.

Shi, Qi and Fang Zhuofen, 'Agricultural change and the spread of cash crops', in Xu Dixin and Wu Chengmin (eds), *Chinese Capitalism, 1522-1840* (Houndmills, London and New York 2000), 113–29.

Shi Zhihong, Xuyi, Ni Yuping and Bas van Leeuwen, 'Chinese national income, ca. 1661-1933', http://www.basvanleeuwen.net/bestanden/ChineseGDP.pdf.

Shimada, Ryuto, *The Intra-Asian Trade in Japanese Copper by the Dutch East India Company during the Eighteenth Century* (Leiden 2005).

Shiue, Carol H. and Wolfgang Keller, 'Markets in China and Europe on the eve of the Industrial Revolution'. *American Economic Review* 97, 4 (2007): 1189–216.

Shovlin, John, 'War and peace: trade, international competition, and political economy', in Philip J. Stern and Carl Wennerlind (eds), *Mercantilism Reimagined. Political Economy in early Modern Britain and its Empire* (Oxford and New York 2013), 305–27.

Shue, Vivian, *The Reach of the State. Sketches of the Chinese Body Politic* (Stanford 1988).

Shulman, Anna, *Copper, Copper Cash and Government Controls in Ch'ing China, 1644-1795* (University of Maryland 1989).

Shupert, Adrian, *A Social History of Modern Spain* (London and New York 1990).

Sieferle, Rolf Peter, *The Subterranean Forest. Energy Systems and the Industrial Revolution* (Cambridge 2001).

Sieferle, Rolf Peter and Helga Breuninger (eds), *Agriculture, Population and Economic Development in China and Europe* (Stuttgart 2003).

Simon, Eugene, *Das Paradies der Arbeit. Ein Weg in eine deutsche Zukunft* (Munich 1920).

Sinor, Denis, 'Horse and pasture in Inner Asian history'. *Oriens Extremis* XIX 1/2 (1972): 171–83.

Smith, Adam, *An Inquiry into the Nature and Causes of the Wealth of Nations*, The Liberty Fund edition (Indianapolis 1981).

Smith, Richard J., *China's Cultural Heritage. The Qing Dynasty, 1644-1912,* second edition (Boulder 1994).

—, *Chinese Maps* (Oxford 1996).

Smith, S. D., 'Accounting for taste: British coffee consumption in historical perspective'. *Journal of Interdisciplinary History* 27 (1996): 183–214.

Sng, Tuan-Hwee, 'Size and dynastic decline. The principal-agent problem in late imperial China, 1700-1850', http://apebhconference.files.wordpress.com/2009/08/sng.pdf.

So, Billy, K. L., 'Institutions in market economies of premodern maritime China', in Billy K. L. So (ed.), *The Economy of Lower Yangzi Delta in late Imperial China. Connecting Money, Markets, and Institutions* (London 2012), 208–32.

—(ed.), *The Economy of Lower Yangzi Delta in late Imperial China. Connecting Money, Markets, and Institutions* (London 2012).

Sokoll, Thomas 'Armut und Familie im Zeitalter der Industrialisierung. England, 1700-1900', *Querschnitte: Einführungstexte zur Sozial- Wirtschafts und Kulturgeschichte* (2010), 57–81.

Soll, Jacob, *The Reckoning. Financial Accountability and the Breaking of Nations* (London 2014).

Solar, Peter M., 'Poor relief and English economic development before the Industrial Revolution'. *The Economic History Review* 48, 1 (1995): 1–22.

—, 'Poor relief and English economic development: a renewed plea for comparative history'. *Economic History Review,* 50 (1997): 369–74.

Solow, Barbara L. (ed.), *Slavery and the Rise of the Atlantic System* (Cambridge 1991).

Solow, Barbara L. and S. L. Engerman (eds), *British Capitalism and Caribbean Slavery: The Legacy of Eric Williams* (Cambridge 1987).

Sombart, Werner, *Krieg und Kapitalismus* (München 1913).

Song, Du-Yul, *Die Bedeutung der asiatischen Welt bei Hegel, Marx und Max Weber* (Frankfurt am Main 1972).

Sonnenscher, Michael, *Before the Deluge: Public Debt, Inequality, and the Intellectual Origins of the French Revolution* (Princeton 2007).

Spadafora, David, *The Idea of Progress in Eighteenth-Century Britain* (New Haven and London 1990).

Spence, Jonathan, *The Chan's Great Continent. China in Western Minds* (New York 1999).

Spierenburg, Pieter, *The Broken Spell: A Cultural and Anthropological History of Pre-Industrial Europe* (Rutgers University Press 1991).

Spoerer, Mark, *Steuerlast, Steuerinzidenz und Steuerwettbewerb: Verteilungswirkungen der Besteuerung in Preußen und Württemberg, 1815-1913* (Berlin 2004).

—, 'The revenue structures of Brandenburg-Prussia, Saxony and Bavaria (fifteenth to nineteenth centuries). Are they compatible with the Bonney-Ormrod model?', in Simonetta Cavaciocchi (ed.), *La fiscalità nell'economia europea secc. XIII-XVIII = Fiscal Systems in the European Economy from the 13th to the 18th Centuries* (Florence 2008), 781–92.

—, 'The evolution of public finance in nineteenth-century Germany', in José Luís Cardoso and Pedro Lains (eds), *Paying for the Liberal State. The Rise of Public Finance in Nineteenth-Century Europe* (Cambridge 2010), 103–31.

Spooner, Frank C., *The International Economy and Monetary Movements in France, 1493-1725* (Cambridge, MA 1972).

Stanislaw, Joseph and Daniel Yergin, *The Commanding Heights. The Battle for the World Economy* (New York 2002).

Stanley, C. John, *Late Ch'ing Finance: Hu Kuang-Yung as an Innovator* (Cambridge, MA 1961).

Stanziani, Alessandro, 'The legal status of labour from the seventeenth to the nineteenth century: Russia in a comparative European perspective'. *International Review of Social History* 54, 3 (2009): 359–89.

Stasavage, David, *Public Debt and the Birth of the Democratic State. France and Great Britain, 1688-1789* (Cambridge and New York 2003).

Bibliography

—, *States of Credit. Size, Power and the Development of European Polities* (Princeton and Oxford 2011).

Steedman, Carolyn, *Labours Lost. Domestic Service and the Making of Modern England* (Cambridge 2009).

Steensgaard, Niels, 'Asia', in Simonetta Cavaciocchi (ed.), *Prodotti e techniche d'oltremare nelle economie Europee secc. XIII-XVIII* (Prato 1998), 81–7.

—, 'Comment', in Simonetta Cavaciocchi (ed.), *Prodotti e techniche d'oltremare nelle economie Europee secc. XIII-XVIII* (Prato 1998), 717.

Steinfeld, Robert J., *The Invention of Free Labour. The Employment Relation in English and American Law* (Chapel Hill 1991).

—, *Coercion, Contract and Free Labour in the Nineteenth Century* (Cambridge 2001).

Stern, Philip J., '"Auspicio Regis et Senatus Angliae". The political foundations of the East India Company's incorporation into the British fiscal-military state', in Torres Sánchez (ed.), *War, State and Development. Fiscal-Military States in the Eighteenth Century* (Pamplona 2007), 385–408.

Stern, Philip J. and Carl Wennerlind, 'Introduction', in Philip J. Stern and Carl Wennerlind (eds), *Mercantilism Reimagined. Political Economy in early Modern Britain and its Empire* (Oxford and New York 2013), 3–22.

—(eds), *Mercantilism Reimagined. Political Economy in early Modern Britain and its Empire* (Oxford and New York 2013).

Steuart, Sir James, *An Inquiry into the Principles of Political Economy. Two Volumes* (London 1767; edited and introduced by A. S. Skinner; London 1966).

Stier, Bernard and Wolfgang von Hippel, 'War, economy and society', in Sheilagh Ogilvie (ed.), *Germany. A New Social and Economic History. Volume II* (London 1996), 233–62.

Stone, Lawrence, 'Introduction', in Lawrence Stone (ed.), *An Imperial State at War* (London 1994), 1–31.

—(ed.), *An Imperial State at War* (London 1994).

Storrs, Christopher (ed.), *The Fiscal-Military State in Eighteenth-Century Europe. Essays in Honour of P.G.M. Dickson* (Farnham, UK and Burlington, US 2009).

Struve, Lynn A. (ed.), *The Qing Formation in World-Historical Time* (Cambridge, MA and London 2004).

Studwell, Joe, *How Asia Works. Success and Failure in the World's most Dynamic Region* (London 2013).

Sudipta, Sen, 'The new frontiers of Manchu China and the historiography of Asian empire. A review essay'. *Journal of Asian Studies* 61 (2002): 165–77.

Sugihara, Kaoru, 'The resurgence of intra-Asian trade', in Giorgio Riello and Tirthankar Roy (ed.), *How India Clothed the World. The World of South Asian Textiles, 1500-1850* (Leiden and Boston 2009), 139–72.

Sun, E-tu Zen, 'Mining labour in the Ch'ing period', in A. Feuerwerker, R. Murphey and M. C. Wright (eds), *Approaches to Modern Chinese History* (Berkeley 1967), 45–67.

—, 'Ch'ing government and the mineral industries before 1800'. *The Journal of Asian Studies* 27, 4 (1968): 835–45.

—, 'The finance ministry (Hubu) and its relationship to the private economy in Qing times', in Leonard and Watt (eds), *To Achieve Security and Wealth. The Qing Imperial State and the Economy, 1644-1911* (Ithaca, NY 1992), 9–20.

Sussman, N. and Y. Yafeh, 'Institutional reforms, financial development and sovereign debt: Britain 1690-1790'. *The Journal of Economic History* 66 (2006): 906–35.

Swart, K. W., *Sale of Offices in the 17th Century* (Utrecht 1980).

Swedberg, Richard (ed.), *The Economics and Sociology of Capitalism* (Princeton 1991).

Swingen, Abigail, 'Labor: employment, colonial servitude, and slavery in the seventeenth-century Atlantic', in Philip J. Stern and Carl Wennerlind (eds), *Mercantilism Reimagined. Political Economy in early Modern Britain and its Empire* (Oxford and New York 2013), 46–73.

Taagepera, R., 'Size and duration of empires: systematics of size'. *Social Science Research* 7 (1978): 180–96.

Tallett, Frank, *War and Society in early Modern Europe 1495-1715* (London 1992).

Talmon, J. L., *The Origins of Totalitarian Democracy* (London 1952).

Teltscher, Kate, *The High Road to China. George Bogle, the Panchen Lama and the first British Expedition to Tibet* (London 2006).

Teng, Emma J., *Taiwan's Imagined Geography: Chinese Colonial Travel Writing and Pictures, 1683-1895* (Cambridge, MA 2004).

Teng, Ssu-yü and John K. Fairbank (eds), *China's Response to the West. A Documentary Survey, 1839-1923* (New York 1966).

Terjanian, Anoush Fraser, *Commerce and Its Discontents in Eighteenth-Century French Political Thought* (Cambridge 2013).

Thier, A., 'Steuergesetzgebeung und Staatsfinanzen in Preussen 1871-1893', in G. Lingelbach (ed.), a.o, *Staatsfinanzen, Staatsverschuldung, Staatsbankrotte in der europäische Staaten- und Rechtsgeschichte* (Cologne 2002), 311–33.

Thomas, R. P. and D. N. McCloskey, 'Overseas trade and empire, 1700-1860', in Roderick Floud and Deirdre McCloskey (eds), *The Economic History of Britain since 1700. Volume 1, 1700-1860,* second edition (Cambridge 1994), 87–100.

Thompson, E. P., 'Time, work-discipline and industrial capitalism'. *Past and Present* 38 (1967): 56–97.

—, *The Making of the English Working Class,* revised edition (Harmondsworth 1968).

—, 'The moral economy of the British crowd in the eighteenth century'. *Past and Present* 50 (1971): 76–136.

Thompson, William R., 'The military superiority thesis and the ascendancy of Western Eurasia in the world system'. *Journal of World History* 10 (1999): 143–78.

Thomson, Janice E., *Mercenaries, Pirates & Sovereigns. State-Building and Extraterritorial Violence in early Modern Europe* (Princeton 1994).

Thornton, Patricia M., *Disciplining the State. Violence and State-Making in Modern China* (Cambridge, MA 2007).

Tilly, Charles, 'Demographic origins of the European proletariat', in David Levine (ed.), *Proletarianization and Family History* (London 1984), 26–52.

—, *Coercion, Capital, and European States, AD 990-1990* (Cambridge, MA and Oxford 1990).

Tilly, Charles and W. P. Blockmans (eds), *Cities & the Rise of States in Europe, A.D. 1000 to 1800* (Boulder 1994).

Tocqueville, Alexis de, *L'Ancien Régime et la Révolution,* fourth edition (Paris 1859).

Torbert, Preston M., *The Ch'ing Imperial Household Department. A Study of Its Organization and Principal Functions, 1662-1796* (Cambridge, MA 1977).

Torr, Dona (ed.), *Marx on China, 1853-1860* (New York 1968).

Torres Sánchez, Rafael, 'The triumph of the fiscal-military state in the eighteenth century. War and mercantilism', in Torres Sánchez (ed.), *War, State and Development. Fiscal-Military States in the Eighteenth Century* (Pamplona 2007), 13–44.

—(ed.), *War, State and Development. Fiscal-Military States in the Eighteenth Century* (Pamplona 2007).

Tortella, Gabriel, *El desarollo de la Espana contemporanea. Historia económica de los siglos XIX y XX* (Madrid 1994)

Tortella, Gabriel and Francisco Comín, 'Fiscal and monetary institutions in Spain, 1600-1900', in Michael D. Bordo and Roberto Cortés-Conde (eds), *Transferring Wealth and Power from the Old to the New World: Monetary and Fiscal Institutions in the 17th through the 19th Centuries* (Cambridge 2001), 140–86.

Toynbee, Arnold, *Toynbee's Industrial Revolution. A Reprint of Lectures on the Industrial Revolution* (New York and Newton Abbot 1969) with a new introduction by the late T. S. Ashton.

Bibliography

Tracy, James D., *A Financial Revolution in the Habsburg Netherlands: 'renten' and 'renteniers' in the County of Holland, 1515-1565* (Berkeley, Los Angeles and London 1985).

—(ed.), *The Rise of Merchant Empires. Long-Distance Trade in the early Modern World 1350-1750* (Cambridge 1990).

—(ed.), *The Political Economy of Merchant Empires. State Power and World Trade, 1350-1750* (Cambridge 1991).

Trentmann, Frank, *Free Trade Nation. Commerce, Consumption and Civil Society in Modern Britain* (New York 2008).

Tribe, Keith, 'Cameralism and the science of government'. *Journal of Modern History* 56 (1984): 263–84.

—, *Strategies of Economic Order. German Economic Discourse, 1750-1950* (Cambridge 1995).

Trocki, Carl A., *Opium, Empire and the Global Political Economy. A Study of the Asian Opium Trade, 1750-1950* (London and New York 1999).

Turchin, Peter, 'A theory for formation of large empires'. *Journal of Global History*, 4, 2 (2009): 191–217.

Tvedt, Terje, 'Why England and not China and India? Water systems and the history of the Industrial Revolution'. *Journal of Global History* 5 (2010): 29–50.

Ullmann, Hans-Peter, *Der deutsche Steuerstaat. Geschichte der öffentlichen Finanzen* (Munich 2005).

Umeno, Yuki, 'Han Chinese immigrants in Manchuria, 1850-1931', in Jan Lucassen and Leo Lucassen (eds), *Globalising Migration History. The Eurasian Experience (16th-21st Centuries)* (Leiden 2014), 307–34.

Van Cauwenberghe, Eddy. (ed.), *Money, Coins, and Commerce: Essays in Monetary History of Asia and Europe (From Antiquity to Modern Times)* (Leuven 1991), 95–118.

Van Creveld, Martin J. R., *Supplying War. Military Logistics from Wallenstein to Patton* (Cambridge 1977).

Van der Linden, Marcel and Karl Heinz Roth (eds), with help of Max Henniger, *Über Marx hinaus. Arbeitsgeschichte und Arbeitsbegriff in der Konfrontation mit den globalen Arbeitsverhältnissen des 21. Jahrhunderts* (Berlin and Hamburg 2009).

Van der Sprenkel, O. B., 'Max Weber on China'. *History and Theory* 8 (1964): 348–70.

Van der Ven, Hans J., 'War in the making of modern China'. *Modern Asian Studies* 30 (1996): 737–56.

—, 'The onrush of modern globalization in China', in A. G. Hopkins (ed.), *Globalization in World History* (London 2002), 167–93.

—, 'Military mobilization in China, 1840-1949', in Jeremy Black (ed.), *War in the Modern World since 1815* (London 2003), 20–40.

—(ed.), *Warfare in Chinese History* (Leiden 2002).

Van Deursen, A. Th., 'Staat van oorlog en generale petitie in de jonge Republiek'. *Bijdragen en Mededelingen betreffende de Geschiedenis der Nederlanden* 91 (1976): 44–55.

Van Dyke, Paul A., *The Canton Trade. Life and Enterprise on the Chinese Coast, 1700-1845* (Hong Kong 2005).

—, *Merchants of Canton and Macao. Politics and Strategies in Eighteenth-Century Chinese Trade* (Hong Kong 2011).

Van Lottum, Jelle, *Across the North Sea. The Impact of the Dutch Republic on International Labour Migration, c. 1550-1850* (Amsterdam 2007).

Van Rooden, Peter, 'Kerk en religie in het confessionele tijdperk', in Willem Frijhoff and Leo Wessels (eds), *Veelvormige dynamiek. Europa in het ancien régime 1450-1800* (Amsterdam and Heerlen 2006), 373–402, (Church and religion in the confessional age' in *Multiple dynamics. Europe during the ancien regime, 1450-1800*).

Van Slyke, Lynman P., *Yangtze. Nature, History and the River* (Reading, MA 1988).

Van Zanden, Jan Luiten, *The Rise and Decline of Holland's Economy. Merchant Capitalism and the Labour Market* (Manchester 1993).

—, 'The road to the Industrial Revolution: hypotheses and conjectures about the medieval origins of the European Miracle'. *Journal of Global History* 3, 3 (2008): 327–59.

—, *The Long Road to the Industrial Revolution. The European Economy in a Global Perspective* (Leiden 2009).

Van Zanden, Jan Luiten and Bozhong Li, 'Before the Great Divergence? Comparing the Yangzi Delta and the Netherlands at the beginning of the nineteenth century'. *The Journal of Economic History*, 72, 4 (2012): 956–89.

Van Zanden, Jan Luiten and Maarten Prak, 'Towards an economic interpretation of citizenship: the Dutch Republic between medieval communes and modern nation-states'. *European Review of Economic History* 10 (2006): 111–45.

Van Zanden, Jan Luiten and Arthur van Riel, *The Strictures of Inheritance. The Dutch Economy in the Nineteenth Century* (Princeton 2004).

—, 'The development of public finance in the Netherlands, 1815-1914', in José Luís Cardoso and Pedro Lains (eds), *Paying for the Liberal State. The Rise of Public Finance in Nineteenth-Century Europe* (Cambridge 2010), 57–80.

Veenendaal, Augustus J. Jr., 'Fiscal crises and constitutional freedom in the Netherlands, 1450-1795', in Philip T. Hoffman and Kathryn Norberg (eds), *Fiscal Crises, Liberty and Representative Government, 1450-1789* (Stanford 1994), 96–139.

Velkar, Aashish, *Markets and Measurement in Nineteenth-Century Britain* (Cambridge 2012).

Verley, Patrick, *L'échelle du monde: essai sur l'industrialisation de l'Occident* (Paris 1997).

Vierhaus, Rudolf, 'The Prussian bureaucracy reconsidered', in John Brewer and Eckhart Hellmuth (eds), *Rethinking Leviathan. The Eighteenth-Century State in Britain and Germany* (Oxford 1999), 149–66.

Viner, Jacob, 'Power versus plenty as objectives of foreign policy in the seventeenth and eighteenth centuries'. *World Politics* 1 (1948): 1–29.

Vogel, Hans Ulrich, 'Chinese central monetary policy, 1644-1800'. *Late Imperial China* 8, 2 (1987): 1–51.

Von Greyerz, Kaspar, 'Confession as a social and economic factor', in Sheilagh Ogilvie (ed.), *Germany. A New Social and Economic History. Volume II* (London 1996), 309–50.

Von Glahn, Richard, *Fountain of Fortune. Money and Monetary Policy in China, 1000-1700* (Berkeley, Los Angeles and London 1996).

—, 'Money use in China and changing patterns of global trade in monetary metals, 1500-1800', in Dennis O. Flynn, Arturo Giráldez and Richard von Glahn (eds), *Global Connections and Monetary History, 1470-1800* (Aldershot and Burlington 2003), 187–205.

—, 'Foreign silver coins and market culture in nineteenth-century China'. *The International Journal of Asian Studies* 4 (2007): 51–78.

—, 'Cycles of silver in Chinese monetary history', in Billy K. L. So (ed.), *Economy of Lower Yangzi Delta in late Imperial China. Connecting Money, Markets, and Institutions* (London 2012), 17–71.

Von Tunzelmann, G. N., *Steam Power and British Industrialization to 1860* (Oxford 1978).

Voth, Hans-Joachim, 'Living standards and urban environment', in Roderick Floud and Paul Johnson (eds), *The Cambridge Economic History of Modern Britain, Volume I, Industrialisation, 1700-1860* (Cambridge 2004), 268–94.

—, *Time and work in England, 1750-1830* (Oxford 2001).

Vries, Peer, 'Culture, clocks, and comparative costs. David Landes on the wealth of the West and the poverty of the rest'. *Itinerario. European Journal of Overseas History* 22, 4 (1998): 67–89.

—, 'Are coal and colonies really crucial? Kenneth Pomeranz and the Great Divergence'. *Journal of World History* 12 (2001): 407–46.

—, 'Governing growth. A comparative analysis of the role of the state in the rise of the West'. *Journal of World History* 13, 1 (2002): 67–138.

—, *Via Peking back to Manchester. Britain, the Industrial Revolution, and China* (Leiden 2003).

—, *Zur politischen Ökonomie des Tees. Was uns Tee über die englische und chinesische Wirtschaft der Frühen Neuzeit sagen kann* (Vienna, Cologne, Weimar 2009).

—, 'Does wealth entirely depend on inclusive institutions and pluralist politics? A review of Daron Acemoglu and James A. Robinson, *Why Nations Fail. The Origins of Power, Prosperity and Poverty'. Tijdschrift voor Sociale en Economische Geschiedenis* 9, 3 (2012): 74–93. The text has also been published on the Internet http://technologygovernance.eu/eng/the_core_faculty/working_papers/

—, *Escaping Poverty. The Origins of Modern Economic Growth* (Göttingen and Vienna 2013).

Wade, Robert, *Governing the Market. Economic Theory and the Role of Government in East Asian Industrialization* (second paperback edition with a new introduction by the author; Princeton 2004).

Wade, T. F., 'The army of the Chinese empire'. *The Chinese Repository* 20, no 5, 6, 7 (1851): 250–80, 300–40, 363–422.

Wagner, Wilhelm, *Die chinesische Landwirtschaft* (Berlin 1926).

Wakefield, Andre, *The Disordered Police State: German Cameralism as Science and Practice* (Chicago 2009).

—, 'Cameralism: a German alternative to mercantilism', in Philip J. Stern and Carl Wennerlind (eds), *Mercantilism Reimagined. Political Economy in early Modern Britain and its Empire* (Oxford and New York 2013), 134–50.

Wakefield, D., *Fenjia. Household Division and Inheritance in Qing and Republican China* (Honolulu 1998).

Wakeman, Frederic Jr., *Strangers at the Gate. Social Disorder in South China, 1839-1861* (Berkeley and Los Angeles 1966).

—, *The Great Enterprise. The Manchu Reconstruction of Imperial Order in Seventeenth-Century China* (Berkeley, Los Angeles and London 1985).

—, 'Voyages'. *The American Historical Review* 98, 1 (1993): 1–17.

Waley-Cohen, Joanna, 'China and western technology in the late eighteenth century'. *American Historical Review* 98 (1993): 1525–44.

—, *The Sextants of Beijing. Global Currents in Chinese History* (New York 1999).

—, *The Culture of War in China. Empire and the Military under the Qing Dynasty* (London 2006).

Wallerstein, Immanuel, *The Modern World-System I. Capitalist Agriculture and the Origins of the European World-Economy in the Sixteenth Century* (New York 1974).

—, *The Modern World-System II. Mercantilism and the Consolidation of the European World-Economy 1600-1750* (New York 1980).

—, *The Modern World-System III. The Second Era of Great Expansion of the Capitalist World-Economy, 1730-1840s* (San Diego 1989).

—, *The Modern World-System IV. Centrist Liberalism Triumphant*, 1789-1914 (Berkeley, Los Angeles, London 2011).

Walvin, James, 'Freedom and slavery and the shaping of Victorian Britain'. *Abolition and Slavery* 15, 2 (1994): 246–59.

Wang, Gungwu, 'Merchants without empire. The Hokkien sojourning communities', in James D. Tracy (ed.), *The Rise of Merchant Empires. Long-Distance Trade in the early Modern World 1350-1750* (Cambridge 1990), 400–22.

—, *Anglo-Chinese Encounters since 1800. War, Trade, Science and Governance* (Cambridge 2003).

Wang, Gungwu and Ng Chin-keong (eds), *Maritime China in Transition 1750-1850* (Wiesbaden 2004).

Wang, Wensheng, *White Lotus Rebels and South China Pirates. Crisis and Reform in the Qing Empre* (Cambridge, MA and London 2004).

Wang, Yeh-chien, *Land Taxation in Imperial China, 1750-1911* (Cambridge, MA 1973).

—, 'Evolution of the Chinese monetary system, 1644-1850', in Chi-ming Hou and Tzong-shian Yu (eds), *Modern Chinese Economic History* (Taipei 1979), 425–52.

—, 'Secular trends of rice prices in the Yangzi delta, 1638-1935', in Thomas G. Rawski and Lillian M. Li (eds), *Chinese History in Economic Perspective* (Berkeley, Los Angeles and Oxford 1992), 35–68.

Ward, W. R., *The English Land Tax in the 18th Century* (London 1957).

Warde, Paul, *Energy Consumption in England and Wales, 1560-2000* (Consiglio Nazionale delle Richerche 2007).

Washbrook, David, 'India in the early modern world economy: modes of production, reproduction and exchange'. *Journal of Global History* 2 (2007): 87–112.

Wawro, Geoffrey, *Warfare and Society in Europe, 1792-1914* (London 2000).

Way, Peter, 'Klassenkrieg: die ursprüngliche Akkumulation, die Militärische Revolution und der britische Kriegsarbeiter'. in Marcel Van der Linden and Karl Heinz Roth (eds), *Über Marx hinaus. Arbeitsgeschichte und Arbeitsbegriff in der Konfrontation mit den globalen Arbeitsverhältnissen des 21. Jahrhunderts* (Berlin and Hamburg 2009), 85–114.

Weber, Max, *The Religion of China* (New York and London 1951). This book is translated from the German and edited by Hans H. Gerth, with an introduction by C. K. Yang. The original text was written in 1920.

—, *Wirtschaftsgeschichte. Abriss der universalen Sozial- und Wirtschaftsgeschichte.* Third revised and expanded edition, edited by J. F. Winckelmann (Berlin 1958). The book is translated into English as *General Economic History*.

—, *Wirtschaft und Gesellschaft. Grundriss der verstehende Soziologie*, fifth, revised edition, edited by Johannes Winckelmann (Tübingen 1976). The book is translated into English as *Economy and society* (Berkeley 1978).

Webster, Anthony, *The Twilight of the East India Company. The Evolution of Anglo-Asian Commerce and Politics 1790-1860* (London 2008).

Weiss, Linda and John M. Hobson, *States and Economic Development. A Comparative Historical Analysis* (Oxford and Cambridge 1995).

Weisser, Michael, *Crime and Punishment in early Modern Europe* (Hassocks 1979).

Weitzel, O., *Die Entwicklung der Staatsausgaben in Deutschland* (Nürnberg 1967).

Wells, Rodger, *Wretched faces: Famine in wartime England 1763-1803* (Sutton 1988; new edition 2011).

Wennerlind, Carl, *Casualties of Credit. The English Financial Revolution, 1620-1720* (Cambridge, MA 2011).

Westad, Odd Arne, *Restless Empire. China and the World since 1750* (London 2012).

Whatley, C. A. and D. J. Patrick, *The Scots and the Union* (Edinburgh 2006).

Wheeler, James Scott, *The Making of a World Power. War and the Military Revolution in Seventeenth-Century England* (Stroud, UK 1999).

White, Eugene N., 'France and the failure to modernize macroeconomic institutions', in Michael D. Bordo and Roberto Cortés-Conde (eds), *Transferring Wealth and Power from the Old to the New World: Monetary and Fiscal Institutions in the 17th through the 19th Centuries* (Cambridge 2001), 59–99.

—, 'Making the French pay'. *European Review of Economic History* 5, 3 (2001): 337–65.

Wiles, R. C., 'The theory of wages in later English mercantilism'. *Economic History Review* 21 (1968): 113–26.

Will, Pierre-Étienne, *Bureaucratie et famine en Chine au 18e siècle* (Paris 1980). This book has been translated into English, substantially revised, and then published as *Bureaucracy and Famine in Eighteenth-Century China* (Stanford 1990).

—, 'Bureaucratie officielle et bureaucratie réelle: sur quelques dilemmes de l'administration impériale à l'époque des Qing'. *Études Chinoises* VIII, 1 (1989): 69–142.

—, 'Chine moderne et Sinologie'. *Annales. Histoire, Sciences Sociales* 49 (1994): 7–26.

Bibliography

—, 'Développement quantitatif et développement qualitatif en Chine à la fin de l'époque impériale'. *Annales. Histoire, Sciences Sociales* 49 (1994): 863–902.

Will, Pierre-Étienne and Roy Bin Wong, with James Lee, *Nourish the People. The State Civilian Granary System in China, 1650-1850* (Ann Arbor 1990).

Williams, Eric, *Capitalism and Slavery* (Chapel Hill 1944).

Williamson, Jeffrey G., *Did British Capitalism Breed Inequality?* (London 1985).

Wills, John E., 'Maritime Asia, 1500-1800: The interactive emergence of European domination'. *American Historical Review* 98 (1993): 83–105.

Wilson, Peter H., 'Prussia as a fiscal-military state, 1640-1806', in Christopher Storrs (ed.), *Fiscal-Military State in Eighteenth-Century Europe. Essays in Honour of P.G.M. Dickson* (Farnham, UK and Burlington, US 2009), 95–124.

Winch, Donald, 'Introduction', in Donald Winch and Patrick K. O'Brien (eds), *The Political Economy of British Historical Experience, 1688-1914* (Oxford 2002), 1–28.

Winch, Donald and Patrick K. O'Brien (eds), *The Political Economy of British Historical Experience, 1688-1914* (Oxford 2002).

Winchester, Simon, *Bomb, Book & Compass. Joseph Needham and the Great Secrets of China* (London 2008). This book was first published as *The Man Who Loved China* (New York 2008).

Winkelbauer, Thomas, 'Territoriale, soziale und nationale Aspekte der Staatsfinanzen der Habsburgermonarchie (vom 16. Jahrhundert bis 1918)', in Jaroslava Panka (ed.), *Per saecula ad tempora nostra* (Prague 2007), 181–94.

Winter, J. M., 'The economic and social history of war', in J. M. Winter (ed.), *War and Economic Development. Essays in the Memory of David Joslin* (Cambridge 1975), 1–10.

—(ed.), *War and Economic Development. Essays in the Memory of David Joslin* (Cambridge 1975).

Wittfogel, Karl, *Wirtschaft und Gesellschaft Chinas. Versuch der wissenschaftlichen Analyse einer großen asiatischen Agrarwirtschaft. Erster Teil. Produktivkräfte, Produktions- und Zirkulationsprozess* (Leipzig 1931).

—, *Oriental Despotism: A Comparative Study of Total Power* (New Haven 1957).

Wolf, Arthur P., 'Europe and China: Two kinds of patriarchy', in Theo Engelen and Arthur P. Wolf (eds), *Marriage and the Family in Eurasia. Perspectives on the Hajnal Hypothesis* (Amsterdam 2005), 215–40.

Wolf, Arthur and Theo Engelen, 'Fertility and fertility control in pre-revolutionary China'. *Journal of Interdisciplinary History* 38, 3 (2008): 345–75.

Wong, J. Y., *Deadly Dreams. Opium and the Arrow War (1856-1860) in China* (Cambridge 1998).

Wong, Roy Bin, 'Qing granaries and world history', in Pierre-Étienne Will and Roy Bin Wong, with James Lee (eds), *Nourish the People. The State Civilian Granary System in China, 1650-1850* (Ann Arbor 1990), 507–25.

—, *China Transformed. Historical Change and the Limits of European Experience* (Ithaca and London 1997).

—, 'The political economy of agrarian empires and its modern legacies', in Timothy Brook and Gregory Blue (eds), *China and Historical Capitalism. Genealogies of Sinological Knowledge* (Cambridge 1999), 210–45.

—, 'The search for European differences and domination in the early modern world: a view from Asia'. *The American Historical Review* 107 (2002): 447–69.

—, 'Relationships between the political economies of maritime and agrarian China', in Gungwu Wang and Ng Chin-Keong (eds), *Maritime China in Transition 1750-1850* (Wiesbaden 2004), 19–32.

—, 'The role of the Chinese state in long-distance commerce'. Global Economic History Network Working Paper 2005/04. http://www.lse.ac.uk/collections/economicHistory/GEHN/GEHNPDF/WorkingPaper05RBW.pdf.

—, 'The changing fiscal regime of Qing dynasty China'. Paper presented at the conference Toward the twentieth century in Asia: Comparative perspectives on politics, economy and society in China and India. 19-22 May 2005, Durham, Duke University. Unpublished.

—, 'Les politiques de dépenses sociales avant ou sans démocratie'. *Annales. Histoire, Sciences Sociales* 62, 6 (2007): 1405–16.

—, 'Taxation and good governance in China, 1500-1914', in Bartolomé Yun-Casalilla and Patrick K. O'Brien (eds), *The Rise of Fiscal States. A Global History, 1500-1914* (Cambridge 2012), 353–77.

Woo-Cumings, Meredith (ed.), *The Developmental State* (Ithaca and London 1999).

Wood, Frances, *The Silk Road. Two Thousand Years in the Hearth of Asia* (London 2002).

Woodside, Alexander, 'The Ch'ien-lung reign', in Willard J. Peterson (ed.), *The Cambridge History of China. Volume 9. Part One. The Ch'ing Dynasty to 1800* (Cambridge 2002), 230–309.

—, *Lost Modernities. China, Vietnam, Korea, and the Hazards of World History* (Cambridge, MA 2006).

Woodward, G. W. O., *The Dissolution of the Monasteries* (London 1966).

Wright, Robert, *Nonzero. The Logic of Human Destiny* (New York 2000).

Wrigley, E. A., *People, Cities and Wealth. The Transformation of Traditional Society* (Oxford and New York 1987).

—, *Continuity, Chance & Change. The Character of the Industrial Revolution in England* (Cambridge 1988).

—, 'Society and the economy in the eighteenth century', in Lawrence Stone (ed.), *An Imperial State at War* (London 1994), 72–95.

—, *Poverty, Progress and Population* (Cambridge 2004).

—, 'The divergence of England: the growth of the English economy in the seventeenth and eighteenth centuries', in E. A. Wrigley (ed.), *Poverty, Progress and Population* (Cambridge 2004), 44–67.

—, "'The great commerce of every civilized society': urban growth in early modern Europe', in E. A. Wrigley (ed.), *Poverty, Progress and Population* (Cambridge 2004), 268–89.

—, 'British population during the "long" eighteenth century, 1680-1840', in Roderick Floud and Paul Johnson (eds), *The Cambridge Economic History of Modern Britain, Volume I, Industrialisation, 1700-1860* (Cambridge 2004), 57–95.

Wrigley, E. A., R. S. Davies, J. E. Oeppen and R. S. Schofield, *English Population History from Family Reconstitution, 1580-1837* (Cambridge 1997).

Xu Dixin and Wu Chengmin (eds), *Chinese Capitalism, 1522-1840* (Houndmills, London and New York 2000).

Xue Yong, 'A "fertiliser revolution"? A critical response to Pomeranz's theory of "geographic luck"'. *Modern China* 33 (2007): 195–229.

Yang, Anand A., 'Indian convict workers in Southeast Asia in the late-eighteenth and early-nineteenth centuries'. *Journal of World History* 14, 2 (2003): 179–208.

Yang, C. K., 'Some characteristics of Chinese bureaucratic behaviour', in David S. Nivison and Arthur F. Wright (eds), *Confucianism in Action* (Stanford 1959), 134–65.

Yang, Lien-sheng, *Money and credit in China. A Short History* (Cambridge, MA 1952).

—, 'Economic justification for spending. An uncommon idea in traditional China'. *Harvard Journal of Asiatic Studies* 20 (1957): 36–52.

Youings, Joyce, 'The Church', in Joan Thirsk (ed.), *The Agrarian History of England and Wales, IV, 1500-1640* (Cambridge 1967), 306–55.

—, *The Dissolution of the Monasteries* (London and New York 1971).

Young, Arthur, *Political Essays Concerning the Present State of the British Empire* (London 1772).

Yun-Casalilla, Bartolomé and Patrick K. O'Brien (eds), with Francisco Comín, *The Rise of Fiscal States. A Global History, 1500-1914* (Cambridge 2012).

Bibliography

Yuping, Ni, 'Steady customs in the Daoguang Depression'. *Essays in Economic and Business History* XXXI (2013): 78–91.

Zelin, Madeleine, *The Magistrate's Tael. Rationalising Fiscal Reform in Eighteenth-Century Ch'ing China* (Berkeley 1984).

—, 'Modernization and the structure of the Chinese economy', in Frederic Wakeman Jr. and Wang Xi (eds), *China's Quest for Modernization. A Historical Perspective* (Berkeley 1997), 87–127.

—, 'The Yung-cheng reign', in Willard J. Peterson (ed.), *The Cambridge History of China. Volume 9. Part One. The Ch'ing Dynasty to 1800* (Cambridge 2002), 183–229.

Zelin, Madeleine, Jonathan K. Ocko and Robert Gardella (eds), *Contract and Property in Early Modern China* (Stanford 2004).

Zerubavel, Eviatar, 'The standardization of time: a socio-historical perspective'. *The American Journal of Sociology* 88, 1(1982): 1–23.

Zhao, Suisheng, *A Nation State by Construction. Dynamics of Modern Chinese Nationalism* (Stanford 2004).

Zheng, Yangwen, *The Social Life of Opium in China* (Cambridge 2005).

Zhuang, Guotu, *Tea, Silver, Opium and War. The International Tea Trade and Western Commercial Expansion into China in 1740-1840* (Xiamen 1993).

Zürcher, Erik-Jan (ed.), *Fighting for a Living. A Comparative History of Military Labour 1500-2000* (Amsterdam 2014).

Zupko, Ronald E., *Revolution in Measurement: Western European Weights and Measurements since the Age of Science* (Philadelphia 1990).

Zurndorfer, Harriet T., 'La sinologie immobile'. *Études Chinoises* VIII, 2 (1989): 99–120.

—, 'Imperialism, globalization and public finance: the case of late Qing China'. Working Papers of the Global Economic History Network (GEHN), 06/04 (2004). Department of Economic History, London School of Economics and Political Science, London.

INDEX OF PERSONS

Index of Persons

Dickson, P. G. M.   58, 58n. 272, 101, 101n. 143
Dincecco, Mark   44, 72, 222, 226, 226n. 41
Dorn, Walter L.   424, 424n. 55
Dundas, Henry   345, 345n. 109

Easterly, William   267
Elliott, John   96, 192, 192n. 43, 192n. 44, 345, 345n. 103
Eltis, David   390, 390n. 30
Elvin, Mark   17, 17n. 78, 150, 150n. 360, 150n. 361, 191, 191n. 39, 316, 316n. 93, 402, 402n. 76
Engels, Friedrich   14, 15, 15n. 63, 15n. 64, 57, 330, 330n. 21
Epstein, Stephan   222, 222n. 19, 222n. 20
Ertman, Thomas   146, 146n. 342
Esherick, Joseph   163, 163n. 417
Etemad, Bouda   384, 384n. 7, 387, 387n. 18, 387n. 21

Fang, Xing   174, 174n. 481, 252, 252n. 148
Fei, Xiaotong   159, 159n. 401
Feinstein, Charles H.   106
Ferguson, Niall   22, 45, 183, 183n. 14, 215, 215n. 150, 223, 223n. 22
Findlay, Ronald   19, 19n. 86, 19n. 87, 21, 21n. 100, 21n. 101, 65, 312
Fischer, David Hackett   57
Fisher, Michael H.   338
Fletcher, Joseph   398, 398n. 65
Flynn, Dennis O.   365, 367
Fortune, Robert   171, 171n. 465, 354
Foucault, Michel   417, 417n. 27, 422, 422n. 44
Frank, Andre Gunder   1, 35, 103, 365 et seq., 370
Fukuyama, Francis   318, 318n. 105
Furber, Holden   387

Gat, Azar   276, 276n. 45
Gates, Hill   17, 17n. 76
Gellner, Ernest   416, 416n. 25
Gernet, Jacques   172, 172n. 474
Gerschenkron, Alexander   35, 412
Giráldez, Arturo   365, 367
Goldstone, Jack A.   1, 22, 26, 26n. 133, 100, 100n. 135, 296, 296n. 4
Gorski, Philip S.   226, 226n. 40, 228, 228n. 50
Goubert, Pierre   250
Greenfeld, Liah   413, 413n. 19, 413n. 20

Hacking, Ian   147, 147n. 350
Hall, John A.   56, 56n. 261
Hall, Thomas   366, 366n. 199
Hanson, Victor Davis   303, 303n. 36
Hao, Yen-p'ing   236, 236n. 81, 357, 357n. 155
Harling, Philip   73, 73n. 13, 269, 269n. 9, 269n. 11

Harris, Joseph   241
Hart, Sir Robert   69, 181
Hayek, Friedrich   252
He, Wenkai   26, 26n. 132, 238, 238n. 91
Headrick, Daniel R.   361, 361n. 178, 361n. 181
Heckscher, Eli   326 et seq., 326n. 2
Heijdra, Martin   54, 54n. 256, 139, 139n. 312
Heinrich, Mathias   30, 197, 197n. 65
Heldernesse, Lord   328
Helpman, Elhanan   413
Ho, Ping-ti   273, 273n. 31
Hobsbawm, Eric   18, 18n. 82
Hobson, John M.   1, 20, 20n. 93, 24, 40, 40n. 203, 55, 125, 125n. 231, 316, 316n. 91, 363, 365, 365n. 194, 406, 406n. 93
Hoffman, Philip T.   30, 30n. 156, 70, 70n. 5, 117, 117n. 183, 125, 125n. 234, 125n. 235, 145, 145n. 339, 224, 224n. 27, 245
Hongmou, Chen   31, 122, 181
Hopkins, A. G.   224, 224n. 29, 391 et seq., 391n. 33
Hoppit, Julian   124, 124n. 228
Horesh, Niv   222, 222n. 14, 257, 257n. 179, 259, 264 et seq., 264n. 214, 264n. 215
Horrell, Sara   106
Hostetler, Laura   33, 33n. 180
Hsü, Immanuel C. Y.   154, 154n. 377, 154n. 379, 357, 357n. 154
Huang, Philip   17, 17n. 77
Hui, Victoria Tin-bor   32, 32n. 173, 36, 429
Hume, David   134, 145, 145n. 340, 205, 215 et seq., 243, 245
Humphries, Jane   106, 106n. 152

Isett, Christopher Mills   17, 17n. 76

Jacobs, Els   387, 387n. 23
Jacques, Martin   30, 30n. 157
James, William   320, 320n. 114, 320n. 116, 415, 415n. 24
Jones, Eric   9, 9n. 27–9, 16, 16n. 71, 34, 65, 65n. 297

Kaske, Elisabeth   90, 90n. 94
Keith, G. S.   128
Kennedy, Paul   295, 295n. 1
Kindleberger, Charles P.   236, 236n. 82
King, Frank H.   63, 63n. 286–8, 256, 256n. 175
Knight, Roger   286
Kozub, Robert   75, 100, 100n. 133
Krugman, Paul   413, 413n. 17
Kuroda, Akinobu   254 et seq.

Landes, David S.   9, 9n. 27, 9n. 30–2, 15, 15n. 67, 24, 409, 413
Lang, James   382, 382n. 4

Index of Persons

INDEX OF PLACES

Index of Persons

INDEX OF SUBJECTS

Index of Persons

Printed in Great Britain
by Amazon